WEBSTER'S DICTIONARY AND ROGET'S THESAURUS

1999 EDITION

Weston, Florida

32033

Cover Design 1999 - Carol-Ann McDonald

Printed in U.S.A. All Rights Reserved.

Copyright © 1999
Paradise Press, Inc.

ISBN #1-884907-00-8

New Webster's Dictionary

All entries are arranged in alphabetical order and appear in bold faced type. Following each entry are related words, derivations, and meanings. Each bold entry also includes a special simplified syllabic pronunciation help. Each entry also displays a symbol indicating the specific part of speech.

ABBREVIATIONS USED IN THIS DICTIONARY

a. adjective.

adv. adverb.

conj. conjunction.

int. interjection.

n. noun.

n. pl. noun plural.

p.a. participial adjective.

pl. plural.

pp. past participle.

prep. preposition.

pret. preterit.

pron. pronoun.

vi. verb intransitive.

vt. verb transitive.

GUIDE TO PRONUNCIATION

ch, *ch*ain; g, *g*o; ng, si*ng*; TH, *th*en; th, *th*in; w, *w*ig; wh, *wh*ig; ah, azure; fāte, fär, fat; mē, met, her; pīne, pin nōte, not, mŏve; tūbe, tub, bůll; oil, pound.

Computer Terms and Definitions

The following is a list of some of the common terms, along with their definitions, used by the computer industry that are unique to that field.

Basic: A high-level interactive programming language that comes with most computers. Basic Is relatively easy to learn to use if you want to try your hand at writing your own computer programs.

Bit: The smallest unit of information that the computer recognizes. A bit is represented in the computer by the presence or absence of an electronic pulse represented by humans as a zero or one.

Byte: A group of bits (usually 8 or 16) which stand for a single letter or number in the computer. Each byte is stored in its own address/location in memory.

CAD/CAM: Short for Computer-Aided Design and Computer-Aided-Manufacturing—encompassing almost every computer-related design, manufacturing and business function.

Cassette: The cheapest ant slowest way to store information when the computer's off. Cassettes transfer 30-120 bytes (characters)per second. That's slow.

Chip (Silicon): A microprocessor that is the complete computer on a single chip of silicon.

COBOL: Common Business Oriented Language—High-level programming language used for business applications.

CP/M: Control Program/Microcomputer. One of several "operating systems" for

CPU: Abbreviation for Central Processing Unit. The portion of a computer, sometimes called the brain, that controls the interpretation/execution of the programs and processing instructions.

CRT: Abbreviation for Cathode Ray Tube. Another name for a picture tube, monitor or video display terminal (VDT).

Data base: Program that files information—names, addresses, amounts owed. Some programs allow the user to sort the information alphabetically, by zip code, etc.

Disk drive: A memory storage device that operates something like a record player, using removable, flexible diskettes (also called floppies or disks).

DOS: Disk Operating System. One of the most popular "operating systems" for computers .

File: A collection of organized records the computer treats as a unit.

Floppy Disk: Single flexible magnetic disk (about the size of a 45-RPM record) that is used with small computers and word processors.

Hardware: The physical components of a computer system.

IC: The abbreviation for Integrated Circuit. The small electronic components that work together on circuit boards to perform a designated task. These components are usually referred to as chips.

I/O: The abbreviation for Input/Output.

Interface: A circuit board (also called a card) that electronically connects a computer to its accessories via a cable.

K: One thousand (actually 1,024), usually referring to memory. A 64K computer has 64,000 (actually 65,536) characters of random access memory. One double-spaced typed page needs about 2K of memory.

Kilobyte (K): Approximately one thousand bytes. This refers to the amount of computer memory in a system. For example: 512K memory equals approximately 512,000 bytes.

Languages: Programming languages. They include: Basic, COBOL, Pascal (business), Fortran (scientific), Forth.

LASER: Acronym for Light Amplification by Stimulated Emission of Radiation. A device that Produces a very narrow beam of coherent light. Lasers are used to produce ultra high resolution images on advanced typesetting systems such as the CG 9600 and Scanner 2000.

Mainframes: Largest, fastest, and most expensive class of computers

Megabyte (MB): Approximately one million bytes or one thousand kilobytes. Often used to measure disk, tape, or larger computer storage capacity. For example: 30 MB hard disk drive.

Microcomputers: Smallest and least expensive class of computers.

Megabyte (MB): Approximately one million bytes or one thousand kilobytes. Often used to measure disk tape, or large computer storage capacity. For example: 30 MB hard disk drive.

Microcomputers: Smallest and least expensive class of computers containing microprocessors on silicon chips.

Microprocessor: The miniature, integrated electronic circuit in the CPU that executes the instructions of a program task.

MODEM: The acronym for MOdulator/DEModulator. A device that uses a telephone hook-up to convert computer signals so that data can be sent or received over telephone lines.

Module: Set of logically related program

Monitor: Video display that gives a higher quality picture than a TV set. Typical size is 12 inches diagonal. Monochrome monitors are available in green, amber, or white displays. Some have non-glare faces. Color monitors are either composite color (so-so for reading words and numbers, fine for graphics and games), or RGB (red-green-blue). Display quality depends heavily on quality of the computer signal.

Operating system: A program or procedure that tells the computer how to operate. The computer you buy determines the operating system you get or have to buy. To operate a computer with disk drives, you need DOS (pronounced doss), a disk operating system.

Pascal: Structured high-level programming language.

Peripheral: An input/output device directed from a controller or computer. Examples: disk drives, printers.

Program: Step-by-step set of instructions that directs the comPuter to perform certain operations to solve a problem preparing for the execution.

Programmer: Person trained to design and test computer programs.

RAM: Random Access Memory. The memory the computer uses to store data. The more the better. Most personal computers store up to 64K bytes (64,000 characters). You lose what's stored in RAM when the computer is turned off, which is why you need a cassette recorder or disk drive.

ROM: Read only memory. ROM provides permanent storage of the computer's operating system and the Basic programming language, and can't be altered. it isn't lost when the computer is off. Caution: some computer makers advertise "total memory' meaning RAM and ROM added up, while most just list RAM, which is more meaningful.

Semiconductor (Silicon): A crystalline substance that conducts electric current when it has been "doped" with chemical impurities shot into the lattice-like structure of the crystal.

Software: A term used to describe the programs, instructions and applications of a computer system.

System: Organized set of related components established to perform a certain task.

Terminal: The peripheral device used to enter or extract data from the computer. It is sometimes referred to as the workstation or human interface. It usually consists of a CRT and keyboard. Sometimes called a monitor.

Word Processing: Computer-based system for inputting, editing, storing and printing of documents.

A

a, the indefinite article, used before a consonant.

abbreviate, ab-brē'vi-āt, *vt.* To shorten.

abbreviation, ab-brē'vi-ā'shon, *n.* A shortening, contraction.

abdomen, ab-dō'men, *n.* The lower belly.

abduct, ab-dukt', *vt.* To entice or lead away wrongly.

aberrant, ab-e'rant, *a.* Wandering from; deviating from an established rule.

ability, a-bil'li-ti, *n.* Power to do anything; talent; skill; in *pl.* the powers of the mind.

abnegate, ab'nē-gāt, *vt.* To deny; to renounce.

aboard, a-bōrd', *adv.* or *prep.* On board, in a ship or vessel.

abode, a-bōd', *n.* Residence; habitation.

abolish, a-bol'ish, *vt.* To destroy; to abrogate.

abortion, a-bor'shon, *n.* A miscarriage.

abound, a-bound', *vi.* To be, or have in great plenty.

about, a-bout', *prep.* Around, near to; relating to; engaged in.—*adv.* Around; round; nearly; here and there.

above, a-buv', *prep.* To or in a higher place than; superior to more than; beyond, before.—*adv.* To or in a higher place; chiefly.

abrasion, ab-rā'zhon, *n.* A rubbing off; substance worn off by rubbing.

abreast, a-brest', *adv.* In a line side by side.

abridge, a-brij', *vt.* To shorten; to condense.

abroad, a-bröd', *adv.* At large; away from home; in a foreign country.

absent, ab'sent, *a.* Being away from; not present; wanting in attention.

absentee, ab-sen-tē', *n.* One who absents himself.

absolute, ab'sō-lūt, *a.* Unlimited; unconditional, certain, despotic.

absolve, ab-solv', *vt.* To free from as from guilt or punishment; acquit, pardon.

absorb, ab-sorb', *vt.* To drink in; to engross.

absorbent, ab-sorb'ent, *a.* Imbibing; swallowing.—*n.* That which absorbs.

absorption, ab-sorp'shon, *n.* Act or process of imbibing or swallowing up.

abstain, ab-stān', *vi.* To keep back from; to refrain; to forbear.

abundant, a-bun'dant, *a.* Abounding, plentiful, ample.

abuse, a-būz, *vt.* (abusing abused). To turn from the proper use; to ill-use; to deceive; to vilify; to violate.

abut, a-but', *vi.* (abutting, abutted). To border, to meet. (With *upon*.)

abyss, a-bis', *n.* A bottomless gulf; a deep pit or mass of waters, hell.

Acacia, a-kä'shi-a, *n.* A genus of ornamental plants, yielding catechu, gum-arabic, etc.

academic, Academical, ak-a-dem'ik, ak-a-dem'ik-al, *a.* Belonging to an academy or university.

academy, a-kad'ē-mi, *n.* A seminary of arts or sciences; a society of persons for the cultivation of arts and sciences.

acaridan a-kar'i-dan, *n.* A mite tick, or allied animal.

accede, ak-sēd', *vi.* (acceding, acceded). To assent to; to comply with.

accelerate, ak-sel'le-rāt, *vt.* (accelerating, accelerated). To hasten; to quicken the speed of.

accent, ak 'sent, *n.* A tone or modulation of the voice; stress of the voice on a syllable or word; the mark which indicates this stress manner of speaking.

accent, ak-sent', *vt.* To express or note the accent of.

accept, ak-sept', *vt.* To receive, to admit; to promise to pay, by attaching one's signature.

acceptable, ak-sept'a-bl, *a.* That may be accepted; pleasing; gratifying.

access, ak'ses, *n.* Approach; admission; means of approach; increase.

accessible, ak-ses'i-bl, *a.* Easy of approach, affable.

accession, ak-se'shon, *n.* The act of acceding; augmentation; succession to a throne.

accessory, ak'ses-sō-ri, *a.* Additional, contributing to.—*n.* An accomplice, an adjunct.

acclamation, ak-kla-mā'shon, *n.* A shout of applause, assent, or approbation.

accolade, ak-kö-lād', *n.* A ceremony used in conferring knighthood, usually a blow on the shoulder with the flat of a sword.

accommodate, ak-kom'mō-dāt, *vt.* (accommodating, accommodated). To make suitable; to adjust, to furnish with.

accompaniment, ak-kum'pa-ni-ment, *n.* That which accompanies; the subordinate part or parts, in music.

accordion, ak-kord'i-on, *n.* A small melodious, keyed wind-instrument.

accost, ak-kost', *vt.* To speak to first; to address.

account, ak-kount ', *n.* A reckoning; a register of facts relating to money; narration; advantage end, importance.—*vt.* To reckon, to consider, to deem, to value.—*vi.* To give or render reasons; to explain (with *for*).

accountant, ak-kount'ant, *n.* One skilled or employed in accounts; one whose profession is to examine accounts.

accumulate, ak-ku'mū-lāt, *vt.* (accumulating, accumulated). To heap up; to amass.—*vi.* To increase.

accumulater ak-ku'mū-lāt-er, *n.* A kind of battery which stores electric energy.

accurate, ak'ku-rät, *a.* Done with care; exact; without error.

accursed, ak-kērs'ed, *a.* Lying under a curse; doomed; wicked.

accusation, ak-kū-zā'shon, *n.* Act of accusing; impeachment, that of which one is accused.

accusative, ak-kūz'at-iv. *a.* or *n.* A case in grammar, in English the objective.

accuse ak-kūz', *vt.* (accusing, accused) To charge with a crime; to impeach, to censure.

accustom, ak-kus'tum, *vt.* To inure to a custom; to make familiar with by use.

ace, äs *n.* A unit, a single point on cards or dice; a distinguished airman, who has destroyed many enemy planes.

aching, āk'ing, *p.a.* Being in continued pain.—*n.* Pain.

achromatic, ak-rō-mat'ik, *a.* Free from color.

acoustic, a-kous'tik, *a.* Pertaining to the sense of hearing, or to the doctrine of sounds.

acoustics, a-kous'tiks, *n.* The science of sound.

acquaint, ak-kwānt', *vt.* To make to know; to make familiar; to inform.

acre, a'kèr, *n.* A quantity of land containing 4840 square yards.

acreage, a'kèr-āj, *n.* A number of acres in a piece of land.

acrid, ak'rid, *a.* Sharp; hot or biting to the taste, corroding, harsh.

acrimony, ak'ri-mo-ni, *n.* Sharpness; harshness; severity.

acrobat, ak'rō-bat, *n.* A rope-dancer; one who practices vaulting, tumbling, etc.

acrogen, ak'rōjen, *n.* A plant increasing by extension of the stem at the top.

Acropolis, a-krop'o-lis, *n.* The citadel of a Greek city, as of Athens.

across, a-kros', *prep.* or *adv.* From side to side; transversely; crosswise.

act, akt, *vi.* To be in action, to exert power; to conduct oneself.—*vt.* To do; to perform, as an assumed part; to counterfeit.—*n.* A deed power, or the effect of power, put forth; a state of reality; a part of a play; law, as an act of parliament.

actinia, ak-tin'i-a, *n.; pl.* -iae. A sea anemone.

actinism, ak'tin-izm, *n.* The chemical action of the sun's rays.

action, ak'shon, *n.* A deed; operation; a series of events; gesture; a suit or process; an engagement, battle.

active, ak'tiv, *a.* That acts or is in action; busy; quick; denoting action.

actor, aktèr *n.* One who acts; an active agent, a stage-player.

adapt, a-dapt', *vt.* To fit; to adjust; to suit.

add, ad, *vt.* To join to; to annex; to say further.

addendum, ad-den'dum, *n., pl.* -da. A thing to be added, an appendix.

additive, ad'it-iv, *a.* That is to be or may be added.

addle, ad'l, *a.* Rotten; barren.—*vt.* (addling, addled). To make corrupt or barren.

address, ad-dres', *vt.* To direct; to apply to by words or writing; to speak to; to apply (oneself) to write a name and destination on.—*n.* Verbal or written application; speech or discourse to a person; tact; courtship (generally in *plural);* direction of a letter.

adduce, ad-dūs', *vt.* (adducing, adduced). To bring forward; to cite.

adhibit, ad-hib'it, *vt.* To attach (one's signature).

adieu, a-dū', *interj.* Farewell.—*n.; pl.* -us or -ux. A farewell.

adit, ad'it, *n.* An approach; the horizontal opening into a mine.

adjacent, ad-jā'sent, *a.* Lying near adjoining; contiguous; neighboring.

adjective, ad'jek-tiv, *n.* A word used with a noun, to express some quality or circumstance.

adjoin, ad-join', *vt.* To join to.—*vi.* To lie or be next, to be contiguous.

adjourn. ad-jèrn', *vt.* To put off to a future day; to postpone.—*vi.* To leave off for a future meeting.

admeasure, ad-me'zhūr, *vt.* To ascertain the size or capacity of.

adminicle, ad-min'i-kl, *n.* Support; aid.

administer, ad-min'is-tèr, *vt.* To manage; to dispense; to distribute.

administration, ad-min'is-trā'shon, *n.* Management, executive part of a government.

admirable, ad'mi-ra-bl, *a.* Worthy of admiration; excellent.

admonish, ad-mon'ish, *vt.* To warn; to reprove solemnly or quietly; to exhort.

admonition, ad-mō̄ni'shon, *n.* Gentle or solemn reproof, instruction; caution.

ado, a-dö', *n.* Stir; bustle; difficulty.

adobe, a-dö'be, *n.* A sun-dried brick.

adolescent, ad-ō̄-les'ent, *a.* Advancing to manhood.

adopt, a-dopt', *vt.* To take and treat as a child, giving a title to the rights of a child; to embrace.

Adorable, a-dō̄r'a-bl, *a.* Worthy to be adored.

Adoration, a-dōr'ā'shon, *n.* Worship paid to God; profound reverence.

adore, a-dō̄r', *vt.* (adoring, adored). To address in prayer; to worship with reverence and awe; to love intensely.

adorn, a-dōrn', *vt.* To deck with ornaments, to embellish, to beautify.

adrift, a-drift', *adv.* Floating at random; at the mercy of any impulse.

adroit, a-droit', *a.* Dexterous; skilful; ready.

adulation, ad-ū-lā'shon, *n.* Servile flattery; excessive praise.

adult, a-dult', *a.* Grown to maturity. —*n.* A person grown to manhood.

adultery, a-dul'tè-ri, *n.* Unfaithfulness to the marriage-bed.

Advent, ad'vent, *n.* Arrival, the coming of Christ; the four weeks before Christmas.

adventitious, ad-ven-ti'shi-us, *a.* Accidental; casual; accessory; foreign.

adventure, ad-ven'tūr, *n.* Hazardous enterprise; a bold undertaking—*vt.* To risk or hazard.—*vi.* To dare, to venture.

adventurous, ad-ven'tū r-us, *a.* Prone to incur hazard; daring; full of hazard.

adverb, ad'vèrb, *n.* A word which modifies a verb, adjective, or another adverb.

adversary, ad'vèr-sa-ri, *n.* An enemy; an antagonist.

adversative, ad-vèrs'at-iv, *a.* Noting or causing opposition.—*n.* A word denoting opposition.

adverse, ad'vèrs, *a.* Hostile; unprosperous.

adversity, ad-vèrs'i-ti, *n.* Misfortune, affliction, calamity, distress.

advise, ad-vīz, *vt.* (advising, advised). To counsel, to warn, to inform.—*vi.* To deliberate or consider.

advised, ad-vīzd', *p.a.* Cautious; done with advice.

advocate, ad'vō̄-kā t, *n.* One who pleads for another, an intercessor.—*vt.* (advocating, advocated). To plead in favor of; to vindicate.

adze, adz, *n.* A kind of axe, with the edge at right angles to the handle.

aegis, e'jis, *n.* A shield; protection.

Aeolian, e-o'li-an, *a.* Pertaining to Aeolus, the god of the winds; played upon by the wind.

aerate, a'er-at, *vt.* (aerating, aerated). To put air into; to combine with carbonic acid.

aerie, e're, *n.* The nest of a bird of prey; a brood of such birds.

affair, af-far', *n.* That which is to do, or which is done; business.

affect, af-fekt', *vt.* To act upon; to move the feelings of; to aim at; to pretend.

affectedly, af-fekt'ed-li, *adv.* In an affected manner feignedly.

affecting, af-fekt'ing, *p.a.* Pathetic; tender; exciting.

affection, af fek'shon, *n.* The state of being affected; fondness, love.

affectionate, af-fek'shon-āt, *a.* Tender; loving; fond.

afferent, af'fè r-ent, *a.* Carrying to or inwards.

affiance, af-fī'ans, *n.* Faith pledged; marriage contract; reliance.—*vt.* (affiancing, affianced). To pledge one's faith to; to betroth.

affidavit, af-fi-dä'vit, *n.* A written declaration ʼupon oath.

affiliate, af-fil'li-āt, *vt.* (affiliating, affiliated). To adopt, to assign to a father; to unite to a chief society or body.

affiliation, af-fil'li-ā'shon, *n.* Act of affiliating, association.

affinity, af-fin'i-ti, *n.* Relation by marriage; resemblance; chemical attraction.

affirm, af-fèrm', *vt.* To assert; to declare; to ratify.—*vi.* To declare solemnly.

affix, af-fiks', *vt.* To fasten to, to subjoin.—*n.* af'fiks. A syllable or letter added to a word.

afield a-fēld', *adv.* To or in the field.

afloat, a-flō̄t ', *adv.* or *a.* Floating; in circulation (as a rumor).

afoot, a-fūt ', *adv.* On foot, in action.

after, äft'èr, *a.* Later in time; subsequent.—*prep.* Later in time than; behind, according to; in imitation of.—*adv.* Later in time.

aftermath, äft'è r-math, *n.* A second crop of grass in the same season, consequences, results.

afternoon, äft'è r-nön, *n.* The part of the

day which follows noon.

age, āj, n. A period of time; an epoch; number of years during which a person has lived; decline of life; oldness; legal maturity.—vi. and t. (aging, aged). To grow or make old; to show signs of advancing age.

agency, ā-jen-si, n. Instrumentality; office or business of an agent.

agenda, a-jen'da, n.pl. Memoranda, business to be transacted at a meeting.

agent, āʹjent, n. One who acts; a deputy, an active cause or power.

Agglutinant, ag-glūʹtin-ant, n. Any viscous or gluey substance.

aggrandize, ag'gran-dī z, vt. To make great; to magnify.

aggravate, ag'gra-vā t, vt. (aggravating, aggravated). To intensify: to exasperate.

aggression, ag-gre'shon, n. The first act of hostility, attack.

aggressor, ag gres'or, n. The person who commences hostilities.

aggrieve, ag-grēv', vt. To pain, oppress, or injure.

aghast, a-gast', a. or adv. Amazed; stupefied. Also agast.

agile, aj'il, a. Ready to act; nimble.

ago, a-go, adv. or a. Past; gone.

agony, ag'ō-ni, n. Extreme pain of body or mind; anguish; the pangs of death.

agrarian, a-grāʹri-an, a. Relating to lands.

agree, a-grē', vi. (agreeing, agreed). To be in concord, to correspond; to suit.

agreement, a-grē'ment, n. Harmony, conformity, stipulation.

agriculture, ag'ri-kul-tūr, n. The art or science of cultivating the ground.

AIDS, ā dz, n. Acquired Immune Deficiency Syndrome. A break down of the human body's immune system.

ail, āl, vt. To pain; to affect with uneasiness.—vi. To be in pain or trouble.

aim, ā m, vi. To point with a missive weapon; to intend; to endeavor.— vt. To level or direct as a firearm.— n. That which is aimed at, direction; purpose; drift.

air, ār, n. The fluid which we breathe; a light breeze, a tune; mien; pl. affected manner.—vt. To expose to the air; to ventilate; to dry.

airport, ār'pōrt, n. An area for landing airplanes, usually having customs houses, servicing facilities, etc.

air pump, ā r'pump, n. A machine for pumping the air out of a vessel.

air-shaft, ār'shaft, n. A passage for air into a mine

air-tight, ār'tīt, a. So tight or compact as not to let air pass.

airy, āʹri, a. Open to the free air; high in air; light; thin; vain; gay.

aisle, īl, n. A wing or side of a church, a passage in a church.

ajar, a-jär', adv. Partly open, as a door.

akin, a-kin', a. Of kin; related to; partaking of the same properties.

alabaster, al'a-bas-tė r, n. A soft marblelike mineral.—a. Made of alabaster.

alacrity, a-lak'ri-ti, n. Liveliness; cheerful readiness, promptitude.

albumen, al-bū 'men, n. The white of an egg; a substance of the same kind found in animals and vegetables.

alburnum, al-bè r'num, n. Sapwood of a tree.

Alchemy, al'ke-mi, n. An obsolete science, aiming at changing metals into gold etc.

alcoholic, al-kō -hol'ik, a. Pertaining to alcohol.

alcoholism, al'kō -hol-izm, n. The condition of habitual drunkards.

alcove, al'kōv, n. A recess.

alga, al 'ga, n.; pl. -gae, A sea-weed.

Algebra, al'je-bra, n. The science of computing by symbols.

alias, ā 'li-as, adv. Otherwise. n.; pl. –ses, An assumed name.

alibi, ali-bī, n. The plea of a person who, charged with a crime, alleges that he was elsewhere when the crime was committed.

alien, ā l'yen, a. Foreign; estranged from.—n. A foreigner.

aliquot, al'i-kwot, a. A part of a number which divides the whole without remainder.

alive, a-līv', a. Living; lively; susceptible.

all, äl, a. Every part; every one.—n. The whole, everything.—adv. Wholly entirely.

Allah, ai'la, n. The Arabic name of God.

allay, al-lā, vt. To repress; to assuage.

allege, al-lej', vt. (alleging, alleged). To adduce; to assert; to plead in excuse.

alley, al 'i, n. A narrow walk or passage.

alliance, al-līʹans, n. State of being allied; confederacy; league.

allied, al-līd', p.a. United by treaty.

allopathy, al-lop'a-thi, n. The ordinary mode of curing diseases, by using medicines which produce a condition contrary to that of the disease.

allot, al-lot' vt. (allotting, allotted). To give by lot; to apportion.

allotrophy, al-lot'ro-pi, n. The capability

of substances of existing in more than one form.

alloy, al-loi', *vt.* To mix with baser metals; to abate by mixture.—*n.* A baser metal mixed with a finer, a metallic compound.

allspice, äl-spīs, *n.* Pimento or Jamaica pepper, supposed to combine many different flavors.

allude, al-lūd', *vi.* (alluding, alluded). To refer to; to hint at.

allusion, al-lūzhon, *n.* The act of alluding, a hint, a reference.

almost, äl'most, *adv.* Nearly, well; nigh; for the greatest part.

alms, ämz, *n.pl.* A charitable gift.

aloft, a-loft', *adv.* In the sky; on high.

alone, a-lōn', *a.* Solitary.—*adv.* Separately.

along, a-long', *adv.* Lengthwise forward.—*prep.* By the side of, lengthwise.

aloof, a-löf', *adv.* At a distance; apart.

aloud, a-loud', *adv.* Loudly.

alpaca, al-pak'a, *n.* A Peruvian animal, with long, soft, and woolly hair; cloth made of its hair, or a similar cloth.

alpha, al'fa, *n.* The first letter in the Greek alphabet; the first or beginning.

alphabet, al'fa-bet, *n.* The letters of a language arranged in the customary order.

already, äl-red'i, *adv.* Before or by this time; even now.

also, äl'sō, *adv.* Likewise; in the same manner, further.

altar, äl'tèr, *n.* An elevated place on which sacrifices were offered, the communion table.

alternation al-tern-ā'shon *n.* Reciprocal succession, interchange.

alternative, al-tė rn'at-iv, *n.* A choice of two things.

altitude, al'ti-tūd, *n.* Height; eminence; elevation.

alto, al'tō, *a.* High.—*n.* In *music,* contralto.

altruism, al'trö-izm, *n.* Devotion to others or to humanity, the opposite of selfishness.

alum, al'um, *n.* An astringent salt of great use in medicine and the arts.

aluminum, a-lu-mi-num, *n.* A very light metal of a silvery white color.

alumnus, a-lum'nus, *n.; pl.* -ni. A pupil, a graduate of a university.

amaranthine, am-a-ran'thin, a. Unfading.

amass, a-mas', *vt.* To form into a mass; to accumulate; to heap up.

amateur, am-a-tūr', *n.* A lover of any art or science, not a professor.

amatory, am'a-tō -ri, *a.* Relating to love;

causing love; amorous.

amaze, a-māz', *vt.* (amazing, amazed). To astonish; to bewilder.

Amazon, am'a-zon, *n.* A warlike or masculine woman; a virago.

ambassador, am-bas'sa-dor, *n.* A representative of a sovereign or state at a foreign court.

ambit, am'bit, *n.* Compass; scope.

ambition, am-bi'shon, *n.* Desire of preferment or power.

ambitious, am-bi'shus, *a.* Aspiring.

ambrosia, am-brōzhi-a, *n.* The imaginary food of the gods, which conferred immortality.

ambulance, am'bū -lans, *n.* An itinerant hospital; a wagon for the sick or wounded.

ambulatory, am'bū-lā-tō-ri *a.* Movable.— *n.* A part of a building to walk in.

amends, a-mendz', *n.pl.* Compensation; satisfaction; recompense.

amenity, a-men'i-ti, *n.* Pleasantness; agreeableness of situation.

American, a-me'ri-kan, n. A native of America.—*a.* Pertaining to America.

amiable, ämi-a-bl, *a.* Lovable; sweet-tempered.

amicable, am'ik-a-bl, *a.* Friendly; kind.

amnesty, am'nes-ti, *n.* A general pardon of offenses against a government.

amnion, am'ni-on, *n.* The innermost membrane surrounding the fetus of mammals, birds, and reptiles.

amoeba, a-mē'ba, *n.;* pl. -bae. A microscopic animal commonly found in fresh water.

among, amongst, a-mung', a-mungst', *prep.* Amidst; throughout; of the number.

amorous, am'or-us, *a.* Inclined to love; enamored; fond; relating to love.

amorphous, a-mor'fus, *a.* Without shape; of irregular shape.

amount, a-mount', *vi.* To mount up to, to result in.—*n.* The sum total effect or result.

ample, am'pl, *a.* Spacious; copious; rich.

amplification, am'pli-fī-kā'shon *n.* Act of amplifying; enlargement, discussion.

amplify, am'plif-ī, *vt.* (amplifying amplified). To enlarge; to treat copiously.— *vi.* To speak copiously; to be diffuse.

amplitude, am'pli-tūd, *n.* Ampleness, extent, abundance.

amply, am'pli, *adv.* Largely; liberally; fully; copiously.

amputate, am'pū -tā t, *vt.* (amputating, amputated). To cut off; as a limb.

amuck, a-muk', *n.* or *adv.* Only in phrase to *run amuck,* to rush about frantically, to attack all and sundry.

amulet, am'ū-let, *n.* A charm against evils or witchcraft.

amuse, a-mūz', *vt.* (amusing amused). To entertain; to beguile.

anagram, an'a-gram, *n.* A transposition of the letters of a name or sentence, by which a new word or sentence is formed.

anal, ā'nal, *a.* Pertaining to the anus.

analogous, an-al'og-us, *a.* Having analogy; corresponding.

analogy, an-al'o-ji, *n.* Likeness; similarity.

analyze, an'a-līz, *vt.* (analyzing, analyzed) To subject to analysis, to resolve into its elements.

ancestor, an'ses-tèr, *n.* A progenitor; forefather.

anchor, ang'kèr, *n.* An iron instrument for holding a ship at rest in water. *vt.* To hold fast by an anchor.—*vi.* To cast anchor.

anchorage, ang'kèr-āj, *n.* A place where a ship can anchor; duty on ships for anchoring.

anchorite, ang'kō-rīt, *n.* A hermit.

anchovy, an-chō'vi, *n.* A small fish of the herring kind, furnishing a fine sauce.

ancient, ān'shent, *a.* That happened in former times; old, antique.

ancillary, an'sil-la-ri, *a.* Pertaining to a maid-servant; subservient or subordinate.

aneroid, an'e-roid, *a.* Dispensing with fluid, said of a kind of barometer.

anesthetic, an-es-thet'ik, *a.* Producing insensibility.—*n.* A sub- stance, as chloroform, which produces insensibility.

aneurysm, an'ū-rizm, *n.* Dilatation of an artery.

angel, ān'jel, *n.* A divine messenger, a spirit, an old English gold coin worth ten shillings.

anger, ang'gèr, *n.* A violent passion, excited by real or supposed injury; resentment.—*vt.* To excite anger; to irritate.

angina, an-ji'na, *n.* Angina pectoris, a fatal disease characterized by paroxysms of intense pain and a feeling of constriction in the chest.

angle, ang'gl, *n.* The inclination of two lines which meet in a point but have different directions; a corner.

angle, ang'gl, *n.* A fishing-hook, or hook with line and rod.—*vi.* (angling, angled). To fish with an angle.

Anglican, ang'glik-an, *a.* Pertaining to England, or to the English Church.

angular, ang'gū-lē r, *a.* Having an angle, stiff.

anile, an'īl, *a.* Aged; imbecile.

aniline, an'i-lin, *n.* A substance obtained from coal-tar, used in dyeing.

animadvert, an'i-mad-vèr", *vi.* To criticize; to censure (with *upon*).

animal, an'i-mal, *n.* A living being having sensation and voluntary motion; a quadruped.—*a.* Belonging to animals; gross.

animus, an'i-mus, *n.* Intention; hostile spirit.

anise, an'is, *n.* An aromatic plant, the seeds of which are used in making cordials.

annals, an'nalz, *n.pl.* A record of events under the years in which they happened.

anneal, an'nēl', *vt.* To temper glass or metals by heat, to fix colors laid on glass.

annelid, an'ne-lid, *n.* An invertebrate animal whose body is formed of numerous small rings, as the worm, leech, etc.

annex, an-neks', *vt.* To unite at the end; to subjoin; to take possession of.

annihilate, an-nī'hil-āt, *vt.* (annihilating, annihilated). To reduce to nothing; to destroy the existence of.

anniversary, an-ni-vè rs'a-rī, *n.* A day on which some event is annually celebrated.

annotate, an'nō-tāt, *vt.* (annotating, annotated). To write notes upon.

annular, an'nu-ler, *a.* Having the form of a ring; pertaining to a ring.

annulose, an'nū-lōs, *a.* Having a body composed of rings; applied to annelids.

annunciation, an-nun'si-ā "shon *n.* The angel's salutation to the Virgin Mary, and its anniversary the 25th of March.

anode, an'ōd, *n.* The positive pole of a voltaic current.

anoint, a-noint', *vt.* To rub over with oil, to consecrate by unction.

anomaly, a-nom'a-li, *n.* Irregularity; deviation from common rule.

anonymous, a-non'im-us, *a.* Name-less; without the real name of the author.

another, an-uTH 'èr, *a.* Not the same different, any other.

answer, an'sèr, *vt.* To reply to; to satisfy; to suit—*vi.* To reply; to be accountable, to succeed.—*n.* A reply, a solution.

antecedent, an-tē-sē'dent, *a.* Going before, prior.—*n.* That which goes before, the noun to which a relative refers; *pl.* a man's previous history, etc.

antechamber, an'tē -chā m-bè r, *n.* An

apartment leading into a chief apartment.

antedate, an'tē-dāt, *n.* Prior date.—*vt.* To date before the true time.

anthem, an'them, *n.* A sacred song sung in alternate parts; a piece of Scripture set to music.

anthology, an-thol'o-ji, *n.* A collection of poems.

anthracite, an'thra-sît, *n.* A hard compact coal which burns almost without flame.

anthropoid, an'thrō-poid, *a.* Resembling man applied to the higher apes.

Anthropology, an-thrō -pol'o-ji, *n.* The science of man and mankind the study of the physical and mental constitution of man.

antidote, an'ti-dōt, *n.* A remedy for poison or any evil.

antinomian, an-ti-nō 'mi-an, *n.* One who opposes the moral law.

antipathy, an-tip'a-thi, *n.* Instinctive aversion; dislike; opposition,

antiphrasis, an-tif'ra-sis, *n.* The use of words in a sense opposite to the proper one.

antipodes, an-tip'o-dē z, *n.pl.* Those who live on opposite sides of the globe; the opposite side of the globe.

antipyrin, an-ti-pî'rin, *n.* A drug used to reduce fever and relieve pain.

antitype, an'ti-tîp, *n.* That which is shadowed out by a type or emblem.

antler, ant'lèr, *n.* A branch of a stag's horn.

antonym, ant'ō-nim, *n.* A word of directly contrary signification to another the opposite of a synonym.

anus, ā'nus *n.* The opening of the body by which excrement is expelled.

anvil, an'vil, *n.* An iron block on which smiths hammer and shape their work.

apathy, ap 'a-thi, *n.* Want of feeling; insensibility, Indifference.

ape, ā p, *n.* A monkey; an imitator.— *vt.* (aping, aped). To imitate servilely, to mimic.

apex, ā 'peks, *n.*; pl. **-exes** and **-ices**. The summit of anything.

aphorism, af-or-izm, *n.* A precept expressed in few words; a maxim.

apiary, ā'pi-a-ri, *n.* A place where bees are kept.

apiece, a-pēs', *adv.* In a separate share; to each; noting the share of each.

Apocalypse, a-pok'a-lips, *n.* Revelation; the last book of the New Testament.

apology, a-pol'ō-ji, *n.* That which is said in defense; vindication; excuse.

apophthegm, **apothegm**, ap'o-them, *n.* A terse pointed saying .

apoplexy, ap'ō-plek'si, *n.* A sudden privation of sense and voluntary motion.

apostasy, a-pos'ta-si, *n.* departure from one's faith; desertion of a party.

apostrophe, a-pos'tro-f ē *n.* An addressing of the absent or the dead as if present; a mark (') indicating contraction of a word, or the possessive case.

Apothecary, a-poth'e-ka-ri, *n.* One who prepares and sells drugs or medicines.

apotheosis, ap-o-thē'ō -sis or -thē -ō' sis, *n.* A deification; a placing among the gods.

appal, ap-päl', *vt.* (appalling, appalled). To depress with fear; to dismay.

apparel, ap-pa'rel, *n.* Equipment; clothing. *vt.* (apparelling, apparelled). To dress; to array.

apparent, ap-pa'rent, *a.* That may be seen; evident; seeming, not real.

apparition, ap-pa-ri'shon, *n.* An appearance; a specter; a ghost or phantom.

appear, ap-pē r', *vi.* To be or become visible; to seem.

appease, ap-pē z', *vt.* (appeasing, appeased). To pacify; to tranquilize.

appetite, ap'pē-tît, *n.* A desire or relish for food or other sensual gratifications.

apple, ap'l, *n.* The fruit of the apple-tree; the pupil of the eye.

appliance, ap-plī'ans, *n.* Act of applying; thing applied; article of equipment.

applicable, ap'pli-ka-bl, *a.* That may be applied, suitable.

appraise, ap-prā z', *vt.* (appraising, appraised). To fix or set a price on; to estimate.

appreciate, ap-prĕshi-āt, *vt.* (appreciating, appreciated). To value; to estimate justly.

apprehend, ap-prē-hend', *vt.* To take hold of; to arrest, to conceive; to fear.—*vi.* To think; to imagine.

appropriate, ap-prōpri-āt, *vt.* (appropriating, appropriated). To take to oneself as one s own; to set apart for.—*a.* Set apart for a particular use or person; suitable; adapted.

appropriateness, ap-prō'pri-āt-nes, *n.* Peculiar fitness.

approval, ap-prōv'al, *n.* Approbation.

approve, ap-prōv', *vt.* (approving approved). To deem good; to like, to sanction.—*vi.* To feel or express approbation (with *of*).

approximate, ap-prok'si-māt, *a.* Near, approaching.—*vt.* (approximating, approximated). To bring near.—*vi.* To come near; to approach.

aquarium, a-kwā'ri-um, *n.*; pl. **-iums or -la.** A vessel or tank for aquatic plants and animals; a collection of such vessels.

aquatic, a-kwat'ik, *a.* Living or growing in water.—*n.* A plant which grows in water; *pl.* sports or exercises in water.

aqueduct, ak 'wē -dukt, *n.* A conduit made for conveying water.

aqueous a'kwē-us, *a.* Watery.

aquiline, ak'wil-ī n, *a.* Belonging to the eagle; hooked like the beak of an eagle.

Arab, a'rab, *n.* A native of Arabia; street urchin, an Arabian horse.

arbiter, är'bit-ėr, *n.* A person appointed by parties in controversy to decide their differences; an umpire.

arbitrate, är'bi-trāt, *vi.* (arbitrating, arbitrated). To act as an arbiter; to decide.

arbor, är'bėr, *n.* A bower; a shelter in a garden, formed of trees, etc.

arboreous, är-bō 'rē -us, *a.* Belonging to trees.

arboretum, är-bo-rē'tum, *n.* A place where trees are cultivated for scientific purposes.

arbutus, är'bu-tūs, *n.* An evergreen shrub, with berries like the strawberry.

arc, ärk, *n.* A part of a circle or curve.

arch, ärch, *a.* Chief; cunning; sly; roguish.

arch, ärch, *n.* A concave structure supported by its own curve, a vault.—*vt.* To cover with an arch; to form with a curve.

archaic, är-kā 'ik, *a.* Antiquated; obsolete.

archaism, är'kā-izm, *n.* Obsolete word or expression.

Archangel, ärk-ā n'jel, *n.* An angel of the highest order.

Archeology, är-kē-ol'o-ji, *n.* The science of antiquities; knowledge of ancient art.

Archipelago, är-ki-pel'a-gō, *n.* The Aegean Sea; a sea abounding in small islands.

architect, är'ki-tekt, *n.* One who plans buildings, etc., a contriver.

architecture, är'ki-tek-tū r, *n.* The art or science of building; structure.

ardor, är'dėr, *n.* Warmth; fervency; eagerness.

arduous, är'du-us, *a.* Difficult; laborious.

are, är, The plural pres. indic. of the verb to be.

area, a'rē-a, *n.* Any open surface; superficial contents; any enclosed space.

argue, är'gū *vi.* (arguing, argued). To offer reasons; to dispute.—*vt.* To show reasons for, to discuss.

argument, är'gūment, *n.* A reason offered, a plea, subject of a discourse; heads of contents; controversy.

Argus, är'gus, *n.* A fabulous being with a hundred eyes; a watchful person.

Arian, ā'ri-an, *a.* Pertaining to Arius, who denied the divinity of Christ.—*n.* One who adheres to the doctrines of Arius.

arid, a'rid, *a.* Dry; dried; parched.

Aries, ā'ri-ē z, *n.* The Ram, the first of the twelve signs of the zodiac.

aristocracy, a-ris-tok'ra-si, *n.* Government by the nobility; the nobility.

aristocrat a'ris-to-krat, *n.* A noble one who favors aristocracy.

Arithmetic, a-rith'met-ik, *n.* The science of numbering; the art of computation.

ark, ärk, *n.* A chest; a large floating vessel.

armadillo, är-ma-dil'1ō, *n.* A quadruped of the southwestern U.S. with a hard bony shell.

armament, ärm'a-ment, *n.* A force armed for war; war-munitions of a ship.

armory, ärm 'e-ri, *n.* A repository of arms.

armpit, ärm'pit, *n.* The hollow place under the shoulder.

army, är'mi, *n.* A body of men armed for war; a great number.

aroma, a-rō 'ma, *n.* Perfume, the fragrant principle in plants, etc.

aromatic, a-rō -mat'ik, *a.* Fragrant; spicy.—*n.* A fragrant plant or drug.

around, a-round', *prep.* About; on all sides of; encircling.—*adv.* On every side.

arrest, a-rest', *vt.* To stop; to apprehend.—*n.* A seizure by warrant; stoppage.

arrive, a-rīv', *vi.* (arriving, arrived). To come, to reach, to attain.

arson, är'son, *n.* The malicious setting on fire of a house, etc.

art, ärt, *n.* Practical skill; a system of rules for certain actions; cunning; profession of a painter, etc.

artery, är'tė-ri, *n.* A tube which conveys blood from the heart.

artful, ärt'ful, *a.* Full of art; skillful; crafty.

arthritis, är-thrī 'tis, *n.* Gout.

article, är'ti-kl, *n.* A separate item; stipulation, a particular commodity; a part of speech used before nouns, as *the.*—*vt.* To bind by articles.—*vi.* To stipulate.

articulate, är-tik'ū-lāt, *a.* Distinct; clear.—*vi.* To utter distinct sound syllables, or words.—*vt.* To speak distinctly.

artifice, ärt'i-fis, *n.* An artful device; fraud; stratagem.

as, az, *adv.* and *conj.* Like, even; equally;

while; since; for example.

asbestos, as-bes'tos, *n.* A mineral fibrous substance which is incombustible.

ascend, as-send', *vi.* To rise; to go backward in order of time.—*vt.* To move upward upon; to climb.

aseptic, a-sep'tik, *a.* Not liable to putrefy.

ash, ash, *n.* A well-known timber tree.

ashamed, a-shāmd', *a.* Affected by shame.

ashes, ash'ez, *n.pl.* The dust produced by combustion; the remains of a dead body.

ashore, a-shōr', *adv.* or *pred.a.* On shore.

askance, askant, a-skans', a-skant', *adv.* Awry, obliquely.

aslant, a-slant'. *Pred.a.* or *adv.* On slant; obliquely; not perpendicular.

asleep, a-slēp', *pred.a.* or *adv.* Sleeping, at rest.

aslope, a-slōp', *pred.a.* or *adv.* On slope; obliquely.

asp, asp, *n.* A small venomous serpent of Egypt.

asparagus, as-pa'ra-gus, *n.* A well-known esculent plant.

aspect, as'pekt, *n.* Appearance; situation.

Aspen, asp'en, *n.* A species of the Poplar.

asperse as-pèrs', *vt.* (aspersing, aspersed). To calumniate; to slander.

asphalt, as-falt', *n.* A bituminous, hard substance, used for pavement, etc.

aspirant, as-pī r'ant, n. A candidate.

asquint, a-skwint', *adv.* Out of the corner or angle of the eye; obliquely.

ass, as, *n.* A well-known animal akin to the horse; a dolt.

assail, as-sāl', *vt.* To attack; to assault.

assemble, as-sem'bl, *vt.* (assembling, assembled). To bring together.—*vi.* To come together.

assembly, as-sem'bli, *n.* An assemblage; a convocation.

assent, as-sent', *n.* Act of agreeing to anything, consent.—*vi.* To agree; to yield.

assert, as-sèrt', *vt.* To affirm; to maintain, to vindicate.

assiduous, as-sid'ū -us, *a.* Constantly diligent.

assign, as-sīn', *vt.* To designate, to allot; to make over to another.—*n.* A person to whom property or any right may bc or is transferred.

assignment, as-sīn'ment, *n.* Act of assigning; thing assigned; a writ of transfer.

assimilate, as-sim'il-āt, *vt.* (assimilating, assimilated). To make like to; to digest.—*vi.* To become similar or of the same substance.

assist, as-sist', *vt.* To help.—*vi.* To lend help, to contribute.

assistance, as-sist'ans, *n.* Help aid.

assuage, as-swā j', *vt.* (assuaging, assuaged). To allay, to calm.—*vi.* To abate or subside.

assume, as-sūm', *vt.* (assuming, assumed). To take for granted, to usurp.—*vi.* To claim more than is due; to be arrogant.

assurance, a-shör'ans, *n.* Act of assuring, secure confidence, impudence; positive declaration; insurance.

assure, a-shör', *vt.* (assuring, assured) To make sure; to confirm; to insure.

astern, a-stè rn', *adv.* In or at the hinder part of a ship.

asteroid, as'tėr-oid, *n.* A small planet.

asthma, as'ma or as'thma, *n.* A disorder of respiration, characterized by difficulty of breathing, cough, and expectoration.

astonish, as-ton'ish, *vt.* To surprise; to astound.

astound, as-tound', *vt.* To astonish; to stun; to strike dumb with amazement.

Astrology, as-trol'o-ji, *n.* The pretended art of foretelling future events from the stars.

Astronomy, as-tron'o-mi, *n.* The science of the heavenly bodies.

astute, as-tūt', *a.* Shrewd; crafty.

asunder, a-sun'dèr, *adv.* or *pred.a.* Apart; into parts; in a divided state.

at, at, *prep.* Denoting presence or nearness; in a state of; employed in, on, or with; with direction towards.

athlete, ath-lēt', *n.* One skilled in exercises of agility or strength.

athletics, ath-let'iks, *n.pl.* Athletic exercises.

Atlantean, at-lan-tē'an, *a.* Gigantic.

Atlantic, at-lan'tik, *a.* Pertaining to the ocean between Europe, Africa, and America.—*n.* This ocean.

atlas, at'las, *n.* A collection of maps.

atmosphere, at'mos-fēr, *n.* The mass of gas around the earth; air pervading influence.

atom, a'tom, *n.* A minute particle of matter; anything extremely small.

atone, a-tōn', *vi.* (atoning, atoned). To make satisfaction.—*vt.* To expiate.

attache, at-ta-shā', *n.* One attached to the suite of an ambassador. **Attache case,** *n.* A small oblong case of leather or fiber, for carrying documents, books, etc.

attack, at-tak', *vt.* To assault; to assail.— *n.* An assault; seizure by a disease.

attain, at-tān', *vi.* To come or arrive. —*vt.* To reach; to gain; to obtain.

attention, at-ten'shon, *n.* Act of attending,

heed; courtesy.

attentive, at-tent'iv, *a*. Heedful.

attenuate, at-ten'ū -āt, *vt*. (attenuating, attenuated). To make slender or thin (as liquids).—*vi*. To diminish.

attest, at-test', *vt*. To bear witness to; to certify; to call to witness.

attestation, at-test-ā'shon, *n*. Testimony.

attic, at'tik, *a*. Pertaining to Attica or to Athens; pure; elegant in style or language.—*n*. The dialect of Attica or Athens; the uppermost story of a building; garret.

attire, at-tī r', *vt*. (attiring, attired) To dress; to array.—*n*. Dress.

attitude, at'ti-tūd, *n*. Posture.

attorney, at-tėr'ni, *n*. One who acts in place of another; one who practices in law-courts.

attractive, at-trakt'iv, *a*. Having the power of attracting; enticing.

attrition, at-tri 'shon, *n*. Act of wearing, or state of being worn, by rubbing.

audit, ä'dit, *n*. An official examination of accounts.—*vt*. To examine and adjust, as accounts.

auditory, ä'di-tō-ri, *a*. Pertaining to the sense or organs of hearing.— *n*. An audience; an auditorium.

auger, ä'gėr, *n*. An instrument for boring holes.

August, ä'gust, *n*. The eighth month of the year.

auk, äk, *n*. A swimming bird found in the British seas, with very short wings.

aunt, änt, *n*. The sister of one's father or mother.

aureate, ä-rē'āt, *a*. Golden.

aurelia, ä-rē 'li-a, *n*. The chrysalis of an insect.

aureola, aureole, ä-rē'ō-la, ä'rē-ōl n. An illumination represented as surrounding a holy person, as Christ, a halo.

Aurora Borealis, ä-rō'ra bō-rē-a'lis *n*. The northern lights or streamers.—**Aurora Australis**, a similar phenomenon in the S. hemisphere.

auspice, ä'spis, *n*. Augury from birds; protection; influence.

auspicious, ä-spi'shus, *a*. Fortunate; propitious.

austere, ä-ster', *a*. Rigid; sour; stern; severe.

autocracy, ätok'ra-si, *n*. Absolute government by one man.

autograph, ä'tō-graf, *n*. A person's own handwriting; signature.

automatic, ä-tō-mat'ik.—*a*. Self-acting; moving spontaneously.— *n*. A pistol which is reloaded by force of the recoil.

automaton, ä-tōm'ā-ton, *n; * pl. **-ta**. A self-moving machine, or one which moves by invisible machinery.

automobile, ä'tō-mo-bĕl", *n*. A motor-car or similar vehicle.

autonomy, ä-ton'o-mi, *n*. The power or right of self-government.

autopsy, ä'top-si, *n*. Personal observation, post-mortem examination.

Autumn, ä'tum, *n*. The third season of the year, between summer and winter.

avail, a-vāl', *vt*. To profit; to promote. —*vi*. To be of use; to answer the purpose.—*n*. Advantage, use.

avalanche, av'a-lansh, *n*. A large body of snow or ice sliding down a mountain.

avarice, av'a-ris, *n*. Covetousness.

average, av'ėr-ā j, *n*. Medium; mean proportion.—*a*. Medial, containing a mean proportion.—*vt*. To find the mean of.—*vi*. To form a mean.

avidity, a-vid'i-ti, *n*. Eager desire; greediness; strong appetite.

avocation, av-ōkäshon, *n*. Business; occupation.

avoid, a-void', *vt*. To shun; to evade; to make void.

avow, a-vou', *vt*. To declare with confidence, to confess frankly.

await, a-wät', *vt*. To wait for; to expect, to be in store for.

award, a-wärd', *vt*. To adjudge.—*vi*. To make an award.—*n*. A judgment; decision of arbitrators.

aware, a-wār', *a*. Informed; conscious.

away, a-wā', *adv*. Absent; at a distance; in motion from; by degrees in continuance.—*exclam*. Begone!

awe, ä, *n*. Fear; fear mingled with reverence.—*vt*. (awing, awed). To strike with fear and reverence.

awhile, a-whīl ', *adv*. For some time.

awkward, ak'wėrd, *a*. Inexpert; inelegant.

awkwardly, ak'wėrd-li, *adv*. In a bungling manner, inelegantly.

awn, än, *n*. The beard of corn or grass.

awning, än'ing, *n*. A cover of canvas, etc.; to shelter from the sun or wind.

awry, arî, *pred.a.* or *adv*. Twisted toward one side; distorted; asquint.

axe, aks, *n*. An instrument for hewing and chopping.

axilla, aks-il'la, *n*. The arm-pit.

axiom, aks'i-om, *n*. A self-evident truth.

azoic, a-zō'ik, *a*. Destitute of organic life.

azure, äzhŭr, *a*. Sky-colored.—*n*. The fine blue color of the sky; the sky.

B

Baccarat, bak-ka-rä, *n.* A game of cards played by any number and a banker.

Bacchanal, bak'ka-nal, *n.* A votary of Bacchus; a revel.—*a.* Characterized by intemperate drinking.

bachelor, bach'el-ėr, *n.* An unmarried man; one who has taken the university degree below that of Master or Doctor.

bacillus, ba-sil'lus, *n.-* *pl.* **-illi.** A microscopic organism which causes disease.

backbite, bak'bīt, *vt.* To speak evil of secretly.

backbone, bak'bō n, *n.* The spine; strength.

bacon, bā 'kn, *n.* Swine's flesh cured and dried.

Bacteriology, bak-tē'ri-ol''o-ji, *n.* The doctrine or study of bacteria.

bacterium, bak-tē'ri-um, *n.; pl.* **-ia.** A disease germ.

bad, bad, *a.* Not good; wicked; immoral; injurious; incompetent.

badge, baj, *n.* A mark or cognizance worn.

badger, baj'ėr, *n.* A burrowing quadruped, nocturnal in habits.— *vt.* To worry; to pester.

bagnio, ban'yō, *n.* A bath; brothel; prison.

bagpipe, bag'pīp, *n.* A musical wind-instrument.

bail, bā l, *vt.* To liberate from custody on security for reappearance, to free (a boat) from water; to bale.—*n.* Security given for release; the person who gives such security.

bailiff, bā 'lif, *n.* A subordinate civil officer, a steward.

bailiwick, bā 'li-wik, *n.* The extent or limit of a bailiffs jurisdiction.

balcony, bal'ko-ni, *n.* A platform projecting from a window.

bald, bäld, *a.* Wanting hair; unadorned; bare; paltry.

bale, bā l, *n.* A bundle or package of goods.—*vt.* (baling, baled). To make up in a bale; to free from water; to bail. **Bale out**, *vi.* To leave aircraft by parachute.

baleful, bāl'fül, *a.* Calamitous, deadly.

balk, bäk, *n.* A bridge of land left unploughed; a great beam; a barrier; a disappointment.—*vt.* To baffle; to disappoint.

ball, bäl, *n.* A round body, a globe; a bullet, an entertainment of dancing.—*vi.* To form, as snow, into balls, as on horses' hoofs.

ballad, bal'lad, *n.* A short narrative poem; a popular song.

ballot, bal'lot, *n.* A ball, paper, etc., used for voting in private; the system of voting by such means.—*vi.* To vote by ballot.

balm, bäm, *n.* Balsam; that which heals or soothes, the name of several aromatic plants.—*vt.* To anoint with balm, to soothe.

balsam, bäl'sam, *n.* An oily, aromatic substance got from trees; a soothing ointment.

band, band, *n.* That which binds, a bond; a fillet; a company; a body of musicians.—*vt.* To bind together, to unite in a troop or confederacy.—*vi.* To unite in a band.

bandage, band'āj, *n.* A band; a cloth for a wound, etc.—*vt.* (bandaging, bandaged). To bind with a bandage.

bandbox, band'boks, *n.* A slight box for caps, bonnets, etc.

bandit, ban'dit, *n.; pl.* **-itti, -its.** An outlaw, a robber, a highwayman.

bandolier, ban-dō-lēr', *n.* A shoulder-belt for carrying cartridges.

bank, bangk, *n.* Ground rising from the side of a river, lake, etc.; any heap piled up; a bench of rowers. place where money is deposited; a banking company.—*vt.* To fortify with a bank; to deposit in a bank.

bankrupt, bangk'rupt, *n.* One who cannot pay his debts.—*a.* Unable to pay debts.

banner, ban'nė r, *n.* A flag bearing a device or national emblem; a standard.

banquet, bang'kwet, *n.* A feast; a sumptuous entertainment.—*vt.* To treat with a feast.—*vi.* To feast.

banshee, ban'shē, *n.* An Irish fairy believed to attach herself to a house or family.

bantam, ban'tam, *n.* A small breed of domestic fowl with feathered shanks.

banter, ban'tėr, *vt.* To attack with jocularity; to rally.—*n.* Raillery; pleasantry.

barb, bärb, *n.* The points which stand backward in an arrow hook, etc.; a Barbary horse.—*vt.* To furnish with barbs or points.

barbarian, bär-ba'ri-an, *a.* Belonging to savages; uncivilized.—*n.* A savage.

barbarous, bär'bär-us, *a.* In a state of barbarism; cruel; inhuman.

barbecue, bär-be-kū , *n.* A hog, etc. roasted whole; a feast in the open air.—*vt.* To dress and roast whole.

barber, bär'bėr, *n.* One who shaves beards and dresses hair.

barge, bärj, n. A boat of pleasure or state; a flat-bottomed boat of burden.

baritone, ba'ri-tōn, a. Having a voice ranging between tenor and bass.—n. A male voice between tenor and bass.

bark, bärk, n. The outer rind of a tree, a barque, the noise made by a dog, wolf, etc.—vt. To strip bark off; to treat with bark; to make the cry of dogs, etc.

barley, bär'li, n. A species of grain used especially for making malt.

barmaid, bär'mād, n. A woman who tends a bar where liquors are sold.

barn, bärn, n. A building for grain, hay, etc.

barnacle, bär'na-kl, n. A shell-fish, often found on ships' bottoms, a species of goose.

barren, ba'ren, a. Sterile; unfruitful; unsuggestive.

barricade, ba-ri-kad', n. A temporary fortification to obstruct an enemy; a barrier.—vt. To obstruct; to bar.

barrier, ba'ri-ėr, n. Fence; obstruction.

barrister, ba'ris-tėr, n. A counselor at law; a lawyer whose profession is to speak in court on behalf of clients.

barrow, ba'rō, n. A small hand or wheel carriage; a sepulchral mound.

barter, bär'tėr, vi. To traffic by exchange.—vt. To exchange in commerce.—n. Traffic by exchange.

basalt, ba-zält', n. A dark volcanic rock, often found in columnar form.

bascule, bas'kūl, n. An arrangement in bridges by which one part balances another.

basilisk, baz'il-isk, n. A fabulous serpent, lizard, or cockatrice; a genus of crested lizards; an old kind of cannon.

basin, bā'sn, n. A broad circular dish, a reservoir, a clock; tract of country drained by a river.

basis, bās'is, n.; pl. -ses. A base; foundation; groundwork.

bask, bask, vt. To lie in warmth, or in the sun, to enjoy ease and prosperity.—vt. To warm by exposure to heat.

basket, bas'ket, n. A domestic vessel made of twigs, etc.- the contents of a basket.—vt. To put in a basket.

bass, bäs, n. The American linden a mat made of bast; a fish allied to the perch.

bass, bās, n. The lowest part in musical harmony; the lowest male voice.

bastion, bas'ti-on, n. A large mass of earth or masonry standing out from a rampart.

bat, bat, n. A flying mammal, like a mouse; a heavy stick; a club used to strike the ball in cricket, etc.— vi. (batting, batted). To play with a bat.

batch, bach, n. Quantity of bread baked at one time; a quantity.

bath, bäth, n. Place to bathe in; immersion in water, etc.; a Jewish measure.

bathe, bā TH, vt. (bathing, bathed). To immerse in water, etc.—vi. To take a bath.

battle, bat'1, n. Encounter of two armies, a combat.—vi. (battling, battled). To contend in fight.

be, bē, vi. substantive (being, been; pres. am, art, is, are; pret. was, wast or wert, were). To exist; to become, to remain.

beach, bēch, n. The shore of the sea.—vt. To run (a vessel) on a beach.

beacon, bē'kn, n. A light to direct seamen, a signal of danger.—vt. To afford light, as a beacon; to light up.

beaker, bēk'ėr, n. A large drinking cup.

beam, bēm, n. A main timber in a building. Part of a balance which sustains the scales; pole of a carriage; a ray of light.—vt. to send forth, as beams: to emit.—vi. To shine.

bean, bēn, n. A name of several kinds of pulse.

bear, bār, n. A large carnivorous plantigrade quadruped; one of two constellations, the Greater and Lesser; an uncouth person; one who tries to bring down the price of stock.

beard, bėrd, n. The hair on the chin, etc.; the awn of corn.—vt. To defy to the face.

beast, bēst, n. Any four-footed animal; a brutal man.

beatify, bē-at'i-fi, vt. (beatifying, beatified). To make happy; to declare a person blessed.

beating, bēt'ing, n. Act of striking; chastisement by blows; a conquering; defeat.

Beatitude, bē-at'i-tūd, n. Blessedness bliss, one of the declarations of blessedness to particular virtues made by Christ.

beauty, bū'ti, n. Loveliness; elegance; grace a beautiful woman.

because, bē-käz', By cause; on this account that.

bed, bed, n. Something to sleep or rest on, the channel of a river, place where anything is deposited; a layer, a stratum.— vt. (bedding, bedded). To lay in a bed; to sow; to stratify.—vi. To go to bed.

Bedouin, bed'ö-in, n. A nomadic Arab living in tents in Arabia, Syria, Egypt, etc.

bedraggle, bē-drag'l, *vt*. To soil by drawing along on mud.

bedrid, bedridden, bed'rid, bed' rid-n, *a*. Confined to bed by age or infirmity.

bedroom, bed'röm, *n*. A sleeping apartment.

bedstead, bed'sted, *n*. A frame for supporting a bed.

bee, bē *n*. The insect that makes honey.

beech, bēch, *n*. A large smoothbarked tree yielding a hard timber and nuts.

beef, bē f, *n*. The flesh of an ox, bull or cow.—*a*. Consisting of such flesh.

befit, bē-fit', *vt*. To suit; to become.

before, bē-fōr', *prep*. In front of; in presence of, earlier than; in preference to.— *adv*. In time preceding further, onward; in front

beforehand, bē-fōr'hand, *a*. In good pecuniary circumstances.— *adv*. In advance.

beg, beg, *vt*. (begging, begged). To ask in charity; to ask earnestly; to take for granted. vi. To ask or live upon alms.

beget, bē-get', *vt*. (begetting, pp. begot, begotten, pret. begot). To procreate; to produce.

beggar, beg'gėr, *n*. One who begs.—*vt*. To impoverish.

begin, bē-gin', *vi*. (pp. begun, pret. began). To take rise; to do the first act, to commence.—*vt*. To enter on to originate.

beige, bā zh, *n*. A fabric made of unbleached or undyed wool; a greyish-brown color.

being, bē'ing, *n*. Existence; a creature.

belabor, bē-lā 'bėr, *vt*. To beat soundly; to thump.

belated, bē-lāt'ed, *p.a*. Made late benighted.

believe, bē-lēv', *vt*. (believing, believed). To give belief to; to credit; to expect with confidence.—*vi*. To have a firm persuasion.

belittle, bē -lit'l, *vt*. To make smaller; to speak disparagingly.

belle, bel, *n*. A lady of great beauty.

bellicose, bel'li-kōs, *a*. Warlike; pugnacious.

belligerent, bel-lij'er-ent, *a*. Waging war.—*n*. A nation or state wag ing war.

bellow, bel'ō , *vi*. To make a hollow loud noise, as a bull; to roar.—*n*. A roar.

bellows, bel'ōz, *n.sing*. and *pl*. An instrument for blowing fires, sup plying wind to organ-pipes, etc.

bell-wether, bel'weTH-ėr, *n*. A sheep which leads the flock with a bell on his neck.

belly, bel'li, *n*. That part of the body which contains the bowels.—*vt*. and *i*. (bellying, bellied). To swell, bulge.

belong, bē -long', *vi*. To be the property; to appertain; to be connected, to have original residence.

below, bē-lō', *prep*. Under in place beneath; unworthy of—*adv*. In a lower place; beneath; on earth; in hell.

belt, belt, *n*. A girdle; a band.—*vt*. To encircle.

bemoan, bē mōn', *vt*. To lament; bewail.

bemused, bē-mū zd', *a*. Muddled stupefied.

bench, bensh, *n*. A long seat; seat of justice; body of judges.—*vt*. To furnish with benches.

bend, bend, *vt*. (pp. and pret. bent and bended). To curve, to direct to a certain point; to subdue.—*vi*. To become crooked; to lean or turn; to yield.—*n*. A curve.

beneath, bē-nē th', *prep*. Under lower in place, rank, dignity, etc., unworthy of.— *adv*. Ina, lower, place, below.

benediction, ben-ē-dik'shon, *n*. Act of blessing; invocation of happiness.

benefaction, ben-ē-fak'shon, *n*. The doing of a benefit; a benefit conferred.

benefactor, ben-ē-fak 'tėr, *n*. He who confers a benefit.

benefit, ben-ē-fit, *n*. An act of kindness; a favor; advantage.—*vt*. To do a service to.—*vi*. To gain advantage.

benevolent, bē -nev'ō-lent, *a*. Kind charitable.

benumb, bē-num', *vt*. To deprive of sensation; to make torpid; to stupefy.

Benzene, ben'zēn, *n*. A liquid used to remove grease spots, etc.

beset, bē-set', *vt*. (besetting beset). To surround, to press on ail sides.

beside, besides, bē-sīd', bē-sīdz' *prep*. By the side of, near, over and above; distinct from.—*adv*. Moreover, in addition.

besiege, bē-sēj', *vt*. (besieging, besieged). To lay siege to; to beset.

besom, be'zum, *n*. A brush of twigs; a broom.

besot, bē-sot', *vt*. (besotting, besotted). To make sottish.

bespangle, bē-spang'gl, *vt*. To adorn with spangles.

bespatter, bēspat'tėr, *vt*. To spatter over.

bespeak, bē-spē k', *vt*. (pp. bespoke, bespoken, pret. bespoke). To speak for beforehand; to indicate.

Bessemer-steel, bes'e-mer-stēl *n*. Steel made directly from molten cast-iron by driving through it air to carry off impurities.

bestial, bes'ti-al, *a*. Belonging to a beast; brutish; vile.

Bestiary, bes'ti-a-ri, *n*. A book of the middle ages treating fancifully of beasts.

bestir, bē-stėr', *vt*. To stir up to put into brisk action. (Usually with refl. pron.)

bestow, bē-stō', *vt*. To lay up; to give; to confer; to dispose of; to apply.

bestride, bē-strid', *vt*. (pp. bestrid, bestridden, pret. bestrid, bestrode). To stride over, to place a leg on each side of.

bet, bet, *n*. A wager; that which is pledged in a contest.—*vt*. (betting, betted). To wager.

betray, bē-trā', *vt*. To disclose treacherously, to entrap.

betroth, bē-trō TH', *vt*. To affiance; to pledge to marriage.

between, bē-twēn', *prep*. In the middle, from one to another of, belonging to two.

beverage, bev'ėr-āj, *n*. Drink; liquor.

bevy, be'vi, *n*. A flock of birds; a company of females.

bewail, bē-wā l', *vt*. To lament.—*vi*. To utter deep grief.

beware, bē-wār', *vi*. To take care (with *of*).

bewilder, bē-wil'dė r *vt*. To confuse; to perplex.

bewitch, bē-wich', *vt*. To enchant; to fascinate; to overpower by charms.

beyond, bē-yond', *prep*. On the further side of; farther onward than; out of the reach of, above.—*adv*. At a distance.

Bible, bī'bl, *n*. The Holy Scriptures.

bibliography, bib-li-og'ra-fi, *n*. A history of books and their editions; list of books by one author or on one subject.

bicycle, bī'si-kl, *n*. A two-wheeled vehicle propelled by the rider.

bid, bid, *vt*. (bidding, pp. bid, bidden, pret. bid, bade). To ask, to order; to offer.—*n*. An offer, as at an auction.

bidding, bid'ing, *n*. Invitation; order; offer.

bide, bīd, *vi*. (biding, bode). To dwell; to remain.—*vt*. To endure; to abide.

bier, bē r, *n*. A carriage or frame for conveying a corpse to the grave.

bile, bīl, *n*. A yellowish bitter liquid secreted in the liver; spleen; anger.

bilingual, bī-lin 'gwal, *a*. In two languages.

biliteral, bī-lit 'er-al, *a*. Consisting of two letters.

bilk, bilk, *vt*. To defraud, to elude.

bimonthly, bī-munth'li, *a*. Occur-ring

every two months.

bin, bin, *n*. A receptacle for corn, etc., a partition in a wine-cellar.

binary, bi'na-ri, *a*. Twofold.

biographer, bī-og'ra-fė r, *n*. A writer of biography.

Biography, bī-og'ra-fi, *n*. An account of one's life and character.

Biology, bī-ol'o-ji, *n*. The science of life.

bioplasm, bī'ō-plazm, *n*. The germinal matter in plants and animals.

bipartite, bī-pärt'-ī, *a*. Having two parts.

biped, bī'ped, *n*. An animal with two feet.

birch, bė rch, *n*. A tree having small leaves, white bark, and a fragrant odor.

bismuth, bis'muth, *n*. A brittle yellowish or reddish-white metal.

bison, bī'zon, *n*. A quadruped of the ox family; the American buffalo.

bisque, bisk, *n*. Unglazed white porcelain; odds given at tennis, etc.

bit, bit, *n*. A morsel, fragment, the metal part of a bridle inserted in a horse's mouth; a boring tool.—*vt*. (bitting, bitted). To put the bit in the mouth.

bitch, bich, *n*. A female dog; a name of reproach for a woman.

biting, bī-t'ing, *p.a*. Sharp; severe; sarcastic.

bitter, bit'ėr, *a*. Sharp to the taste severe; painful; calamitous; distressing.

biweekly, bī-wek'li, *a*. Occurring every two weeks.

bizarre, bi-zär', *a*. Odd, fantastical.

blab, blab, *vt*. (blabbing, blabbed). To tell indiscreetly.—*vi*. To talk indiscreetly.

blackberry, blak'be-ri, *n*. A plant of the bramble kind, and its fruit.

blackbird, blak'bė rd, *n*. A species of thrush.

blackboard, blak'bō-rd, *n*. A board for writing on with chalk for instruction.

blacken, blak'n, *vt*. To make black; to defame.—*vi*. To grow black or dark.

blackguard, blak'gärd or bla'gärd, *n*. A scoundrel.—*vt*. To revile in scurrilous language.

black-sheep, blak'shēp, *n*. One whose conduct is discreditable.

blacksmith, blak'smith, *n*. A smith who works in iron.

blackthorn, blak'thorn, *n*. The sloe.

bladder, blad'ėr, *n*. A thin sac in animals containing the urine, bile, etc.; a blister; anything like the animal bladder.

blade, blā d, *n*. A leaf; cutting part of a sword, knife, etc.; flat part of an oar.

blame, blā m, *vt*. (blaming, blamed). To censure, to reprimand.—*n*. Censure;

fault.

blanch, blansh, *vt.* To make white.—*vi.* To grow white; to bleach.

blare, blā r, *vi.* (blaring, blared). To give forth a loud sound.—*vt.* To sound loudly; to proclaim noisily.—*n.* Sound like that of a trumpet; roar.

blarney, blär'ni, *n.* Excessively complimentary language; gammon.—*vt.* To flatter.

blase, blä-zā , *a.* Satiated; used up; bored.

blaspheme, blas-fēm', *vt.* (blaspheming, blasphemed). To speak irreverently of, as of God; to speak evil of.—*vi.* To utter blasphemy.

blatant, blā̆tant, *a.* Bellowing; noisy.

blemish, blem'ish, *vt.* To mar, to tarnish.—*n.* A mark of imperfection; dishonor.

blend, blend, vt. To mix together.— *vi.* To be mixed.—*n.* A mixture.

blindfold, blīnd'fō ld, *a.* Having the eyes covered.—*vt.* To cover the eyes of.

blindness, blīnd'nes, *n.* Want of sight or discernment, ignorance.

blink, blingk, *vi.* To wink; to twinkle.—*vt.* To shut the eyes upon; to avoid.—*n.* A twinkle; a glimpse or glance.

blinker, bling'kẻr, *n.* A flap to prevent a horse from seeing sideways.

bliss, blis, *n.* Blessedness; perfect happiness.

blister, blis 'tẻr, *n.* A thin bladder on the skin; a pustule, something to raise a blister.—*vi.* To rise in blisters.—*vt.* To raise a blister or blisters on, to apply a blister to.

blithe, blīTH, *a.* Joyful; gay; mirth.

blockade, blok-ā d', *n.* A close siege by troops or ships.—*vt.* (blockading, blockaded). To besiege closely.

blockhead, blok'hed, *n.* A stupid fellow.

blond, blonde, blond, *a.* Of a fair complexion.—*n.* A person of fair complexion.

blood-hound, blud'hound, *n.* A hound of remarkably acute smell.

blossom, blos 'om, *n.* The flower of a plant.—*vi.* To bloom: to flower; to flourish.

blot, blot, *vt.* (blotted, blotting). To spot, to stain, to cancel (with out) to dry.—*n.* A spot or stain; an obliteration.

blotch, bloch, *n.* Pustule upon the skin; an eruption; a confused patch of color.

blotter, blot'ẻr, *n.* One who blots; a piece of blotting-paper.

blouse, blouz, *n.* A light loose upper garment.

bluebell, blü'bel, *n.* The wild hyacinth (in England), the harebell (in Scotland).

blue-stocking, blü'stok-ing, *n.* A learned and pedantic lady.

blue-stone, blü'stōn, *n.* Sulphate of copper.

bluff, bluf, *a.* Steep; blustering; burly, hearty.—*n.* A steep projecting bank.—*vt.* and *i.* To impose on by a show of boldness or strength.

blunder, blun'dẻ r, *vi.* To err stupidly; to stumble.—*vt.* To confound.—*n.* A gross mistake, error.

blunt, blunt, *a.* Dull on the edge or point; not sharp; dull in understanding, unceremonious.—*vt.* To make blunt or dull.

blur, blẻr, *n.* A stain; a blot.—*vt.* (blurring, blurred). To stain, to obscure; to render indistinct.

boarder, bord'ẻr, *n.* One who receives food and lodging at a stated charge; one who boards a ship in action.

boarding-school, bō rd'ing-sköl, *n.* A school which supplies board as well as tuition.

boast, bō st, *vi.* To brag; to talk ostentatiously.—*vt.* To brag of; to magnify.—*n.* A vaunting; the cause of boasting.

boat, bō t, *n.* A small open vessel usually impelled by oars, a small ship.—*vt.* To transport in a boat.— *vi.* To go in a boat.

boatswain, bō'sn, *n.* A ship's officer who has charge of boats, sails, etc.

body, bo'di, *n.* The trunk of an animal; main part, matter, a persona system; strength; reality; any solid figure.—*vt.* (bodying, bodied). To give a body to; to embody (with *forth*).

boisterous, bois'tẻr-us, *a.* Stormy; noisy.

bold, bō ld, *a.* Daring; courageous; impudent, steep and abrupt.

bole, bōl, *n.* The body or stem of a tree; a kind of fine clay.

Bolero, bō-lār'ō, *n.* A Spanish dance.

bolster, bō l'stẻr, *n.* A long pillow; a pad.—*vt.* To support with a bolster; to hold up; to maintain.

bondage, bond'āj, *n.* Slavery; thraldom.

bonded, bond'ed, *a.* Secured by bond; under a bond to pay duty containing goods liable to duties.

bonfire, bon'fīr, *n.* A large fire in the open air expressive of joy.

book-maker, bük'mak-ẻr, *n.* One who compiles books, one who bets systematically.

bookworm, bük'wẻrm, *n.* A worm that eats holes in books, a close student of books.

boomerang, bōm'e-rang, *n.* An Australian missile of hard wood, which can return to hit an object behind the thrower.

boon, bön, *n.* Answer to a prayer; a favor, gift, or grant.—*a.* Merry; pleasant.

boor, bör, *n.* A rustic; an ill-mannered or illiterate fellow.

boot, böt, *vt.* To benefit; to put on boots.—*n.* Profit, a covering for the foot and leg; *pl.* a male servant in a hotel.

bore, bōr, *vt.* (boring, bored). To make a hole in, to weary.—*vi.* To pierce.—*n.* The hole made by boring; the diameter of a round hole; a person or thing that wearies; a sudden rise of the tide in certain estuaries.

bosky, bosk'i, *a.* Woody or bushy.

bosom, bö'zum, *n.* The breast; the seat of the affections.—*vt.* To conceal.—*a.* Much beloved; confidential.

boss, bos, *n.* A knob; an ornamental projection; a master.

Botany, bot'a-ni *n.* The science which treats of plants.

botch, boch, *n.* A swelling on the skin; a clumsy patch; bungled work.—*vt.* To mend or perform clumsily.

both, bōth, *a.* and *pron.* The two taken by themselves; the pair.— *conj.* As well; on the one side.

bother, boTH'er, *vt.* To annoy.—*vi.* To trouble oneself.—*n.* A trouble, vexation.

bothersome, boTH'èr-sum, *a.* Causing trouble.

bott, **bot**, bot, *n.* A maggot found in the intestines of horses, etc.: generally in *pl.*

bound, bound, *n.* A boundary; a leap.—*vt.* To limit, to restrain.—*vi.* To leap, to rebound.—*p.a.* Obliged; sure.—*a.* Ready; destined.

boundary, bound'a-ri, *n.* A mark designating a limit, border.

bountiful, boun'ti-ful, *a.* Munificent, generous.

bounty, boun'ti, *n.* Liberality; generosity; a gratuity; premium to encourage trade.

bow, bō , *n.* An instrument to shoot arrows; the rainbow; a curve; a fiddle-stick an ornamental knot.

bowel, bou'el, *n.* One of the intestines; *pl.* the intestines; the seat of pity, compassion.

bower, bou'èr, *n.* An anchor carried at the bow; a shady recess; an arbor.

Bowie-knife, bō'i-nīf, *n.* A knife from 10 to 15 inches long and about 2 inches broad.

bowler, bō l'è r, *n.* One who bowls; a round-shaped felt hat.

bowling, bōl'ing, *n.* Act or art of playing with bowls; art or style of a bowler.

bowman, bō'man, *n.* An archer.

bowsprit, bō'sprit, *n.* A large spar which projects over the bow of a ship.

boxwood, boks'wüd, *n.* The hardgrained wood of the box-tree; the plant itself.

boy, boi, *n.* A male child, a lad.

brackish, brak'ish, *a.* Salt; saltish.

bract, brakt, *n.* An irregularly developed leaf at the base of a flower.

brad, brad, *n.* A small nail with no head.

brag, brag, *vi.* (bragging, bragged). To bluster; to talk big.—*n.* A boast.

brake, brāk, *n.* A place overgrown with brushwood, etc., a thicket; the bracken; an instrument to break flax; a harrow for breaking clods; a contrivance for retarding the motion of wheels; a large wagonette.

bramble, bram'bl, *n.* A prickly shrub of the rose family; its berry.

bran, bran, *n.* The husks of ground corn.

branch, bransh, *n.* The shoot of a or plant; the offshoot of anything, as of a river, family, etc.; a limb.—*vi.* To spread in branches.—*vt.* To divide or form into branches.

bravado, bra-vä'dō, *n.* A boast or rag; would-be boldness.

brave, brāv, *a.* Daring; bold; valiant; noble.—*n.* A daring person, a savage warrior.—*vt.* (braving, braved). To challenge; to defy; to encounter with courage.

brawl, bräl, *vi.* To quarrel noisily.—*n.* A noisy quarrel, uproar.

brawn, brän, *n.* The flesh of a boar; the muscular part of the body; muscle.

bray, brā, *vt.* To beat or grind small.—*vi.* To make a loud harsh sound, as an ass.—*n.* The cry of an ass.

braze, brā z, *vt.* (brazing, brazed). To cover with brass; to solder with brass.

breaker, brā k'er, *n.* One who or that which breaks; a rock; a wave broken by rocks.

breakwater, brā k 'wa-tè r, *n.* A mole to break the force of the waves.

bream, brēm, *n.* A fish.—*vt.* To clean a ship's bottom by means of fire.

breath, breth *n.* The air drawn into and expelled from the lungs; life; a single respiration; pause; a gentle breeze.

breech, brē ch, *n.* The lower part of the body behind; the hinder part of a gun, etc.—*vt.* To put into breeches.

bribe, brīb, *n.* A gift to corrupt the conduct or judgment.—*vt.* (bribing bribed).

To gain over by bribes.

bric-a-brac, brik-a-brak, *n.* Articles of interest or value from rarity, antiquity, etc.

brick, brik, *n.* A rectangular mass of burned clay, used in building, etc., a loaf shaped like a brick.—*a.* Made of brick.—*vt.* To lay with bricks.

bridal, brī d'al, *n.* A wedding-feast a wedding.—*a.* Belonging to a bride or to a wedding.

bride, brīd, *n.* A woman about to be or newly married.

bridegroom, brī d'gröm, *n.* A man about to be or newly married.

bride's-maid, brīdz'mād, *n.* A woman who attends on a bride at her wedding.

bridge, brij, *n.* A structure across a river, etc., to furnish a passage; the upper part of the nose.—*vt.* (bridging, bridged). To build a bridge over.

brier, brī'ėr, *n.* A prickly shrub, species of the rose.

brig, brig, *n.* A vessel with two masts, square-rigged.

brigand, bri'gand, *n.* A freebooter.

brigantine, brig'an-tīn, *n.* A light swift vessel two-masted and square-rigged.

bright, brīt, *a.* Clear; shining; glittering; acute; witty; lively; cheer-

brim, brim, *n.* The rim of anything; the upper edge of the mouth of a vessel.—*vi.* (brimming, brimmed). To be full to the brim.

brimstone, brim'stön, *n.* sulphur.

brindled, brind'ld, *a.* Marked with brown streaks.

brine, brīn, *n.* Salt water, the sea.

bring, bring, *vt.* (bringing, brought). To lead or cause to come; to fetch; to produce; to attract; to prevail upon.

brink, bringk, *n.* The edge of a steep place.

broach, brōch, *n.* A spit a brooch.—*vt.* To pierce, as with a spit; to tap; to open up; to publish first.

broad, bräd, *a.* Having extent from side to side; wide; unrestricted; indelicate.

broaden, bräd'n, *vi.* To grow broad.—*vt.* To make broad.

broadside, brad'sīd, *n.* A discharge of all the guns on one side of a ship; a sheet of paper printed on one side.

brocade, brō-kād', *n.* A silk or satin stuff variegated with gold and silver.

broccoli, brok'o-li, *n.* A kind of cauliflower.

bronchial, brong'ki-al, *a.* Belonging to the tubes branching from the windpipe

through the lungs.

bronchitis, brong-kī'tis *n.* Inflammation of the bronchial tubes.

brother, bruTH'ėr, *n.; pl.* **brothers, brethren**, bruTH'ėrz, breTH'ren. A male born of the same parents, an associate a fellow-creature.

browse, brouz, *vt.* (browsing, browsed). To pasture or feed upon.—*vi.* To crop and eat food.

bruin, brö'in, *n.* A familiar name of a bear.

brusque, brusk, *a.* Abrupt in manner, rude.

brussels-sprouts, brus'elz-sprouts, *n.pl.* A variety of cabbage.

brutal, bröt'al, *a.* Cruel, ferocious.

brute, bröt, *a.* Senseless; bestial; uncivilized.—*n.* A beast; a brutal person.

bubo, bū'bö , *n.,* pl. **-oes**. A swelling or abscess in a glandular part of the body.

bubonic, bū-bon'ik, *a.* Pertaining to bubo.

buccaneer, buk-a-nēr', *n.* A pirate.

buck, buk, *n.* The male of deer goats, etc., a gay young fellow; a lye for steeping clothes in.—*vt.* To steep in lye.—*vi.* To leap, as a horse, so as to dismount the rider.

bucket, buk 'et, *n.* A vessel in which water is drawn or carried.

buck-shot, buk'shot, *n.* A large kind of shot used for killing large game.

buckwheat, buk'whēt, *n.* A plant bearing small seeds which are ground into meal.

bucolic, bū-kol'ik, *a.* Pastoral.—*n.* A pastoral poem.

buffalo, buf'fa-lö, *n.* A species of ox larger than the common ox; the American bison.

buffer, buf'ėr, *n.* An apparatus for deadening concussion.

buffet, buf'et, *n.* A cupboard for wine, glasses, etc.; a place for refreshments (pron. bu-fe).

buffet, buf'et, *n.* A blow; a slap.—*vt.* To beat; to box; to contend against.

buffoon, buf-fön', *n.* One who makes sport by low jests and antic gestures; a droll.

bug, bug, *n.* A name for various insects, particularly one infesting houses and inflicting severe bites.

bulb, bulb, *n.* A round root; a round protuberance.

bulbul, bül'bül, *n.* The Persian nightingale.

bulge, bulj, *n.* A swelling, bilge.—*vi.* (bulging, bulged). To swell out, to be protuberant.

bulk, bulk, *n.* Magnitude; the majority; extent.

bull-frog, bül'frog, *n.* A large species of frog in N. America, with a loud bass voice.

bullion, bül'yon, *n.* Uncoined gold or silver.

bull's-eye, bülz'ī, *n.* A circular opening for light or air; the center of a target.

bully, bül'i, *n.* An overbearing quarrelsome fellow.—*vt.* (bullying bullied). To insult and overbear.— *vi.* To bluster or domineer.

bulrush, bül'rush, *n.* A large strong kind of rush.

bulwark, bül'werk, *n.* A bastion, a fortification; a means of defense or safety.

bumble-bee, bum'bl-bē, *n.* A large bee.

bumpkin, bump'kin, *n.* An awkward rustic; a lout.

bun, bun, *n.* A kind of cake or sweet bread.

bunch, bunsh, *n.* A knob or lump; a cluster.—*vi.* To swell out in a protuberance; to cluster.

bundle, bun'dl, *n.* A number of things bound together; a package.—*vt.* (bundling, bundled). To tie in a bundle; to dispose of hurriedly.—*vt.* To depart hurriedly.

bung, bung, *n.* The stopper of a cask.—*vt.* To stop with a bung; to close up.

bungalow, bung'ga-lō, *n.* A single-storied house.

buoy, boi, *n.* A floating mark to point out shoals, etc.; something to keep a person or thing up in the water.—*vt.* To keep afloat; to bear up.—*vi.* To float.

buoyant, boi'ant, *a.* Floating; light; elastic.

burglar, berg'ler, *n.* One who robs a house by night.

burgundy, ber'gun-di, *n.* A kind of wine, so called from Burgundy in France.

burnish, ber'nish, *vt.* To polish.—*vi.* To grow bright or glossy.—*n.* Gloss; luster.

burr, ber, *n.* A guttural sounding of the letter r; a rough or projecting ridge; bur

burrow, bu'rō , *n.* A hole in the earth made by rabbits, etc.— *vi.* To excavate a hole underground; to hide.

bury, be'ri, *vt.* (burying, buried). To put into a grave; to overwhelm; to hide.

bush, büsh, *n.* A shrub with branches; a thicket; the backwoods of Australia, a lining of hard metal in the nave of a wheel, etc.—*vi.* To grow bushy.

bushel, büsh'el, *n.* A dry measure containing eight gallons or four pecks.

business, biz'nes, *n.* Occupation concern; trade.—*a.* Pertaining to traffic, trade, etc.

butter, but'ter, *n.* An oily substance obtained from cream by churning, any substance resembling butter. —*vt.* To spread with butter; to flatter grossly.

butterfly, but'ter-flī, *n.* The name of a group of winged insects.

buttermilk, but'er-milk, *n.* The milk that remains after the butter is separated.

buttock, but'tok, *n.* The protuberant part of the body behind; the rump.

button, but'n, *n.* A knob to fasten the parts of dress; a knob or stud; *pl.* a page-boy.—*vt.* To fasten with buttons.

buxom, buks'um, *a.* Gay; brisk; wanton.

buy, bī, *vt.* (buying, bought). To acquire by payment' to purchase; to bribe.—*vi.* To negotiate or treat about a purchase.

buzz, buz, *vi.* To hum, as bees; to whisper.—*vt.* To whisper.—*n.* The noise of bees, a confused humming noise.

by, bī, *prep.* Used to denote the instrument, agent, or manner, at near, beside, through or with, in, for; according to; at the rate of; not later than.—*adv.* Near; passing. In *composition,* secondary, side.

Byzantine, biz-an'tīn or biz', *a.* Pertaining to Byzantium or Constantinople and the Greek Empire of which it was the capital.

C

cabal, ka-bal', *n.* An intrigue; persons united in some intrigue. —*vi.* (caballing, caballed). To combine in plotting.

cabaret, kab-a-ret, ka-ba-rā, *n.* A tavern; a restaurant in which singing and dancing performances are given.

cabbage, kab'ā j, *n.* A culinary vegetable.—*vt.* (cabbaging, cabbaged). To purloin, especially pieces of cloth.

cabin, kab'in, *n.* A hut; an apartment in a ship.—*vt.* To confine, as in a cabin.

cabinet, kab'in-et, *n.* A closet; a small room; a set of drawers for curiosities; the ministers of state.

cacophony, ka-kof'ō -ni, *n.* Unpleasant vocal sound; a discord.

cactus, kak'tus, *n.*; pl. **-tuses** or **-ti**. A spiny shrub of numerous species.

caisson, kas'son, *n.* An ammunition chest; a structure to raise sunken vessels; a structure used in laying foundations in deep water.

cajole, ka-jōl', *vt.* (cajoling, cajoled). To coax; to court; to deceive by flattery.

Caledonian, kal-i-dō'ni-an, *a.* Pertaining to Scotland.—*n.* A Scot.

Calends, ka'lendz, *n.pl.* Among the Romans, the first day of each month.

calf, käf, *n.*, pl. **calves**, kävz. The young of the cow, a kind of leather the fleshy part of the leg below the knee.

calico, ka'li-kō, *n.* Cotton cloth.

calligraphy, kal-lig'ra-fi, *n.* The art of beautiful writing; penmanship.

calling, käl'ing, *n.* Vocation; profession.

calipers, kal'i-pè rz, *n.pl.* Compasses for measuring caliber.

callosity, ka-los'i-ti, *n.* Hardness of skin; horny hardness.

callous, kal'us, *a.* Hardened; unfeeling; obdurate.

caloric, ka-lo'rik, *n.* The principle or simple element of heat, heat.

calumet, kal'ū -met, *n.* The North American Indians' pipe of peace.

camera, kam'è -ra, *n.* An arched roof; a council chamber; an apparatus for taking photographs.

camomile kam'ō-mil, *n.* A bitter medicinal plant.

camouflage, kam-ö-fläzh, *n.* The art of disguising; especially the art of disguising material in warfare.

camp, kamp, *n.* The ground on which an army pitch their tents; an encampment.—*vi.* To pitch a camp; to encamp.

campaign, kam-pän', *n.* The time an army keeps the field every year, during a war; its operations.—*vi.* To serve in a campaign.

campanile, kam-pa-nē'lā or kam' pa-nīl, *n.*; pl. **-ili** or **-iles**. A belltower.

campion, kam'pi-on, *n.* A popular name of certain plants of the Pink family.

can, kan, *n.* A cup or vessel for liquors.

can, kan, *vi.* (pret. could). To be able, to have sufficient moral or physical power.

canal, ka-nal', *n.* A channel; an artificial water-course for boats; a duct of the body.

canard, ka-när or ka-närd', *n.* An absurd story; a false rumor.

cancel, kan'sel, *vt.* (cancelling cancelled). To obliterate, to revoke, to set aside.—*n.* Act of cancelling.

Cancer, kan'sèr, *n.* One of the signs of the zodiac, a malignant growth in the body.

candid, kan'did, *a.* Sincere; ingenuous.

candidate, kan'di-dā t, *n.* One who proposes himself, or is proposed for some office; one who aspires after preferment.

candied, kan'did, *a.* Preserved with sugar, or incrusted with it.

candle, kan'dl, *n.* A cylindrical body of tallow wax, etc., surrounding a wick and used for giving light.

candlestick, kan'dl-stik, *n.* An instrument to hold a candle.

cane, kān, *n.* A reed; a walking-stick.—*vt.* (caning, caned). To beat with a cane.

canine, ka'nīn, *a.* Pertaining to dogs.

cannon, kan'un, *n.* A great gun the striking of a ball on two other balls successively.—*vi.* To strike with rebounding collision; to make a cannon at billiards.

canny, cannie, kan'i, *a.* Cautious; wary.

canoe, ka-nö', *n.* A boat made of the trunk of a tree, or of bark or skins; a light boat propelled by Paddles.

cantankerous, kan-tang'kèr-us, *a.* Ill-natured; cross; contentious.

cantata, kan-tä'ta, *n.* A short musical composition in the form of an oratorio.

canteen, kan-tēn', *n.* A vessel used by soldiers for carrying liquor, a place in barracks where provisions, etc., are sold.

canvas, kan'vas, *n.* A coarse cloth; sailcloth, sails of ships, cloth for painting on, a painting.

canvass, kan'vas, *vt.* To scrutinize; to solicit the votes of—*vi.* To solicit votes or interest, to use efforts to obtain.—*n.*

Scrutiny; solicitation of votes.

capable, kā'pa-bl, *a.* Having sufficient skill or power; competent; susceptible.

capacious, ka-pā'shus, *a.* Wide; large; comprehensive.

capacitate, ka-pas'i-tāt, *vt.* To make able; to qualify.

capacity, ka-pas'i-ti, *n.* Power of holding; extent of space; ability; state.

capital, kap'it-al, *a.* First in importance, metropolitan, affecting the head, punishable with death.—*n.* The uppermost part of a column; the chief city, the stock of a bank tradesman, etc.; a large letter or type.

capitalist, kap'it-al-ist, *n.* A man who has a capital or wealth.

capsicum, kap'si-kum, *n.* The generic name of some tropical plants yielding chilies and cayenne pepper.

capsize, kap-sīz', *vt.* (capsizing, capsized). to upset or overturn.

captain, kap'tin, *n.* A head officer the commander of a ship, troop of horse, or company of infantry; a leader.

caption, kap'shon, *n.* Seizure; arrest; heading or short title of a division of a book, or of a scene in a cinematograph film.

captious, kap'shus, *a.* Ready to find fault; carping.

captive, kap'tiv, *n.* One taken in war, one ensnared by love, beauty etc.—*a.* Make prisoner; kept in bondage.

capture, kap'tūr, *n.* Act of taking the thing taken.—*vt.* (capturing' captured). To take by force or stratagem.

caravan, ka'ra-van, *n.* A company of travelers associated together for safety, a large close carriage.

caraway, ka'ra-wā, *n.* A biennial, aromatic Plant whose seeds are used in baking, etc.

carbide, kär'bīd, *n.* A compound of carbon with a metal.

carbine, kär'bīn, *n.* A short-barreled rifle used by cavalry, police, etc.

carbolic, kär-bol'ik, *a.* An antiseptic and disinfecting acid obtained from coal-tar.

carbon, kär'bon, *n.* Pure charcoal an elementary substance, bright and brittle.

carbonate, kär'bon-āt, *n.* A salt formed by the union of carbonic acid with a base.

carbuncle, kär'bung-kl, *n.* A fiery red precious stone; an inflammatory tumor.

carburetor, kär'bū-ret-ėr, *n.* A device for vaporizing the light oil fuel used in the engines of motorcars, airplanes, etc.

carcas, kär'kas, *a.* A dead body anything decayed; a framework; a kind of bomb

care, kār, *n.* Solicitude; attention; object of watchful regard.—*vi.* (caring, cared). To be solicitous; to be inclined; to have regard.

caress, ka-res', *vt.* To fondle, to embrace affectionately.—*n.* An act of endearment.

caret, ka'ret, *n.* In writing, this mark, A, noting insertion.

carious, kā'ri-us, *a.* Ulcerated; decayed.

carminative, kär'min-āt-iv, *n.* A medicine for flatulence, etc.

carmine, kär'min, *n.* A bright crimson color.

carnage, kär'nāj, *n.* Great slaughter in war, massacre, butchery.

carnal, kär'nal, *a.* Fleshly; sensual.

carotid, ka-rot'id, *a.* Pertaining to the two great arteries in the neck conveying the blood to the head.

carrion, ka'ri-on, *n.* Dead and putrefying flesh.—*a.* Relating to putrefying carcasses; feeding on carrion.

carrot, ka'rot, *n.* A yellowish or reddish esculent root of a tapering form.

carry, ka'ri, *vt.* (carrying, carried). To bear, convey, or transport, to gain, to capture, to import, to behave.—*vi.* To convey; to propel.—*n.* Onward motion.

cart, kärt, *n.* A carriage of burden with two wheels.—*vt.* To carry or place on a cart.

carte-blanche, kärt-blänsh, *n.* A blank paper; unconditional terms.

cartel, kär'tel, *n.* A challenge; an agreement for the exchange of prisoners.

cartography, kär-tog'ra-fi, *n.* The art or practice of drawing up charts.

cartoon, kär-tön', *n.* A drawing for a fresco or tapestry; a pictorial sketch relating to a prevalent topic.

cartouch, kär-tösh', *n.* A cartridge or cartridge-box; a sculptured ornament.

cartridge, kär'trij, *n.* A case containing the charge of a gun or any firearm.

carve, kärv, *vt.* (carving, carved). To cut, to engrave, to shape by cutting.—*vi.* To cut up meat; to sculpture.

cash, kash, *n.* Money; ready money; coin.—*vt.* To turn into money.

cashmere, kash'mēr *n.* A rich kind of shawl, a fine woolen stuff.

casino, ka-sē'nō, *n.* A public dancing, singing, or gaming saloon.

castor, kas'tėr, *n.* A small cruet, a small wheel on the leg of a table, etc.

castor-oil, kas'tėr-oil, *n.* A medicinal oil obtained from a tropical Plant.

castrate, kas'trāt, *vt.* (castrating, castrated). To geld; to emasculate; to expurgate.

cast-steel, kast'stēl, *n.* Steel melted and cast into ingots and rolled into bars.

casual, ka'zhūal, *a.* Happening by chance; occasional; contingent.

casualty, ka'zhū-al-ti, *n.* Accident, especially one resulting in death or injury; death or injury caused by enemy action.

casuistry, ka'zū -is-tri, *n.* The science of determining cases of conscience; sophistry.

cataclysm, kat'a-klizm, *n.* A deluge; a sudden overwhelming catastrophe.

catapult, kat'a-pult, *n.* An apparatus for throwing stones, etc.

cataract, kat'a-rakt, *n.* A great waterfall; a disease of the eye.

catarrh, ka-tär', *n.* A flow of mucus from the nose, etc.; a cold.

catastrophe, ka-tas'trō-fē, *n.* Calamity or disaster, final event.

catechism, ka'tē-kizm, *n.* A manual of instruction by questions and answers, especially in religion.

catgut, kat'gut, *n.* The intestines of a cat; intestines made into strings for musical instruments, etc.; a kind of linen or canvas.

cathartic, ka-thär'tik, *a.* Purging.—*n.* A medicine that purges.

cathedral, ka-thē'dral, *n.* The principal church in a diocese.

catheter, kath'e-tėr, *n.* A tubular instrument, to be introduced into the bladder.

cathode, kath'ōd, *n.* The negative pole of an electric current.

cattle, kat'til, *n.pl.* Domestic quadrupeds serving for tillage or food; bovine animals.

caucus, kä'kus, *n.* A Private committee to manage election matters.

caudal, kä'dal, *a.* Pertaining to a tail.

caul, käl, *n.* A net for the hair; a membrane investing some part of the intestines.

caulk, käk, *vt.* To drive oakum into the seams of (a ship) to prevent leaking.

causative, käz'a-tiv, *a.* That expresses a cause or reason that effects.

cause, käz, *n.* That which produces an effect, reason, origin, sake, purpose, a suit in court; that which a person or party espouses.—*vt.* (causing, caused). To effect; to bring about.

causeway, causey, käz'wā , käz'i, *n.* A raised road, a paved way.

caustic, käs'tik, *a.* Burning; corroding; cutting.—*n.* A substance which burns the flesh.

cauterization, kä'ter-īz-ā"shon, *n.* Act of cauterizing.

cavern, ka'vėrn, *n.* A large cave.

caviare, caviar, ka-vi-är', *n.* The roe of the sturgeon salted and prepared for food.

cavil, ka'vil, *vi.* (caviling, caviled). To carp, to find fault with insufficient reason.—*n.* A captious objection.

cavity, ka'vi-ti, *n.* A hollow place.

cayenne, kā-en', *n.* A pepper made from capsicum seeds.

cease, sēs, *vi.* (ceasing, ceased). To leave off, to fail, to stop, to become extinct.—*vt.* To put a stop to.

celestial, sē-les'ti-al, *a.* Heavenly pertaining to heaven.—*n.* An inhabitant of heaven.

celibacy, se'li-ba-si, *n.* The unmarried state; a single life.

celibate, se'li-bāt, *n.* One who intentionally remains unmarried.— *a.* Unmarried.

cell, sel, *n.* A small room, a cave, a small mass of protoplasm forming the structural unit in animal tissues.

cemetery, se'mē-te-ri, *n.* A burial place.

cenotaph, sen'ō-taf, *n.* A monument to one who is buried elsewhere.

censorious, sen-sō'ri-us, *a.* Addicted to censure.

census, sen'sus, *n.* An enumeration of the inhabitants of a country.

cent, sent, *n.* A hundred; a copper coin in America etc., the hundredth part of a dollar. *Per cent,* a certain rate by the hundred.

centipede, sen'ti-pēd, *n.* An insect having a great number of feet.

central, sen'tral, *a.* Placed in the center, relating to the center.

centripetal, sen-trip'et-al, *a.* Tending toward the center.

cereal, sē'rē-al, *a.* Pertaining to corn.—*n.* A grain plant.

cerebral, se're-bral, *a.* Pertaining to the brain.

ceremony, se're-mō-ni, *n.* Outward rite, form, observance, formality.

cerise, se-rēz', *n.* Cherry-color.

certain, sėr'tān, *a.* Sure; undeniable; decided; particular; some; one.

certificate, sėr-tif'i-kāt, *n.* A written testimony a credential.

certify, sėr-ti-fī, *vt.* (certifying, certified). To give certain information to testify to in writing.

chafe, chāf, *vt.* (chafing, chafed). To make

warm by rubbing; to fret by rubbing, to enrage.—*vi.* To be fretted by friction; to rage.—*n.* A heat; a fretting.

chaff, chaf, *n.* The husk of corn and grasses; banter.—*vt.* To banter.

chagrin sha-grēn', *n.* Ill-humor; vexation.—*vt.* To vex, to mortify.

chain, chān, *n.* A series of links; a line of things connected, that which binds, a line formed of links 66 feet long; (*pl.*) bondage; slavery. —*vt.* To bind with a chain; to confine.

chairman, chā r'man, *n.* The presiding officer of an assembly; a President.

chalybeate, ka-lib'ē-āt, *a.* Impregnated with particles of iron.—*n.* A liquid into which iron or steel enters.

chameleon, ka-mē'lē-on, *n.* A species of lizard, whose color changes.

chamfer, cham'fėr, *n.* A small furrow in wood, etc., a bevel.—*vt.* To cut a chamfer in, to bevel

chamois, sham'i or sham'wä, *n.* A species of antelope; a soft leather.

champ, champ, *vt.* To devour with violent action of the teeth, to bite the bit, as a horse.—*vi.* To keep biting.

champagne, sham-pān', *n.* A kind of brisk sparkling wine.

champion, cham'pi-on, *n.* A combatant for another, or for a cause; a hero, one victorious in contest.— *vt.* To fight for.

chance, chans, *n.* That which happens; accident; possibility of an occurrence, opportunity.—*vi.* (chancing, chanced). To happen.—*a.* Happening by chance, casual.

changeling, chānj'ling, *n.* A child substituted for another; a fool; one apt to change.

chaplain, chap'lān, *n.* A clergyman of the army, navy, court, etc.

chapter, chap'tėr, *n.* Division of a book; a society of clergymen belonging to a cathedral or collegiate church; an organized branch of some fraternity.

charade, sha-räd', *n.* A species of riddle upon the syllables of a word.

charcoal, chär'kōl, *n.* Coal made by charring wood, the residue of animal, vegetable, and many mineral substances, when heated to redness in close vessels.

charity, cha'ri-ti, *n.* A disposition to relieve the wants of others; benevolence; alms; a charitable institution.

charlatan, shär 'la-tan, *n.* A quack.

charm, chärm, *n.* A spell; fascination; a locket, etc.—*vt.* To enthrall; to delight.

chart, chärt, *n.* A map, delineation of coasts, etc., tabulated facts.

charter, chär'tė r, *n.* A writing given as evidence of a grant, contract etc.—*vt.* To establish by charter; to hire or to let (a ship).

chauffeur, shō'fėr, *n.* A person regularly employed to drive a private motor-car.

cheap, chēp, *a.* Of a low price; common, not respected.

cheat, chēt, *vt.* To defraud; to deceive.—*n.* A deceitful act; a swindler.

checkmate, chek'māt, *n.* A move in chess which ends the game; defeat.—*vt.* to give checkmate to, to frustrate; to defeat.

cheddar, ched'ėr, *n.* A rich English cheese.

cheek, chēk, *n.* The side of the face below the eyes on each side; impudence.

Chemistry, kem'ist-ri, *n.* The science which treats of the properties and nature of elementary substances.

cherish, che'rish, *vt.* To treat with tenderness; to encourage.

cheroot, shē-röt', *n.* A kind of cigar with both ends cut square off.

cherry, che'ri, *n.* A tree and its fruit, of the plum family.—*a.* Like a cherry in color.

cherub, che'rub, *n.*; pl. **-ubs** and **-ubim.** An angel of the second order, a beautiful child.

chicory, chik'o-ri, *n.* A common English plant, often used to mix with coffee.

chide, chīd, *vt.* and *i.* (chiding, pret. chid, pp. chid, chidden). To reprove, to scold.

chief, chēf, *a.* Being at the head first; leading.—*n.* A principal person; a leader.

chilblain, chil'blān, *n.* A blain or sore produced on the hands or feet by cold.

childbirth, child'bė rth, *n.* The act of bringing forth a child; travail; labor.

chill, chil, *n.* A shivering with cold; a cold fit, that which checks or disheartens.—*a.* Cold, tending to cause shivering, dispiriting.—*vt.* To make cold; to discourage.

chime, chīm, *n.* A set of bells tuned to each other; their sound; harmony; the brim of a cask.—*vi.* (chiming, chimed). To sound in consonance; to agree.—*vt.* To cause to sound in harmony; to cause to sound.

chin, chin, *n.* The lower part of the face, the point of the under jaw.

china, chī'na, *n.* A species of fine porcelain.

chinchilla, chin-chil'la, *n.* A genus of S. American rodent animals; their fur.

chiropodist, kī-rop'od-ist, *n.* One who

extracts corns, removes bunions, etc.

chirp, chẽrp, *vi.* To make the lively noise of small birds.—*n.* A short, shrill note of birds.

chisel, chiz'el, *n.* A cutting tool used in wood-work, masonry, sculpture, etc.—*vt.* (chiselling chiselled). To cut gouge, or engrave with a chisel.

chit, chit, *n.* A note; an order or pass.

chlorophyll, klŏ'rō-fil, *n.* The green coloring matter of plants.

chocolate, cho 'ko-lā t, *n.* A preparation from the kernels of the cacaonut.—*a.* Dark, glossy brown.

choice, chois, *n.* Act of choosing oPtion, the thing chosen, best part of anything; the object of choice.—*a.* Select, Precious.

chop, chop, *vt.* (chopping chopped). To cut into small pieces, to barter or exchange.—*vi.* To change; to turn suddenly.—*n.* A piece chopped off; a small piece of meat, a crack or cleft, a turn or change; the jaw; the mouth.

chopsticks, chop'stiks, *n.* Two sticks of wood, ivory, etc., used by the Chinese in eating.

chord, kord, *n.* String of a musical instrument, the simultaneous combination of different sounds; a straight line joining the ends of the arc of a circle or curve.

chorus, kō'rus, *n.* A company of singers, a piece performed by a company in concert; verses of a song in which the company join the singer; any union of voices in general.

chosen, chōz'n, *a.* Select, eminent.

chrism, krizm, *n.* Consecrated oil.

christen, kris'n, *vt.* To baptize; to name.

Christian, kris'ti-an, *n.* A professed follower of Christ.—*a.* Pertaining to Christ or Christianity.

Christmas, kris'mas, *n.* The festival of Christ's nativity, observed annually on 25th December.—*a.* Belonging to Christmas time.

chromatic, krō-mat'ik, *a.* Relating to color; proceeding by semitones.

chrome, chromium, krōm, krō 'mium, *n.* A steel-gray, hard metal, from which colored preparations are made.

chronic, kron'ik, *a.* Continuing a long time, lingering, continuous.

chronology, kro-nol'o-ji, *n.* Arrangement of events according to their dates.

chrysalis, kris'a-lis, *n.*, pl. **-ides** or **-ises**. The form of certain insects before they arrive at their winged state.

chrysanthemum, kri-san'thē-mum, *n.* The name of numerous composite plants.

chub, chub, *n.* A small river fish of the carp family.

cider, sī'dẽr, *n.* A fermented drink prepared from the juice of apples.

cigar, si-gär', *n.* A roll of tobacco for smoking.

cigarette, sig-a-ret', *n.* A little cut tobacco rolled up in rice paper, used for smoking.

cilia, sil'i-a, *n.pl.* Minute hairs on plants or animals.

ciliary, sil'i-a-ri, *a.* Belonging to or of the nature of eyelashes.

Cimmerian, sim-mē'ri-an, *a.* Pertaining to the fabulous Cimmerians, who dwelt in perpetual darkness; extremely dark.

cinnamon, sin'na-mon, *n.* The inner bark of a tree, a native of Ceylon; a spice.

circle, sẽr'kl, *n.* A plane figure contained by a curved line, every point of which is equally distant from a point within the figure, called the center the curved line itself, a ring; enclosure; a class; a coterie.—*vt.* (circling circled). To move round, to enclose.—*vi.* To move circularly.

circuit, sẽr'kit, *n.* Act of going round; space measured by travelling round; the journey of judges to hold courts the district visited by judges; path of an electric current.

circular, sẽr'kū-lẽr, *a.* Round; addressed to a number of persons.—*n.* A paper addressed to a number of persons.

circulate, sẽr'kū-lāt, *vi.* (circulating, circulated). To move in a circle, to have currency.—*vt.* To spread; to give currency to.

circumcise, sẽr'kum-sīz *vt.* (circumcising, circumcised). To cut off the foreskin, according to Jewish and Mohammedan law.

circumference, sẽr-kum'fẽ-rens, *n.* The bounding line of a circle.

circumstance, sẽr'kum-stans, *n.* Something attending, or relative to a main fact or case; event; *(pl.)* state of affairs, condition.

circumvent, sẽr-kum-vent', *vt.* To encompass; to outwit.

circus, sẽr'kus, *n.*; pl. **-ses**. Among the Romans, a place for horseraces; a place for feats of horsemanship and acrobatic displays.

cirrus, sir'rus, *n.*; pl. **cirri**. A tendril; a light fleecy cloud at a high elevation.

cistern, sis'tẽrn, *n.* An artificial receptacle for water, etc.; a natural reservoir.

citadel, si'ta-del, *n.* A fortress in or near a city.

citation, sī-tā'shon, *n.* Quotation; a summons.

citizen, si'ti-zen, *n.* An inhabitant of a city; one who has full municipal and political privileges.—*a.* Having the qualities of a citizen.

civilian, si-vil'i-an, *n.* One skilled in the civil law, one engaged in civil, not military or clerical pursuits.

civility, si-vil'i-ti, *n.* Quality of being civil; good breeding; (pl.) acts of politeness.

civilize, si'vil-īz, *vt.* (civilizing, civilized). To reclaim from a savage state.

clamp, klamp, *n.* A piece of timber or iron, used to strengthen or fasten, a heavy footstep.—*vt.* To fasten or strengthen with clamps; to tread heavily.

clan, klan, *n.* A family; a tribe; a sect.

clandestine, klan-des'tin, *a.* Secret; underhand.

clang, klang, *vt.* or *i.* To make a sharp sound, as by striking metallic substances.—*n.* A loud sound made by striking together metallic bodies.

clank, klangk, *n.* The loud sound made by the collision of metallic bodies.—*vi.* or *t.* To sound or cause to sound with a clank.

clasp, klasp, *n.* An embrace; a hook for fastening; a catch; a bar added to a military medal to commemorate a particular battle or campaign.—*vt.* To fasten together with a clasp, to inclose in the hand; to embrace closely.

clasp-knife, klasp'nīf, *n.* A knife the blade of which folds into the handle.

class, klas, *n.* A rank of persons or things; an order; a group.—*vt.* To arrange in classes.

clause, kläz, *n.* A member of a sentence; a distinct part of a contract, will, etc.

claustrophobia, kläs'trō-fo"bē-a, *n.* Morbid fear of confined spaces.

clavicle, klav'i-kl, *n.* The collarbone.

claw, klä, *n.* The sharp hooked nail of an animal; that which resembles a claw.—*vt.* To scrape, scratch, or tear.

clay, klā, *n.* A tenacious kind of earth, earth in general; the body. —*vt.* To cover with clay; to purify and whiten with clay, as sugar.

clean, klēn, *a.* Free from dirt; pure. —*adv.* Quite; fully.—*vt.* To purify; to cleanse.

cleat, klēt, *n.* A piece of wood or iron in a ship to fasten ropes upon; a wedge.

clement, kle'ment, *a.* Mild; humane.

clench, klensh, *vt.* To secure; to confirm; to grasp.

clergy, klėr'ji, *n.pl.* The body or order of men set apart to the service of God, in the Christian church.

clericalism, kle'rik-al-izm, *n.* Clerical power to influence; sacerdotalism.

clerk, klärk, *n.* A clergyman; one who reads the responses in church; one who is employed under another as a writer.

cliche, klē'shā, *n.* A hackneyed phrase.

click, klik, *vi.* To make a small sharp noise, or a succession of such sounds.—*n.* A small sharp sound.

client, klī'ent, *n.* A person under patronage; one who employs a lawyer.

cliff, klif, *n.* A precipice; a steep rock.

climacteric, kli-mak-te'rik, *n.* A critical period in human life.

climate, klī'māt, *n.* The condition of a country in respect of temperature, dryness, wind, etc.

climb, klīm, *vi.* To creep up step by step; to ascend.—*vt.* To ascent.

clock, klok, *n.* An instrument which measures time.

clod, klod, *n.* A lump of earth; a stupid fellow.—*vt.* (clodding, clodded). To pelt with clods.

clog, klog, *vt.* (clogging, clogged). To hinder; to impede; to trammel.—*vi.* To be loaded.—*n.* Hindrance; a shoe with a wooden sole.

cloister, klois'tėr, *n.* A monastery or nunnery; an arcade round an open court.—*vt.* To shut up in a cloister; to immure.

close, klōs, *a.* Shut fast; tight; dense; near; stingy, trusty, intense; without ventilation; disposed to keep secrets.—*adv.* Tightly, in contact, or very near.—*n.* An inclosed place; precinct of a cathedral.

clot, klot, *n.* A mass of soft or fluid matter concreted.—*vi.* (clotting, clotted). To become thick; to coagulate.

cloud, kloud, *n.* A collection of visible vapor, suspended in the air; something similar to this; what obscures, threatens, etc.; a great multitude, a mass.—*vt.* To obscure; to darken; to sully; to make to appear sullen.—*vi.* To grow cloudy.

cloy, kloi, *vt.* To glut; to fill to loathing.

club-footed, klub'fut-ed, *a.* Having short, crooked, or deformed feet.

cluck, kluk, *vi.* To make the noise of the hen when calling chickens.—*n.* Such a sound.

clue, klö, *n.* A ball of thread; a thread serving to guide; something helping to unravel a mystery.

coast, kōst, *n*. The sea-shore; the country near the sea.—*vi*. To sail along a shore; to sail from port to port.

coax, kōks, *vt*. To wheedle; to persuade by fondling and flattering.

cob, kob, *n*. A round knob; the head of clover or wheat; a smallish thick-set horse; a mile swan.

cobalt, kō'bält, *n*. A mineral of grayish color, and a metal obtained from it yielding a permanent blue; the blue itself.

cobble, kob'l, *vt*. (cobbling, cobbled). To mend coarsely, as shoes; to botch.—*n*. A roundish stone.

coco, cocoa, kō'kō, *n*. A tropical palm-tree.

cocoa, kō'kō, *n*. The seed of the cacao prepared for a beverage; the beverage itself.

cocoon, kō'kön', *n*. The silky case in which the silkworm involves itself when still a larva; the envelope of other larvae.

cod, kod, *n*. A species of sea fish allied to the haddock; a husk; a pod.

coddle, kod'l, *vt*. (coddling, coddled). To fondle.

code, kōd, *n*. A digest of laws; a collection of rules; a system of signals, etc.

codicil, ko'di-sil, *n*. A writing by way of supplement to a will.

coffee, kof'i, *n*. A tree and its fruit or berries; a beverage made from the seeds.

coffee-house, kof'i hous, *n*. A house where coffee and refreshments are supplied.

coffer, kof'ėr, *n*. A chest for holding gold, jewels etc.

coffin, kof'fin, *n*. The chest in which a dead human body is buried.—*vt*. To inclose in a coffin.

cog, kog, *n*. The tooth of a wheel.—*vt*. (cogging, cogged). To furnish with cogs; to trick, deceive; to manipulate dice unfairly.—*vi*. To cheat; to lie.

cogent, kō'jent, *a*. Forcible; convincing.

cogitate, ko'jit-āt, *vi*. (cogitating cogitated) To ponder; to meditate.

cognac, kō'nyak, *n*. A kind of brandy.

cognate, kog'nāt, *a*. Born of the same stock; akin; of the same nature.

cognition, kog-ni'shon, *n*. Knowledge from personal view or experience.

cohesion, kō-hē'zhon, *n*. Act of sticking together; the attraction by which bodies are kept together; coherence.

coiffure, koif'ūr, *n*. Mode of dressing the hair in women.

coil, koil, *vt*. To wind into a ring.

—*n*. A ring or rings into which a rope, etc., is wound.

coin, koin, *n*. A piece of metal stamped, as money, that which serves for payment.—*vt*. To stamp and convert metal into money; to mint; to invent; to fabricate.

coition, kō-i'shon, *n*. Sexual intercourse.

colitis, kō-lī'tis, *n*. Inflammation of the large intestine, especially of its mucous membrane.

collar, kol'ėr, *n*. A part of dress that surrounds the neck, something worn round the neck.—*vt*. To seize by the collar; to put a collar on; to roll up and bind with a cord.

collect, kol'ekt, *n*. A short comprehensive prayer; a short prayer adapted to a particular occasion.

collected, kol-lekt'ed, *p.a*. Cool; self-possessed.

collectivism, kol-lek'tiv-izm, *n*. The doctrine that the state should own or control the land and all means of production.

collide, kol-līd', *vi*. (colliding, collided). To strike against each other; to meet in opposition.

collie, kol'i, *n*. A dog common in Scotland, much used for sheep.

colophon, ko'lo-fōn, *n*. An inscription or device formerly on the last page of a book, now usually in its preliminary pages.

color-blindness, kul'ėr-blī nd-nes, *n*. Inability to distinguish colors.

colossal, kō-los'al, *a*. Huge; gigantic.

colure, kō-lūr', *n*. Either of two great circles of the heavens, passing through the solstitial and the equinoctial points of the ecliptic.

coma, kō'ma, *n*. Deep sleep; stupor; the hair-like envelope round the nucleus of a comet.

comb, kōm, *n*. An instrument for separating hair, wool, etc.; the crest of a cock, honeycomb.—*vt*. To separate and adjust with a comb.

combine, kom-bīn', *vt*. (combining, combined). To cause to unite; to join.—*vi*. To come into union, to coalesce; to league together.—kom' bin, *n*. A union.

combustible, kom-bust'i-bl, *a*. Capable of catching fire; inflammable.—*n*. A substance easily set on fire.

come, kum, *vi*. (coming, pret. came, pp. come). To move hitherward; to draw nigh; to arrive; to happen, to appear; to rise, to result.

comedian, ko-mē'di-an, *n*. An actor in or

writer of comedies.

coming, kum'ing, *p.a.* Future.—*n.* Approach.

comity, ko'mi-ti, *n.* Courtesy; civility.

comma, kom'ma, *n.* A mark of punctuation, thus (,) an interval in music.

commend, kom-mend', *vt.* To commit to the care of; to recommend; to praise.

commensal, kom-men'sal, *n.* One that eats at the same table; one living with another.

commensurate kom-men'sūr-āt *a.* Proportional; having equal measure.

comment, kom-ment', *vi.* To make remarks or criticisms.—*vt.* To annotate.—*n.* kom'-ment. An explanatory note; criticism.

commentary, kom'ment-a-ri, *n.* Book of comments, an historical narrative.

commerce, kom'mẽrs, *n.* Exchange of goods by barter or purchase; trade; intercourse.

commercial, kom-mẽr'shal, *a.* Pertaining to commerce, trading; mercantile.

commissure, kom'mis-sūr, *n.* A joint or seam; juncture.

commit, kom-mit', *vt.* (committing, committed). To intrust; to consign; to send to prison, to perpetrate; to endanger or compromise (oneself).

committee, kom-mit'tē, *n.* A body of persons appointed to manage any matter.

commix, kom-miks', *vt.* To blend; to mix.

commodious, kom-mō'di-us, *a.* Convenient; spacious and suitable.

commodore, kom'mo-dōr, *n.* A captain in the navy who is discharging duties rather more important than those usually assigned to a captain.

communicable, kom-mū'ni-ka-bl *a.* Capable of being imparted to another.

communicant, kom-mūni-kant, *n.* One who communicates, a partaker of the Lord's supper.

communicate, kom-mū'ni-kāt, *vt.* (communicating, communicated). To cause to be common to others; to impart, as news disease, etc. to bestow, to reveal.—*vi.* To share with others; to partake of the Lord's supper; to have intercourse, to correspond.

communion, kom-mūn'yon, *n.* A mutual participation in anything mutual intercourse; concord; celebration of the Lord's supper.

Communism, kom'mūn-izm, *n.* The doctrine of a community of property by which the state owns and controls all means of production.

Communist, kom'mūn-ist, *n.* One who holds the doctrines of communism; member of the communist party.

community, kom-mū'ni-ti, *n.* Mutual participation; the public; a society of persons under the same laws.

company, kum'pa-ni, *n.* Companionship; an assembly of persons; partners in a firm; a division of a battalion, consisting of four platoons, and commanded by a major or mounted captain, with a captain as second-in-command the crew of a ship.—*vi.* To associate with.

comparative, kom-pa'ra-tiv, *a.* Estimated by comparison; not positive or absolute.

compatriot, kom-pā'tri-ot, *n.* One of the same country.

compete, kom-pēt', *vi.* (competing, competed). To strive for the same thing as another; to contend.

competent, kom'pē-tent *a.* Suitable, sufficient, qualified, having adequate right.

competition, kom-pē-ti'shon, *n.* Contest for the same object, rivalry.

complacence, complacency, komplā'sens, komplā'sen-si, *n.* A feeling of quiet satisfaction; complaisance.

complain, kom-plān', *vi.* to express grief or distress, to lament to express dissatisfaction; to make a formal accusation.

complaisance, kom'plā-zans, *n.* A pleasing deportment; courtesy; urbanity.

complement, kom'plē-ment, *n.* That which fills up; full quantity or number.

complete, kom-plēt', *a.* Having no deficiency; finished; total; absolute.—*vt.* (completing, completed). To make complete; to finish; to fulfill.

complexion, kom-plek'shon, *n.* The color of the face; general appearance.

comply, kom-plī', *vi.* (complying, complied). To yield; to assent; to acquiesce.

component, kom-pōn'ent, *a.* Composing; forming an element of a compound.—*n.* A constituent part; ingredient.

composer, kom-pōz'ẽr, *n.* An author, especially a musical author.

compost, kom'pōst, *n.* A mixture for manure.

compress, kom-pres', *vt.* To press together; to squeeze; to condense.—*n.* kom'pres. A soft mass or bandage used in surgery.

compressible, kom-pres'i-bl, *a.* Capable of being compressed.

comprise, kom-prīz, *vt.* (comprising, comprised). To embrace; to contain; to inclose.

compromise, kom'prō-mīz, *n.* An amicable agreement to settle differences, mutual concession.—*vi.* To settle by mutual concessions; to involve; to endanger the interests of.

comptroller, kon-trōl'er, *n.* A controller, an officer who examines the accounts of collectors of public money.

compulsion, kom-pul'shon, *n.* Act of compelling; state of being compelled; force.

compulsory, kom-pul'so-ri, *a.* Constraining; coercive; obligatory.

compunction, kom-pungk'shon, *n.* Remorse; contrition.

concave, kon'kāv, *a.* Hollow, as the inner surface of a sphere; opposed to convex.—*n.* A hollow; an arch or vault.

conceal, kon-sēl', *vt.* To hide; to secrete; to disguise.

concede, kon-sēd', *vt.* (conceding, conceded). To yield; to grant.—*vi.* To make concession.

conceit, kon-sēt', *n.* Conception; fancy; self-flattering opinion; vanity.

concentrate, kon'sen-trāt, *vt.* (concentrating, concentrated). To bring together; to direct to one object, to condense.

concentric, kon-sen'trik, *a.* Having a common center.

concept, kon'sept, *n.* An object conceived by the mind; a general notion of a class of objects.

concert, kon-sert', *vt.* to plan together; to contrive.—*n.* kon'sert. Agreement in a design; harmony; performance of a company of players, singers, etc.

concise, kon-sīs', *a.* Brief; abridged; comprehensive.

conclave, kon'klāv, *n.* A private apartment; the assembly of cardinals for the election of a pope; a close assembly.

conclude, kon-klūd', *vt.* (concluding, concluded). To end; to decide; to deduce.—*vt.* To end; to form a final judgment.

concomitance, concomitancy, kon-kom'i-tans, kon-kom'i-tan-si, *n.* A being together or in connection with another thing.

concubine, kong'kū-bīn, *n.* A woman who cohabits with a man; a mistress.

concupiscence, kon-kū'pis-ens, *n.* Lust.

concur, kon-ker', *vt.* (concurring, concurred). To unite; to agree; to assent.

concussion, kon-ku'shon, *n.* A violent shock.

concussive, kon-kus'iv, *a.* Having the power or quality of shaking; agitating.

condemn, kon-dem', *vt.* To pronounce to be wrong; to censure; to sentence.

conditionally, kon-di'shon-al-li, *adv.* With certain limitations.

condone, kon-don', *vt.* (condoning condoned). To pardon; to imply forgiveness of.

condor, kon'dor, *n.* A S. American vulture.

conduce, kon-dūs', *vi.* (conducing conduced). To lead; to tend, to contribute.

conduct, kon'dukt, *n.* Personal behavior, management; escort.—*vt.* kon-dukt'. To read or guide; to escort; to manage; to behave (oneself), to transmit, as heat, etc.

confection, kon-fek'shon, *n.* A mixture; a sweetmeat.

confectioner, kon-fek'shon-er, *n.* One who makes or sells sweetmeats.

Confederacy, kon-fe'de-ra-si, *n.* A confederation; the parties united by a league.

confederate, kon-fe'de-rāt, *a.* Allied by treaty.—*n.* One united with others in a league.—*vt.* and *i.* (confederating, confederated). To unite in a league.

confederation, kon-fe'de-rā"shon, *n.* A league; alliance, particularly of states, etc.

conference, kon'fer-ens, *n.* A meeting for consultation, or for the adjustment of differences; bestowal.

confidence, kon'fi-dens, *n.* Firm belief or trust; self-reliance; boldness; assurance; a secret.

confidential, kon-fi-den'shal, *a.* Enjoying confidence; trusty; private; secret.

confirm, kon-ferm', *vt.* To make firm or more firm; to establish; to make certain; to administer the rite of confirmation to.

confirmation, kon-ferm-ā'shon, *n.* Act of confirming; additional evidence; ratification; the laying on of a bishop's hands in the rite of admission to the privileges of a Christian.

confiscate, kon'fis-kāt, *vt.* (confiscating, confiscated). To seize as forfeited to the public treasury.

conflagration, kon-fla-grā'shon, *n.* A great fire.

conflict, kon'flikt, *n.* a struggle; clashing of views or statements.—*vi.* kon-flikt'. To meet in opposition; to be antagonistic.

confluence, kon'flū-ens, *n.* A flowing together; meeting, or place of meeting, of rivers; a concourse; a crowd.

conform, kon-form', *vt.* To cause to be of the same form; to adapt.—*vi.* To comply.

conformation, kon-for-mā'shon, *n.* The act of conforming; structure; configuration.

conformist, kon-for'mist, *n.* One who conforms; one who complies with the worship of the established church.

confound, kon-found', *vt.* To confuse; to astound; to overthrow; to mistake.

confute, kon-fū't', *vt.* (confuting confuted). To prove to be false; to refute.

congeniality, kon-jē 'ni-al''i-ti, *n.* Natural affinity; suitableness.

congenital, kon-jen'it-al, *a.* Pertaining to an individual from his birth.

congeries, kon-jē 'ri-ēz, *n.* A head or pile; a collection of several bodies in one mass.

congest, kon-jest', *vt.* and *i.* To accumulate to excess, as blood, population, etc.

congestion kon-jest'shon *n.* Excessive accumulation; undue fullness of blood-vessels in an organ.

Congregation, kong-grē -gā'shon, *n.* Act of congregating; an assembly; an assembly met for divine worship.

Congregationalist, kong-grē-gā' shon-al-ist, *n.* One who adheres to the system in which each separate congregation or church forms an independent body

congress, kong'gres, *n.* An assembly; a meeting of ambassadors etc., for the settlement of affairs between different nations; the legislature of the United States.

congruence, congruency, kong' grü-ens, kong'grü-en-si, *n.* Accordance; consistency.

congruity, kon-grü'i-ti, *n.* Suitableness accordance; consistency.

conic, conical, kon'ik, kon'ik-al, *a.* Having the form of a cone; pertaining to a cone.

conjugate, kon'jū-gā t, *vt.* (conjugating, conjugated). To join together; to inflect (a verb) through its several forms.—*a.* Joined in pairs; kindred in origin and meaning.

conjunction, kon-jungk'shon, *n.* Act of joining; state of being joined; connection; a connecting word.

connect, kon-nekt', *vt.* To conjoin; to combine, to associate.—*vi.* To unite or cohere together; to have a close relation.

connection, kon-nek'shon, *n.* Act of connecting; state of being connected; a relation by blood or marriage; relationship.

connective, kon-nekt'iv, *a.* Having the power of connecting; tending to connect.—*n.* A word that connects other words and sentences; a conjunction.

connivance, kon-nīv'ans, *n.* Voluntary blindness to an act; pretended ignorance.

connive, kon-nīv', *vi.* (conniving connived). To wink; to pretend ignorance or blindness, to forbear to see (with at).

conscience, kon'shens, *n.* Internal knowledge or judgment of right and wrong; the moral sense; morality.

conscionable, kon'shon-a-bl, *a.* Reasonable.

conscious, kon 'shus, *a.* Knowing in one's own mind; knowing by sensation or perception; aware; sensible; self-conscious.

consciousness, kon'shus-nes, *n.* State of being conscious; perception of what passes in one's own mind; sense of guilt or innocence.

consequence, kon'sē-kwens, *n.* That which follows as a result, inference; importance.

consequent, kon'sē-kwent, *a.* Following, as the natural effect, or by inference.— *n.* Effect; result; inference.

consequential, kon-sē -kwen'shal, *a.* Following as the effect; pompous.

conservation, kon-sē rv-ā 'shon, *n.* Preservation, the keeping of a thing entire.

considerable, kon-si'dèr-a-bl, *a.* Worthy of consideration; moderately large.

considerate, kon-si'dèr-āt, *a.* Given to consideration; mindful of others; deliberate.

considerately, kon-si'dèr-āt-li, *adv.* In a considerate manner.

consideration, kon-si'dèr-ā "shon *n.* Mental view; serious deliberation; importance; motive of action; an equivalent.

considering, kon-si'dèr-ing, *prep.* Taking into account; making allowance for.

consign, kon-sīn', *vt.* To deliver over to another by agreement; to intrust; to commit; to deposit.

consolation, kon-sōl-ā'shon, *n.* A solace; alleviation of misery, what helps to cheer; what gives comfort.

console, kon-sōl', *vt.* (consoling, consoled). To comfort; to soothe; to cheer.

consolidate, kon-sol'id-āt, *vt.* (consolidating, consolidated). To make solid or firm, to unite into one; to compact.—*vi.* To grow firm and solid.

conspiracy, kon-spi'ra-si, *n.* A plot; a treasonable combination.

conspire, kon-spīr', *vi.* (conspiring, conspired). To plot; to combine for some evil purpose; to tend to one end.

constable, kun 'sta-bl, *n.* An officer of the peace; policeman.

constant, kon'stant, *a.* Stead-fast; perpetual; assiduous; resolute.—*n.* That which remains unchanged; a fixed quantity.

constellation, kon-stel-lā'shon, *n.* A group of fixed stars; an assemblage of splendors or excellences.

constipate, kon'sti-pāt, *vt.* (constipating, constipated). To make costive.

constituent, kon-stit'ū-ent, *a.* Forming; existing as an essential part.—*n.* An elector; an essential part.

constitute, kon'sti-tūt, *vt.* (constituting, constituted). To set up or establish; to compose; to appoint; to make and empower.

constitution, kon-sti-tū'shon, *n.* The particular frame or character of the body or mind, established form of government, a system of fundamental laws; a particular law.

constitutional, kon-sti-tū'shon-al, *a.* Adherent in the human constitution, consistent with the civil constitution; legal.—*n.* A walk for the sake of health.

constrain, kon-strān', *vt.* To urge by force; to necessitate; to restrain.

constructive, kon-strukt'iv, *a.* Having ability to construct; created or deduced by construction; inferred.

construe, kon'strū , *vt.* (construing, construed). To arrange words so as to discover the sense of a sentence to interpret.

consult, kon-sult', *vi.* To seek the opinion of another; to deliberate in common; to consider.—*vt.* To ask advice of; to refer to for information; to have regard to.

consume, kon-sūm', *vt.* (consuming, consumed). To reduce to nothing; to burn up; to squander.—*vi.* To waste away slowly; to be exhausted.

consummate, kon'sum-āt, *vt.* To finish; to perfect.—*a.* kon-sum'at. Complete; perfect.

consumption, kon-sum'shon, *n.* Act of consuming; quantity consumed; a gradual wasting away of the body.

contact, kon'takt, *n.* A touching together; close union or juncture of bodies.

contagion, kon-tā'jon, *n.* Communication of a disease by contact; poisonous emanation; infection.

contain, kon-tān', *vt.* To hold, to be able to hold; to comprise; to restrain.

contaminate, kon-tam'in-āt, *vt.* To corrupt; to taint; to vitiate.

contemptible, kon-tem'ti-bl, *a.* Worthy of contempt; despicable; vile; mean.

contemptuous, kon-tem'tū -us, *a.* Manifesting contempt; scornful; insolent.

contend, kon-tend', *vi.* To strive; to vie; to dispute; to wrangle.

contest, kon-test', *vt.* To call in question; to strive for.—*vi.* To strive; to contend; to emulate.—*n.* kon'test. Struggle for victory; encounter; debate; competition.

context, kon'tekst, *n.* The parts which precede or follow a passage quoted.

contiguous, kon-tig'ū-us, *a.* Touching one another; in contact; adjacent.

continence, continency, kon'ti-nens, kona-ti-nen-si, *n.* Restraint of the desires and passions; chastity; temperance.

continent, kon'ti-nent, *a.* Chaste; moderate.—*n.* A connected tract of land of great extent; the mainland of Europe.

contingence, contingency, kon-tin'jens, kon-tin'jen-si, *n.* Quality of being contingent; an event which may occur; chance; juncture.

continue, kon-tin'ū, *vi.* (continuing continued). To remain in a state or place; to be durable; to persevere; to be steadfast.—*vt.* To prolong; to extend, to persevere in.

continuity, kon-ti-nū 'i-ti, *n.* Close union of parts; unbroken texture; cohesion.

continuous, kon-tin'ū-us, *a.* Joined together closely; conjoined; continued.

contort, kon-tort', *vt.* To twist; to writhe, to draw or pull awry.

contortionist, kon-tor'shon-ist, *n.* An acrobat who practices contortions of the body.

contour, kontör', *n.* The line that bounds a body; outline.

contractile, kon-traktīl, *a.* Having the power of contracting, as living fibers.

contraction, kon-trak'shon, *n.* Shrinking; shortening; abbreviation.

contractor, kon-trakt'ér, *n.* One who contracts to perform any work or service, or to furnish supplies, at a certain price or rate.

contradict, kon-tra-dikt', *vt.* To assert to be the contrary; to deny; to oppose.

contradiction, kon-tra dik 'shon, *n.* A contrary assertion; inconsistency with itself.

contradictory, kon-tra-dik'to-ri, *a.* Implying contradiction; inconsistent.

contradistinction, kon'tra-distingk"shon, *n.* Distinction by opposites.

contravene, kon-tra-vēn' *vt.* (contravening, contravened). To oppose; to transgress.

contribute, kon-trib'ūt, vt. (contributing, contributed). To give in common with others.—vi. To give a part; to conduce.

contribution, kon-tri-bū'shon, n. Act of contributing; that which is contributed; an article sent to a periodical, etc.

contrite, kon'trīt, a. Brokenhearted for sin; penitent.

contrition, kon-tri'shon, n. Grief of heart for sin.

contrivance, kon-trīv'ans, n. Scheme; invention; artifice.

control, kon-trōl', n. Restraint; superintendence, authority.—vt. (controlling, controlled). To restrain; to regulate.

controller, kon-trōl'ėr, n. An officer who checks the accounts of collectors of public moneys.

controversy, kon'trō-vėr-si, n. A disputation, particularly in writing; litigation.

controvert, kon'trō-vėrt, vt. To dispute by reasoning; to attempt to disprove or confute.

conundrum, kō-nun'drum, n. A sort of riddle turning on some odd resemblance between things quite unlike.

convalesce, kon-va-les', vi. (convalescing, convalesced). To recover health.

convalescence, kon-va-les'ens, n. The state of one convalescent; gradual recovery after illness.

convene, kon-vēn', vi. (convening convened). To assemble.—vt. To cause to assemble, to convoke.

convenience, conveniency, kon-vē' niens, kon-vē'ni-en-si, n. Ease; comfort; suitable opportunity; an appliance or utensil.

convenient, kon-vē'ni-ent, a. Suit-able, adapted opportune.

convent, kon-vent, n. A body of monks or nuns; a monastery; a nunnery.

conventicle, kon-ven'ti-kl, n. A secret meeting, a meeting of religious dissenters; their meeting place.

convention, kon-ven'shon, n. An assembly; an agreement; recognized social custom.

conventional, kon-ven'shon-al, a. Formed by agreement, tacitly understood; resting on mere usage.

convergent, kon-vėrj'ent, a. Tending to one point or object; approaching.

conversant, kon'vėrs-ant, a. Having intercourse or familiarity; versed in; proficient; occupied or concerned.

conversation, kon-vė r-sā 'shon, n.

Familiar intercourse; easy talk.

converse, kon-vėrs', vi. (conversing, conversed). To hold intercourse; to talk familiarly; to commune.—n. kon'vers. Conversation, familiarity, something forming a counterpart.—a. Put the opposite or reverse way.

conversion, kon-vėr'shon, n. Change from one state, religion, or party to another; interchange of terms in logic.

convert, kon-vėrt', vt. and i. To change from one state, use, religion, or party to another; to turn from a bad life to a good; to interchange conversely.—n. kon'vert. One who has changed his opinion, practice, or religion.

convict, kon-vikt', vt. To prove or decide to be guilty.—n. kon'vikt. A person found guilty; one undergo ing penal servitude.

convince, kon-vins', vt. (convincing, convinced). To persuade by argument; to satisfy by evidence or proof.

convocation, kon-vō-ka'shon, n. Act of convoking; an assembly, particularly of clergy or heads of a university.

convoke, kon-vōk', vt. (convoking, convoked). To call together; to summon to meet.

convolution, kon-vō-lū'shon, n. Act of rolling together or on itself, a winding; a spiral.

convolve, kon-volv', vt. To roll together or on itself, to coil up.

cool, kōl, a. Moderately cold, dispassionate; self-possessed; impudent.—n. A moderate degree or state of cold.—vt. To make cool; to moderate; to calm; to render indifferent.—vi. To lose heat, ardor, affection, etc.

cope, kōp, n. A sacerdotal cloak; the arch of the sky; the roof of a house; the arch over a door, etc.— vt. (coping, coped). To cover, as with a cope, to strive, or contend to oppose with success (with with).

Copernican, kō-pėr'ni-kan, a. Pertaining to Copernicus, or to his astronomical system.

copper, kop'ėr, n. A reddish colored ductile and malleable metal; a large boiler; a copper coin.—a. Consisting of or resembling copper.—vt. To cover with sheets of copper.

copulate, kop'ū-lāt, vi. (copulating, copulated). To come together, as different sexes.

copulative, kop'ū-lāt-iv, a. That unites. n. A conjunction.

copy, ko'pi, n. An imitation; a transcript; a pattern; a single example of a book, etc.; matter to be set up in type.—vt. (copying copied). To imitate; to transcribe.

copyright, kop'i-rît, n. The exclusive right to print or produce, given for a limited number of years to an author, artist, etc., or his assignee.—a. Relating to, or protected by copyright.—vt. To secure by copyright.

coralline, ko'ral-în, a. Consisting of, like, or containing coral.—n. A sea-weed; an orange-red color; a coral zoophyte.

corbel, kor'bel, n. A piece projecting from a wall as a support.—vt. (corbelling, corbelled). To support on corbels; to provide with corbels.

cord, kord, n. A small rope; a band; a sinew; a pile of wood, 8 feet long, 4 high, and 4 broad.—vi. To bind with a cord.

corduroy, kor-dè-roi', n. A thick cotton stuff corded or ribbed.

core, kōr, n. The heart or inner part; the central part of fruit.

co-respondent, kō-rē-spond'ent, n. A joint respondent; a man charged with adultery in a divorce case.

corn, korn, n. Grain; the seeds of plants which grow in ears, and are made into bread; a horny excrescence on a toe or foot.—vt. To preserve with salt in grains; to granulate.

cornea, kor'nē-a, n. The horny transparent membrane in the fore part of the eye.

corned, korned, a. Cured by salting.

corner, kor'nèr, n. A projecting extremity; angle; a secret or retired place; a nook.—vt. To buy up the whole stock of a commodity.

corner-stone, kor'nèr-stōn, n. The stone which lies at the corner of two walls, and unites them; the principal stone.

cornet, kor'net, n. A sort of trumpet, formerly a cavalry officer, of the lowest commissioned rank, who bore the standard.

cornice, kor'nis, n. A molded projection crowning a part; uppermost molding of a pediment, room, etc.

Cornish, korn'ish, a. Pertaining to Cornwall.—n. The language of Cornwall.

cornucopia, kor-nū-kō'pi-a, n. The representation of a horn filled with fruit, flowers, and grain, a symbol of plenty and peace.

coronet, ko'rō-net, n. A small crown worn by peers and peeresses; an ornamental headdress; something that surmounts.

corporal, kor'po-ral, n. A non-commissioned officer ranking below a sergeant.—a. Belonging or relating to the body; material.

corporate, kor'po-rāt, a. Formed into a legal body, and empowered to act in legal processes as an individual.

corporation, kor-po-rā'shon, n. A body corporate, empowered to act as an individual; the human body or frame.

corporeal, kor-pō'rē-al, a. Having a body; material; opposed to spiritual.

corps, kōr, n., pl. **corps**, kōrz. A body of troops. Army Corps. Two or more divisions.

corpse, korps, n. The dead body of a human being; a carcass; remains.

corpulence, corpulency, kor'pū-lens, kor'-pū-len-si, n. The state of being corpulent; excessive fatness.

corpuscle, kor'pus-l, n. A minute particle or physical atom; a minute animal cell.

corral, kor-räl', n. A pen for cattle; an inclosure formed by wagons; a stockade for capturing elephants.

correct, ko-rekt', a. Right; accurate; exact.—vt. To make right; to chastise; to counteract.

correction, ko-rek'shon, n. Act of correcting; state of being corrected; discipline; chastisement; counteraction.

correctness, ko-rekt'nes, n. Freedom from faults or errors; accuracy; exactness.

correlate, kor'ē-lāt, n. A correlative.—vi. (correlating, correlated). To be reciprocally related.—vt. To place in reciprocal relation; to determine the relations between.

correlative, ko-rel'at-iv, a. Having a mutual relation, as father and son.—n. One who or that which stands in reciprocal relation.

correspond, ko-rē-spond', vi. To answer one to another, to be congruous; to fit; to hold intercourse by letters.

correspondence, ko-rē-spond'ens n. Act or state of corresponding, fitness; congruity; intercourse by letters; the letters interchanged.

correspondent, ko-rē-spond'ent, a. Corresponding; suitable; congruous.—n. One who has intercourse by letters.

corridor, ko'ri-dör, n. A passage in a building, or round a court.

corrosion, ko-rō'zhon, n. Action of corroding; state of being corroded.

corrugate, ko'rū-gāt, vt. To wrinkle; to contract into folds or furrows.

corrugation, ko-rū-gā'shon, *n.* A wrinkling; contraction into wrinkles.

corrupt, ko-rupt', *vt.* To make putrid; to deprave; to taint; to bribe; to infect with errors.—*vi.* To become putrid or vitiated.—*a.* Tainted; depraved; infected with errors.

corruptible, ko-rupt'i-bl, *a.* That may be corrupted; subject to decay, destruction, etc.

corruption, ko-rup'shon, *n.* Act or process of corrupting; depravity; pollution, taint of blood, bribe-taking; bribery.

corset, kor'set *n.* An article of dress laced closely round the body; stays.

cortege, kor'tāzh, *n.* A train of attendants.

cortex, kor'teks, *n.* The bark of a tree; a membrane enveloping part of the body.

cortical, kor'tik-al, *a.* Belonging to consisting of, or resembling bark, belonging to the external covering.

coruscate, ko-rus'kā t *vi.* (coruscating, coruscated). To flash intermittently; to glitter.

cosmetic, koz-met'ik, *a.* Improving beauty.—*n.* An application to improve the complexion.

cosmic, cosmical, koz'mik, koz' mik-al, *a.* Relating to the whole frame of the universe.

Cosmos, koz'mos, *n.* The universe; the system of order and harmony in creation.

cost, kost, *vt.* (costing, cost). To be bought for; to require to be laid out or borne.—*n.* That which is paid for anything; expenditure; loss *(pl.)* expenses of a lawsuit.

cough, kof *n.* A violent convulsive effort of the lungs to throw off offending matter.—*vi.* To make a violent effort, with noise, to expel the airs from the lungs, and throw off any offensive matter.—*vt.* To expel from the lungs by a violent effort with noise; to expectorate.

could, küd, *pret.* of *can.* Was able.

council, koun'sil, *n.* An assembly for consultation, a body of men designated to advise a sovereign or chief magistrate; a convocation.

counter, count-ėr *n.* One who or that which counts; anything used to reckon, as in games; a shop table.—*adv.* Contrary; in an opposite direction.—*a.* Adverse; opposing.

counteract, koun-tėr-akt', *vt.* To act in opposition to; to render ineffectual.

counterbalance, koun-tėr-bal'ans, *vt.* To weigh against with an equal weight; to act against with equal power.—*n.* Equal weight, power, or agency, acting in opposition.

countercheck, koun-tėr-chek', *vt.* To oppose by some obstacle; to check.—*n.* Check, check that controls another check.

counterfeit, koun'tėr-fit, *vt.* and *i.* To forge; to copy; to feign.—*a.* Made in imitation; fraudulent.—*n.* An imposter; a forgery.

counterpoise, koun'tėr-poiz, *vt.* To counterbalance.—*n.* A weight which balances another; equivalence of power or force; equilibrium.

countryman, kun'tri-man, *n.* One born in the same country with another; one who dwells in the country; a rustic.

county, koun'ti, *n.* A particular portion of a state or kingdom; a shire.—*a.* Pertaining to a county.

couplet, kup'let, *n.* Two lines that rhyme.

coupling, kup'ling, *n.* The act of one who couples; that which couples; a hook, chain, or other contrivance forming a connection.

courage, ku'rij, *n.* Intrepidity; dauntlessness; hardihood.

courageous, ku-rā'jē-us. *a.* Bold; brave, heroic, fearless.

courier, kö'rē-er, *n.* A messenger sent express with dispatches; a travelling attendant.

courthouse, kört'hous, *n.* A house in which established courts are held.

cove, kōv, *n.* A small inlet or bay; a sheltered recess in the sea-shore a concave molding; a man, fellow.—*vt.* To arch over.

covenant, kuv'en-ant, *n.* A contract; compact; a writing containing the terms of an agreement.— *vi.* To enter into a formal agree ment; to stipulate.—*vt.* To grant by covenant.

coverlet, kuv'ėr-let, *n.* The cover of a bed.

covert, kuv'ėrt, *a.* Kept secret; private; insidious.—*n.* A shelter; a thicket.

cowardice, kou'ėrd-is, *n.* Want of courage to face danger.

cow-catcher, kou'kach-ėr, *n.* A frame in front of locomotives to remove obstructions.

cower, kou'ėr, *vi.* To crouch; to sink by bending the knees; to shrink through fear.

cowhide, kou'hĭd. *n.* The hide of a cow; a leather whip.—*vt.* To flog with a leather whip.

crab, krab, *n.* A crustaceous fish with strong claws, a portable windlass, etc.; Cancer, a sign of the zodiac; a wild sour apple; a morose person.

crabbed, krab'ed, *a.* Perverse; peevish, perplexing.

crack, krak, *n.* A chink or fissure, a sudden or sharp sound; a sounding blow, a chat.—*vt.* and *i.* To break with a sharp, abrupt sound; to break partially: to snap: to boast of, to utter with smartness; to chat.

cracked, krakt, *a.* Having fissures but not in pieces, impaired, crazy.

cracker, krak'ẽr, *n.* One who or that which cracks, a small firework; a hard biscuit.

crackle, krak'l, *vi.* (crackling, crackled). To make small abrupt noises rapidly repeated.

crackling, krak'ling, *n.* The act or noise of the verb to crackle, the brown skin of roasted pork.

cradle, krā'dl, *n.* A small bed in which infants are rocked, a frame to support or hold together.—*vt.* (cradling, cradled). To lay or rock in a cradle.

Craniology, krā-ni-ol'o-ji, *n.* The knowledge of the cranium or skull.

cranium, krā'ni-um, *n.* The skull; the bones which inclose the brain.

crank, krangk, *n.* A contrivance for producing a horizontal or perpendicular motion by means of a rotary motion, or the contrary; a bend or turn.—*a.* Liable to be overset, loose.

cravat, kra-vat', *n.* A neck-cloth.

craven, krā'vn, *n.* A coward; a weak-hearted, spiritless fellow.—*a.* Cowardly.

craw, krä, *n.* The crop or first stomach of fowls.

crawl, kräl, *vi.* To creep; to advance slowly, slyly, or weakly.

crayfish, crawfish, krā'fish. krä'fish, *n.* A crustacean found in streams; also the spiny lobster, a sea crustacean.

crayon, krā'on, *n.* A pencil of colored clay, chalk, or charcoal, used in drawing; a drawing made with crayons.—*vt.* To sketch.

craze, krāz, *vt.* (crazing, crazed). To shatter; to impair the intellect of —*vi.* To become crazy.—*n.* An inordinate desire.

crazy, krā z'i, *a.* Decrepit; deranged; weakened or disordered in intellect.

create, kre-āt', *vt.* (creating, created). To bring into being from nothing; to cause to be; to shape; to beget, to bring about; to invest with a new character; to constitute or appoint.

creation, krē-ā'shon, *n.* Act of creating; the aggregate of created things; the universe; conferring of a title or dignity.

creature, krē'tur, *n.* Something created; a human being, something imagined; a person who owes his rise to another; a mere tool.

credential, krē-den'shi-al, *n.* That which gives a title to credit; *(pl.)* documents showing that one is entitled to credit, or is invested with authority.

credit, kred'it, *n.* Reliance on testimony; faith, reputed integrity; transfer of goods, etc., in confidence of future payment; reputation for pecuniary worth; time given for payment of goods sold on trust, side of an account in which payment is entered; money possessed or due.—*vt.* To trust, to believe; to sell or lend to, in confidence of future payment; to procure credit or honor to, to enter on the credit side of an account; to attribute.

credulity, kred-du'li-ti, *n.* A disposition to believe on slight evidence.

creed krēd, *n.* A system of principles believed or professed; a brief summary of the articles of Christian faith.

creek, krēk, *n.* A small bay; a small harbor, a brook.

creep, krēp, *vi.* (creeping, crept). To move as a reptile; to crawl; to grow along the ground, or on another body; to move secretly, feebly, or timorously; to be servile; to shiver.

cress, kres, *n.* The name of various plants, mostly cruciferous, used as a salad.

crib, krib, *n.* A child's bed; a small habitation; a rack a stall for oxen a framework; a literal translation.—*vt.* (cribbing, cribbed). To shut up in a narrow habitation; to pilfer.

Cribbage, krib'āj, *n.* A game of cards.

crick, krik, *n.* A local spasm or cramp; a stiffness of the neck.

cricket, krik'et, *n.* An insect which makes a creaking or chirping sound; an open-air game played with bats, ball, and wickets.

cringe, krinj, *vi.* (cringing, cringed). To bend, to bend with servility; to fawn.—*n.* A bow; servile civility.

crinkle, kring'kl, *vi.* (crinkling, crinkled). To bend in little turns; to wrinkle.—*vt.* To form with short turns or wrinkles.—*n.* A winding or turn; a wrinkle.

criterion, krī-tē'ri-un, *n.;* pl. **-ia**. Standard of judging; a measure, test.

critic, kri'tik, *n*. One skilled in judging literary or artistic work; a reviewer; a severe judge.—*a*. Relating to criticism.

critical, kri'tik-al, *a*. Relating to or containing criticism; nicely judicious, inclined to find fault, relating to a crisis; momentous.

crochet, krō'shā, *n*. A species of knitting performed by means of a small hook.

crockery, krok'e-ri, *n*. Earthenware, vessels formed of clay glazed and baked.

crop, krop, *n*. The first stomach of birds; the craw; harvest; corn, etc., while growing; act of cutting, as hair; a short whip without a lash.—*vt*. (cropping, cropped). To cut off the ends of; to cut close; to browse, to gather before it falls; to cultivate.

crop-eared, krop'ērd, *a*. Having the ears cut short.

croquet, krō'kā, *n*. An open-air game played with mallets, balls, hoops, and pegs.

cross, kros, *n*. An instrument of death, consisting of two pieces of timber placed transversely; the symbol of the Christian religion; the religion itself, a monument or sign in the form of a cross; anything that thwarts; a hybrid.—*a*. Athwart, adverse; fretful.—*vt*. To draw a line or lay a body across; to mark with a cross, to cancel; to pass from side to side of, to thwart; to perplex; to interbreed.—*vi*. To be athwart; to move across.

crotch, kroch, *n*. A fork or forking.

crotchet, kroch'et, *n*. A note in music, half the length of a minim; a whim; a perverse conceit; a bracket in printing.

crow, krō, *n*. A black bird of the genus Corvus, including the raven, rook, jackdaw, etc., a crowbar, the sound which a cock utters.—*vi*. (crowing, *pret*. crew, crowed, *pp*. crowed). To cry as a cock; to exult; to boast.

crowbar, krō'bar, *n*. A bar of iron with a bent or forked end, used as a lever.

crowd, kroud, *n*. A number of persons or things; a throng; the populace.—*vt*. To fill by pressing together, to fill to excess.—*vi*. To press in numbers; to throng.

crowded, kroud'ed, *a*. Filled by a promiscuous multitude.

crow's-feet, krōz'fēt, *n.pl*. The wrinkles at corners of the eyes, the effects of age.

crucial, krō'shi-al, *a*. Relating to a cross, severe searching, decisive.

crucible, krō'si-bl, *n*. A melting pot, used by chemists and others.

Crucifix, krō'si-fiks, *n*. A cross with the figure of Christ crucified on it.

Crucifixion, krō-si-fik'shon, *n*. The act of crucifying; the death of Christ.

crucify, krō'si-fī, *vt*. (crucifying crucified). To put to death by nailing the hands and feet of to a cross, to mortify; to torment.

crude, krōd, *a*. Raw, unripe; in its natural state; not brought to perfection.

cruel, krō'el, *a*. Unmerciful; hardhearted; ferocious; brutal; severe.

cruet, krō'et, *n*. A vial or small glass bottle for holding vinegar, oil, etc.

cruise, krōz, *vi*. (cruising, cruised). To sail hither and thither.—*n*. A sailing to and fro in search of an enemy's ships, or for pleasure.

cruiser, krōz'ėr, *n*. A person or a ship that cruises; a swift armed vessel to protect or destroy shipping.

crumb, krum, *n*. A fragment; a small piece of bread broken off the soft part of bread.—*vt*. To break into small pieces with the fingers; to cover with breadcrumbs.

crush, krush, *vt*. To squeeze; to bruise; to pound; to overpower; to oppress.—*vi*. To be pressed; to force one's way amid a crowd.—*n*. A violent pressing or squeezing; a crowding.

crust, krust, *n*. The hard outer coat of anything; the outside of a loaf, a piece of hard bread; a deposit from wine.—*vt*. and *i*. To cover with a crust or hard coat.

cry, krī, *vi*. (crying, cried). To utter the loud shrill sounds of weeping joy, fear, surprise, etc.; to clamor; to weep.—*vt*. To shout; to proclaim.—*n*. The loud voice of man or beast; a shriek or scream; acclamation, weeping, importunate call, a political catchword.

crypt, kript, *n*. A subterranean cell for burying purposes; a subterranean chapel.

ctenoid, ten'oid, *a*. Comb-shaped; having the posterior edge with teeth: said of the scales of fishes; having scales of this kind.

cub, kub, *n*. The young of certain quadrupeds, as the bear and fox.—*vi*. (cubbing, cubbed). To bring forth cubs.

cube, kūb, *n*. A regular solid body, with six equal square sides, the third power, or the product from multiplying a number twice by itself.—*vt*. To raise to the third power.

cubicle, kū-bi-kl, *n.* A sleeping place, a compartment for one bed in a dormitory.

cubit, kū'bit, *n.* The forearm; the length from the elbow to the extremity of the middle finger, usually taken as 18 inches.

cuckold, kük'öld, *n.* A man whose wife is false to his bed.—*vt.* To make a cuckold of.

cuckoo, kü'kö, *n.* A migratory bird so named from the sound of its note.

cucumber, kū'kum-bér, *n.* An annual plant of the gourd family.

cud, kud, *n.* The food which ruminating animals bring up from the first stomach to chew.

cue, kū, *n.* The last words of an actor's speech, catch-word, hint, the part which any man is to play in his turn; humor; the straight rod used in billiards.

cuff, kuf, *n.* A blow; slap; part of a sleeve near the hand.—*vt.* To beat; to strike with talons or wings, or with fists.

culprit, kul'prit, *n.* A person arraigned in court for a crime, or convicted of a crime; a criminal; an offender.

cult, kult, *n.* A system of belief and worship; a subject of devoted study.

cultivate, kul'ti-vät, *vt.* To till; to refine, to foster, to improve.

culture, kul'tūr, *n.* Cultivation, the rearing of certain animals, as oysters; the application of labor, or other means of improvement, the result of such efforts; refinement.—*vt.* To cultivate.

culvert, kul'vért, *n.* An arched drain under a road, railway, etc., for the passage of water.

cumulation, kū-mu-lā'shon, *n.* A heaping up; a heap; accumulation.

cumulus, kū'mū-lus, *n.*, pl. -**li.** A cloud in the form of dense convex or conical heaps.

cuneiform, kū-nē'i-form, *a.* Wedge-shaped; applied to the arrowheaded characters on old Babylonian and Persian inscriptions.

cunning, kun'ing, *a.* Astute; artful.—*n.* Faculty or act of using stratagem; craftiness; artifice.

cupboard, kup'bōrd, *n.* A case or inclosure for cups, plates, dishes, etc.

curate, kū'rāt, *n.* One to whom the cure of souls is committed, a clergyman employed to assist in the duties of a rector or vicar.

curative, kū'rāt-iv, *a.* Relating to the cure of diseases; tending to cure.

curb, kérb, *vt.* To control; to check; to restrain with a curb, as a horse to strengthen by a curb-stone.—*n.* Check; restraint; part of a bridle; a curb-stone.

curio, kū'ri-ō, *n.;* pl. -**os,** A curiosity; an interesting and curious article.

curiosity, kūri-os'i-ti, *n.* Inquisitiveness; a thing unusual; a rarity.

curl, kérl, *vt.* To form into ringlets, —*vi.* To take a twisted or coiled form; to play at the game of curling.—*n.* A ringlet of hair, or anything of a like form, a waving; flexure.

curriculum, ku-rik'ū-lum, *n.* A course of study in a university, school, etc.

currier, ku'ri-ér, *n.* A man who dresses leather after it is tanned.

curry, ku'ri, *n.* A highly spiced sauce or mixture; a dish cooked with curry.—*vt.* (currying, curried). To flavor with curry, to dress leather; to rub and clean (a horse) with a comb, to seek (favor).

curse, kérs, *vt.* (cursing, cursed). To utter a wish of evil against; a blight, to torment with calamities. —*vi.* To utter imprecations, to blaspheme.—*n.* Imprecation of evil, execration, torment.

curve, kérv, *a.* Bending, inflected. —*n.* A bending without angles; a bent line.—*vt.* (curving, curved). To bend.

cushion, kush'on, *n.* A pillow for a seat, something resembling a pillow.—*vt.* To seat on a cushion; to furnish with cushions.

cusp, kusp, *n.* The point of the moon, or other luminary; a point formed by the meeting of two curves.

custodian, kus-tō'di-an, *n.* One who has care of a library, public building, etc.

custody, kus'tō-di, *n.* A keeping; guardianship; imprisonment; security.

custom, kus'tum, *n.* Habit, established practice, fashion, a buying of goods; business support; a tax on goods, *pl.* duties on merchandise imported or exported.

custom-house, kus'tum-hous, *n.* The office where customs are paid.

cut, kut, *vt.* (cutting, cut). To divide into pieces, to fell or mow, to clip to carve; to affect deeply; to intersect, to castrate, to divide, as cards, to refuse to recognize.—*vi.* To make an incision; to be severed by a cutting instrument, to pass straight and rapidly.—*a.* Gashed carved; intersected; deeply affected.—*n.* The action of an edged instrument; a wound; a stroke with a whip, a severe remark; a channel; any small piece; a lot; a near passage, a carving or engraving; act of dividing a pack of cards; form; fashion; refusal to recognize a person.

cyanide, sī'an-id, *n.* A combination of cyanogen with a metallic base.

cyanogen, sī-an'ō-jen, *n.* A poisonous gas of a strong and peculiar odor.

cycle, sī'kl, *n.* An orbit in the heavens; a circle of years; a bicycle or tricycle.—*vi.* To recur in a cycle, to ride a bicycle.

cylinder, si'lin-dėr, *n.* An elongated round body of uniform diameter.

cymbal, sim'bal, *n.* A basin-shaped musical instrument of brass, used in pairs.

cynic, sin'ik, *n.* One of a sect of Greek philosophers who professed contempt of riches, arts, etc.; a morose man.

cypress, sī'pres, *n.* An evergreen tree, the emblem of mourning.

cyst, sist, *n.* A bag in animal bodies containing matter.

D

dabble, dab'bl, vt. (dabbling, dabbled). To wet, to sprinkle.—vi. To play in water, to do anything in a superficial manner, to meddle.

dais, dā'is, n. The high table at the upper end of the dining-hall, the raised floor on which the table stood; a canopy.

damage, dam'āj, n. Hurt; injury; money compensation (generally in pl.).—vt. (damaging, damaged). To injure, to impair.

damn, darn, vt. To send to hell; to condemn.

damnation, dam-nā'shon, n. Condemnation; sentence to punishment in the future state.

dandelion, dan'di-lī-un, n. A composite plant bearing a bright yellow flower.

dandle, dan'dl, vt. (dandling, dandled). To shake on the knee, as an infant, to fondle, to trifle with.

dandruff, dan'druff, n. A scurf on the head.

danger, dān'jer, n. Exposure to injury; jeopardy; risk.

dangerous, dān'jer-us, a. Perilous causing risk of harm; unsafe; insecure.

dangle, dang'gl, vi. (dangling, dangled). To hang loose, to follow officiously.— vt. To carry suspended loosely, to swing.

darkness, därk'nes, n. Absence of light; blackness; gloom; ignorance, privacy.

darling, där'ling, a. Dearly beloved.—n. One much beloved; a favorite.

darn, därn, vt. To mend by imitating the texture of the stuff with thread and needle, to sew together.—n. A place so mended.

dauby, däb'i, a. Viscous; glutinous.

daybreak, dā'brak, n. The dawn; first appearance of light in the morning.

daydream, dā'drēm, vt. A vision to the waking senses, a reverie.

daylight, dā'līt, n. The light of the day.

daze, dāz, vt. (dazing, dazed). To stupefy, to stun.

dead, ded, a. Without life; deceased, perfectly still, dull, cold tasteless; spiritless; utter; unerring.

deaden, ded'n, vt. To abate in vigor force, or sensation; to darken, dull or dim.

deaf, def, a. Wanting the sense of hearing, not listening or regarding.

dearth, derth, n. Scarcity; want; famine.

debauch, dē-bäch', vt. To corrupt to pervert.—vi. To riot; to revel.—n. Excess in eating or drinking; lewdness.

debit, deb'it, n. A recorded item of debt, the left-hand page or debtor side of a ledger or account.—vt. To charge with debt.

debonair, de-bō-nār', a. Gracious; courteous.

debouch, dē-bösh', vi. To issue or march out of a narrow place.

debris, dē-brē', n.sing. or pl. Fragments; rubbish.

debt, det, n. That which is due from one person to another; obligation; guilt.

debut, dā-bü', n. First appearance in public.

decade, de'kād, n. The number of ten, a period of ten Years.

decapod, dek'a-pod, n. A crustacean having ten feet, as a crab; also a cuttle-fish with ten prehensile arms.

deceit, dē-sēt', n. Fraud; guile; cunning.

deceitful, dē-sēt'ful, a. Fraudulent delusive; false; hollow.

December, dē-sem'ber, n. The twelfth and last month of the year.

decency, dē'sen-si, n. The state or quality of being decent; decorum; modesty.

decennial, dē-sen'ni-al, a. Consisting of ten years; happening every ten years.

decent, dē'sent, a. Becoming seemly; respectable; modest, moderate.

decentralize, dē-sen'tral-īz, vt. To remove from direct dependence on a central authority.

decide, dē-sīd', vt. (deciding, decided). To determine, to settle, to resolve.—vi. To determine; to pronounce a judgment.

deck, dek, vt. To clothe; to adorn; to furnish with a deck, as a vessel.—n. The platform or floor of a ship.

declaim, dē-klam', vi. To make a formal speech; to harangue; to inveigh.

declamation, de-kla-mā'shon, n. The art or act of declaiming; a harangue.

declaration, de-kla-rā'shon, n. Act of declaring, that which is declared; an explicit statement; a solemn affirmation.

declarative, dē-klār'at-iv, a. Explanatory; making proclamation.

decoration, dek'ō-rā'shon, n. Act of decorating; that which adorns; a badge or medal.

decorum, dē-kō'rum, n. Propriety of speech or behavior; seemliness.

decoy, dē-koi', n. An enclosure for catching ducks or wild fowls, a lure.—vt. To lure into a snare; to entice.

decrement, de'krē-ment, *n*. De-crease; quantity lost by diminution or waste.

decrepit, dē-krep'it, *a*. Broken down with age; being in the last stage of decay.

dedicate, ded'i-kāt, *vt*. (dedicating, dedicated). To consecrate to a sacred purpose, to devote (often refl.); to inscribe to a friend.

dedication, ded-i-kā'shon, *n*. Act of devoting to some person, use, or thing; inscription or address.

deem, dēm, *vt*. To judge, to think.— *vi*. To judge; to be of opinion; to estimate.

deface, dē'fās', *vt*. To destroy or mar the surface of a thing; to disfigure; to erase.

defeat, dē-fet', *n*. Frustration; overthrow, loss of battle.—*vt*. To frustrate; to foil, to overthrow; to conquer.

defect, dē-fekt', *n*. Want, a blemish fault; flaw.

defective, dē-fekt'iv *a*. Having a defect; deficient; faulty.

defendant, dē-fen'dant, *n*. A defender; in law, the person that opposes a charge, etc.

defer, dē-fèr', *vt*. (deferring, deferred). To put off to a future time; to postpone.— *vi*. To yield to another's opinion, to submit courteously or from respect.

deference, de'fer-ens, *n*. A yielding in opinion; regard; respect; submission.

deferment, dē-fer-ment, *n*. Postponement.

defiance, dē-fī'ans, *n*. Act of defying; a challenge to fight; contempt of opposition or danger.

deficient, de-fi'shent, *a*. Defective; imperfect; not adequate.

defunct, dē-fungkt', *a*. Dead; deceased.— *n*. A dead person; one deceased.

defy, dē-fī', *vt*. (defying, defied). To provoke to combat, to dare, to challenge, to set at nought.

degrade, dē-grād', *vt*. (degrading, degraded). To reduce to a lower rank; to strip of honors, to debase; to depose; to dishonor.

dehydration, dē-hī-drā'shon, *n*. Process of freeing a compound from water.

delectable, dē-lekt'a-bl, *a*. Delightful.

deliberation, dē'-lib'é -rā "shon, *n*. Thoughtful consideration, prudence, discussion of reasons for and against a measure.

delicacy, de'li-ka-si, *n*. The quality of being delicate- fineness of texture; tenderness; minute accuracy, refined taste, a dainty.

deliverance, dē-liv'ér-ans, *n*. Re-lease; rescue; an authoritative judgment.

delusive, de-lū"siv, *a*. Apt to deceive.

delve, delv, *vt*. and *i*. (delving delved). To dig.

demagnetize, dē-mag'net-īz, *vt*. To deprive of magnetic polarity.

demagogue, dem'a-gog, *n*. A leader of the people; a factious orator.

demarcation, de-mär-kā'shon, *n*. Act of setting a limit; a limit fixed.

demean, dē-mēn', *vt*. To conduct, to behave, to debase (oneself).

demeanor, dē-mēn'èr, *n*. Manner of conducting oneself; behavior.

demobilize, dē-mō'bil-īz, *vt*. To disband.

demolish, dē-mol'ish, *vt*. To pull down; to destroy.

demon, dē'mon, *n*. A spirit, holding a place below the celestial deities of the pagans, an evil spirit, a devil; a fiendlike man.

demoralize, dē-mo'ral-īz, *vt*. To corrupt the morals of, to deprave.

demoralizing, dē-mo'ral-īz-ing, *p.a*. Tending to destroy morals or moral principles.

demure, dē-mūr', *a*. Consciously grave, affectedly modest.

den, den, *n*. A cave; a dell; a haunt.

denary, dē-na-ri, *a*. Containing ten; proceeding by tens.—*n*. The number ten.

dendriform, den'dri-form, *a*. Having the form or appearance of a tree.

denial, dē-nī'al, *n*. Act of denying contradiction; refusal to grant or acknowledge.

denigrate, den'i-grāt, *vt*. To blacken; to sully.

denim, den'im, *n*. A coarse cotton drill used for making aprons, overalls, etc.

denizen, de'ni-zn, *n*. A stranger admitted to residence in a foreign country.

denominate, dē-nom'in-āt, *vt*. (denominating, denominated). To name, to designate.

denomination, dē-nom'in-ā"shon, *n*. Act of naming; title; class; religious sect.

denominationalism, dē-nom'in-ā" shonal-izm, *n*. A class spirit; system of religious sects having each their own schools.

denominative, dē-nom'in-āt-iv, *a*. That confers a distinct appellation.

denote, dē-not', *vt*. To indicate; to imply.

denouement, dā-nō'mäng, *n*. The winding up of a plot in a novel or drama; solution of a mystery; issue, the event.

denounce, dē-nouns', *vt*. (denouncing, denounced). To threaten; to accuse publicly, to stigmatize.

dentition, den-ti'shon, *n.* The cutting of teeth in infancy; the system of teeth peculiar to an animal.

denture, den'tūr, *n.* A set of false teeth.

denude, dē-nūd', *vt.* (denuding, denuded). To make bare; to divest; to uncover.

denunciation, dē-nun'si-ā"shon, *n.* Act of denouncing; public menace; arraignment.

deodorize, dē-ō'dėr-īz, *vt.* (deodorizing, deodorized). To deprive of fetid odor.

deoxidate, deoxidize, dē-ok'sid-āt, de-ok'sĭd-iz, *vt.* To reduce from the state of an oxide.

depart, de-pärt', *vi.* To go away; to desist, to abandon; to deviate; to die.

department, dē-pärt'ment, *n.* A separate part; a division of territory; a distinct branch, as of science, etc.

depend, dē-pend, *vi.* To hang from; to be contingent or conditioned; to rest or rely solely; to trust.

deplorable, dē-plō r'a-bl, *a.* To be deplored; lamentable; grievous; pitiable.

deplore, dē-plōr', *vt.* (deploring, deplored). To feel or express deep grief for; to bewail.

deploy, dē-ploi', *vt.* To open out; to extend from column to line as a body of troops.—*vi.* To form a more extended front or line.

deportation, dē-pōrt-ā'shon, *n.* Removal from one country to another; exile.

depot, dep'ō, *n.* A place of deposit; headquarters of a regiment; a railway-station.

deprave, dē-prā v', *vt.* (depraving, depraved). To make bad or worse to impair the good qualities of; to corrupt; to vitiate.

depredate, de'pre-dāt, *vt.* To plunder, to waste.

depress, dē-pres', *vt.* To press down; to lower; to humble; to deject.

derangement, dē-rānj'ment, *n.* A putting out of order; disorder; insanity.

derelict, de're-likt, *a.* Abandoned.—*n.* Anything forsaken or left, especially a ship.

dereliction, de-re-lik 'shon, *n.* Act of forsaking; state of being forsaken; neglect.

deride, dē-rīd', *vt.* (deriding, derided). To laugh at in contempt; to ridicule, to jeer.

derision, dē-ri'zhon, *n.* Act of deriding; scorn; ridicule, mockery.

derivation, de-ri-vā'shon, *a.* Act of deriving, the tracing of a word from its root; deduction.

derivative, de-riv'āt-iv, *a.* Derived sec-

ondary.—*n.* That which is derived; a word which takes its origin in another word.

derive, de-rĭv', *vt.* (deriving, derived). To draw or receive, as from a source or origin, to trace the etymology of.—*vi.* To come from.

derma, dermis, derm, dėr'ma, dėr'mis, dė rm, *n.* The true skin, or under layer of the skin.

descant, des'kant, *n.* A discourse discussion, a song or tune with various modulations.—*vi.* deskant'. To discourse or animadvert freely; to add a part to a melody.

descend, dē-send, *vi.* To pass or move down, to invade, to be derived; to pass to an heir.—*vt.* To pass or move down, on, or alone.

desecrate, de'se-krāt, vt. (desecrating, desecrated). To divert from a sacred purpose, to profane.

desiderate, dē-sid'er-āt, *vt.* To desire; to want, to miss.

despair, dē-spār', *n.* A hopeless state, despondency, that which causes despair; loss of hope.—*vi.* To give up all hope; to despond.

despite, dē-spît', *n.* Extreme malice, defiance with contempt, an act of malice. — *vt.* To despise, to spite. —*prep.* In spite of; notwithstanding.

despoil, dē-spoil', *vt.* To take from by force; to rob; to bereave; to rifle.

despond, dē-spond', *vi.* To be cast down or dejected; to lose heart, hope, or resolution.

dessert, dē-zėrt', *n.* That which is served at the close of a dinner, as fruits, etc.

destination, des-tin-ā'shon, *n.* Act of destining; ultimate design; predetermined end.

destine, des'tin, *vt.* (destining, destined). To set or appoint to a purpose; to design; to doom; to ordain.

destroy, dē-stroi', *vt.* To pull down to overthrow; to devastate; to annihilate.

detain, dē-tān', *vt.* To keep back or from; to withhold; to arrest, to check, to retard.

detect, dē-tekt', *vt.* To discover, to bring to light.

detergent, dē-tėrj'ent, *a.* Cleansing; purging.—*n.* That which cleanses.

deteriorate, dē-tē'ri-ō-rā t, *vi.* (deteriorating, deteriorated). To grow worse, to degenerate.—*vt.* To reduce in quality.

detest, dē-test', *vt.* To abhor; to loathe.

detestable, dē-test'a-bl, *a.* Extremely hateful; abominable; odious.

D

dethrone, dē-thrōn', *vt.* (dethroning dethroned). To divest of royal authority and dignity; to depose.

detonate, de'tō-nāt, *vt.* (detonating, detonated). To cause to explode, to cause to burn with a sudden repot.—*vi.* To explode.

detract, dē-trakt', *vt.* To draw away, to disparage.—*vi.* To take away from (especially reputation).

devastate, de'vas-tāt, *vt.* (devastating, devastated). To lay waste; to ravage.

deviate, de'vi-āt, *vi.* (deviating, deviated). To stray; to wander; to swerve, to err.

device, dē-vīs', *n.* That which is devised, contrivance; scheme; an emblem.

devotee, dev-o-tē', *n.* One wholly devoted, particularly to religion; a votary.

devout, dē-vout', *a.* Pious, expressing devotion; earnest; solemn.

diagnose, dī-ag-nōs', *vt.* To ascertain from symptoms the true nature of.

diagnosis, dī-ag-nō'sis, *n.* The ascertaining from symptoms the true nature of diseases.

diagram, dī'a-gram, *n.* A drawing to demonstrate the properties of any figure; an illustrative figure in outline.

dial, dī'al, *n.* An instrument for showing the hour by the sun's shadow; face of a clock, etc.

dialect, dī'a-lekt, *n.* The idiom of a language peculiar to a province; language; manner of speaking.

diapason, dī-a-pā'zon, *n.* The entire compass of a voice or instrument; an organ stop.

diaphanous, dī-af'an-us, *a.* Having power to transmit rays of light transparent.

diarrhea, dī-a-rē'a, *n.* A morbidly frequent evacuation of the intestines.

diary, dī'a-ri, *n.* A register of daily events or transactions; a journal.

dibble, dib'bl, *n.* A pointed instrument to make holes for planting seeds, etc.—*vt.* (dibbling, dibbled). To make holes for planting seeds, etc.

dickey, **dicky**, dik'i, *n.* A false shirtfront; the driver's seat in a carriage.

dicotyledon, dī'kot-i-lē"don, *n.* A plant whose seeds contain a pair of cotyledons.

dictaphone, dik'ta-fon, *n.* Trade name for an instrument into which correspondence is dictated to be transcribed afterwards.

dictator, dik-tāt'èr, *n.* One invested with absolute authority.

diction, dik'shon, *n.* Choice of words; mode of expression, style.

die, dī, *vi.* (dying, died). To cease to live, to expire; to sink gradually; to vanish.

dietetics, dī-et-et'iks, *n.* Principles for regulating the diet.

differ, dif'èr, *vi.* To be unlike or distinct; to disagree; to be at variance.

digit, di'jit, *n.* A finger; three-fourths of an inch, the twelfth part of the diameter of the sun or moon; any integer under 10.

dignify, dig'ni-fi, *vt.* (dignifying, dignified). To invest with dignity, to exalt in rank or office; to make illustrious.

digress, di-gres' or di'gres, *vi.* To depart from the main subject; to deviate.

diligence, di'li-jens, *n.* Steady application; assiduity; a four-wheeled stage-coach.

diluvium, di-lū'vi-um, *n.* A deluge or inundation; a deposit of sand, gravel, etc., caused by a flood.

dim, dim, *a.* Not seeing clearly; not clearly seen; mysterious; tarnished. —*vt.* (dimming, dimmed). To dull, to obscure, to sully.

dime, dim, *n.* A silver coin the tenth of a dollar.

diminish, di-min'ish, *vt.* To reduce to abate, to degrade.—*vi.* To become less.

dinner, din'nèr, *n.* The principal meal of the day.

diocese, dī'ō-sēs, *n.* An ecclesiastical division of a state, subject to a bishop.

diorama, dī-ō-rä'ma, *n.* A contrivance for giving a high degree of optical illusion to painted scenes.

diphtheria, dif-thē'ri-a, *n.* An epidemic inflammatory disease of the throat.

diphthong, dif'thong, *n.* A union of two vowels pronounced in one syllable.

diploma, di-plō-ma, *n.* A document conferring some power, privilege, or honor.

disagree, dis-a-grē', *vi.* To be of a different opinion, to dissent; to be unfriendly, to be unsuitable.

disapprove, dis-ap-pröv', *vt.* To censure as wrong, to regard with dislike; to reject.

disarrange, dis-a-ranj', *vt.* To put out of arrangement or order; to derange.

disarray, dis-a-rā', *vt.* To undress; to throw into disorder.—*n.* Disorder, undress.

disband dis-band', *vt.* To dismiss from military service; to dis perse.—*vi.* To retire from military service; to dissolve connection.

disbar, dis-bär', *vt.* To expel from being a member of the bar.

discard, dis-kärd', *vt*. To throw away; to cast off; to dismiss; to dis charge.

discernment, dis-sẽrn'ment, *n*. Act or power of discerning; judgment; sagacity.

disciple, dis-sī'pl, *n*. A learner, a pupil, an adherent to the doctrines of another.

disconsolate, dis-kon'sō-lāt, *a*. Comfortless, hopeless; gloomy, cheerless.

discontent, dis-kon-tent', *n*. Want of content, uneasiness of mind dissatisfaction.

discontinuance, dis-kon-tin'ū-ans, *n*. A breaking off- cessation.

discord, dis'kord, *n*. Want of concord; disagreement; disagreement of sounds.

discountenance, dis-koun'ten-ans *vt*. To restrain by censure, cold treatment, etc.

discourage, dis-ku'rāj, *vt*. (discouraging, discouraged). To dishearten, to dissuade.

discouragement, dis-ku'rāj-ment, *n*. Act of discouraging; that which discourages.

discourse, dis-kōrs', *n*. A speech; treatise, sermon- conversation.— *vi*. (discoursing, discoursed). To talk; to converse; to treat of formally, to expatiate.—*vt*. To utter.

discourtesy, dis-kõr'te-si, *n*. In-civility, rudeness, act of disrespect.

discovery, dis-kuv'ẽri, *n*. Act of discovering; disclosure; that which is discovered.

discreet, dis-krēt, *a*. Prudent; wary; judicious.

discrete, dis'kret, *a*. Separate; distinct.

disembroil, dis-em-broil', *vt*. To disentangle, to free from perplexity.

disentangle, dis-en-tang'gl, *vt*. To free from entanglement; to clear.

disfavor, dis-fa'vėr, *n*. Want of favor, unfavorable regard.—*vt*. To withhold favor from; to discountenance.

disfigure, dis-fi'gūr, *vt*. (disfiguring, disfigured). To mar the figure of; to impair the beauty, symmetry, or excellence of.

disfranchise, dis-fran'chiz, *vt*. To deprive of the rights of a free citizen.

disgust, dis-gust', *n*. Distaste; loathing; repugnance.—*vt*. To cause distaste in; to offend the mind or moral taste of

dishearten, dis-härt'n, *vt*. To discourage to depress.

dishevel, di-she'vel, *vt*. (dishevelling, dishevelled). To put out of order, or spread loosely, as the hair.

disjoint, disjoint', *vt*. To separate as parts united by joints; to put out of joint; to make incoherent.

dislocate, dis'lō-kāt, *vt*. To displace, to put out of joint.

disloyal, dis-loi'al, *a*. Void of loyalty, false to a sovereign, faithless.

dismal, diz'mal, *a*. Dark; gloomy; doleful, calamitous sorrowful.

dismantle, dis-man'tl, *vt*. To strip; to divest, to unrig; to deprive or strip, as of military equipment or defenses, to break down.

disobedience, dis-ō-bē'di-ens, *n*. Neglect or refusal to obey.

disobey, dis-ō-bā', *vt*. To neglect or refuse to obey; to violate an order.

disorganize, dis-or'gan-īz, *vt*. To destroy organic structure or connected system in; to throw into confusion.

disperse, dis-pẽrs', *vt*. To scatter; to dispel, to diffuse, to distribute.— *vi*. To be scattered; to vanish.

displease, dis-plēz, *vt*. To offend, to dissatisfy; to provoke.—*vi*. To disgust.

displeasure, dis-ple'zhŭr, *n*. Dissatisfaction, resentment.

disproportionate, dis-prō-pōr' shon-āt, *a*. Not proportioned; unsymmetrical, inadequate.

disprove, dis-pröv', *vt*. To prove to be false, to confute.

disputation, dis-pūt-ā'shon, *n*. Act of disputing; controversy in words; debate.

disqualify, dis-kwo'li-fī, *vt*. To divest of qualifications; to incapacitate.

disquiet, dis-kwī'et, *n*. Uneasiness anxiety.—*vt*. To make uneasy or restless.

disreputable, dis-rē'pūt-a-bl, *a*. Discreditable, low, mean.

disrepute, dis-rē-pūt', *n*. Loss or want of reputation; disesteem; disgrace.

disrespect, dis-rē-spekt', *n*. Want of respect; incivility.—*vt*. To show disrespect to.

disroot, dis-rōt', *vt*. To tear up the roots.

dissatisfaction, dis-sa'tis-fak''shon, *n*. Want of satisfaction; discontent.

dissatisfy, dis-sa'tis-fī, *vt*. To fail to satisfy, to render discontented.

dissect, dis-sekt', *vt*. To cut up; to anatomize, to divide and examine minutely.

dissertation, dis-sẽr-tā'shon, *n*. A formal discourse; treatise; disquisition.

disservice, dis-sẽr'vis, *n*. An ill-service, injury, harm, mischief

dissever, dis-sev'er, *vt*. To part in two; to disunite.

dissident, dis'si-dent, *a*. Dissenting. —n. A dissenter.

dissimilitude, dis-si-mil'i-tū d, *n*. Unlikeness; want of resemblance.

dissolvent, diz-zolv'ent, *a*. Having power

D

to dissolve.—*n*. That which has the power of melting; a solvent.

distaste, dis-tāst', *n*. Aversion of the taste or mind, dislike.—*vt*. To dislike.

distend, dis-tend', *vt*. To stretch by force from within, to swell.—*vi*. To swell; to dilate.

distinguish, dis-ting'gwish, *vt*. To mark out by some peculiarity; to perceive, to make eminent, to signalize.—*vi*. To make a distinction; to find or show the difference.

distort, dis-tort', *vt*. To twist; to pervert.

distortion, dis-tor'shon, *n*. Act of distorting, a writhing motion, deformity; perversion of the true meaning of words.

distract, dis-trakt', *vt*. To draw towards different objects; to perplex; to disorder the reason of; to render furious.

distraught, dis-trät', *a*. Distracted.

distress, dis-tres', *n*. Anguish of body or mind, affliction, state of danger or destitution; act of distraining.—*vt*. To afflict with pain or anguish; to perplex.

distributive, dis-tri'būt-iv, *a*. That distributes; expressing separation or division.—*n*. A word that divides or distributes, as *each, every, either*.

district, dis'trikt, *n*. A limited extent of country; a circuit; a region.

distrust, dis-trust', *vt*. To have no trust in; to doubt; to suspect.—*n*. Want of trust; doubt; suspicion; discredit.

disturb, dis-térb ', *vt*. To throw into disorder; to agitate; to hinder; to move.

disturbance, dis-térb'ans, *n*. State of being disturbed; commotion; excitement- interruption of a right.

ditch, dich, *n*. A trench in the earth for drainage or defense.—*vi*. To dig a ditch.—*vt*. To dig a ditch in; to drain by a ditch; to surround with a ditch.

ditto, dit'tō, *n*. A word used in lists, etc., meaning same as above; often written *Do*.

dive, dīv, *vi*. (diving, dived). To plunge into water head-foremost; to go under water to execute some work- to go deep.

diverge, di-vèrj', *vi*. (diverging, diverged). To proceed from a point in different directions; to deviate; to vary.

diversity, di-vérs'i-ti, *n*. State of being diverse; contrariety, variety.

divert, di-vért', *vt*. To turn aside; to amuse.

divide, di-vīd', *vt*. (dividing, divided). To part asunder; to separate; to keep apart; to distribute, allot; to set at variance.—*vi*. To part; to be of different opinions;

to vote by the division of a legislative house into parties.

dividend, di'vi-dend *n*. A number which is to be divided; share of profit; share divided to creditors.

divination, di-vin-ā'shon, *n*. Act of divining; a foretelling future events, or discovering things secret, by magical means.

divulsion, di-vul'shon, *n*. A pulling tearing, or rending asunder, or separating.

dizziness, diz'zi-nes, *n*. Giddiness; vertigo.

dizzy, diz'zi, *a*. Having a sensation of whirling in the head; giddy causing giddiness.—*vt*. (dizzying dizzied). To make giddy.

docket, dok'et, *n*. A summary; a bill tied to goods; a list of cases in a court.—*vt*. To make an abstract of; to mark the contents of papers on the back; to attach a docket to.

dockyard, dok'yärd, *n*. A yard near a dock for naval stores.

doctor, dok'ter, *n*. A person who has received the highest degree in a university faculty, one licensed to practice medicine; a physician.—*vt*. To treat medically; to adulterate.

dodge, doj, *vt*. (dodging, dodged). To start aside; to quibble.—*vt*. To evade by a sudden shift of place.—*n*. An artifice, an evasion.

dodo, dō'dō, *n*. An extinct bird of Mauritius, having a massive, clumsy body, short strong legs and wings useless for flight.

doe, dō, *n*. A female deer.

dogmatism, dog'mat-izm, *n*. Positiveness in assertion; arrogance in opinion.

dogmatize, dog'mat-īz, *vi*. (dogmatizing, dogmatized). To assert with undue confidence; to advance principles with arrogance.

doily, doi'li, *n*. A small ornamental mat for glasses, etc.

doldrums, dol'drumz, *n.pl*. The dumps.

dole, dōl, *n*. That which is dealt out share; gratuity, grief, sorrow.—*vt*. (doling, doled). To deal out to distribute.

doleful, dōl'fül, *a*. Full of pain grief, etc.; expressing or causing grief; gloomy.

dolomite, dōl'o-mīt, *n*. A granular crystalline or schistose rock compounded of carbonate of magnesia and carbonate of lime.

dolor, dō'lèr, *n*. Sorrow; lamentation.

dolorous, dō'lèr-us, *a*. Sorrowful; doleful.

dolphin, dol'fin, *n*. A small species of

whale remarkable for gambolling in the water; a fish celebrated for its changes of color when dying.

dolt, dōlt, n. A blockhead.

domain, dō-mān', n. Territory governed; estate, a demesne.

dome, dōm, n. A hemispherical roof of a building; a large cupola.

domestic, dō-mes'tik, a. Belonging to the house or home tame, not foreign.—n. A household servant.

domesticate, do-mes'tik-āt, vt. To accustom to remain much at home; to tame.

domicile, do'mi-sil, n. A habitation; family residence.—vt. (domiciling domiciled). To establish in a residence.

dominant, dom'in-ant, a. Governing; predominant; ascendant.

dominate, dom'in-āt, vt. (dominating, dominated). To rule; to predominate over.

Don, don, n. A Spanish title, corresponding to Eng. Mr.; an important personage, a resident Fellow of a college at Oxford or Cambridge.—vt. (donning, donned). To put on; to invest with.

donate, dō'nāt, vt. To bestow.

donation, dō-nā'shon, n. Act of giving; that which is given; a gift; a present.

donkey, dong'ki, n. An ass.

donna, don'na, n. A lady, as, *prima donna*, the first female singer in an opera, etc.

doomsday, dömz'dā, n. The day of judgment.

door, dōr, n. The entrance of a house or room, the frame of boards that shuts such an entrance; avenue; means of approach.

dossier, dos'ē-ā, n. A collection of documents of information about a person or incident.

dot, dot, n. A small point, as made with a pen, etc.; a speck.—vt. (dotting, dotted). To mark with a dot to diversify with small objects.—vi. To make dots.

dotal, dōt'al, a. Pertaining to dower.

dotard, dōt'érd, n. One whose mind is impaired by age; one foolishly fond.

dote, dōt, vi. (doting, doted). To have the intellect impaired by age; to be foolishly fond.

doubling, du'bl-ing, n. Act of making double, a fold, a lining.

doubt, dout, vi. To waver in opinion or judgment; to question; to suspect.—vt. To deem uncertain; to distrust.—n. A wavering in opinion; uncertainty; suspicion.

dowager, dou'ā-jėr, n. A title given to the widow of a person of title provided that she is mother grandmother, or stepmother of the successor.

dowdy, dou'di, n. An awkward, illdressed woman.—a. Ill-dressed vulgar-looking.

dowel, dou'el, n. A pin of wood or iron to join boards, etc.—vt. (dowelling, dowelled). To fasten by dowels.

downy, doun'i, a. Covered with, or pertaining to, down, soft; soothing.

dowry, dou'ri, n. The property which a woman brings to her husband in marriage; a dower; gift.

dozen, du'zn, n. Twelve things regarded collectively.

Draconic, Draconian, drā-kon'ik, drā-kō'ni-an, a. Relating to Draco, the Athenian lawgiver; extremely severe.

draft, dräft, n. A detachment of men or things; an order for money; the first sketch of any writing; a sketch.—vt. To make a draft of; to sketch, to select.

drake, drāk, n. The male of ducks.

dram, dram, n. The eighth part of an ounce, or sixty grains apothecaries' measure; the sixteenth part of an ounce avoirdupois; as much spirituous liquor as is drunk at once.

drama, drä'ma, n. A representation on a stage; a play; dramatic literature.

dramatist, drä'mat-ist, n. The author of a dramatic composition.

dramaturgy, dräm'a-ter-ji, n. The science of dramatic composition and representation.

drape, drāp, vt. (draping, draped). To cover with cloth or drapery.

drapery, drāp'ė-ri, n. The occupation of a draper; fabrics of wool or linen; clothes or hangings.

drastic, dras'tik, a. Acting with strength or violence.—n. A strong purgative.

drawer, drä'ėr, n. One who or that which draws; he who draws a bill; a sliding box in a case, etc., pl. an under-garment for the lower limbs.

drawing, drä'ing, n. Act of one who draws; representation of objects by lines and shades; delineation.

drawl, dräl, vi. To speak with slow prolonged utterance.—vt. To utter in a slow tone.—n. A lengthened utterance.

dread, dred, n. Fear, united with respect; terror; the person or the thing dreaded.—a. Exciting great fear; terrible; venerable.—vt. and i. To fear in a great degree.

drill, dril, n. A kind of coarse linen or cotton cloth.

drone, drōn, *n.* The male or nonworking bee, an idler, a low humming sound; a large tube of the bagpipe.—*vi.* (droning, droned). To give a low dull sound; to hum.

drowse, drouz, *vi.* (drowsing drowsed). To nod in slumber; to doze, to look heavy.—*vt.* To make heavy with sleep, or stupid.

dual, dū'al, *a.* Expressing the number two; existing as two; twofold.

dubious, dū'bi-us, *a.* Wavering in opinion, doubtful; uncertain.

duel, dū'el, *n.* A premeditated combat between two persons, single combat; contest.

duet, dū'et, *n.* A piece of music for two performers, vocal or instrumental.

dugout, dug-out, *n.* A rudely hollowed-out canoe from trunk of tree, an underground shelter from shells, an elderly officer recalled to duty from retirement.

dull, dul, *a.* Stupid, slow, blunt drowsy, cheerless, not bright or clear; tarnished; uninteresting.— *vt.* To make dull, to stupefy, to blunt, to make sad to sully.—*vi.* To become dull, blunt or stupid.

dulness, dullness, dul'nes, *n.* Stupidity; heaviness; slowness; dimness.

duly, dū'li, *adv.* Properly; fitly.

dumb, dum, *a.* Incapable of speech, mute, silent, not accompanied with speech.

dump, dump, *n.* A heap of refuse; a place where refuse is deposited, a large concentration of military stores especially of ammunition.

dumpling, dump'ling, *n.* A pudding of boiled suet paste, with or without fruit.

dumpy, dump'i, *a.* Short and thick.

dunce, duns, *n.* One slow at learning, a dullard, a dolt.

dune, dūn, *n.* A sand-hill on the sea-coast.

dung, dung, *n.* The excrement of animals.—*vt.* To manure; to immerse (calico) in cow-dung and water.—*vi.* To void excrement.

dungeon, dun'jon, *n.* A strong tower in the middle of a castle; a deep, dark place of confinement.

durable, dūr'a-bl, *a.* Having the quality of lasting long; permanent, firm.

dust, dust, *n.* Fine dry particles of earth, etc.; powder; earth as symbolic of mortality; a low condition.—*vt.* To free from dust, to sprinkle, as with dust.

Dutch, duch, *a.* Pertaining to Holland, or to its inhabitants.—*n.pl.* The people of Holland; sing. their language.

duty, dū'ti, *n.* That which a person is bound to perform; obligation; act of reverence or respect; business, service, or office; tax, impost or customs.

dwell, dwel, *vi.* (pret. and pp. dwelled). To live in a place; to reside; to hang on with fondness; to continue.

dwindle, dwin'dl, *vi.* (dwindling dwindled). To diminish gradually to shrink; to sink.

dye, dī, *vt.* (dyeing, dyed). To stain; to give a new and permanent color to.—*n.* A coloring liquid or matter; tinge.

dying, dī'ing, *a.* Mortal; destined to death uttered, given, etc., just before death, pertaining to death fading away.

dynamics, dī-nam'iks, *n.* The science which investigates the action of force

dynamite, din'a-mīt, *n.* An explosive substance consisting of some powdery matter impregnated with nitro-glycerine.

dynamo, dī'na-mō, *n.* A machine for producing an electric current by mechanical power.

dynasty, di'nas-ti, *n.* A race of kings of the same family.

dyne, din, *n.* A unit of force, being that force which, acting on a gram for one second, generates a velocity of a centimeter per second.

dysentery, dis'en-te-ri, *n.* A disorder of the intestines; a flux in which the stools consist chiefly of blood and mucus.

E

each, ĕch, *a.* and *pron.* Every one of any number considered individually.

eager, ē'gėr, *a.* Sharp; ardent; keenly desirous; impetuous; earnest, intense.

eagle, ē'gl, *n.* A large bird of prey, of great powers of flight and vision; a military standard.

ear, ēr, *n.* The organ of hearing power of distinguishing musical sounds; heed; regard; anything resembling an ear or ears; a spike, as of corn—*vi.* To form ears, as corn.—*vt.* To plow or till.

earnest, ėrn'est, *a.* Ardent in the pursuit of an object; eager; zealous, serious—*n.* Seriousness, a reality first-fruits, a part given beforehand as a pledge for the whole, indication, token.

earnest-money, ėrn'est-mun-i, *n.* Money paid as earnest, to bind a bargain, etc

Earth, ėrth, *n.* The globe we inhabit, the world; the fine mold on the surface of the globe; dry land; the ground, the hiding hole of a fox, etc.—*vt.* To cover with earth.— *vi.* To retire underground; to burrow.

east, ēst, *n.* That part of the heavens where the sun rises, the countries east of Europe.—*a.* In or toward the east, easterly.—*adv.* Eastwards.

Easter, ēs'tėr, *n.* A festival of the Christian church in March or April, in commemoration of Christ's resurrection.

easy, ēz'i, *a.* Being at ease free from pain or anxiety; not difficult; gentle; complying; affluent; not stiff or formal.

ebony, eb'on-i, *n.* A hard, heavy dark wood admitting of a fine polish.

ebullient, ē-bul'yent, *a.* Boiling over, as a liquor; over enthusiastic.

eccentric, ek-sen'trik, *a.* Not having its axis in the center; not having the same center; deviating from usual practice, etc., anomalous; whimsical.—*n.* An eccentric person; mechanical contrivance for converting circular into reciprocating rectilinear motion.

echelon, esh'e-lon, *n.* The position of troops or ships in parallel lines each line being a little to the right or left of the preceding one.

eclectic, ek-lek'tik, *a.* Proceeding by the method of selection, applied to certain philosophers who selected from the principles of various schools what they thought sound.—*n.* One who follows an eclectic method in philosophy, etc.

economic, economical, ē-kon-om'ik, e-kon-om'ik-al, *a.* Pertaining to economy or economics; frugal; careful.

edify, ed'i-fī, *vt.* (edifying, edified). To build up, in a moral sense; to instruct or improve generally.

edition, ēdi'shon, *n.* A published book as characterized by form or editorial labors, the whole number of copies of a work published at once.

editorial, ed-i-tō'ri-al, *a.* Pertaining to or written by an editor.—*n.* A leading article in a newspaper.

educate, ed'ū-kāt, *vt.* (educating educated). To teach, to cultivate and train; to enlighten.

education, ed'ū-kā'shon, *n.* Act of educating; instruction and discipline; schooling.

efficiency, ef-fi'shen-si, *n.* The state or character of being efficient; effectual agency.

efficient, ef-fi'shent, *a.* Effecting; capable, qualified for duty.

effusion, ef-fū'zhon, *n.* Act of pouring out, that which is poured out; in *pathology,* the escape of fluid out of its proper vessel into another part; cordiality of manner; a literary production.

egotism, eg'ot-izm or ē', *n.* The practice of too frequently using the word I; an exaggerated love of self, self-exaltation.

egotist, eg'ot-ist or ē', *n.* One always talking of himself, one who magnifies his own achievements.

either, ē'THėr or ī'THėr, *a.* or *pron.* One or the other; one of two; each; *conj.* or *adv.* Used disjunctively as correlative to or.

elaborate, ē-lab'o-rāt, *vt.* (elaborating, elaborated). To produce with labor; to refine by successive operations.—*a.* Wrought with labor; studied, high-wrought.

elaboration, ē-lab'o-rā''shon, *n.* Refinement by successive operations, the process in animal and vegetable organs by which something is produced.

elastic, ē-las'tik, *a.* Having the power of returning to the form from which it is bent or distorted; rebounding.—*n.* Cord or ribbon made of cotton or silk, etc., with strands of rubber.

elate, ē-lāt', *a.* Elevated in mind; flushed, as with success.—*vt.* (elating, elated). To exalt; to puff up; to make proud.

elect, ē-lekt', *vt.* To pick or choose; to select for an office.—*a.* Chosen; chosen to an office, but not yet in office.—*n. sing.* or *pl.* One or several chosen, those favored by God.

election, ē-lek'shon, *n.* Act of choosing, choice, voluntary preference; divine choice; predestination.

electricity, ē-lek-tris'i-ti, *n.* The force that manifests itself in lightning and in many other phenomena; the science which deals with these phenomena.

electrify, ē-lek'tri-fī, *vt.* (electrifying, electrified). To communicate electricity to, to thrill.—*vi.* To become electric.

electrolyte, ē-lek'tro-līt, *n.* A compound decomposable by electricity.

electron, ē-lek'tron, *n.* One of the extremely small particles of negative electricity, which form essential constituents of atoms, and by which, according to the electron theory, heat and electricity are conducted.

eleemosynary, el-ē-mos'i-na-ri, *a.* Given in or relating to charity; founded to dispense some gratuity.—*n.* One who subsists on charity.

elegance, elegancy, el'ē-gans, el'ē-gan-si, *n.* Quality of being elegant; beauty resulting from propriety; refinement.

elegiac, el'ē-ji'ak, *a.* Belonging to elegy; plaintive.—*n.* Elegiac verse.

elegy, el'ē-ji, *n.* A poem or a song expressive of sorrow and lamentation.

element, el'ē-ment, *n.* A fundamental part or principle, an ingredient; proper sphere; suitable state of things; *pl.* first principles of an art or science; data employed in a calculation; the bread and wine used in the Lord's supper.

elementary, el-ē-ment'ar-i, *a.* Primary; uncompounded; teaching first principles or rudiments.

elephant, el'ē-fant, *n.* A huge quadruped, having a long trunk and tusks.

elevate, el'ē-vāt, *vt.* (elevating, elevated). To raise; to refine or dignify, to elate, to cheer.

elevator, el'ē-vāt-ėr, *n.* One who or that which elevates; a hoist.

elicit, ē-lis'it, *vt.* To draw out by reasoning, discussion, etc.; to educe.

eligibility, el'i-ji'bil''i-ti, *n.* Worthiness or fitness to be chosen.

elongation, ē-long-gā'shon, *n.* Act of lengthening; state of being extended; continuation; apparent distance of a planet from the sun.

elope, ē-lōp', *vi.* (eloping, eloped). To escape privately; to run away with a lover.

eloquence, e'lō-kwens, *n.* The quality or faculty of being eloquent; oratory.

eloquent, e'lō-kwent, *a.* Having the power of fluent, elegant, or forcible speech; characterized by eloquence.

emaciate, ē-mā'shi-āt, *vi.* and *t.* (emaciating, emaciated). To become or make lean.

emaciation, ē-mā'shi-ā''shon, *n.* Act of emaciating, leanness.

emancipate, ē-man'si-pāt, *vt.* (emancipating, emancipated). To set free from slavery; to liberate.

emancipation, ē-man'si-pā''shon, *n.* Liberation; freedom; enfranchisement.

emasculate, ē-mas'kū-lāt, *vt.* To castrate; to render effeminate; to expurgate.

embark, em-bärk', *vt.* To put on board a ship, to engage in.—*vi.* To go on board of a ship; to engage in, to take a share.

embarrass, em-ba'ras, *vt.* To involve in difficulties; to entangle; to disconcert.

embarrassment, em-ba'ras-ment, *n.* Entanglement; trouble; abashment.

embezzlement, em-bez'l-ment, *n.* Act of fraudulently appropriating money, etc., intrusted to one's care.

embitter, em-bit'ėr, *vt.* To make bitter or more bitter, to exasperate.

emblem, em 'blem, *n.* A picture representing one thing and suggesting another; a symbol; type; device.

embower, em-bou'ėr, *vt.* To inclose in or cover with a bower; to shade.

embrace, em-brā s', *vt.* (embracing embraced). To take within the arms; to press to the bosom; to seize ardently, to include; to accept.—*vi.* To join in an embrace.— *n.* Clasp with the arms; a hug; conjugal endearment.

emerald, e'me-rald, *n.* A precious stone, akin to the beryl, usually green; a small printing type.—*a.* Of a bright-green color.

emerge, ē-merj', *vi.* (emerging, emerged). To rise out of a fluid or other substance; to issue; to rise into view; to reappear.

emeritus, ė'-mer'i-tus, *a.* Dis-charged from duty with honor on account of infirmity, age, or long service.

emersion, ē-mėr'shon, *n.* Act of rising out of a fluid or other substance, reappearance of a heavenly body after eclipse, etc.

emetic, ē-met'ik, *a.* Causing vomiting.— *n.* A medicine that provokes vomiting.

emigrant, em'i-grant, *a.* Emigrating; pertaining to emigration or emigrants.—*n.* One who emigrates.

emigrate, em'i-grāt, *vi.* (emigrating, emigrated). To remove from one country or state to another for the purpose of residence.

eminence, em'in-ens, *n.* A rising ground; elevation; top; distinction; fame; a title of honor given to cardinals, etc.

emotion, ē-mō'shon, *n.* Any agitation of mind, feeling.

empale, em-pāl', *vt.* (empaling, empaled). To put to death by fixing on a stake.

emperor, em'pèr-èr, *n.* The sovereign of an empire.

emphasis, em'fa-sis, *n.* A stress laid on a word or clause to enforce a meaning; impressiveness; weight.

emphasize, em'fa-sīz, *vt.* (emphasizing, emphasized). To place emphasis on.

empire, em'pīr, *n.* Supreme power in governing; sway; dominion of an emperor; region over which dominion is extended.

employ, em-ploi', *vt.* To occupy; to engage in one's service, to keep at work, to make use of.—*n.* Business, occupation; engagement.

employee, em-ploi'ē, *n.* One who works for an employer.

employer, em-ploi'èr, *n.* One who employs; one who keeps men in service.

emporium, em-pō'ri-um, *n.;* pl. **-ia** or **-iums.** A commercial center; a warehouse or shop.

empower, em-pou'èr, *vt.* To give legal or moral power to; to authorize.

empress, em'pres, *n.* The consort of an emperor; a female invested with imperial power.

empty, em'ti, *a.* Containing nothing, or nothing but air; void; unsatisfactory; unburdened; hungry; vacant of head.— *vt.* (emptying, emptied). To make empty.—*vi.* lo become empty.—*n.* An empty packing case, etc.

enamel, en-am'el, *n.* A substance of the nature of glass, used as a coating; that which is enameled; a smooth glossy surface of various colors; the smooth substance on a tooth.—*vt.* (enameling, enameled). To lay enamel on, to paint in enamel; to form a surface like enamel; to adorn with different colors.—*vi.* To practice the art of enameling.

enamor, en-am'èr, *vt.* To inspire with love, to charm; to fill with delight.

enceinte, äng-sangt, *n.* The rampart which surrounds a fortress; the area thus surrounded.—*a.* Pregnant, with child.

encompass, en-kum'pas, *vt.* To encircle; to hem in; to go or sail round.

encounter, en-koun'tèr, *n.* A meeting in contest; a conflict; a meeting, controversy, debate.—*vt.* To meet face to face; to meet suddenly; to strive against.—*vi.* To meet unexpectedly, to conflict.

encourage, en-ku'rä j, *vt.* (encouraging, encouraged). To give courage to; to stimulate; to embolden; to countenance.

encroach, en-krōch', *vi.* To trespass on the rights and Possessions of another; to intrude; to infringe, with on or *upon.*

encroachment, en-krōch-ment, *n.* Act of encroaching; invasion; inroad; that which is taken by encroaching.

encumber, en-kum'bèr, *vt.* To impede the motion of with a load, to embarrass; to load with debts or legal claims.

endanger, en-dān'jér, *vt.* To bring into danger; to expose to loss or injury.

endear, en-der', *vt.* To make dear; to make more beloved

endeavor, en-dev'èr, *n.* Effort, attempt; exertion; essay; aim.—*vi.* To try; to strive; to aim.—*vt.* To try to effect, to strive after.

endemic, endemical, en-dem'ik, en-dem'ik-al, *a.* Peculiar to a people or region, as a disease.—*n.* A disease of endemic nature.

endive, en'div, *n.* A plant allied to chicory; garden succory.

endless, end'les, *a.* Without end everlasting, infinite, incessant.

endogen, en'dō-jen, *n.* A plant whose stem grows by additions developed from the inside, as palms and grasses.

endogenous, en-doj'e-nus, *a.* Pertaining to endogens; developing from within.

endorse, en-dors', *vt.* (endorsing, endorsed). To write on the back of, as one's name òn a bill; to assign by endorsement, to ratify

endorsement, en-dors'ment, *n.* The act of endorsing; a docket; signature of one who endorses; sanction or approval

enema, en'e-ma, *n.* A liquid or gaseous medicine injected into the rectum; a clyster.

enemy, en'e-mi, *n.* One who is unfriendly; an antagonist; a hostile army.

energetic, energetical, en-èr-jet'ik, en-èr-jet'ik-al *a.* Acting with energy; forcible; potent; active; vigorous.

energy, en'èr-ji, *n.* Inherent power to operate or act; power exerted; force; vigor; strength of expression; emphasis, in physics, power to do work; it may be mechanical, electrical, thermal, chemical, etc.

enforcement, en-fōrs'ment, *n.* Act of enforcing; compulsion; a giving of force or effect to; a putting in execution, as law.

enfranchise, en-fran'chĭz, *vt.* (en-franchising, enfranchised). To set free; to admit to the privileges of a citizen; to endow with the franchise.

engineer, en-ji-nēr', *n.* One who constructs or manages engines one who plans works for offense or defense; one who constructs roads, railways, etc.—*vt.* To direct the making of in the capacity of engineer.

English, ing'glish, *a.* Belonging to England, or to its inhabitants.—*n.* The people or language of England.—*vt.* To translate into English.

engulf, en-gulf', *vt.* To engulf; to swallow up.

enhance, en-hans', *vt.* (enhancing enhanced). To raise to a higher point; to increase; to aggravate. —*vi.* To grow larger.

enigma, ē-nig'ma, *n.* An obscure statement or question, riddle, anything inexplicable.

enjoin, en-join', *vt.* To order with urgency, to admonish, to prescribe.

enjoy, en-joi', *vt.* To feel gladness in to have, use, or perceive with pleasure.

enjoyment, en-joi'ment, *n.* State of enjoying; pleasure; satisfaction; fruition.

enlarge, en-lärj', *vt.* (enlarging, enlarged). To make large or larger; to set free.—*vi.* To grow large or larger; to expatiate.

enlargement, en-lärj'ment, *n.* Act of enlarging, state of being enlarged; expansion; release; addition.

enlighten, en-līt'en, *vt.* To make clear; to enable to see more clearly, to instruct.

enlist, en-list', *vt.* To enter on a list to engage in public service, especially military; to engage the services of—*vi.* To engage voluntarily in public service; to enter heartily into a cause.

enough, ē-nuf', *a.* That satisfies desire, that may answer the purpose.—*n.* A sufficiency, that which is equal to the powers or abilities.—*adv.* Sufficiently, tolerably.

enrage, en-rāj', *vt.* To excite rage in; to incense.

enrapture, en-rap'tūr, *vt.* To transport with rapture; to delight beyond measure.

enroll, enrol, en-rōl', *vt.* To write in a roll

or register, to record.

ensign, en'sīn, *n.* A mark of distinction; the flag of a company of soldiers or a vessel, formerly the lowest rank of commissioned officer in the infantry.

entail, en-tāl', *vt.* To cut off an estate from the heirs general; lo settle, as the descent of lands by gift to a man and to certain heirs, to devolve as a consequence or of necessity.—*n.* The act of entailing; an estate entailed, rule of descent settled for an estate.

entangle, en-tang'gl, *vt.* To knit or interweave confusedly; to involve; to hamper.

enter, en'tėr, *vt.* To go or come into; to begin; to set down in writing; to register; to take possession of.—*vi.* To go or come in; begin; engage in; be an ingredient in.

enterprise, en'tėr-prĭz, *n.* That which is undertaken, a bold or hazardous attempt; adventurous spirit; hardihood.—*vt.* To undertake.

entertain, en-tėr-tān', *vt.* To receive as a guest; to cherish; to treat with conversation, to please; to admit with a view to consider.—*vi.* To give entertainments.

entire, en-tīr', *a.* Whole, unshared complete; sincere; hearty; in full strength.

entirely, entīr'li, *adv.* Wholly; fully.

entitle, en-tī'tl, *vt.* (entitling, entitled). To give a title to, to style, to characterize; to give a claim to; to qualify.

entrail, en'trāl, *n.* One of the intestines; generally in *pl.;* the bowels.

entrain, en-trān', *vt.* To put on board a railway train.—*vi.* To take places in a train.

entrance en'trans, *n.* Act or power of entering into a place, the door or avenue by which a place may be entered; beginning; act of taking possession.

entrance, en-trans', *vt.* To put in a trance or ecstasy; to enrapture; to transport.

enumerate, ē-nu'me-rāt, *vt.* (enumerating, enumerated). To count number by number; to reckon or mention a number of things, each separately.

enunciation, ē-nun'si-ā"shon, *n.* Act or manner of enunciating, expression; declaration; public attestation.

envelop, en-vel'op, *vt.* To cover by wrapping or folding; to lie around and conceal.

envelope, en'vel-ō p, *n.* That which infolds; a wrapper; a covering for a letter, etc.; an investing integument.

environ, en-vī'ron, *vt.* To encompass; to

encircle; to besiege; to invest.

environment, en-vī'ron-ment, *n.* Act of environing, state of being environed; that which environs conditions under which one lives.

envoy, en'voi, *n.* One sent on a mission; a person next in rank to an ambassador deputed to transact business with a foreign power.

epic, ep'ik, *a.* Composed in a lofty narrative style, heroic.—*n.* A poem of elevated character, describing the exploits of heroes.

epicure, ep 'i-kūr, *n.* One devoted to sensual enjoyments; a voluptuary.

epidemic, epidemical, ep-i-dem'ik ep-i-dem'ik-al, *a.* Affecting a whole community, as a disease prevalent.—**epidemic,** ep-i-dem' ik, *n.* A disease which attacks many people at the same period.

epigram, ep'i-gram, *n.* A short poem, usually keenly satirical; a pointed or antithetical saying.

epigraph, ep'i-graf, *n.* An inscription; quotation; motto.

epilepsy, ep'i-lep-si, *n.* The falling sickness, a disease characterized by spasms and loss of sense.

epilogue, ep'i-log, *n.* A speech or short poem spoken by an actor at the end of a play.

Epiphany, ē-pif'a-ni, *n.* A church festival on January 6th, celebrating the manifestation of Christ to the wise men of the East.

epitaph, ep'i-taf, *n.* That which is written on a tomb; an inscription, or a composition, in honor of the dead.

epithalamium, ep'i-tha-lā'mi-um, *n.*; pl. **-iums** or **-ia.** A nuptial song or poem.

epithet, ep'i-thet, *n.* Any word implying a quality attached to a person or thing.

epitome, e-pit'o-mi, *n.* A brief summary; abridgment; compendium.

epoch, ē'pok, *n.* A fixed point of time from which years are numbered; period; era; date.

equal, ē'kwal, *a.* The same in extent, number, degree, rank, etc., same in qualities, uniform, proportionate; adequate; just.— *n.* One not inferior or superior to another.—*vt.* (equalling, equalled). To make equal to; to become or be equal to.

equanimity, ē-kwa-nim'i-ti or ek-, *n.* Evenness of mind; steadiness of temper.

equate, ē-kwāt, *vt.* (equating equated). To make equal; to reduce to an equation; to reduce to mean time or motion.

equation, ē-kwā'shon, *n.* The act of equating; an expression asserting the equality of two quantities; a quantity to be taken into account in order to give a true result.

Equator, ē-kwā'tèr, *n.* The great circle of our globe which divides it into the northern and southern hemispheres; a circle in the heavens coinciding with the plane of the earth's equator

equilibrium, ē-kwi-li'bri-um or ek-, *n.* State of rest produced by the counteraction of forces; balance.

equinoctial, ē-kwi-nok'shal, or ek-, *a.* Pertaining to the equinoxes.—*n.* The celestial equator when the sun is on it, the days and nights are of equal length.

Equinox, ē'kwi-noks or ek', *n.* The time when the day and night are of equal length, about March 21st and September 23rd.

equip, ē-kwip', *vt.* (equipping, equipped). To fit out or furnish, as for war, to dress, to array.

equipment, ē-kwip'ment, *n.* Act of equipping; habiliments; warlike apparatus; necessary adjuncts.

equitable, ek'wit-a-bl, *a.* Distributing equal justice; just; upright; impartial.

equity, ek'wi-ti, *n.* The giving to each man his due; impartiality; uprightness; a system of supplementary law founded upon precedents and established principles.

equivalent, ē-kwiv'a-lent or ek-, *a.* Equal in excellence, worth, or weight, of the same import or meaning.—*n.* That which is equal in value, etc., compensation.

equivocate, ē-kwiv'ō-kāt, *vi.* To use ambiguous expressions to mislead to quibble.

erect, ē-rekt', *a.* Upright; bold; undismayed.—*vt.* To raise and set upright, to build, to found, to cheer.

erode, ē-rōd', *vt.* (eroding, eroded). To gnaw off or away, to corrode.

erotic, ē-rot'ik *a.* Pertaining to or prompted by love; treating of love.

err, er, *vi.* To wander; to stray; to depart from rectitude, to blunder.

errand, e'rand, *n.* A message; mandate, business to be transacted by a messenger.

erratic, e-rat'ik, *a.* Wandering; irregular eccentric.

erratum; e-rā'tum, *n.*; pl. **-ata.** An error or mistake in writing or printing.

error, e'rèr, *n.* A deviation from truth or what is right; a mistake; a blunder, fault;

offense.

escapade, es-ka-pād', *n.* A runaway adventure; a freak; a mad prank.

escape, es-kāp', *vt.* (escaping, escaped). To get out of the way of; to pass without harm, to pass unobserved; to avoid.—*vi.* To be free; to avoid, to regain one's liberty.—*n.* Flight, to shun danger; an evasion of legal restraint or custody.

escarpment, es-kärp'ment, *n.* A steep declivity, ground cut away nearly vertically

eschew, es-chö', *vt.* To shun; to avoid.

escort, es'kort, *n.* A guard attending an officer or baggage, etc.; persons attending as a mark of honor.—*vt.* es-kort'. To attend and guard.

espionage, es'pi-on-ā j, *n.* Practice or employment of spies; practice of watching others without being suspected.

espousal, es-pouz'al, *n.* Betrothal; nuptials: in this sense generally in *pl;* the adopting of a cause.

espouse, es-pouz', *vt.* (espousing, espoused). To give or take in marriage; to betroth; to wed; to embrace or adopt, to uphold.

esprit, es-prē, *n.* Soul; spirit; mind; wit.

essential, es-sen'shal, *a.* Relating to or containing the essence; necessary to the existence of, indispensable, highly rectified, volatile diffusible (oils).—*n.* Something necessary; the chief point; constituent principle.

establish, es-tab'lish, *vt.* To make stable; to found permanently; to institute; to enact; to sanction; to confirm; to make good.

esteem, es-tēm', *vt.* To set a value on; to regard with respect; to prize.—*n.* Judgment of merit or demerit, estimation, great regard.

estimate, es'tim-āt, *vt.* (estimating, estimated). To form an opinion regarding, to calculate, to appraise to esteem,—*n.* Valuation; calculation of probable cost.

estrange, es-trā nj', *vt.* (estranging, estranged). To alienate, as the affections.

estuary, es'tū-a-ri, *n.* The mouth of a river where the tide meets the current; a firth.

etching, ech'ing, *n.* The act or art of the etcher; a mode of engraving; the impression taken from an etched plate.

eternal, ē-tèrn'al, *a.* Everlasting without beginning or end of existence; unchangeable.—*n.* An appellation of God.

eternity, ē-tèrn'i-ti, *n.* Continuance without beginning or end; duration without end, the state or time after death.

ethereal, ē-thē'rē-al, *a.* Formed of ether; heavenly; aerial; intangible.

ethic, ethical, eth'ik, eth'ik-al, *a.* Relating to morals; treating of morality; delivering precepts of morality.

ethics, eth'iks *n.* The doctrine of morals, moral philosophy, a system of moral principles.

ethnic, ethnical, eth'nik, eth'nik-al, *a.* Pertaining to the gentiles; pagan; ethnological.

etymology, et-i-mol'o-ji, *n.* that part of philology which traces the origin of words; the derivation or history of any word.

eulogy, ū'lo-ji, *n.* A speech or writing in commendation; praise; panegyric.

euphemism, ū'fem-izm, *n.* A mode of speaking by which a delicate word or expression is substituted for one which is offensive, a word or expression so substituted.

evade, ē-vād', *vt.* (evading, evaded). To avoid by dexterity; to slip away from; to elude; to baffle.—*vi.* To practice evasion.

evaluate, ē-val'ū-āt, *vt.* To value carefully; to ascertain the amount of.

evanesce, ev-a-nes', *vi.* To vanish.

evaporate, ē-va'per-āt, *vi.* (evaporating, evaporated). To pass off in vapor, to exhale, to be wasted.—*vt.* To convert into vapor; to disperse in vapors.

evasion, ē-vā'zhon, *n.* Act of evading; artifice to elude; shift; equivocation.

even, ē'vn, *a.* Level, smooth, equable; on an equality; just; settled; balanced; capable of being divided by 2 without a remainder.— *vt.* To make even or level, to equalize; to balance.—*adv.* Just, exactly; likewise; moreover.—*n.* The evening.

evening, ē'vn-ing, *n.* The close of the day; the decline of anything.— *a.* Being at the close of day.

ever, ev'èr *adv.* At all times; at any time; continually; in any degree.

evergreen, ev'èr-grēn, *n.* A plant that always retains its greenness.—*a.* Always green.

evict, ē-vikt', *vt.* To dispossess by judicial process, to expel from lands, etc., by law.

evidence, ev'i-dens, *n.* That which demonstrates that a fact is so, testimony; proof; witness.—*vt.* To make evident, to prove.

evince, ē-vins', *vt.* (evincing evinced). To show in a clear manner; to manifest.

evolve, ē-volv', *vt.* (evolving evolved). To unfold, to develop, to open and expand.—*vi.* To open or disclose itself.

exaggerate, egz-aj'e-rāt, *vt.* (exaggerating, exaggerated). To increase beyond due limits; to depict extravagantly.

exalt, egz-ält', *vt.* To raise high; to raise to power or dignity; to extol.

examination, egz-am'in-ā'shon, *n.* Act of examining; inquiry into facts, etc., by interrogation; scrutiny by study.

examine, egz-am'in, *vt.* (examining, examined). To inspect carefully; to inquire into, to interrogate, as a witness, a student, etc.; to discuss.

example, egz-am'pl, *n.* A sample; pattern; model; precedent; instance.

exasperate, egz-as'pē-rāt, *vt.* (exasperating, exasperated). To irritate; to enrage; to make worse; to aggravate.

excavate, eks'ka-vāt, *vt.* (excavating, excavated). To hollow out.

excel, ek-sel', *vt.* (excelling, excelled). To surpass; to transcend; to outdo.—*vi.* To be eminent or distinguished.

exception, ek-sep 'shon, *n.* Act of excepting; state of being excepted; that which is excepted; an objection; offense.

excerpt, ek-sèrpt', *n.* An extract; a passage selected from an author.—*vt.* To pick out from a book etc.; to cite.

excess, ek-ses', *n.* That which exceeds, super-abundance; intemperate conduct; that by which one thing exceeds another.

exchange, eks-chānj', *vt.* To change one thing for another; to commute, to bargain.—*n.* Act of exchanging; interchange; barter; the thing interchanged; place where merchants, etc., of a city meet to transact business; a method of finding the equivalent to a given sum in the money of another country.

excise, ek-sīz', *n.* A tax on certain commodities of home production and consumption, as beer, etc.; also for licenses to deal in certain commodities.—*vt.* (excising, excised). To impose a duty on articles produced and consumed at home, to cut out.

exclamation, eks-klam-ā'shon, *n.* A loud outcry, a passionate sentence, a note by which emphatical utterance is marked, thus, !; an interjection.

exclude, eks-klūd', *vt.* (excluding, excluded). To shut out; to thrust out; to debar; to prohibit; to except.

excrement, eks'krē-ment, *n.* That which is separated from the nutriment by digestion, and discharged from the body; ordure; dung.

excrete, eks-krēt', *vt.* (excreting, excreted). To separate and discharge from the body by vital action.

excruciate, eks-krö'shi-āt, *vt.* To torture; to rack.

execrate, ek'sē-krāt, *vt.* (execrating, execrated). To curse; to abominate.

execute, ek'sē-kūt, *vt.* (executing executed). To effect to achieve, to inflict capital punishment on, to make valid, as by signing and sealing; to perform.—*vi.* To perform.

executioner, ek-sēkū'shon-èr, *n.* One who puts to death by law.

executive, egz-ek'ūt-iv, *a.* That executes; carrying laws into effect, or superintending their enforcement.—*n.* The person or persons who administer the government.

exempt, egz-emt', *vt.* To free from to privilege; to grant immunity from.—*a.* Free by privilege; not liable.

exemption, egz-em'shon, *n.* Act of exempting; state of being exempt; immunity.

exfoliate, eks-fō'li-āt, *vt.* and *i.* To scale off.

exhaust, egz-äst', *vt.* To drain off contents; to expend entirely; to treat thoroughly; to tire.

exhibit, egz-ib 'it, *vt.* To show, to display; to administer by way of remedy.—*n.* Anything exhibited.

exhibition, eks-i-bi'shon, *n.* Act of exhibiting; display; any public show, a benefaction for students in English universities.

exhilarate, egz-il'a-rāt, *vt.* (exhilarating, exhilarated). To make cheerful; to inspirit.

exist, egz-ist', *vi.* To be; to live; to endure.

existence, egz-ist'ens, *n.* State of being; life; continuation; anything that exists.

exit, eks'it, *n.* A going out; the departure of a player from the stage; death, a way out.

exonerate, egz-on'ē-rāt, *vt.* To exculpate; to acquit; to justify.

exorable, eks'ōr-a-bl, *a.* That can be persuaded; placable.

exorbitant, egz-or'bit-ant, *a.* Excessive; extravagant.

expand, ek-spand', *vt.* and *i.* To spread out; to enlarge; to distend; to dilate.

expect, ek-spekt', *vt.* To wait for; to look

for to happen, to anticipate.

expectance, expectancy, ek-spek' tans, ek-spek'tan-si, *n.* Act or state of expecting; expectation; hope.

expectation, ek-spek-tā'shon, *n.* Act or state of expecting; prospect of good to come; prospect of reaching a certain age.

expectorate, eks-pek'tō-rāt, *vt.* (expectorating, expectorated). To expel, as phlegm, by coughing; to spit out.

expeditious, eks-pē-di'shus, *a.* Speedy, prompt, nimble, active.

expend, ek-spend', *vt.* To spend; to use or consume, to waste.

expenditure, ek-spend'i-tūr, *n.* Act of expending; a laying out, as of money; money expended; expense.

expense, ek-spens', *n.* That which is expended; cost; charge; price.

experiment, eks-pe'ri ment, *n.* A trial; an operation designed to discover something unknown, or to establish it when discovered.—*vi.* To make trial or experiment.

expert, eks-pèrt', *a.* Skillful; dexterous, adroit.—*n.* eks'pert. An expert person; a scientific witness.

explanation, eks-pla-nā'shon, *n.* Act of explaining, interpretation clearing up of matters between parties at variance.

expletive, eks'plēt-iv, *a.* Serving to fill out; superfluous.—*n.* A word or syllable inserted to fill a vacancy or for ornament; an oath or interjection.

explicate, eks'pli-kāt, *vt.* To unfold the meaning of, to explain.

explode, eks-plō d', *vt.* (exploding, exploded). To drive out of use or belief, to cause to burst with violence and noise.—*vi.* To burst with noise; to burst into activity or passion.

exploit, eks-ploit', *n.* A deed; a heroic act; a deed of renown.—*vt.* To make use of; to work.

exploitation, eks-ploi-tā 'shon, *n.* Successful application of industry on any object, as land, mines, etc.

exploration, eks-plo-rā'shon, *n.* Act of exploring; strict or careful examination.

explore, eks-plōr', *vt.* (exploring, explored) To travel with the view of making discovery; to search; to examine closely.

explosion, eks-plō'zhon, *n.* Act of exploding; a bursting with noise; a violent outburst of feeling.

explosive, eks-plō'siv, *a.* Causing explosion; readily exploding.—*n.* Anything liable to explode, as gunpowder; a mute or non-continuous consonant, as k, t, b.

exponent, eks-pō'nent, *n.* One who explains or illustrates; that which indicates; the index of a power in algebra.

expound, eks-pound', *vt.* To explain; to interpret; to unfold.

express, eks-pres', *vt.* To press out to set forth in words; to declare; to make known by any means; (refl.) to say what one has got to say.—*a.* Clearly exhibited; given in direct terms, intended or sent for a particular purpose; traveling with special speed.—*n.* A messenger or vehicle sent on a particular occasion; a message specially sent, a specially fast railway train.—*adv.* For a particular purpose; with special haste.

expression, eks-pre'shon, *n.* Act of expressing; a phrase or mode of speech; manner of utterance; a natural and lively representation in painting and sculpture; musical tone, grace, or modulation; play of features; representation of a quantity in algebra.

expropriate, eks-prō'pri-āt , *vt.* To take for public use, to dispossess.

extemporize, eks-tem'pō-rīz, *vi.* To speak without preparation.—*vt.* To make without forethought; to prepare in haste.

extend, eks-tend', *vt.* To stretch out; to spread; to prolong; to bestow on.—*vi.* To stretch; to reach; to become larger.

extenuate, eks-ten'ū-ā t, *vt.* To lessen; to weaken the force of; to palliate.

exterior, eks-tē'ri-èr, *a.* External; on the outside; foreign.—*n.* The outward surface; that which is external.

extirpation, eks-tèrp-ā 'shon, *n.* Act of rooting out; eradication; total destruction.

extortion eks-tor'shon, *n.* Act of extorting; illegal or oppressive exaction.

extract, eks-trakt', *vt.* To draw out or forth; to select; to draw or copy out, to find the root of a number.— *n.* eks'trakt. That which is extracted; a quotation; an essence, tincture, etc.

extraction, eks-trak'shon, *n.* Act of extracting; lineage; operation of drawing essences, tinctures; etc.; operation of finding the roots of numbers.

extradite, eks'tra-dīt, *vt.* To deliver up (a criminal) to the authorities of the country from which he has come.

extradition, eks-traä-di'shon, *n.* The delivery, under a treaty, of a fugitive from justice by one government to another.

extreme, eks-trēm', *a.* Outermost; furthest; most violent, last; worst or best; most pressing.—*n.* The utmost point or verge of a thing; end; furthest or highest degree; *(pl.)* points at the greatest distance from each other.

extremist, eks-trēm'ist, *n.* A supporter of extreme doctrines or practice.

extremity, eks-trem'i-ti, *n.* That which is extreme, utmost point part, or degree; utmost distress or violence.

extricate, eks'tri-kā t, *vt.* (extricating, extricated). To disentangle; to set free.

extrinsic, extrinsical, eks-trin'sik, eks-trin'-sik-al, *a.* Being on the outside; extraneous; accessory.

extrusion, eks-trö'zhon, *n.* Act of extruding; a driving out; expulsion.

exude, eks-ūd, *vt.* (exuding, exuded). To discharge through the pores; to let ooze out.—*vi.* To flow through pores; to ooze out like sweat.

exult, egz-ult', *vi.* To rejoice exceedingly; to triumph.

exultation, egz-ult-ā'shon, *n.* Lively joy; triumph; rapture; ecstasy.

eyrie, eyry, ī'ri, *n.* An aerie; nest of a bird of prey.

E

F

fable, fā'bl, *n*. A fictitious narrative to instruct or amuse, often to enforce a precept; falsehood; an idle story, the plot in a poem or drama.—*vi*. (fabling, fabled). To tell fables or falsehoods. —*vt*. To feign, to invent.

fabric, fab'rik, *n*. Frame or structure of anything; a building; texture; cloth.

fabricate, fab'rik-āt, *vt*. (fabricating, fabricated). To make or fashion, to form by art or labor; to devise falsely.

fabulous, fa'bū-lus, *a*. Containing or abounding in fable; feigned; mythical, incredible.

facade, facade, fa-säd', fa-sād', *n*. Front view or elevation of an edifice.

face, fās, *n*. The front part of an animal's head, particularly of the human head; the visage, front, effrontery, assurance, dial of a watch, etc.—*vt*. (facing; faced). To meet in front; to stand opposite to; to oppose with firmness; to finish or protect with a thin external covering, to dress the face of (a stone etc.).—*vi*. To turn the face; to look.

facsimile, fak-sim'i-lē, *n*. An exact copy or likeness.

faction, fak'shon, *n*. A party in political society in opposition to the ruling power, a party unscrupulously promoting its private ends; discord, dissension.

factor, fak'tėr, *n*. An agent, particularly a mercantile agent; in Scotland, one appointed to manage an estate; one of two or more numbers or quantities, which, when multiplied together, form a product; one of several elements which contribute to a result.

factory, fak'to-ri, *n*. An establishment where factors in foreign countries reside to transact business for their employers; buildings appropriated to the manufacture of goods, a manufactory.

fairy, fā' ri, *n*. An imaginary being of human form, supposed to play a variety of pranks.—*a*. Belonging to fairies; given by fairies.

faith, fāth, *n*. Belief; trust, confidence, conviction in regard to religion; system of religious beliefs; strict adherence to duty and promises, word or honor pledged.

falcon, fä'kn, or fäl'kon, *n*. The name of various small or medium-sized raptorial birds, a hawk of any kind trained to sport.

fall, fäl, *vi*. (pret. fell, pp. fallen). To sink to a lower position, to drop down, to empty or disembogue; to sink into sin, weakness, or disgrace; to come to an end suddenly; to decrease; to assume an expression of dejection, etc., to happen to pass or be transferred; to belong or appertain; to be uttered carelessly.—*n*. Descent; tumble; death; ruin; cadence; a cascade or cataract; extent of descent; declivity, autumn. that which falls; a kind of ladies' veil; lapse or declension from innocence or goodness; *naut*. the part of a tackle to which the power is applied in hoisting.

false, fäls, *a*. Not true; forged; feigned, fraudulent; treacherous; inconstant; constructed for show or a subsidiary purpose.

falsehood, fäls'höd, *n*. Quality of being false; untruth; fiction; a lie.

falsetto, fäl-set'tō, *n*. A false or artificial voice; the tones above the natural compass of the voice.

familiar, fa-mil'i-ėr, *a*. Well acquainted; intimate; affable; well known, free, unconstrained.—*n*. An intimate; one long acquainted; a demon supposed to attend at call.

family, fam'i-li, *n*. Household; the parents and children alone, the children as distinguished from the parents; kindred; line of ancestors; honorable descent; a group or class of animals or plants.

famine, fam'in, *n*. Scarcity of food; dearth.

famish, fam'ish, *vt*. To kill or exhaust with hunger, to starve, to kill by denial of anything necessary.—*vi*. To die of hunger; to suffer extreme hunger or thirst.

fan, fan, *n*. An instrument for winnowing grain, an instrument to agitate the air and cool the face; something by which the air is moved a wing.—*vt*. (fanning fanned). To cool and refresh by moving the air with a fan; to winnow, to stimulate.

fanatic, fanatical, fa-nat'ik, fanat'ik-al, *a*. Wild in opinions, particularly in religious opinions, excessively enthusiastic.—**fanatic**, fa-nat'ik, *n*. A person affected by excessive enthusiasm, particularly on religious subjects; an enthusiast, a visionary.

fancy, fan'si, *n* A phase of the intellect of a lighter cast than the imagination;

thought due to this faculty; embodiment of such in words, opinion or notion, liking caprice; false notion.—*vi.* (fancying, fancied). To imagine; to suppose without proof.—*vt.* To imagine; to like; to be pleased with.—*a.* Fine, ornamental, adapted to please the fancy; beyond intrinsic value.

fantasy, fan'ta-si, *n.* Fancy, a vagary of the imagination; a fanciful artistic production.—*vt.* To picture in fancy.

farce, färs, *n.* A play full of extravagant drollery; absurdity; mere show.—*vt.* To stuff with forcemeat or mingled ingredients.

fare, fär, *vi.* (faring, fared). To go; to travel; to be in any stale, good o bad, to be entertained with food to happen well or ill.—*n.* Sun charged for conveying a person person conveyed; food; provisions of the table.

fascinate, fas'si nät, *vt.* (fascinating, fascinated). To bewitch, to charm; to captivate.

fashion, fa'shon, *n.* The make or form of anything; external appearance; form of a garment; prevailing mode, custom, genteel life.—*vt.* To give shape to; to mold; to adapt.

fast, fäst, *a.* Firmly fixed; closely adhering; steadfast; durable swift dissipated.—*adv.* Firmly rapidly; durably; near; with dissipation.—*vi.* To abstain from eating and drinking, or from particular kinds of food.—*n.* Abstinence from food; a religious mortification by abstinence; the time of fasting.

fasten, fäs'n, *vt.* To fix firmly closely, or tightly to hold together to affix.—*vi.* To become fixed; t seize and hold on.

fastidious, fas-tid'i-us. *a.* Squeamish; delicate to a fault; difficult to please

fat, fat, *a.* Fleshy; plump, unctuous heavy; stupid; rich; fertile.—*n.* solid oily substance found in parts of animal bodies; the best or rich est part of a thing.—*vt.* (fatting, fat ted). To make fat.

fatal, fät'al, *a.* Proceeding from fate; causing death; deadly; calamitous.

fate, fat, *n.* Destiny; inevitable necessity; death; doom; lot; *pl.* the three goddesses supposed to preside over the birth and life of men.

father, fä'THėr, *n.* A male parent; the first ancestor, the oldest member of a society or profession; the first to practice any art; a creator; a name given to God, a dignitary of the church; one of the early expounders of Christianity.—*vt.* To

become a father to, to adopt, to profess to be the author of; to ascribe to one as his offspring or production.

fathom, faTH'um, *n.* A measure of length containing six feet.—*vt.* To try the depth of; to sound; to master, to comprehend.

fatigue, fa-tēg', *vt.* (fatiguing, fatigued) To employ to weariness; to tire, to harass with toil or labor.—*n.* Weariness from bodily or mental exertion; exhaustion; toil; labors of soldiers distinct from the use of arms.

fatten, fat'n, *vt.* To make fat; to feed for slaughter; to make fertile.—*vi.* To grow fat.

fauna, fä'na, *n.* A collective term for the animals peculiar to a region or epoch.

faux-pas, fō-pä, *n.* A false step; a breach of manners or moral conduct.

fear, fär, *n.* Painful emotion excited by apprehension of impending danger; dread; the object of fear; filial regard mingled with awe; reverence.—*vt.* To feel fear, to apprehend; to dread; to reverence.— *vi.* To be in apprehension of evil, to be afraid.

feasibility, fēz-i-bil 'i-ti, *n.* Quality of being feasible; practicability.

feasible, fēz-i-bl, *a.* That may be done, practicable.

feast, fēst, *n.* A festal day, a sumptuous entertainment; a banquet; a festival, that which delights and entertains.—*vi.* To partake of a feast; to eat sumptuously; to be highly gratified.—*vt.* To entertain sumptuously.

feather, feTH'ėr, *n.* One of the growths which form the covering of birds, a plume, projection on a board to fit into another board; kind of nature, birds collectively, a trifle.—*vt.* To cover or fit with feathers; to turn (an oar) horizontally over the water.

feature, fē'tur, *n.* The make or cast of any part of the face; any single lineament; a prominent part or characteristic.

federal, fed'ėr-al, *a.* Pertaining to a league or contract; confederated; founded on alliance between states which unite for national purposes.—*n.* One who upholds federal government.

federation, fed-e' r-a'shon, *n.* Act of uniting in a league; confederacy.

fee, fē, *n.* A reward for services; recompense for professional services; a fief; a freehold estate held by one who is absolute owner.—*vt.* (feeing, feed). To pay a fee to; to engage in one's service by advancing a fee to.

feeble, fē'bl, *a*. Weak; impotent; deficient in vigor, as mental powers sound, light, etc.

feed, fēd, *vt*. (feeding, fed). To give food to; to furnish with anything of which there is constant consumption; to fatten.—*vi*. To take food, to eat; to prey, to graze, to grow fat.—*n*. That which is eaten; fodder; portion of provender given to a horse, cow, etc.

feel, fēl, *vt*. (feeling, felt). To perceive by the touch, to have the sense of; to be affected by; to examine by touching.—*vi*. To have perception by the touch; to have the sensibility moved; to have perception mentally.—*n*. Act of feeling; perception caused by the touch.

feign, fān, *vt*. To pretend, to counterfeit; to simulate.—*vi*. To represent falsely; to pretend.

felicitate, fē-lis'it-āt, *vt*. To congratulate.

felon, fe'lon, *n*. One who has committed felony, a culprit, a whitlow.—*a*. Fierce; malignant; malicious.

felony, fe'lon-i, *n*. Any crime which incurs the forfeiture of lands or goods, a heinous crime.

female, fē'māl, *n*. One of that sex which conceives and brings forth young. *a*. Belonging to the sex which produces young; feminine; weak.

feminine, fem'in-in, *a* Pertaining to females; womanly; effeminate; denoting the gender of words which signify females.

femur, fē'mėr, *n*. The thigh-bone.

fence, fens, *n*. That which defends or guards, a wall, railing, etc. forming a boundary, etc.—*vi*. To practice the swordsman's art; to parry arguments, to prevaricate.

fencing, fens'ing, *n*. The art of using a sword or foil in attack or defense, material used in making fences; that which fences.

fenestration, fen-es-trā'shon, *n*. The arrangement of windows in a building.

fennel, fen'el, *n*. A plant cultivated for the aromatic flavor of its seeds and for its leaves.

fermentation, fé r-ment-ā'shon, *n*. Decomposition or conversion of an organic substance into new compounds by a ferment, indicated by the development of heat, bubbles etc., process by which grape juice is converted into wine agitation; excitement.

ferocious, fē-rō'shus, *a*. Fierce; savage; cruel.

ferry, fe'ri, *vt*. (ferrying, ferried). To carry over a river or other water in a boat.—*n*. Place where boats pass over to convey passengers; regular conveyance provided at such a place; a boat that plies at a ferry.

fertile, fėr'til, *a*. Fruitful, prolific, inventive; able to produce abundantly.

fertility, fėr-til'i-ti, *n*. Fruitfulness; richness, fertile invention.

fertilize, fėr'til-īz, *vt*. To make fertile or fruitful; to enrich; to impregnate.

fervent, fėr'vent, *a*. Burning; vehement; ardent; earnest.

fever, fē'vėr, *n*. A disease characterized by an accelerated pulse, heat, thirst, and diminished strength, agitation; excitement.— *vt*. To put in a fever.—*vt*. To be seized with fever.

fiasco, fē-as'kō, *n*. An ignominious failure.

fiber, fī bėr, *n*. A thread; a fine, slender body which Constitutes a part of animals, plants, or minerals.

fiction, fik'shon, *n*. A feigned story; literature in the form of novels, tales, etc., a falsehood; fabrication.

fidelity, fi-del'i-ti, *n*. Faithfulness; trustiness; loyalty; integrity.

fiduciary, fi-dū'shi-a-ri, *a*. Held in trust; having the nature of a trust.—*n*. One who holds a thing in trust, a trustee.

field, fēld, *n*. A piece of land suitable for tillage or pasture; piece of enclosed land; place of battle, battle; open space for action; sphere; blank space on which figures are drawn, those taking part in a hunt or race.—*vi*. and *t*. To watch and catch the ball, as in cricket.

fiend, fēnd, *n*. A demon; the devil; a wicked or cruel person

fierce, fērs, *a*. Wild; savage; outrageous; violent.

fight, fit, *vi*. (fighting, fought). To strive for victory; to contend in arms.—*vt*. To war against; to contend with in battle, to win by struggle.—*n*. A struggle for victory; a battle; an encounter.

fighter, fī t'ėr, *n*. One who fights; a combatant; a warrior; an aeroplane designed for aerial combat.

figment, fig'ment, *n*. A fiction; fabrication.

figure-head, fig'ūr-hed, *n*. The ornamental figure on a ship under the bowsprit.

filament, fil'a-ment, *n*. A slender thread, a fine fiber.

file, fil, *n*. A line or wire on which papers are strung; the papers so strung, a row of soldiers one behind another, a steel instrument for cutting and smoothing iron wood, etc.—*vt.* (filing, filed). To arrange or place on or in a file; to bring before a court by presenting the proper papers; to rub or cut with a file; to polish.—*vi.* To march in a line one after the other.

fill, fil, *vt.* To make full; to occupy; to pervade; to satisfy; to surfeit; to supply with an occupant, to hold to possess and perform the duties of.—*vi.* To grow or become full.—*n.* As much as fills or supplies want.

fillet, fil'et, *n.* A little band to tie about the hair, the fleshy part of the thigh in veal, meat rolled together and tied round; something resembling a fillet or band.—*vt.* (filleting, filleted). To bind with a little band.

filter, fil'tėr, *n.* A strainer; any substance through which liquors are passed—*vt.* To purify by passing through a filter.—*vi.* To percolate to pass through a filter.

finance, fi-nans', *n.* The science of public revenue and expenditure; management of money matters; pl. public funds or resources of money, private income. —*vi.* (financing, financed). To conduct financial operations.—*vt.* To manage the financial affairs of.

finch, finsh, *n.* A small singing bird.

finding, find'ing, *n.* Discovery; act of discovering: that which is found, a verdict.

finery, fin'ė-ri, *n.* Fine things, showy articles of dress; a furnace where cast-iron is converted into malleable iron.

finger, fing'gėr, *n.* One of the five members of the hand; something resembling a finger; skill in playing on a keyed instrument.—*vt.* To handle with the fingers; to touch lightly, to pilfer.—*vi.* To dispose the fingers aptly in playing on an instrument.

finis, fi'nis, *n.* An end, conclusion.

finish, fin'ish, *vt.* To bring to an end; to perfect; to polish to a high degree.—*vi.* To come to an end; to expire.—*n.* Completion; the last touch to a work, polish.

finite, fi'nīt, *a.* Limited; bounded; circumscribed, not infinite.

fire, fīr, *n.* Heat and light emanating from a body; fuel burning; a conflagration; discharge of firearms; splendor; violence of passion; vigor of fancy animation; ardent affection: affliction.—*vt.* (firing, fired). To set on fire; to irritate; to animate; to bake, to cause to explode, to discharge (firearms).—*vi.* To take

fire; to be inflamed with passion, to discharge firearms.

firmament, fėrm'a-ment, *n.* The sky or heavens; region of the air; an expanse.

first, fėrst, *a.* Foremost in time, place, rank, value, etc., chief, highest; the ordinal of one.—*adv.* Before all others in time, place, etc.

fiscal, fis'kal, *a.* Pertaining to the public treasury.—*n.* A treasurer; a public prosecutor, as in Scotland.

fisherman, fish'ér-man, *n.* One whose occupation is to catch fish.

fistular, fis'tū-lėr, *a.* Hollow like a pipe.

fixation, fiks-ā'shon, *n.* Act of fixing; state in which a body resists evaporation.

fixture, fiks'tūr, *n.* That which is fixed; that which is permanently attached, an appendage.

flabby, flab'i, *a.* Soft; yielding to the touch; languid; feeble.

flaccid, flak 'sid, *a.* Flabby; soft and weak, drooping, limber.

flake, flāk, *n.* A loose, filmy mass of anything, a scale; a fleecy or feathery particle, as of snow; a flock, as of wool.—*vt.* (flaking flaked). To form into flakes.—*vi.* To break in layers; to peel off.

flamboyant, flam-boi'ant, *a.* Noting that style of gothic architecture characterized by wavy tracery in the windows; florid.

flame, flām, *n.* Light emitted from fire, a blaze, fire, heat of passion; ardor of temper or imagination; ardent love; rage; one beloved.—*vi.* (flaming, flamed). To blaze; to glow; to rage.

flamingo, fla-ming'gō, *n.* A webfooted, long-necked bird about 5 to 6 feet high.

flank, flangk, *n.* The part of the side of an animal, between the ribs and the hip, the side of an army; the extreme right or left; the side of any building.—*vt.* To be situated at the side of; to place troops so as to command or attack the flank, to pass round the side of

flannel, flan'el, *n.* A soft, nappy, woolen cloth of loose texture; garment made of flannel.

flask, flask, *n.* A kind of bottle; a bottle for the pocket; a vessel for powder.

flatter, flat'ėr, *vt.* To gratify by praise; to compliment; to praise falsely.

flattery, flat'ė-ri, *n.* False praise; sycophancy, cajolery.

flaunt, flänt, *vi.* and *t.* To display ostentatiously.—*n.* Bold or impudent parade.

flavor, flā'vėr, *n.* The quality of a substance which affects the smell or taste;

F

relish; zest.—*vt.* To give a flavor to.

flawless, flä'les, *a.* Without defect; perfect.

flesh, flesh, *n.* The muscular part of an animal; animal food; beasts and birds used as food; the body, as distinguished from the soul mankind, corporeal appetites kindred, family.—*vt.* To feed with flesh; to initiate to the taste of flesh.

fleshly, flesh'li, *a.* Carnal, worldly lascivious; human; not spiritual.

flicker, flik'e˙r, *vi.* To flutter; to waver, as an unsteady flame.—*n.* A wavering gleam.

flight, flīt, *n.* Act of fleeing or flying; power or manner of flying; a flock of birds; a volley, as of arrows; pace passed by flying; a soaring; lofty elevation, as of fancy; extravagant sally; a series of steps or stairs.

flimsy, flim'zi, *a.* Thin; slight; weak; without force, shallow.

flinch, flinsh, *vi.* to shrink; to withdraw, to wince, to fail.

fling, fling, *vi.* (flinging, flung). To cause to fly from the hand; to hurl; to scatter, to throw to the ground.—*vi.* To fly into violent and irregular motions; to flounce; to rush away angrily.—*n.* A throw; a gibe; a lively Scottish dance.

flint, flint, *n.* A very hard siliceous stone, which strikes fire with steel anything proverbially hard.

flirt, flė rt, *vt.* To throw with a jerk to make coquettish motions with (a fan). *vi.* To run and dart about; to coquette, to play at courtship.—*n.* A sudden jerk; one who plays at courtship; a coquette.

float, flōt, *n.* That which is borne on water or any fluid; a raft.—*vi.* To be borne on the surface of a fluid; to be buoyed up, to move with a light, irregular course.— *vt.* To cause to be conveyed on water; to flood; to get (a company, scheme, etc.) started.

flock, flok, *n.* A lock of wool or hair; stuffing for mattresses, etc., a company, as of sheep, birds, etc; a Christian congregation in relation to their pastor.—*vi.* To gather in companies; to crowd; to move in crowds.

flood flud, *n.* A great flow of water a deluge; a river; the flowing of the tide; a great quantity; abundance.—*vt.* To overflow; to deluge; to overwhelm.

floor, flōr, *n.* That part of a building on which we walk, bottom of a room; story in a building; a flat, hard surface of loam, lime, etc. used in some kinds of business, as in malting.—*vt.* Tò lay a floor upon; to strike down.

flounder, floun'dėr, *n.* A flat fish found in the sea near the mouths of rivers.—*vi.* To struggle, as in mire, to roll, toss, and tumble.

flour, flour, *n.* Finely ground meal of wheat or other grain; fine powder of any substance.—*vt.* To convert into flour; to sprinkle with flour.

flourish, flu'rish, *vi.* To grow luxuriantly, to thrive; to live; to use florid language, to make ornamental strokes in writing, etc.; to move in bold and irregular figures.—*vt.* To adorn with flowers or figures, to ornament with anything showy, to brandish.—*n.* Showy splendor, parade of words and figures; fanciful stroke of the pen; decorative notes in music; brandishing.

flow, flō, *vi.* To move, as water; to issue; to abound; to glide smoothly; to hang loose and waving; to rise, as the tide; to circulate, as blood.—*vt.* To flow over, to flood.—*n.* A moving along, as of water; stream; current; rise of water; fullness; free expression, feeling.

flower, flou'e˙r, *n.* The delicate and gaily-colored leaves or petals on a plant, a bloom or blossom; youth; the prime; the best part; one most distinguished, an ornamental expression; *pl.* a powdery substance.—*vi.* To blossom, to bloom.—*vt.* To embellish with figures of flowers.

flowing, flō'ing, *p.a.* Moving as a steam; abounding; fluent; undulating.

fluctuate, fluk'tū-āt, *vi.* To move as a wave, to waver, to hesitate; to experience vicissitudes.

fluctuation, fluk-tū-ā'shon, *n.* A rising and falling; change, vicissitude.

fluff, fluf, *n.* Light down or nap such as rises from beds, cotton, etc

fluid, flü'id, *a.* Capable of flowing; liquid or gaseous.—*n.* Any substance whose parts easily move and change their relative position without separation; a liquid.

flurry, flu'ri, *n.* Bustle, hurry, a gust of wind; light things carried by the wind.— *vt.* (flurrying, flurried). To agitate or alarm.

fluster, flus'tėr, *vt.* To agitate; to make hot with drink.—*n.* Agitation, confusion, heat.

flute, flöt, *n.* A small wind-instrument with holes and keys, a channel cut along the shaft of a column; a similar channel.—*vi.* (fluting, fluted). To play on a flute.—*vt.* To play or sing in notes like those of a flute; to form flutes or channels in.

flutist, flöt'ist, *n.* A performer on the flute.

flutter, flut'èr, *vi.* To move or flap the wings rapidly; to be in agitation; to fluctuate.—*vt.* To agitate; to throw into confusion.—*n.* Quick confused motion; agitation; disorder.

flux, fluks, *n.* Act of flowing, any flow of matter; dysentery; flow of the tide; anything used to promote fusion; fusion; liquid state from the operation of heat.—*vt.* To melt; to fuse.

fly, flī', *vi.* (flying, pret, flew, pp. flown). To move through air by wings, to move in air by the force of wind, etc., to rise in air, to move rapidly; to pass away; to depart suddenly; to spring; to flutter.—*vt.* To flee from; to cause to float in the air.—*n.* A winged insect; a revolving mechanism to regulate the motion of machinery; a light carriage, a cab.

foal, fōl, *n.* The young of a mare she-ass etc.; a colt or filly.—*vt.* To bring forth, as a colt or filly.—*vi.* To bring forth a foal.

foam, fōm, *n.* Froth; spume.—*vt.* To froth, to show froth at the mouth to rage.—*vt.* To cause to give out foam; to throw out with rage or violence.

fob, fob, *n.* A little pocket for a watch in the waistband of the breeches.

focus, fō'kus, *n.*; pl. **-cuses** or **-ci.** A point in which rays of light meet after being reflected or refracted point of concentration.—*vt.* To bring to a focus.

fodder, fod'èr, *n.* Food for cattle, etc.—*vt.* To furnish with fodder.

foe, fō, *n.* An enemy; an opposing army; one who opposes anything.

fog, fog, *n.* A dense vapor near the surface of the land or water, mental confusion; dimness; second growth of grass; long grass that remains in pastures till winter.

fogey, fō'gi, *n.*; pl. **-eys, -ies,** A stupid fellow; an old-fashioned person.

foible, foi'bl, *n.* A weak point in character; a failing; the weak part of a sword.

folio, fō'li-ō, *n.* A book of the largest size, formed by sheets of paper once doubled; a page; number appended to each page; a written page of a certain number of words.

follicle, fol'li-kl, *n.* A little bag or vesicle in animals or plants.

follow, fol'ō, *vt.* To go or come after; to chase, to accompany, to succeed; to result from; to understand; to copy; to practice; to be occupied with, to be guided by.—*vi.* To come after another; to ensure, to result.

folly, fol'i, *n.* Foolishness; imbecility; a weak or foolish act; criminal weakness.

foment, fō-ment', *vt.* To apply warm lotions to; to abet; to stir up (in a bad sense).

fondle, fon'dl, *vt.* (fondling, fondled). To treat with fondness; to caress.

foolish, föl'ish, *a.* Void of understanding; acting without judgment or discretion; silly; ridiculous; unwise.

football, füt'bäl, *n.* An inflated leather ball to be driven by the foot; a game played with such a ball.

footstep, füt'step, *n.* A track, the mark of the foot; vestige; *pl.* example; course.

forbear, for-bär', *vi.* To keep away; to cease; to delay; to refrain.—*vt.* To abstain from; to avoid doing.

forbid, for-bid', *vt.* To prohibit; to oppose; to obstruct.—*vi.* To utter a prohibition.

forcible, fōrs'i-bl, *a.* Efficacious, *potent*, cogent; done by force; suffered by force.

forcing, fōrs'ing, *n.* Art of raising plants or fruits, at an earlier season than the natural one, by artificial heat.

foreign, fo'rin, *a.* Belonging to another nation or country; alien; not to the purpose; irrelevant.

forensic, fō-ren'sik *a.* Belonging to courts of justice, or to public debate; used in courts or legal proceedings.

forest, fo'rest, *n.* An extensive wood; a district devoted to the purposes of the chase; a tract once a royal forest.—*a.* Relating to a forest; sylvan; rustic.—*vt.* To convert into a forest.

forever, for-ev'èr, *adv.* At all times; through endless ages, eternally.

forewarn, fōr-warn', *vt.* To warn beforehand, to give previous notice to.

foreword, for'wèrd, *n.* A preface.

forfeiture, for'fit-ūr, *n.* Act of forfeiting, loss of some right, estate, honor, etc., by a crime or fault; fine; penalty.

forgery, fōrj'è-ri, *n.* The crime of counterfeiting, that which is forged or counterfeited.

forget, for-get', *vt.* (forgetting, pret, forgot, pp. forgot, forgotten). To lose the remembrance of; to slight; to neglect.

forlorn, for-lorn', *a.* Deserted; abandoned; miserable.—**Forlorn hope, a**

body of men appointed to perform some specially perilous service.

former, form'èr, *n.* He who forms. — *a comp. deg.* Before in time; long past; mentioned before another.

formidable, for'mid-a-bl, *a.* Exciting fear or apprehension; difficult to deal with or undertake.

formula, for'mū la, *n.*, pl. **-lae.** A prescribed form; a confession of faith, expression for resolving certain problems in mathematics; expression of chemical composition.

formulate, for'mū-lāt, *vt.* To express in a formula; to put into a precise and comprehensive statement.

fornicate, for'ni-kāt, *vi.* To have unlawful sexual intercourse.

forthcoming, fōrth-kum'ing, *a.* Coming forth; making appearance, ready to appear.

fortification, for'ti-fi-kā''shon, *n.* The art or science of fortifying places; the works erected in defense; a fortified place; additional strength.

fortify, for'ti-fī , *vt.* (fortifying, fortified). To make strong; to strengthen by forts, batteries, etc.; to invigorate, to increase the strength of.

fortunate, for'tu-nāt, *a.* Having good fortune; successful, coming by good luck.

fortune, for'tūn, *n.* Chance, luck the good or ill that befalls man means of living; estate; great wealth; destiny, the power regarded as determining the lots of life.

forum, fō'rum, *n.* A public place in ancient Rome, where causes were tried; a tribunal; jurisdiction.

forward, for'wèrd, *adv.* Toward a place in front, onward.—*a.* Near or towards the forepart; in advance of something; ready; bold; pert; advanced beyond the usual degree; too ready.—*vt.* To help onward, to hasten, to send forward to transmit.—*n.* In football hockey, etc., one of the players in the front line.

found, found, *vt.* To lay the base of; to establish, to institute, to form by melting metal and pouring it into a mold, to cast.—*vi.* To rest or rely (with on or *upon*). Pret. and pp. of *find.*

foundation, found-ā'shon, *n.* Act of founding; base of an edifice, base; endowment; endowed institution.

founder, found'èr, *n.* One who lays a foundation; an originator, an endower, one who casts metal.—*vi.* To fill with water and sink, to miscarry; to go lame, as a horse.

foundry, found'ri, *n.* An establishment for casting metals.

fountain, fount'ān, *n.* A spring or source of water, an artificial jet or shower; head of a river; original; source.

fraction, frak'shon, *n.* A fragment a very small part, one or more of the equal parts into which a unit of number is divided.

fracture, frak'tūr, *n.* A breach or break, breaking of a bone, manner in which a mineral breaks.—*vt.* (fracturing, fractured). To break.

fragility, fra-jil'i-ti, *n.* Quality of being fragile; delicacy of substance.

fragment, frag'ment, *n.* A part broken off; an imperfect thing.

fragrant, frā'grant, *a.* Sweet-smelling; spicy; balmy; aromatic.

frail, frāl, *a.* Easily broken; weak; liable to fail and decay.—*n.* A kind of basket.

frame, frām, *vt.* (framing, framed). To make, to construct, to devise, to adjust; to shape; to place in a frame.—*n.* Anything composed of parts fitted together; structure; bodily structure; framework; particular state, as of the mind; mood or disposition.

framing, frām'ing, *n.* Act of constructing a frame frame thus constructed; rough timber-work of a house.

fratricide, fra'tri-sīd, *n.* Murder of a brother; one who murders a brother.

fraud, fräd, *n.* Artifice by which the right or interest of another is injured, deception.

freak, frēk, *n.* A sudden causeless turn of the mind; a caprice; a sport.—*vt.* To variegate.

freckle, frek'l, *n.* A yellowish spot in the skin any small snot or discoloration.— *vt.* or *i.* (freckling, freckled). To give or acquire freckles.

free, frē, *a.* Being at liberty; instituted by a free people; not arbitrary or despotic; open; clear; disjoined; licentious; candid; generous, gratuitous; guiltless.—*vt.* (freeing, freed). To set free; to liberate; to disentangle; to exempt; to absolve from some charge.

freedom, frē'dum, *n.* State of being free, liberty, particular privilege: facility of doing anything: frankness, undue familiarity.

free-will, frē'wil, *n.* The power of directing our own actions, without restraint by necessity or fate.—*a.* Spontaneous.

freeze, frēz, *vi.* (freezing,pret. froze, pp. frozen or froze). To be congealed by cold; to be hardened into ice; to be of that degree of cold at which water congeals; to stagnate; to shiver or stiffen with cold.—*vt.* To congeal; to chill; to make credits, etc., temporarily unrealizable.

freight, frāt, *n.* The cargo of a ship lading; hire of a ship; charge for the transportation of goods.—*vt.* To load with goods; to hire for carrying goods.

frenzy, fren'zi, *n.* Madness, distraction; violent agitation of the mind.

fresh, fresh, *a.* Full of health and strength, vigorous; brisk; bright; not faded; in good condition; not stale; cool and agreeable; clearly remembered, new, not salt; unpracticed; unused.

friction, frik'shon, *n.* A rubbing effect of rubbing; resistance which a moving body meets with from the surface on which it moves.

Friday, frī'dā, *n.* The sixth day of the week.—**Good Friday,** the Friday preceding Easter, sacred as the day of Christ's crucifixion.

frighten, frīt'n, *vt.* To strike with fright or fear; to terrify; to scare; to alarm.

frigid, fri'jid, *a.* Cold; wanting spirit or zeal, stiff, formal lifeless.

frigidity, fri-jid'i-ti, *n.* Coldness coldness of affection; dullness.

frill, fril, *n.* A crisp or plaited edging on an article of dress a ruffle.—*vt.* To decorate with frills.

frolic, fro'lik, *a.* Joyous; merry; frisky; poetic.—*n.* A merry prank merry-making.—*vi.* To play merry pranks, to gambol.

frond, frond, *n.* The leaf of a fern or other cryptogamic plant.

front, frunt, *n.* The forehead; the whole face; the fore part, boldness impudence; the area of military operations.—*a.* Relating to the front or face.—*vt.* To stand with the front opposed to; to oppose; to face; to supply with a front.—*vi.* To face; to look.

frontage frunt'āj, *n.* The front part of an edifice, quay, etc.

frontal, frunt'al, *a.* Belonging to the forehead.—*n.* An ornament for the forehead; a frontlet; a small pediment.

frontier, fron'tēr, *n.* That part of a country which fronts another country, extreme part of a country.—*a.* Bordering; conterminous.

frontispiece, fron'tis-pēs, *n.* The principal face of a building, an illustration facing the title page of a book.

froward, frō'wėrd, *a.* Perverse; ungovernable; disobedient. peevish.

frown, froun, *vi.* To express displeasure by contracting the brow; to look stern; to scowl.—*n.* A wrinkling of the brow; a sour or stern look; any expression of displeasure.

fruit, frōt, *n.* Whatever of a vegetable nature is of use to man or animals; the reproductive produce of a plant; such products collectively; the seed or matured ovary that which is produced; offspring, effect; outcome.—*vi.* To produce fruit.

frustrate, frus'trāt, *vt.* (frustrating, frustrated). To balk, to foil, to bring to nothing; to render of no effect.

frustration, frus-trā'shon, *n.* Disappointment; defeat.

fry, frī, *vt.* (frying, fried). To cook by roasting over a fire.—*vi.* To be cooked as above; to simmer; to be in agitation.—*n.* A dish of anything fried; state of mental ferment; young fishes at an early stage, swarm of small fishes, etc. insignificant objects.

fuchsia, fū'shi-a, *n.* A beautiful flowering shrub.

fuddle, fud'l, *vt.* (fuddling, fuddled). To make stupid by drink, to spend in drinking.—*vi.* To drink to excess.

fugitive, fū-jit-iv, *a.* Apt to flee away; volatile; fleeting; vagabond; temporary.—*n.* One who flees from duty or danger, refugee.

full, fül, *a.* Having all it can contain; abounding; crowded; entire; strong, loud, clear, mature, perfect; ample.—*n.* Complete measure, the highest state or degree (usually with the).—*adv.* Quite, altogether; exactly; directly.—*vt.* To scour and thicken, as woolen cloth, in a mill.

fumble, fum'bl, *vi.* (fumbling, fumbled). To grope about awkwardly to attempt or handle something bunglingly.

fumigate, fūm'i-gāt, *vt.* (fumigating, fumigated). To smoke, to purify from infection, etc.

function, fungk'shon, *n.* Performance; office; duty; proper office of any organ in animals or vegetables; a ceremonial; a mathematical quantity connected with and varying with another.

fundamental, fun-da-ment'al, *a.* Pertaining to the foundation; essential, primary.—*n.* A leading principle which serves as the groundwork of a system; an essential.

funeral, fū'nė-ral, *n.* Burial; ceremony of burying a dead body.—*a.* Used at the interment of the dead.

funereal, fū-ne'rē-al, *a.* Suiting a funeral; dark; dismal; mournful.

funny, fun'i, *a.* Making fun; droll; comical.

furnace, fėr'nas, *n.* A structure in which a vehement fire may be maintained for melting ores, heating water, etc.; place or occasion Or torture or trial.

furniture, fėr'ni-tūr, *n.* That with which anything is furnished equipment; outfit; movable wooden articles in a house.

furrow, fu'rō, *n.* A trench made by a plow, a groove, a wrinkle.—*vt.* To make furrows in; to groove; to wrinkle.

further, fėr'THėr, *adv.* More in advance; besides; farther.—*a.* More distant, farther.—*vt.* To help forward; to advance.

furtive, fėr'tiv, *a.* Stolen; sly; stealthy.

fusion, fū'zhon, *n.* Act or operation of fusing; state of being melted or blended; complete union.

futile, fū'til *a.* Serving no useful end, trivial, worthless.

futility, fū-til'i-ti, *n.* Quality of being futile; worthlessness; unimportance.

future, fū'tūr, *a.* That is to be, pertaining to time to come.—*n.* The time to come, all that is to happen the future tense.

G

gab, gab, *vi.* (gabbling, gabbed). To talk much: to chatter.—*n.* Idle talk.

gabble, gab'l, *vi.* (gabbling, gabbled). To talk fast, or without meaning.—*n.* Rapid talk without meaning; inarticulate sounds rapidly uttered.

gadget, gad'jet, *n.* A tool, appliance, or contrivance.

gain, gān, *vt.* To obtain; to get, as profit or advantage; to receive, as honor, to win to one's side, to conciliate; to reach, arrive at.—*vi.* To reap advantage or profit; to make progress.—*n.* Something obtained as an advantage; profit; benefit.

gall, gäl, *n.* A bitter fluid secreted in the liver; bile; rancor; malignity; an excrescence produced by the egg of an insect on a plant, especially the oak; a sore place in the skin from rubbing.—*vt.* To make a sore in the skin of by rubbing; to fret, to vex; to harass.

gallant, gal'ant, *a.* Gay in attire; handsome; brave, showing politeness and attention to ladies (in this sense also pron. ga-lant').—*n.* A gay sprightly man; a daring spirit; (pron. also ga-lant') a man attentive to ladies, suitor paramour.—*vt.* To act the gallant towards; to be very attentive to (a lady).

gallantry, gal'ant-ri, *n.* Show; bravery; intrepidity; polite attentions to ladies, vicious love or pretentions to love.

gallery, gal'é-ri, *n.* A long apartment serving as a passage of communication, or for the reception of pictures, etc.; upper floor of a church, theatre, etc.; a covered passage; frame like a balcony projected from a ship.

gallop, gal'up, *vi.* To move or run with leaps; to ride at this pace; to move very fast.—*n.* The pace of a horse, by springs or leaps.

gallows, gal'ōz, *n. sing* or *pl.;* also **gallowses**, gal'oz-ez, in *pl.* A structure for the hanging of criminals; one of a pair of braces for the trousers.

gambit, gam'bit, *n.* An opening in chess incurring the sacrifice of a pawn.

gamble, gam'bl, *vi.* (gambling, gambled). To play for money.

gambling, gam'bl-ing, *n.* The act or practice of gaming for money or anything valuable.

gambol, gam'bol, *vi.* (gamboling, gam-boled). To skip about in sport; to frisk; to frolic.—*n.* A skipping about in frolic, a prank.

game, gām, *n.* Sport of any kind; exercise for amusement, testing skill, etc., scheme pursued, fieldsports, animals hunted.—*vi.* (gaming, gamed). To play at any sport; to play for a stake or prize, to practice gaming. To die game. to maintain a bold spirit to the last.

gamester, gām'ster, *n.* A person addicted to gaming; a gambler.

gamin, gam'in, *n.* A street arab; a neglected street-boy.

gaming, gām'ing, *n.* The act or practice of gambling.

gangrene, gang'grēn, *n.* An eating away of the flesh; first stage of mortification.—*vt.* (gangrening, gangrened). To mortify.—*vi.* To become mortified.

gangster, gang'stėr, *n.* A member of a criminal organization.

gap, gap, *n.* An opening; breach; hiatus; chasm.

gape, gāp, *vi.* (gaping, gaped). To open the mouth wide, to yawn, to open in fissures; to stand open.— *n.* A gaping; the width of the mouth when opened, as of a bird fish, etc.

garage, gar'aj, *n.* A place for housing or repairing motor-cars.

garb, gärb, *n.* Dress; clothes; mode of dress.—*vt.* To dress.

garbage, gärb'äj, *n.* Waste matter; offal; vegetable refuse.

garlic, gär'lik, *n.* A plant allied to the onion, with a pungent taste and strong odor.

garment, gär'ment, *n.* An article of clothing, as a coat, a gown, etc.

garner, gär'nėr, *n.* A granary; a store.—*vt.* To store in a granary; to store up.

garnet, gär'net, *n.* A precious stone, generally of a red color.

garnish, gär'nish, *vt.* To adorn; to embellish (a dish) with something laid round.—*n.* Ornament; an embellishment round a dish.

garret, ga'ret, *n.* A room in a house on the uppermost floor, immediately under the roof

garrison, ga'ri-sn, *n.* A body of troops stationed in a fort or town.—*vt.* To place a garrison in.

garrotte, ga-rot', *vt.* To rob by seizing a person and compressing his windpipe till he become helpless.

garrulity, ga-rū'li-ti, *n.* Loquacity; practice or habit to talking much.

garter, gär'tėr, *n*. A band to hold up a stocking; the badge of the highest order or knighthood in Great Britain, the order itself.—*vt*. To bind with a garter.

gasteropod, gastropod, gas'tėr-opod, gas'trō-pod, *n*. A mollusk such as snails, having a broad muscular foot attached to the ventral surface.

gastric, gas'trik, *a*. Belonging to the stomach.

Gastronomy, gas-tron'o-mi, *n*. The art or science of good eating; epicurism.

gate, gāt, *n*. A large door or entrance; a frame of timber, iron, etc., closing an entrance, etc., a way or passage; the frame which stops the passage of water through a dam, lock, etc.

gate-crasher, gāt-krash'ėr, *n*. An uninvited guest, one who obtains admission to a public entertainment without a ticket.

gateway, gāt'wā, *n*. A way through the gate of some enclosure; the gate itself.

gazette, ga-zet', *n*. A newspaper, especially an official newspaper.—*vt*. (gazetting, gazetted). To insert in a gazette, to announce or public officially.

gazetteer, ga-zet-tēr', *n*. A writer or publisher of news, a dictionary of geographical information.

gear, gēr, *n*. Dress; ornaments; apparatus, harness, tackle, a train of toothed wheels.—*vt*. To put gear on to harness.

gelatine, jel'a-tin, *n*. A concrete transparent substance obtained by boiling from certain parts of animals; the principle of jelly; glue.

geld, geld, *vt*. To castrate; to emasculate.

gelid, je'lid, *a*. Icy cold; frosty or icy.

gem, jem, *n*. A precious stone of any kind; a jewel; anything remarkable for beauty or rarity.—*vt*. (gemming, gemmed). To adorn, as with gems; to bespangle; to embellish.

Gemini, jem'i-nī, *n.pl*. The twins, a sign of the zodiac, containing the two stars Castor and Pollux.

general, jen'ė-ral, *a*. Of or belonging to a genus; not special; public; common; extensive, though not universal; usual; taken as a whole.—*n*. The whole a comprehensive notion; a military officer of the highest rank.

generous, jen'ė-rus, *a*. Noble, bountiful; liberal; full of spirit, as wine; courageous, as a steed.

genetic, genetical, jen-net'ik, jenet'ik-al, *a*. Relating to origin or production.

genial, jē'ni-al, *a*. Cordial kindly; con-

tributing to life and cheerfulness.

genitals, jen'it-alz, *n.pl*. the parts of generation, sexual organs.

genitive, jen'it-iv, *a*. and *n*. Applied to a case of nouns, pronouns, etc., in English called the possessive.

genre, zhäng-r, *n*. A term applied to the department of painting which depicts scenes of ordinary life.

genteel, jen-tēl, *a*. Having the manners of well-bred people; refined; elegant.

gentle, jen'tl, *a*. Well-born; refined in manners, mild placid not rough, violent, or wild; soothing.— *n*. A person of good birth.

gentleman, jen'tl-man, *n*. A man of good social position; technically any man above the rank of yeoman, comprehending noblemen; a man of good breeding or of high honor; a polite equivalent for 'man'

genuflection, jen-ū-flek'shon, *n*. The act of bending the knee, particularly in worship.

genuine, jen'ū-in, *a*. Belonging to the original stock, real, pure true.

genus, jē'nus, *n.; pl*. **genera**, jen'ė-ra. A kind, class, or sort; an assemblage of species having distinctive characteristics in common.

Geometry, jē-om'e-tri, *n*. The science of magnitude; that branch of mathematics which treats of the properties and relations of lines, angles, surfaces, and solids.

gerrymander, ge'ri-man-dėr, *vt*. To arrange so as to get an unfair result from the distribution of voters in political elections.

gerund, je'rund, *n*. A kind of verbal noun in Latin; a verbal noun, such as 'teaching' in 'fit for teaching boys.'

gestation, jest-ā'shon, *n*. The carrying of young in the womb from conception to delivery; pregnancy.

gesture, jes'tūr, *n*. A posture or motion of the body of limbs; action intended to express an idea or feeling; or to enforce an argument.

get, get, *vt*. (getting, pret, got, pp. got, gotten). To obtain; to gain; to reach, to beget, to learn; to induce.—*vi*. To arrive at any place or state by degrees; to become; to make gain.

geyser, gī'zėr, *n*. A hot-water spring, the water rising in a column.

ghastly, gast'li, *a*. Deathlike in looks; hideous; frightful, as wounds.

giant, jī'ant, *n*. A man of extraordinary

stature, a person of extraordinary powers, bodily or intellectual.—*a*. Like a giant; extraordinary in size.

gibberish, gib'bėr-ish, *n*. Rapid and inarticulate talk; unmeaning words.

gibbet, jib'bet, *n*. A gallows; the projecting beam of a crane. on which the pulley is fixed.—*vt*. To hang on a gibbet; to expose to scorn infamy, etc.

gift, gift, *n*. Anything given; act of giving; power of giving; talent or faculty.—*vt*. To endow with any power or faculty.

giggle, gig'l, *n*. A kind of laugh, with short catches of the voice or breath.—*vi.*(giggling, giggled). To laugh with short catches of the breath; to titter.

gigot, jig'ot, *n*. A leg of mutton.

gild, gild, *vt*. (pret. and pp. gilded or gilt). To overlay with gold in leaf or powder; to illuminate; to give a fair and agreeable appearance to.

gill, gil, *n*. The organ of respiration in fishes the flap below the beak of a fowl, the flesh on the lower part of the cheeks.

gin, jin. *n*. A distilled spirit flavored with juniper berries; a machine for driving piles, raising great weights, etc.; a machine for separating the seeds from cotton; a trap, snare.—*vt*. (ginning, ginned). To clear of seeds by a cotton-gin; to catch in a trap.

ginger, jin'jėr, *n*. A tropical plant, the root of which has a hot, spicy quality.

giraffe, ji-raf', *n*. The camelopard, the tallest of animals.

gird, gėrd, *vt*. (pp. girded or girt). To bind; to make fast by binding, to invest; to encompass.—*vi*. To gibe; to sneer.—*n*. A stroke with a whip; a twitch; a sneer.

girder, gėrd'ėr, *n*. One who girds; a main beam supporting a superstructure.

girdle, gėr'dl, *n*. That which girds; a band or belt, something drawn round the waist and tied or buckled.—*vt*. (girdling, girdled). To bind with a girdle; belt, or sash; to gird.

girl, gėrl, *n*. A female child; young woman.

girth, gėrth, *n*. That which girds; band fastening a saddle on a horse's back, measure round a person's body or anything cylindrical.

gist, jist, *n*. The main point of a question; substance or pith of a matter.

give, giv, *vt*. (giving, pret, gave, pp. given). To bestow; to deliver; to impart, to yield to afford; to utter; to show; to send forth; to devote (oneself); to pledge; to allow; to ascribe.—*vi*. To make gifts; to yield to pressure; to recede.

gizzard, giz'ėrd, *n*. The muscular stomach of a bird.

glacier, glä'shi-ėr, *n*. An immense mass of ice formed in valleys above the snowline, and having a slow movement downwards.

glad, glad, *a*. Affected with pleasure; pleased; cheerful; imparting pleasure.— *vt*. (gladding, gladded). To make glad, to gladden.

glance, gläns, *n*. A sudden shoot of light or splendor; a glimpse or sudden look.— *vi*. (glancing, glanced). To shine; to gleam; to dart aside; to look with a sudden rapid cast of the eye; to move quickly, to hint.—*vt*. To shoot or dart suddenly or obliquely, to cast for a moment.

gland, gland, *n*. An acorn, any acorn-shaped fruit; a roundish organ in many parts of the body secreting some fluid; a secreting organ in plants.

glare, glär, *n*. A bright dazzling light, a fierce piercing look.—*vi*. (glaring, glared). To shine with excessive luster; to look with fierce piercing eyes.

glass, gläs, *n*. A hard transparent substance; a small drinking vessel of glass; a mirror; quantity of liquor that a glass vessel contains; a lens; a telescope; a barometer pl. spectacles.—*a*. Made of glass, vitreous.

glazier, glä'zhėr, *n*. One whose business is to set window-glass.

gleam, glēm, *n*. A small stream of light; brightness.—*vi*. To shoot or dart, as rays of light; to shine; to flash.

glider, glīd'ėr, *n*. A modification of the airplane, which can travel through the air for a certain time without engine power.

glimmer, glim'ėr, *vi*. To shine faintly, and with frequent intermissions; to flicker.— *n*. A faint light; a twinkle.

glimpse, glimps, *n*. A gleam or flash of light, short transitory view; faint resemblance, slight tinge.—*vi*. To appear by glimpses.

globe, glōb, *n*. A round solid body; a sphere; the earth; an artificial sphere on whose surface is drawn a map of the earth or heavens.—*vt*. To gather into a round mass.

globule, glob'ūl, *n*. A little globe a small spherical particle, one of the red particles of the blood

globulin, glob'ū-lin, *n*. The main ingredient of blood globules and resembling albumen.

gloom, glöm, *n.* Obscurity, thick shade; sadness; aspect of sorrow darkness of prospect or aspect.— *vi.* To shine obscurely, to be cloudy or dark; to be sullen or sad.

glorify, glō'ri-fī, *vt.* (glorifying, glorified). to make glorious, to ascribe glory or honor to; to extol.

glorious, glō'ri-us, *a.* Full of glory; renowned; celebrated; grand; brilliant.

glory, glō'ri, *n.* Praise, honor, admiration, or distinction, renown magnificence, celestial bliss; the divine presence; the divine perfections, that of which one may be proud.— *vi.* (glorying, gloried). To boast; to rejoice; to be proud with regard to something.

gloss, glos, *n.* Brightness from a smooth surface; sheen; specious appearance, an interpretation comment.— *vt.* To give superficial luster to; to give a specious appearance to; to render plausible to comment; to annotate.

glossary glos'a-ri, *n.* A vocabulary explaining antiquated or difficult words or phrases.

glow, glō, *vi.* To burn with intense heat, especially without flame; to feel great heat of body; to be flushed; to be ardent to rage.— *n.* White heat; brightness of color; animation.

glowworm, glō'wĕrm, *n.* A wingless female beetle which emits a greenish light.

glucose, glö'kō s, *n.* Grape-sugar, a sugar produced from grapes, starch, etc.

glue, glö, *n.* A tenacious, viscid matter which serves as a cement.— *vt.* (gluing, glued). To join with glue; to unite.

glum, glum, *a.* Sullen; moody; dejected.

glycerine, glis'ĕr-in, *n.* A transparent, colorless, sweet liquid obtained from fats.

glyphic, glif'ik, *a.* Of or pertaining to carving or sculpture.

glyptic, glip'tik, *a.* Pertaining to the art of engraving on precious stones.

gnarl, närl, *n.* A protuberance on the outside of a tree a knot.

gnash, nash, *vt.* To strike together, as the teeth.— *vi.* To strike or dash the teeth together, as in rage or pain.

gnat, nat, *n.* A small two-winged fly, the female of which bites.

gnaw, nä, *vt.* To bite by little and little; to bite in agony or rage; to fret; to corrode.— *vi.* To use the teeth in biting; to cause steady annoying pain.

gneiss, nîs, *n.* A species of rock composed of quartz, feldspar, and mica, and having a slaty structure.

gnome, nōm, *n.* A sprite supposed to inhabit the inner parts of the earth; a dwarf; a maxim, aphorism.

go, gō, *vi.* (going, pret, went, pp. gone). To move; to proceed, to depart; to be about to do; to circulate, to tend, to be guided, to be alienated or sold; to reach; to avail; to conduce; to die; to fare; to become.

goad, gōd, *n.* A pointed instrument to make a beast move faster; anything that stirs into action.— *vt.* To drive with a goad; to instigate.

goal, gōl, *n.* The point set to bound a race; a mark that players in some outdoor sport must attain; a success scored by reaching this; final purpose; end.

goat, gōt, *n.* A ruminant quadruped with long hair and horns.

gobble, gob'l, *vt.* (gobbling, gobbled). To swallow in large pieces or hastily.— *vi.* To make a noise in the throat, as a turkey.

goggle, gog'l, *vi.* (goggling, goggled). To roll or strain the eyes.— *a.* Prominent, rolling, or staring *(eyes).*—*n.* A strained or affected rolling of the eye; *pl.* a kind of spectacles to protect the eyes or cure squinting.

going, gō'ing, *n.* Act of one who goes; departure; way; state of roads.—**goings-on**, actions; behavior

goiter, goi'tĕr, *n.* A morbid enlargement of the thyroid gland, forming a mass on the front of the neck.

gold, gōld, *n.* A precious metal of a bright yellow color; money; something pleasing or valuable, a bright yellow color— *a.* Made or consisting of gold.

golden, gōld'n, *a.* Made of gold; like gold; splendid; most valuable; auspicious.

gong, gong, *n.* A kind of metallic drum; a similar article used instead of a bell.

good, güd, *a.* The opposite of bad; wholesome. useful, fit, virtuous valuable; benevolent, clever, adequate; valid; able to fulfill engagements, considerable, full or complete; immaculate.—*n.* What is good or desirable; advantage; welfare; virtue *pl.* commodities, chattels, movables.—**For good**, to close the whole business, finally.—*interj.* Well; right.

goose, gös, *n.*; pl. **geese**, gēs. A swimming bird larger than the duck; a tailor's smoothing-iron; a silly person.

gooseberry, gös'be-ri, *n.* The fruit of a prickly shrub, and the shrub itself.

gopher, gō'fė r, n. The name given in America to several burrowing animals.

gordian knot, gor'di-an not. An inextricable difficulty, *to cut the gordian knot,* to remove a difficulty by bold measures.

gore, gōr, n. Blood that is shed thick or clotted blood; a wedgeshaped piece of land or cloth; a gusset.—*vt.* (goring, gored). To cut in a triangular form; to pierce with a pointed instrument, or an animal s horns.

gorge, gorj, n. The throat; the gullet a narrow passage between hills or mountains; entrance into a bastion.—*vt.* and *i.* (gorging, gorged). To swallow with greediness; to glut; to satiate.

gory, gō'ri, a. Covered with gore; bloody; murderous.

gosling, goz'ling, n. A young goose.

Gospel, gos'pel, n. The history of Jesus Christ any of the four records of Christ's life by his apostles; scheme of salvation as taught by Christ, any general doctrine.— a. Relating to the gospel; accordant with the gospel.

gossamer, gos'a-mėr, n. A fine filmy substance, like cobwebs, floating in the air in calm, sunny weather, a thin fabric.

gossip, gos'ip, n. An idle tattler; idle talk. vi. To prate; to run about and tattle.

gourd, görd, n. The popular name of the family of plants represented by the melon, cucumber, etc.; a cup made from the rind of a gourd.

gourmet, gör-mā or gör'met, n. A connoisseur in wines and meats, a nice feeder.

gout, gout, n. A painful disease, affecting generally the small joints a drop; a clot or coagulation.

govern, gu'vėrn, vt. To direct and control; to regulate; to steer; to affect so as to determine the case etc., in grammar.— vi. To exercise authority; to administer the laws.

governess, gu'vėrn-es, n. A female who governs or instructs.

government, gu'vėrn-ment, n. Rule, control, administration of public affairs; system of polity in a state; territory ruled by a governor, executive power, the influence of a word in grammar in regard to construction.

governor, gu'vėrn-ėr, n. One who governs; one invested with supreme authority, a tutor, a contrivance in machinery for maintaining a uniform velocity.

gown, goun, n. A woman's outer garment; a long, loose garment worn by professional men, as divines.—*vt.* To put on a gown.

grab, grab, vt. (grabbing, grabbed). To seize; to snatch.—*n.* A sudden grasp; implement for clutching objects.

grace, grās, n. Favor, kindness love and favor of God; state of reconciliation to God, pardon, license or privilege; expression of thanks before or after meals; title of a duke or archbishop, elegance with appropriate dignity; an embellishment, one of three ancient goddesses in whose gift were grace and beauty; in music, a trill, shake, etc.—*vt.* (gracing, graced). To lend grace to; to adorn; to favor.

gracious, grā'shus, a. Full of grace, favorable, disposed to forgive offenses and impart blessings; benignant; condescending.

gradation, gra-dā'shon, n. Arrange-ment by grades; regular advance step by step; rank; series; regular process by degrees.

grade, grād, n. A step; degree; rank; gradient.—*vt.* (grading, graded). To arrange in order of rank, etc.; to reduce to a suitable slope.

gradient, grā'di-ent, a. Moving by steps; rising or descending by regular degrees.—*n.* The degree of ascent or descent in a road, etc.; part of a road which slopes.

graduate, grad'ū-āt, vt. (graduating, graduated). To divide into regular intervals or degrees, to mark with such; to arrange by grades; to confer a university degree on; to reduce to a certain consistency by evaporation.—*vi.* To receive a university degree; to change gradually.—*n.* One who has received a degree of a university, etc.

graft, graft, n. A small scion of a tree inserted in another tree which is to support and nourish the scion, corrupt gains or practices in politics.—*vt.* To insert a graft on; to propagate by a graft; to join on as if organically; a part.

Grail, Graal, grāl, n. The holy vessel containing the last drops of Christ's blood, brought to England by Joseph of Arimathea, and, being afterwards lost, eagerly sought for by King Arthur's knights.

grain, grān, n. A single seed of a plant; corn in general; a minute particle, a small weight, fibers of wood with regard to their arrangement substance of a thing with respect to the size, form, or direction of the constituent particles; texture;

dye.—*vt*. To paint in imitation of fibers; to granulate.

gram, gram, *n*. The French unit of weight, equal to 15.43 grains troy.

grammar, gram'ér, *n*. A system of principles and rules for speaking or writing a language; propriety of speech; an outline of any subject.

grammatical, grammatic, gram-mat'ik-al, gram-mat'ik, *a*. Belong-ing to grammar; according to the rules of grammar.

granary, gra'na-ri, *n*. A storehouse for grain after it is thrashed.

grand, grand, *a*. Great, figuratively majestic; magnificent; noble.

grandchild, grand'chîld, *n*. A son's or daughter's child.

granddaughter, grand'dä-tér, *n*. The daughter of a son or daughter.

grandeur, grand'yūr, *n*. Greatness sublimity; splendor; magnificence.

granulate, gran'ū-lāt, *vt*. and *i*. (granulating, granulated). To form into grains, to make or become rough on the surface.

granulation, gran-ū-lā'shon, *n*. Act of forming into grains; a process by which minute fleshy bodies are formed on wounds during healing, the fleshy grains themselves

grasp, gräsp, *vt*. To seize and hold by the fingers or arms, to take possession of, to comprehend.—*vi*. To make a clutch or catch.—*n*. Gripe of the hand, reach of the arms; power of seizing or comprehending.

grass, gräs *n*. Herbage; any plant of the family to which belong the grain-yielding and pasture plants.—*vt*. To cover with grass; to bleach on the grass.

grasshopper, gräs'hop-ér, *n*. An insect that hops among grass, allied to the locusts.

grate, grät, *n*. A frame composed of parallel or cross-bars; grating; iron frame for holding coals used as fuel.—*vt*. (grating, grated). To furnish or make fast with crossbars to wear away in small particles by rubbing; to offend. as by a discordant sound.—*vi*. To rub roughly on; to have an annoying effect; to sound harshly.

grateful, grät'fül, *a*. Pleasing, gratifying; feeling or expressing gratitude.

grave, gräv, *vt*. (graving, pret. graved, pp. graven, graved). To make incisions on, to engrave, to impress deeply, as on the mind; to clean, as a ship's bottom, and cover with pitch.—*n*. A pit for the dead, a tomb.—*a*. Weighty; serious; staid;

thoughtful; not gay; not tawdry, in music, low.

gravel, gra'vel, *n*. Small pebbles; a disease produced by small concretions in the kidneys and bladder.—*vt*. (gravelling, gravelled). To cover with gravel, to cause to stick in the sand or gravel; to puzzle.

gravely, gräv'li, *adv*. In a grave, solemn manner; soberly; seriously.

gravid, grav'id, *a*. Being with young; pregnant.

gravitation, grav-i-tā'shon, *n*. The force by which bodies are drawn towards the center of the earth tendency of all matter toward all other matter.

gravity, grav'i-ti, *n*. The tendency of matter toward some attracting body, particularly toward the center of the earth, state or character of being grave; weight; enormity.

gravy, grä'vi, *n*. The juice that comes from flesh in cooking.

gray, grä, *a*. Of the color of hair whitened by age, white with a mixture of black; having gray hairs.—*n*. A gray color; a gray animal, as a horse, early morning twilight

graze, grä z, *vt*. (grazing, grazed). To rub or touch lightly in passing; to feed with growing grass, as cattle to feed on.—*vi*. to pass so as to rub lightly; to eat grass; to supply grass.—*n*. A slight rub or brush.

grease, grēs, *n*. Animal fat in a soft state; oily matter.—*vt*. (greasing, greased). To smear with grease.

great, grä t, *a*. Large in bulk or number; long-continued; of vast power and excellence, eminent majestic; pregnant; distant by one more generation, as great-grandfather, etc.

greet, grē t, *vt*. To salute; to meet and address with kindness.—*vi*. To meet and salute.

grenade, gre-nä d', *n*. A small bomb, thrown by hand or fired from a rifle.

greyhound, grä'hound, *n*. A tall, slender, fleet dog kept for the chase.

griddle, grid'l, *n*. A circular plate of iron, or a shallow pan, for baking cakes.

grief, grēf, *n*. Pain of mind produced by loss, misfortune, etc.; sorrow; cause of sorrow; trouble.

grievance, grēv'ans, *n*. A wrong suffered; cause of complaint; trouble.

grieve, grēv, *vt*. (grieving, grieved). To cause grief to; to deplore.—*vi*. To feel grief; to sorrow; to lament.

grim, grim, *a.* of a forbidding or fear-inspiring aspect; stern; sullen; surly; ugly.

grimace, gri-mās', *n.* A distortion of the countenance; air of affectation.—*vi.* To make grimaces.

grime, grīm, *n.* Foul matter.—*vt.* (griming, grimed). To sully or soil deeply.

grin, grin, *vi.* (grinning, grinned). To show the teeth, as in laughter, scorn, or anguish—*n.* Act of showing the teeth; a forced smile or restrained laugh.

grind, grīnd, *vt.* (grinding, ground). To reduce to fine particles; to sharpen or polish by friction, to rub together; to oppress; to crush in pieces.—*vi.* To turn a mill, to be moved or rubbed together, to be pulverized by friction; to study hard.—*n.* Act of one who grinds; a laborious spell of work.

grindstone, grīnd'stōn, *n.* A circular stone, made to revolve, to sharpen tools.

groan, grōn, *vi.* To utter a mournful voice, as in pain or sorrow, to moan.—*n.* A deep, mournful sound, uttered in pain, sorrow, or disapprobation; any low rumbling sound.

groin, groin, *n.* The part of the human body between the belly and thigh in front; the angular projecting curve made by the intersection of simple vaults at any angle.

gross, grōs, *a.* Thick; coarse; obscene; palpable; dense; shameful; dull, whole.— *n.* Main body, bulk the number of twelve dozen.

grotesque, grō-tesk', *a.* Wildly formed; extravagant, fantastic.—*n.* Whimsical figures or scenery.

grotto, grot'tō, *n.* A natural cave an artificial ornamented cave.

ground, ground, *n.* Surface of the earth, soil, land, basis, reason, foil or background; predominating color; *pl.* dregs, sediment; ornamental land about a mansion—*vt.* To set on the ground; to found; to fix firmly; to instruct in first principles.—*vi.* To strike the bottom and remain fixed, as a ship.

grove, grōv, *n.* A shady cluster of trees; a small wood.

grovel, gro'vel, *vi.* (grovelling, grovelled). To lie prone, or creep on the earth; to be low or mean.

grow, grō, *vi.* (pret. grew, pp. grown). To be augmented by natural process; to increase; to make progress, to become; to accrue, to swell.—*vt.* To raise from the soil, to produce.

growl, groul, *vi.* To murmur or snarl, as a dog; to utter an angry, grumbling sound.—*vt.* to express by growling.—*n.* Angry sound of a dog; grumbling murmur.

grown, grōn, *p.a.* Increased in growth; having arrived at full size or stature.

growth, grōth, *n.* Act or process of growing; product; increase; advancement.

grub, grub, *vi.* (grubbing, grubbed). To dig; to be employed meanly.— *vt.* To dig, to root out by digging.— *n.* The larva of an insect; caterpillar; maggot.

gruel, grū'el, *n.* A light food made by boiling meal in water.

gruesome, grö'sum, *a.* Causing one to shudder; frightful, horrible; repulsive.

guarantee, ga-ran-tē', *n.* An undertaking by a third person that a covenant shall be observed by the contracting parties or by one of them; one who binds himself to see the stipulations of another performed.—*vt.* (guaranteeing, guaranteed). To warrant; to pledge oneself for.

guard, gärd, *vt.* To keep watch over; to secure against injury, loss, or attack.— *vi.* To watch, by way of caution or defense; to be in a state of caution or defense.—*n.* Defense; protector; sentinel; escort; attention; caution; posture of defense. Conjecture; surmise.

guest, gest, *n.* A visitor or friend entertained in the house or at the table of another.

guffaw, guf-fä', *n.* A loud burst of laughter.—*vi.* To burst into a loud laugh.

guidance, gīd'ans, *n.* The act of guiding; direction; government; a leading.

guide, gīd, *vt.* (guiding, guided). To lead; to direct; to influence; to regulate.—*n.* A person who guides a director; a regulator; a guidebook.

guise, gīz, *n.* External appearance dress; mien; cast of behavior.

guitar, gi-tär', *n.* A musical instrument having six strings.

gulch, gulch, *n.* A gully; dry bed of a torrent.

gull, gul, *vt.* To cheat.—*n.* One easily cheated; a simpleton, a marine swimming bird.

gullet, gul'et, *n.* The passage in the neck of an animal by which food and liquor are taken into the stomach.

gully, gul'i, *n.* A channel worn by water; a ravine.—*vt.* To wear into a gully.

gulp, gulp, *vt.* To swallow eagerly. —*n.* Act of taking a large swallow.

gum, gum, *n.* The fleshy substance of the

jaws round the teeth: a juice which exudes from trees, etc., and thickens; a viscous substance.— *vt.* (gumming, gummed). To smear with or unite by a viscous substance.

gunshot, gun'shot, *n.* Range of a cannon-shot, firing of a gun.—*a.* Made by the shot of a gun.

gunwale, gunnel, gun'wăl, gun'el, *n.* The upper edge of a ship's side.

gurgle, gêr'gl, *vi.* (gurgling, gurgled). To run or flow in a broken noisy current.— *n.* Sound produced by a liquid flowing from or through a narrow opening.

gush, gush, *vi.* To issue with violence and rapidity, as a fluid; to be effusively sentimental.—*n.* A sudden and violent issue of a fluid, the fluid thus emitted; effusive display of sentiment.

gutter, gut'êr, *n.* A channel at the side of a road, etc., for water.—*vt.* To cut or form gutters in.—*vi.* To become channeled.

guttural, gut'tėr-al, *a.* Pertaining to the throat; formed in the throat.—*n.* A letter pronounced in the throat; any guttural sound.

guzzle, guz'l, *v.* and *t.* (guzzling, guzzled). To swallow greedily or frequently.—*n.* A debauch.

gymnasium jim-nā'zi-um, *n.*, *pl.* **-ia** or **-iums**. A place for athletic exercises; a school for the higher branches of education.

gymnast, jim'nast, *n.* One who teaches or practices gymnastic exercises.

H

haberdasher, ha'bèr-dash-èr, *n*. A dealer in drapery goods, as woollens, silks, ribbons, etc.

habilitate, ha-bil'i-tat, *vi*. To qualify.

habitat, ha'bit-āt, *n*. The natural abode or locality of a plant or animal.

habitation, ha-bit-ā'shon, *n*. Occupancy; abode; residence.

Hades, ha'dez, *n*. The abode of the dead, state of departed souls.

haft, haft, *n*. A handle; that part of an instrument which is taken into the hand.—*vt*. To set in a haft.

hag, hag, *n*. An ugly old woman; a witch; an eel-shaped fish that eats into other fishes.

haggard, hag'ärd, *a*. Wild; intractable, having the face worn and pale; gaunt.—*n*. An untrained or refractory hawk.

haggle, hag'l, *vt*. (haggling, haggled). To cut into small pieces; to mangle.—*vi*. To be difficult in bargaining; to stick at small matters; to chaffer.

hail, hāl *n*. Frozen drops of rain; a wish of health, a call.—*vi*. To pour down hail; to have as one's residence, or belong to (with *from*).—*vt*. To pour down in the manner of hail; to salute; to call to; to designate as.—*interj*. A salutation expressive of well-wishing.

hailstone, hāl'stōn, *n*. A single pellet of hail falling from a cloud.

hair, hār, *n*. A small filament issuing from the skin of an animal, the mass of filaments growing from the skin of an animal; anything similar a very small distance.

hale, hā, *a*. Sound; healthy; robust.—*n*. A violent pull.—*vt*. (haling, haled). To take, pull, or drag by force.

hall, häl, *n*. A large room, especially a large public room; a large room at the entrance of a house, a manor-house; The name of certain colleges at Oxford and Cambridge.

Halleluiah, Hallelujah, hal-lē-lü'ya, *n*. and *interj*. A word used in sacred songs of praise, signifying *praise ye, Jehovah*.

Halloween, Hallow-even, hal'ō-ēn, hal'o-ē-vn, *n*. The eve or vigil of All-Hallows' or All-Saints' Day.

hallucination, hal-lū'si-nā''shon *n*. A mistaken notion; mere dream or fancy; morbid condition in which objects are believed to be seen and sensations experienced object or sensation thus erroneously perceived.

halo, hā'lō, *n*. A luminous ring round the sun or moon; any circle of light, as the glory round the head of saints; an ideal glory investing an object.—*vi*. To form itself into a halo.—*vt*. To surround with a halo.

halt, hält, *vi*. To limp; to be lame; to hesitate; to cease marching.—*vt*. To stop; to cause to cease marching.—*a*. Lame: limping.—*n*. A limp; a stopping; stoppage on march.

hammer, ham'ér, *n*. An instrument for driving nails, beating metals, and the like.—*vt*. To beat or forge with a hammer, to contrive by intellectual labor.—*vi*. To work with a hammer; to labor in contrivance.

hammock, ham'ok, *n*. A kind of hanging bed.

hamstring, ham'string, *n*. One of the tendons of the ham.—*vt*. (pp. hamstrung or hamstringed). To cut the tendons of the ham, and thus to lame or disable.

handcuff, hand'kuf, *n*. A fetter for the hands or wrists.—*vt*. To manacle with handcuffs.

handful, hand'fül, *n* As much as the hand will grasp or hold, a small quantity or number.

handicap, hand'i-kap, *n*. In racing, games, etc., an allowance to bring superior competitors to an equality with the others, a race or contest so arranged.—*vt*. To put a handicap on; to equalize by a handicap.

handle, hand'dl, *vt*. (handling, handled). To feel, use, or hold with the hand; to discuss; to deal with to treat or use well or ill.—*n*. That part of an instrument, etc., held in the hand; instrument for effecting a purpose.

hangar, hang'ar, *n*. A shed for housing airplanes.

hanging, hang'ing, *n*. Act of suspending; death by the halter; *pl*. linings for rooms, of tapestry, paper, etc.

happy, hap'i, *a*. Being in the enjoyment of agreeable sensations from the possession of good, fortunate, propitious; well suited, apt.

harangue, ha-rang', *n*. A noisy or pompous address, a declamatory public address; a tirade—*vi*. (haranguing, harangued). To make a harangue.—*vt*. To address by a harangue.

harass, ha'ras, *vt*. To vex, to tire with

labor; to fatigue with importunity.

harbinger, här'bin-jėr, *n.* A forerunner, that which precedes and gives notice of something else.—*vt.* To precede as harbinger

harbor, här'bėr, *n.* A shelter, a haven for ships; an asylum.—*vt.* To shelter, to entertain in the mind.— vi. To take shelter; to lodge or abide for a time.

hard, härd. *a.* Not easily penetrated or separated; firm; difficult to understand; arduous; unfeeling; severe; unjust; harsh; stiff; grasping applied to certain sounds, as sibilants contrasted with gutturals applied to water not suitable for washing, from holding minerals.—*adv.* Close, diligently; with difficulty; fast; copiously; with force.

hardy, härd'i, *a.* Bold; intrepid; full of assurance; inured to fatigue, capable of bearing exposure.

harm, härm, *n* Injury; hurt; evil.— *vt.* To hurt; to damage; to impair.

harmless, härm'les, *a.* Free from harm; not causing harm; inoffensive; uninjured.

harmonic, harmonical, här-mon' ik, här-mon'ik-al, a Pertaining to harmony; concordant; musical.— **harmonic,** här-mon'ik, *n.* A less distinct tone accompanying a principal tone.

harmony, här'mo-ni, *n.* The just adaptation of parts to each other musical concord; agreement, peace and friendship.

harness, här'nes, *n.* Armor; furniture of a carriage or draft horse.— *vt.* To dress in armor; to put harness on.

harp, harp, *n.* A stringed musical instrument of triangular form played with the fingers.—*vi.* To play on the harp; to dwell on tediously.

harpoon, här-pön', *n.* A spear or javelin, used to strike whales etc.—*vt.* To strike, catch, or kill with a harpoon.

harpy, här'pi, *n.* A fabulous winged monster with the face of a woman, any rapacious animal, an extortioner

harridan, ha'ri-dan, *n.* A hag; an odious old woman, a vixenish woman; a trollop.

harrow, ha'rō, *n.* A frame set with spikes, to prepare plowed land for seed or to cover the seed.—*vt.* To draw a harrow over; to lacerate; to torment.

harrowing, ha'rō-ing, *p.a.* Causing acute distress to the mind.

hasp, hasp, *n.* A clasp that passes over a staple to be fastened by a padlock.—*vt.* To fasten with a hasp.

hassock, has'ok, *n.* A thick mat or cushion used for kneeling on, etc.

haste, hā st, *n.* Speed, hurry, sudden excitement of passion; precipitance.—*vt.* (hasting, hasted). To drive or urge forward, to hurry.— *vi.* To move with celerity; to be speedy.

hate, hāt, *vt.* (hating, hated). To detest, to loathe to abhor.—*n.* Great dislike hatred.

haughty, hät'i, *a.* Proud and disdainful; lofty and arrogant.

haul, häl, *vt.* To pull or draw with force; to drag; to compel to go.—*n.* A violent pull; draught of fish in a net; that which is taken or gained at once.

have, hav, *vt.* (having, had). To possess; to accept; to enjoy; to hold in opinion; to be under necessity, or impelled by duty; to procure; to bring forth.

haven, hā'vn, *n.* A harbor; port; shelter.

haversack, hav'ėr-sak, *n.* A soldier's bag for provisions on the march.

having, hav'ing, *n.* What one has; possession, goods.

havoc, hav'ok, *n.* Devastation; wide and general destruction, slaughter.

hawk, häk, *n.* A rapacious bird of the falcon family.—*vi.* To catch birds by means of hawks, to practice falconry, to take prey on the wing; to force up phlegm with noise.—*vt.* To carry about for sale from place to place.

hazel, hā'zl, *n.* A small tree of the oak family that bears edible nuts.—*a.* Pertaining to the hazel of a light-brown color.

hazy, hāz'i, *a.* Thick with haze mentally obscure or confused.

he, hē, *pron.* of the third person, nominative. A substitute for the third person masculine, representing the man or male named before, prefixed to names of animals to specify the male.

head, hed, *n.* The anterior part of animals; uppermost part of the human body; seat of the brain; etc., intellect; an individual; a chief; first place; top; chief part; principal source; crisis; height; promontory, division of discourse headway.—*vt.* To form a head to; to behead; to lead; to go in front of in order to stop; to oppose.— *vi.* To form a head; to be directed, as a ship.

heading, hed'ing, *n.* That which stands at the head, title of a section; passage excavated in the line of an intended tunnel.

heal, hēl, *vi.* To make hale or sound; to cure; to reconcile.—*vt.* To grow whole or sound, to recover.

health, helth, *n.* A sound state of body or mind, freedom from disease; bodily conditions; wish of health and happiness (used in drinking).

healthy, helth'i, *a.* Being in health; sound; hale; salubrious; wholesome.

heap, hē p, *n.* A mass, large quantity; pile.—*vt.* To raise in a heap; to amass, to pile.

hearing, hėr'ing, *n.* The faculty or sense by which sound is perceived; audience opportunity to be heard; judicial trial; reach of the ear

hearsay, hėr'sā, *n.* Report; rumor—*a.* Given at second hand.

hearse, hėrs *n.* A carriage for conveying the dead to the grave; bier.

heart, härt, *n.* The primary organ of the blood's motion, the inner, vital, or most essential part; seat of the affections, will, etc., disposition of mind, conscience, courage spirit; what represents a heart, one of a suit of playing cards marked with such a figure.

hearty, härt'i, *a.* Warm; cordial; healthy; having a keen appetite; large to satisfaction.

heat, hēt, *n.* The sensation produced by bodies that are hot, hot air; hot weather; high temperature; degree of temperature; a single effort; a course at a race, animal excitement; rage; ardor, animation in thought or discourse fermentation.—*vt.* To make hot, to warm with passion or desire, to rouse into action.—*vi.* To grow warm or hot.

heath, hēth, *n.* A small flowering shrub growing on waste or wild places; a place overgrown with heath; waste tract.

heather, heTH'ėr, *n.* Common heath, a low shrub with clusters of rose-colored flowers.

heave, hēv, *vt.* (heaving, pret. and pp. heaved, hove). To lift to move upward; to cause to swell; to raise or force from the breast, as a groan; to throw; to turn in some direction.—*vi.* To rise; to swell, as the sea, to pant to retch, *to heave in sight,* to appear, as a ship.—*n.* A rising or swell, an effort upward, a throw; a swelling, as of the breast.

Heaven, hev'n, *n.* The blue expanse surrounding the earth, the sky; the abode of God and of his angels, God or Providence, supreme felicity; bliss.

heavenly, hev'n-li, *a.* Pertaining to heaven, divine, inhabiting heaven enchanting.—*adv.* In a heavenly manner.

heavy, he'vi, *a.* That is heaved or lifted with difficulty; weighty; sad; grievous; burdensome; drowsy; wearisome, not easily digested; soft and miry; difficult; large in amount; dense; abundant; forcible.

hedge, hej, *n.* A fence consisting of thorns or shrubs.—*vt.* (hedging hedged). To enclose with a hedge to surround or restrain.—*vi.* To hide oneself, to bet on both sides to skulk, to dodge or trim.—*a.* Pertaining to a hedge; mean; rustic.

Hedonism, hē'don-izm. *n.* The doctrine that the chief good of man lies in pursuit of pleasure.

Hedonist, hē'don-ist, *n.* One who professes hedonism.

heed, hēd, *vt.* To look to or after, to regard with care, to notice.—*vi.* To mind; to consider—*n.* Care; attention, regard.

heel, hēl, *n.* The hind part of the foot; a cant.—*vt.* To add a heel to; to furnish with heels, as shoes.— *vi.* To cant over from a vertical position.

height, hīt, *n.* The condition of being high; distance of anything above its base or above the earth eminence; any elevated ground, extent, degree, utmost degree.

heighten, hī t'n, *vt.* To raise higher; to improve; to increase.

heir, ār, *n.* One who succeeds or is to succeed another in the possession of property.

helium, hē'li-um, *n.* An inert gas present in the air in small quantities, the lightest element next to hydrogen.

helix, hē'liks, *n;* pl. helices, hel'isez. A spiral line, as of wire in a coil; something that is spiral.

Hell, hel, *n.* The place or state of punishment for the wicked after death; the abode of the devil and his angels; the infernal powers; a gambling-house.

help, help, *vt.* To lend strength or means towards effecting a purpose, to aid, to relieve, to remedy; to prevent; to avoid.—*vi.* To lend aid.—*n.* Aid, remedy, an assistant.

hem, hem, *n.* The border of a garment, doubled and sewed to strengthen it, edge, border.—*interj.* and *n.* A sort of half cough, suggested by some feeling.—*vt.* (hemming, hemmed). To form a hem or border on; to enclose and confine; to make the sound expressed by the word hem.

hematite, he'ma-tit, *n.* A name of two ores of iron, red hematite and brown hematite.

hemisphere, he'mi-sfēr, *n*. One half of a sphere, half the celestial or terrestrial sphere.

hemlock, hem'lok, *n*. An umbelliferous plant whose leaves and root are poisonous.

hemorrhage, he'mor-āj, *n*. A bursting forth of blood, any discharge of blood from the blood-vessels.

hemorrhoids, he'mor-oidz, *n.pl*. Piles.

hemp, hemp, *n*. An annual herbaceous plant of the nettle family the fiber of which, also called hemp, is made into sail-cloth, ropes, etc.

hen, hen, *n*. The female of the domestic fowl; any female bird.

herald, he'rald, *n*. An officer whose business was to proclaim war or peace, bear messages, etc.; a forerunner, an officer who regulates matters relating to public ceremonies; one who records and blazons arms, etc.—*vt*. To introduce, as by a herald, to proclaim.

herbarium, hér-bā'ri-um, *n.; pl. -iums* and *-ia*. A collection of herbs or plants dried and preserved.

herbivorous, hérb-iv'or-us, *a*. Eating herbs; subsisting on herbaceous plants.

Herculean, hèr-kū'lē-an, *a*. Belong-ing to or resembling Hercules, of extraordinary strength; very great or difficult.

herd, hèrd, *n*. A number of animals feeding or driven together; flock; crowd, rabble, a keeper of cattle or sheep.—*vi*. and *t*. To unite into a herd, as beasts; to congregate.

hereafter, hèr-af'tèr, *adv*. After this time, in a future state.—*n*. The time after this; a future state.

heresy, he're-si, *n*. A fundamental error in religion; error in doctrine; heterodoxy.

heretic, he're-tik, *n*. One guilty of heresy.

heritage, he'rit-āj, *n*. Inheritance lot or portion by birth.

hermit, her 'mit, *n*. One who lives in solitude, a recluse.

hernia, hèr'ni-a, *n*. A protrusion of some organ of the abdomen through an interstice; a rupture.

heroin, her'o-in, *n*. A narcotic drug derived from morphia.

heroine, he'rō-in, *n*. A female hero.

heroism, he'rō-izm, *n*. The qualities of a hero; intrepidity; magnanimity.

heron, her'un, *n*. A wading bird with a long bill, long slender legs and neck.

herpes, hèr'pez, *n*. A skin disease characterized by eruption or inflamed vesicles.

herpetology, hèr-pe-tol'o-ji, *n*. The natural history of reptiles.

herring, he'ring, *n*. One of those small food fishes which go in shoals in northern seas.

herring-bone, he'ring-bōn, *a*. Applied to masonry, sewing, etc., which bears resemblance to the backbone of a herring.

hesitate, he'zi-tāt, *vi*. (hesitating, hesitated). To pause respecting decision or action; to stop in speaking; to stammer.

hesitation, he-zi-tā'shon, *n*. Act of hesitating; doubt; a stopping in speech.

hew, hū, *vt*. (*pret*. hewed, *pp*. hewed or hewn). To cut with an axe, etc.; to cut; to hack; to make smooth, as stone; to shape.

high-pressure, hī'pre-shŭr, *a*. Having or involving a pressure exceeding that of the atmosphere, or having a pressure greater than 50 lbs. to the square inch.

highway, hī'wā, *n*. A public road; direct course, train of action.

hike, hīk, *vi*. To tramp; to go on a long or fairly long walking expedition.

hilarity, hi-la'ri-ti, *n*. Cheerfulness; merriment, good humor, jollity.

hill, hil, *n*. A natural elevation of less size than a mountain; an eminence.

hilt, hilt, *n*. A handle, particularly of a sword.

himself, him-self', *pron*. The emphatic and reflexive form of he and him.

hind, hīnd, *n*. The female of the reddeer or stag; a farm servant; a rustic.—*a*. Backward, back, pertaining to the backward part.

hinder, hīnd'èr, *a*. Posterior; in the rear, latter, after.

hinder, hin'dèr, *vt*. To prevent from moving or acting; to obstruct; to thwart to check.—*vi*. To interpose obstacles or impediments.

hint, hint, *vt*. To suggest indirectly; to insinuate.—*vi*. To make an indirect allusion.—*n*. A distant allusion; a suggestion.

hip, hip, *n*. The fleshy projecting part of the thigh; the haunch; the joint of the thigh; the fruit of the dog-rose or wild brier.—*interj*. Exclamation expressive of a call to anyone. *Hip, hip, hurrah!* the signal to cheer.

hire, hīr, *vt*. (hiring, hired). To procure for temporary use, at a certain price; to engage in service for a stipulated reward; to let; to lease (with out).—*n*. Price paid for temporary use of anything; recompense for personal service;

wages; pay.

hirsute, hėr-sūt', *a.* Hairy; shaggy.

history, his'to-ri, *n.* An account of facts, particularly respecting nations or states; that branch of knowledge which deals with past events, narration; a story; an account of existing things, as animals or plants.

histrionics, his-tri-on'iks, *n.* The art of theatrical representation.

hit, hit, *vt.* (hitting, hit). To strike or touch with some force to give a blow to; not to miss; to reach; to light upon; to suit.—*vi.* To strike; to come in contact, to reach the intended point; to succeed.—*n.* A stroke; a blow; a lucky chance; happy thought or expression.

hitch, hich, *vi.* To move by jerks; to be entangled, hooked, or yoked.—*vt.* To fasten; to hook, to raise by jerks.—*n.* A catch; act of catching, as on a hook, etc., knot or noose in a rope; a jerk; a temporary obstruction.

hither, hiTH'ėr, *adv.* To this place.— *a.* Nearer; toward the person speaking.

hive, hīv, *n.* A box or receptacle for honey-bees; the bees inhabiting a hive; a place swarming with busy occupants.—*vt.* (hiving, hived). To collect into a hive; to lay up in store.—*vi.* To take shelter together; to reside in a collective body.

hoar, hōr, *a.* White or whitish; hoary.—*vi.* To become moldy or musty.

hoard, hōrd, *n.* A store, stock, or large quantity of anything, a hidden stock.—*vt.* To collect; to store secretly.—*vi.* To form a hoard; to lay up in store.

hoar frost, hōr'frost, *n.* The white particles of frozen dew, rime.

hoarse, hŏrs, *a.* Having a grating voice, as when affected with a cold, discordant, rough, grating.

hobby, hob'i, *n.* A small but strong British falcon; an active, ambling nag; a hobbyhorse; any favorite object or pursuit.

hod, hod, *n.* A kind of trough for carrying mortar and brick on the shoulder.

hodge-podge, hoj'poj, *n.* A mixed mass; a medley of ingredients; a hotch-potch.

hoe, hō, *n.* An instrument to cut up weeds and loosen the earth.—*vt.* (hoeing, hoed). To dig or clean with a hoe.—*vi.* To use a hoe.

hog, hog, *n.* A swine; a castrated boar; a sheep of a year old; a brutal or mean fellow.—*vi.* To bend, as a ship's bottom.

hogshead, hogz'hed, *n.* A large cask; an old measure of capacity, containing about 52-1/2 imperial gallons.

hoist, hoist, *vt.* To heave up, to lift upward by means of tackle.—*n.* Act of raising; apparatus for raising goods, etc., an elevator

hold, hōld, *vt.* (pret. held, pp. held,). To have in the grasp; to keep fast; to confine; to maintain; to consider; to contain; to possess; to withhold, to continue, to celebrate.—*vi.* To take or keep a thing in one's grasp; to stand as a fact or truth, not to give way or part, to refrain, to adhere; to derive title (with *of*).—*n.* A grasp; something which may be seized for support power of keeping, seizing, or directing; influence; place of confinement, stronghold, interior cavity of a ship.

hole, hōl, *n.* A hollow place in any solid body, a perforation, crevice, etc.; a den, a subterfuge.—*vt.* (holing, holed). To make a hole or holes in to drive into a hole.

holiday, ho'li-dā, *n.* A holy or sacred day; a festival; day of exemption from labor.—*a.* Pertaining to a festival.

holiness, hō'li-nes, *n.* State or quality of being holy; moral goodness, sanctity.— **His Holiness,** a title of the pope.

holometabolic, hol'o-met-a-bol"ik, *a.* Applied to insects which undergo a complete metamorphosis.

holster, hōl'ster, *n.* A leathern case for a pistol.

holy, hō'li, *a.* Free from sin; immaculate, consecrated, sacred.

homage, hom'āj, *n.* An act of fealty on the part of a vassal to his lord; obeisance, reverential worship.

home, hōm, *n.* One's own abode; the abode of one's family; residence; one' own country; an establishment affording the comforts of a home.—*a.* Domestic; close; severe, poignant.—*adv.* To one's own habitation or country; to the point; effectively.

homestead, hōm'sted, *n.* A house with the grounds and buildings contiguous; a home; native seat.

homeward, hōm'wėrd, *adv.* Toward one's habitation or country.—*a.* Being in the direction of home.

homiletics, ho-mi-let'iks, *n.* The art of preaching.

homily, ho'mi-li, *n.* A sermon, a familiar religious discourse; a serious discourse or admonition.

homologous, hō-mol'o-gus, *a.* Having the same relative position, proportion, or

H

structure; corresponding.

homonym, ho'mō-nim, *n.* A word which agrees with another in sound, and perhaps in spelling but differs in signification.

hone, hōn, *n.* A stone of a fine grit used for sharpening instruments—*vt.* (honing, honed). To sharpen on a hone.

honest, on'est, *a.* Free from fraud; upright; just; sincere; candid; virtuous.

honey, hun'i, *n.* A sweet viscous juice collected by bees from flowers, sweetness, a word of tenderness.—*vt.* To sweeten.

honorary, on'èr-a-ri, *a.* Relating to honor, conferring honor, possessing a title or place without performing services or without receiving a reward.

honor, on'èr, *n.* Respect; esteem; testimony of esteem; dignity; good name; a nice sense of what is right, scorn of meanness, a title of respect or distinction, one of the highest trump cards; *pl.* civilities paid, public marks of respect, academic and university distinction.—*vt.* To regard or treat with honor, to bestow honor upon, to exalt; to accept and pay when due, as a bill.

honorable, on'èr-a-bl, *a.* Worthy of honor; actuated by principles of honor; conferring honor, consistent with honor; performed with marks of honor, not base, honest fair; a title of distinction.

hood, hüd, *n.* A soft covering for the head; a cowl; a garment worn as part of academic dress, which indicates by its colors, material and shape the degree and University of its wearer; anything resembling a hood.—*vt.* To dress in a hood; to cover; to blind.

hoodwink, hüd'wingk, *vt.* To blind by covering the eyes of; to impose on.

hoof, hōf, *n.*, *pl.* **hoofs,** rarely hooves. The horny substance that covers the feet of certain animals, as the horse.

hook, hök, *n.* A bent piece of iron or other metal for catching; that which catches, a sickle.—*vt.* To catch with a hook, to ensnare.—*vi.* To bend; to be curving.

hoot, höt, *vi.* To shout in contempt; to cry as an owl.—*vt.* To utter contemptuous cries at.—*n.* A cry or shout in contempt.

hop, hop, *n.* A leap on one leg; a spring, a bitter plant of the hemp family used to flavor malt liquors.—*vi.* To leap or spring on one leg, to skip, to limp, to pick hops.—*vt.* To impregnate with hops.

hope, hōp, *n.* A desire of some good, accompanied with a belief that it is attainable; trust, one in whom trust or confidence is placed, the object of hope.—*vi.* (hoping, hoped). To entertain hope; to trust.—*vt.* To desire with some expectation of attainment.

horde, hōrd, *n.* A tribe or race of nomads; a gang; migratory crew; rabble.—*vi.* (hording, horded). To live together like migratory tribes.

horizon, ho-rī'zon, *n.* The circle which bounds the part of the earth's surface visible from given point; the apparent junction of the earth and sky.

hormones, hor'mōnz, *n.pl.* Products of the ductless glands, affecting other organs by way of the blood stream.

horn, horn, *n.* A hard projection on the heads of certain animals, the material of such horns; wind-instrument of music; extremity of the moon; drinking-cup; powder-horn, something resembling a horn; the feeler of a snail, etc.

horror, hor'rèr, *n.* A powerful feeling of fear and abhorrence, that which may excite terror, something frightful or shocking.

horse, hors, *n.* A well-known quadruped, used for draft and carriage in war; the male animal; cavalry; a name of various things resembling or analogous to a horse.—*vt.* (horsing, horsed). To supply with a horse; to carry on the back; to bestride.

horseradish, hors'rad-ish, *n.* A perennial plant, having a root of a pungent taste.

horseshoe, hors'shö, *n.* A shoe for horses, commonly of iron shaped like the letter U; anything shaped like a horse-shoe.—*a.* Having the form of a horse-shoe.

hortatory, hort'a-to-ri, *a.* Giving exhortation or advice, encouraging.

horticulture, hor'ti-kul-tūr, *n.* The art of cultivating gardens.

Hosanna, hō-zan'na, *n.* An exclamation of praise to God, or an invocation of blessings.

hose, hōz, *n. sing.* or *pl.* A covering for the thighs, legs, or feet; closefitting breeches, stockings, in these senses plural; a flexible pipe used for conveying water.

host, hōst, *n.* One who entertains a stranger or guest; an innkeeper; an army; any great number or multitude, the consecrated bread in the R. Catholic sacrament of the mass.

hostage, host'āj, *n.* A person delivered to an enemy, as a pledge to secure the performance of conditions.

hostel, hostelry, hos'tel, hos'tel-ri. *n.* An inn, a lodging-house.

hostile, hos'fil *a.* Belonging to an enemy; unfriendly; antagonistic; adverse.

hostility, hos-til'i-ti, *n.* State or quality of being hostile; state of war between nations or states, the actions of an open enemy (in *pl.*); animosity, enmity, opposition.

hot, hot, *a.* Having sensible heat burning; glowing; easily exasperated; vehement; eager; lustful; biting; pungent in taste.

hour, our, *n.* The twenty-fourth part of a day, consisting of sixty minutes, the particular time of the day; an appointed time; *pl.* certain prayers in the R. Catholic Church.

house, hous *n.,* pl. **houses,** hou'zez. A building or erection for the habitation or use of man; any building or edifice, a dwelling a household; a family; a legislative body of men; audience or attendance, a commercial establishment.—*vt.* (housing, housed). To put or receive into a house, to shelter.—*vi.* To take shelter; to take up abode.

housing, houz'ing, *n.* A horsecloth, *pl.* the trappings of a horse.—*p.n.* Placing in houses; sheltering.

hovel, ho'vel, *n.* A mean house; an open shed for cattle, etc.—*vt.* To put in a hovel.

hover, ho'vèr, *vi.* To hang fluttering in the air; to be in doubt; to linger near.

how, hou, *adv.* In what manner; to what extent; for what reason; by what means, in what state.

however, hou-ev'èr, *adv.* In whatever manner or degree, in whatever state.—*conj.* Nevertheless yet; still; though.

howl, houl, *vi.* To cry as a dog or wolf; to utter a loud mournful sound; to roar, as the wind.—*vt.* To utter or speak with outcry.—*n.* A loud protracted wail; cry of a wolf, etc.

hub, hub, *n.* The central cylindrical part of a wheel in which the spokes are set.

hubbub, hub'bub, *n.* A great noise of many confused voices; tumult; uproar.

huckster, huk'ster, *n.* A retailer of small articles; a hawker.—*vi.* To deal in small articles; to higgle.— *vt.* To hawk.

huddle, hud'l, *vi.* (huddling, huddled). To crowd or press together promiscuously.—*vt.* To throw or crowd together in confusion, to put on in haste and disorder.—*n.* A confused mass; confusion.

huff, huf, *n.* A fit of peevishness or petulance; anger.—*vt.* To treat with inso-

lence, to bully; to make angry.—*vi.* To swell up; to bluster to take offense.

hug, hug, *vt.* (hugging, hugged). To press close in an embrace; to hold fast; to cherish; to keep close to.— *n.* A close embrace, a particular grip in wrestling.

Huguenot, hū'ge-not, *n.* A French Protestant of the period of the religious wars in France in the 16th century.

hulk, hulk, *n.* the body of an old vessel; anything bulky or unwieldy.

hull, hul, *n.* The outer covering of anything particularly of a nut or of grain; husk; frame or body of a ship.—*vt.* To strip off the hull or hulls; to pierce the hull of a ship with a cannon-ball.

hum, hum, *vi.* (humming, hummed). To utter the sound of bees, to make an inarticulate buzzing sound.—*vt.* To sing in a low voice; to sing or utter inarticulately.—*n.* The noise of bees or insects, a low, confused noise, a low, inarticulate sound.—*interj.* A sound with a pause, implying doubt and deliberation.

human, hū'man, *a.* Belonging to man or mankind; having the qualities of a man.

humble, hum'bl, *a.* Of a low, mean, or unpretending character, lowly modest; meek.—*vt.* (humbling, humbled). To make humble, to abase, to lower.

humidity, hū-mid'i-ti, *n.* State of being humid moisture.

humiliate, hū-mil'i-āt, *vt.* To humble; to depress; to mortify.

humility, hū-mil'i-ti, *n.* Humbleness of mind; modesty; sense of insignificance.

humming-bird, hum'ing-bèrd, *n.* A family of minute but richly-colored birds that make a humming sound with their wings.

hummock, hum'ok. *n* A rounded knoll.

humorist, hu'mèr-ist or u', *n.* One that makes use of a humorous style in speaking or writing; a wag.

humor, hu'mèr or u'mèr, *n.* Moisture or moist mater, fluid matter in an animal body, not blood, disposition; mood; a caprice; jocularity; a quality akin to wit, but depending for its effect less on point or brilliancy of expression.—*vt.* To comply with the inclination of, to soothe by compliance; to indulge.

hundred, hun'dred, *a.* Ten times ten.—*n.* The sum of ten times ten the number 100; a division or part of a county in England.

hundredweight, hun'dred-wat, *n.* A weight of a hundred and twelve pounds avoirdupois, twenty of which make a ton.

hunger, hung'ger, *n.* An uneasy sensation occasioned by the want of food, a craving of food, a strong or eager desire.— *vi.* To feel the uneasiness occasioned by want of food; to desire with great eagerness.

hungry, hung'gri, *a.* Feeling uneasiness from want of food; having an eager desire; lean; barren.

hunt, hunt, *vt.* To chase or search for, for the purpose of catching or killing; to follow closely; to use or manage, as hounds; to pursue animals over.— *vi.* To follow the chase, to search.— *n.* The chase of wild animals for catching them pursuit; an association of huntsmen, a pack of hounds.

hunter, hunt'er, *n.* One who hunts a horse used in the chase; a kind of watch with a hinged case which protects the glass.

hurdle, her'dl, *n.* A movable frame made of twigs or sticks, or of bars or rods.— *vt.* (hurdling, hurdled). To make up, cover, or close with hurdles.

hurl, herl, *vt.* To send whirling through the air, to throw with violence; to utter with vehemence.— *n.* Act of throwing with violence.

hurricane, hu'ri-kan, *n.* A violent storm of wind traveling over 75 miles per hour.

hurry, hu'ri, *vt.* (hurrying, hurried). To drive or press forward with more rapidity, to urge to act with more celerity, to quicken.— *vi.* To move or act with haste; to hasten.— *n.* Act of hurrying; urgency; bustle.

hurt, hert, *n.* A wound; bruise; injury; harm.— *vt.* (pret. and pp. hurt) To cause physical pain to, to bruise; to harm; to impair; to injure; to wound the feelings of.

hurtle, her'tl, *vi.* (hurtling, hurtled). To meet in shock, to clash, to fly with threatening noise; to resound.

husband, huz'band, *n.* A married man; the correlative of wife, a good manager; a steward.— *vt.* To manage with frugality; to use with economy.

hush, hush, *a.* Silent; still; quiet.— *n.* Stillness; quiet.— *vt.* To make quiet; to repress, as noise.— *vi.* To be still, to be silent.

hut, hut, *n.* A small house, hovel, or cabin; a temporary building to lodge soldiers.— *vt.* (hutting, hutted); To place in huts, as troops.— *vi.* To take lodgings in huts.

hutch, huch, *n.* A chest or box, a corn bin; a box for rabbits, a low wagon used in coal-pits; a measure of 2 bushels.

hyacinth, hi'a-sinth, *n.* A flowering, bulbous plant, of many varieties; a red variety of zircon tinged with yellow or brown: also applied to varieties of garnet, sapphire, and topaz.

hydrogen, hi'dro-jen, *n.* The gaseous elementary substance which combines with oxygen to form water.

hydrophobia, hi-dro-fo'bi-a, *n.* A morbid dread of water; a disease produced by the bite of a mad animal, especially a dog.

hyena, hi-e'na, *n.* A carnivorous quadruped of Asia and Africa feeding chiefly on carrion.

hygiene, hi'ji-en, *n.* A system of principles designed for the promotion of health, sanitary science.

hymnal, him'nal, *n.* A collection of hymns, generally for use in public worship.

hyperbola, hi-per'bo-la, *n.* A conic section, a curve formed by a section of a cone, when the cutting plane makes a greater angle with the base than the side of the cone makes.

hyperbole, hi-per'bo-le, *n.* Exaggeration, a figure of speech exceeding the truth.

hyperborean, hi-per-bo're-an, *a.* Being in the extreme north, arctic frigid.— *n.* An inhabitant of the most northern regions.

hypercritic, hi-per-krit'ik, *n.* One critical beyond measure; a captious censor.

hyphen, hi'fen, *n.* A character, thus (-), implying that two words or syllables are to be connected.

hypnotism, hip'no-tizm, *n.* A sleeplike condition caused by artificial means.

hypochondria, hi-po-kon'dri-a, *n.* An ailment characterized by exaggerated anxiety, mainly as to the health; low spirits.

hypocrisy, hi-pok'ri-si, *n.* A feigning to be what one is not, insincerity; a counterfeiting of religion.

hypocrite, hi'po-krit, *n.* One who feigns to be what he is not; a dissembler.

hysteria, hysterics, his-te'ri-a, hister'iks. *n.* A nervous affection chiefly characterized by laughing and crying, convulsive struggling, sense of suffocation, etc.

I

I, ĭ, *pron.* The pronoun of the first person in the nominative case; the word by which a speaker or writer denotes himself

ice, ĭs, *n.* Water or other fluid congealed; ice-cream.—*vt.* (icing, iced). To cover with ice; to convert into ice; to cover with concreted sugar, to freeze.

iconoclast, ĭ-kon'o-klast, *n.* A breaker of images; one who attacks cherished beliefs.

iconography, ĭ-ko-nog'ra-fi, *n.* The knowledge of ancient statues, paintings, gems, etc.

icy, ĭs'i, *a.* Abounding with ice; made of ice, resembling ice, chilling; frigid; destitute of affection or passion.

idea, ĭ-dē'a, *n.* That which is seen by the mind's eye; an image in the mind; object of thought; notion; conception; abstract principle; ideal view.

ideal, ĭ-dē'al, *a.* Existing in idea or fancy; visionary; imaginary; perfect.—*n.* An imaginary model of perfection.

idealism, ĭ'dē'al-izm, *n.* The system that makes everything to consist in ideas, and denies the existence of material bodies, or which denies any ground for believing in the reality of anything but percipient minds and ideas.

idealize, ĭ-dē'al-iz, *vt.* To make ideal, to embody in an ideal form.

identical, ĭ-den'tik-al, *a.* The same.

identify, ĭ-den'ti-fi, *vt.* To make to be the same, to consider as the same in effect; to ascertain or prove to be the same.

identity, ĭ-den'ti-ti, *n.* Sameness, as distinguished from similitude and diversity; sameness in every possible circumstance.

idiopathy, id-i-op'a-thi, *n.* A morbid state not produced by any preceding disease.

idiosyncrasy, id'i-o-sin"kra-si, *n.* Peculiarity of temperament or constitution; mental or moral characteristic distinguishing an individual.

idle, ĭ'dl, *a.* Not engaged in any occupation; inactive; lazy; futile; affording leisure; trifling; trivial.— *vi.* (idling, idled). To be idle; to lose or spend time in inaction.—*vt.* To spend in idleness.

idol, ĭ'dol, *n.* An image or symbol of a deity consecrated as an object of worship, a person honored to adoration; anything on which we set our affections inordinately.

ignorance, ig-nō-rans, *n.* State of being illiterate, uninformed, or uneducated; want of knowledge.

ignore, ig-nōr', *vt.* (ignoring, ignored). to pass over or overlook as if ignorant of, to disregard.

iguana, ig-wä'na, *n.* An American reptile of the lizard family.

ill, il, *a.* Bad or evil; producing evil, unfortunate, cross, crabbed, sick or indisposed; impaired; ugly; unfavorable, rude.—*n.* Evil, misfortune; calamity; disease, pain.— *adv.* Not well; badly; with pain or difficulty.

illegitimate, il-lē-jit'i-māt, *a.* Not legitimate, born out of wedlock, illogical; not authorized.—*vt.* To render illegitimate.

illuminate, il-lūm'in-āt, *vt.* (illuminating, illuminated). To light up; to adorn with festal lamps or bonfires, to enlighten intellectually, to adorn with colored pictures, etc., as manuscripts.

illustrate, il-lus'trāt or il'lus-trāt, *vt.* (illustrating, illustrated). To make clear or obvious, to explain, to explain and adorn by means of pictures: drawings. etc.

illustration, il-lus-trā'shon, Act of illustrating; that which illustrates; an example; design to illustrate the text of a book.

illustrious, il-lus'tri-us, *a.* Renowned; celebrated; noble; conferring honor or renown, glorious.

image, im'ā j, *n.* A representative of any person or thing, a statue; an idol; embodiment; a picture drawn by fancy; the appearance of any object formed by the reflection or refraction of the rays of light.—*vt.* (imaging, imaged). To represent by an image; to mirror; to form a likeness of in the mind.

imagination, im-aj'in-ā"shon, *n.* The act of imagining; the faculty by which we form a mental image or new combinations of ideas, mental image; a mere fancy; notion.

imagine, im-aj'in, *vt.* (imagining, imagined). To picture to oneself, to fancy, to contrive, to think; to deem.—*vi.* To conceive; to have a notion or idea.

imbroglio, im-brō'lyō, *n.* An intricate and perplexing state of affairs, a misunderstanding of a complicated nature.

imitate, im'i-tāt, *vt.* (imitating, imitated). To follow as a model or example; to copy; to mimic; to counterfeit.

imitation, im-i-tā'shon, *n.* Act of imitating; that which is made or produced as a copy, resemblance, a counterfeit

immediate, im-mē'di-āt, *a.* Without anything intervening; acting without a medium; direct; not acting by secondary causes; present; without intervention of time.

immemorial, im-me-mō'ri-al, *a.* Beyond memory; extending beyond the reach of record or tradition.

immerge', im-merj', *vt.* (immerging, immerged). To dip or plunge; to immerse.—*vi.* To disappear by entering into any medium.

immerse, im-mėrs', *vt.* (immersing, immersed). to plunge into water or other fluid; to overwhelm; to engage deeply.

immigrate, im'mi-grāt, *vi.* To come into a country for permanent residence .

immolate, im'mō-lā t, *vt.* (immolating, immolated). To sacrifice, to kill, as a victim offered in sacrifice; to offer in sacrifice.

immunity, im-mū'ni-ti, *n.* Freedom from service or obligation, particular privilege or prerogative; state of not being liable.

imp, imp, *n.* A young or little devil; a mischievous child.—*vt.* (imping, imped). To graft, to mend a deficient wing by the insertion of a feather, to strengthen.

impact, im'pakt, *n.* A forcible touch; a blow; the shock of a moving body that strikes against another.

impale, im-pāl', *vt.* (impaling, impaled). To put to death by fixing on a stake; to join, as two coats of arms on one shield, with an upright line between.

impalpable, im-pal'pa-bl, *a.* Not to be felt; so fine as not to be perceived by the touch; not easily or readily apprehended by the mind.

impassive, im-pas'iv, *a.* Not susceptible of pain or suffering; impassible, unmoved.

impatient, im-pā'shent, *a.* Not patient; uneasy under given conditions and eager for change, not suffering quietly; not enduring de lay.

impeach, im-pēch', *vt.* To charge with a crime; to bring charges of maladministration against a minister of state, etc., to call in question; to disparage

impediment, im-ped'i-ment, *n.* That by which one is impeded; obstruction.

impel, im-pel', *vt.* (impelling, impelled). To drive or urge forward to press on; to instigate; to incite, to actuate.

imperceptible, im-pėr-sep'ti-bl, *a.* Not perceptible; not easily apprehended by the senses; fine or minute.

imperfect, im-pėr'fekt, *a.* Not perfect; not complete; not perfect in a moral view; faulty; *imperfect tense,* a tense expressing an uncompleted action or state, especially in time past.

imperforate, im-pėr'fo-rāt, *a.* Not perforated or pierced; having no opening or pores.

imperial, im-pē'ri-al, *a.* Pertaining to an empire or emperor, supreme; suitable for an emperor; of superior excellence.—*n.* A tuft of hair beneath a man's lower lip; a size of paper measuring 30 by 22 inches.

impersonal, im-pėr'son-al, *a.* Not having personal existence; not endued with personality; not referring to any particular person; *impersonal verb,* a verb (such as *it* rains) used only with an impersonal nominative.—*n.* That which wants personality; an impersonal verb.

impersonate, im-pėr'son-āt, *vt.* To invest with personality, to assume the character of; to represent in character, as on the stage.

impetuous, im-pe'tū-us, *a.* Rushing with great force; forcible; precipitate; vehement of mind; hasty; passionate.

impiety, im-pī-e-ti, *n.* Want of piety; irreverence toward the Supreme Being; ungodliness; an act of wickedness.

impinge, im-pinj', *vi.* (impinging, impinged). To dash against; to clash.

implicate, im'pli-kāt, *vt.* (implicating, implicated). To involve or bring into connection with; to prove to be connected or concerned, as in an offense.

implication, im-pli-kā'shon, *n.* Act of implicating; state of being implicated, entanglement, a tacit inference; something to be understood though not expressed.

implicit, im-pli'sit, *a.* Implied; fairly to be understood, though not expressed in words; trusting to another; unquestioning.

implore, im-plōr, *vt.* and *i.* (imploring, implored). To call upon or for, in supplication; to beseech, entreat.

imply, im-plī', *vt.* (implying, implied). To involve or contain in substance or by fair inference; to signify indirectly; to presuppose.

importance, im-pōrt'ans, *n.* Quality of being important; weight; moment, rank or standing; weight in self-estimation.

importune, im-pōr-tūn', *vt.* (importuning importuned). To press with solicitation;

to urge with frequent application.—*vi.* To solicit earnestly and repeatedly.

impose, im-pōz', *vt.* (imposing, imposed). To place, set, or lay on; to lay on, as a tax, penalty, duty, etc.; to lay on, as hands; to obtrude fallaciously, to palm or pass off.—*vi.* Used in phrase to *impose on* or *upon*, to deceive; to victimize.

impotent, im-pō-tent, *a.* Entirely wanting vigor of body or mind feeble, destitute of the power of begetting children.

impound, im-pound', *vt.* To confine in a pound or close pen, to confine to take possession of for use when necessary.

impoverish, im-po'vėr-ish, *vt.* To make poor, to reduce to indigence; to exhaust the strength or fertility of, as of soil.

impress, im-pres', *vt.* To press into; to imprint, to stamp on the mind to inculcate; to compel to enter into public service, as seamen; to take for public use.—*n.* im'press. That which is impressed; mark made by pressure, impression character, act of compelling to enter into public service.

impression, im-pre'shon, *n.* Act of impressing, that which is impressed; mark; effect produced on the mind, an indistinct notion idea, copy taken by pressure from type, etc.; edition; copies forming one issue of a book.

impressionist, im-pre'shon-ist, *n.* One who lays stress on impressions, an artist who depicts scenes by their most striking characteristics as they first impress the spectator.

impromptu, im-promp'tū, *n.* A saying, poem, etc., made off-hand; an extemporaneous composition.—*a.* Off-hand; extempore.—*adv.* Offhand.

improper, im-pro'pér, *a.* Not proper; unfit; not decent; erroneous; wrong.

impropriety, im-prō-prī'e-ti, *n.* Quality of being improper, that which is improper; an unsuitable act, expression, etc.

improve, im-prōv', *vt.* (improving improved). To better; to ameliorate; to mend; to rectify; to use to good purpose; to apply to practical purposes.—*vi.* To grow better.

improvement, im-prōv'ment, *n.* Act of improving; state of being improved, a change for the better that which improves, a beneficial or valuable addition or alteration.

improvise, im-pro-vīz', To form on the spur of the moment to compose and recite, etc., without previous prepara-

tion.

impulse, im'puls, *n.* Force communicated instantaneously, effect of a sudden communication of motion, influence acting on the mind motive; sudden determination.

in, in, *prep.* Within; inside of; surrounded by, indicating presence or situation within limits, whether of place, time, circumstances, etc.—*adv.* In or within some place state, circumstances, etc.; not out.

inadvertence, inadvertency, in-ad-vėrt-ens, in-ad-vėrt'en-si, *n.* Quality of being inadvertent; any oversight or fault which proceeds from negligence or want of attention.

inadvertent, in-ad-vėrt'ent, *a.* Not paying strict attention; heedless; unwary; negligent.

inappropriate, in-ap-prō'pri-āt, *a.* Not appropriate; unsuited; not proper.

inarticulate, in-är-tik'ū-lāt, *a.* Not articulate, not jointed or articulated; not uttered distinctly.

inaugurate, in-ä'gū-rāt, *vt.* To induct into an office with suitable ceremonies, to perform initiatory ceremonies in connection with.

incalculable, in-kal'kū-la-bl, *a.* Not calculable; very great.

incandescent, in-kan-des'ent, *a.* White or glowing with heat.—**incandescent light,** a form of gas light, a form of electric light given forth from a filament of carbon inclosed in an airless glass globe.

incantation, in-kan-tā'shon, *n.* The act of using certain words and ceremonies to raise spirits, etc.; the form of words so used; a magical charm or ceremony.

incapable, in-kā'pa-bl, *a.* Not capable; possessing inadequate power or capacity; not susceptible; incompetent, unqualified or disqualified.—*n.* One physically or mentally weak.

incarnate, in-kär'nāt, *vt.* To clothe with flesh; to embody in flesh.—*a.* Invested with flesh; embodied in flesh.

incense, in'sens, *n.* Aromatic substance burned in religious rites odors of spices and gums, burned in religious rites; flattery or agreeable homage.—*vt.* (incensing, incensed). To perfume with incense.

inceptive, in-sep'tiv, *a.* Pertaining to inception; beginning, applied to a verb which expresses the beginning of an action.—*n.* An inceptive verb.

incessant, in-ses'ant, *a.* Unceasing unintermitted; continual; constant.

incest, in 'sest, *n.* Sexual commerce between near blood relations.

inch, insh, *n.* The twelfth part of a foot in length, a small quantity or degree.—*vt.* To drive or force by inches.

incite, in-sīt', *vt.* (inciting, incited). To move to action by impulse or influence, to instigate, to encourage.

inclination, in-klin-ā'shon, *n.* The act of inclining; deviation from a normal direction; a leaning of the mind or will; tendency; bent; bias; predilection liking.

incline, in-klīn', *vi.* (inclining, inclined). To deviate from a direction regarded as normal, to slope; to be disposed; to have some wish or desire.—*vt.* To cause to lean or bend towards or away from; to give a leaning to; to dispose.—*n.* An ascent or descent; a slope.

inclose, in-klōz', *vt.* (inclosing, inclosed). To shut up or confine on all sides; to environ; to cover with a wrapper or envelope.

inclosure, in-klō'zhūr, *n.* Act of inclosing, what is inclosed, a space inclosed or fenced; something inclosed with a letter, etc.

inclusive, in-klō'siv *a.* Inclosing; comprehended in the number or sum; comprehending the stated limit.

incognito, in-kog'ni-tō, *pred.a.* or *adv.* In disguise.—*n.* (fem. being **incognita**). One passing under an assumed name; assumption of a feigned character.

incoherent, in-kō-hēr'ent, *a.* Not coherent; wanting rational connection, as ideas, language, etc.; rambling and unintelligible.

incombustible in-kom-bust'i-bl, *a.* Not combustible; that cannot be burned.

income, in'kum, *n.* Receipts or emoluments regularly coming in from property or employment; annual receipts; revenue.

incomparable, in-kom'pa-ra-bl, *a.* Not comparable, that admits of no comparison with others; matchless.

incompatibility, in-kom-pat'i-bil"iti, *n.* State or quality of being incompatible; inconsistency; disposition or temper entirely out of harmony.

incompatible, in-kom-pat'i-bl, *a.* Not compatible; inconsistent; irreconcilably different; that cannot be made to accord.

incompetence, incompetency, inkom'pē-tens, in-kom'pē-ten-si, *n.* State or quality of being incompetent, want of suitable faculties, adequate means, or proper qualifications.

incompetent, in-kom'pē-tent, *a.* Not competent; incapable; wanting legal qualifications, not admissible.

incondite, in-kon'dīt, *a.* Rude; unpolished, said of literary compositions.

inconsistence, inconsistency, in-kon-sist'ens, in-kon-sist'en-si, *n.* The condition or quality of being inconsistent; opposition or disagreement of particulars; self contradiction; incongruity; discrepancy.

inconstant, in-kon'stant, *a.* Not constant, subject to change of opinion or purpose, not firm in resolution; fickle.

incontinent, in-kon'ti-nent, *a.* Not continent; not restraining the passions or appetites, unchaste, unable to restrain discharges.

inconvenience, in-kon-vē'ni-ens, *n.* The quality of being inconvenient annoyance; molestation; trouble disadvantage.—*vt.* To put to inconvenience; to trouble.

inconvertible, in-kon-vért'i-bl, *a.* Not convertible, that cannot be changed into or exchanged for something else.

incorporate, in-kor'pō-rāt, *vt.* To form into one body; to unite; to blend; to associate with another whole, as with a government, to form into a legal body or corporation.—*vi.* To unite; to grow into or coalesce.—*a.* Incorporated; united m one body.

incorruptible, in-ko-rupt'i-bl, *a.* Not corruptible; that cannot corrupt or decay; inflexibly just and upright.

increase, in-krēs', *vi.* (increasing, increased). To become greater; to augment, to advance in any quality, good or bad; to multiply by the production of young.—*vt.* To make greater or larger, to add to.—*n.* in'kres. A growing larger in size, quantity, etc.; augmentation; addition; increment; profit; interest; offspring.

incredulous, in-kred'ū-lus, *a.* Not credulous; refusing or withholding belief

increment, in'krē-ment, *n.* Act or process of increasing; increase; increase in the value of real property from adventitious causes.

incubator, in'kū-bā t-ėr, *n.* One who or that which incubates, an apparatus for hatching eggs by artificial heat.

incubus, in'kū-bus, *n.*, pl. **-buses** or **-bi**. A name of nightmare; something that weighs heavily on a person; burden or incumbrance, dead weight.

inculpate, in-kul'pāt, *vt.* To show to be in

fault; to impute guilt to; to incriminate.

incumbent, in-kum'bent, *a.* Lying on; resting on a person, as duty or obligation.—*n.* One in possession of an ecclesiastical benefice or other office.

indecency, in-dē'sen-si, *n.* The quality of being indecent; what is indecent in language, actions, etc.; indecorum; immodesty.

indelicate, in-de'li-kāt, *a.* Wanting delicacy; offensive to modesty or nice sense of propriety; somewhat immodest.

indemnify, in-dem'ni-fī, *vt.* To make safe from loss or harm; to reimburse or compensate.

indemnity, in-dem'ni-ti, *n.* Security given against loss, damage, or punishment; compensation for loss or injury sustained.

indent, in-dent', *vt.* To notch, to cut into points or inequalities, to bind by indenture.—*n.* A cut or notch; an indentation.

indenture, in-den'tūr, *n.* That which is indented; a deed under seal between two or more parties each having a duplicate.—*vt.* To indent, to bind by indenture.

independence, in-dē-pend'ens, *n.* State of being independent; complete exemption from control, self-reliance; political freedom.

index, in'deks, *n.; pl.* **indexes** or **indices,** in'dek-sez, in'di-sez. Something that points out; the hand ☞ used by printers, etc.; a table of contents, list of books disapproved of by R. Catholic authorities; the forefinger; the figure denoting to what power any mathematical quantity is involved.—*vt.* To provide with an index; to place in an index.

Indian, In'di-an, *a.* Pertaining to India, or to the Indies, East or West pertaining to the aborigines of America.

indicative, in-dik'a-tiv, *a.* That serves to point out, serving as an indication; designating a mood of the verb that declares directly or asks questions.—*n.* The indicative mood.

indigestion, in-di-jest'yon, *n.* Incapability of or difficulty in digesting; dyspepsia.

indignation, in-dig-nā'shon, *n.* A feeling of displeasure at what is unworthy or base; anger, mingled with contempt, disgust, or abhorrence; violent displeasure.

indigo, in 'di-go, *n.* A blue vegetable dye, from India and other places the leguminous plant that produces the dye.

indirect, in-di-rekt', *a.* Not direct; circuitous; not tending directly to a purpose or end, not straightforward; not resulting directly.

indissoluble, in-dis'sō-lū-bl, *a.* Not capable of being dissolved, perpetually binding or obligatory; not to be broken.

indistinct, in-dis-tingkt', *a.* Not distinct; faint; confused; imperfect or dim.

individual, in-di-vid'ū-al, *a.* Subsisting as one indivisible entity; pertaining to one only, peculiar to a single person or thing.—*n.* A being or thing forming one of its kind, a person.

indoor, in'dōr, *a.* Being within doors, being within the house.

indoors, in'dorz, *adv.* Within doors, inside a house.

indubitable, in-dū'bit-a-bl, *a.* Not to be doubted, too plain to admit of doubt, evident.

induce, in-dūs', *vt.* (inducing, induced). To lead by persuasion or argument; to prevail on; to actuate, to produce or cause.

induct, in-dukt', *vt.* To lead or bring into; to put in possession of an ecclesiastical living or office, with customary ceremonies.

indulge, in-dulj', *vt.* (indulging, indulged). To give free course to, to gratify by compliance, to humor to excess.—*vi.* To indulge oneself; to practice indulgence.

indulgence, in-dulj'ens, *n.* The act or practice of indulging; a favor; intemperance, gratification of desire; tolerance; remission of the penance attached to certain sins.

indurate, in'dū-rāt, *vi.* To grow hard.—*vt.* To make hard; to deprove of sensibility.

industrious, in-dus'tri-us, *a.* Given to or characterized by industry; diligent, active.

industry, in'dus-tri, *n.* Habitual diligence steady attention to business; the industrial arts generally. or any one of them; manufacture; trade.

ineptitude, in-ept'i-tūd *n.* Condition or quality of being inept; unfitness, silliness.

inequality, in-ē-kwol'i-ti, *n.* Condition of being unequal; want of equality, an elevation or depression in a surface; diversity.

inert, in-ėrt', *a.* Destitute of the power of moving itself, or of active resistance to motion impressed; lifeless; sluggish; inactive.

inertia, in-ėr'shi-a, *n.* Passiveness inactivity; the property of matter by which it tends to retain its state of rest or of uniform rectilinear motion.

inexorable, in-eks'ōr-a-bl, *a.* Not to be persuaded by entreaty or prayer; unbending; unrelenting; implacable.

inexpedient, in-eks-pē'di-ent, *a.* Not expedient; not advisable or judicious.

inexplicable, in-eks'pli-ka-bl, *a.* That cannot be explained or interpreted; unaccountable; mysterious.

infamous, in'fa-mus, *a.* Notoriously vile; detestable, branded with infamy.

infamy, in'fa-mi, *n.* Total loss of reputation; public disgrace; qualities detested and despised; extreme vileness.

infancy, in'fan-si, *n.* State of being an infant, early childhood, period from birth to the age of twenty-one; first age of anything.

infant, in'fant, *n.* A very young child; one under twenty-one years of age.—*a.* Pertaining to infants.

infatuate, in-fa'tū-āt, *vt.* To make foolish; to inspire with an extravagant passion.

infatuation, in-fa'tū- ā"shon, *n.* Act of infatuating, state of being infatuated; foolish passion.

inferior, in-fē'ri-ėr, *a.* Lower in place, station, age, value, etc., subordinate.—*n.* A person lower in rank, importance, etc.

infernal, in-fėr 'nal, *a.* Pertaining to the lower regions or hell; very wicked and detestable, diabolical.—**infernal machine**, an explosive apparatus contrived for assassination or other mischief.

infidel, in'fi-del, *n.* A disbeliever; a skeptic, one who does not believe in God or in Christianity.—*a.* Unbelieving, skeptical.

infinitive, in-fin'it-iv, *a.* Designating a mood of the verb which expresses action without limitation of person or number, as, to love.— *n.* The infinitive mood.

infinity, in-fin'i-ti, *n.* State or quality of being infinite, unlimited extent of time, space, quantity, etc.; immensity.

infirmary, in-fėrm'a-ri *n.* A place where the sick and injured are nursed, a hospital.

infirmity, in-fėrm'i-ti, *n.* State of being infirm; unsound state of the body; weakness of mind or resolution; failing; malady.

inflame, in-flām', *vt.* To set on fire; to kindle; to excite or increase, to incense; to make morbidly red and swollen.—*vi.* To grow hot, angry, and painful, to take fire.

inflammation, in-flam-ā'shon, *n.* Act of inflaming, state of being inflamed; a redness and swelling attended with heat, pain, and feverish symptoms.

inflection, in-flek'shon, *n.* Act of inflecting; state of being inflected; grammatical variation of nouns verbs, etc.; modulation of the voice, deflection or diffraction.

inflexibility, in-fleks'i-bil"i-ti *n.* Firmness of purpose; unbending pertinacity or obstinacy.

inflexible, in-fleks'i-bl, *a.* That cannot be bent; firm in purpose; pertinacious, inexorable.

inflow, in'flō, *n.* The act of flowing in or into; that which flows in; influx.

influence, in'flü-ens, *n.* Agency or power serving to affect, modify, etc.; sway; effect; acknowledged ascendency with people in power.—*vt.* To exercise influence on, to bias, to sway.

informal, in-form'al, *a.* Not in the usual form or mode, not with the official or customary forms; without ceremony.

information. in-form-ā'shon, *n.* The act of informing; intelligence communicated or gathered; a charge or accusation before a magistrate.

infringe, in-frinj', *vt.* (infringing, infringed) To break, as laws, agreements, etc., to violate, to contravene.—*vi.* To encroach (with *on* or *upon*).

infuse, in-fūz', *vt.* (infusing, in-fused). To pour in, as a liquid, to instill, as principles, to steep in liquor without boiling, in order to extract solutions, etc.

infusion, in-fū'zhon, *n.* Act or process of infusing; that which is infused; liquor obtained by infusing or steeping.

ingenious, in-jē'ni-us, *a.* Possessed of cleverness or ability, apt in contriving; contrived with ingenuity; witty or well conceived.

ingenuity, in-jen-ū'i-ti, *n.* Quality of being ingenious; ready invention; skill in contrivance.

ingredient, in-grē'di-ent, *n.* That which is a component part of any mixture; an element, component, or constituent.

inhabit, in-ha'bit, *vt.* To live or dwell in, to occupy as a place of settled resident.—*vi.* To dwell, to live, to abide.

inherit, in-he'rit, vt. To come into possession of as an heir, to receive by nature from a progenitor, to hold as belonging to one's lot.—*vi.* To take or have possession of property.

inheritance, in-he'rit-ans, *n.* Act of inheriting, that which is or may be inherited; what falls to one's lot; possession.

inhospitable, in-hos'pit-a-bl, *a.* Not hospitable; incapable of being satisfied or appeased.

inscribe, in-skrīb', *vt.* (inscribing inscribed). To write down, to imprint on, as on the memory; to address or dedicate, to mark with letters or words; to draw a figure within another.

inscrutable, in-skrö'ta-bl, *a.* Unsearchable, that cannot be penetrated or understood by human reason.

insect, in'sekt, *n.* One of those small animals that have three divisions of the body—head, thorax, and abdomen—and usually three pairs of legs and two pairs of wings, as flies, etc.; a puny, contemptible person.—*a.* Pertaining to insects; like an insect; mean.

insensible, in-sens'i-bl *a.* Not perceived or perceptible by the senses; void of feeling; unfeeling; callous, indifferent.

inseparable, in-sep'a-ra-bl, *a.* Not separable; not to be parted; always together.

insert, in-sèrt', *vt.* To put, bring, or set in; to thrust in; to set in or among.

insertion, in-sèr'shon, *n.* Act of inserting; thing inserted; place or mode of attachment of a part or organ to its support.

inside, in'sīd, *n.* The interior side or part of a thing.—*a.* Interior; internal.—*prep.* In the interior of; within.

insinuate, in-sin'u-āt, *vt.* To introduce by windings or gently; to work gradually into favor; to introduce by gentle or artful means, to hint.—*vi.* To creep or wind; to make an insinuation, to wheedle.

insolvent, in-sol'vent, *a.* Not solvent; not having money, etc., sufficient to pay debts.—*n.* One unable to pay his debts.

inspiration, in-spi-rā'shon *n.* The act of inspiring; the drawing in of breath, the divine influence by which the sacred writers were instructed; influence emanating from any object; the state of being inspired, something conveyed to the mind when under extraordinary influence.

inspire, in-spīr', *vt.* (inspiring, inspired). To breathe in; to breathe into, to communicate divine instructions to; to infuse ideas or poetic spirit into; to animate in general.—*vi.* To draw in breath; to inhale air into the lungs.

instant, in'stant, *a.* Pressing or urgent; immediate; making no delay; present or current.—*n.* A moment.

instill, in-stil', *vt.* (instilling, instilled). To pour in, as by drops; to infuse by degrees; to insinuate imperceptibly.

instinct, in'stingkt, *n.* Spontaneous or natural impulse the knowledge and skill which animals have without experience; intuitive feeling.—*a.* in-stingkt'. Animated or stimulated from within; inspired.

institute, in'sti-tūt, *vt.* To set up or establish; to found; to begin; to appoint to an office; to invest with a benefice.—*n.* That which is instituted, established law, principle, a literary or scientific body; an institution, *pl.* a book of elements or principles.

insulate, in'sū-lāt, *vt.* To make into an island, to detach, to separate as an electrified body, by interposition of nonconductors.

insulator, in 'sū-lāt-èr, *n.* One who or that which insulates; a body that interrupts the communication of electricity; nonconductor.

insulin, ins'ū-lin, *n.* A substance extracted from the pancreas of animals, and found beneficial in diabetes.

insult, in'sult, *n.* Any gross affront or indignity; act or speech of insolence or contempt.—*vt.* in-sult'. To treat with insult or insolence.—*vi.* To behave with insolent triumph.

insure, in-shör', *vt.* (insuring, insured). To make sure; to contract for the receipt of a certain sum in the event of loss, death, etc.

insurgent, in-sèr'jent, *a.* Rising in opposition to lawful authority, rebellious.—*n.* One who rises in opposition to authority.

integral, in'ti-gral, *a.* Whole; forming a necessary part of a whole not fractional.—*n.* A whole; an entire thing.

intelligent, in-tel'i-jent, *a.* Endowed with the faculty of understanding or reason; endowed with a good intellect well informed.

intelligible, in-tel'i-ji-bl, *a.* Capable of being understood; comprehensible; clear.

intemperate, in-tem'pèr-ēt, *a.* Not temperate; addicted to an excessive use of alcoholic liquors, excessive or immoderate.—*n.* One not temperate.

intercede, in-tèr-sēd', *vi.* (interceding, interceded). To mediate; to plead in favor of one; to make intercession.

intercept, in-tèr-sept', *vt.* To take or seize on by the way; to stop on its passage; to obstruct the progress of; to cut or shut off.

intercession, in-tèr-se'shon, *n.* Act of interceding; mediation; prayer or solicitation to one party in favor of another.

interest, in'tèr-est, *vt.* To concern; to engage the attention of.—*n.* Concern or regard, advantage, profit profit per cent from money lent or invested influence with a person.

interfere, in-ter-fēr', *vi.* (interfering, interfered). To clash; to interpose, to take a part in the concerns of others.

interior, in-tē'ri-èr, *a.* Internal, being within; inland.—*n.* The inner part of a thing, the inside; the inland part of a country, etc.

interlude, in'tèr-lūd, *n.* A short entertainment between the acts of a play, or between the play and the afterpiece; a piece of music between certain more important passages.

interminable, in-tèr'min-a-bl, *a.* Admitting no limit; boundless; endless.

international, in-tèr-na'shon-al, *a.* Relating to or mutually affecting nations, regulating the mutual intercourse between nations.

interpretation, in-tèr'pret-ā"shon *n.* Act of interpreting; explanation, representation of a character on the stage.

interregnum, in-tèr-reg'num, *n.* The time between reigns; intermission or break in succession.

interrogate, in-te'rō-gāt, *vt.* To question; to examine by asking questions.

interrogation, in-te'rō-gā"shon, *n.* Act of interrogating; question put; a sign that marks a question, thus (?).

interrupt, in-tèr-rupt', *vt.* To break in upon the progress of; to cause to stop in speaking.

interstice, in-tèrs'tis, *n.* A narrow space between things closely set; a chink.

interval, in'tèr-val, *n.* A space between things; amount of separation between ranks, degrees, etc.; difference in gravity or acuteness between sounds.

interview, in'tèr-vū, *n.* A meeting between persons; a conference.— *vt.* To have an interview with to get information for publication.

interweave, in-tèr-wēv', *vt.* To weave together; to unite intimately; to interlace.

intestate, in-test'āt, *a.* Dying without having made a will; not disposed of by will.—*n.* A person who dies without making a will.

intestine, in-tes'tin, *a.* Internal; domestic; not foreign. *n.* The canal extending from the stomach to the anus; *pl.* entrails or viscera in general.

intimate, in'ti-māt, *a.* Inward or internal; close in friendship; familiar, close.—*n.* An intimate or familiar friend.—*vt.* (intimating, intimated). To hint or indicate; to announce.

intolerable, in-tol'èr-a-bl, *a.* That cannot be borne, unendurable; insufferable.

intolerant, in-tol'èr-ant, *a.* That cannot bear, not enduring difference of opinion or worship; refusing to tolerate others.

intone, in-tōn', *vi.* To use a musical monotone in pronouncing. *vt.* To pronounce with a musical tone; to chant.

intoxicate, in-toks'i-kāt, *vt.* To make drunk; to elate to enthusiasm or madness.—*vi.* To cause intoxication.

intrigue, in-trēg', *n.* An underhand plot or scheme, plot of a play, etc.; an illicit intimacy between a man and woman.— *vi.* (intriguing, intrigued). To engage in an intrigue; to carry on forbidden love.

intrinsic, intrinsical, in-trin'sik, intrin'sik-al, *a.* Being within; inherent; essential.

introduce, in-trō-dūs', *vt.* To lead or bring in; to insert; to bring to be acquainted; to present; to make known, to import; to bring before the public.

introduction, in-trō-duk'shon, *n.* Act of introducing, act of making persons known to each other; act of bringing something into notice; a preliminary discourse.

introspection, in-trō-spek'shon, *n.* The act of looking inwardly; examination of one's own thoughts or feelings.

intrude, in-trōd', *vi.* (intruding, intruded). to thrust oneself in, to force an entry or way in without permission, right, or invitation; to encroach.—*vt.* To thrust in.

intuition, in-tū-i'shon, *n.* A looking on; direct apprehension of a truth without reasoning.

intuitive, in-tū'it-iv, *a.* Perceived by the mind immediately without reasoning; based on intuition; self-evident.

invalid, in'va-lēd, *n.* One weak or infirm; a person disabled for active service.—*a.* In ill health; infirm disabled.—*vt.* To render an invalid; to enroll on the list of invalids.

invention, in-ven'shon, *n.* Act of inventing, contrivance of that which did not before exist; device; power of inventing; ingenuity; faculty by which an author produces plots, etc.

inventory, in'ven-to-ri, *n*. An account of catalogue of the goods and chattels of a deceased person; a catalogue of particular things.— *vt.* to make an inventory of.

inverse, in'vèrs or in-ve˙ rs', *a*. Opposite in order or relation; inverted

invest, in-vest', *vt.* To clothe, to array, to clothe with office or authority; to endow; to besiege; to lay out as money in some species of property.—*vi.* To make an investment.

investigate, in-ves'ti-gāt, *vt.* To search into, to make careful examination of.

invincible, in-vin'si-bl, *a*. Not to be conquered or overcome, insurmountable.— *n*. One who is invincible.

invitation, in-vi-tā'shon, *n*. Act of inviting; bidding to an entertainment, etc.

invite, in-vīt', *vt.* (inviting, invited). To ask to do something; to ask to an entertainment, etc., to allure or attract.—*vi.* To give invitation; to allure.

involute, in'vō-lūt, *n*. A curve traced by any point of a tense string when it is unwound from a given curve.—*a*. Involved; rolled inward from the edges.

involve, in-volv', *vt.* (involving, involved). To roll up; to envelop to imply; to include; to implicate; to complicate, in algebra, etc., to raise a quantity to any assigned power.

inward, in'wèrd, *a*. Internal; being within; intimate; in the mind, soul, or feelings.—*adv*. Toward the inside; into the mind.—*n.pl*. The inner parts of an animal; the viscera.

iron, ī'ern, *n*. The most common and useful metal, an instrument made of iron; a utensil for smoothing cloth, *pl.* fetters; chains, handcuffs.—*a*. Made of iron; consisting of or like iron, harsh, severe, binding fast, vigorous; inflexible.—*vt.* To smooth with an iron; to fetter; to furnish or arm with iron.

irony, ī'ron-i, *n*. A mode of speech which expresses a sense contrary to that conveyed by the words; a subtle kind of sarcasm.

irradiation, ir-rā'di-ā"shon. *n*. Act of irradiating; illumination; apparent enlargement of an object strongly illuminated.

irregular, ir-re'gū-lèr, *a*. Not regular; not according to rule or custom; anomalous, vicious, crooked variable; deviating from the common rules in its inflections.—*n*. A soldier not in regular service.

irrepressible, ir-rē-pres'i-bl, *a*. Not repressible; incapable of being repressed.

irreproachable, ir-rē-prōch'a-bl, *a*. Incapable of being reproached upright; faultless.

irresistible, ir-rē -zist'i-bl, *a*. Not resistible; that cannot be resisted; resistless.

irrigate, ir'ri-gāt, *vt.* To bedew or sprinkle; to water by means of channels or streams.

irritant, ir'rit-ant, *a*. Irritating, producing inflammation.—*n*. That which irritates; a medical application that causes pain or heat.

irritation, ir-rit-ā 'shon, *n*. Act of irritating; exasperation, annoyance; vital action in muscles or organs caused by some stimulus.

isolationist, ī s-ō-lā'shon-ist, *n*. One who favors keeping aloof from other countries politically.

isometric, isometrical, ī-sō-met'rik, ī-sō-met'rik-al, *a*. Pertaining to or characterized by equality of measure.

isosceles, ī-sos'e-lēz, *a*. Having two legs or sides only that are equal (an *isosceles* triangle).

issue, ish'ū, *n*. The act of passing or flowing out; delivery; quantity issued at one time, event; consequence; progeny; offspring; an artificial ulcer to promote a secretion of pus; matter depending in a lawsuit.—*vi.* (issuing, issued). To pass or flow out; to proceed, to spring to grow or accrue; to come to an issue in law, to terminate.—*vt.* To send out; to put into circulation, to deliver for use

isthmus, ist'mus or is'mus, *n*. A neck of land connecting two much larger portions.

italic, i-ta'lik, *a*. Pertaining to Italy the name of a printing type sloping towards the right.—*n*. An italic letter or type.

itch, ich, *n*. A sensation in the skin causing a desire to scratch, a constant teasing desire; —*vi.* To feel an itch; to have a teasing sensation impelling to something.

itinerant, i- or ī-tin'èr-ant, *a*. Passing or travelling from place to place; not settled.—*n*. One who travels from place to place.

itinerary, i- or ī-tin'èr-a-ri, *n*. A work containing notices of places of a particular line of road; a travel route; plan of a tour.—*a*. Travelling; pertaining to a journey.

ivory, ī'vo-ri, *n*. The substance composing the tusks of the elephants, etc. something made of ivory.—*a*. Consisting or made of ivory.

I

J

jabber, jab'ėr, *vi.* To gabble; to talk rapidly or indistinctly; to chatter.*vt* To utter rapidly with confused sounds.—*n.* Rapid and indistinct talk.

jacket, jak'et, *n.* A short outer garment; a casing of cloth, felt, wood etc.

jag, jāg, *vt.* (jagging, jagged). To cut into notches or teeth; to notch.—*n.* A notch; a ragged protuberance.

jaguar, ja-gwär', *n.* The American tiger, a spotted carnivorous animal, the most formidable feline quadruped of the New World.

jail, jāl, *n.* A prison; place of confinement.

jailer, jailor, jāl'er, *n.* The keeper of a jail.

jam, jam, *n.* A conserve of fruits boiled with sugar and water.—*vt.* (jamming, jammed). To crowd; to squeeze tight, to wedge in.

jargon, jär'gon, *n.* Confused, unintelligible talk; gibberish; phraseology peculiar to a sect, profession, etc.; a variety of zircon.

jasmine, jas'min, *n.* A fragrant shrub, bearing white or yellow flowers.

jaunt, jänt, *vi.* To ramble here and there; to make an excursion.—*n.* A trip; a tour; an excursion; a ramble.

jaunty, jän'ti, *a.* Gay and easy in manner or actions; airy; sprightly; showy.

javelin, jav'lin, *n.* A light spear thrown from the hand.

jaw, jä, *n.* The bones of the mouth in which the teeth are fixed.

jazz, jaz, *n.* Syncopated or rag-time music, originally of Negro origin.

Jehovah, jē-hō'va, *n.* An old Hebrew name of the Supreme Being.

jelly, je'li, *n.* Matter in a glutinous state; the thickened juice of fruit boiled with sugar, transparent matter obtained from animal substances by boiling.—*vi.* To become a jelly.

jelly-fish, jel'i-fish, *n.* A gelatinous marine animal.

jeopardy, je'pėrd-i, *n.* Hazard; risk exposure to death, loss, or injury.

Jesus, jē'zus, *n.* The Savior of men; Christ.

jettison, jet'i-son, *n.* Jetsam.—*vt.* To throw overboard

Jew, jū, *n.* A Hebrew or Israelite.

jewel, jū'el, *n.* A personal ornament of precious stones, a precious stone.—*vt.* (jewelling, jewelled). To adorn with jewels.

jilt, jilt, *n.* A woman who gives her lover hopes and capriciously disappoints him.—*vt.* To deceive in love.—*vi.* To play the jilt.

jingle, jing'gl, *vi.* and *t.* (jingling, jingled). To sound with a tinkling metallic sound, to clink.—*n.* A rattling or clinking sound.

jockey, jok'i, *n.* A man who rides horses in a race; a dealer in horses; one who takes undue advantage in trade.—*vt.* To play the jockey to; to ride in a race; to jostle by riding against; to cheat.

joiner, join'ėr, *n.* A mechanic who does the wood-work of houses; a carpenter.

joist, joist, *n.* One of the pieces of timber to which the boards of a floor or the laths of a ceiling are nailed.—*vt.* To fit with joists.

joke, jōk, *n.* A jest; something said to excite a laugh, raillery, what is not in earnest.—*vi.* (joking, joked). To jest; to sport.—*vt.* To cast jokes at; to rally.

jot, jot, *n.* An iota; a tittle.—*vt.* (jotting, jotted). To set down in writing.

journal, jėr'nal, *n.* A diary; an account of daily transactions, or the book containing such; a daily or periodical paper, a narrative of the transactions of a society, etc.; that part of an axle which moves in the bearings.

journalist, jėr'nal-ist, *n.* The writer of a journal; a newspaper editor or contributor.

journey, jėr'ni, *n.* A traveling from one place to another; tour; excursion; distance traveled.—*vi.* To travel from place to place.

Judaism, jū'dā-izm, *n.* The religious doctrines and rites of the Jews, conformity to the Jewish rites and ceremonies.

Judaize, jū'da-iz, *vi.* and *t.* To conform to the religious doctrines and rites of the Jews.

Judas, jū'das, *n.* A treacherous person.

judgment, juj'ment, *n.* Act of judging; good sense; discernment; opinion or estimate; mental faculty by which man ascertains the relations between ideas; sentence pronounced, a calamity regarded as a punishment of sin; final trial of the human race.

jug, jug, *n.* A vessel for liquors, generally with a handle; a mug; a pitcher.—*vt.* (jugging, jugged). To put in a jug; to cook by Putting into a jug, and this into boiling water (*jugged* hare).

jumble, jum'bl, *vt.* (jumbling, jumbled). To mix in a confused mass.—*vi.* To meet, mix, or unite in a confused manner.—*n.* Confused mass disorder, confusion.

jump, jump, *vi.* To leap; to skip; to spring; to agree, tally, coincide.—*vt.* To pass over by a leap; to pass over hastily.—*n.* Act of jumping; leap; spring; bound.

junction, jungk'shon, *n.* Act or operation of joining; state of being joined; point of union; place where railways meet.

juncture, jungk'tūr, *n.* A joining or uniting; line or point of joining; point of time; point rendered critical by circumstances.

June, jūn, *n* The sixth month of the year.

jungle, jung'gl, *n.* Land covered with trees, brushwood, etc., or coarse, reedy vegetation.

junior, jū'ni-ėr, *a.* Younger, later or lower in office or rank.—*n.* A per son younger than another or lower in standing.

juniper, jū'ni-pėr, *n.* A coniferous shrub, the berries of which are used to flavor gin.

junket, jung'ket, *n.* Curds mixed with cream, sweetened and flavored, a sweetmeat, a feast.—*vi.* and *t.* To feast.

juridical, jū-rid'ik-al, *a.* Relating to the administration of justice or to a judge.

jurisdiction, jū-ris-dik'shon, *n.* Judicial power, right of exercising authority; district within which power may be exercised.

jurisprudence, jū-ris-prö'dens, *n.* The science of law; the knowledge of the laws, customs, and rights of men necessary for the due administration of justice.

jurist, jū'rist, *n.* A man who professes the science of law; one versed in the law, or more particularly, in the civil law.

just, just, *a.* Right; acting rightly; upright, impartial, fair, due, merited; exact.—*adv.* Exactly, precisely; near or nearly; almost; merely; barely.

justice, jus'tis, *n.* Quality of being just, rectitude, propriety, impartiality; fairness; just treatment; merited reward or punishment, a judge holding a special office.

J

K

kaleidoscope, ka-lī'dos-kōp, n. An optical instrument which exhibits an endless variety of colored figures.

kangaroo, kang'ga-rö, n. An Australian marsupial quadruped that moves forward by leaps.

keel, kēl, n. The principal timber in a ship, extending from stem to stern at the bottom; the corresponding part in iron vessels; the whole ship, something resembling a keel, a coal-barge.—vi. To capsize.

keen, kēn, a. Acute of mind; shrewd; sharp; eager; piercing; severe, bitter.

keep, kēp, vt. (keeping, kept). To hold, to preserve; to guard; to detain, to attend to; to continue any state, course, or action; to obey; to perform; to observe or solemnize; to confine to one's own knowledge; not to betray; to have in pay.—vi. To endure; not to perish or be impaired.—n. Care; guard; sustenance; a donjon or strong tower.

kettle, ket'l, n. A vessel of iron or other metal, used for heating and boiling water, etc.

key, kē, n. An instrument for shutting or opening a lock; a little lever by which certain musical instruments are played on by the fingers; fundamental tone in a piece of music, that which serves to explain a cipher, etc.—vt. To furnish or fasten with a key.

kick, kik, vt. To strike with the foot; to strike in recoiling, as a gun.—vi. To strike with the foot or feet; to manifest opposition to restraint; to recoil.—n. A blow with the foot or feet recoil of a firearm.

kid, kid, n. A young goat; leather made from its skin, a small wooden tub.—vt. (kidding, kidded). To bring forth a kid.

kidnap, kid'nap, vt. (kidnapping, kidnapped). To steal or forcibly abduct a human being.

kidney, kid'ni, n. Either of the two glands which secret the urine; sort or character.

kill, kil, vt. To deprive of life; to slay; to slaughter for food; to deaden (pain), to overpower.

kiln, kil, n. A fabric of brick or stone, which may be heated to harden or dry anything.

kin, kin, n. Race; family, consanguinity or affinity, kindred.—a. Kindred; congenial.

kind, kīnd, n. Race; genus; variety; nature, character.—**In kind**, to pay with produce or commodities.—a. Humane, having tenderness or goodness of nature; benevolent, friendly.

kindergarten, kin'd'ér-gär-tn, n. An infants' school in which amusements are systematically combined with instruction.

kindle, kin'dl, vt. (kindling, kindled). To set on fire; to light; to rouse, to excite to action.—vi. To take fire; to be roused or exasperated.

kindly, kīnd'li, a. Of a kind disposition, congenial, benevolent mild.—adv. In a kind manner; favorably.

kink, kingk, n. A twist in a rope or thread, a crotchet.—vi. To twist or run into knots.

kinsfolk kinz'fōlk n. People of the same kin; kindred; relations.

kinsman, kinz'man, n. A man of the same kin, a relative.

kipper, kip'ér, n. A salmon at the spawning season, a fish split open, salted, and dried or smoked.—vt. To cure (fish) by splitting open, salting, and drying.

kismet, kis'met, n. Fate or destiny.

kiss, kis, vi. To touch with the lips to caress by joining lips; to touch gently.—vi. To join lips; to come in slight contact.—n. A salute given with the lips.

kitchen, ki'chen, n. The room of a house appropriated to cooking.

kitchen-garden, ki'chen-gär-dn, n. A garden for raising vegetables for the table.

kite, kīt, n. A bird of the falcon family; a light frame of wood and paper constructed for flying in the air.

kith, kith, n. Relatives or friends collectively.

kitten, kit'n, n. A young cat.—vi. To bring forth young, as a cat.

kleptomania, klep-tō-mā'ni-a, n. An irresistible mania for pilfering.

knack, nak, n. Facility of performance; dexterity.

knap, nap, vt. (knapping, knapped). To break short (as flints); to snap; to bite off.—n. A short sharp noise; a snap.

knapsack, nap'sak, n. A bag for necessaries borne on the back by soldiers, etc.

knave, nāv, n. A petty rascal; a dishonest man, a card with a soldier or servant on it.

knead, nēd, vt. To work into a mass or suitable consistency for bread, etc.

knee, nē, *n.* The joint connecting the two principal parts of the leg a similar joint; piece of bent timber or iron used in a ship, etc

knife, nīf, *n.;* pl. **knives,** nīvz. A cutting instrument consisting of a blade attached to a handle, cutting part of a machine.

knob, nob, *a.* A hard protuberance; a boss; a round ball at the end of anything.

knock, nok, *vt.* To strike with something thick or heavy; to strike against; to clash.—*vi.* To strike.—*n.* A stroke, a blow, a rap.

knocker, nok'ér, *n.* One who knocks; something on a door for knocking.

knoll, nōl, *n.* A little round hill; ringing of a bell, knell.—*vt.* and *i.* To sound, as a bell.

knot, not, *n.* A complication of threads or cords; a tie, ornamental bunch of ribbon, etc.; hard protuberant joint of a plant, a knob bunch; group; a difficult question a nautical mile (= 1.151 ordinary mile).—*vt.* (knotting, knotted). To tie in a knot; to unite closely.—*vi.* To become knotted, to knit knots.

know, nō, *vt.* (pret. knew, pp. known). To perceive with certainty, to understand, to be aware of; to distinguish, to be acquainted with; to have experience of—*vi.* To have knowledge; not to be doubtful.

knowledge, nol'ej, *n.* The result or condition of knowing; clear perception; learning; information; skill; acquaintance.

K

L

label, lā'bel, *n*. A slip of paper, etc. affixed to something and stating name, contents, etc., a slip affixed to deeds to hold the seal.—*vt*. (labeling, labeled). To affix a label to.

labor, lā'bėr, *n*. Exertion, physical or mental, toil, work done or to be done; laborers in the aggregate the pangs and efforts of childbirth.—*vi*. To engage in labor, to work; to proceed with difficulty, to be burdened.—*vt*. To cultivate; to prosecute with effort.

laborer, lā'bėr-ėr, *n*. One who labors; a man who does work that requires little skill, as distinguished from an artisan.

labyrinth, lab'i-rinth, *n*. A place full of intricacies, a maze, an inexplicable difficulty; a part of the internal ear

lace, lās, *n*. A cord used for fastening boots, etc., ornamental cord or braid; a delicate fabric of interlacing threads.—*vt*. (lacing, laced). To fasten with a lace; to adorn with lace; to interlace; to mingle in small quantity.

lack, lak, *vt*. To want; to be without; to need, to require.—*vi*. To be in want—*n*. Want; deficiency; need; failure.

ladder, lad'er, *n*. An article of wood rope, etc., consisting of two long side-pieces connected by crosspieces forming steps; means of rising to mienence; vertical flaw in stocking, etc.

lag, lag, *a*. Coming behind, sluggish; tardy.—*n*. Quantity of retardation of some movement.—*vi*. (lagging, lagged). To loiter, tarry.

laity, lā'i-ti, *n*. The people, as distinguished from the clergy; non-professional people.

lake, lāk, *n*. A body of water wholly surrounded by land; a pigment of earthy substance with red (or other) coloring matter.

lamb, lam, *n*. The young of the sheep one as gentle or innocent as a iamb.—*vi*. To bring forth young, as sheep.

lame, lām, *a*. Crippled in a limb or limbs; disabled; limping; defective, not satisfactory, not smooth.—*vt*. (laming, lamed). To make lame; to render imperfect and unsound.

lamp, lamp, *n*. A vessel for containing oil to be burned by means of a wick, any contrivance for supply artificial light.

lampoon, lam-pōn', *n*. A scurrilous or personal satire in writing, a satiric attack.—*vt*. To write a lampoon against.

lamprey, lam'prā, *n*. The name of eel-like, scaleless fishes with suctorial mouths, inhabiting fresh and salt waters.

lance, lans, *n*. A weapon consisting of a long shaft with a sharp-pointed head, a long spear.—*vt*. (lancing, lanced). To pierce with a lance, to open with a lancet.

land, land, *n*. The solid matter which constitutes the fixed part of the surface of the globe; soil; estate, country, people of a country or region.—*vt*. and *i*. To set or go on the land, to disembark.

landscape, land'skāp, *n*. A portion of land which the eye can comprehend in a single view; a country scene; picture representing a piece of country.

landslip, landslide, land'slip, land'slīd, *n*. A portion of a hill which slips down, the sliding down of a piece of land.

land-surveying, land'sėr-vā-ing, *n*. Act of surveying land, art of determining the boundaries and extent of land.

languid, lang'gwid, *a*. Wanting energy; listless; dull or heavy; sluggish.

languish, lang'gwish, *vi*. To be or become faint, feeble or spiritless to fade; to sink under sorrow or any continued passion, to look with tenderness.

languor, lang'gér, lang'gwer, *n*. Languidness; lassitude; a listless or dreamy state.

lanolin, lan'ō-lin, *n*. A greasy substance obtained from unwashed wool, used as an ointment.

lantern, lan'tėrn, *n*. A case in which a light is carried; part of a lighthouse in which is the light; erection on the top of a dome, etc., to give light, a tower with the interior open to view.—*vt*. To provide with a lantern.

lanyard, lan'yärd, *n*. A short piece of rope or line, used in ships.

lap, lap, *n*. The loose lower part of a garment; the clothes on the knees of a person when sitting; the knees in this position part of a thing that covers another; single round of a course in races; a lick, as with the tongue, sound as of water rippling on the beach.—*vt*. (lapping, lapped). To lap; to infold, to lick up, to wash gently against.—*vi*. To lie or be turned over; to lick up food; to ripple gently.

larceny, lär'se ni, *n*. Theft of goods or personal property.

lard, lärd, *n.* The fat of swine, after being melted and separated from the flesh.—*vt.* To apply lard to; to fatten, to stuff with bacon, to interlard.

large, lärj, *a.* Great in size, number etc., not small, copious, big; bulky; wide.—**At large**, without restraint, with all details.

lariat, lä'ri-at. *n.* The lasso a long cord or thong of leather with a noose used in catching wild horses, etc.

larva, lär'va, *n.*, pl. **larvae**. An insect in the caterpillar or grub state.

larynx, la'ringks, *n.*, pl. **larynxes, larynges**, la'ringks-ez, la-rin'jēz; The upper part of the windpipe, a cartilaginous cavity serving to modulate the sound of the voice.

lascivious, las-si'vi-us, *a.* Wanton; lewd; lustful.

lash, lash, *n.* The thong of a whip, a whip; a stroke with a whip; a stroke of satire; a cutting remark.—*vt.* To strike with a lash, to satirize; to dash against, as waves; to tie with a rope or cord.— *vi.* To ply the whip; to strike at.

lasso, las'sō, *n.* A rope with a running noose, used for catching wild horses, etc.—*vt.* To catch with a lasso.

last, läst, *a.* That comes after all the others; latest, final, next before the present; utmost.—*adv.* The last time in conclusion.—*vi.* To continue in time; to endure; not to decay or perish.—*vt.* To form on or by a last.—*n.* A mold of the foot on which boots are formed; a weight of 4000 lbs.

late, lāt, *a.* Coming after the usual time; slow; not early; existing not long ago, but not now, deceased recent; modern; last or recently in any place, office, etc.—*adv.* At a late time or period; recently.

Latin, la'tin, *a.* Pertaining to the Latins, a people of Latium, in Italy; Roman.—*n.* The language of the ancient Romans

latitude, la'ti-tūd, *n.* Breadth; width; extent from side to side scope, laxity; distance north or south of the equator, measured on a meridian; distance of a star north or south of the ecliptic.

laud, läd, *n.* Praise; a hymn of praise; *pl.* a service of the church comprising psalms of praise.—*vt.* To praise; to celebrate.

laudanum, lä'da-num, *n.* Opium prepared in spirit of wine; tincture of opium.

laugh, läf, *vi.* To make the involuntary noise which sudden merriment excites; to treat with some contempt; to appear gay, bright, or brilliant.—*vt.* To express by laughing; to affect or effect by laughter.—*n.* The act of laughing; short fit of laughing.

laughter, läf'tèr, *n.* Act or sound of laughing, expression of mirth peculiar to man

launch, länsh, *vt.* To throw, to cause to slide into the water, to put out into another sphere of duty, etc. —*vi.* To glide, as a ship into the water, to enter on a new field of activity, to expatiate in language.—*n.* Act of launching the largest boat carried by a man-of-war.

laundry, län'dri, *n.* Place where clothes are washed and dressed.

lavish, lav'ish, *a.* Profuse, liberal to a fault; extravagant; superabundant.—*vt.* To expend with profusion, to squander.

law, lä, *n.* A rule prescribed by authority; a statute; a precept; such rules or statues collectively, legal procedure; litigation; a principle deduced from practice or observation; a formal statement of facts observed in natural phenomena.

lax, laks, *a.* Loose; flabby; soft; slack; vague; equivocal; not strict remiss; having too frequent discharges from the bowels.

laxative, laks'at iv, *a.* Having the power of relieving from constipation.—*n.* A gentle purgative.

lay, lä, *vt.* (pret. and pp. laid). To place in a lying position; to set or place in general, to impose, to bring into a certain state; to settle; to allay; to place at hazard; to wager; to contrive.—*vi.* To bring forth eggs; wager.—*n.* A stratum; a layer; one rank in a series reckoned upward, a song a narrative poem.—*a.* Not clerical; not professional.

layer, lä'èr, *n.* One who or that which lays, a stratum; a coat, as of paint; a row of masonry, etc.; a shoot of a plant, not detached from the stalk, partly laid underground for growth.—*vt.* To propagate by bending a shoot into the soil.

lead, lēd, *vt.* (pret. and pp. led). To guide or conduct, to direct and govern; to precede, to entice; to influence, to spend, to begin.—*vi.* To go before and show the way; to be chief or commander; to draw; to have a tendency.—*n.* Guidance; precedence.

leader, lēd'èr, *n.* One who leads; a guide; captain; head of a party; editorial article in a newspaper.

leaf, lēf, *n.*; pl. **leaves**, lēvz. One of the thin, expanded, deciduous growths of a plant, a part of a book containing two pages; a very thin plate, the movable side of a table, one side of a double door.—*vi.* To shoot out leaves; to produce leaves.

league, lēg, *n.* A combination between states for their mutual aid; an alliance, a compact, a measure of three miles or knots.—*vi.* (leaguing, leagued). To form a league; to confederate.

leak, lēk, *n.* A fissure in a vessel that admits water, or permits it to escape; the passing of fluid through an aperture.—*vi.* To let water in or out of a vessel through a crevice.

lean, lēn, *vi.* (pret. and pp. leaned). To slope or slant, to incline, to tend; to bend so as to rest on something; to depend.—*vt.* To cause to lean; to support or rest.

learn, lėrn, *vt.* (pret. and pp. learned). To gain knowledge of or skill in, to acquire by study.—*vi.* To gain knowledge; to receive instruction.

least, lēst, *a.* Smallest.—*adv.* In the smallest or lowest degree.—**At least, at the least,** to say no more; at the lowest degree.

leave, lēv, *n.* Permission; liberty granted; a formal parting of friends.—*vt.* (leaving, left). To let remain; to have remaining at death; to bequeath, to quit, to abandon to refer.—*vi.* To depart; to desist.

leaven, lev'n, *n.* A substance that produces fermentation, as in dough; yeast; barm.—*vt.* To mix with leaven; to excite fermentation in, to imbue.

lecher, lech'ėr, *n.* A man given to lewdness.—*vi.* To practice lewdness, to indulge lust.

lecture, lek'tūr, *n.* A discourse on any subject; a reprimand; a formal reproof.—*vi.* (lecturing, lectured). To deliver a lecture or lectures.—*vt.* To reprimand; to reprove.

leer, lēr, *n.* A side glance, an arch or affected glance.—*vi.* To give a leer; to look meaningly.—*vt.* To turn with a leer, to affect with a leer.

leeway, lē'wā, *n.* The drifting of a ship to the leeward.—**To make up leeway,** to overtake work in arrears.

left, left, *a.* Denoting the part opposed to the right of the body.—*n.* The side opposite to the right.

left-handed, left'hand-ed, *a.* Using the left hand and arm with more dexterity than the right; sinister; insincere; awkward.

leg, leg, *n.* The limb of an animal, a lower or posterior limb; the long or slender

support of anything.

legal, lē'gal, *a.* According to, pertaining to, or permitted by law lawful; judicial.

legion, lē'jon, *n.* A Roman body of infantry soldiers, in number from 3000 to above 6000; a military force, a great number.

legislation le-jis-lā'shon, *n.* Act of making a law or laws; laws or statutes enacted.

leisure, lē'zhur or lezh'ūr, *n.* Freedom from occupation; vacant time.—*a.* Not spent in labor; vacant.

lemon, le'mon, *n.* An acid fruit of the orange kind; the tree that produces this fruit.

lemonade, le-mon-ād', *n.* A beverage, usually aerated, consisting of lemon-juice mixed with water and sweetened.

lemur, lē'mėr, *n.* A quadrumanous mammal, allied to monkeys and rodents.

lend, lend, *vt.* (lending, lent). To furnish on condition of the thing being returned; to afford or grant *refl.* to accommodate.

length, length, *n.* State or quality of being long; extent from end to end, extension, long duration, extent or degree.—**At length,** at full extent; at last.

leprosy, lep'rō-si, *n.* A foul cutaneous disease characterized by dusky red or livid tubercles on the face or extremities.

less, les, *a.* Smaller; not so large or great.—*adv.* In a smaller or lower degree.—*n.* A smaller quantity.

lessen, les'n, *vt.* To make less, to lower to depreciate.—*vi.* To become less; to abate.

lesson, les'n, *n.* Portion which a pupil learns at one time; portion of scripture read in divine service; something to be learned, severe lecture; truth taught by experience.

let, let, *vt.* (letting, let). To permit; to allow, to lease.—*vi.* To be leased or let.

let, let, *vt.* To hinder; to impede.—*n.* A hindrance, impediment.

letter, let'ėr, *n.* A mark used as the representative of a sound; a written message, an epistle, the literal meaning; in *printing,* a single type; *pl.* learning; erudition.—*vt.* To impress or form letters on.

level, le'vel, *n.* An instrument for detecting variation from a horizontal surface; an instrument by which to find a horizontal line; a horizontal line or plane; a surface without inequalities, usual elevation; equal elevation with something else; horizontal gallery in a mine.—*a.* Horizontal, even, flat having no degree of superiority.— *vt.* (leveling leveled).

To make level, to lay fiat on the ground, to reduce to equality; to point, in taking aim.—*vi*. To point a gun, etc.; to aim.

lexicon, leks'i-kon, *n*. A word-book; a dictionary a vocabulary containing an alphabetical arrangement of the words in a language with the definition of each.

liable, lī'a-bl, *a*. Answerable for consequences; responsible; subject; exposed: with *to*.

liaison, lē-ā-zōng, *n*. A bond of union; an illicit intimacy between a man and woman.

libation, lī-bā'shon, *n*. Act of pouring a liquor, usually wine, on the ground or on a victim in sacrifice in honor of some deity; the wine or other liquor so poured.

libel, lī'bel, *n*. A defamatory writing; a malicious publication; the written statement of a plaintiff's ground of complaint against a defendant.—*vt*. (libeling, libeled). To frame a libel against, to lampoon to exhibit a charge against in court.

liberal, lī'bér-al, *a*. Generous; ample; profuse; favorable to reform or progress; not too literal or strict; free.—*n*. One who advocates great political freedom.

liberty, lī'bėr-ti, *n*. State or condition of one who is free; privilege; immunity; license, district within which certain exclusive privileges may be exercised; freedom of action or speech beyond civility or decorum; state of being disengaged.

library, lī'bra-ri, *n*. A collection of books, edifice or apartment for holding books.

librate, lī'brāt, *vt*. To poise; to balance.—*vi*. To move, as a balance to be poised.

lick, lik, *vt*. To draw the tongue over the surface of, to lap, to take in by the tongue, to beat.—*n*. A drawing of the tongue over anything; a slight smear or coat; a blow.

lie, lī, *vi*. (lying, lied). To utter falsehood with deceitful intention.—*n*. A falsehood; an intentional violation of truth.

lie, lī, *vi*. (lying, pret. lay, pp. lain). To occupy a horizontal position; to rest on anything lengthwise; to be situated, to remain, to be incumbent; to exist; to depend; to be sustainable in law.—**To lie in**, to be in childbed.—**To lie to**, to stop and remain stationary.—*n*. Relative position of objects; general bearing or direction.

life, līf, *n.;* pl. **lives**, līvz. State of animals and plants in which the natural functions are performed; vitality; present state of existence; time from birth to death; manner of living; animal being; spirit; vivacity, the living form, exact resemblance; rank in society; human affairs, a person, narrative of a life, eternal felicity.

lift, lift, *vt*. To raise to a higher position to hoist, to elevate, to raise in spirit; to collect when due.; vi. To raise; to rise.—*n*. Act of lifting; assistance, that which is to be raised; an elevator or hoist.

ligament, li'ga-ment, *n*. That which unites one thing to another; a band; a substance serving to bind one bone to another.

light, līt, *n*. That by which objects are rendered visible; day; that which gives or admits light; illumination of mind knowledge, open view; explanation; point of view; situation, spiritual illumination.—*a*. Bright, clear, not deep, as color; not heavy; not difficult; easy to be digested, active, not laden, slight moderate; unsteady; gay; trifling, wanton, sandy, having a sensation of giddiness; employed in light work.—*adv*. Lightly; cheaply.—*vt*. (pret. and pp. lighted or lit). To give light to, to enlighten to ignite.—*vi*. To brighten; to descend, as from a horse, etc., to alight, to come by chance.

like, līk, *a*. Equal; similar; resembling; likely; feeling disposed.—*adv*. or *prep*. In the same manner similarly; likely.—*vt*. (liking, liked). To be pleased with; to approve.—*vi*. To be pleased, to choose.—*n*. Some person or thing resembling another; a counterpart; a liking; a fancy.

lilt, lilt, *vt*. and *i*. To sing cheerfully; to give musical utterance.—*n*. A song; a tune.

limb, lim, *n*. The arm or leg, especially the latter; a branch of a tree; graduated edge of a quadrant etc.; border of the disc of the sun moon, etc.—*vt*. To supply with limbs, to tear off the limbs of.

limber, lim'bėr, *a*. Flexible, pliant.—*n*. A carriage with ammunition boxes attached to the guncarriage.—*vt*. and *i*. To attach the limber to the gun-carriage.

limbo, lim'bo, *n*. A supposed region beyond this world for souls of innocent persons ignorant of Christianity; any similar region; a prison of confinement.

lime, līm, *n*. Any viscous substance, calcareous earth used in cement; mortar made with lime; the linden-tree, a tree producing an inferior sort of lemon.—*vt*.

L

(liming, limed). To smear or manure with Lime, to ensnare, to cement.

line, līn. *n.·* A small rope or cord; a thread-like marking; a stroke or score, a row of soldiers, ships words, etc.; a verse; an outline; a short written communication; course of procedure, etc., connected series, as of descendants; series of public conveyances, as steamers, the twelfth part of an inch; the equator; the regular infantry of an army; *pl.* works covering extended positions and presenting a front in only one direction to the enemy.—*vt.* (lining lined). To draw lines upon; to set with men or things in lines; to cover on the inside, to put in the inside of.

lineament, lin'ē-a-ment, *n.* One of the lines which mark the features feature; form.

linen, lin'en, *n.* Cloth made of flax under clothing.—*a.* Made of flax, resembling linen cloth.

linger, ling'gèr, *vi.* To delay; to loiter; to hesitate; to remain long.— *vt.* To spend wearily.

link, lingk, *n.* A single ring of a chain anything closed like a link; anything connecting; a measure of 7.92 inches; a torch.—*vi.* To be connected.—*vt.* To join or connect, as by links to unite.

linseed, lin'sēd, *n.* Flax-seed.

lintel, lin'tel, *n.* The horizontal part of the door or window frame.

lion, lī'on, *n.* A carnivorous animal of the cat family; a sign in the zodiac Leo; an object of interest and curiosity.

liquefy, lik'wē-fī, *vt.* To melt, to dissolve by heat.—*vi.* To become liquid.

liqueur, li-kūr' or li-kör', *n.* An alcoholic beverage sweetened and containing some infusion of fruits or aromatic substances.

liquid, lik'wid, *a.* Fluid; not solid; soft, smooth, devoid *of* harshness.—*n.* A fluid; a letter with a smooth flowing sound, as l and r.

liquidate, lik'wid-āt, *vt.* To clear from obscurity; to adjust; to settle, adjust, and apportion, as a bankrupt's affairs.

lisp, lisp, *vi.* To pronounce the sibilant letters imperfectly, as in pronouncing th for s, to speak imperfectly, as a child.— *vt.* To pronounce with a lisp, or imperfectly.—*n.* The habit or act of lisping.

list, list, *n.* The selvedge of cloth; a limit or border, a roll or catalogue: inclination to one side, *pl.* a field inclosed for a combat.—*vt.* To enroll, to enlist.—*vi.*

To enlist, as in the army; to desire; to be disposed; to hearken.

literature, li'tèr-a-tū r, *n.* Learning; literary knowledge; collective writings of a country or period belles-lettres; the literary profession.

lithology, li-thol'o-ji, *n.* The knowledge of rocks; study of the mineral structure of rocks.

litigant, li'ti-gant, *a.* Disposed to litigate; engaged in a lawsuit.—*n.* One engaged in a lawsuit.

litigate, li'ti-gāt, *vt.* To contest in law. *vi.* To carry on a suit by judicial process.

little, lit'1, *a.* Small in size or extent; short in duration; slight; mean.—*n.* A small quantity, space, etc.—A **little,** somewhat.—*adv.* In a small degree or quantity.

liturgy, li'ter-ji, *n.* A ritual or established formulas for public worship.

live, liv, *vi.* (living, lived). To exist; to be alive, to dwell, to conduct oneself in life; to feed or subsist; to acquire a livelihood, to be exempt from spiritual death—*vt.* To lead, pass or spend.

live, līv, *a.* Having life, alive, not dead, ignited; vivid, as color.

load, lōd, *vt.* To charge with a load; to burden; to encumber, to bestow in great abundance; to charge, as a gun.—*n.* A burden, cargo, a grievous weight; something that oppresses.

loaf, lōf, *n.;* pl. **loaves,** lōvz. A mass of bread formed by the baker; a conical lump of sugar.—*vi.* To lounge.—*vt.* To spend idly.

loath, loth, lōth, *a.* Disliking; unwilling; averse; not inclined; reluctant.

loathe, lōTH, *vt.* (loathing, loathed). To feel disgust at, to abhor, to abominate.—*vi.* To feel nausea or abhorrence.

loathing, lōTH'ing, *n.* Extreme disgust or aversion; abhorrence; detestation.

loathness, lōTH'sum, *a.* Exciting disgust; disgusting; detestable; abhorrent.

lob, lob, *n.* A dolt, a lout.—*vt.* (lobbing, lobbed). To throw or toss slowly.

lobby, lob'i, *n.* An apartment giving admission to others; an entrance-hall.

lobe, lōb, *n.* A round projecting part of something; such a part of the liver, lungs, brain, etc., the lower soft part of the ear.

lobster, lob'stèr, *n.* A ten-footed crustacean with large claws, allied to the crab.

local, lō'kal, *a.* Pertaining to a particular place, confined to a spot or definite district.—*n*. A local item of news; a local railway train.

lock, lok, *n*. An appliance for fastening doors, etc.; mechanism by which a firearm is discharged; a fastening together, inclosure in a canal, with gates at either end; a tuft or ringlet of hair.—*vt*. To fasten with a lock and key, to shut up or confine; to join firmly; to embrace closely.—*vi*. To become fast, to unite closely by mutual insertion.

lodge, loj, *n*. A small country house, a temporary abode, place where members of a society, as freemasons, meet; the society itself.—*vt*. (lodging, lodged). To furnish with temporary accommodation; to set or deposit for keeping; to beat down (growing crops).—*vi*. To have a temporary abode; to settle, to reside.

loft, loft, *n*. The space below and between the rafters; a gallery raised within a larger apartment or in a church.

log, log, *n*. A bulky piece of timber unhewed; a floating contrivance for measuring the rate of a ship's velocity; a log-book.

loiter, loi'tèr, *vi*. To be slow in moving; to spend time idly; to hang about.—*vi*. To waste carelessly with *away*.

loll, lol, *vi*. (lolling, lolled). To lean idly, to lie at ease, to hang out, as the tongue of a dog.—*vt*. To suffer to hang out.

lone, lōn, *a*. Solitary; unfrequented; single.

long, long, *a*. Drawn out in a line; drawn out in time, tedious protracted; late; containing much verbal matter.—*n*. Something that is long.—*adv*. To a great extent in space or in time, at a point of duration far distant.—*vi*. To desire eagerly; with *for*.

longitude, lon'ji-tūd, *n*. Length; distance on the surface of the globe east or west, measured by meridians.

look, lük, *vi*. To direct the eye so as to see; to gaze; to consider; to expect; to heed; to face; to appear.— *vt*. To see, to express by a look.—*n*. Act of looking; sight; gaze; glance; mien, aspect.

loose, lös, *a*. Not attached; untied not dense or compact; vague, careless, having lax bowels, unchaste.—*vt*. (loosing, loosed). To untie or unbind; to detach; to set free; to relax; to loosen.

loot, löt, *n*. Booty; plunder, especially such as is taken in a sacked city.—*vt*. To plunder.

lord, lord, *n*. A master; a ruler; proprietor of a manor, a nobleman, a British title applied to peers, sons of dukes and mar-

quises, and the eldest sons of earls; honorary title of certain high officials, (with *cap*.) the Supreme Being.—*vi*. To act as a lord; to rule with arbitrary or despotic sway.

lose, löz, *vt*. (losing, lost). To cease to possess, as through accident, to fail to keep; to forfeit; not to gain or win, to miss, to cease or fail to see or hear; to misuse.— *vi*. To suffer loss; not to win.

lost, lost, *p.a*. Gone from our hold, view, etc., not to be found, ruined wasted; forfeited; perplexed; alienated.

lot, lot, *n*. A person's part or share fate which falls to one; part in life allotted to a person a distinct portion, a considerable quantity or number; something used to decide what is yet undecided.— *vt*. (lotting, lotted). To assign by lot; to sort; to portion.

lounge, lounj, *vi*. (lounging lounged). To loiter; to loll.—*n*. An idle gait or stroll; act of reclining at ease; a place for lounging.

love, luv, *vt*. (loving loved). To regard with affection, to like, to delight in.—*vi*. To be in love; to be tenderly attached.— *n*. Warm affection; fond attachment; the passion between the sexes, the object beloved a word of endearment, Cupid, the god of love; the score of nothing at tennis, etc.

low, lō, *a*. Depressed below any given surface or place; not high; deep; below the usual rate; not loud, wanting strength, mean, dishonorable; not sublime; plain.— *adv*. Not aloft, under the usual price; near the ground, not loudly.

luck, luk, *n*. That which happens to a person; chance; hap; fortune; success.

lucky, luk'i, *a*. Meeting with good luck or success; fortunate; auspicious.

ludicrous, lū'di-krus, *a*. That serves for sport; laughable; droll ridiculous.

luggage, lug'āj, *n*. Anything cumbersome and heavy; a traveller's baggage.

lull, lul, *vt*. To sing to, as to a child; to soothe.—*vi*. To subside, to become calm.—*n*. A season of quiet or cessation.

lumber, lum'bèr, *n*. Anything useless and cumbersome, in America timber sawed or split for use.—*vt*. To fill with lumber; to heap together in disorder.—*vi*. To move heavily, as a vehicle, in America to cut and prepare timber.

lump, lump, *n*. A small mass of matter; a mass of things.—*vt*. To throw into a mass; to take in the gross.

L

lunge, lunj, *n.* A sudden thrust or pass, as with a sword.—*vi.* (lunging, lunged). To make a thrust.

lurch, lėrch, *vi.* To lurk; to roll or sway to one side.—*n.* A sudden roll or stagger; a difficult or helpless position.

lure, lūr, *n.* Something held out to call a trained hawk; a bait; any enticement.— *vt.* (luring, lured). To attract by a lure or bait; to entice.

lust, lust, *n.* Longing desire; carnal appetite; depraved affections.—*vi.* To desire eagerly; to have carnal desire.

luster, lus'ter, *n.* Brightness; brilliancy, renown, a branched chandelier ornamented with cut glass a glossy fabric for dress.

luxury, luks'ū-ri, *n.* Extravagant indulgence; that which gratifies a fastidious appetite; anything delightful to the senses.

lymphatic, lim-fat'ik, *a.* Pertaining to lymph; phlegmatic; sluggish.— *n.* A vessel in animal bodies which contains or conveys lymph.

lynx, lingks, *n.* A carnivorous anima;resembling the cat, noted for its keen sight.

lyric, lyrical, li'rik, li'rik-al, *a.* Pertaining to a lyre; designating that species of poetry which has reference to the individual emotions of the poet, such as songs.—**lyric,** li'rik, *n.* A lyric poem; an author of lyric poems.

M

Machiavelian, ma'ki-a-vē l"i-an, *a*. Pertaining to *Machiavelli*, or denoting his principles; cunning in political management.

machine, ma-shēn', *n*. Any contrivance which serves to regulate the effect of a given force or to produce or change motion, an organized system; a person who acts as the tool of another.—*vt*. To apply machinery to; to produce by machinery.

mad, mad, *a*. Disordered in intellect; insane; crazy; frantic; furious; infatuated.—*vt*. (madding, madded). To make mad.

Magi, mā'jī, *n.pl*. The caste of priests among the ancient Medes and Persians; holy men or sages of the East.

magic, ma'jik, *n*. The art of producing effects by superhuman means, sorcery, enchantment; power similar to that of enchantment. —*a*. Pertaining to magic working or worked by or as if by magic.

magnesia, mag-nē'si-a, *n*. Oxide of magnesium, a white slightly alkaline powder.

magnet, mag'net, *n*. The loadstone, which has the property of attracting iron; a bar of iron or steel to which the properties of the loadstone have been imparted.

magnificence, mag-nif'i-sens, *n*. Grandeur of appearance; splendor, pomp.

magnify, mag'ni-fī, *vt*. To make great or greater, to increase the apparent dimensions of; to extol; to exaggerate.—*vi*. To possess the quality of causing objects to appear larger.

maiden, mād'n, *n*. A maid or virgin, an old Scottish instrument of capital punishment resembling the guillotine.—*a*. Pertaining to maidens; unpolluted; unused; first.

mail, māl, *n*. A bag for conveying letters, etc.; letters conveyed; person or conveyance carrying the mail; armor of chain-work, etc.—*vt*. (mailing, mailed). To send by mail; to post; to arm with mail.

main, mān, *a*. Chief, or most important mighty; vast; directly applied; used with all one's might.—*n*. Strength; great effort; chief or main portion; the ocean; a principal gas or water pipe in a street;

a hand at dice, a match at cockfighting.

major, mā'jėr, *a*. The greater in number, quantity, or extent; the more important.—*n*. A military officer next above a captain; a person aged twenty-one years complete.

majority, ma-jo'ri-ti, *n*. The greater number; excess of one number over another; full age; rank or commission of a major.

make, māk, *vt*. (making, made). To produce or effect; to cause to be; to compose; to constitute; to perform; to cause to have any quality to force; to gain; to complete; to arrive at, to have within sight.—*vi*. To act or do; to tend; to contribute; to flow toward land.—*n*. Form; structure texture.

malcontent, mal'kon-tent, *n*. A discontented person.—*a*. Discontent-ed with the rule under which one lives.

male, māl, *a*. Pertaining to the sex that begets young; masculine.—*n*. One of the sex that begets young; a plant which has stamens only.

malt, mält, *n*. Barley or other grain steeped in water till it germinates, then dried in a kiln and used in brewing.—*vt*. To make into malt.—*vi*. To become malt.

man, man, *n*., *pl*. **men**, men. A human being; a male adult of the human race; mankind; the male sex; a male servant; a piece in a game as chess, etc.—*vt*. (manning, manned). To furnish with men, to guard with men; *refl*. To infuse courage into.

manacle, man'a-kl, *n*. An instrument of iron for fastening the hands; a handcuff; used chiefly in the plural.—*vt*. (manacling, manacled). To put manacles on; to fetter.

manage, man'āj, *vt*. (managing, managed). To wield, to direct in riding; to conduct or administer; to have under command, to treat with judgment.—*vi*. To conduct affairs.

mandatory, man'da-to-ri, *a*. Containing a command; preceptive directory.

maneuver, ma-nū'vėr or ma-nö'vėr, *n*. A regulated movement, particularly of troops or ships; management with address; stratagem.—*vi*. (maneuvering, maneuvered). To perform military or naval maneuvers; to employ stratagem; to manage with address.—*vt*. To cause to perform maneuvers.

mangle, mang'gl, *vt*. (mangling mangled). To mutilate; to lacerate, to smooth, as linen.—*n*. A rolling press or small calender for smoothing cotton or linen.

manicure, man'i-kūr, n. One whose occupation is to trim the nails, etc., of the hand.

manifest, man'i-fest, a. Clearly visible; evident; obvious.—vt. To make manifest; to display or exhibit.—n. A document stating a ship's cargo, destination, etc.

manifold, man'i-fōld, a. Numerous and various, of divers kinds.—vt. To multiply impressions of, as by a copying apparatus.

manipulate, ma-nip'ū-lāt, vt. To treat with the hands: to handle; to operate upon so as to disguise.

manner, man'ėr n. The mode in which anything is done; method; bearing or conduct; pl. carriage or behavior; civility in society; sort or kind

mannerism, man'ėr-izm, n. Adherence to the same manner; tasteless uniformity of style; peculiarity of personal manner.

mantle, man'tl, n. A kind of cloak worn over other garments; something that covers and conceals; incandescent hood for gas jet.—vt. (mantling, mantled). To cloak; to cover as with a mantle.—vi. To become covered with a coating; to cream; to display superficial changes of hue.

manual, man'ū-al, a. Performed by the hand; used or made by the hand.—n. A small book; a compendium, the servicebook of the R. Catholic Church; keyboard of an organ.

manufacture, man-ū-fak'tūr, n. The process of making anything by hand or machinery; something made from raw materials.—vt. (manufacturing, manufactured). To fabricate from raw materials; to fabricate without real grounds.—vi. To be occupied in manufactures.

manure, man-ūr', vt. (manuring, manured). To fertilize with nutritive substances.—n. Any substance added to soil to accelerate or increase the production of the crops.

manuscript, man'ū-skript, n. A paper written with the hand often contracted to MS pl. MSS.—a. Written with the hand.

many, me'ni, a. Forming or comprising a number; numerous.— **The many,** the great majority of people; the crowd..— **So many,** the same number of; a certain number indefinitely.

marble, mär'bl, n. A calcareous stone of compact texture; a little hard ball used

by boys in play; an inscribed or sculptured marble stone.—a. Made of or like marble.—vt. (marbling, marbled). To stain like marble.

march, märch, vi. To move by steps and in order, as soldiers; to walk in a stately manner; to progress; to be situated next. vt. To cause to march.—n. The measured walk of a body of men; a stately walk; distance passed over; a musical composition to regulate the march of troops etc., a frontier or boundary (usually in pl.); the third month of the year.

marine, ma-rēn', a. Pertaining to the sea; found in the sea; used at sea naval, maritime.—n. A soldier who serves on board of a man-of-war; collective shipping of a country; whole economy of naval affairs.

maritime, ma'ri-tīm, a. Relating to the sea; naval; bordering on the sea; having a navy and commerce by sea.

mark, märk, n. A visible sign or impression on something; a distinguishing sign; indication or evidence, preeminence or importance, a characteristic; heed or regard, object aimed at; proper standard, extreme estimate; a German coin.—vt. To make a mark or marks on, to denote (often with out), to regard, observe, heed.—vi. To note; to observe critically; to remark.

market, mär'ket, n. An occasion on which goods are publicly exposed for sale; place in which goods are exposed for sale; rate of purchase and sale; demand for commodities; privilege of keeping a public market.—vi. To deal in a market.—vt. To offer for sale in a market.

maroon, ma-rön, n. A fugitive slave in the W. Indies; a brownish crimson or claret color.—vt. To land and leave on a desolate island.

marrow, ma'rō, n. A soft substance in the cavities of bones; the best part; a kind of gourd, also called vegetable marrow.

marry, ma'ri, vt. (marrying, married). To unite in wedlock, to dispose of in wedlock; to take for husband or wife.—vi. To take a husband or a wife.—interj. Indeed; forsooth.

marshal, mär'shal, n. One who regulates rank and order at a feast, procession, etc.; a military officer of the highest rank, Generally called field-marshal.— vt. (marshalling, marshalled). To dispose in order, to array.

masculine, mas'kū-lin, a. Male manly;

robust; bold or unwomanly; designating nouns which are the names of male animals, etc.

mash, mash, *n*. A mixture of ingredients beaten or blended together; a mixture of ground malt and warm water yielding wort.—*vt*. To mix; to beat into a confused mass.

mask, mask, *n*. A cover for the face; a masquerade; a sort of play common in the 16th and 17th centuries; pretense.—*vt*. To cover with a mask; to disguise; to hide.

masquerade, mas-kėr-ā d', *n*. An assembly of persons wearing masks; a disguise.—*vi*. To assemble in masks; to go in disguise.

mass, mas, *n*. A body of matter, a lump; magnitude; an assemblage collection; the generality; the communion service in the R. Catholic Church.—**The masses**, the populace.—*vt*. and *i*. To form into a mass; to assemble in crowds.

massacre, mas'sa-kėr, *n*. Ruthless, unnecessary, or indiscriminate slaughter—*vt*. (massacring, massacred) To kill with indiscriminate violence, to slaughter.

massage, ma-säzh' or mas'ā j, *n*. A process of kneading, rubbing, pressing, etc., parts of a person s body to effect a cure.—*vt*. (massaging, massaged). To treat by this process.

massive, mas'iv, *a*. Bulky and heavy; ponderous; pertaining to a mass; not local or special.

mast, mäst, *n*. A long upright timber in a vessel, supporting the yards, sails, and rigging, the fruit of the oak, beech, etc. (no *pl*.).—*vt*. To supply with a mast or masts.

master, mäs'tėr, *n*. One who rules or directs; an employer; owner; captain of a merchant ship teacher in a school; a man eminently skilled in some art; a word of address for men (written Mr. and pron. mis'ter) and boys (written in full); a vessel having masts.—*vt*. To bring under control to make oneself master of.—*a*. Belonging to a master, chief.

mat, māt, *n*. An article of interwoven rushes, twine, etc., used for cleaning or protecting, anything growing thickly or closely interwoven.—*vt*. (matting, matted). To cover with mats, to entangle.—*vi*. To grow thickly together.

matador, ma-ta-dōr', *n*. The man appointed to kill the bull in bullfights; a card in ombre and quadrille

match, mach, *n*. A person or thing equal to another, union by marriage, one to be married; a contest; a small body that catches fire readily or ignites by friction.—*vt*. To equal; to show an equal to; to set against as equal in contest; to suit, to marry.—*vi*. To be united in marriage; to suit; to tally.

mate, māt, *n*. A companion; a match, a husband or wife; second officer in a ship.—*vt*. (mating, mated). To equal; to match, to marry; to checkmate.

material, ma-tē'ri-al, *a*. Consisting of matter not spiritual, important; essential; substantial.—*n*. Anything composed of matter, substance of which anything is made.

materialize, ma-tē'ri-al-īz, *vt*. To reduce to a state of matter; to regard as matter.

mathematics, ma-thē-ma'tiks, *n*. The science of magnitude and number, comprising arithmetic, geometry, algebra, etc.

matron, mā'tron *n*. An elderly married woman or an elderly lady; head nurse or superintendent of a hospital, etc.

matter, mat'ėr, *n*. Not mind; body; that of which anything is made; substance as distinct from form; subject, business, circumstance; import; moment; pus.—*vi*. To be of importance; to signify; to form pus.

May, mā, *n*. The fifth month of the year, hawthorn blossom—*vi*. To celebrate the festivities of Mayday.—*v*. *aux*. (pret. might, mit). Used to imply possibility, opportunity, permission, desire, etc.

mead, mēd, *n*. A fermented liquor made from honey and water; a meadow: *poet*.

meadow, me'dō, *n*. A low level tract of land under grass.—*a*. Belonging to a meadow.

meal, mēl, *n*. Portion of food taken at one time; a repast; ground grain, flour.

mealy-mouthed, mē l'i-mouTHd, *a*. Unwilling to tell the truth in plain language; soft-spoken; inclined to hypocrisy.

mean, mēn, *a*. Low in rank or birth; humble, base contemptible; occupying a middle position; middle; intermediate.—*n*. What is intermediate average rate or degree; medium; *pl*. measure or measures adopted; agency (generally used as *sing*.), income or resources.—*vt*. (pret. and pp. *meant*). To have in the mind, to intend; to signify; to import.—*vi*. To have thought or ideas, or to have meaning.

M

measure, me'zhŭr, *n.* The extent or magnitude of a thing; a standard of size, a measuring rod or line; that which is allotted; moderation; just degree; course of action; legislative proposal; musical time; meter; a grave solemn dance; *pl.* beds or strata.—*vt.* (measuring, measured). To ascertain the extent or capacity of; to estimate; to value; to pass through or over, to proportion; to allot.—*vi.* To have a certain extent.

measurement, me'zhŭr-ment, *n.* Act of measuring; amount ascertained.

meat, mēt, *n.* Food in general; the flesh of animals used as food; the edible portion of something (the *meat* of an egg).

mechanic, me-kan'ik, *a.* Mechanical.—*n.* An artisan, an artisan employed in making and repairing machinery.

mechanical, me-kan'ik-al, *a.* Pertaining to mechanism or machinery, resembling a machine; done by the mere force of habit; pertaining to material forces, physical.

medicate, med'i-kāt, *vt.* (medicating, medicated). To treat with medicine; to impregnate with anything medicinal.

medicine, med'sin, *n.* Any substance used as a remedy for disease; a drug; the science and art of curing diseases.

mediocrity, mē-di-ok'ri-ti, *n.* State of being mediocre, a moderate degree or rate; a person of mediocre talents or abilities.

meditate, med'i-tāt, *vi.* (meditating, meditated). To dwell on anything in thought, to cogitate.—*vt.* To think on; to scheme; to intend.

Mediterranean, med'i-te-rā'nē-an, *a.* Surrounded by land: now applied exclusively to the *Mediterranean* Sea.

medium, mē 'di-um, *n.*; pl. **-ia**, **-iums**. Something holding a middle position; a mean; means of motion or action, agency of transmission; instrumentality.—*a.* Middle; middling.

meet, mēt, *vt.* (meeting, met). To come face to face with; to come in contact with, to encounter, to light on, to receive; to satisfy.—*vi.* To come together; to encounter; to assemble.—*n.* A meeting, as of huntsmen.—*a.* Fit; suitable; proper.

mellow, mel'ō, *a.* Soft with ripeness; soft to the ear, eye, or taste; toned down by time; half-tipsy.— *vt.* To make mellow, to soften.—*vi.* To become mellow.

melodrama, me-lō-dra'ma, *n.* Properly a musical drama, a serious play, with startling incidents, exaggerated sentiment, and splendid decoration.

melody, me'lō-di, *n.* An agreeable succession of sounds; sweetness of sound the particular air or tune of a musical piece.

melt, melt, *vt.* To reduce from a solid to a liquid state by heat; to soften; to overcome with tender emotion.—*vi.* To become liquid; to dissolve; to be softened to love, pity, etc.; to pass by imperceptible degrees.

member, mem'bér, *n.* An organ or limb of an animal body, part of an aggregate; one of the persons composing a society, etc.; a representative in a legislative body.

memoir, mem'oir, mem'wär, *n.* A written account of events or transactions; a biographical notice; recollections of one's life (usually in the *pl.*).

memorial, mē-mō'ri-al, *a.* Pertaining to memory or remembrance; serving to commemorate.—*n.* That which preserves the memory of something; a monument; memorandum, a written representation of facts, made as the ground of a petition.

memory, mem'ō-ri, *n.* The faculty of the mind by which it retains knowledge or ideas, remembrance, recollection; the time within which a person may remember what is past; something remembered.

mend, mend, *vt.* To repair; to restore to a sound state, to amend.— *vi.* To advance to a better state; to improve.

meningitis, men-in-jī'tis, *n.* Inflammation of the membranes of the brain or spinal cord.

mercenary, mèr'se-na-ri, *a.* Hired venal, that may be hired; greedy of gain; sordid.—*n.* One who is hired; a soldier hired into foreign service.

merchant, mèr'chant *n.* One who carries on trade on a large scale; a man who exports and imports goods.—*a.* Relating to trade; commercial.

mercy, mèr'si, *n.* Willingness to spare or forgive; clemency; pity; a blessing, benevolence, unrestrained exercise of authority.

mere, mēr, *a.* This or that and nothing else, simple absolute, entire, utter.—*n.* A pool or small lake; a boundary.

meretricious, me-rē-tri'shus, *a.* Pertaining to prostitutes; alluring by false show, gaudy.

merge, mèrj, *vt.* (merging, merged). To cause to be swallowed up or incorporated.—*vi*. To be sunk, swallowed, or lost.

meridian, mē-rid'i-an, *n*. Pertaining to midday or noon, pertaining to the acme or culmination.—*n*. Mid-day; point of greatest splendor, any imaginary circle passing through both poles, used in marking longitude; a similar imaginary line in the heavens passing through the zenith of any place.

mermaid, mėr'mād, *n*. A fabled marine creature, having the upper part like a woman and the lower like a fish.

mesentery, me'sen-te-ri, *a*. A membrane retaining the intestines in a proper position.

mesh, mesh, *n*. The space between the threads of a net; something that entangles, implement for making nets.—*vt*. To catch in a net.

mess, mes, *n*. A dish of food, food for a person at one meal; a number of persons who eat together, especially in the army or navy, a disorderly mixture; muddle.—*vi*. To take meals in common with others.

metabolism, me-tab'ol-izm, *n*. Change or metamorphosis; chemical change of nutriment taken into the body.

metal, me'tal, *n*. An elementary substance, such as gold, iron, etc., having a peculiar luster and generally fusible by heat; the broken stone for covering roads.

metallurgy, me'tal-ėr-ji, *n*. Art of working metals; art or operation of separating metals from their ores by smelting.

metaphysics, me-ta-fi'ziks, *n*. The science of the principles and causes of all things existing; the philosophy of mind as distinguished from that of matter.

meteor, mē'tē-ėr, *n*. An atmospheric phenomenon; a transient luminous body; something that transiently dazzles.

meteoric, mē-tē-or'ik, *a*. Pertaining to or consisting of meteors; proceeding from a meteor; transiently or irregularly brilliant.

mew, mū, *n*. A sea-mew, a gull moulting of a hawk; a coop for fowls, a place of confinement, the cry of a cat.—*vt*. To moult, to shut up, as in a cage.—*vi*. To moult; to cry as a cat.

miasma, mī-az'ma, *n*., pl. **miasmata**, miaz'ma-ta. The effluvia of any putrefying bodies; noxious emanation, malaria.

middle, mid'l, *a*.; no compar.; *superl*. middlemost. Equally distant from the extremes, intermediate intervening.—
Middle Ages, the period from the fall of the Roman Empire to about 1450.—*n*. Point or part equally distant from the extremities; something intermediate.

mildew, mil'dū, *n*. A minute parasitic fungus that causes decay in vegetable matter, condition so caused.—*vt*. and *i*. To taint with mildew.

militarism, mil'i-ta-rizm, *n*. The system that leads a nation to pay excessive attention to military affairs.

military, mil'i-ta-ri, *a*. Pertaining to soldiers or war, martial; soldierly belligerent.—*n*. The whole body of soldiers, the army.

milk, milk, *n*. A whitish fluid secreted in female animals, serving as nourishment for their young what resembles milk; white juice of plants.—*vt*. To draw milk from.

mill, mil, *n*. A machine for making meal or flour; a machine for grinding, etc.; building that contains the machinery for grinding, etc.— *vt*. To pass through a mill; to stamp in a coining press, to throw as silk; to full, as cloth.

milling, mil'ing, *n*. The process of grinding or passing through a mill, the transverse grooves on the edge of a coin.

mimic, mim'ik, *a*. Imitative; consisting of imitation.—*n*. One who imitates or mimics.—*vt*. (mimicking, mimicked). To imitate, especially for sport; to ridicule by imitation.

mind, mīnd, *n*. The intellectual power in man, understanding cast of thought and feeling; inclination; opinion; memory.— *vt*. To attend to, to observe, to regard.

mindful, mīnd'ful, *a*. Bearing in mind; attentive; regarding with care; heedful.

mine, mīn, *adj. pron. My;* belonging to me.—*n*. A pit from which coal, ores, etc. are taken an underground passage in which explosives may be lodged for destructive purposes, a contrivance floating on or near the surface of the sea, to destroy ships by explosion; a rich source or store of wealth.—*vi*. (mining, mined). To dig a mine; to dig for ores, etc.; to burrow.—*vt*. To undermine; to sap.

mineral, mi'ne-ral, *n*. An inorganic body existing on or in the earth.—*a*. Pertaining to or consisting of minerals; impregnated with mineral matter.

mingle, ming'gl, *vt*. (mingling, mingled). To mix up together; to blend; to debase by mixture.—*vi*. To be mixed; to join.

miniature, min'i-a-tūr, *n*. A painting of very small dimensions, usually in water-

M

colors, on ivory, vellum, etc.; anything represented on a greatly reduced scale a small scale.—*a.* On a small scale; diminutive.

minister, min'is-tèr, *n.* A servant; attendant, agent, a member of a government; a political representative or ambassador, the pastor of a church.—*vt.* To give, to supply.—*vi.* To perform service; to afford supplies, to contribute.

minnow, min'ō, *n.* A very small British fish inhabiting fresh-water streams.

minor, mī'nor, *a.* Lesser, smaller, of little importance; petty; in music. Less by a lesser semitone.—*n.* A person not yet 21 years of age.

minority, mi-no'ri-ti, *n.* State of being a minor, period from birth until 21 years of age, the smaller number or a number less than half; the party that has the fewest votes.

minute, mi-nūt *a.* The sixtieth part of an hour or degree; short sketch of an agreement, etc., in writing; a note to preserve the memory of anything.—*vt.* (minuting, minuted). To write down a concise state or note of.

mirror, mi'rèr, *n.* A looking-glass; any polished substance that reflects images; an exemplar—*vt.* To reflect, as in a mirror

misadventure, mis-ad-ven'tūr, *n.* An unlucky accident; misfortune; ill-luck.

misalliance, mis-al-lī'ans, *n.* Improper association; an unequal marriage.

misanthrope, misanthropist, mis'an-thr'ōp, mis-an'thr'ōp-ist, *n.* A hater of mankind.

misapprehend, mis-ap'pē-hend", *vt.* To misunderstand; to take in a wrong sense.

misbecome, mis-bē-kum', *vt.* Not to become, to suit ill.

miscalculate, mis-kal'kū-lāt, *vt.* To calculate erroneously.

miscarry, mis-ka'ri, *vi.* To fail to reach its destination, to fail of the intended effect, to bring forth young before the proper time.

miscellaneous, mis-sel-lā'nē-us, *a.* Consisting of several kinds, promiscuous; producing written compositions of various sorts.

miserly, mī'zèr-li, *a.* Like a miser in habits; penurious; sordid; niggardly.

misery, miz'èr-i, *n.* Great unhappiness; extreme distress; wretchedness.

misfeasance, mis-fē'zans, *n.* In *law*, a wrong done; wrong-doing in office

misfit, mis-fit', *n.* A bad fit.—*vt.* To make

(a garment, etc.) of a wrong size; to supply with something not suitable.

misfortune, mis-for'tūn, *n.* Ill fortune; calamity; mishap.

misinform, mis-in-form', *vt.* To give erroneous information to.

misinterpret, mis-in-t ér 'pret, *vt.* To interpret erroneously.

misjudge, mis-juj', *vt.* To judge erroneously.—*vi.* To err in judgment.

misplace, mis-plās, *vt.* To put in a wrong place; to set on an improper object.

misprint, mis-print', *vt.* To print wrongly.—*n.* A mistake in printing.

missile, mis'ī l *a.* Capable of being thrown.—*n.* A weapon or projectile thrown with hostile intention as an arrow, a bullet.

mission, mi'shon, *n.* A sending or delegating, duty on which one is sent; destined end or function; persons sent on some political business or to propagate religion, a station of missionaries.

missive, mis'iv, *a.* Such as is sent proceeding from some authoritative source.—*n.* A message; a letter or writing sent.

misspell, mis-spel', *vt.* To spell wrongly.

misspent, mis-spent', *p.a.* Ill-spent; wasted.

misstatement, mis-stāt'ment, *n.* A wrong statement.

mist, mist, *n.* Visible watery vapor aqueous vapor falling in numerous but almost imperceptible drops; something which dims or darkens.

mistake, mis-tāk', *vt.* To misunderstand or misapprehend; to regard as one when really another.—*vi.* To err in opinion or judgment.—*n.* An error in opinion or judgment; blunder, fault.

mistress, mis'tres, *n.* The female appellation corresponding to *master,* a woman who has authority, ownership, etc.; a female teacher, a concubine, a title of address applied to married women (written *Mrs.* and pronounced mis'iz).

mite, mīt, *n.* A minute animal of the class Arachnida (cheese-mite, etc.); a very small coin formerly current; a very little creature.

mixture, miks'tūr, *n.* Act of mixing state of being mixed; a compound, a liquid medicine of different ingredients.

moan, mōn, *vi.* To utter a low dull sound through grief or pain.—*vt.* To bewail or deplore.—*n.* A low dull sound due to grief or pain; a sound resembling this.

moat, mōt, *n.* A deep trench round a castle

or other fortified place.—*vt*. To surround with a ditch for defense.

mob, mob, *n*. A crowd, disorderly assembly; rabble.—*vt*. (mobbing mobbed). To attack in a disorderly crowd, to crowd round and annoy.

moccasin, mok'a-sin, *n*. A shoe of deerskin or soft leather, worn by N. American Indians; a venomous serpent of the United States.

mock, mok, *vt*. To mimic in contempt or derision; to flout, to ridicule; to set at naught; to defy.—*vi*. To use ridicule, to gibe or jeer.—*n*. A derisive word or gesture; ridicule; derision.—*a*. Counterfeit; assumed.

mockery, mok'é-ri, *n*. Derision; sportive insult; counterfeit appearance, vain effort.

model, mo'del, *n*. A pattern, an image, copy, facsimile; standard, plan, or type; a person from whom an artist studies his proportions, postures, etc.—*vt*. (modelling, modelled). To plan after some model; to form in order to serve as a model; to mold.—*vi*. To make a model.

moderate, mo'de-rāt, *vt*. To restrain from excess; to temper, lessen, allay.—*vi*. To become less violent or intense; to preside as a moderator.—*a*. Not going to extremes; temperate, medium, mediocre.—*n*. One not extreme in opinions.

modulus, mod'ū-lus, *n*. In *mathematics, etc.*, a constant quantity used in connection with some variable quantity.

mohair, mō'hār, *n*. The hair of the Angora goat; cloth made of this hair; an imitation wool and cotton cloth.

mold, mōld, *n*. Fine soft earth; mustiness or mildew, dust from incipient decay, form in which a thing is cast; model; shape; character.—*vt*. To cause to contract mold, to cover with mold or soil, to model; to shape; to fashion.—*vi*. To become moldy.

molding, mōld'ing, *n*. Anything cast in a mold; ornamental contour or form in wood or stone along an edge or a surface.

mole, mōl, *n*. A small discolored protuberance on the human body; a mound or break-water to protect a harbor from the waves, a small burrowing insectivorous animal.

molecule, mo'le-kūl, *n*. A very minute particle of matter.

mole-hill, mōl'hil, *n*. A little hillock of earth thrown up by moles; a very small hill.

mollify, mol'i-fī, *vt*. (mollifying, mollified). To soften; to assuage; to appease; to reduce in harshness; to tone down.

mollusc, mollusk, mol'usk, *n*. An animal whose body is soft, as mussels, snails, cuttle-fish, etc.; one of the *Mollusca*.

monarch, mon'ärk, *n*. A supreme governor of a state, a sovereign one who or that which is chief of its kind.—*a*. Supreme, ruling.

monarchy, mon'är-ki, *n*. Govern ment in which the supreme power is lodged in a single person, actually or nominally; a kingdom.

monastery, mon'as-te-ri, *n*. A house for monks, sometimes for nuns abbey; priory; convent.

monatomic, mon-a-tom'ik, *a*. Said of an element one atom of which will combine with only one atom of another element.

money, mun'i, *n*. Coin; pieces of gold, silver, or other metal, stamped by public authority and used as the medium of exchange a circulating medium; wealth; affluence.

Mongol, Mongolian, mon'gol, mongō'li-an, *n*. A native of Mongolia.— *a*. Belonging to Mongolia.

monitor, mo'ni-tè r, *n*. One who admonishes; one who warns of faults or informs of duty, a senior pupil in a school appointed to instruct and look after juniors; a lizard.

monk, mungk, *n*. A male inhabitant of a monastery, bound to celibacy.

monogamy, mon-og'a mi, *n*. The practice or principle of marrying only once; the marrying of only one at a time.

monopoly, mo-nop'o-li, *n*. An exclusive trading privilege; assumption of anything to the exclusion of others.

monotony, mon-ot'o-ni, *n*. Uniformity of sound; a dull uniformity, an irksome sameness or want of variety.

monsoon, mon-sön', *n*. The trade-wind of the Indian seas, blowing from N.E. from November to March, and s.w. from April to October.

monster, mon'stèr, *n*. An animal of unnatural form or of great size; one unnaturally wicked or evil.—*a*. Of inordinate size.

month, munth, *n*. The period measured by the moon's revolution (the lunar month, about 29-1/2 days), one of the twelve parts of the year (the calendar month, 30 or 31 days).

M

monthly, munth'li, *a.* Done or happening once a month, or every month.—*n.* A publication appearing once a month.—*adv.* Once a month; in every month.

monument, mon'ū-ment, *n.* Any-thing by which the memory of a person or of an event is preserved; a memorial; a singular or notable instance.

mood, mōd, *n.* Temper of mind; disposition, a fit of sullenness, a form of verbs expressive of certainty contingency, etc.; a form of syllogism.

moon, mön, *n.* The changing luminary of the night; the heavenly body next to the earth, revolving round it in about 29-1/2 days; a satellite of any planet, a month.

moonlight, mön'līt, *n.* The light afforded by the moon.—*a.* Illuminated by the moon, occurring during moonlight.—**moon-lit,** mön 'lit *a.* Illuminated by the moon.

moonshine, mön'shīn, *n.* The light of the moon; show without substance; pretense; illegally distilled corn whiskey.

moonstone, mön'stōn, *n.* A translucent variety of felspar used in trinkets, etc.

moor, mör, *n.* A tract of waste land or of hilly ground on which game is preserved, a native of the northern coast of Africa.—*vt.* To secure a ship in a particular station, as by cables and anchors.—*vi.* To be confined by cables.

mooring, mör'ing, *n.* Act of one who moors; *pl.* the anchor, etc., by which a ship is moored; the place where a ship is moored.

mop, mop, *n.* A cloth or collection of yarns fastened to a handle, and used for cleaning; a grimace.—*vt.* (mopping mopped). To rub with a mop; to wipe.—*vi.* To grimace.

mope, mōp, *vi.* (moping, moped). To show a downcast air; to be spiritless or gloomy.—*n.* One who mopes.

moral, mo'ral, *a.* Relating to morality or morals; ethical; virtuous; supported by reason and probability. —*n.* The practical lesson inculcated by any story; *pl.* general conduct as right or wrong, mode of life; ethics.

moralist, mo'ral-ist, *n.* One who teaches morals; a writer or lecturer on ethics; one who inculcates or practices moral duties.

morality, mō-ral'i-ti, *n.* The doctrine of moral duties; ethics; moral character or quality; quality of an action in regard to right and wrong, an old form of drama in which the personages were allegorical representations of virtues, vices, etc.

morass, mō-ras', *n.* A tract of low soft, wet ground; a marsh; a swamp, a fen.

Mormon, mor'mon, *n.* A member of a sect founded in the United States in 1830, who practice polygamy; a Latter-day Saint. Also **Mormonite, Mormonist.**

morning, morn'ing, *n.* The first part of the day; the time between dawn and the middle of the forenoon; the first or early part. Often used as an *adj.*

Morocco, mō-rok'ō, *n.* A fine kind of leather prepared from goat skin.

mortality, mor-tal-i-ti, *n.* State of being mortal; actual death of great numbers of men or beasts; deathrate.

mortise, mor'tis, *n.* A hole cut in one piece of material to receive the tenon of another piece.—*vt.* To cut a mortise in; to join by a tenon and mortise.

mortuary, mor'tū-a-ri, *n.* A place for the temporary reception of the dead.—*a.* Pertaining to the burial of the dead.

mosaic, mō-zā'ik, *n.* Inlaid work of marble, precious stones, etc., disposed on a ground of cement so as to form designs.—*a.* Pertaining to or composed of mosaic.

moss, mos, *n.* A small plant with simple branching stems and numerous small leaves, a bog, a place where peat is found,—*vt.* To cover with moss by natural growth.

most, mōst, *a.* superl. of more. Greatest in any way.—*adv.* In the greatest degree, quantity, or extent; mostly; chiefly.—*n.* The greatest number; the majority; greatest amount; utmost extent, degree, etc.

mother, muTH'ėr, *n.* A female parent; a woman who has borne a child, source or origin, an abbess or other female at the head of a religious institution; a slimy substance that gathers in vinegar etc.—*a.* Native; natural; inborn, vernacular.

mother-country, muTH'ėr-kun-tri *n.* A country which has sent out colonies, a country as the producer of anything.

motion, mō'shon, *n.* Act or process of moving; power of moving; movement, internal impulse, proposal made; evacuation of the intestines.—*vi.* To make a significant gesture with the hand.

motive, mō'tiv, *n.* That which incites to action; cause, inducement; purpose, theme in a piece of music; prevailing idea of an artist.—*a.* Causing motion.—*vt.* To supply a motive to or for, to prompt.

motley, mot'li, *a.* Variegated in color, parti colored, heterogeneous; diversified—*n.* A dress of various colors.

motor, mō'tor, *n.* A moving power; force or agency that sets machinery in motion; a motor-car—*a.* Imparting motion.

mottle, mot'l, *n.* A blotched or spotted character of surface.—*vt.* (mottling, mottled). To mark with spots or blotches as if mottled.

motto, mot'tō, *n.; pl.* -oes, or -os. A short sentence or phrase, or a single word, adopted as expressive of one's guiding idea.

moult, mōlt. *vi.* and *t.* To shed or cast the hair, feathers, skin, horns, etc., as birds and other animals.— *n.* Act or process of changing the feathers, etc.; time of moulting.

mound, mound. *n.* An artificial elevation of earth; a bulwark, a rampart; the globe which forms part of the regalia.

mount, mount, *n.* A hill; a mountain, that with which something is fitted, a setting, frame, etc.; opportunity or means of riding on horseback, a horse.—*vi.* To rise; to get on horseback or upon any animal; to amount.—*vt.* To raise aloft, to climb to place oneself upon, as on horseback; to furnish with horses; to set in or cover with something; to set off to advantage.

mountain, moun'tin, *n.* An elevated mass larger than a hill, anything very large.— *a.* Pertaining to a mountain; found on mountains.

mountaineer, moun-tin-ēr', *n.* An inhabitant of a mountainous district a climber of mountains.—*vi.* To practice the climbing of mountains.

mountebank, moun'ti-bangk, *n.* One who mounts a bench or stage in a public place, and vends medicines or nostrums, a quack: any boastful and false pretender.

mounting, mount 'ing, *n.* Act of one who mounts: that with which an article is mounted or set off; trimming, setting, etc.

mourn, mōrn, *vi.* To sorrow: to lament; to wear the customary habit of sorrow.— *vt.* To grieve for: to deplore.

mourning, mōrn'ing, *n.* Lamentation, dress worn by mourners.—*a.* Employed to express grief.

mouse, mous, *n.*, pl. **mice**, mîs, A small rodent quadruped that infests houses, fields, etc.—*vi.* mouz (mousing, moused). To hunt for or catch mice.

mouth, mouth, *n.; pl.* **mouths**, mouTHz. The opening in the head of an animal into which food is received, and from which voice is uttered; opening of anything hollow, as of a pitcher. or of a cave, pit, etc., the part of a river, etc., by which it joins with the ocean.—*vt.* mouTH. To take into the mouth; to utter with a voice affectedly big.—*vi.* To speak with a loud, affected voice; to vociferate.

mouth-organ, mouth-or'gan, *n.* A small popular wind-instrument, flat in shape, with openings for the various notes, which are produced by inhalation and exhalation.

move, möv, *vt.* (moving, moved). To cause to change place, posture, or position, to set in motion, to affect; to rouse, to prevail on; to propose, as a resolution.—*vi.* To change place or posture; to stir; to begin to act; to shake; to change residence to make a proposal to a meeting.—*n.* The act of moving; a movement; proceeding; action taken.

movement, möv'ment, *n.* Act of moving; motion; change of position, manner of moving; gesture; an agitation to bring about some result desired, wheel-work of a clock.

mow, mō, *vt.* (pret. mowed, pp. mowed or mown). To cut down, as grass, etc.; to cut the grass from; to cut down in great numbers.—*vi.* To cut grass; to use the scythe.

much, much, *a.;* comp. more, superl. most. Great in quantity or amount, abundant.—*adv.* In a great degree; by far; greatly.—*n.* A great quantity; something strange or serious.

mucilage, mū'si-lāj, *n.* A solution in water of gummy matter, a gummy substance found in certain plants.

muck muk, *n.* Dung in a moist state, something mean, vile, or filthy.—*vt.* To manure with muck; to remove muck from.

mucous, mucose, mū'kus, *a.* Pertaining to mucus, or resembling it; slimy.— **mucous membrane**, a membrane that lines all the cavities of the body which open externally, and secretes mucus.

mud, mud, *n.* Moist and soft earth; sediment from turbid waters mire.—*vt.* (mudding, mudded). To soil with mud; to make turbid.

muddle, mud'l, *vt.* (muddling, muddled). To make muddy; to intoxicate partially, to confuse, to make a mess of.—*vi.* To become muddy to act in a confused manner.—*n.* A mess, confusion, bewilderment.

muffle, muf'l, *vt.* (muffling, muffled). To cover close, particularly the neck and face; to conceal; to deaden the sound of by wrapping cloth, etc., round.—*n.* The tumid and naked portion of the upper lip and nose of ruminants and rodents.

muffler, muf'lėr, *n.* A cover for the face or neck; a stuffed glove for lunatics.

multiple, mul'ti-pl, *a.* Manifold; having many parts or divisions.—*n.* A number which contains another an exact number of times.

multiplication, mul'ti-pli-kā"shon, *n.* Act or process of multiplying state of being multiplied; reproduction of animals.

multiply, mul'ti-plī, *vt.* (multiplying, multiplied). To increase in number; to add to itself any given number of times.—*vi.* To increase in number, or to become more numerous by reproductive; to extend.

multitude, mul'ti-tūd, *n.* State of being many; a great number, collectively or indefinitely, a crowd.— **The multitude,** the populace.

mumble, mum'bl, *vi.* (mumbling, mumbled). To mutter; to speak with mouth partly closed, to eat with the lips close.—*vt.* To utter with a low, inarticulate voice.

mummy, mum'i, *n.* A dead human body embalmed after the manner of the ancient Egyptians, with wax, balsams, etc.

mumps, mumps, *n.* Silent displeasure, sullenness, a disease consist ing in an inflammation of the salivary glands.

municipality, mū-ni'si-pal"i-ti, *n.* A town possessed of local self-government; community under municipal jurisdiction.

munificence, mū-ni'fi-sens, *n.* A be-stowing liberally; liberality; generosity.

munition, mū-ni'shon, *n.* Military stores; ammunition; material for any enterprise.

murder, mėr'dėr, *n.* Act of killing a human being with premeditated malice.—*vt.* To kill (a human being) with premeditated malice; to mar by bad execution.

murmur, mėr'mėr, *n.* A low continued or repeated sound, a hum, a grumble or mutter.—*vi.* To utter a murmur or hum, to grumble.—*vt.* To utter indistinctly, to mutter.

Muscadel, Muscatel, Muscadine,

mus'ka-del, mus'ka-tel, mus'ka-dīn, *a.* and *n.* A sweet and strong Italian or French wine; the grapes which produce this wine; a delicious pear.

muscle, mus'l, *n.* A definite portion of an animal body consisting of fibers susceptible of contraction and relaxation, and thus effecting motion, a mussel.

muscular, mus'ku-lėr, *a.* Pertaining to or consisting of muscle; performed by a muscle; strong; brawny; vigorous.

muse, mūz, *n.* One of the nine sister goddesses of the Greeks and Romans presiding over the arts; poetic inspiration; a fit of abstraction.—*vi.* (musing mused). To ponder; to meditate in silence; to be absent in mind.—*vt.* To meditate on.

mushroom, mush'röm, *n.* An edible fungus; an upstart,—*a.* Pertaining to mushrooms; resembling mushrooms in rapidity of growth.

music, mū'zik, *n.* Melody of harmony, the science of harmonious sounds; the written or printed score of a composition.

muster, mus'tėr, *vt.* To collect, as troops; to assemble or bring together—*vi.* To assemble, to meet in one place.—*n.* An assembling of troops; register of troops mustered an array

mutation, mū-tā'shon, *n.* Act or process of changing, change, alteration, either in form or qualities, modification.

mute, mūt, *a.* Silent, incapable of speaking; dumb; not pronounced, or having its sound checked by a contact of the vocal organs, as certain consonants (*t, p, k, etc.*).—*n.* A dumb person; a hired attendant at a funeral, a mute consonant.—*vi.* (muting, muted). To eject the contents of the bowels as birds.

myself, mī-self', *compd. pron.*, pl. **Ourselves,** our-selvz'. As a nominative it is used, generally after I, to express emphasis—I, and not another; in the objective often used reflexively and without any emphasis.

mysterious, mis-tē'ri-us, *a.* Containing mystery, beyond human comprehension; untelligible; enigmatical.

mystery, mis'tėr-i, *n.* Something above human intelligence; a secret, an old form of drama in which the characters and events were drawn from sacred history; a trade craft, or calling.

myth, mith, *n.* A tradition or fable embodying the notions of a people as to their gods, origin early history etc., an invented story.

N

nab, nab, *vt.* (nabbing, nabbed). To catch or seize suddenly or unexpectedly.

nail, nāl, *n.* The horny substance at the end of the human finger and toes; a claw; a small pointed piece of metal, to be driven into timber etc., a stud or boss, a measure of 2-1/4 inches.—*vt.* To fasten or stud with nails; to hold fast or make secure.

naked, nā'ked, *a.* Not having clothes on; bare; nude; open to view; mere, bare, simple; destitute, unassisted.

name, nǎm, *n.* That by which a person or thing is designated; appellation; title, reputation, eminence sound only; not reality; authority, behalf; a family.—*vt.* (naming, named). To give a name to; to designate; to style; to nominate; to speak of or mention as.

namely, nǎm'li, *adv.* By name; particularly; that is to say.

nap, nap *n.* The woolly substance on the surface of cloth, etc.; the downy substance on plants, a short sleep.—*vi.* (napping napped). To have a short sleep; to drowse.

nape, nāp, *n.* The prominent joint of the neck behind; the back part of the neck.

nard, nārd, *n.* An aromatic plant, usually called spikenard; an unguent prepared from the plant.

narrative, nar'a-tiv, *a.* Pertaining to narration.—*n.* That which is narrated or related; a relation orally or in writing.

narrow, na'rō, *a.* Of little breadth not wide or broad, very limited straitened; not liberal; bigoted, near; close; scrutinizing.—*n.* A narrow channel, a strait: usually in *pl.*—*vt.* To make narrow.—*vi.* To become narrow, to contract in breadth.

nasal, nā'zal, *a.* Pertaining to the nose, formed or affected by the nose, as speech.—*n.* An elementary sound uttered partly through the nose.

national, na'shon-al, *a.* Pertaining to a nation; public; attached to one's own country.

nationality, na-shon-al'i-ti, *n.* Quality of being national; national character; strong attachment to one's own nation; a nation.

native, nā'tiv, *a.* Pertaining to the place or circumstances of one's birth; indigenous; inborn; occurring in nature pure or unmixed.— *n.* One born in a place or country; an indigenous animal or plant; an oyster raised in an artificial bed.

natural, na'tūr-al, *a.* Pertaining to nature; produced or effected by nature consistent with nature not artificial; according to the life, not revealed; bastard; unregenerated.—*n.* An idiot; a fool.

naturalization, na'tūr-al-izā"shon, *n.* Act of investing an alien with the privileges of a native citizen.

nature, nā'tūr, *n.* The universe, the total of all agencies and forces in the creation; the inherent or essential qualities of anything, individual constitution; sort; natural human instincts; reality as distinct from that which is artificial.

navigate, na'vi-gat, *vi.* To conduct or guide a ship, to sail.—*vt.* To manage in sailing, as a vessel; to sail or guide a ship over.

navy, nā'vi, *n.* All the ships of a certain class belonging to a country; the whole of the ships of war belonging to a nation.

near, nēr, *a.* Not distant in place, time, or degree, intimate, affecting one's interest or feelings, parsimonious; narrow; on the left of a horse, not circuitous.—*prep.* Close to; nigh.—*adv.* Almost; within a little; close to the wind.—*vt.* and *i.* To approach, to come near.

neat, nēt, *n.* Cattle of the bovine genus.— *a.* Pure; clean; trim; tidy; clever; smart, without water added

nebula, neb'ū-la, *n. pl.* -ae. Celestial objects like white clouds, generally clusters of stars.

necessary, ne'ses-sa-ri, *a.* Such as must be, inevitable, essential acting from necessity.—*n.* Anything indispensably requisite.

necrology, nek-rol 'o-ji, *n.* A register of deaths; a collection of obituary notices.

necromancy, nek'rō-man-si, *n.* The revealing of future events through pretended communication with the dead, sorcery.

Necropolis, nek-rō'po-lis, *n.* A city of the dead, a cemetery.

need, nēd, *n.* A state that requires supply or relief; urgent want; necessity; poverty; destitution.—*vt.* To have necessity or need for, to lack, require.—*vi.* To be necessary: used impersonally.

needle, nē'dl, *n.* An instrument for interweaving thread; a small steel instrument for sewing, a magnetized piece of steel

N

in a compass attracted to the pole; anything in the form of a needle.

needless, nĕd'les, *a.* No needed or wanted; unnecessary; not requisite; useless.

needle-work, nē'dl-wėrk, *n.* Work done with a needle; business of a seamstress.

negative, neg'at-iv, *a.* That denies; implying denial or negation; implying absence, the opposite of positive.—*n.* A word which denies, as *not, no,* a proposition by which something is denied; a veto, a photographic picture on glass or celluloid, in which the lights and shades are the opposite of those in nature.—*vt.* To prove the contrary of; to reject by vote.

negotiate, nē-gō'shi-āt, *vi.* To treat with another respecting purchase and sale; to hold diplomatic intercourse; to conduct communications in general.—*vt.* To procure or bring about by negotiation to pass into circulation (as a bill of exchange).

neighborhood, nā'bėr-hud, *n.* Condition of being neighbors; neighbors collectively, vicinity, locality.

neither, nē'THėr or nī'THėr, *pron.* and *pron. adj.* Not either; not the one or the other—*conj.* Not either; nor.

nematoid, nem'a-toid, *n.* A roundworm; one of an order of entozoa or intestinal worms.—*a.* Pertaining to or resembling the nematoids.

Nemesis, nem'e-sis, *n.* A female Greek divinity personifying retributive justice; just retribution or punishment.

nerve, nėrv, *n.* One of the fibrous threads in animal bodies whose function is to convey sensation and originate motion; fortitude; courage; energy; something resembling a nerve.—*vt.* (nerving, nerved). To give strength or vigor to; to steel.

nervous, nėrv'us, *a.* Pertaining to the nerves, affecting the nerves having the nerves easily affected, easily agitated; having nerve or bodily strength, vigorous; sinewy.

nest, nest, *n.* The place or bed formed by a bird for laying and hatching her eggs; a number of persons frequenting the same haunt; a snug abode.—*vi. To* build a nest, to nestle.

nestle, nes'l, *vi.* (nestling, nestled). To make or occupy a nest; to lie close and snug.—*vt.* To shelter, as in a nest, to cherish.

net, net, *n.* A texture of twine, etc., with meshes, commonly used to catch fish,

birds, etc.; a snare.—*vt.* (netting, netted). To make into a net; to take in a net; to capture by wile.

net, nett, net, *a.* Being clear of all deductions, estimated apart from all expenses.—*vt.* (netting, netted). To gain as clear profit.

neuter, nū'tėr, *a.* Neutral; neither masculine nor feminine; neither active nor passive, as a verb.—*n.* An animal or neither sex; a plant with neither stamens nor pistils; a noun of the neuter gender.

neutral, nū'tral, *a.* Not siding with any party in a dispute; indifferent; neither acid nor alkaline.—*n.* A person or nation that takes no part in a contest between others.

neutralize, nū'tral-īz, *vt.* To render neutral or inoperative; to counteract.

neutron, nū'tron, *n.* An uncharged particle of the same mass as a proton.

nevertheless, nev'ėr-THe-les", *adv.* Not the less, notwithstanding; yet; however.

new, nū, *a.* Recent in origin, novel not before known; different; unaccustomed, fresh after any event not second-hand.—*adv.* Newly; recently.

newel, nū'el, *n.* The upright structure in a winding staircase supporting the steps.

Newfoundland, nū-found'land or nu'found-land, *n.* A large dog, remarkable for sagacity and swimming powers.

newspaper, nūz'pa-per, *n.* A sheet of paper printed periodically for circulating news.

next, nekst, *a.* superl. of nigh. Nearest in place, time rank, or degree.—*adv.* At the time or turn nearest.

nick, nik, *n.* The exact point of time, the critical time; a notch; a score.—*vt.* To hit upon exactly; to make a nick in, to mark with nicks.

nickel, nik'el, *n.* A valuable metal of a white color and great hardness, magnetic, and when pure malleable and ductile.

nickel-silver, nik'el-sil-vėr, *n.* An alloy composed of copper, zinc, and nickel.

nickname, nik'nām, *n.* A name given in contempt or jest.—*vt.* To give a nickname to.

nicotine, nik'ō-tin, *n.* A volatile alkaloid from tobacco, highly poisonous.

night, nīt, *n.* The daily period of darkness; the time from sunset to sunrise, a state or time of darkness, depression, etc.; ignorance; obscurity, death.

nihilism, nī'hil-izm, *n.* Nothingness; the doctrine that nothing can be known; principles of a Russian secret society of communists.

nimble, nim'bl, *a.* Quick in motion; moving with ease and celerity; agile, prompt.

nimbus, nim'bus, *n.* A rain-cloud; a halo surrounding the head in representations of divine or sacred personages.

niter, nī'tėr, *n.* Nitrate of potassium or saltpeter, used for making gunpowder, in dyeing, medicine, etc.

nitrogen, nī'tro-gen. *n.* The elementary unflammable gas constituting about four-fifths of the atmospheric air.

nitro-glycerine, nī-trō-glis'ėr-in, *n.* A powerful explosive produced by the action of nitric and sulphuric acids on glycerine.

nitrous, nī'trus, *a.* Pertaining to niter; applied to compounds containing less oxygen than those called nitric.

nival, nī'val, *a.* Snowy; growing among snow, or flowering during winter.

no, nō, *adv.* A word of denial or refusal; not in any degree; not.—*n.* A denial; a negative vote.—*a.* Not any; none.

noble, nō'bl, *a.* Of lofty lineage; belonging to the peerage, illustrious, lofty in character; magnanimous, magnificent; stately.—*n.* A person of rank; a peer; an old English gold coin.

nocturn, nok'tėrn, *n.* A religious service formerly used in the R. Catholic Church at midnight, now a part of matins.

nod, nod, *vi.* (nodding, nodded). To make a slight bow, to let the head sink from sleep; to incline the head, as in assent or salutation, etc.—*vt.* To incline; to signify by a nod.—*n.* A quick inclination of the head.

node, nōd, *n.* A knot, a protuberance; a sort of knot on a stem where leaves arise, one of the two points in which two great circles of the celestial sphere intersect.

nominal, no'mi-nal, *a.* Pertaining to a name; titular; not real; merely so called.

nonagon, non'a-gon, *n.* A plane figure having nine sides and nine angles.

non-conductor, non-kon-dukt'ėr, *n.* A substance which does not conduct, or transmits with difficulty heat, electricity, etc.

nonconformist, non-kon-form'ist, *n.* One who does not conform to the established church.

nonconformity, non-kon-form'i-ti, *n.* Neglect or failure of conformity, refusal to unite with an established church.

nondescript, non'dē-skript, *a.* That has not been described, abnormal; odd; indescribable.—*n.* A person or thing not easily described or classed.

nonentity, non-en'ti-ti, *n.* Non-existence; a thing not existing; a person utterly without consequence or Importance.

nonesuch, nun'such, *n.* A person or thing that has not its equal or parallel.

noonday, nōn'dā, *n.* Mid-day noon.—*a.* Pertaining to mid-day, meridional.

noose, nös or nöz, *n.* A running knot, which binds the closer the more it is drawn.—*vt.* (noosing. noosed). To tie or catch in a noose, to entrap.

nor, nor, *conj.* A word used to render negative a subsequent member of a clause or sentence, correlative to neither or other negative; also equivalent to *and not.*

Nordic, nor'dik *a.* Of or belonging to those peoples of Northern Europe who are long-headed, tall blue-eyed and fair-haired.

normal, nor'mal, *a.* According to a rule, conforming with a certain type or standard; regular; perpendicular.—**normal school,** a training-college for teachers. *n.* A perpendicular.

nose, nōz, *n.* The organ of smell employed also in respiration and speech; the power of smelling; scent, sagacity, a nozzle.—*vt.* and *i.* (nosing, nosed). To smell; to wange through the nose; to pry officiously.

nostalgia, nos-tal'ji-a, *n.* Vehement desire to revisit one's native country, homesickness.

nostrum, nos'trum, *n.* A quack medicine, the ingredients of which are kept secret.

note, nōt, *n.* A mark, sign, or token; an explanatory or critical comment, a memorandum; a bill, account; a paper promising payment, a communication in writing notice, reputation; distinction; a character representing a musical sound, or the sound itself.—*vt.* (noting, noted). To observe carefully; to mark; to set down in writing.

noteworthy, nōt'wėr-THi, *a.* Deserving notice; worthy of observation or notice.

notice, nōt'is, *n.* Act of noting; regard; information; order; intimation; civility; a brief critical review.—*vt.* (noticing, noticed). To take note of; to perceive; to make observations on; to treat with attention.

notify, nōt'i-fī, *vt.* To make known; to declare; to give notice to; to inform.

notoriety, nō-tō-rī'e-ti, *n.* State of being notorious; discreditable publicity; one

N

who is notorious.

novel, no'vel, *a.* Of recent origin or introduction, new and striking unusual.—*n.* A fictitious prose narrative picturing real life.

novelist, no'vel-ist, *n.* A writer of novels.

noxious, nok'shus, *a.* Hurtful, pernicious, unwholesome; corrupting to morals.

nozzle, noz'l, *n.* The projecting spout of something; terminal part of a pipe.

nucleus, nū'klē-us, *n.;* pl. **-lei.** A kernel or something similar, a mass about which matter is collected, body of a comet.

number, num'ber, *n.* An aggregate of units, or a single unit; a numeral; many; one of a numbered series of things, part of a periodical, metrical arrangement of syllables; difference of form in a word to express unity or plurality.—*vt.* To reckon; to enumerate; to put a number on; to reach the number of.

numeral, nū'mėr-al, *a.* Pertaining to number; consisting of or representing number.—*n.* A figure used to express a number.

numerate, nū'me˙ r-āt, *vt.* (numerating, numerated). To count; to enumerate.

numerator, nū'mėr-āt-er, *n.* One who numbers; the number (above the line) in vulgar fractions which shows how many parts of a unit are taken.

numerous, nū'mėr-us, *a.* Consisting of a great number of individuals, many.

nurse, nėrs, *n.* One who suckles or nourishes a child, one who tends the young, sick, or infirm; an attendant in a hospital, one who or that which nurtures or protects.— *vt.* (nursing, nursed). To act as nurse to, to suckle, to rear, to tend in sickness or infirmity; to foment; to foster.

nursery, nėr'sē-ri, *n.* The place in which children are nursed and taken care of; a place where trees, plants, etc., are propagated.

nurture, nėr'tūr, *n.* Upbringing education, nourishment.—*vt.* (nurturing, nurtured). To nourish, to educate; to bring or train up.

nut, nut, *n.* A fruit containing a seed or kernel within a hard covering; a small block of metal or wood with a grooved hole, to be screwed on the end of a bolt.—*vi.* (nutting, nutted). To gather nuts.

nutation, nū-tā'shon, *n.* A nodding a slight gyratory movement of the earth's axis.

nutmeg, nut'meg, *n.* The aromatic kernel of the fruit of a tree of the Malay Archipelago.

nymph, nimf, *n.* A goddess of the mountains, forests, meadow, or waters, a young and attractive woman; a maiden; the chrysalis of an insect.

O

O, ō, An exclamation used in earnest or solemn address; often distinguished from *Oh,* which is more strictly expressive of emotion.

obedience, ō-bē'di-ens, *n.* Act of obeying; quality of being obedient, submission to authority.

obelisk o'be-lisk, *n.* A tall four-sided pillar, tapering as it rises and terminating in a small pyramid, a mark (†) used in printing.

obey, ō-bā', *vt.* To comply with, as commands or requirements; to be ruled by; to yield to.—*vi.* To submit to authority.

obituary, ō-bit'ū-a-ri, *n.* An account of a person or persons deceased, list of the dead.—*a.* Relating to the decease of a person.

object, ob'jekt *n.* That about which any faculty of the mind is employed; end; purpose; a concrete reality; the word, clause, etc., governed by a transitive verb or by a preposition.—*vt.* ob-jekt'. To oppose, to offer as an objection.— *vi.* To oppose in words or arguments.

objective, ob-jek'tiv, *a.* Pertaining to an object; relating to whatever is exterior to the mind (also *pron.* ob'jek-tiv), belonging to the case which follows a transitive verb or preposition.—*n.* The objective case, object, place, etc., aimed at.

oblige, ō-blīj', *vt.* (obliging, obliged). To constrain, to bind by any restraint; to lay under obligation of gratitude; to render service or kindness to.

oblivion, ob-li'vi-on, *n.* State of being forgotten; forgetfulness; act of forgetting.

obscure, ob-skūr', *a.* Darkened dim; not easily understood; abstruse; unknown to fame; indistinct.—*vt.* (obscuring obscured). To darken; to make less visible, legible, or intelligible; to tarnish.

observe, ob-zė rv', *vt.* (observing observed). To take notice of, to behold with attention; to remark; to keep religiously; to celebrate; to comply with; to practice.—*vi.* To remark; to be attentive.

obsession, ob-sesh'on, *n.* Act of besieging; persistent attack; state of being beset.

obstruction, ob-struk'shon, *n.* Act of obstructing, that which impedes progress; obstacle; impediment; check.

obstruent, ob'strü-ent, *a.* Obstructing.— *n.* Anything that obstructs the natural passages in the body.

obtain, ob-tān', *vt.* To get possession of; to acquire; to earn.—*vi.* To be received in common use, to prevail; to hold good.

obverse, ob'vėrs, *n.* and *a.* That side of a coin or medal which has the face or head or principal device on it.

obviate, ob'vi-ā t, *vt.* (obviating, obviated). To meet, as difficulties or objections; to get over, to remove.

occupancy, ok'kū-pan-si, *n.* Act of occupying; a holding in possession; term during which one is occupant.

occupation, ok-kū-pā'shon, *n.* Act of occupying; act of taking possession; tenure; business; employment; vocation.

occupy, ok'kū-pî, *vt.* (occupying, occupied). To take possession of; to hold and use; to cover or fill; to employ; to engage: often *refl.*—*vi.* To be an occupant.

occur, ok-kėr', *vi.* (occurring, occurred). To come to the mind; to happen; to be met with; to be found here and there.

occurrence, ok-ku'rens, *n.* The act of occurring or taking place; any incident or accidental event, an observed instance.

ocean, ō'shan, *n.* The vast body of water which covers more than three-fifths of the globe; the sea; one of the great areas into which the sea is divided, any immense expanse.—*a.* Pertaining to the great sea.

odd, od, *a.* Not even, not exactly divisible by 2; not included with others; incidental; casual; belonging to a broken set, queer

odds, odz, *n. sing.* or *pl.* Inequality excess; difference in favor of one, advantage; amount by which one bet exceeds another.

off, of, *adv.* Away, distant, not on from; not toward.—**Well off, ill off,** in good or bad circumstances. *a.* Distant, farther away, as applied to horses; right hand— *prep.* Not on; away from; to seaward from.— *interj.* Begone!

offense, of-fens', *n.* Injury, an affront, insult, or wrong; displeasure; transgression of law; misdemeanor.

offend, of-fend', *vt.* To displease; to shock; to cause to sin or neglect duty.— *vi.* To sin, to commit a fault to cause dislike or anger.

offensive, of-fens'iv, *a.* Causing offense; causing displeasure or annoyance; disgusting; impertinent; used in attack, aggressive.—*n.* Act or posture of attack

offer, of'er, *vt.* To present for acceptance or rejection; to tender; to bid, as a price or wages.—*vi.* To present itself; to declare a willingness, to make an attempt.—*n.* Act of offering; act of bidding a price; the sum bid.

offertory, of'er-to-ri, *n.* Sentences read or repeated in church while the alms or gifts are collecting the alms collected.

off-hand, of'hand, *a.* Done without thinking or hesitation, unpremeditated.—*adv.* On the spur of the moment; promptly.

office, of'is, *n.* Special duty or business; high employment or position under government; function; service, a formulary of devotion, a place where official or professional business is done; persons entrusted with certain duties, persons who transact business in an office; pl. kitchens, outhouses, etc., of a mansion or farm.

officer, of'is-er, *n.* A person invested with an office one who holds a commission in the army or navy.—*vt.* To furnish with officers.

official, of-fi'shal, *a.* Pertaining to an office or public duty, made by virtue of authority.—*n.* One invested with an office of a public nature.

officiate, of-fi'shi-āt, *vi.* To perform official duties, to act in an official capacity.

oil, oil, *n.* An unctuous inflammable liquid drawn from various animal and vegetable substances, a similar substance of mineral origin; an oil-color.—*vi.* To smear or rub over with oil.

oleander, ö-lē-an'der, *n.* An evergreen flowering shrub.

olfactory ol-fak'to-ri, *a.* Pertaining to smelling; having the sense of smelling.—*n.* An organ of smelling.

oligarchy, o'li-gär-ki, *n.* Govern-ment in which the supreme power is in a few hands, those who form such a class or body.

olive, o'liv, *n.* An evergreen tree its fruit, from which a valuable oil is expressed; the color of the olive; the emblem of peace.—*a.* Relating to, or of the color of the olive.

Olympiad, ö-lim'pi-ad, *n.* A period of four years reckoned from one celebration of the Olympic games to another,

the first Olympiad beginning 776 B.C.

omen, ö'men, *n.* An event thought to portend good or evil; an augury; presage.—*vi.* To augur, to betoken.—*vt.* To predict.

ominous, o'min-us, *a.* Containing an omen, and especially an ill omen; inauspicious.

omission, ö-mi'shon, *n.* Act of omitting; neglect or failure to do something required; failure to insert or mention, something omitted.

omit, ö-mit', *vt.* (omitting, omitted) To pass over or neglect; not to insert or mention.

omnivorous, om-niv'or-us, *a.* All-devouring; eating food of every kind.

on, on, *prep.* Above and touching by contact with the surface or upper part; in addition to; at or near; immediately after and as a result in reference or relation to, toward or so as to affect; at the peril of among the staff of; pointing to a state, occupation, etc.—*adv.* On ward; in continuance, adhering not off

once, wuns, *adv.* One time, formerly; immediately after; as soon as.—**At once,** all together; suddenly, forthwith.

one, wun, *a.* Being but a single thing or a unit, closely united forming a whole; single.—*n.* The first of the simple units; the symbol representing this (= 1).—**At one,** in union or concord.—*pron.* Any single person; any man; any person, a thing, particular thing.

only, ön'li, *a.* Single; sole; alone.— *adv.* For one purpose alone; simply; merely; solely.—*conj.* But; excepting that.

onomatopoeia, on'o-ma-tō-pē"a, *n.* The formation of words by imitation of sounds.

ooze, öz, *n.* A soft flow, as of water; soft mud or slime; liquor of a tanvat.—*vi.* (oozing, oozed). To flow or issue forth gently; to percolate.— *vt.* To emit in the shape of moisture.

opal, ö-pal, *n.* A precious stone, which exhibits changeable reflections of green, blue, yellow, and red.

open, ö'pn, *a.* Not shut, covered, or blocked; not restricted, accessible; public; spread out; free, liberal, bounteous, candid, clear, exposed, fully prepared, attentive amenable; not settled; enunciated with a full utterance.—*n.* An open or clear space.—*vt.* To make open; to unclose; to cut into; to spread out; to begin; to make public; to declare open; to reveal.—*vi.* To unclose itself; to be parted; to begin. **opening,** ō'pn-ing, *a.* First in order; beginning.—*n.* Act of one who or that which opens; an open place; aperture; beginning; vacancy; opportunity of commencing a business, etc.

opera, o'pe-ra, *n.* A dramatic composition set to music and sung and acted on the stage; a theater where operas are performed.

opossum, ō-pos'um, *n.* The name of several marsupial mammals of America.

opponent, op-pō'nent, *a.* Opposing; antagonistic; opposite.—*n.* One who opposes; an adversary; an antagonist.

opposition, op-pō-zi'shon, *n.* Act of opposing; attempt to check or defeat; contradiction, inconsistency; the collective body of opponents of a ministry.

oppressive, op-pres'iv, *a.* Burden-some, unjustly severe, tyrannical.

optics, op'tiks, *n.* The science which treats of the nature and properties of light and vision, optical instruments, etc.

optimism, op'tim-izm, *n.* The opinion or doctrine that everything is for the best, tendency to take the most hopeful view.

or, or, *conj.* A particle that marks an alternative, and frequently corresponds with *either* and *whether.*—*adv.* Ere before.—*n.* Heraldic name for gold.

oracle, o'ra-kl, *n.* Among the Greeks and Romans, the answer of a god to an inquiry respecting some future event, place where the answers were given, the sanctuary of the ancient Jews; any person reputed uncommonly wise, a wise or authoritative utterance.

orange, o'ranj *n.* An evergreen fruit-tree and also its fruit, the color of this fruit, a reddish yellow.—*a.* Belonging to an orange; colored as an orange.

orange-peel, o'ranj-pēl, *n.* The rind of an orange separated from the fruit, the peel of the bitter orange dried and candied.

orchestra, or'kes-tra, *n.* That part of the Greek theater allotted to the chorus; that part of a theater, etc. appropriated to the musicians; a body of musicians.

order, or'dėr, *n.* Regular disposition; proper state; established method, public tranquillity, command; instruction to supply goods or to pay money; rank, class, division, or dignity, a religious fraternity; division of natural objects; *pl.* clerical character, specially called holy orders.—**In order,** for the purpose.—*vt.* To place in order; to direct; to command; to give an order or com-

mission for—*vi.* To give command.

ordinal, or'din-al, *a.* Expressing order or succession.—*n.* A number denoting order (as *first);* a book containing an ordination service.

ordinance, or'din-ans, *n.* That which is ordained; law, statute, edict, decree.

ordinary, or'din-a-ri, *a.* Con-formable to order; regular; customary; common; of little merit.—*n.* An ecclesiastical judge; a judge who takes cognizance of causes in his own right; an eating-house where the prices are settled.—**In ordinary,** in actual and constant service; statedly attending, as a physician: but a ship *in ordinary* is one laid up.

ordinate, or'din-āt, *a.* Regular, methodical.—*n.* In geometry, a line of reference determining the position of a point.

organ, or'gan, *n.* An instrument or means; a part of an animal or vegetable by which some function is carried on; a medium of conveying certain opinions; a newspaper; the largest wind instrument of music.

organization, or'gan-i-zā"shon, *n.* Act or process of organizing suitable disposition of parts for performance of vital functions.

organize, or'gan-īz, *vt.* To give an organic structure to; to establish and systematize, to arrange so as to be ready for service.

Orient, ō'ri-ent, *a.* Rising, as the sun; eastern; oriental; bright.—*n.* The East, luster as that of a pearl.—*vt.* To define the position of; to cause to lie from east to west.

orientation, ōr'i-en-tā"shon, *n.* A turning towards the east; position east and west.

origin, o'ri-jin, *n.* Source, beginning; derivation; cause; root; foundation.

original, ō-ri'jin-al, *a.* Pertaining to origin; primitive, first in order; having the power to originate, not copied.—*n.* Origin; source; first copy; model; that from which anything is translated or copied, a person of marked individuality.

originate, ō-ri'jin-āt, *vt.* (originating, originated). To give origin to; to produce.—*vi.* To have origin; to be begun.

Orthodox, or'thō-doks, *a.* Sound in opinion or doctrine; sound in religious doctrines; in accordance with sound doctrine.

orthography, or-thog'ra-fi, *n.* The art of writing words with the proper letters; spelling.

O

Orthopter, Orthopteran, or-thop'tèr, or-thop'tèr-an, *n.* One of an order of insects including cockroaches, grasshoppers, and locusts.

osmose, os'mōs, *n.* The tendency of fluids to pass through porous partitions and mix.

osprey, os'prā, *n.* A kind of hawk or eagle which feeds on fish; one of its feathers.

Osteopathy, os-tē-op'a-thi, *n.* A system of medical treatment, based on the view that the proper adjustment of the vital mechanism is a more important factor than chemical intake in the maintenance of health.

ostrich, os'trich, *n.* A large running bird of Africa, Arabia, and S. America, the largest of existing birds.

other, uTH'èr, *a.* and *pron.* Not the same; second of two; not this; opposite; often used reciprocally with each.

ounce, ouns, *n.* The twelfth part of a pound troy, and the sixteenth of a pound avoirdupois; an Asiatic animal like a small leopard.

our, our, *a.* or *pron.* Pertaining or belonging to us. Ours is used when no noun follows.

out, out, *adv.* On or towards the outside, not in or within forth, beyond usual limits; not in proper place; public; exhausted; deficient; not in employment; loudly; in error, at a loss, having taken her place as a woman in society.—*n.* One who is out, a nook or corner.— *vt.* To put out.—*interj.* Away! begone!

outbreak, out'brāk, *n.* A breaking forth; eruption; sudden manifestation as of anger, disease, etc.

outer, out'èr, *a.* Being on the outside, external.—*n.* That part of a target beyond the circles surrounding the bull's-eye; a shot which hits this part.

outermost, out'èr-mōst, *a.* Being farthest out; being on the extreme external part.

outgrow, out-grō', *vt.* To surpass in growth; to grow too great or old for anything.

outlaw, out'lä, *n.* A person excluded from the benefit of the law—*vt.* To deprive of the benefit and protection of law; to proscribe.

out-patient, out'pā-shent, *n.* A patient not residing in a hospital, but who receives medical advice, etc., from the institution.

outpost, out'pōst, *n.* A station at a distance from the main body of an army; troops placed at such a station.

outrage, out'rāj, *vt.* (outraging, outraged). To do extreme violence or injury to; to abuse; to commit a rape upon.—*n.* Excessive abuse injurious violence.

outskirt, out'skèrt, *n.* Parts near the edge of an area, border, purlieu; generally in *pl.*

outspoken, out'spō-kn, *a.* Free or bold of speech, candid, frank.

outspread, out-spred', *vt* To spread out, to diffuse.—*a.* Extended; expanded.

outstanding, out-stand'ing, *a.* Projecting outward; prominent; unpaid; undelivered.

oval, ō'val, *a.* Shaped like an egg elliptical.—*n.* A figure shaped like an egg or ellipse.

ovation, ō-vā'shon, *n.* A lesser triumph among the ancient Romans; triumphal reception; public marks of respect.

over, ō'vèr, *prep.* Above; denoting motive, occasion, or superiority; across; throughout; upwards of.— *adv.* From side to side; in width; on all the surface, above the top or edge; in excess, completely, too.— *a.* Upper; covering.—*n.* (*cricket*) The number of balls (six or eight) which the bowler delivers in succession from one end of the pitch before a change is made to the other side.

overcharge, ō'vèr-chärj', *vt.* To charge or burden to excess; to fill too numerously.—*n.* o'ver-charj. An excessive charge.

overflow, ō'vèr-flō', *vt.* (pp. overflowed and overflown). To flow or spread over; to flood; to overwhelm.—*vi.* To be so full that the contents run over; to abound.—*n.* o'ver-flo. An inundation; superabundance.

overhaul, ō'vèr-häl', *vt.* To examine thoroughly with a view to repairs, to re-examine; to gain upon or overtake.—*n.* o'ver-hal. Examination, inspection, repair.

overlook, ō'vèr-lük', *vt.* To oversee to superintend; to view from a higher place; to pass by indulgently.

overnight, ō'vèr-nīt, *adv.* Through or during the night; in the night before.

overpower, ō'vèr-pou'èr, *vt.* To be too powerful for; to bear down by force; to overcome; to subdue; to crush.

overreach, ō'vèr-rēch', *vt.* To reach over or beyond, to deceive by artifice; to outwit.

overrule, ō'vèr-röl', *vt.* To control; to govern with high authority; to disallow.

overrun, ō'vėr-run', *vt.* To run or spread over; to ravage; to outrun.—*vi.* To overflow, to run over.

oversea, ō'vėr-sē, *a.* Foreign, from beyond sea.—**overseas,** ō'vėr-sēz *adv.* Abroad.

overtake, ō'vėr-tāk', *vt.* To come up with; to catch; to take by surprise.

overthrow, ō'vėr-thrō', *vt.* To throw or turn over, to overset, to defeat to destroy.—*n.* o'ver-thro. Ruin defeat.

overturn, ō'vėr-tėrn', *vt.* To overset or overthrow; to capsize; to subvert; to ruin.

overweening, ō'vėr-wēn'ing, *a* Haughty; arrogant; proud; conceited.

overwork, ō'vėr-wėrk', *vt.* To work beyond strength, to tire with labor.—*n.* o'ver-werk. Work done beyond one's strength or beyond the amount required.

overwrought, ō'vėr-rat', *p.a.* Wrought to excess; excited to excess, tasked beyond strength.

owe, ō, *vt.* (owing, owed). To be indebted in; to be obliged or bound to pay; to be obliged for.

own, ōn, *a.* Belonging to: used, distinctively and emphatically, after a possessive pronoun, or a noun in the possessive.—*vt.* To hold or possess by right; to acknowledge or avow, to concede.

oxygen, oks'i-jen, *n.* A gaseous element, a component of atmospheric air and water, and essential to animal and vegetable life and combustion.

O

P

pabulum, pab'ū-lum, *n*. Food; that which feeds either mind or body.

pace, pās, *n*. A step; space between the two feet in walking; distance of 2-1/2 feet or 5 feet, gait rate of progress.—*vi*. (pacing, paced). To step, to walk slowly; to move by lifting the legs on the same side together; as a horse.—*vt*. To measure by steps; to accompany and set a proper rate of motion; to race.

pacific, pa-sif'ik, *a*. Suited to make peace; pacifying; calm.—**The Pacific Ocean**, the ocean between America, Asia, and Australia.

package, pak'āj, *n*. A bundle or bale; a packet; charge for packing goods.

pack-horse, pak'hors, *n*. A horse employed in carrying goods and baggage on its back

pack-saddle, pak'sad-l, *n*. The saddle of a pack-horse, made for bearing burdens.

pact, pakt, *n*. A contract; an agreement or covenant.

pad, pad, *n*. An easy-paced horse; a robber who infests the road on foot; a soft saddle; a cushion; a quantity of blotting paper.—*vi*. (padding, padded). To walk or go on foot; to rob on foot.—*vt*. To furnish with padding.

padlock, pad'lok, *n*. A lock with a link to be fastened through a staple.—*vt*. *To* fasten or provide with a padlock

padre, päd'rä, *n*. A chaplain.

paean, pē'an, *n*. A war-song; song of triumph.

pagan, pā'gan, *n*. A heathen.—*a*. Heathenish; idolatrous.

page, pāj, *n*. A young male attendant on persons of distinction; one side of a leaf of a book, a written record.—*vt*. (paging, paged). To number the pages of

pain, pān, *n*. A penalty, bodily suffering, distress, anguish; *pl*. The throes of childbirth; labor; diligent effort.—*vt*. To cause pain to; to afflict, to distress.

painstaking, pānz'tāk-ing, *a*. Giving close application, laborious and careful.—*n*. The taking of pains; careful labor.

paint, pānt, *vt*. To represent by colors and figures; to cover with color, to portray, to delineate.—*vi*. To practice painting.—*n*. A substance used in painting; a pigment; rouge.

painting, pānt'ing, *n*. Art or employment of laying on colors; art of representing objects by colors; a picture, colors laid on.

pair, pār, *n*. Two things of like kind suited, or used together; a couple, a man and his wife, two members on opposite sides in parliament, etc., who agree not to vote for a time.—*vi*. To join in pairs, to mate.—*vt*. To unite in pairs.

pajamas, pā-jäm-az, *n.pl*. A sleeping-suit.

palace, pa'lās, *n*. The house in which an emperor, king, bishop etc., resides, a splendid residence.

palatable, pa'lat-a-bl, *a*. Agreeable to the palate or taste; savory.

palate pa'lāt *n*. The roof of the mouth; taste relish; intellectual taste.

palatial, pa-lā'shal, *a*. Pertaining to a palace; becoming a palace; magnificent.

palaver, pa-la'vė r, *n*. A long or serious conference; idle talk.—*vt*. To flatter or humbug.—*vi*. To talk idly; to engage in a palaver.

pale, pāl, *n*. A pointed stake, an inclosure; sphere or scope.—*vt*. (paling, paled). To inclose with pales to fence in.—*vi*. To turn pale.—*a*. Whitish; wan; deficient in color; not bright, dim.

paleography, pal-ē-og'ra-fi, *n*. The art of deciphering ancient writing.

paleolithic, pal'ē-ō-lith''ik, *a*. Belonging to the earlier stone period, when rude unpolished stone implements were used.

paleontology, pal'ē-on-tol''o-ji, *n*. The science of fossil organic remains.

paleozoic pal'ē-ō-zō''ik, *a*. In *geology*, applied to the lowest division of stratified groups.

pall, päl, *n*. An outer mantle of dignity, a cloth thrown over a coffin at a funeral; a linen cloth to cover a chalice; a covering.—*vt*. To cover with a pall, to shroud to make vapid; to cloy.—*vi*. To become vapid or cloying.

palladium, pal-lä'di-um. *n*. A statue of the goddess Pallas; bulwark; safeguard; a grayish-white hard malleable metal.

pallet, pal'et, *n*. A palette; a tool used by potters, etc.; a small rude bed.

palliate, pal'i-āt, *vt*. To extenuate; to mitigate; to lessen, abate, alleviate.

pallid, pal'id, *a*. Pale, wan.

pallor, pal'or, *n*. Paleness.

palm, päm, *n*. The inner part of the hand, a measure of 3 or 4 inches, name of plants constituting an order of endogens; a branch or leaf of such a plant, victory; triumph.—*vt*. To conceal in the palm of the hand, to impose by fraud.

palpitate, pal 'pi-tāt, *vi.* (palpitating, palpitated). To pulsate rapidly; to throb, to tremble.

palpitation, pal-pi-tā'shon, *n.* Act of palpitating; violent pulsation of the heart.

palsy, päl'zi, *n.* Paralysis, especially of a minor kind.—*vt.* (palsing, palsied). To affect with palsy; to paralyze.

paltry, päl'tri, *a.* Mean and trivia] trifling; worthless; contemptible.

paludal, pal'ū-dal, *a.* Pertaining to marshes. Also *paludine, palustral, palustrine.*

pampas, pam'pas, *n.pl.* The immense grassy treeless plains of South America.

pamper pam'pėr, *vt.* To gratify to the full; to furnish with that which delights.

pamphlet, pam'flet *n.* A small book, stitched but not bound; short treatise.

pan, pan, *n.* A broad and shallow vessel, of metal or earthenware, pond for evaporating salt water to make salt part of a gun-lock hold ing the priming: the skull; the Greek and Roman god of flock and herds.

panacea, pan-a-sē'a, *n.* A remedy for all diseases; a universal medicine.

pancake, pan'kāk, *n.* A thin cake fried in a pan or baked on an iron plate.

panel, pa'nel, *n.* A surface distinct from others adjoining in a piece of work; a sunk portion in a door, etc.; a piece of wood on which a picture is painted, list of Health Insurance doctors for a district; a doctor's list of insured persons; list of those summoned to serve on a jury, in Scotland, the accused.—*vt.* (paneling, paneled). To form with panels.

pang, pang, *n.* A sharp and sudden pain; painful spasm; throe.

panic, pan'ik, *n.* A sudden fright; terror inspired by a trifling cause.—*a.* Extreme, sudden, or causeless: said of fright.

pant, pant, *vi.* To breathe quickly, to gasp; to desire ardently.—*n.* A gasp, a throb.

pantaloons, pan'ta-lönz, *n.pl.* Tightly fitting trousers; trousers in general.

pantheism, pan'thē-izm, *n.* The doctrine that the universe is God or that all things are manifestations of God.

Pantheon, pan'thē-on, *n.* A temple dedicated to all the gods, all the divinities collectively worshiped by a people.

papacy, pā'pa-si, *n.* The office and dignity of the pope; the popes collectively; papal authority or jurisdiction; popedom.

paper, pā'pėr, *n.* A substance formed into thin sheets used for writing, printing, etc.; a leaf, or sheet of this; a journal; an essay or article, promissory notes, bills of exchange, etc.—*a.* Made or consisting of paper; appearing merely in documents without really existing; slight.—*vt.* To cover with paper; to inclose in paper

par, pär, *n.* State of equality; equality in condition or value state of shares or stocks when they may be purchased at the original price.

parable, pa'ra-bl, *n.* An allegorical representation of something real in life or nature, embodying a moral.

parabola, pa-ra'bō-la, *n.* A conic section, shown when a cone is cut by a plane parallel to one of its sides, the curve described theoretically by a projectile.

parachute, pa'ra-shöt, *n.* An apparatus like a large umbrella, enabling a safe drop to the ground from an aircraft.

paraclete, pa'ra-klēt; *n.* One called to aid or support; the Holy Spirit.

parade, pa-rād', *n.* Ostentation show; military display; place where such display is held.—*vt.* (parading, paraded). To exhibit in ostentatious manner; to marshal in military order.—*vi.* To walk about for show; to go about in military procession.

paragraph, pa'ra-graf, *n.* The character ¶ used as a reference, etc.; a distinct section of a writing, distinguished by a break in the lines; a brief notice.

parallax, pa'ral-laks, *n.* The apparent change of position of an object when viewed from different points; the difference between the place of a heavenly body as seen from the earth's surface and its center at the same time.

parallel, pa'ral-lel, *a.* Extended in the same direction, and in all parts equally distant, as lines or surfaces; running in accordance with something, equal in all essential parts.—*n.* A line which throughout its whole length is equidistant from another line; conformity in all essentials; likeness, comparison, counterpart.— *vt.* To place so as to be parallel; to correspond to; to compare.

parallelogram, pa-ral-lel'ō-gram, *n.* A quadrilateral, whose opposite sides are parallel and equal.

parapet, pa'ra-pet *n.* A wall or rampart breast-high, a wall on the edge of a bridge, quay, etc.

paraphernalia, pa'ra-fèr-nā''li-a, *n.pl.* That which a bride brings besides her dowry, as clothing, jewels, etc.; personal attire; trappings.

paraphrase, pa'ra-frāz, *n.* A statement giving the meaning of another statement; a loose or free translation, a sacred song based on a portion of Scripture.—*vt.* To make a paraphrase of; to explain or translate with latitude.

parasite, pa'ra-sīt, *n.* One who frequents the rich, and earns his welcome by flattery; a sycophant: an animal that lives upon or in another; a plant which grows on another.

parasol, pa'ra-sol *n.* A small umbrella used to keep off the sun's rays.

parcel, pär'sel, *n.* A portion of anything, a small bundle or package a collection.—*vt.* (parceling, parceled). To divide into portions, to make up into packages.

parcel-post, pär'sel-pōst, *n.* Depart-ment of a post-office by which parcels are sent.

parch, pärch, *vt.* To dry to extremity; to scorch.—*vi.* To become very dry; to be scorched.

parenthesis, pa-ren'the-sis, *n.;* pl. -theses. A sentence or words inserted in another sentence, usually in brackets. thus, ( ).

parhelion, pär-hē'li-on, *n.,* pl. -lia. A mock sun or meteor, appearing as a bright light near the sun.

park, pärk, *n.* A piece of ground inclosed; ornamental ground adjoining a house; ground in a town for recreation; an assemblage of heavy ordnance.—*vt.* To inclose in a park; to bring together as artillery; to draw up motorcars and leave them for a time in an inclosed space, or at the side of the road.

parody, pa'rod-i, *n.* An adaptation of the words of an author, etc., to a different purpose; a burlesque imitation.—*vt.* (parodying, parodied). To imitate in parody.

parole, pa-rōl', *n.* Words or oral declarations, word of honor, a promise by a prisoner of war not to bear arms against his captors for a certain period, or the like, a military countersign.

paroxysm, pa'roks-izm, *n.* A violent access of feeling (as of rage) convulsion; spasm.

parsimony, pär'si-mō-ni, *n.* The habit of being sparing in expenditure of money; excessive frugality; miserliness; closeness.

parsley, pärs'li, *n.* A garden vegetable, used for flavoring in cooking.

parsnip, pärs'nip, *n.* An umbelliferous plant with a fleshy esculent root.

parson, pär'sn, *n.* The priest or incumbent of a parish; a clergyman.

part, pärt, *n.* A portion or piece of a whole; a section; a constituent or organic portion; share; lot; party; duty; business; character assigned to an actor in a play; *pl.* faculties, superior endowments, regions' locality.—*vt.* To divide; to sever; to share; to distribute; to separate; to intervene.—*vi.* To become separated, broken, or detached; to quit each other; to depart.

partake, pär-tāk', *vi.* (partaking, pret. partook, pp. partaken). To take or have a part with others; to share, to have something of the nature, claim, or right.—*vt.* To share.

partial, pär'shal, *a.* Belonging to or affecting a part only, not general biased to one party; having a fondness.

partiality, pär'shi-al''i-ti, *n.* Unfair bias; undue favor shown; a liking or fondness.

particularize, pär-tik'ū-lèr-īz, *vt.* To make particular mention of; to specify in detail.—*vi.* To be particular to details.

parting, pärt'ing, *p.a.* Serving to part or divide, given at separation departing.—*n.* Division; separation; leave-taking.

partisan, pär'ti-zan, *n.* An adherent of a party or faction; a party man.—*a.* Adhering to a faction.

partition, pär-ti'shon, *n.* Act of parting or dividing; division; a division-wall, part where separation is made.—*vt.* To divide by partitions to divide into shares.

partner, pärt'nèr, *n.* One who shares with another; an associate in business, a husband or wife.

partnership, pärt'nèr-ship, *n.* Fellowship; the association of two or more persons in any business; joint interest or property

partridge, pär'trij, *n.* A game bird of the grouse family.

parturition, pär-tū-ri'shon, *n.* The act of bringing forth young.

pass, päs, *vi.* (pret. and pp. passed or past). To go by or past, to change; to die; to elapse; to be enacted, to be current, to thrust in fencing or fighting; to go success.

patrol, pa-trōl', *n.* The marching round by

a guard at night to secure the safety of a camp; the guard who go such rounds; on active service, a small party sent out to harass the enemy (fighting patrol), or to get information (reconnaissance patrol).—*vi.* (patrolling, patrolled). To go the rounds as a patrol.—*vt.* To pass round, as a guard.

patron, pā 'tron, *n.* A protector; one who supports or protects a person or a work; one who has the disposition of a church-living, professorship, or other appointment, a guardian saint.

patronize, pat'ron-īz or pā ', *vt.* To act as patron of; to countenance or favor; to assume the air of a superior to.

paunchy, pänsh'i, *a.* Big-bellied.

pauper, pä'pėr, *n.* A poor person; one dependent on the public for maintenance.

pause, päz, *n.* A temporary cessation cessation proceeding from doubt; suspense.—*vi.* (pausing, paused). To make a short stop, to delay; to deliberate; to hesitate

pave, pā v, *vt.* (paving, paved). To cover with stone, brick, etc., so as to make a level and solid surface for carriages or foot-passengers.

pavement, pā v'ment, *n.* The solid floor of a street, courtyard, etc. paved part of a road used by footpassengers, material with which anything is paved.

pavilion, pa-vil'yon, *n.* A tent; a small building having a tent-formed roof; a building of ornamental character for entertainments the outer ear.—*vt.* To furnish with pavilions; to shelter with a tent.

pay, pā , *vt.* (paying, paid). To give money, etc., for goods received or service rendered, to reward, to discharge, as a debt; to give, to cover with tar or pitch.—*vi.* To make a payment; to be profitable or remunerative.—*n.* An equivalent for money due, goods, or services; salary, wages; reward.

pea, pē, *n.; pl.* **peas, pease.** A well-known flowering plant cultivated for its seeds; one of the seeds of the plant.

peace, pēs, *n.* A state of quiet; calm; repose; public tranquillity; freedom from war; concord.

peak, pēk, *n.* A projecting point; the top of a mountain ending in a point; the upper corner of a sail extended by a yard, also, the extremity of the yard or gaff.—*vi.* To look sickly; to be emaciated.

peal, pēl, *n.* A series of loud sounds as of bells, thunder, etc.; a set of bells tuned to each other; chime.—*vi.* To give out a peal.—*vt.* To cause to ring or sound.

pear, pār, *n.* A well-known fruit-tree: one of the fruits of the tree.

pearl, pėrl, *n.* A smooth lustrous whitish gem produced by certain mollusks' something resembling a pearl; a small printing type; what is choicest and best.—*a.* Relating to or made of pearl or mother-of-pearl.—*vt.* To set or adorn with pearls.

peck, pek, *n.* A dry measure of eight quarts.—*vt.* and *i.* To strike with the beak, or something pointed; to pick up, as food, with the beak.

pectic, pek'tik, *a.* Having the property of forming a jelly.

pectinate, pek'tin-at, *a.* Toothed like a comb.

pectoral, pek'to-ral, *a.* Pertaining to the breast.—*n.* A breastplate, a medicine for the chest and lungs.

peculate, pe'kū-lā t, *vi.* To appropriate money or goods entrusted to one's care.

peculiar, pē-kū'li-ėr, *a.* One's own; characteristic; particular; unusual, odd.

peculiarity, pē-kū'li-a''ri-ti, *n.* Quality of being peculiar; something peculiar to a person or thing.

pecuniary, pē-kū'ni-a ri, *a.* Relating to or connected with money; consisting of money.

pedagogue, ped'a-gog, *n.* A teacher of children; a schoolmaster.

pedal, pēd'al, *a.* Pertaining to a foot or to a pedal.—*n.* pe'dal. A lever to be pressed by the foot; a part of a musical instrument acted on by the feet.

peel, pēl, *vt.* To strip off, as bark or rind; to flay; to pare; to pillage.— *vi.* To lose the skin, bark or rind, to fall off, as bark or skin—*n.* The skin or rind, a baker's wooden shovel.

peep, pēp, *vi.* To chirp as a chicken; to begin to appear, to look through a crevice.—*n.* A chirp, a look through a small opening; first appearance.

pelt, pelt, *n.* A raw hide; a blow; a heavy shower.—*vt.* To strike with something thrown.—*vi.* To throw missiles; to fall in a heavy shower.

pelvis, pel'vis, *n.* The bony cavity forming the framework of the lower part of the abdomen.

pen, pen *n.* An instrument for writing with ink, style or quality of writing; a small inclosure for cows, etc.; a fold.—*vt.* (penning, penned). To write; to com-

P

pose; to coop or shut up.

penal, pē'nal, *a.* Relating to, enacting, or incurring punishment.

penalty, pen'al-ti, *n.* Punishment for a crime or offense forfeit for non-fulfillment of conditions; sum to be forfeited; a fine.

penance, pen'ans, *n.* An ecclesiastical punishment imposed for sin; voluntary suffering as an expression of penitence.

penchant, päng'shäng, *n.* Strong inclination, bias.

pencil, pen'sil, *n.* A small brush used by painters; an instrument of black-lead, etc., for writing and drawing, a converging or diverging aggregate of rays of light.—*vt.* (penciling, penciled). To write or mark with a pencil.

pend, pend, *vi.* To impend; to wait for settlement.

pendant, pen'dant, *n.* Anything hanging down by way of ornament, a hanging apparatus for giving light, etc.; an appendix or addition; a flag borne at the masthead.

pendent, pen'dent, *a.* Hanging; pendulous; projecting.—*n.* Something hanging.

pendulous, pen'dū-lus, *a.* Hanging; hanging so as to swing; swinging.

pendulum, pen'dū-lum, *n.* A body suspended and swinging; the swinging piece in a clock which regulates its motion.

penetrable, pen'e-tra-bl, *a.* That may be entered or pierced, susceptible of moral or intellectual impression.

penetrate, pen'e-trāt, *vt.* and *i.* To enter or pierce, as into another body; to affect, as the mind; to cause to feel; to understand.

penitentiary, pe-ni-ten'sha-ri, *a.* Relating to penance.—*n.* One who does penance; an office or official of the R. Catholic church connected with the granting of dispensations, etc.; a house of correction.

penumbra, pen-urn'bra, *n.* The partial shadow on the margin of the total shadow in an eclipse; the point of a picture where the shade blends with the light.

people, pē'pl, *n.* The body of persons who compose a community, race, or nation persons indefinitely.—*vt.* (peopling, peopled). To stock with inhabitants; to populate.

pepper, pep'ėr, *n.* A plant and its aromatic pungent seed, much used in seasoning, etc.—*vt.* To sprinkle with pepper; to pelt with shot or missiles; to drub

thoroughly.

peppermint, pep'ėr-mint, *n.* A plant of the mint genus having a penetrating aromatic smell and a strong pungent taste.

per, pėr, *prep.* A Latin preposition used in the sense of by or *for* chiefly in certain Latin phrases, as *per annum,* by or for the year.

perceive, pėr-sēv', *vt.* (perceiving perceived). To apprehend by the organs of sense or by the mind; to observe, to discern.

percentage, pėr-sent'āj, *n.* The allowance duty, rate of interest, proportion, etc., reckoned on each hundred.

perception, pėr-sep'shon, *n.* Act, process, or faculty of perceiving; discernment.

perch, pėrch, *n.* A spiny fresh-water fish, a roost for fowls, an elevated place or position; 51/2 yards, also called a rod or pole, 301/4 square yards, a square rod.—*vi.* To sit on a perch; to light, as a bird.—*vt.* To place on a perch.

perennial, pe-ren'i-al, *a.* Lasting through the year; perpetual; unceasing.—*n.* A plant whose root remains alive more years than two.

perfect, pėr'fekt, *a.* Finished; complete; fully informed; completely skilled; faultless; in *grammar,* denoting a tense which expresses an act completed.—*vt.* To accomplish, to make perfect, to make fully skilful.

performance, pėr-form'ans, *n.* Act of performing, deed; achievement; a literary work; exhibition on the stage; entertainment at a place of amusement.

perfume, pėr'fūm or pėr-fūm', *n.* A pleasant scent or smell, fragrance. —*vt.* (perfuming, perfumed). To scent with perfume; to impregnate with a grateful odor.

period, pē'ri-od, *n.* The time taken up by a heavenly body in revolving round the sun; the time at which anything ends, end, an indefinite portion of any continued state or existence, a complete sentence, the point that marks the end of a sentence, thus (.).

periodical, pē-ri-od'ik-al, *n.* A magazine, newspaper, etc., published at regular periods.—*a.* Periodic.

peripatetic, pe'ri-pa-tet''ik, *a.* Walking about; itinerant; pertaining to Aristotle's system of philosophy, taught while walking.—*n.* One who walks, a follower of Aristotle.

periscope, pe'ri-skōp, *n.* An apparatus or

structure rising above the deck of a submarine vessel, giving by means of mirrors, etc., a view of outside surroundings, though the vessel itself remains submerged; a similar device used in trenches.

perish, pe'rish, *vi.* To die; to wither and decay; to be destroyed; to come to nothing.

peritoneum, pe'ri-tō-nē''um, *n.* A membrane investing the internal surface of the abdomen, and the viscera contained in it.

perjure, pėr'jūr, *vt.* (perjuring, perjured). To forswear, wilfully to make a false oath when administered legally.

permit, pėr-mit' *vt.* and *i.* (permitting, permitted). To allow; to grant; to suffer; to concede.—*n.* per'mit. A written permission or license given by competent authority.

permutation, per-mū-tā 'shon *n.* Interchange, in *mathematics,* any of the ways in which a set of quantities can be arranged.

pernicious, pėr-ni'shus, *a.* Having the quality of destroying or injuring; destructive; deadly; noxious.

perpetuity, pėr-pe-tū'i-ti, *n.* State or quality of being perpetual; endless duration; something of which there will be no end.

perplexity, pėr-pleks'ī-ti, *n.* State of being puzzled, or at a loss; bewilderment; state of being intricate or involved.

persecute, pėr'se-kūt, *vt.* (persecuting, persecuted). To harass with unjust punishment, to afflict for adherence to a particular creed.

persevere, pėr-se-vėr', *vi.* (persevering, persevered). To continue steadfastly in any business; to pursue steadily any design.

persist, pėr-sist', *vi.* To continue steadily in any business or course; to persevere; to continue in a certain state.

personal, pėr'son-al, *a.* Pertaining to a person; peculiar or proper to him or her, belonging to face and figure; denoting the person in a grammatical sense.

personality, pėr-son-al'i-ti *n.* State of being personal; that which constitutes an individual a distinct person; disparaging remark on one's conduct and character; in *law,* personal estate.

perspective, pėr-spek'tiv, *n.* The art of representing objects on a flat surface so that they appear to have their natural dimensions and relations; a representa-

tion of objects in perspective view.—*a.* Pertaining to the art of perspective.

perspicacious, pėr-spi-kā'shus, *a.* Quicksighted; of acute discernment.

persuasive, pėr-swā'siv *a.* Having the power of persuading; calculated to persuade.—*n.* That which persuades; an incitement.

pertinent, pėr'ti-nent, *a.* Related to the subject or matter in hand; opposite; fit.

peruse, pe-rūz', *vt.* (perusing, perused). To read through to read with attention; to examine carefully.

pervade, pėr-vād', *vt.* (pervading pervaded). To pass or flow through; to permeate; to be diffused through.

perverse, pėr-vėrs', *a.* Obstinate in the wrong; stubborn; untractable; petulant.

pervert, pėr-vert', *vt.* To turn from truth or proper purpose; to corrupt, to misinterpret. to misapply.—*n.* per'vert. One who has been perverted.

pestilence, pes'ti-lens *n.* Any contagious disease that is epidemic and fatal; something morally evil or destructive.

pestle, pes'l, *n.* An instrument for pounding substances in a mortar.—*vt.* and *i.* (pestling, pestled). To pound with a pestle.

pet, pet, *n.* A darling any little animal fondled and indulged; fit of peevishness.— *vt.* (petting, petted). To fondle, to indulge.

petition, pē-ti'shon, *n.* An entreaty, supplication, or prayer; a written application in legal proceedings.—*vt.* To supplicate; to solicit.

petrify, pet-ri-fī, *vt.* To turn into stone or a fossil; to paralyze or stupefy.—*vi.* To become stone, or of a stony hardiness.

petulant, pe'tū-lant, *a.* Irritable; peevish, fretful; saucy; pert; capricious.

pewter, pū'tėr, *n.* An alloy mainly of tin and lead, a vessel made of pewter.—*a.* Relating to or made of pewter.

phallus, fal'lus, *n.* The emblem of the generative power in nature, especially in certain religious usages.

pharmaceutic, pharmaceutical, fär-ma-sū'tik, fär-ma-sū'tik-al, *a.* Pertaining to the knowledge or art of pharmacy.

pharynx, fā'ringks *n.* The muscular sac between the mouth and the esophagus.

phase, fāz, *n.* A particular stage of the moon or a planet in respect to illumination; state of a varying phenomenon, one of the various aspects of a question.

phenomenon, fē-no'me-non, *n.;* pl. **-mena.** An appearance; anything visi-

P

ble, an appearance whose cause is not immediately obvious; something extra-ordinary.

philanthropist, fi-lan'throp-ist, *n*. One devoted to philanthropy; one who exerts himself in doing good to his fel-lowmen.

philosophy, fi-los'o-fi, *n*. The science which tries to account for the phenome-na of the universe; metaphysics; the general principles underlying some branch of knowledge; practical wisdom.

phonetics, fō-net'iks, *n.pl*. The doctrine or science of sounds especially of the human voice; the representation of sounds.

phonograph, fō'nō-graf, *n*. An instrument for registering and reproducing sounds; a predecessor of the gramophone.

phosgene, fos'jēn, *n*. A poison gas, car-bon oxychloride.

phosphate, fos'fāt, *n*. A salt of phosphoric acid.

photography, fō-tog'ra-fi, *n*. The art or practice of producing representations of scenes and objects by the action of light on chemically prepared surfaces.

photology, fō-tol'o-ji, *n*. The doctrine or science of light.

photometer, fō-tom'et-ėr, *n*. An instru-ment for measuring the intensity of lights.

phrase, frāz, *n*. A short sentence or expression, an idiom, style, diction.—*vt*. and *i*. (phrasing, phrased). To style, to express.

phraseology, frā-zē-ol'o-ji, *n*. Manner of expression; peculiar words used in a sentence. diction; style.

physics, fi'ziks, *n*. That branch of science which deals with mechanics, dynamics, light, heat, sound, electricity, and mag-netism; natural philosophy.

physiognomy, fi-zi-og'no-mi, *n*. The art of perceiving a person's character by his countenance; particular cast or expression of countenance.

physiography, fi-zi-og'ra-fi, *n*. The sci-ence of the earth's physical features and phenomena; physical geography.

physiology, fi-zi-ol'o-ji, *n*. The science of the phenomena of life, the study of the functions of living beings.

pick, pik, *vt*. To strike at with something pointed; to peck at, to clean by the teeth, fingers, etc.; to select; to pluck, to gather.—*vi*. To eat slowly; to nibble, to pilfer.—*n*. A pointed tool; a pick-axe; choice; selection.

picket, pik'et, *n*. A pointed stake used in fortification; a pale; an advanced guard or outpost, a game at cards.—*vt*. To for-tify with pickets; to post as a guard of observation.

pickle, pik'l, *n*. Brine; a solution of salt and water for preserving flesh, fish, etc., vegetables preserved in vinegar; a state of difficulty or disorder, a trouble-some child.—*vt*. (pickling, pickled). To preserve in or treat with pickle.

picture, pik'tūr, *n*. A painting drawing, etc., exhibiting the resemblance of any-thing; any resemblance or representa-tion, *pl*. the moving photographs shown in cinematography; the cinema.—*vt*. To represent pictorially, to present an ideal likeness of; to describe in a vivid man-ner.

picturesque, pik-tūr-esk', *a*. Form-ing, or fitted to form, a pleasing picture; abounding with vivid imagery; graphic.

pie, pī, *n*. A paste baked with something in or under it; a mass of types unsorted, the magpie.

piece, pēs, *n*. A portion of anything; a dis-tinct part, a composition or writing of no great length; a separate performance; a picture; a coin; a single firearm.—*vt*. (piecing, pieced). To patch, to join.—*vi*. To unite or join on.

piety, pī'e-ti, *n*. Reverence or veneration towards God, godliness; devotion; reli-gion.

pig, pig, *n*. A young swine; a swine in general, an oblong mass of unforged metal.—*vt*. or *i*. (pigging, pigged). To bring forth pigs; to act like pigs.

pigeon-hole, pi'jon-hōl, *n*. A hole for pigeons to enter their dwelling a divi-sion in a desk or case for holding papers.

pigment, pig'ment, *n*. Paint; any prepara-tion used by painters, dyers, etc., to impart colors to bodies, coloring matter.

pill, pil, *n*. A medicine in the form of a lit-tle ball, anything nauseous to be accept-ed.—*vt*. To dose with pills; to form into pills; to rob; to plunder.

pillow, pil'ō, *n*. A long soft cushion; something that bears or supports.—*vt*. To rest or lay on for support.

pilot, pī'lot, *n*. One whose occupation is to steer ships, a guide, a director of one's course.—*vt*. To act as pilot of, to guide through dangers or difficulties.

pimp, pimp, *n*. A man who provides grati-fications for others' lusts; a procurer.—*vi*. To pander, to procure women for others.

pin, pin, *n*. A longish piece of metal, wood, etc., used for a fastening, or as a support; a peg; a bolt.—*vt*. (pinning, pinned). To fasten with a pin or pins; to hold fast.—*vt*. To inclose, to pen or pound.

pinch, pinsh, *vt*. To press hard or squeeze, to nip, to afflict.—*vi*. To press painfully; to be sparing.—*n*. A close compression, as with the fingers; a nip; a pang; straits; a strong iron lever; as much as is taken by the finger and thumb; a small quantity.

pinion, pin'yon, *n*. A bird's wing; the joint of a wing remotest from the body; a large wing-feather; a small toothed wheel; a fetter for the arms.—*vt*. To bind the wings of, to cut off, as the first joint of the wing; to fetter.

pink, pingk, *n*. A garden flower; a light rose-color or pigment; the flower or something supremely excellent.—*a*. Of a fine light rose color.—*vt*. To work in eyelet holes; to scallop; to stab.—*vi*. To wink or blink.

pioneer, pī-on-ēr', *n*. One whose business is to prepare the road for an army, make entrenchments etc., one who leads the way.—*vt*. To prepare a way for.—*vi*. To act as pioneer.

pipe, pîp, *n*. A wind-instrument of music; a long tube; a tube with a bowl at one end for tobacco, the windpipe; a call of a bird; a wine measure containing about 105 imperial gallons.—*vi*. (piping, piped). To play on a pipe, to whistle.—*vt*. To utter in a high tone; to call by a pipe or whistle.

piracy, pî'ra-si, *n*. The act or practice of robbing on the high seas; infringement of the law of copyright.

pirate, pî'rat, *n*. A robber on the high seas; a ship engaged in piracy; one who publishes others' writings without permission.—*vi*. (pirating, pirated). To rob on the high-seas.—*vt*. To take without right, as writings.

pistachio, pis-tā'shi-ō, *n*. The nut of a small tree cultivated in S. Europe for its fruit, the tree itself also called *pistacia*.

pistol, pis'tol, *n*. A small firearm fired with one hand.—*vt*. (pistoling, pistolled). To shoot with a pistol.

piston, pis'ton, *n*. a cylindrical piece of metal which fits exactly into a hollow cylinder, and works alternately in two directions.

piston-rod, pis'ton-rod, *n*. A rod which connects a piston to some other piece, and either moved by the piston or moving it.

pit, pit, *n*. A hollow in the earth; the shaft of a mine, a vat in tanning, dyeing, etc.; a concealed hole for catching wild beasts; a small cavity or depression, part of the floor of a theater.—*vt*. (pitting, pitted). To lay in a pit or hole; to mark with little hollows, to set in competition.

pitch, pich, *vt*. To thrust, as a pointed object; to fix; to set; to throw; to set the key-note of; to set in array; to smear or cover with pitch.—*vi*. To settle; to fall headlong, to fix choice, to encamp, to rise and fall, as a ship.—*n*. A throw; degree of elevation; highest rise, descent; elevation of a note; (cricket) prepared ground between wickets, a thick dark resinous substance obtained from tar.

pith, pith, *n*. The spongy substance in the center of exogenous plants the spinal cord or marrow of an animal; strength or force; energy; cogency, essence.

pity, pi'ti, *n*. Sympathy or compassion; ground of pity; thing to be regretted.—*vt*. (pitying, pitied). To feel pain or grief for; to sympathize with.—*vi*. To be compassionate.

pivot, pi'vot, *n*. A pin on which something turns; a turning-point; that on which important results depend.—*vt*. To place on or furnish with a pivot.

placard, plak'ėrd or pla-kärd', *n*. A written or printed bill posted in a public place; a poster.—*vt*. To post placards.

place, pläs, *n*. An open space in a town; a locality, spot, or site; position; room; an edifice; quarters; a passage in a book; rank; office; calling; ground or occasion; stead.—*vt*. (placing, placed). To put or set, to locate, to appoint or set in an office, rank, or condition to invest; to lend.

placenta, pla-sen'ta, *n*. The afterbirth; an organ developed in mammals during pregnancy, connecting the mother and fetus, the part of the seed-vessel to which the seeds are attached.

plait, plāt, *n*. A fold; a doubling of cloth, etc., a braid, as of hair, etc.— *vt*. To fold, to double in narrow strips; to braid.

plan, plan, *n*. The representation of anything on a flat surface; sketch; scheme; project; method; process.—*vt*. (planning, planned). To form a plan or repre-

P

sentation of to scheme.—*vi*. To form a scheme.

plane, plane-tree, plān, plān'trē, *n*. A forest tree with a straight smooth stem and palmate leaves a kind of maple.

plant, plant, *n*. One of the living organisms of the vegetable kingdom; a herb; a shoot or slip; the machinery, etc., necessary to carry on a business.—*vt*. To set in the ground for growth; to set firmly; to establish; to furnish with plants, to set and direct, as cannon.—*vi*. To set plants in the ground.

plasma, plas'ma or plaz'ma, *n*. Formless matter; the simplest form of organized matter in the vegetable and animal body.

plaster, pläs'tèr, *n*. An adhesive substance used in medical practice, a mixture of lime, water sand etc., for coating walls; calcined gypsum, used with water for finishing walls, for casts, cement, etc.—*vt*. To overlay with plaster; to lay on coarsely.

plastic, plas'tik, *a*. Having the power to give form to matter; capable of being molded, applied to sculpture, as distinguished from painting, etc.—**plastics**, plas'tiks, *n*. The science or craft of converting various resins into durable materials; the articles so made.

plat, plat, *vt*. (platting, platted). To plait; to weave; to make a groundplan of—*n*. A plot of ground devoted to some special purpose.

plate, plāt, *n*. A flat piece of metal; gold and silver wrought into utensils, a shallow flattish dish for eatables; an engraved piece of metal for printing; a page of stereotype for printing.—*vt*. (plating, plated). To cover with a thin coating of metal, as of silver.

plating, plāt'ing, *n*. The art of covering articles with gold or silver; the coating itself.

plea, plē, *n*. A suit or action at law; that which is alleged in support, justification, or defense; an excuse; a pleading.

plead, plēd, *vi*. (pleading, pleaded or pled). To argue in support of or against a claim, to present an answer to the declaration of a plaintiff; to supplicate with earnestness, to urge.—*vt*. To discuss and defend; to argue; to offer in excuse; to allege in a legal defense.

pleasant, ple'zant, *a*. Pleasing; agreeable; grateful; humorous; sportive.

please, plēz, *vt*. (pleasing, pleased). To excite agreeable sensations or emotions in; to delight, to gratify; to seem good to.—*vi*. To give pleasure; to be kind enough.

pleasurable, ple'zhŭr-a-bl, *a*. Pleasing, giving pleasure; affording gratification.

pleasure, ple'zhŭr, *n*. The gratification of the senses or of the mind; agreeable emotion; delight; joy; approbation; choice; will; purpose; command; arbitrary will or choice.

plebeian, ple-bē'an, *a*. Pertaining to the common people; vulgar; common.—*n*. One of the lower ranks of men, one of the common people of ancient Rome.

plenipotentiary, ple'ni-pō-ten"shia-ri, *n*. A person with full power to act for another, an ambassador with full power.—*a*. Containing or invested with full power.

plight, plīt, *vi*. To pledge, as one's word or honor, to give as a security; never applied to property or goods.—*n*. A pledge, a solemn promise; predicament; risky or dangerous state.

plod, plod, *vi*. (plodding, plodded). To trudge or walk heavily; to toil; to drudge.—*vt*. To accomplish by toilsome exertion.

plot, plot, *n*. A small piece of ground; a plan, as of a field, etc., on paper; a scheme; a conspiracy; the story of a play, novel, etc.—*vt*. (plotting, plotted). To make a plan of; to devise.—*vi*. To conspire; to contrive a plan.

plow, plou, *n*. An instrument for turning up the soil.—*vt*. To turn up with the plow, to make grooves in; to run through, as in sailing.—*vi*. To turn up the soil with a plow; to use a plow.

plum, plum, *n*. A fleshy fruit containing a kernel; the tree producing it, a raisin, a handsome sum or fortune generally.

plumb, plum, *n*. A plummet; a perpendicular position.—*a*. Perpendicular.—*adv*. In a perpendicular direction.—*vt*. To set perpendicularly, to sound with a plummet; to ascertain the capacity of; to sound.

plump, plump, *a*. Fat, stout; chubby.—*vt*. To make plump, to dilate.—*vi*. To plunge or fall like a heavy mass; to fall suddenly; to vote for only one candidate.—*adv*. Suddenly; at once; flatly.

plunder, plun'dèr, *vt*. To deprive of goods or valuables; to pillage; to spoil.—*n*. Robbery; pillage; spoil; booty.

plunge, plunj, *vt*. (plunging, plunged). To thrust into water or other fluid; to immerse; to thrust or push; to cast or involve.—*vi.* To dive or rush into water, etc., to pitch or throw oneself head-long; to throw the body forward and the hind-legs up, as a horse.—*n.* Act of plunging into water, etc.; act of throwing oneself headlong, like an unruly horse.

plutonium, plö-tōn'i-um, *n.* An element got from uranium by bombarding it with neutrons.

ply, plī, *vt.* (plying, plied). To employ with diligence; to work at, to assail briskly; to beset; to press.—*vi.* To work steadily; to go in haste; to run regularly between any two ports, as a vessel.—*n.* A fold; a plait.

pneumatic, nū-mat'ik, *a.* Pertaining to air; moved or played by means of air, filled with or fitted to contain air.

pneumatics, nū-mat'iks, *n.* That branch of physics which treats of the mechanical properties of elastic fluids and particularly of air.

poach, pōch, *vt.* To cook (eggs) by breaking and pouring among boiling water; to pierce; to tread or stamp.—*vt.* To encroach on another's ground to steal game, to kill game contrary to law; to be or become swampy.

poetic, poetical, pō-et'ik, pō-et'ik-al, *a.* Pertaining or suitable to poetry; expressed in poetry or measure; possessing the peculiar beauties of poetry.

poetry, pō'et-ri, *n.* The language of the imagination or emotions expressed rhythmically; the artistic expression of thought in emotional language; whatever appeals to the sense of ideal beauty; verse; poems.

point, point, *n.* The sharp end of anything; a small headland; sting of an epigram; telling force of expression; exact spot; verge; stage; degree; a mark of punctuation; a mark or dot; end or purpose; characteristic; argument; (cricket) fielder square with wicket on off side; *pl.* The movable guiding rails at junctions on railways.—*vt.* To make pointed, to aim, to indicate to punctuate; to fill the joints of with mortar.—*vi.* To direct the finger to an object, to indicate the presence of game, as dogs do; to show distinctly.

poise, poiz, *n.* Weight; balance; that which balances.—*vt.* (poising poised). To balance in weight, to hold in equilibrium.—*vi.* To be balanced or suspended, to depend.

poison, poi'zn, *n.* Any agent capable of

producing a morbid effect on anything endowed with life.— *vi.* To infect with poison, to taint, impair, or corrupt.

pole, pōl, *n.* A long piece of wood; a measure of 5-1/2 yards or 30-1/4 square yards; one of the extremities of the axis of the celestial sphere or the earth; the pole-star one of the two points in a magnet in which the power seems concentrated, (with cap.) a native of Poland.—*vt.* (poling, poled). To furnish with poles; to impel by poles.

police, pō-lēs', *n.* The internal government of a community; a body of civil officers for enforcing order, cleanliness, etc.— *vt.* (policing, policed). To guard or regulate by police.

policy, po'li-si, *n.* The governing a city, state, or nation; line of conduct with respect to foreign or internal affairs; dexterity of management; pleasure-grounds around a mansion; contract of insurance.

polytechnic, po-li-tek'nik, *a.* Comprehending many arts; designating a school teaching many branches of art or science.—*n.* A school of instruction in arts.

pomegranate, pōm'gran-āt, *n.* A fruit of the size of an orange, containing numerous seeds, the tree producing the fruit.

pommel, pum'el, *n* A knob or ball the knob on the hilt of a sword; the protuberant part of a saddlebow.—*vt.* (pommeling, pommelled). To beat; to belabor.

pontifical, pon-tif'ik-al, *a.* Belonging to a high-priest or to the pope.—*n.* A book containing rites performable by a bishop; *pl.* the dress of a priest or bishop.

pontoon, pon-tön, *n.* A kind of boat for supporting temporary bridges, a watertight structure to assist in raising submerged vessels.

pop, pop, *n.* A small, smart sound.—*vi.* (popping, popped). To make a small, smart sound; to enter or issue forth suddenly.—*vt.* To offer with a quick sudden motion, to thrust or push suddenly.—*adv.* Suddenly.

popular, po'pū-lėr, *a.* Pertaining to the common people; familiar; plain; liked by people in general; prevalent.

popularize, po'pū-lėr-īz, *vi.* To make popular or suitable to the common mind; to spread among the people.

populate, po'pū-lā t, *vt.* To people; to furnish with inhabitants.

P

population, po-pū-lā 'shon, *n.* Act or process of populating; number of people in a country, etc.; the inhabitants.

porcelain, por'sē-lā n, *n.* The finest species of pottery ware.

porch, pōrch, *n.* A portico; covered approach at the entrance of buildings.

porcine pōr'sĭn *a.* Pertaining to swine like a swine; hog-like.

porcupine, por'kū-pĭn, *n.* A rodent animal, about 2 feet long, with erectile spines.

pore, pōr, *n.* A minute opening in the skin, through which the perspirable matter passes, a small interstice.—*vi.* (poring, pored). To look with steady attention; to read or examine with perseverance.

portal, pōrt'al, *n.* A door or gate; the main entrance of a cathedral, etc.—*a.* Belonging to a vein connected with the liver.

Portuguese, por'tū-gēz, *a.* Pertaining to Portugal.—*n.* The language of Portugal; the people of Portugal.

pose, pōz, *n.* Attitude or position an artistic posture.—*vi.* (posing posed). To attitudinize; to assume characteristic airs.—*vt.* To cause to assume a certain posture; to state or lay down; to perplex or puzzle.

positive, poz'it-iv, *a.* Definitely laid down explicit, absolute, actual, confident, dogmatic, affirmative noting the simple state of an adjective; applied to the philosophical system of Auguste Comte, which limits itself to human experience, applied to electricity produced by rubbing a vitreous substance.—*n.* That which is positive; the positive degree.

possess, po-zes', *vt.* To have and hold; to own; to affect by some power or influence, to pervade, to put in possession; to furnish or fill.

post, pōst, *n.* A piece of timber, etc., set upright, a place assigned, a military or other station; office or employment; a carrier of letters, messages, etc., a system for the public conveyance of letters, etc.; a post-office; a size of paper, about 18 or 19 inches by 15.—*vt.* To travel with post-horses; to hasten on.— *vt.* To place, to place in the post-office to transfer (accounts or items) to the ledger; to make master of full details, to fix up in some public place.—*a.* Used in travelling quickly.—*adv.* Travelling as a post, swiftly.

postage, pōst'āj, *n.* The charge for conveying letters or other articles by post.

posterior, pos-tē'ri-or, *a.* Later or subsequent; hinder.—*n.* A hinder part; *pl.* the hinder parts of an animal.

post-office, pōst'of-is, *n.* An office where letters are received for transmission, a government department that has the duty of conveying letters, etc.

postpone, pōst-pōn, *vt.* (postponing postponed). To put off to a later time; to set below something else in value.

pot, pot, *n.* A metallic or earthenware vessel more deep than broad; the quantity contained in a pot; a sort of paper of small-sized sheets.—*vt.* (potting, potted). To put in a pot; to preserve in pots; to plant in a pot of earth.

potter, pot'ėr, *n.* One who makes earthenware vessels or crockery.—*vi.* To busy oneself about trifles; to move slowly.

poultice, pōl'tis, *n.* A soft composition applied to sores.—*vt.* (poulticing, poulticed). To apply a poultice to.

pounce, pouns, *n.* A fine powder to prevent ink from spreading on paper; the claw or talon of a bird.—*vt.* (pouncing pounced). To sprinkle or rub with pounce.—*vi.* To fall on and seize with the pounces or talons, to fall on suddenly.

pound, pound, *n.* A standard weight of 12 ounces troy or 16 ounces avoirdupois; a money of account, an inclosure for cattle.— *vt.* To confine in a public pound; to beat, to pulverize.

powder, pou'dėr, *n.* A dry substance of minute particles; dust; gunpowder.—*vt.* To reduce to fine particles, to sprinkle with powder to corn, as meat. vi. To fall to dust; to use powder for the hair or face.

power, pou'ėr, *n.* Ability to act or do; strength; influence; talent; command, authority, one who exercises authority; a state or government; warrant; a mechanical ad vantage or effect, product of the multiplication of a number by itself.

practical, prak'ti-kal, *a.* Pertaining to practice, action, or use; not merely theoretical; skilled in actual work.

practice, prak'tis, *n.* A doing or effecting; custom; habit; actual performance, exercise of any profession; medical treatment; training; drill, dexterity.

practice, prak'tis, *vt.* (practicing, practiced). To put in practice; to do or perform frequently or habitually; to exercise, as any profession; to commit;

to teach by practice.— vi. To perform certain acts frequently for instruction or amusement; to exercise some profession.

prance, prans, vt. (prancing, pranced). To spring, leap, or caper, as a horse; to strut about ostentatiously.

prank, prangk, vt. To adorn in a showy manner; to dress up.—vi. To have a showy appearance.—n. A merry trick; a caper.

prate, prāt, vi. (prating, prated). To babble, chatter, tattle.—vt. To utter foolishly.—n. Trifling talk; unmeaning loquacity.

prattle, prat'l, vi. (prattling, prattled). To talk much and idly, like a child; to prate.—n. Trifling or puerile talk.

prayer, prā'er, n. One who prays; the act of praying; a petition; a solemn petition to G;od; a formula of worship, public or private; that part of a written petition which specifies the thing desired to be granted.

preach, prēch, vi. To deliver a sermon, to give earnest advice.—vt. To proclaim; to publish in religious discourses; to deliver in public, as a discourse.

precedent, prē-sē d'ent, a. Preceding; going before in time; anterior.

precept, prē'sept, n. Anything enjoined as an authoritative rule of action; injunction; doctrine; maxim.

precipitate, prē'si'pi-tā t, vt. and i. To throw or hurl headlong; to has ten excessively; to cause to sink or to fall to the bottom of a vessel, as a substance in solution.—a. Headlong, overhasty.—n. A substance deposited from a liquid in which it has been dissolved.

precognition, prē -kog-ni'shon, n. Previous knowledge; preliminary examination, as of a witness before a trial (Scots law).

preconceive, prē-kon-sēv', vt. To form a conception or opinion of beforehand.

predicable, pre'di-ka-bl, a. That may be attributed to something.— n. Anything that may be affirmed of another.

predicate, pre'di-kāt, vt. and i. To affirm one thing of another; to assert.—n. In logic, that which is affirmed or denied of the subject; in grammar, the word or words which express what is affirmed or denied of the subject.

prefabricate, prē-fab'ri-kāt, vt. To manufacture separately parts, of a building, etc., designed to be easily fitted together afterwards.

preface, pre'fās, n. Introduction to a discourse or book, etc.—vt. (prefacing, prefaced). To introduce by preliminary remarks.

prefect, prē'fekt, n. One placed over others, a governor, chief magistrate; a senior pupil entrusted with the maintenance of discipline.

prefer, prē-fer', vt. (preferring, preferred). To bring or lay before; to present, as a petition, etc.; to exalt; to set higher in estimation; to choose rather.

preference, pre'fer-ens, n. Act of preferring; state of being preferred, choice.

prehensible, prē-hen'si-bl, a. That may be seized.

prejudice, pre'jū-dis, n. An unwarranted bias; prepossession; detriment; injury.— vt. To bias the mind of, to do harm to.

preliminary, prē-lim'in-a-ri, a. Introductory; preparatory; prefactory.— n. Something introductory; preface, prelude.

prelude, prel'ūd or prē-lūd', vt. (preluding, preluded). To introduce, to preface.—vi. To form a prelude.—n. prel'ud or pre'lud. Something preparatory; a musical introduction.

premium, prē'mi-um, n. A reward or prize; a bonus; a bounty; sum paid for insurance; increase in value.

preoccupation, prē-ok'kū-pā ''shon, n. Act of preoccupying; prior possession; state of being preoccupied.

preoccupy, prē-ok'kū-pī, vt. To occupy before another; to engross before another; to engross beforehand.

preparation, pre-pa-rā 'shon, n. Act or operation of preparing; that which is prepared; state of being prepared.

prepare, prē-pā r', vt. and i. (preparing, prepared). To make ready; to adjust; to provide; to procure as suitable.

preposterous, prē-pos'ter-us, a. Absurd; irrational; monstrous; utterly ridiculous.

prerogative, prē-ro'ga-tiv, n. A prior claim or title; an exclusive privilege; an official and hereditary right.

presage, prē'sā j or pres'aj, n. A presentiment; a prognostic, omen, or sign.—vt. and i. prē-sā j', (presaging, presaged). To betoken; to forebode, to predict.

prescribe, prē-skrīb', vt. (prescribing, prescribed). To lay down authoritatively for direction, to appoint; to direct to be used as a remedy.—vi. To give directions, to give medical directions to become of no validity through lapse of time.

P

prescription, prĕ-skrip'shon, *n.* Act of prescribing; that which is prescribed; a claim or title based on long use; the loss of a legal right by lapse of time.

presence, pre'zens, *n.* State of being present; existence in a certain place; company; sight; port; mien; the person of a great personage; an appearance or apparition; readiness.

present, pre'zent, *a.* Being at hand, in view, or in a certain place; now existing; ready at hand; quick in emergency.—*n.* Present time; *pl.* term used in a legal document for the document itself.

present, prĕ-zent', *vt.* To introduce to or bring before a superior; to show, to give or bestow; to nominate to an ecclesiastical benefice; to lay before a public body for consideration, to point or aim, as a weapon.—*n.* pre'zent. A donation; a gift.

preside, prĕ-zĭd', *vi.* (presiding, presided). To exercise authority or superintendence; to have the post of chairman.

president, pre'zi-dent, *n.* One who presides, the head of a province or state; the highest officer of state in a republic.

press, pres, *vt.* To bear or weigh heavily upon; to squeeze; to urge to enforce; to emphasize, to solicit earnestly; to force into service.— *vi.* To bear heavily or with force; to crowd; to push with force.—*n.* A pressing; a crowd; an instrument for squeezing or crushing; a machine for printing, the art or business of printing; periodical literature; an upright cupboard for pressing.

presume, prĕ-zūm', *vt.* (presuming, presumed). To take for granted; to take the liberty, to make bold.—*vi.* To infer, to act in a forward way.

pretend, prĕ-tend', *vt.* To feign; to simulate; to assume or profess to feel, use as a pretext.—*vi.* To assume a false character; to sham; to put in a claim.

prevail, pĕ-vāl', *vi.* To gain the victory or superiority; to be in force; to succeed; to gam over by persuasion.

prey, prā, *Property* taken from an enemy; spoil; booty; a victim.—*vi.* To take prey or booty; to get food by rapine; to cause to pine away: with *on.*

price, prĭs, *n.* The value which a seller sets on his goods; cost; value; worthy.—*vt.* (pricing, priced). To set a price on; to ask the price of.

prick, prik, *n.* A slender pointed thing that can pierce; a thorn; a puncture by a prick; a sting; tormenting thought.—*vt.* To pierce with a prick; to erect, as ears; to spur; to sting with remorse, to trace by puncturing.—*vi.* To spur on; to ride rapidly; to feel a prickly sensation.

prickle, prik'l, *n.* A small sharppointed shoot; a thorn; a small spine.—*vt.* To prick, to cause a prickly feeling in.

pride, prĭd, *n.* State or quality of being proud, inordinate self-esteem a cause of pride; glory or delight, highest pitch; splendid show.—*vt.* To indulge pride, to value (oneself).

priest, prĕst, *n.* A man who officiates in sacred offices; a clergyman above a deacon and below a bishop.

primary, prī'ma-ri, *a.* First, chief first in time; original; elementary, radical.—*n.* That which stands first or highest in importance, a large feather of a bird's wing.

prime, prîm, *a.* Foremost, first, original; first in rank, excellence, or importance; not divisible by any smaller number.— *n.* The earliest stage; full health; strength; or beauty; the best part.—*vt.* (priming, primed). To make ready for action; to supply with powder for communicating fire to a charge; to instruct or prepare beforehand to lay on the first color in painting.

priming, prîm'ing, *n.* The powder used to ignite a charge; a first layer of paint; water carried over with the steam into the cylinder.

primitive, prim'it-iv, *a.* Being the first or earliest of its kind; original; antiquated, primary radical, not derived.—*n.* That which is original; an original word.

principal, prin'si-pal, *a.* First, chief most important or considerable.— *n.* A chief or head, the president governor, or chief in authority, one primarily engaged; a capital sum lent on interest.

principle, prin'si-pl, *n.* Cause or origin, a general truth, a fundamental law; a ule of action; uprightness, an element.

print, print, *vt.* To mark by pressure; to stamp; to form or copy by pressure; as from types, etc.—*vi.* To use or practice typography, to publish.—*n.* A mark made by pressure; an engraving, etc.; state of being printed; a newspaper; printed calico.

private, prī'vat, *a.* Separate from others, solitary, personal, secret not having a public or official character.—**In private**, secretly.—*n.* A common soldier.

privy, pri'vi, *a.* Private; assigned to private uses; secret; privately knowing (with *to*).—*n.* A watercloset or necessary house.

prize, prīz, *n.* That which is seized that which is deemed a valuable acquisition; a reward.—*vt.* (prizing, prized). To value highly.

prize-fight, prīz'fīt, *n.* A boxing match for a prize.

probability, pro-ba-bil'i-ti, *n.* Likelihood; appearance of truth.

probate, prō‾ 'bāt, *n.* The proceeding by which a person's will is established and registered; official proof of a will.

proboscis, prō-bos'is, *n.*, *pl.* **proboscides,** prō-bos'i-dĕz. The snout or trunk of an elephant, etc.; the sucking-tube of insects.

proceed, prō-sēd', *vi.* To go forth or forward; to issue, arise, emanate; to prosecute any design; to carry on a legal action; to take a university degree.

procrastinate, prō-kras'ti-nat, *vt.* and *i.* To put off from day to day; to postpone.

prod, prod, *n.* A pointed instrument, as a goad; a stab.—*vt.* (prodding, prodded). To prick with a pointed instrument; to goad.

prodigal, prod'i-gal, *a.* Lavish; wasteful.—*n.* A waster; a spendthrift.

produce, prō-dūs', *vt.* (producing, produced). To bring forward; to exhibit; to bring forth, bear, yield; to supply, to cause; to extend, as a line.—*n.* prō'dūs, What is produced; outcome; yield; agricultural products.

productive, prō-duk'tiv, *a.* Having the power of producing; fertile; causing to exist; producing commodities of value.

profane, prō-fān', *a.* Not sacred; secular, irreverent, blasphemous; impure.—*vt.* (profaning, profaned). To treat with irreverence; to desecrate.

profanity, prō-fan'i-ti, *n.* Quality of being profane; profane language or conduct.

profess, prō-fes', *vt.* To avow; to acknowledge; to declare belief in; to pretend, to declare oneself versed in.— *vi.* To declare openly.

profession, prō-fe'shon, *n.* Act of professing, declaration; vocation; such as medicine, law; etc.; the body of persons engaged in such calling

professional, prō-fe'shon-al, *a.* Pertaining to a profession.—*n.* A member of any profession; one who makes a living by arts, sports, etc., in which amateurs engage.

profit, pro'fit', *n.* Any advantage, benefit, or gain, pecuniary gain.— *vt.* To benefit; to advance.—*vi.* To derive profit; to improve; to be made better or wiser.

profitable, pro'fit-a-bl, *a.* Bringing profit or gain; lucrative; beneficial; useful.

profound, prō-found', *a.* Deep; deep in skill or knowledge; far-reaching; bending low; humble.—*n.* The ocean, the abyss.

program, prō'gram, *n.* A plan of proceedings; statement of the order of proceedings in any entertainment.

progress, prō'gres, *n.* A going forward, a journey of state; a circuit; advance; development.—*vi.* progres'. To advance; to improve.

progressive, prō-gres'iv, *a.* Making steady progress; advancing; advocating progress.

prolapse, prolapsus, prō-laps', prō-lap'sus, *n.* A falling down of some internal organ from its proper position.

prolegomenon, prō-le-gom'e-non, *n.; pl.* **-mena.** A preliminary observation, *pl.* an introduction.

prolepsis, prō-lep'sis, *n.* Something of the nature of an anticipation, a rhetorical figure.

proletarian, prō-lē-ta'ri-an, *n.* and *a.* Applied to a member of the poorest class.

promenade, pro-me-näd', *n.* A walk for pleasure, a place set apart for walking.—*vi.* (promenading, promenaded). To walk for pleasure.

promise, pro'mis, *n.* A statement binding the person who makes it; ground or basis of expectation pledge.—*vt.* (promising, pro-mised). To make a promise of; to afford reason to expect.—*vi.* To make a promise; to afford expectations.

promote, prō-mōt', *vt.* (promoting, promoted). To forward or further; to advance; to encourage; to exalt; to form (a company).

pronounce, prō-nouns', *vt.* and *i.* (pronouncing, pronounced). To articulate by the organs of speech; to utter formally; to declare or affirm.

proof, prōf, *n.* Something which tests; trial; what serves to convince; evidence; firmness; a certain standard of strength in spirit; an impression in printing for correction, early impression of an engraving.—*a.* Impenetrable; able to resist.

prop, prop, *n.* A body that supports a weight, a support.—*vt.* (propping, propped). To support by a prop; to sustain generally.

propagate, pro'pa-gāt, *vt.* To multiply by generation or reproduction; to diffuse to increase.—*vi.* To have young or issue; to be multiplied by generation, etc.

prophylactic, prō-fi-lak'tik, *a.* Preventive of disease—*n.* A medicine which preserves against disease.

propitiatory, prō-pi'shi-a-to-ri, *a.* Having the power to make propitious; conciliatory.—*n.* Among the Jews, the mercy-seat.

proportion, pro-pō r'shon, *n.* Comparative relation; relative size and arrangement symmetry, just or equal share, lot, that rule which enables us to find a fourth proportional to three numbers.—*vt.* To adjust in due proportion; to form with symmetry.

prosecute, pro'se-kūt, *vt.* and *i.* (prosecuting, prosecuted). To persist in; to carry on; to pursue at law.

prosecution, pro-se-kū'shon, *n.* Act of prosecuting; the carrying on of a suit at law, the party by whom criminal proceedings are instituted.

proselyte, pro'se-līt, *n.* A convert to the Jewish faith; a new convert.— *vt.* To make a convert of.

prospect, pros'pekt, *n.* A distant view; sight; scene; outlook; exposure, expectation.—*vt.* and *i.* prospekt'. To make search for precious stones or metals.

prostitute, pros'ti-tūt, *vt.* (prostituting, prostituted). To offer publicly for lewd purposes for hire, to devote to anything base.—*a.* Openly devoted to lewdness.—*n.* A female given to indiscriminate lewdness.

prostitution, pros-ti-tū'shon, *n.* Practice of offering the body to indiscriminate intercourse with men, debasement.

prostrate, pros'trāt, *a.* Lying with the body flat; lying at mercy.—*vt.* (prostrating, prostrated). To lay flat or prostrate; to bow in reverence, to overthrow, to ruin.

protect, prō-tekt', *vt.* To shield from danger, injury, etc.; to guard against foreign competition by tariff regulations.

protection, prō-tek'shon, *n.* Act of protecting; shelter; defense; the system of favoring articles of home production by duties on foreign articles.

protest, prō-test', *vi.* To affirm with solemnity, to make a formal declaration of opposition.—*vt.* To assert; to mark for non-payment, as a bill.—*n.* pro'test.

A formal declaration of dissent; a declaration that payment of a bill has been refused.

Protestant, pro'test-ant, *n.* One of the party who adhered to Luther at the Reformation, a member of a reformed church.—*a.* Belonging to the religion of the Protestants.

protocol, prō'tō-kol, *n.* A diplomatic document serving as a preliminary to diplomatic transactions.

protrude, prō-trōd', *vt.* and *i.* (protruding, protruded). To thrust forward, to project.

proud, proud, *a.* Having a high opinion of oneself, haughty; of fearless spirit; ostentatious; magnificent.—**proud flesh,** an excessive granulation in wounds or ulcers.

prove, prōv, *vt.* (proving, proved). To try by experiment; to test; to establish the truth or reality of; to demonstrate, to obtain probate of.—*vi.* To be found by experience or trial, to turn out to be.

province, pro'vins, *n.* A territory at some distance from the metropolis; a large political division; sphere of action, department.

provincial, prō-vin'shal, *a.* Pertaining to or forming a province; characteristic of the people of a province; rustic.—*n.* A person belonging to a province.

provision, prō-vi'zhon, *n.* Act of providing; preparation; stores provided, victuals, stipulation; proviso.—*vt.* To supply with provisions.

provisional, prō-vi'zhon-al, *a.* Provided for present need; temporary.

proviso, prō-vī'zō *n.* An article or clause in any statute or contract; stipulation.

provocative, prō-vok'a-tiv, *a.* Serving to provoke; exciting. —*n.* A stimulant.

provoke, prō-vōk', *vt.* (provoking provoked). To incite; to stimulate, to incense; to irritate.—*vi.* To produce anger.

prowl, proul, *vi.* and *t.* To roam or wander stealthily.—*n.* Act of one who prowls.

prune, prōn, *vt.* (pruning, pruned). To trim; to cut or lop off; to clear from superfluities.—*n.* A plum particularly a dried plum.

psychic, psychical, sī'kik, sī'kik-al, *a.* Belonging to the soul, psychological; pertaining to that force by which spiritualists aver they produce "spiritual" phenomena.

psychology, sī-kol'o-ji, *n.* That branch o knowledge which deals with the mind;

mental science.

ptomaine, tō'mā n, *n.* A name of certain substances generated during putrefaction or morbid conditions prior to death.

public, pub'lik, *a.* Not private, pertaining to a whole community; open or free to all, common, notorious.—*n.* The people, indefinitely.—**In public**, in open view.

publication, pub-li-kā'shon, *n.* Act of publishing; announcement; promulgation; act of offering a book, etc., to the public by sale any book, etc., published.

publish, pub'lish, *vt.* To make public; to proclaim, promulgate, to cause to be printed and offered for sale.

puff, puf, *n.* A sudden emission of breath, a whiff; a short blast of wind; a puff-ball; piece of light pastry; a consciously exaggerated commendation.—*vi.* To give a quick blast with the mouth; to breathe hard after exertion.—*vt.* To drive with a blast; to inflate; to praise extravagantly.

puff-adder, puf'ad-ėr, *n.* A venomous snake which swells out the upper part of its body.

pull, pül, *vt.* To draw towards one; to tug; to rend; to pluck; to gather.—*vi.* To draw; to tug.—*n.* Act of pulling, a twitch, act of rowing a boat; a drink; a struggle.

pulse, puls, *n.* The beating of the heart or an artery; vibration; leguminous plants or their seeds, as beans, etc.—*vi.* (pulsing, pulsed) To beat or throb.

pulverize, pul'vėr-īz, *vt.* To reduce to dust or fine powder.

puma, pū'ma, *n.* A carnivorous quadruped of the cat kind; the cougar.

pumice, pū'mis or pum'is, *n.* A light and spongy stone, used for polishing.

pump, pump, *n.* A machine for raising water or extracting air; a shoe used in dancing.—*vi.* To work a pump.—*vt.* To raise with a pump; to free from liquid by a pump; to put artful questions to extract information.

pun, pun, *n.* A play on words like in sound, but different in meaning; a kind of quibble.—*vi.* (punning, punned) To make a pun or puns.

punch, punsh, *n.* An instrument for driving holes in metal, etc., a blow or thrust, a beverage of spirits, lemon-juice, water, etc.; a buffoon; a short-legged, barrel-bodied horse, a short fat fellow.—*vt.* To stamp or perforate with a punch; to hit with the fist.

punitive, pū-ni-tiv, *a.* Pertaining to, awarding, or involving punishment.

punning, pun'ing, *p.a.* Given to make puns; containing a pun or puns.

pupil, pū'pil, *n.* A young person under the care of a tutor, the aperture in the iris through which the rays of light pass.

pupilary, (or **-ll-**), pū'pil-a-ri, *a.* Pertaining to a pupil or ward, or to the pupil of the eye.

puppet, pup'et, *n.* A small figure in the human form mechanically worked; a person who is a mere tool.

purchase, pėr'chās, *vt.* (purchasing purchased). To buy; to obtain by labor, danger, etc.—*n.* Acquisition of anything by money, what is bought; mechanical advantage.

purify, pū'ri-fī, *vt.* (purifying, purified). To make pure or clear; to free from admixture; to free from guilt.—*vi.* To become pure or clear.

puritan, pūr'i-tan, *n.* One very strict in religious matters or in conduct, an early Protestant dissenter from the Church of England. *a.* Pertaining to the Puritans.

purple, pėr'pl, *n.* A color produced by mixing red and blue; a purple robe, the badge of the Roman emperors, regal power.—*a.* Of a color made of red and blue, dyed with blood.—*vt.* (purpling, purpled). To make purple.

P

Q

quack, kwak, *vi*. To cry like a duck; to boast; to practice quackery.—*n*. The cry of a duck, a pretender to skill or knowledge, especially medical.—*a*. Pertaining to quackery.

quackery, kwak'ė-ri, *n*. Practice or boastful pretenses of a quack, particularly in medicine.

quadragesima, kwod-ra-je'si-ma, *n*. Lent.

quadrangle, kwod-rang-gl, *n*. A plane figure, have four angles and sides; an inner square of a building.

quadrennial, kwod-ren'ni-al, *a*. Comprising four years; occurring once in four years.

quadrilateral, kwod-ri-lat''ėr-al, *a*. Having four sides and four angles.—*n*. A plane figure having four sides and angles.

quadrillion, kwod-ril'yon, *n*. The fourth power of a million; a number represented by a unit and 24 ciphers.

quadruped, kwod'rü-ped, *n*. An animal with four legs or feet.

quadruple, kwod'rü-pl, *a*. Fourfold.—*n*. Four times the sum or number.—*vt*. To make fourfold.—*vi*. To become fourfold.

quaff, kwaf, *vt*. and *i*. To drain to the bottom, to drink copiously.

qualification, kwo'li-fi-kā''shon, *n*. Act of qualifying, state of being qualified, suitable quality or characteristic; legal power; ability; modification, restriction.

qualify, kwo'li-fī, *vt*. (qualifying, qualified). To give proper or suitable qualities to, to furnish with the knowledge, skill, etc., necessary; to modify or limit; to soften or moderate, to dilute.—*vi*. To become qualified or fit.

quality, kwo'li-ti, *n*. Sort, kind, or character, a distinguishing property or characteristic; degree of excellence, high rank.

qualm, kwäm *n*. A sudden fit of nausea; a twinge of conscience; compunction.

quandary, kwon-dā'ri or kwon'dari, *n*. A state of perplexity; a predicament.

quarrel, kwo'rel, *n*. An angry dispute; a brawl; cause of dispute; a dart for a crossbow, a glazier's diamond.—*vi*. (quarreling, quarreled). To dispute violently; to disagree.

quarry, kwo'ri, *n*. A place where stones are dug from the earth; any animal pursued for prey, game killed.—*vt*. (quarrying, quarried). To dig or take from a quarry.

quart, kwärt, *n*. The fourth part of a gallon, two pints.

quarter, kwär't'ėr, *n*. The fourth part of anything, 28 lbs., 8 bushels; any direction or point of the compass; a district; locality; division of a heraldic shield, proper position; mercy to a beaten foe; *pl*. shelter or lodging; encampment.—*vt*. To divide into four equal parts; to cut to pieces; to furnish with lodgings or shelter, to add to other arms on an heraldic shield.—*vi*. To lodge.

quash, kwosh, *vt*. To subdue or quell; to suppress; to annul or make void.

quasi, kwā'sī, A prefix implying appearance without reality; sort of, sham.

quatercentenary, kwa-t'ėr-sen' tena-ri, *n*. A four hundredth anniversary.

quaternary, kwa-t'ėr'na-ri, *a*. Consisting of four; arranged in fours; applied to the strata above the tertiary.

quaternion, kwa-t'ėr'ni-on, *n*. A set of four; a quantity employed in mathematics.

quaver, kwā'v'ėr, *vi*. To have a tremulous motion; to vibrate.—*vt*. To utter with a tremulous sound.—*n*. A shake or rapid vibration of the voice, or on a musical instrument; a musical note equal to half a crotchet.

quay, kē, *n*. A built landing-place for vessels, a wharf.

querimonious, kwe-ri-mō'ni-us, *a*. Apt to complain; complaining; querulous.

quern kw'ėrn, *n*. A stone hand-mill for grinding grain.

querulous, kwe'rü-lus, *a*. Complaining, murmuring peevish.

query, kwē'ri, *n*. A question; the mark of interrogation (?).—*vi*. (querying, queried). To ask a question or questions.—*vt*. To question; to mark with a query.

quest, kwest, *n*. Act of seeking: search; pursuit; inquiry; solicitation.

question, kwest'yon, *n*. Act of asking; an interrogation; inquiry; discussion, subject of discussion.—*vi*. To ask a question; to doubt.—*vt*. To interrogate; to doubt; to challenge.

quick, kwik, *a*. Alive; brisk; swift; keen, sensitive; irritable.—*n*. A growing plant, usually hawthorn, for hedges, the living flesh; sensitiveness.—*adv*. Quickly, soon.

quicken, kwik'n, *vt*. To revive or resuscitate, to cheer, to increase the speed of, to sharpen, to stimulate.—*vi*. To become alive; to move quickly or more quickly.

quicksand, kwik'sand, *n*. A movable sandbank under water; sand yielding under the feet; something treacherous.

quilt, kwilt, *n*. A padded bedcover.—*vt*. To form into a quilt, to sew pieces of cloth with soft substance between.

quince, kwins, *n*. The fruit of a tree allied to the pear and apple; the tree itself.

quintuple, kwin'tü-pl, *a*. Fivefold.—*vt*. To make fivefold.

quip, kwip, *n*. A sharp sarcastic turn; a severe retort; a gibe.

quirk, kw'èrk, *n*. An artful turn for evasion a shift; a quibble.

quit, kwit, *a*. Discharged; released free; clear.—*vt*. (quitting, quitted). To discharge; to rid; to acquit; to leave; to abandon.

quite, kwĩt, *adv*. Completely wholly; entirely, altogether, very.

quiver, kwi'v'èr, *n*. A case or sheath for arrows.—*vi*. To shake with small rapid movements, to tremble, to shiver

quixotic, kwiks-ot 'ik, *a*. Chivalrous to extravagance; aiming at visionary ends.

quiz, kwiz, *n*. A hoax a jest, one who quizzes; one liable to be quizzed; a game or test in which two or more persons or teams compete in answering questions.—*vt*. (quizzing, quizzed). To make fun of, as by obscure questions; to look at inquisitively; to tease, to test by questioning.

quote, kwōt, *vt*. (quoting, quoted). To adduce or cite, as from some author; to name as the price of an article.

quotient, kwō'shent, *n*. The number obtained by dividing one number by another.

Q

R

rabbi, rab'bĭ, *n*. A Jewish teacher or expounder of the law.

rabbit, rab'it, *n*. A burrowing rodent allied to the hare.

rabble, rab'l, *n*. A crowd of vulgar noisy people; the mob, the lower class of people.

rabid, ra'bid, *a*. Raving; furious; mad.

rabies, rā'bi-ēs, *n*. A disease affecting certain animals, especially dogs, from which hydrophobia is communicated.

raccoon, racoon, ra-kön', *n*. An American carnivorous animal.

race, rās, *n*. A body of individuals sprung from a common stock, a breed or stock; a running; a con test in speed a course or career, a rapid current or channel.—*vi*. (racing, raced). To run swiftly; to contend in running.—*vt*. To cause to contend in speed.

radar, rā'där, *n*. A method of finding the position of an object (ship aircraft, etc.) by reflection of radio waves.

radiance, rā'di-ans, *n*. Brightness shooting in rays; luster; brilliancy; splendor.

radiate, rā'di-āt, *vi*. To emit rays of light; to shine; to spread about as in rays.—*vt*. To emit in divergent lines; to enlighten.—*a*. Having rays or lines resembling radii.

radical, ra'di-kal, *a*. Pertaining to the root; original thorough-going; native, underived, relating to radicals in politics.—*n*. A root, a simple, underived word; one who advocates extreme political reform.

radix, rā'diks, *n*. A root, as of a plant or a word; source, origin.

raffle, raf'l, *n*. A kind of lottery.—*vi*. (raffling, raffled). To engage in a raffle.—*vt*. To dispose of by raffle.

raft, räft, *n*. Logs fastened together and floated; a floating structure.

raid, rād, *n*. A hostile incursion, a foray.—*vi*. To engage in a raid.—*vt*. To make a raid on.

rail, rāl, *n*. A horizontal bar of wood or metal, a connected series of posts; a railing; one of the parallel iron bars forming a track for locomotives, etc.; a railway; a grallatorial bird.—*vt*. To inclose with rails; to furnish with rails.—*vi*. To use abusive language; to scold; to inveigh.

rainbow, rān'bō, *n*. An arc of a circle, consisting of all the prismatic colors, appearing in the heavens opposite the sun.

raise, rāz, *vt*. (raising, raised). To cause to rise to lift upward, to excite; to recall from death; to stir up; to construct; to levy; to breed; to originate; to give vent to; to inflate; to cause to be relinquished (a siege).

raisin, rā'zn, *n*. A dried grape.

rake, rāk, *n*. An implement for collecting hay or straw, smoothing earth, etc., a dissolute, lewd man slope.—*vt*. (raking, raked). To apply a rake to, to gather with a rake, to ransack, to enfilade.—*vi*. To use a rake; to search minutely; to incline, to slope, aft, as masts.

rally, ral'i, *vt*. (rallying, rallied). To reunite, as disordered troops, to collect, as things scattered, to attack with raillery; to banter.—*vi*. To recover strength or vigor.—*n*. A stand made by retreating troops; recovery of strength

ram, ram, *n*. The male of the sheep a battering-ram, the loose hammer of a pile-driving machine; a heavy steel beak of a war-vessel; an iron-clad ship with such a beak; one of the signs of the zodiac.—*vt*. (ramming, rammed). To strike with a ram; to batter; to cram.

ramble, ram'bl, *vi*. (rambling, rambled). To roam carelessly about; to talk incoherently; to have parts stretching irregularly.—*n*. An irregular excursion.

rampant, ram'pant, *a*. Rank in growth, exuberant, unrestrained; in *heraldry*, standing up on the hind-legs.

ranch, ranch, *n*. In North America, a farming establishment for rearing cattle and horses.

rancid, ran'sid, *a*. Having a rank or stinking smell; strong-scented; sour; musty.

random, ran'dum, *n*. Action without definite object, chance; caprice.—**At random**, in a haphazard manner.—*a*. Left to chance; done without previous calculation.

range, rānj, *vt*. (ranging, ranged). To set in a row; to dispose systematically; to wander through or scour.—*vt*. To rank; to rove about; to fluctuate.—*n*. A row, a rank; compass or extent; a kitchen grate, distance to which a projectile is carried; a place for gun practice.

rank, rangk, *n*. A row, a line; a social class; comparative station; titled dignity.—*vt*. To place in a line; to classify.—*vi*. To belong to a class; to put in a claim against a bankrupt.—*a*. Luxuriant in growth; strong-scented; utter; coarse, disgusting.

rap, rap, *n*. A quick smart blow;a knock.—*vi*. (rapping, rapped). To strike a quick, sharp blow.—*vt*. To strike with a quick blow.

rapacious, ra-pā'shus, *a*. Greedy of plunder; subsisting on prey; extortionate.

rape, rāp, *n*. A seizing by violence; carnal knowledge of a woman against her will; a plant of the cabbage kind, whose seeds yield an oil.—*vt*. (raping, raped). To carry off violently; to ravish.

rapid, ra'pid, *a*. Very swift; speedy; hurried.—*n*. A swift current in a river.

rash, rash, *a*. Precipitate, hasty; overbold; incautious.—*n*. An eruption on the skin.

ratchet, rach'et, *n*. A catch which abuts against the teeth of a wheel to prevent it running back.

rate, rāt, *n*. Proportion, standard; degree; degree of speed; price; a tax, assessment.—*vt*. (rating, rated). To fix the value, rank, or degree of; to appraise; to reprove; to scold.—*vi*. To be classed in a certain order.

rather, räTH'ér, *adv*. More readily; preferably; more properly; somewhat.

ratify, ra'ti-fī, *vt*. (ratifying, ratified). To confirm, to approve and sanction.

rattle, rat'l, *vi*. and *t*. (rattling, rattled). To clatter, to chatter fluently.—*n*. A rapid succession of clattering sounds; an instrument or toy which makes a clattering sound; one who talks much and rapidly.

rattlesnake, rat'l-snāk, *n*. A venomous American snake, with horny pieces at the point of the tail which rattle.

raucous, rä'kus, *a*. Hoarse, harsh.

ravage, ra'vāj, *n*. Devastation; havoc.—*vt*. (ravaging, ravaged). To lay waste, to pillage.

rave, rāv, *vi*. (raving, raved). To be delirious, to speak enthusiastically; to dote.

raw, rä, *a*. Not cooked or dressed not manufactured, unfinished; not diluted; bare, as flesh; galled, sensitive; inexperienced; cold and damp

ray, rā, *n*. A line of light; a gleam of intellectual light, one of a number of diverging radii; a flat-fish.—*vt*. and *i*. (raying, rayed). To shine forth, to radiate, to streak.

raze, rāz, *vt*. (razing, razed). To graze; to lay level with the ground; to efface.

reach, rēch, *vt*. To extend, to hand to extend or stretch from a distance; to arrive at; to gain.—*vi*. To extend, to stretch out the hand in order to touch; to make efforts at attainment.—*n*. Act or power of extending to; straight course of a river; scope.

react, rē-akt', *vi*. To act in return; to return an impulse, to act reciprocally upon each other.—*vt*. To perform anew.

reaction, rē-ak'shon, *n*. A reacting; reciprocal action; tendency to revert to a previous condition, exhaustion consequent on activity and *vice versa*.

read, rēd, *vt*. (reading, read). To peruse; to utter aloud, following something written or printed, to explain.—*vi*. To peruse, to study to stand written or printed; to make sense.—*a*. red, Instructed by reading; learned.

realize, rē'al-īz, *vt*. (realizing, realized). To make real, to convert into money, to impress on the mind as a reality; to render tangible or effective; to acquire; to gain.

realm, relm, *n*. The dominions of a sovereign; a region, sphere, or domain.

realty, rē'al-ti, *n*. The fixed nature of property termed *real;* real property.

ream, rēm, *n*. A package of paper consisting generally of 20 quires or 480 sheets.

reanimate, rē-an'i-māt, *vt*. To animate again; to revive; to infuse new life into.

reap, rēp, *vt*. and *i*. To cut with a scythe, etc., as grain; to gather; to clear of a grain crop; to receive as a reward of labor, etc.

rear, rēr, *n*. The part behind; the part of an army behind the rest; the background.—*vt*. To raise; to bring up, as young; to breed, as cattle, to build up.—*vi*. To rise on the hind-legs, as horse; to become erect.

reasonable, rē'zn-a-bl, *a*. Having the faculty of reason; rational; conformable to reason, moderate fair; tolerable.

reasoning, rē'zn-ing, *n*. The act or process of exercising the faculty of reason; arguments employed.

reassurance, rē-a-shōr'ans, *n*. Act of reassuring; a second assurance against loss.

reassure, rē-a-shōr', *vt*. To assure anew; to free from fear or terror; to reinsure.

rebuff, rē-buf', *n*. A sudden check; a repulse, refusal.—*vt*. To beat back; to check; to repel the advances of

rebuke, rē-būk', *vt*. (rebuking, rebuked). To reprimand; to reprove sharply.—*n*. A direct and severe reprimand, reproof.

rebus, rē'bus, *n*. A set of words represented by pictures of objects, a kind of puzzle made up of such pictures.

rebut, rē-but', *vt.* (rebutting, rebutted). To repel; to refute; in *law,* to oppose by argument, plea, or countervailing proof.

receipt, rē-sēt', *n.* Act of receiving; that which is received, a written acknowledgment of something received; a recipe.—*vt.* To give a receipt for; to discharge, as an account.

receive, rē-sēv', *vt.* (receiving, received). To take, as a thing offered; to admit, to entertain, to contain to be the object of; to take stolen goods.

recess, rē-ses', *n.* A withdrawing; place or period of retirement, time during which business is suspended; a niche in a wall; an alcove.

recipe, re'si-pē, *n.* A medical prescription; a statement of ingredients for a mixture.

reciprocal, rē-sip'rō-kal, *a.* Reciprocating; alternate; done by each to the other; mutual; interchangeable.

reciprocate, rē-sip'rō-kāt, *vi.* To move backward and forward, to alternate.—*vt.* To exchange, to give in requital.

reciprocity, re-si-pros'i-ti, *n.* Reciprocation; interchange; reciprocal obligation, equal commercial rights mutually enjoyed.

reckoning, rek'n-ing, *n.* Calculation; a statement of accounts with another, landlord's bill, calculation of a ship's position.

reclaim, rē-klām', *vt.* To claim back, to reform; to tame; to re cover; to reduce to a state fit for cultivation.

recline, rē-klīn', *vt.* and *i.* (reclining, reclined). To lean; to rest or repose.

recluse, rē-klös', *a.* Retired; solitary.—*n.* A person who lives in seclusion; a hermit.

recognition, re-kog-ni'shon, *n.* Act of recognizing; avowal; acknowledgment.

recognizance, rē-kog'niz-ans or re-kon'i-zans, *n.* Recognition, an obligation, as to appear at the assizes, keep the peace, etc.

recognize, re'kog-nīz, *vt.* (recognizing, recognized). To know again: to admit a knowledge of; to acknowledge formally; to indicate one's notice by a bow, etc., to indicate appreciation of.

recoil, rē-koil', *vi.* To move or start back, to retreat, to shrink, to rebound—*n.* A starting or falling back, rebound, as of a gun.

recommend, re-kom-mend', *vt.* To praise to another; to make acceptable; to commit with prayers; to advise.

recompense, re'kom-pens, *vt.* (recompensing, recompensed). To compensate; to requite; to make amends for.—*n.* Compensation; reward; amends.

reconcile, re'kon-sîl, *vt.* (reconciling, reconciled). To make friendly again; to adjust or settle; to harmonize.

record, rē-kord', *vt.* To preserve in writing; to register, to chronicle.— *n.* rek'ord. A written memorial; a register; a public document; memory; one's personal history; best results in contests.

recount, rē-kount', *vt.* To relate in detail; to count again.—*n.* A second counting.

recourse, rē-kōrs', *n.* A going to with a request, as for aid; resort in perplexity.

recover, rē-kuv'ėr, *vt.* To get back; to regain; to revive; to rescue; to obtain in return for injury or debt.—*vi.* To grow well; to regain a former condition.

recriminate, rē-krim'in-āt, *vi.* To return one accusation with another.—*vt.* To accuse in return.

recruit, rē-kröt', *vt.* To repair, to supply with new soldiers.—*vi.* To gain new supplies of anything; to raise new soldiers.—*n.* A soldier newly enlisted.

rectification, rek'ti-f-kā"shon, *n.* Act or operation of rectifying; process of refining by repeated distillation.

recur, rē-kėr', *vi.* (recurring, recurred). To return; to be repeated at a stated interval.

red, red, *a.* Of a color resembling that of arterial blood.—*n.* A color resembling that of arterial blood; a red pigment.

redemption, rē-dem'shon, *n.* The act of redeeming; state of being redeemed; ransom; release; deliverance.

redraw, rē-drä', *vt.* To draw again.—*vi.* To draw a new bill of exchange.

redress, rē-dres', *vt.* To set right; to adjust to repair; to relieve.—*n.* Relief, deliverance, reparation.

red-tape, red'tāp, *n.* Excessive official routine and formality.—*a.* Characterized by excessive routine or formality.

reduce rē-dūs', *vt.* (reducing, reduced). To bring down; to decrease; to degrade; to subdue; to bring under rules or within categories; to restore to its proper place.

reduction, rē-duk'shon, *n.* Act of reducing; diminution; conversion into another state or form; subjugation.

redundant, rē-dun'dant, *a.* Super-fluous; having more words than necessary.

reduplication, rē-dū'pli-kā"shon *n.* Act of reduplicating; the repetition of a root or initial syllable.

reed, rēd, *n.* A tall broad-leaved grass growing in marshy places, or its hollow stems; a musical instrument; a rustic pipe.

reek, rēk, *n.* Vapor; steam; exhalation; smoke.—*vi.* To smoke; to exhale.

reel, rēl, *n.* A bobbin for thread; a revolving appliance for winding a fishing line; a staggering motion; a lively Scottish dance.—*vt.* To wind upon a reel, to stagger.

refer, rē-fėr', *vt.* (referring, referred). To trace or carry back, to attribute, to appeal; to assign—*vi.* To respect or have relation; to appeal; to apply, to allude.

referendum, ref-ėr-en'dum, *n.* The referring of a measure passed by a legislature to the people for final approval.

refine, rē-fīn', *vt.* (refining, refined). To increase the fineness of; to purify; to make elegant; to give culture to.—*vi.* To become purer; to indulge in hair-splitting.

reflection, rē-flek'shon, *n.* Act of reflecting, that which is produced by being reflected; meditation; a censorious remark, reproach.

reflexive, rē-flek'siv, *a.* Reflective; having respect to something past; in *grammar*, having for its object a pronoun which stands for the subject; also applied to such pronouns.

reflux, rē'fluks, *n.* A flowing back; ebb.

reform, rē-form', *vt.* and *i.* To change from worse to better; to amend; to form anew.—*n.* A beneficial change, amendment; a change in the regulations of parliamentary representation.

refrain, rē-frān', *vt.* To restrain; to keep (oneself from action.—*vi.* To forbear, to abstain.—*n.* The burden of a song; part repeated at the end of every stanza.

refuge, re'fūj, *n.* Protection from danger or distress, a retreat, a shelter; a device; contrivance; shift.—*vt.* and *i.* To shelter.

refugee, re-fū-jē', *n.* One who flees for refuge; one who flees to another country or place for safety.

refuse, re-fūz', *vt.* (refusing, refused). To deny, as a request or demand, to decline, to reject.—*vi.* To decline a request or offer.

regale, rē-gāl', *vt.* and *i.* (regaling, regaled). To refresh sumptuously; to feast. *n.* A splendid feast; a treat.

regality, rē-gal'i-ti, *n.* Royalty; kingship.

regard, rē-gärd', *vt.* To notice carefully; to

observe; to respect; to heed; to view in the light of; to relate to.—*n.* Look or gaze; respect; notice; heed; esteem; deference; *pl.* good wishes.

regeneration, rē-jen'ė-rā''shon, *n.* Act of regenerating; that change by which love to God is implanted in the heart.

regret, rē-gret', *n.* Grief at something done or undone; remorse; penitence.—*vt.* (regretting, regretted). To be sorry for, to lament.

regular, re'gū-lėr, *a.* Conformed to a rule, law, or principle; normal; methodical, uniform; having the parts symmetrical; thorough.—*n.* A monk who has taken the vows in some order; a soldier of a permanent army.

regulate, re'gū-lāt, *vt.* (regulating, regulated). To adjust by rule; to put or keep in good order; to direct.

rehabilitate, rē-ha-bil'i-tāt, *vt.* To restore to a former capacity or position; to reestablish in esteem.

rein, rān, *n.* The strap of a bridle, by which a horse is governed; an instrument for restraining, restraint.—*vt.* To govern by a bridle; to restrain.—*vi.* To obey the reins.

reindeer, rān'dēr, *n.* A deer of northern parts, with broad branched antlers.

reinforce, rē-in-fōrs', *vt.* To strengthen by new assistance, as troops.—*n.* An additional thickness given to an object to strengthen it.

reject, rē-jekt', *vt.* To cast off; to discard, to repel; to forsake; to decline.

relation, rē-lā'shon, *n.* Act of relating; account; reference; connection; kindred; a relative; proportion.

relative, re'lat-iv, *a.* Having relation or reference, not absolute or existing by itself, relevant.—*n.* Something considered in its relation to something else; one allied by blood; a word which relates to or represents another word or sentence.

relax, rē-laks', *vt.* To slacken, to loosen or weaken; to unbend.—*vi.* To become loose, feeble, or languid, to abate in severity.

release, rē-lēs', *vt.* (releasing, released). To liberate; to disengage; to acquit.—*n.* Liberation, discharge; acquittance.

relic, re'lik, *n.* A remaining fragment; the body of a deceased person (usually in *pl.*); a memento or keepsake.

relief, rē-lēf', *n.* Ease or mitigation of pain; succor; remedy; redress; assistance given to a pauper; one who relieves another by taking duty; prominence of figures above a plane surface in sculpture, carving, etc.; prominence or distinctness.

relieve, rē-lēv', *vt.* (relieving, relieved). To remove or lessen, as anything that pains; to ease; to succor; to release from duty; to give variety to; to set off by contrast; to give the appearance of projection to.

religion, rē-li'jon, *n.* An acknowledgment of our obligation to God practical piety; devotion; any system of faith and worship.

remain, rē-mān', *vi.* To continue in a place or condition; to abide; to be left, to last.—*n.* That which is left *pl.* a dead body; literary works of one who is dead.

remainder, rē-mān'dėr, *n.* That which remains; residue; remnant; an estate limited so as to be enjoyed after the death of the present possessor or otherwise.— *a.* Left over.

remark, rē-märk', *n.* Notice; an observation in words; a comment.—*vt.* To observe; to utter by way of comment.

remember, rē-mem'bėr, *vt.* To have in the memory; to think of; to observe; to give a gratuity for service done.—*vi.* To have something in remembrance.

remembrance, rē-mem'brans, *n.* The keeping of a thing in mind; memory; what is remembered; a memorial, a keepsake.

remnant, rem'nant, *n.* That which is left; a scrap, fragment.—*a.* Remaining.

remonstrance, rē-mon'strans, *n.* Act of remonstrating; expostulation, strong representation against something.

remonstrate, rē-mon'strāt, *vi.* To present strong reasons against an act, to expostulate.

remorse, rē-mors', *n.* Reproach of conscience, compunction for wrong committed.

remove, rē-möv', *vt.* (removing, removed) To move from its place; to take away; to displace from an office, to banish or destroy.—*vi.* To be moved from its place; to change the place of residence.—*n.* A removal; departure.

rend, rend, *vt.* (rending, rent). To force asunder, to tear away, to sever.—*vi.* To be or become torn, to split.

render, ren'dėr, *vt.* To give in return; to give back; to present; to afford; to invest with qualities; to translate; to interpret; to clarify, as tallow.

rendezvous, ren'de-vö, *n.* A place of meeting.—*vi.* To meet at a particular place.

renew, rē-nū', *vt.* To make new again; to repair; to repeat; to grant anew; to transform.—*vi.* To grow or begin again.

rent, rent, *n.* Money, etc., payable yearly for the use of lands or tenements, a tear a schism.—*vt.* To let on lease; to hold on condition of paying rent.—*vi.* To be leased or let for rent.

renunciation, rē-nun'si-ā"shon, *n.* Act of renouncing; disavowal; abandonment.

repair, rē-pār', *vt.* To restore; to refit, to mend to retrieve.—*vi.* To betake oneself; to resort.—*n.* Restoration; supply of loss; state as regards repairing; a resorting; abode.

repel, rē-pel', *vt.* (repelling, repelled). To drive back; to resist successfully.—*vi.* To cause repugnance, to shock.

repellent, rē-pel'ent, *a.* Having the effect of repelling; repulsive; deterring.

repent, rē-pent', *vi.* To feel regret for something done or left undone to be penitent.—*vt.* To remember with self-reproach or sorrow.

repetition, re-pē-ti'shon, *n.* Act of repeating; recital; that which is repeated.

replace, rē-plās', *vt.* (replacing. replaced). To put again in the former place; to put in the place of another, to take the place of.

report, rē-pōrt', *vt.* and *i.* To bring back, as an answer; to relate; to give an official statement of, to take down from the lips of a speaker, etc.; to lay a charge against.—*n.* An account, rumor repute; noise of explosion; official statement; account of proceedings.

reporter, rē-pōrt'ėr, *n.* One who reports; one of a newspaper staff who gives accounts of public meetings, events, etc.

repose, rē-pōz', *vt.* (reposing, reposed). To lay at rest.—*vi.* To lie at rest; to rely.—*n.* A lying at rest; tranquillity, composure, absence of show of feeling.

reprehension, re-prē-hen'shon, *n.* Act of reprehending; reproof; censure, blame. Containing reprehension or reproof.

represent, re-prē-zent', *vt.* To exhibit by a likeness of; to typify; to act the part of; to describe; to be a substitute for, to exemplify.

reprieve, rē-prē v', *vt.* (reprieving, reprieved). To grant a respite to; to relieve temporarily.—*n.* Suspension of the execution of a criminal's sentence, respite.

reprimand, rep'ri-mand, *n*. A severe reproof for a fault.—*vt*. rep-rimand'. To administer a sharp rebuke to.

reprint, rē-print', *vt*. To print again.—*n*. re'print. A second or new edition.

reproach, rē-prōch', *vt*. To charge severely with a fault, to censure.—*n*. Censure; blame; source of blame; disgrace.

reptile, rep'til, *a*. Creeping; grovelling.—*n*. An animal that moves on its belly, or by means of small short legs.

republic, rē-pub'lik, *n*. A common wealth, a state in which the supreme power is vested in elected representatives.

repulse, rē-puls', *n*. Act of repelling, a check or defeat, refusal, denial.—*vt*. (repulsing, repulsed). To repel.

reputation, re-pūt-ā'shon, *n*. Character derived from public opinion; repute; good name; honor; fame.

repute, rē-pūt', *vt*. (reputing, reputed). To estimate; to deem.—*n*. Reputation; character; good character.

request, rē-kwest', *n*. An expressed desire, a petition, thing asked for, a state of being asked for.—*vt*. To ask; to beg.

rescue, res'kū, *vt*. (rescuing, rescued). To deliver from confinement, danger, or evil.—*n*. Act of rescuing; deliverance.

research, rē-sėrch', *n*. A diligent seeking of facts or principles; investigation.—*vt*. To search again.

resemblance, rē-zem'blans, *n*. Likeness; similarity; something similar, similitude.

resemble, rē-zem'bl, *vt*. (resembling, resembled). To be like; to liken, to compare.

reservoir, re'zėr-vwär, *n*. A place where anything is kept in store; an artificial lake to supply a town with water.

reside, rē-zīd', *vi*. (residing, resided). To have one's abode, to dwell; to inhere.

residential, re-zi-den'shal, *a*. Pertaining to or suitable for residence.

resin, re'zin, *n*. An inflammable vegetable substance; the hardened juice of pines.

resistant, resistent, rē-zis'tent, *a*. Making resistance.—*n*. One who or that which resists.

resolute, re'zō-lūt, *a*. Having fixedness of purpose; determined; steadfast.

resolution, re-zō-lū'shon, *n*. Character of being resolute. determination, a formal decision; operation of separating the component parts, solution.

resolve, rē-zolv', *vt*. (resolving, resolved). To separate the component parts of, to

analyze, to solve to determine; to decide.—*vi*. To separate into component parts, to melt, to determine; to decide. *n*. Fixed purpose of mind; resolution.

resort, rē-zort', *vi*. To have recourse; to go; to repair frequently.—*n*. Recourse; concourse; a haunt.

resound, rē-zound', *vt*. To give back the sound of; to echo; to praise.—*vi*. To sound again; to echo, to be much praised.

respite, res'pit, *n*. Temporary intermission, interval, a reprieve.—*vt*. (respiting, respited). To grant a respite to; to reprieve.

rest, rest, *n*. Cessation of action peace; sleep; an appliance for support; a pause; remainder; the others.—*vi*. To cease from action to lie for repose; to be supported, to be in a certain state, remain, to be left.—*vt*. To lay at rest; to place, as on a support.

restaurant, res'tō-rong, *n*. An establishment for the sale of refreshments.

restriction, re-strik'shon, *n*. Act of restricting; limitation; a reservation.

result, rē-zult', *vi*. To rise as a consequence; to issue; to ensue; to end.—*n*. Consequence; effect; issue, outcome.

resurrection, re-zėr-rek'shon, *n*. A rising again; the rising of the dead at the general judgment.

retail, rē-tāl', *vt*. To sell in small quantities, to tell to many.—*n*. re' tal. The sale of commodities in small quantities; used also as *adj*.

retainer, rē-tān'ėr, *n*. One who retains, an adherent or dependent; a fee to engage a counsel.

retaliate, rē-ta'li-āt, *vi*. and *t*. To return like for like; to repay; to take revenge.

retire, rē-tīr', *vi*. (retiring, retired). To go back; to withdraw from business or active life; to go to bed.—*vt*. To remove from service, to pay when due, as a bill of exchange.

retiring, rē-tīr'ing, *a*. Reserved; unobtrusive; granted to one who retires from service.

retort, re-tort', *vt*. To retaliate; to throw back.—*vi*. To return an argument or charge.—*n*. A severe reply, a repartee, a chemical vessel for distilling.

retributive, retributory, re-tri'bu-tiv, re-tri'bu-to-ri, *a*. Making retribution; entailing justly deserved punishment.

retrieve, re-trev', *vt*. (retrieving, retrieved). To recover; to regain; to repair.

retriever, re-trev'er, n. A dog that brings in game which a sportsman has shot.

return, re-tern', vi. To come or go back; to recur.—vt. To send back; to repay, to report officially to elect, to yield.—n. Act of returning; repayment; election of a representative; profit, an official statement; pl. tabulated statistics; a light tobacco.

revelation, re-ve-la'shon, n. Act of revealing; that which is revealed; divine communication; the Apocalypse.

revenge, re-venj', vt. and i. (revenging, revenged). To take vengeance for, to avenge.—n. Act of revenging; retaliation; deliberate infliction of injury in return for injury; vindictive feeling.

reverence, rev'er-ens, n. Awe combined with respect, veneration; an obeisance; a reverend personage; a title of the clergy.—vt. To revere; to pay reverence to.

reverse, ra-vèrs', vt. (reversing, reversed). To alter to the opposite; to annul.—n. A reversal; a complete change or turn; a check; a defeat; the contrary, the back or undersurface.—a. Turned backward; opposite.

revert, rē-vėrt', vt. To reverse.—vi. To return to a former position, habit, statement, etc.; to return to the donor.

review, rē-vū', vt. To view again; to reconsider; to write a critical notice of; to inspect.—vi. To write reviews.—n. A re-examination; a criticism, a periodical containing criticisms; official inspection of troops.

revise, rē-vīz', vt. (revising, revised). To go over with care for correction.—n. A revision; a second proof-sheet in printing.

revolt, rē-vōlt', vi. To renounce allegiance, to rebel, to be disgusted: with at.—vt. To shock.—n. Rebellion; mutiny.

revolution, re-vō-lū'shon, n. Act of revolving, rotation; a turn; circuit; a cycle of time; a radical change; overthrow of existing political institutions.

revue, rē-vū', n. A loosely-constructed and spectacular theatrical exhibition, depending on music and scenic and staging effects.

reward, rē-wärd', n. What is given in return for good done; recompense; punishment.—vt. To repay; to requite.

rhapsody, rap 'so-di, n. A short epic poem, or portion of an epic, a confused series of extravagantly enthusiastic statements.

rhetoric, re'to-rik, n. The art of using language effectively; the art which teaches oratory; eloquence; flashy oratory declamation.

rhomb, rhombus, rom, rom'bus, n. A quadrilateral whose sides are equal, but the angles not right angles.

rhyme, rīm, n. A correspondence of sound in the ends of words or verses; a short poem; a word rhyming with another.—vi. (rhyming, rhymed). To make verses; to accord in sound.—vt. To put into rhyme.

rhythm, rithm, n. Periodical emphasis in verse or music; metrical movement; harmony; rhyme; meter, verse.

rib, rib, n. One of the curved bones springing from the backbone; something resembling a rib, a long ridge on cloth.—vt. (ribbing, ribbed). To furnish with ribs, to inclose with ribs.

ricochet, rik'o-shet, n. A rebounding from a flat, horizontal surface.—vt. and i. rik-o-shet'. To operate upon by ricochet firing; to rebound.

rid, rid, vt. (ridding, rid). To make free; to clear; to disencumber—a. Free clear.

riddle, rid'l, n. A puzzling question; an enigma; a coarse sieve.— vt. (riddling, riddled). To solve, to sift, to make many holes in.

ride, rīd, vi. (riding, pret. rode, pp. ridden). To be borne on horseback, in a vehicle, etc.; to have ability as an equestrian, to be at anchor.— vt. To sit on, so as to be carried; to go over in riding; to domineer over.—n. An excursion on horseback, or in a vehicle; a road for the amusement of riding.

ridge, rij, n. A long narrow prominence; strip thrown up by a plow; a long crest of hills; upper angle of a roof.—vt. (ridging, ridged). To form into ridges.

right, rīt, a. Straight; upright; just; suitable, proper real, correct, belonging to that side of the body farther from the heart; to be worn outward perpendicular, formed by one line perpendicular to another.—adv. Justly; correctly; very; directly, to the right hand.—n. What is right; rectitude; a just claim; authority; side opposite to the left.—vt. To put right, to do justice to; to restore to an upright position.—vi. To resume a vertical position.

ring, ring, n. Anything in the form of a circle; a circle of gold, etc., worn on the finger; an area in which games, etc., are performed; a group of persons, sound of a bell a metallic sound.—vt. To encircle to cause to sound, to repeat often or loudly.—*vi.* To sound, to resound; to tingle.

riotous, rī'ot-us, *a.* Indulging in riot or revelry; tumultuous; seditious; excessive.

rip, rip, *vt.* (ripping, ripped). To tear or cut open; to take out by cutting or tearing. —*n.* A rent; a scamp.

ripe, rīp, *a.* Brought to perfection in growth; mature; complete ready for action or effect.—*vt.* and *i.* (riping, riped). To mature.

ripple, rip'l, *vi.* (rippling, rippled). To show a ruffled surface, as water; to make a gentle sound, as running water.—*vt.* To clean the seeds from, as flax.—*n.* A ruffle of the surface of water, a comb for separating the seeds from flax.

rise, rīz, *vi.* (rising pret. rose, pp. risen). To pass to a higher position to stand up; to bring a session to an end, to arise, to swell by fermentation; to slope upwards, to become apparent; to come into existence, to rebel.—*n.* Act of rising ascent, elevation; origin; beginning; appearance above the horizon; increase; advance.

rivet, ri'vet *n.* A metallic bolt whose end is hammered broad after insertion.—*vt.* (riveting, riveted). To fasten with rivets, to clinch, to make firm.

road, rōd, *n.* An open way or public passage; a highway; a means of approach; a roadstead (usually in *plural*).

roast, rōst, *vt.* To cook by exposure to a fire, to parch by heat, to banter severely.—*vi.* To become roasted.—*n.* Roasted meat, part selected for roasting.—*a.* Roasted.

robe, rōb, *n.* A gown, or long, loose garment, worn over other dress an elegant dress.—*vt.* (robing, robed). To put a robe upon; to in vest.

robot, rōb'ot, *n.* Any mechanical contrivance designed to perform work normally requiring the exercise of human intelligence.

rock, rok, *vt.* To move backwards and forwards without displacing to swing.—*vi.* To sway; to reel. *n.* A large mass of stone; defense; source of peril or disaster, a kind of solid sweetmeat.

rod, rod, *n.* A straight slender stick a badge of office; an enchanter's wand; a fishing-rod; a measure of 5-1/2 lineal yards.

rodent, rō'dent, *a.* Gnawing, belonging to the gnawing animals (Rodentia).—*n.* An animal that gnaws, as the squirrel.

roll, rōl, *vt.* To turn on its surface; to wrap on itself by turning; to involve in a bandage or the like; to press with a roller.—*vi.* To turn over and over, to run on wheels, to be tossed about; to sound with a deep prolonged sound.—*n.* Act of rolling, something rolled up; an official document; a catalogue; a cake of bread, a roller, a prolonged deep sound.

roller, rōl'ėr, *n.* One who or that which rolls, a cylinder for smoothing, crushing, etc.; that on which something may be rolled up; a long, heavy, swelling wave.

Roman, rō'man, *a.* Pertaining to Rome or its people and to the Roman Catholic religion; applied to the common upright letter in printing.

romance, rō-mans', *n.* A tale in verse in a Romance dialect; a popular epic or tale in prose or verse of some length; a tale of extraordinary adventures, tendency to the wonderful or mysterious; a fiction.—*a.* (with *cap.*). A term applied to the languages sprung from the Latin.—*vi.* To tell fictitious stories.

roost, rōst, *n.* The pole on which birds rest at night, a collection of fowls resting together.—*vi.* To occupy a roost; to settle.

root, rōt, *n.* That part of a plant which fixes itself in the earth; lower part of anything; origin; a form from which words are derived.—*vi.* To fix the root, to be firmly fixed.—*vt.* To plant deeply; to impress durably; to tear up or out, to eradicate.

rope, rōp, *n.* A cord or line of some thickness; a row or string of things united.—*vi.* (roping, roped). To draw out in threads.—*vt.* To pull by a rope; to fasten or inclose with a rope.

rosin, ro'zin, *n.* The resin left after distilling off the volatile oil from turpentine; resin in a solid state.—*vt.* To rub with rosin.

rostrum, ros'trum, *n.*; pl. **-tra.** The beak or bill of a bird; the ram of an ancient ship; *pl.* a platform or pulpit.

rot, rot, *vi.* (rotting, rotted). To become rotten, to decay.—*vt.* To make rotten.— *n.* Putrid decay; a fatal distemper of sheep; a disease injurious to plants; nonsense.

rouge, rözh, *n.* A cosmetic to impart ruddiness to the complexion.—*vt.* and *i.* (rouging, rouged). To paint with rouge.

R

rough, ruf, *a*. Not smooth; rugged; boisterous, harsh, rude; cruel; vague; hasty.—*vt*. To make rough; to roughhew.—**To rough it,** to submit to hardships.—*n*. State of being rough or unfinished; a rowdy.

roulette, rö-let', *n*. A game of chance; an engraver's tool with a toothed wheel.

round, round, *a*. Circular; spherical; large; open; candid; brisk, as a trot, not minutely accurate, as a number.—*n*. That which is round; rung of a ladder; a circular course or series, circuit made by one on duty; a vocal composition in parts; ammunition for firing once; a turn or bout.—*vt*. To make round; to encircle; to make full and flowing; to pass round.—*vi*. To become round or full, to make a circuit.—*adv*. In a circle; around; not directly.— *prep*. About; around.

rove, rōv, *vt*. (roving, roved). To move about aimlessly; to roam; to ramble.—*vt*. To wander over; to card into flakes, as wool.

row, rō, *n*. A series in a line; a rank; a line of houses, an excursion in a boat with oars.—*vt*. To impel by oars, as a boat, to transport by rowing.—*vi*. To work with the oar

rub, rub, *vt*. (rubbing, rubbed). To move something along the surface of with pressure; to scour; to remove by friction; to chafe.—*vi*. To move along with pressure; to fret.—*n*. Act of rubbing; friction; obstruction; difficulty; a gibe.

rubber, rub'ėr, *n*. One who rubs; thing used in polishing or cleaning; india-rubber; obstruction or difficulty; contest of three games in whist.

rudiment, rö'di-ment, *n*. The original of anything; a first principle; an undeveloped organ; *pl* . first elements of a science or art.

rudimentary, rö-di-ment'a-ri, *a*. Pertaining to rudiments; consist ing in first principles; initial; in an undeveloped state.

rue, rö, *vt*. (ruing, rued). To repent of; to regret.—*vi*. To become sorrowful or repentant. n. An acrid ill-smelling plant.

ruffle, ruf'l, *vt*. (ruffling, ruffed) To rumple, to derange; to disturb.— *vi*. To bluster.—*n*. A plaited cambric, etc., attached to one's dress; frill, state of being agitated; low vibrating beat of a drum.

rug, rug, *n*. A heavy fabric used to cover a bed, protect a carpet, etc.; a mat

rugby, rug'bi, *n*. One of the two principal varieties of football, played by fifteen men a side, with an oval ball, handling being permitted.

ruin, rö'in, *n*. Destruction; fall; overthrow; anything in a state of decay; that which destroys; *pl*. remains of a city, house, etc.; state of being destroyed.—*vt*. To bring to ruin, to destroy, to impoverish.

rule, röl, *n*. A ruler or measure; a guiding principle or formula; a precept, law, maxim; government; control, regulation, order; method.—*vt*. (ruling, ruled). To govern, to manage; to decide; to mark with lines by a ruler.—*vi*. To exercise supreme authority; to maintain a level, as the market price; to settle, as a rule of court.

rumble, rum'bl, *vi*. (rumbling, rumbled). To make a dull, continued sound.—*n*. A low, heavy, continued sound, a seat for servants behind a carriage.

run, run, *vi*. (running, pret. ran, pp. run). To move by using the legs more quickly than in walking; to take part in a race; to flee; to spread; to ply; to move or pass; to become fluid; to continue in operation, to have a certain direction; to have a certain purport to be current; to continue in time.—*vt*. To cause to run, to pursue, as a course; to incur; to break through (a blockage); to smuggle; to pierce; to melt; to carry on.—*n*. Act of running; course or distance run; a trip; course, tenor, etc.; general demand, as on a back, place where animals may run; generality.

runner, run'ėr, *n*. One who runs; a messenger; a bird of the order Cursores, a stem running along the ground and taking root; that on which something runs or slides.

rustic, rus'tik, *a*. Pertaining to the country; rural; homely; unpolished.—*n*. A country-man, a peasant; a clown.

rustle, rus'l, *vi*. and *t*. (rustling, rustled). To make the noise of things agitated, as straw, leaves, etc.—*n*. The noise of things that rustle; a slight sibilant sound.

rut, rut, *n*. The track of a wheel; a line cut with a spade; line of routine time during which certain animals are under sexual excitement.—*vt*. (rutting, rutted). To cut in ruts.—*vi*. To be in heat, as deer.

S

Sabbath, sa'bath, *n*. The day of rest; Sunday.

saber, sā'bèr, *n*. A sword with one edge, a cavalry sword.—*vt*. (sabering, sabered). To strike or kill with a saber.

sable, sā'bl, *n*. A small animal of the weasel family; the fur of the sable; black.—*a*. Black; dark.

sabotage, sä-bǒ-täzh, *n*. Malicious destruction of employers, property or national plant by employees on strike or during war-time.

sack, sak, *n*. A bag for flour, wool, etc., that which a sack holds; a sort of jacket; a dry wine; pillage of a town.—*vt*. To put in sacks, to pillage, as a town.

sacrament, sa'kra-ment, *n*. A solemn religious ordinance observed by Christians, as baptism or the Lord's Supper.

sacred, sā'kred, *a*. Set apart for a holy purpose; consecrated; religious; set apart to some one in honor, venerable.

sacrifice, sa'kri-fīs, *n*. The offering of anything to God; anything offered to a divinity, surrender made in order to gain something else.—*vt*. (sacrificing, sacrificed). To make an offering or sacrifice of.—*vi*. To offer up a sacrifice to some deity.

saddle, sad'l, *n*. A seat for a rider on a horse's back; something like a saddle in shape or use.—*vt*. (saddling, saddled). To put a saddle on; to burden.

Sadducee, sad'ū-sē, *n*. One of a sect among the Jews who denied the resurrection and the existence of angels or spirits.

Sadism, sād'ism, *n*. A form of sexual perversion, in which pleasure is taken in the cruel treatment of the companion.

safe, sāf, *a*. Secure; free from danger; unharmed; no longer dangerous; trustworthy.—*n*. A strong box or chamber for securing valuables, a cool receptacle for meat.

safeguard, sāf'gärd, *n*. One who or that which guards; a defense; protection, a passport.—*vt*. To guard.

sagacity, sa-gas'i-ti, *n*. Quickness of discernment; shrewdness, high intelligence.

sage, sāj, *a*. Wise; sagacious; well-judged; grave.—*n*. A wise man; a man venerable for years, and of sound judgment, a

labiate plant.

sailing, sāl'ing, *p.a*. Moved by sails and not by steam.—*n*. Act of setting sail; art or rules of navigation.

saint, sānt, *n*. One eminent for piety and virtue; one of the blessed; a person canonized.—*vt*. To canonize.

saliva, sa-lī'va, *n*. The fluid secreted by certain glands, which moistens the mouth and assists digestion.

salivate, sa'li-vāt, *vt*. To produce an unusual secretion and discharge of saliva.

sallow, sal'ō, *a*. Having a pale, sickly, yellowish color.—*n*. A kind of willow.

sally, sal'i, *n*. A leaping forth; a rush of troops from a besieged place, a dart of intellect, fancy etc.; frolic.—*vi*. (sallying, sallied). To leap forth; to issue suddenly.

salon, sä-long, *n*. An apartment for the reception of company; a saloon.

salt, sält, *n*. A substance for seasoning and preserving food; a compound produced by the combination of a base with an acid taste, savor, piquancy, an old sailor.—*a*. Impregnated with salt; pungent.—*vt*. To sprinkle or season with salt.

salute, sa-lūt', *vt*. (saluting, saluted). To greet; to greet by a bow, etc., to kiss, to honor.—*vi*. To perform a salutation; to greet each other.—*n*. Act of saluting; greeting; a kiss; a bow; discharge of artillery, etc.

salvage, sal'väj, *n*. Act of saving a ship or goods from shipwreck, fire, etc.; allowance for the saving of property; goods thus saved.

salvation, sal-vā'shon, *n*. Act of saving; redemption of man from sin, that which saves.

salve, salv or säv, *n*. A healing ointment; remedy.—*vt*. (salving, salved). To apply salve to; to remedy.

sanatorium, san-a-tǒ'ri-um, *n*. A place to which people go for the sake of health.

sanctify, sangk'ti-fī, *vt*. (sanctifying sanctified). To make holy, to hallow; to make pure from sin.

sanctimonious, sangk-ti-mǒ'ni-us *a*. Making a show of sanctity; hypocritical.

sanction, sangk'shon, *n*. Confirmation; ratification; authority.—*vt*. To ratify; to authorize; to countenance.

sanctity, sangk'ti-ti, *n*. State of being sacred; holiness; inviolability.

sanctuary, sangk'tū-a-ri, *n*. A sacred place; a place of worship; part of a church where the altar is placed, a place of protection to criminals, debtors, etc.; shelter.

sandstone sand'stŏn, *n.* A stone composed of agglutinated grains of sand.

sandwich sand'wich, *n.* Slices of bread, with meat or something savory between.—*vt.* To insert like the meat in a sandwich, to fit between two other pieces

sanguine, sang'gwin, *a.* Consisting of blood; full of blood; of the color of blood cheerful, confident.

sanitary, san'i-ta-ri, *a.* Pertaining to or designed to secure health; hygienic.

saponify, sa-pon'i-fī, *vt.* To convert into soap by combination with an alkali.

Sapphic, saf'fik, *a.* Pertaining to *Sappho,* a Grecian poetess, or to a kind of verse invented by her. *n.* A Sapphic verse.

sapphire, saf'fīr, *n.* A precious stone of very great hardness, and of various shades of blue; a rich blue color; blue.

sarcastic, sär-kas'tik, *a.* Containing sarcasm; scornfully severe; taunting

sarcode, sär'kod, *n.* Structureless gelatinous matter forming the bodies of animals belonging to the protozoa.

sash, sash, *n.* A long band or scarf worn for ornament; the frame of a window; a frame for a saw.—*vt.* To furnish with sashes or sash windows.

sassafras, sas'a-fras, *n.* A kind of laurel, the root of which has medicinal virtues.

Satan, sā'tan, *n.* The devil or prince of darkness; the chief of the fallen angels.

satchel, sa'chel, *n.* A little sack or bag; a bag for a school-boy's books.

sate, sāt, *vt.* (sating, sated). To satiate, to satisfy the appetite of; to glut.

satellite, sa'tel-līt, *n.* An attendant; an obsequious dependent; a small planet revolving round another.

satiate, sā'shi-āt, *vt.* (satiating, satiated). To fully satisfy the desire of; to surfeit; to glut.—*a.* Filled to satiety.

satisfy, sa'tis-fī, *vt.* and *i.* (satisfying, satisfied). To gratify fully; to content; to fulfill the claims of; to answer, to free from doubt.

saturate, sa'tūr-āt, *vt.* To imbue till no more can be received; to soak thoroughly.

saunter, sän'tèr, *vi.* To stroll about idly; to loiter.—*n.* A stroll; a leisurely pace.

saurian, sä'ri-an, *a.* Pertaining to the lizards.—*n.* A scaly reptile, as the lizard.

sausage, sä'sāj, *n.* The prepared intestine of an ox, etc., stuffed with minced meat.

savage, sa'väj, *a.* wild uncultivated, barbarous, brutal.—*n.* One who is uncivilized; a barbarian.

savant, sä-väng', A man of learning; a man eminent for his scientific acquirements.

save, sāv, *vt.* (saving, saved). To preserve; to protect; to rescue; to spare; to keep from doing or suffering, to reserve, to obviate.—*vi.* To be economical.—*prep.* Except.

saving, sāv'ing, *a.* Thrifty; that secures from evil; containing some reservation.—*n.* What is saved; sums accumulated by economy: generally *pl.*—*prep.* Excepting.

savior, sāv'yèr, *n.* One who saves from evil, destruction, or danger; Christ.

savor, sā'vor, *n.* Taste, flavor, odor distinctive quality.—*vi.* To have a particular taste; to partake of some characteristic of something else. vt. To taste or smell with pleasure, to like.

say, sā, *vt.* (saying, said). To utter in words, to speak, to declare, to assume.—*vi.* To speak; to relate.—*n.* A speech statement.

saying, sā'ing, *n.* Something said; speech; an adage; a maxim; a proverb.

scab, skab, *n.* An encrusted substance over a sore in healing; a disease of sheep; the mange in horses.

scale, skāl, *n.* A thin flake on the skin of an animal, dish of a balance; balance itself (generally *pl.*) anything graduated used as a measure; series of steps or ranks; relative dimensions; succession of notes; gamut.—*vt.* (scaling, scaled). To weigh, as in scales, to strip of scales; to clean, to climb, as by a ladder.—*vi.* To come off in thin layers.

scalene, skā'lĕn, *a.* A term applied to a triangle of which the three sides are unequal.

scallop, skal'op or skol'op, *n.* Edible bivalve of the oyster family; a curving on the edge of anything.—*vt.* To cut the edge of into scallops or segments of circles

scalp, skalp, *n.* The skin of the top of the head, with the hair on it.—*vt.* To deprive of the scalp.

scamp, skamp, *n.* A knave; swindler; rogue.—*vt.* To do in a perfunctory manner.

scan, skan, *vt.* (scanning, scanned). To measure by the metrical feet, as a verse; to scrutinize; to eye.

scandal, skan'dal, *n*. Public reproach; shame; defamatory talk; slander.

scandalize, skan'dal-īz, *vt*. To fend by some action deemed disgraceful, to shock.

scapular, scapulary, skap'ū-lèr, skap'ū-la-ri, *n*. A monastic garment resting on the shoulders, with a flap hanging down in front and another behind.

scar, skär, *n*. The mark of a wound or ulcer, a cicatrix, a cliff, a bare place on the side of a hill.—*vt*. (scarring, scarred). To mark with a scar, to wound.

scarcity, skärs'i-ti, *n*. State or condition of being scarce: deficiency; dearth.

scare, skā r, *vt*. (scaring, scared). To strike with sudden terror; to frighten.—*n*. A sudden fright, a causeless alarm.

scarlet, skär'let, *n*. A bright-red color.—*a*. Of a bright-red color.

scathe, skā th. *n*. Damage, injury.—*vt*. (scathing, scathed). To injure; to harm.

scatter, skat'èr, *vt*. To disperse; to spread; to strew; to disunite.—*vi*. To be dispersed; to straggle apart.

scattered, skat'èrd, *p.a*. Thinly spread; loose and irregular in arrangement.

scene, sēn, *n*. A stage; a distinct part of a play, a painted device on the stage; place of action or exhibition; general appearance of any action, a view, display of emotion.

scenery, sēn'è-ri, *n*. The painted representations on the stage, pictorial features, landscape characteristics.

schedule, shed'ūl, sed'ūl, *n*. A paper containing a list, and annexed to a larger writing, as to a will, deed, etc., an inventory.—*vt*. (scheduling, scheduled). To place in a schedule.

scheme, skēm, *n*. A combination of things adjusted by design; a system, project, diagram.—*vt*. and *i*. (scheming, schemed). To plan, contrive, project.

school, sköl, *n*. A place of instruction; a body of pupils; disciples; sect or body; a system or custom; a shoal (of fishes).—*a*. Relating to a school; scholastic.—*vt*. To instruct; to reprove.

schooner, skön'èr, *n*. A vessel with two or more masts, her chief sails fore-and-aft.

sciatic, sciatical, sī-at'ik, sī-at'ik-al *a*. Pertaining to the hip or to sciatica.

sciatica, sī-at'i-ka, *n*. Neuralgia or inflammation of the sciatic nerve or great nerve of the thigh.

science, sī'ens, *n*. Knowledge reduced to a system; the facts pertaining to any department of mind or matter in their due connections; skill resulting from training.

scientific, sī-en-tif'ik, *a*. Pertaining to science; versed in science; according to the rules or principles of science.

scleroma, sclerosis, sklē-rō'ma skle-ro'sis, *n*. Induration of the cellular tissue.

scoff, skof, *n*. An expression of derision or scorn; a gibe.—*vi*. To utter contemptuous language; to jeer, to mock.—*vt*. To mock at.

scold, skōld, *vi*. To find fault with rude clamor; to utter harsh, rude rebuke.—*vt*. To reprimand loudly: to chide.—*n*. A clamorous, foul mouthed woman.

scorch, skorch, *vt*. To burn superficially, to singe, to parch.—*vi*. To be as hot as to burn a surface; to be dried up; to ride a cycle at excessive speed.

score, skōr, *n*. A notch; a long scratch or mark, an account or reckoning, the number twenty; a debt; the number of points made in certain games, motive, ground draft of a musical composition.— *vt*. (scoring, scored). To make scores or scratches on; to record; to get for oneself, as points, etc., in games.

scoria, skō'ri-a, *n*.; pl. -ae. Dross; cinder; the cellular, slaggy lavas of a volcano.

scorn, skorn, *n*. Extreme contempt; subject of contempt. *vt*. To hold in extreme contempt, to despise.—*vi*. To feel or show scorn.

scorpion, skor'pi-on, *n*. An animal of the class Arachnida, with a jointed tail terminating with a venomous sting; a sign of the zodiac.

Scottish, skot'ish, *a* Pertaining to Scotland, its inhabitants, or language.

scoundrel, skoun'drel, *n*. A mean, worthless fellow; a rascal.—*a*. Base, unprincipled.

scout, skout, *n*. A person sent to obtain intelligence regarding an enemy; a college servant.—*vi*. To act as a scout.—*vt*. To watch closely, to treat with disdain.

scowl, skoul, *vi*. To wrinkle the brows, as in displeasure, to frown.—*n*. A deep angry frown; gloom.

scrape, skrāp, *vt*. (scraping, scraped). To rub with something hard; to clean by a sharp edge; to act on with a grating noise; to erase; to collect laboriously.— *vi*. To roughen or remove a surface by rubbing; to make a grating noise.—*n*. Act of scraping; an awkward bow; an

S

awkward predicament.

scraper, skrāp'ér, n. One who or that which scrapes; an instrument for scraping or cleaning.

scratch, skrach, vt. and i. To mark or wound with something sharp; to tear with the nails; to withdraw from the list of competitors.—n. A score in a surface; a slight wound; a line from which runners start etc.; one most heavily handicapped in a contest.—a. Taken at random, hastily collected.

scrawl, skräl, vt. and i. To write or draw carelessly or awkwardly.—n. Inelegant or hasty writing.

scream, skrēm, vi. To shriek; to utter a shrill cry.—n. A sharp, shrill cry.

screw, skrö, n. A cylinder with a spiral ridge which enables it when turned to enter another body, a screw-propeller; a twist or turn; a niggard.—vt. To fasten by a screw; to twist; to oppress.

screw-propeller, skrö'prö-pel-ėr, n. An apparatus on the principle of the common screw, for propelling boats and ships.

scribble, skrib'l, vt. and i. (scribbling, scribbled). To write with haste or without care; to tease coarsely, as cotton or wool.—n. Careless writing; a scrawl.

scribe, skrīb, n. A writer, notary copyist; doctor of the law among the Jews.

scrimmage, skrim'āj, n. A tussle; a confused, close struggle in football.

scrimp, skrimp, vt. To make too small or short; to scant; to limit.— a. Scanty.

scrofula, skro'fū-la, n. A disease, a variety of consumption, often showing itself by glandular tumors in the neck which suppurate.

scroll, skröl, n. A roll of paper or parchment, a draft or first copy, a spiral ornament; a flourish added to a person's name.

scrub, skrub, vt. (scrubbing scrubbed). To rub hard with something rough, to make clean or bright.—vi. To be diligent and penurious.—n. One who labors hard and lives sparingly; a mean fellow; a worn-out brush; low underwood.—a. Mean.

scruple, skrö'pl, n. A weight of 20 grains; doubt, hesitation, backwardness.—vi. (scrupling, scrupled). To doubt, to hesitate.

scuffle, skuf'l, n. A confused struggle.— vi. (scuffling, scuffled). To strive confusedly at close quarters.

scull, skul, n. A short oar, used in pairs.— vt. To propel by sculls, or by moving an oar at the stern.

sculptor, skulp'tor, n. One who works in sculpture; an artist who carves or models figures.

sculpture, skulp'tūr, n. The art of carving wood or stone into images; an image in stone, etc.— vt. (sculpturing, sculptured). To carve; to form, as images on stone, etc.

scum, skum, n. Impurities which rise to the surface of liquors refuse.—vt. (scumming scummed). To take the scum from.—vi. To throw up scum.

scurvy, skėr'vi, n. A disease caused by insufficiency of vegetable food.—a. Vile; mean; malicious.

scuttle, skut'l, n. A broad basket; a pail for coals; a hatchway in a ship's deck, a short run, a quick pace.—vt. (scuttling, scuttled). To sink by making holes in (a ship).— vi. To scurry.

scythe, sīTH, n. An implement for mowing grass, etc.—vt. To cut with a scythe.

sea, sē, n. The mass of salt water covering most of the earth, some portion of this, a name of certain lakes; a large wave; a surge; a flood.

sea-anemone, sē'a-nem'o-nē, n. A beautiful sea-shore, plant-like animal.

sea-breeze, sē'brēz, n. A wind or current of air blowing from the sea upon land.

seal, sē l, n. A hard substance bearing some device, used to make impressions, the wax stamped with a seal; assurance; that which makes fast, a carnivorous marine mammal.—vt. To set a seal to, to confirm; to fasten; to shut or keep close.

seamanship, sē'man-ship, n. The art or skill of a seaman; art of managing a ship.

seamstress, sēm'stres, n. A woman whose occupation is sewing, a sempstress.

seamy, sēm'i, a. Having a seam; showing seams; showing the worst side. disagreeable.

seance, sä-ängs, n. A session, as of some public body; a sitting with the view of evoking spiritual manifestations.

sea-port, sē'pört, n. A harbor on the seacoast; a town on or near the sea.

sear, sėr, n. A catch in the mechanism of a rifle which holds back the cocking-piece.

search, sėrch, vt. To look through to find something; to examine.—vi. To seek diligently, to inquire.—n. Act of searching; examination; inquiry.

sea-shore, sē'shŏr, n. The shore of the sea; ground between high and low water mark.

sea-sick, sē'sik, *a*. Affected with sickness caused by the motion of a vessel at sea.

season, sē'zn, *n*. A division of the year, a suitable time a time. time of the year marked by special activity; seasoning.— *vt*. To accustom, to acclimatize, to flavor.—*vi*. To become suitable by time.

seasonable, sē'zn-a-bl, *a*. Natural to the season, opportune, timely.

seasoning, sē'zn-ing, *n*. Something added to food to give it relish, relish, condiment.

seat, sēt, *n*. That on which one sits a chair, stool, etc., place of sitting a right to sit, residence; station— *vt*. To place on a seat; to settle; to locate; to assign seats to; to fit up with seats.

secessionist, sē-se'shon-ist, *n*. One who advocates or engages in a secession.

seclude sē-klöd', *vt*. (secluding, secluded). To shut up apart; to separate; *refl*. to withdraw into solitude.

seclusion, sē-klö'zhon, *n*. Act of secluding: retired mode of life; privacy.

second, se'kund, *a*. Next after the first; repeated again; inferior; other.—*n*. One who or that which comes next a first, one who supports another; attendant in a duel; sixtieth part of a minute; a lower part in music, *pl*. a coarse kind of flour.—*vt*. To follow in the next place; to support; to join with in proposing some measure.

secret, sē'kret, *a*. Hidden; concealed, private; unseen.—*n*. Something hidden or not to be revealed; a mystery

secretary, se'krē-ta-ri, *n*. A person employed to write orders, letters, etc., an escritoire, one who manages the affairs of a department of government.

secrete, sē-krēt', *vt*. (secreting, secreted). To hide, to separate from the blood in animals or from the sap in vegetables.

section, sek'shon, *n*. Act of cutting; a distinct part, subdivision of a chapter, etc., representation of an object as if cut asunder by an intersecting plane, a quarter of a platoon of infantry, the normal fire-unit.

sector, sek'tor, *n*. A part of a circle between two radii; a mathematical instrument useful in making diagrams.

secular, se'kū-lèr, *a*. Pertaining to things not spiritual or sacred worldly; temporal; coming once in a century.

secularism, sek'ū-lèr-izm, *n*. The elimination of the religious element from life.

secure, sē-kūr', *a*. Free from care or danger; heedless; undisturbed; safe; confident.—*vt*. (securing, secured). To make safe or certain, to seize and confine; to guarantee, to fasten.

security, sē-kū'ri-ti, *n*. Safety; confidence; protection; a guarantee; a surety, an evidence of property, as a bond, a certificate of stock, etc.

sedate, sē-dāt', *a*. Composed in manner; staid; placid; sober; serious.

sedition, sē-di'shon, *n*. A commotion in a state, insurrection, civic discord.

seduce, sē-dūs', *vt*. (seducing, seduced).To lead astray; to corrupt; to entice to a surrender of chastity.

seduction, sē-duk'shon, *n*. Act of seducing; allurement; the persuading of a female to surrender her chastity.

see, sē, *vt*. (seeing, pret, saw, pp. seen). To perceive by the eye; to notice; to discover; to understand; to receive, to experience, to attend.—*vi*. To have the power of sight; to understand, to consider.—*interj*. Lo! look!—*n*. A seat of episcopal power; a diocese.

seed, sēd, *n*. That product of a plant which may produce a similar plant; seeds collectively; the semen, first principle, offspring.— *vi*. To produce seed; to shed the seed.—*vt*. To sow; to supply with seed.

seeming, sēm'ing, *p.a*. Appearing; specious.—*n*. Appearance; semblance.

seemly, sēm'li, *a*. Becoming, suitable; decorous.—*adv*. In a suitable manner.

see-saw, sē'sä, *n*. A swinging movement up and down; a game in which children swing up and down on the two ends of a balanced piece of timber.—*vi*. and *t*. To move up and down or to and fro.

seethe, sēTH, *vt*. (seething, seethed). To boil, to soak.—*vi*. To be in a state of ebullition, to be hot.

segment, seg'ment, *n*. A part cut off, a section; a natural division of a body (as an orange).

seize, sēz, *vt*. (seizing, seized). To lay hold of suddenly; to take by force or legal authority; to attack, as a disease, fear, etc.; to comprehend to put in possession.—*vi*. To take hold or possession.

select, sē-lekt', *vt*. To choose; to pick out; to cull.—*a*. Chosen; choice, exclusive.

selection, sē-lek'shon, *n*. Act of selecting; a collection of things selected.

selenium, se-lē'ni-um, *n*. A non-metallic element akin to sulphur and tellurium.

selenology, sel-ē-nol'o-ji, *n*. That branch of astronomy which treats of the moon.

S

self, self, *n.;* pl. **selves,** selvz. One's individual person; personal interest; a blossom of a uniform color (with *pl.* selfs).—*a.* or *pron.* Same. Affixed to pronouns and adjectives to express emphasis or distinction, or reflexive usage.

self-control, self-kon-trōl', *n.* Control exercised over oneself; self-command.

self-denial, self-dē-nī'al, *n.* The forebearing to gratify one's own desires.

self-denying, self-dē-nī'ing, *a.* Denying oneself; forbearing to indulge one's own desires.

self-esteem, self-es-tēm', *n.* The esteem or good opinion of oneself; vanity.

self-evident, self-ev'i-dent, *a.* Evident in its own nature; evident without proof.

self-government, self-gu'vèrn-ment, *n.* The government of oneself, government by rulers appointed by the people.

self-important, self-im-pōrt'ant, *a.* Important in one's own esteem; pompous.

self-imposed, self'im-pōzd, *a.* Imposed or voluntarily taken on oneself.

selfish, self'ish, *a.* Devoted unduly to self, influenced by a view to private advantage.

self-sufficient, self-suf-fi'shent, *a.* Having too much confidence in oneself; conceited; assuming; overbearing.

sell, sel, *vt.* (selling, sold). To give in exchange for money, etc., to betray.— *vi.* To practice selling; to be sold.

selvedge, selvage, sel'vej, sel'vāj, *n.* The edge of cloth; border of close work.

semaphore, se'ma-för, *n.* An apparatus for signalling at a distance, usually a pole supporting a movable arm.

seminary, se'min-a-ri, *n.* A school or academy; a place for educating for the priesthood.

semination, se-min-ā'shon, *n.* Act of sowing; the natural dispersion of seeds.

Semite, sem'īt, *n.* A descendant of Shem; one of the Semitic race, a Shemite.

semi-vowel, se'mi-vou-el, *n.* A sound partaking of the nature of both a vowel and a consonant, as *l, m, r.*

senile, sē'nīl, *a.* Pertaining to old age; characterized by the failings of old age.

senior, sē'ni-or, sēn'yor, *a.* Older; older or more advanced in office.—*n.* One older in age or office.

senna, sen'na, *n.* The dried leaves of certain plants used as a purgative; the plant itself.

sensation, sen-sā'shon, *n.* Impression made through the senses feeling; power of feeling; what produces excited interest.

sensational, sen-sā'shon-al, *a.* Relating to sensation; producing excited interest.

sense, sens, *n.* The faculty of receiving impressions; a separate faculty of perception; sight; hearing, taste, smell, or touch, consciousness; discernment; understanding; good judgment; meaning.

sensorium, sen-sō'ri-um, *n.* The common center at which all the impressions of sense are received; the brain.

sensual, sens'ū-al *a.* Pertaining to the senses, as distinct from the mind; carnal; voluptuous; indulging in lust.

sentient, sen'shi-ent, *a.* Having the capacity of sensation; perceptive; sensible.

sentiment, sen'ti-ment, *n.* Thought prompted by emotion; tenderness of feeling; sensibility; a thought or opinion.

sentimental, sen-ti-men'tal, *a.* Having sentiment, apt to be swayed by emotional feelings; mawkishly tender.

sentinel, sen'ti-nel, *n.* One who is set to keep watch; a sentry (now archaic or poetical).

sentry, sen'tri, *n.* A soldier placed on guard; guard; watch; sentinel's duty.

separate, se'pa-rāt, *vt.* (separating, separated). To put or set apart, to disjoin.— *vi.* To go apart, to cleave or split.—*a.* Detached; distinct; individual.

separation, se pa-rā'shon, *n.* Act of separating; disunion; incomplete one's abode, to subside, to become calm; to adjust differences or accounts.

settlement, set'l-ment, *n.* Act of settling, establishment in life; colonization; a colony; adjustment; liquidation; arrangement; settling of property on a wife.

severalty, se'vèr-al-ti, *n.* A state of separation from the rest, or from all others

severe, sē-vēr', *a.* Serious; grave; harsh; stern; austere; rigidly exact, keen.

severity, sē-ve 'ri-ti, *n.* State or quality of being severe; rigor; intensity; austerity.

Sevres, sā-vr, *n.* A kind of beautiful porcelain, made of *Sevres,* near Paris.

sewer, sū'èr, *n.* A subterranean drain, as in a city, to carry off water, filth, etc.

sewing, sō'ing, *n.* Act of using a needle, that which is sewed; stitches made.

sexual, seks'ū-al, *a.* Pertaining to, proceeding from, characterized by sex.

shabby, shab'i, *a.* Poor in appearance;

threadbare; mean; paltry; stingy.

shackle, shak'l, *n*. A fetter; a manacle; that which obstructs free action.—*vt*. (shackling, shackled). To bind with shackles; to hamper.

shade, shād, *n*. Obscurity caused by the interception of light; obscure retreat; twilight dimness; a screen; darker part of a picture; gradation of light; a scarcely perceptible degree or amount; a ghost.—*vt*. (shading, shaded). To screen from light, to obscure; to protect; to darken; to mark with gradations of color

shadow, sha'dŏ, *n*. A figure projected by the interception of light; shade; an inseparable companion, an imperfect representation; a spirit; protection.—*vt*. To shade; to cloud, to screen, to represent faintly, to follow closely.

shake, shāk, *vt*. (shaking, pret, shook, pp. shaken). To cause to move with quick vibrations; to agitate, to move from firmness; to cause to waver; to trill.—*vi*. To tremble; to shiver; to quake.—*n*. A wavering or rapid motion, tremor; shock; a trill in music; a crack in timber.

shallow, shal'ŏ, *a*. Not deep; superficial; simple, silly.—*n*. A place where the water is not deep; a shoal.

sham, sham, *n*. That which appears to be what it is not; imposture, humbug.—*a*. False; counterfeit.—*vt*. and *i*. (shamming, shammed). To feign, pretend.

shame, shām, *n*. A painful sensation excited by guilt, disgrace, etc.; reproach; disgrace.—*vt*. (shaming, shamed). To make ashamed; to disgrace.

shamefaced, shām'fāst, *a*. Easily put out of countenance; modest; bashful.

shameful, shām'ful, *a*. Full of shame; disgraceful; scandalous; infamous.

shampoo, sham-pö', *vt*. (shampooing, shampooed). To press and rub the body after a hot bath; to wash and rub thoroughly the head.

shamrock, sham'rok, *n*. A trefoil plant, the national emblem of Ireland.

shank, shangk, *n*. The leg; the shinbone, the part of a tool connecting the acting part with a handle; the stem of an anchor.

shanty, shan'ti, *n*. A hut or mean dwelling; song sung by sailors working together.

shape, shāp, *vt*. (shaping, shaped). To form; to mold; to adjust.—*vi*. To suit.—*n*. Form or figure; make; a model; a dish of blancmange, etc.

shard, shärd, *n*. A fragment of an earthen vessel; the wing-case of a beetle.

share, shār, *n*. A part bestowed or contributed; lot or portion; a plowshare.—*vt*. (sharing, shared). To part among two or more, to participate in.—*vi*. To have part.

shareholder, shār'hŏld-ėr, *n*. One who holds shares in a joint property.

shark, shärk, *n*. A voracious seafish; an unscrupulous person; a sharper.

shave, shāv, *vt*. (shaving, shaved). To cut off the hair from the skin with a razor; to cut off thin slices from, to skim along; to fleece.—*vi*. To cut off the beard with a razor.—*n*. A cutting off of the beard; a thin slice; an exceedingly narrow escape.

sheath, shēth, *n*. A case for a sword, etc.; a scabbard; wing-case of an insect.

sheathe, shēTH, *vt*. (sheathing, sheathed). To put into a sheath, to protect by a casing.

shed, shed, *vt*. (shedding, shed). To cast or throw off; to emit or diffuse; to let fall in drops; to spill.— *vi*. To let fall seed, a covering, etc.—*n*. A watershed; the opening between threads in a loom through which the shuttle passes; a penthouse; a hut; a large open structure.

sheep, shēp, *sing*. and *pl*. A ruminant animal valued for its wool and flesh; a silly or timid fellow— **sheep's eye,** a loving or wistful glance.

sheet, shēt, *n*. A broad, thin piece of anything broad expanse, piece of linen or cotton spread on a bed; piece of paper, a rope fastened to the lower corner of a sail.—*vt*. To furnish with sheets; to shroud.

shelf, shelf, *n*. pl. **shelves,** shelvz. A board fixed along a wail to support articles; a ledge; a ledge of rocks in the sea.

shell, shel, *n*. A hard outside covering, an outside crust, framework any slight hollow structure; a projectile containing a bursting charge.—*vt*. To strip off the shell of, to throw bomb-shells into or among.—*vi*. To cast the exterior covering.

sherbet, sher'bet, *n*. An Eastern drink of water, the juice of fruits, and sugar.

sheriff, she'rif, *n*. An officer in each county to whom is entrusted the administration of the law; in Scotland, the chief judge of a county.

shibboleth, shib'bŏ-leth. *n*. The watchword of a party; a cry or motto.

shield, shēld, *n*. A broad piece of armor carried on the arm protection, an

S

escutcheon with a coat of arms.—*vt.* To cover, as with a shield; to protect.

shift, shift, *vi.* To change; to change place or direction; to manage; to practice indirect methods.—*vt.* To remove, to alter to dress in fresh clothes.—*n.* A change; expedient; evasion, an under garment; a squad of workmen; the working time of a relay of men; the spell of work.

shingle, shing'gl, *n.* A thin piece of wood used in covering roofs, loose gravel and pebbles.—*vt.* To cover with shingles; to hammer so as to expel slag or scoriae from in puddling iron.

shingles, shing'glz, *n.* An eruptive disease which spreads around the body.

shiny, shīn'i, *a.* Bright; brilliant; clear.

ship, ship, *n.* A vessel of some size adapted to navigation, a three-masted, square-rigged vessel.—*vt.* (shipping, shipped). To put on board of a ship; to transport in a ship, to hire for service in a ship; to fix in its place.—*vi.* To engage for service on a ship; to embark.

shipwreck, ship'rek, *n.* The wreck or loss of a ship; destruction; ruin.—*vt.* To wreck; to cast away; to ruin.

shipwright, ship'rīt, *n.* A builder of ships or other vessels; a ship-carpenter.

shirt, shėrt, *n.* A man's loose under garment of linen etc., a lady's blouse.—*vt.* To clothe with a shirt.

shiver, shi'vėr, *vt.* To shatter.—*vi.* To fall into many small pieces; to tremble, as from cold, to shudder.—*n.* A small fragment, a shaking fit, shudder.

shoal, shōl, *n.* A multitude; a crowd, a sandbank or bar, a shallow.—*vi.* To become more shallow.—*a.* Shallow.

shock, shok, *n.* A violent striking against; violent onset; a sudden disturbing emotion; a stook; a thick mass of hair.—*vt.* To give a shock to; to encounter violently; to disgust; to make up into shocks or stooks.

shook, shük, pret. and pp. of *shake.*—*n.* The staves for a single barrel made into a package.

shoot, shōt, *vt.* (shooting shot). To cause to fly forth; to discharge; to hit or kill with a missile, to empty out suddenly, to thrust forward; to pass rapidly under, over, etc.—*vi.* To charge a missile; to dart along; to sprout; to project.—*n.* A shooting; a young branch; a sloping trough; a place for shooting rubbish.

shooting, shōt'ing, *n.* Sport of killing game with firearms; tract over which game is shot, sensation of a darting

pain.—*a.* Pertaining to one who shoots.

shop, shop *n.* A place where goods are sold by retail; a building in which mechanics work; one's special business.—*vi.* (shopping, shopped) To visit shops for purchasing goods.

shot, shot, *n.* Act of shooting; a projectile; a bullet; bullets collectively; range or reach; a marksman; the number of fish caught in one haul; a reckoning.—*vt.* (shotting, shotted). To load with shot.—*a.* Having a changeable color, as silk, interwoven.

should, shüd, the pret. of *shall,* denoting present or past duty or obligation, or expressing a hypothetical case.

shoulder, shō l'dė r, *n.* The joint by which the arm or the fore-leg is connected with the body; a projection; support.—*vt.* To push with the shoulder, to put upon the shoulder.—*vi.* To push forward.

shoulder-strap, shōl'dėr-strap, *n.* A strap worn on the shoulder, either to support dress, or as a badge of distinction.

shout shout, *vi.* To utter a loud and sudden cry.—*vt.* To utter with a shout.—*n.* A loud sudden cry.

shove, shuv, *vt.* and *i.* (shoving, shoved). To push forward; to press against; to jostle.—*n.* Act of shoving, a push.

shovel, shu'vel, *n.* An instrument with a broad shallow blade for lifting earth, etc.—*vt.* (shoveling, shoveled). To throw with a shovel.

show, shō, *vt.* (pret. showed, pp. (shown or showed). To display to the view of others: to let be seen; to make known; to prove; to bestow, afford.—*vi.* To appear—*n.* Act of showing; exhibition; appearance; pretense; pageant; things exhibited for money.

shrew, shrö, *n.* A peevish, ill-tempered woman; a scold; a shrew-mouse.

shrine, shrīn, *n.* A case, as for sacred relics, a tomb altar, a place hallowed from its associations.— *vt.* (shrining, shrined). To enshrine.

shrink, shringk, *vi.* (pret. shrank or shrunk, pp. shrunk or shrunken). To contact spontaneously, to shrivel; to withdraw, as from danger; to flinch.—*vt.* To cause to contract.—*n.* contraction.

shrub, shrub, *n.* A woody plant less than a tree, a plant with several woody stems from the same root a beverage containing the juice of fruit, etc.

shrubbery, shrub'er-i, *n.* An ornamental plantation of shrubs shrubs collectively.

shrug, shrug, *vt.* and *i.* (shrugging, shrugged) To draw up or to contract as the shoulders.—*n.* A drawing up of the shoulders.

shudder, shud'er, *vi.* To tremble with fear, horror, etc.; to quake.—*n.* A tremor.

shuffle, shuf'l, *vt.* (shuffling; shuffled). To shove one way and the other, to confuse, to change the position of cards.—*vi.* To change position, to quibble, to move with a dragging gait; to scrape the floor in dancing.—*n.* An evasion; mixing cards; scraping movement in dancing.

shunt, shunt, *vi.* and *t.* In railways; to turn from one line of rails into another, to free oneself of.

shut, shut, *vt.* (shutting, shut). To close or stop up, to bar, to preclude, to exclude, to confine.—*vi.* To close itself; to be closed.—*a.* Made close, closed, not resonant.

shutter, shut'er, *n.* One who shuts; a moveable covering for a window or aperture.

shuttle, shut'l, *n.* An instrument used by weavers for shooting the thread of the woof between the threads of the warp.

shuttle-cock, shut'l-kok, *n.* A cork stuck with feathers, and struck by a battledore.—*vt.* To throw backwards and forwards.

sick, sik, *a.* Affected with disease of any kind; ill; inclined to vomit; disgusted or weary; pertaining to those who are sick.

sicken, sik'n, *vt.* To make sick; to disgust.—*vi.* To become sick, to be disgusted; to languish.

sickle, sik'l, *n.* An instrument for cutting grain, used with one hand; a reaping-hook.

side, sīd, *n.* The broad or long surface of a body, edge, border, right or left half of the body; part between the top and bottom; any party or interest opposed to another.—*a.* Being on, from, or toward the side, indirect.—*vi.* (siding, sided). To embrace the opinions of one party.

sienna, sē-en'na, *n.* An earth of a fine yellow color, used as a pigment.

sieve, siv, *n.* A utensil for separating the smaller particles of a loose substance.

sift, sift, *vt.* To separate by a sieve to examine minutely.—*vi.* To pass as if through a sieve.

sigh, sī, *vi.* To make a long breath audibly, as from grief; to make a melancholy sound.—*n.* A long breath made audibly, as in grief.

signal, sig'nal, *n.* A sign to communicate intelligence, orders, etc., at a distance. *a.* Worthy of note; remarkable.—*vt.* or *i.* (signalling, signalled). To communicate by signals.

signet, sig'net, *n.* A seal; seal used by the sovereign in sealing private letters.

significant, sig-ni'fi-kant, *a.* Signifying something; indicative; important.

signification, sig'ni-fi-kā"shon, *n.* Act of signifying; meaning; import; sense.

signify, sig'ni-fī, *vt.* (signifying, signified). To make known either by signs or words; to betoken; to mean; to imply; to import.

silent, sī'lent, *a.* Not speaking; mute; dumb; taciturn; making no noise.

sill, sil, *n.* The timber or stone at the foot of a door or window; the threshold; the floor of a gallery in a mine.

silo, sī'lō, *n.* The pit in which green fodder is preserved in the method of ensilage.

silurian, sī-lū'ri-an, *a.* Applied to the lowest division of the paleozoic strata.

silver, sil'ver, *n.* A precious metal of a white color, money: plate made of silver.—*a.* Made of silver; silvery.—*vt.* and *i.* To cover with a coat of silver, to tinge with gray.

silversmith, sil'ver-smith, *n.* One whose occupation is to work in silver.

simper, sim'per, *vi.* To smile in a silly manner.—*n.* A silly or affected smile.

simple, sim'pl, *a.* Not complex single; not involved; clear; artless; mere, plain, sincere, silly.—*n.* Something not mixed, a medicinal herb.

simpleton, sim'pl-ton, *n.* A simple or silly person; one easily deceived.

simplicity, sim-plis'i-ti, *n.* State or quality of being simple; singleness; artlessness; sincerity; plainness, foolishness.

since, sins, *adv.* From that time; from then till now; ago.—*prep.* Ever from the time of; after.—*conj.* From the time when; because that.

sincere, sin-sēr', *a.* Pure, unmixed; real; genuine; guileless; frank; true.

sincerity, sin-se'ri-ti, *n.* Honesty of mind or intention; freedom from hypocrisy.

sinful, sin'fūl, *a.* Full of sin; wicked; iniquitous; wrong.

singe, sinj, *vt.* (singeing, singed). To burn slightly; to burn the surface of—*n.* A burning of the surface.

single, sing'gl, *a.* Being one or a unit; individual; unmarried; performed by

S

one person simple, sincere.—*vt*. (sin-gling, singled). To select individually; with out.

singular, sing'gū-lẻr, *a*. That is single, expressing one person or thing; remark-able; rare; odd.—*n*. The singular num-ber

sip, sip, *vt*. (sipping, sipped). To drink in small quantities; to drink out of.—*vi*. To take a fluid with the lips.—*n*. A small quantity of liquid taken with the lips.

siren, sī'ren, *n*. A sea-nymph who enticed seamen by songs, and then slew them; a woman dangerous from her fascina-tions; a fog-signal; a signal used as an air-raid warning.—*a*. Bewitching.

size, sīz, *n*. Comparative magnitude; big-ness; bulk; a glutinous substance used by painters, etc.—*vt*. (sizing, sized). To arrange according to size; to take the size of; to cover with size.

skeleton, ske'le-ton, *n*. The bony frame-work of an animal; general structure or frame; outline.—*a*. Resembling a skele-ton.

sketch, skech, *n*. An outline or general delineation; a first rough draft.—*vt*. To draw a sketch of; to give the chief points of; to plan.—*vi*. To practice sketching.

skim, skim, *vt*. (skimming, skimmed). To remove the scum from; to take off from a surface; to pass lightly over; to glance over superficially.—*vi*. To glide along.

skirmish, skẻr'mish, *n*. A slight battle; a brief contest.—*vi*. To fight in short con-tests or in small parties.

slack, slak, *a*. Not tight or tense; loose; remiss; backward; not busy.—*adv*. In a slack manner; partially; insufficiently.—*n*. The part of a rope that hangs loose; small broken coal.—*vt*. and *i*. To slack-en; to slake.

slake, slāk, *vt*. (slaking, slaked). To quench, as thirst or rage; to extinguish.*vi*. To abate; to become extinct.—*n*. A muddy tract adjoining the sea.

slang, slang, *n*. and *a*. A class of expres-sions not generally approved of, as being inelegant or undignified.—*vt*. To address with slang; to abuse vulgarly.

slant, slant, *a*. Sloping.—*vt*. and *i*. To turn from a direct line, to slope to incline.—*n*. A slope

slaughter, slä'tẻr, *n*. A slaying; carnage, massacre, a killing of beasts for market.—*vt*. To slay; to kill for the mar-ket.

slavish, slāv'ish, *a*. Pertaining to slaves; servile, mean; oppressively laborious.

sleazy, slē'zi, *a*. Thin, flimsy, want-ing firmness of texture, as silk. Also *sleezy*.

sled, sled, *n*. A sledge.—*vt*. (sledding, sledded). To convey on a sled.

sledge, sledge-hammer, slej, slej' ham-ẻr, *n*. A large, heavy hammer, used by iron-workers.

sleep, slē p, *vi*. (sleeping, slept). To take rest by a suspension of voluntary exer-cise of the powers of body and mind; to be dormant or inactive.—*vt*. To pass in sleeping; to get rid of by sleeping, with *off*—*n*. That state in which volition is suspended; slumber; death; dormant state.

sleight, slīt, *n*. A sly artifice; an artful trick, dexterity.

slice, slīs *vt*. (slicing, sliced). To cut into thin pieces; to divide.—*n*. A thin, broad piece cut off; a broad flat utensil.

slide, slīd, *vi*. (sliding, pret. slid, pp. slid, slidden). To move along a surface by slipping: to pass smoothly or gradually.—*vt*. To thrust smoothly along a surface.—*n*. A smooth and easy passage, that part of an apparatus which slides into place.

slime, slīm, *n*. A soft or glutinous sub-stance moist earth or mud; viscous sub-stance exuded by certain animals.—*vt*. (sliming, slimed). To cover with slime, to make slimy.

sling, sling, *vt*. (slinging, slung). To throw, to hang so as to swing, to place in a sling.—*n*. An instrument for throwing stones, a bandage to support a wounded limb; a rope for raising heavy articles.

slink, slingk, *vi*. (slinking, slunk). To sneak; to steal away.—*vt*. To cast pre-maturely.—*n*. A premature calf.

slip, slip, *vi*. (slipping, slipped). To move smoothly along; to glide; to depart secretly; to have the feet slide; to err; to escape insensibly.—*vt*. To put or thrust secretly. to omit; to disengage oneself from; to make a slip of for planting.—*n*. A sliding of the feet, an unintentional error; a twig cut for planting or grafting; a long narrow piece, a leash by which a dog is held; a long strip of printed mat-ter, a loose covering, an inclined plane upon which a ship is built.

slipper, slip'ẻr, *n*. One who slips or lets slip; a loose light shoe for household wear.

slipshod, slip'shod, *a*. Shod with slippers; having shoes down at heel; slovenly.

slope, slōp, *n.* An oblique direction; a declivity.—*vt.* and *i.* (sloping sloped). To form with a slope; to incline.

slot, slot, *n.* A bolt or bar; an oblong hole; track of a deer.—*vt.* (slotting, slotted). To make a slot in

sloth, slōth or sloth, *n.* Indolence: laziness; idleness; a South American mammal.

slouch, slouch. *n.* A stoop in walking; an ungainly gait: a droop.—*vi.* To hang down; to have a drooping gait.—*vt.* To cause to hang down.

slue, slö, *vt.* (sluing, slued). To turn or swing round (as the yard of a ship).

slump, slump, *n.* The whole number taken in one lot; a sudden fall in prices or values.—*vt.* To throw into one lot.—*vi.* To sink in walking, as in snow.

slur, slėr, *vt.* (slurring, slurred). To soil; to traduce; to pass lightly over, to pronounce in a careless indistinct manner.—*n.* A slight reproach; a stain or stigma.

smack, smak, *vi.* To make a sharp noise with the lips; to taste; to savor.—*vt.* To make a sharp noise with, to slap.—*n.* A loud kiss, a sharp noise; a smart blow; a slap; a slight taste; a smattering; a fishing-vessel.

small, smäl, *a.* Little; petty; short; weak, gentle, not loud, narrow-minded; mean.—*n.* The small part of a thing; *pl.* small-clothes.

smart, smärt, *n.* A quick, keen pain, pungent grief.—*a.* Keen; quick; sharp; brisk; witty; spruce; well dressed.—*vt.* To feel a sharp pain, to be acutely painful; to be punished.

smell, smel, *vt.* (smelling, smelled). To perceive by the nose; to perceive the scent of, to detect.—*vi.* To give out an odor.—*n.* The faculty by which odors are perceived; scent, perfume.

smelt, smelt, *vt.* To melt, as ore, to separate the metal.—*n.* A small fish allied to the salmon.

smile, smîl, *vi.* (smiling, smiled). To show pleasure, sarcasm, pity, etc., by a look, to appear propitious.— *vt.* To express by a smile; to affect by smiling.—*n.* A set of the features expressing pleasure, scorn, etc.; favor.

smock, smok, *n.* A chemise; a smock; frock.—*vt.* To clothe with a smock; to pucker diagonally.

smocking, smok'ing, *n.* An ornamental diagonal puckering, in form of a honeycomb, and capable of being expanded.

smoke, smōk, *n.* The exhalation from a burning substance; vapor; idle talk; nothingness; a drawing in and puffing out of tobacco fumes.—*vi.* (smoking, smoked). To emit smoke, to use tobacco.—*vt.* To apply smoke to; to befoul by smoke; to fumigate; to use in smoking.

smooth, smōTH, *a.* Even on the surface; glossy; moving equably; not harsh, bland.—*n.* Smooth part of anything.—*vt.* To make smooth; to level; to make easy; to palliate; to soothe.

smother, smuTH'èr, *n.* Stifling smoke; suffocating dust.—*vt.* To stifle, to suffocate to suppress.— *vi.* To be suffocated or suppressed; to smoulder.

smoulder, smōl'dèr, *vi.* To burn and smoke without flame; to exist in a suppressed state.

snaffle, snaf'l, *n.* A bridle consisting of a slender bitmouth without a curb.—*vt.* To bridle, to manage with a snaffle.

snag, snag, *n.* A short projecting stump, a shoot; the tine of a deer's antler; a tree in a river dangerous to vessels.

snail, snāl, *n.* A slimy, slow-creeping mollusk; a slug; a sluggard.

snap, snap, *vt.* (snapping, snapped). To bite or seize suddenly, to break with a sharp sound, to break short.—*vi.* To try to seize with the teeth, to break suddenly or without bending.—*n.* A quick eager bite; a sudden breaking; a sharp noise; a kind of biscuit.

snare, snār, *n.* A line with a noose for catching animals; anything that entraps.—*vt.* (snaring, snared). To catch with a snare; to ensnare.

snarl, snärl, *vi.* To growl, as an angry dog, to talk in rude murmuring terms.—*vt.* To entangle.—*n.* A sharp angry growl; a knot; embarrassment.

snatch, snach, *vt.* To seize hastily or abruptly.—*vi.* To make a grasp.—*n.* A hasty catch; a short fit or turn; a small portion; a snack.

sneak, snēk, *vt.* To creep privately; to go furtively; to crouch.—*n.* A mean fellow, one guilty of under hand work.

snip, snip, *vt.* (snipping, snipped). To cut off at a stroke with shears; to clip.—*n.* A single cut with shears; a bit cut off.

snore, snōr, *vi.* (snoring, snored). To breathe with a rough, hoarse noise in sleep.—*n.* A breathing with a hoarse noise in sleep.

snort, snort, *vi.* To force air with violence through the nose.—*n.* A loud sound produced by forcing the air through the nostrils.

S

snow, snō, *n.* Watery particles congealed in the air, and falling in flakes.—*vi.* To fall in snow; used impersonally.—*vt.* To scatter like snow.

snow-plow, snō'plou, *n.* An implement for clearing away the snow from roads, etc.

snub, snub, *vt.* (snubbing, snubbed). To stop or rebuke with a tart, sarcastic remark, to slight designedly.—*n.* A check; a rebuke.

snuff, snuf, *vt.* To draw up through the nose; to smell; to crop, as the snuff of a candle.—*vi.* To draw up air or tobacco through the nose; to take offense.—*n.* A drawing up through the nose; resentment; burned wick of a candle; pulverized tobacco.

so, sō, *adv.* In this or that manner; to that degree; thus; extremely; very; the case being such; thereby.—*conj.* Provided that in case that, therefore; accordingly.

soak, sōk, *vt.* To let lie in a fluid till the substance has imbibed all that it can; to steep; to wet thoroughly.—*vi.* To steep; to enter by pores; to tipple.

soap, sōp, *n.* A compound of oil or fat with an alkali, used in washing.—*vt.* To rub or cover with soap.

soar, sōr, *vi.* To mount upon the wing, to rise high; to tower.—*n.* A towering flight; a lofty ascent.

sob, sob, *vi.* (sobbing, sobbed). To sigh or weep convulsively; to make a similar sound.—*n.* A convulsive catching of the breath in weeping or sorrow.

sober, sō'bėr, *a.* Temperate; not drunk; calm; cool; staid; grave; dull-looking.—*vt.* To make sober.—*vi.* To become sober

society, sō-sī'e-ti, *n.* Fellowship; company; a body of persons united for some object; persons living in the same circle, those who take the lead in social life.

sociology, sō-shi-ol'o-ji, *n.* The science which treats of society, its development, the progress of civilization, etc.

sock, sok, *n.* The shoe of the ancient actors of comedy; a short woven covering for the foot.

sod, sod, *n.* That layer of earth which is covered with grass; piece of turf

soda, sō'da, *n.* The alkali carbonate of sodium used in washing, glass-making, etc., and extensively made from salt.

soft, soft, *a.* Easily yielding to pressure, delicate, mild, effeminate not loud or harsh; not strong or glaring.—*adv.* Softly.—*interj.* Be soft, stop, not so fast.

soften, sof'n, *vt.* To make soft or more soft; to mollify; to alleviate; to tone down.—*vi.* To become soft; to relent; to become milder.

soil, soil, *vt.* To sully; to tarnish; to manure; to feed (cattle) indoors with green fodder.—*vi.* To tarnish.—*n.* Dirt; ordure; tarnish; the upper stratum of the earth; mould; loam; earth; land; country.

solder, sol'dėr, *vt.* To unite metals by a fused metallic substance, to patch up.—*n.* A metallic cement.

soldier, sōl'jėr, *n.* A man in military service; a man of distinguished valor

sole, sōl, *n.* The under side of the foot; the bottom of a shoe, a marine fish allied to the flounder.—*vt.* (soling, soled). To furnish with a sole, as a shoe.—*a.* Single; individual, only, alone.

solid, so'lid, *a.* Resisting pressure not liquid or gaseous; not hollow, cubic, sound, not frivolous.—*n.* A body that naturally retains the same shape.

soliloquy, sō-lil'ō-kwi, *n.* A speaking to oneself; discourse of a person alone.

solitaire, so'li-tär, *n.* A solitary, an article of jewelry in which a single gem is set; a game for a single person.

soluble, so'lū-bl, *a.* Susceptible of being dissolved in a fluid, capable of being solved, as a problem.

solution, so-lū'shon, *n.* A dissolving; preparation made by dissolving a solid in a liquid; act of solving; explanation; termination or crisis of a disease.

solvent, sol'vent, *a.* Having the power of dissolving; able to pay all debts. *n.* A fluid that dissolves any substance.

somehow, sum'hou, *adv.* In some way not yet known; one way or another.

somersault, somerset, sum'ėr-sält sum'ėr-set, *n.* A leap in which the heels turn over the head; a turn of the body in the air.

something, sum'thing, *n.* A thing quantity, or degree indefinitely; a person or thing of importance.— *adv.* somewhat.

somewhat, sum'whot, *n.* Something, more or less.—*adv.* In some degree; a little.

sonorous, sō-nō'rus, *a.* Giving sound when struck, resonant high-sounding.

soon, sön, *adv.* In a short time; shortly; early; quickly; promptly; readily; gladly.

soot, söt, *n.* A black substance formed from burning matter.—*vt.* To cover or foul with soot.

soothe, sö̈TH, *vt.* (soothing, soothed). To

please with soft words; to flatter, to pacify; to assuage, to soften.

soporiferous, sō-pō-rif'ik, *a*. Causing sleep.—*n*. A drug or anything that induces sleep.

soprano, sō-prä'nō, *n*. The highest female voice; a singer with such a voice.

sore, sōr, *a*. Painful; severe; distressing, tender, galled.—*n*. An ulcer; wound, etc.—*adv*. Severely; sorely.

sorrel, so'rel, *n*. A plant allied to the locks, a reddish or yellow-brown color.—*a*. Of a reddish color.

sorrow, so'rō, *n*. Affliction or distress of mind; grief; regret.—*vi*. To feel sorrow; to grieve.

sort, sort, *n*. Nature or character kind; species; manner; a set.—*vt*. To assort; to arrange; to reduce to order.—*vi*. To consort; to agree.

soul, sōl, *n*. The spiritual principle in man the moral and emotional part of man's nature; elevation of mind; fervor; essence; an inspirer or leader; a person.

sound, sound, *a*. Not in any way defective healthy valid, free from error; orthodox; just; heavy.—*n*. A narrow channel of water; a strait; air-bladder of a fish, that which is heard; noise.—*vt*. To measure the depth of; to examine medically; to try to discover the opinion, etc., of to cause to give out a sound, to pronounce.—*vi*. To give out a sound; to appear on narration, to be spread or published.

soundings, sound'ingz, *n.pl*. The depths of water in rivers, harbors, etc.

soundness sound'nes, *n*. Healthiness; solidity; validity, orthodoxy.

sour, sour, *a*. Acid or sharp to the taste; tart; peevish; morose.—*vt*. To make sour; to make cross or discontented; to embitter.—*vi*. To become sour or peevish.

source, sōrs, *n*. That from which anything rises; the spring, etc., from which a stream proceeds first cause; origin.

Soviet, sov'i-et, *n*. The method of government in Russia since the Revolution, local soviets (elected councils) sending delegates to larger bodies, and these, in their turn, to the Supreme Congress, which elects the Supreme Council.

sow, sō, *vt*. (pret. sowed, pp. sowed or sown). To scatter seed over, to spread abroad.—*vi*. To scatter seed for growth.

spa, spä, *n*. A place to which people go on account of a spring of mineral water

space, spās, *n*. Extension; room; interval between points or objects quantity of time; a while.—*vt*. (spacing, spaced). To arrange at proper intervals; to arrange the spaces in.

spade, spād, *n*. An instrument for digging; a playing card of a black suit.—*vt*. (spading, spaded). To dig with a spade; to use a spade on.

span, span, *n*. Reach or extent in general; space between the thumb and little finger, nine inches; a short space of time; the stretch of an arch; a yoke of animals.—*vt*. (spanning, spanned). To extend across; to measure with the hand with the fingers extended.

spar, spär, *n*. A long piece of timber; a pole, a crystalline mineral, boxing-match; flourish of the fists.— *vi*. (sparring, sparred). To fight in show; to box; to bandy words.

spare, spär, *a*. Scanty; thin; sparing or chary; superfluous; held in reserve.—*vt*. (sparing, spared). To use frugally; to dispense with; to omit, to use tenderly, to withhold from.—*vi*. To be frugal; to use mercy or forbearance.

spark, spärk, *n*. A particle of ignited substance, which flies off from burning bodies; a small transient light; a gay man; a lover.—*vi*. To emit particles of fire, to sparkle.

sparkle, spär'kl, *n*. A little spark; luster.— *vi*. (sparkling, sparkled). To emit sparks; to glitter; to be animated.

speak, spēk, *vi*. (pret. spoke, spake, pp. spoken). To utter words; to talk; to deliver a speech; to argue; to plead to be expressive.—*vt*. To utter with the mouth, to pronounce; to accost; to express.

spear, spēr, *n*. A long, pointed weapon; a lance.—*vt*. To pierce or kill with a spear.

special, spe'shal, *a*. Pertaining to a species; particular; distinctive; having a particular purpose or scope.

specialize, spe-shal-īz, *vt*. To assign a specific use to.—*vi*. To apply oneself to a particular subject.

specific, spe-sif'ik, *a*. Pertaining to, designating or constituting a species; definite; precise.—*n*. A remedy which exerts a special action in the cure of a disease, an infallible remedy.

specification, spe'si-fi-kā''shon, *n*. The act of specifying, details of particulars; particular mention; statement.

specify, spe'si-fī, *vt*. (specifying, specified). To make specific; to state in

S

detail.

speckle, spek'l, *n.* A speck; a small colored marking.—*vt.* (speckling, speckled). To mark with small specks.

spectacle, spek'ta-kl, *n.* A show; a sight, an exhibition, a pageant, *pl.* glasses to assist or correct defective vision.

speculate, spek'ū-lāt, *vi.* (speculating, speculated). To meditate, to engage in risky financial transactions with a view to profit.

speculator, spek'ū-lāt-or, *n.* A theorizer; one who speculates in business.

speech, spēch, *n.* The faculty of speaking; language; talk; a formal discourse, oration.

speed, spēd, *n.* Success; velocity; haste.—*vi.* (speeding, sped). To make haste; to prosper.—*vt.* To dispatch in haste; to help forward; to dismiss with good wishes.

sphere, sfēr, *n.* An orb, a ball, a globe; a sun, star, or planet; circuit of motion, action, etc.; range; province, rank.—*vt.* (sphering, sphered). To place in a sphere or among the spheres.

sphincter, sfingk'tėr, *n.* A ring-like muscle closing the external orifices of organs, as the mouth or anus.

spice, spīs, *n.* A vegetable production, aromatic to the smell and pungent to the taste; something piquant, flavor, smack.—*vt.* (spicing, spiced). To season with spice; to flavor.

spill, spil, *vt.* (pret. and pp. spilled or split). To suffer to fall, flow over, etc., to shed.—*vi.* To be shed, to be suffered to fall, be lost, or wasted.—*n.* A spigot; piece of wood or paper used to light a lamp, etc.; a fall.

spin, spin, *vt.* (spinning, spun). To draw out and twist into threads to protract; to whirl; to make threads, as a spider.—*vi.* To work at drawing and twisting threads; to rotate; to go quickly.—*n.* Act of spinning; a rapid run.

spindle, spin'dl, *n.* A pin carrying a bobbin in a spinning machine; a small axis; a long, slender stalk; a measure of yarn.—*vi.* To grow in a long slender stalk.

spine, spīn, *n.* A prickle a thorn a thin, pointed spike in animals; the backbone or spinal column.

spire, spīr, *n.* A winding line like a screw; a spiral; a wreath; a convolution, a steeple, a stalk or blade of grass, etc.—*vi.* (spiring, spired). To taper up.

spirit, spi'rit, *n.* The breath of life; the

soul; a spectre; vivacity; courage; mood; essence; real meaning; intent, a liquid obtained by distillation, *pl.* alcoholic liquor.—*vt.* To infuse spirit into; to encourage.

spirt, spėrt, *vt.* To force out in a jet; to squirt.—*vi.* To gush out in a jet.—*n.* A jet of fluid.

spit, spit, *n.* A prong on which meat is roasted; low land running into the sea.—*vt.* (spitting, spitted). To put on a spit: to pierce.

spit, spit, *vt. and i.* (spitting, spat). To eject from the mouth, as saliva.—*n.* What is ejected from the mouth; spittle.

spite, spīt, *n.* A feeling of ill-will; malice rancor—**In spite of**, notwithstanding.—*vt.* (spiting, spited). To mortify or chagrin; to thwart.

splash, splash, *vt. and i.* To bespatter with liquid matter.—*n.* A quantity of wet matter thrown on anything; a noise from water dashed about; a spot of dirt.

splice, splīs, *vt.* (splicing, spliced). To unite, as two ropes, by interweaving the strands; to unite by overlapping, as timber.—*n.* Union of ropes by interweaving; piece added by splicing.

splinter, splint'ėr, *n.* A piece of wood, or other solid substance, split off.—*vt.* To split into splinters, to shiver.

split, split, *vt.* (splitting, split). To divide lengthwise; to cleave; to rend; to burst.—*vi.* To part asunder; to burst; to crack; to differ in opinion.—*n.* A rent; fissure, breach or separation.—*a.* Divided; rent. deeply cleft

splutter, splut'ėr, *n.* A bustle, a stir.—*vi.* To speak confusedly; to sputter

spode, spōd, *n.* A material composed of calcined ivory, of which vases, etc., are made.

spoil, spoil, *n.* Pillage; booty; plunder.—*vt.* To plunder; to impair; to ruin; to injure by over-indulgence.—*vi.* To grow useless; to decay.

spoke, spōk, *n.* A bar of a wheel, the round of a ladder, a bar.—*vt.* (spoking, spoked). To furnish with spokes. Pret. of *speak.*

sponge, spunj, *n.* A soft porous marine substance which readily imbibes liquids, a mean parasite.—*vt.* (sponging, sponged). To wipe with a sponge; to wipe out completely, to harass by extortion to get by mean arts.—*vi.* To imbibe; to act as a hanger-on

sport, spōrt, *n.* A game; a merrymaking; out-of-door recreation, as shooting, horse-racing, etc.; jest; object of mockery; a plant or animal that differs from the normal type.—*vt.* To divert (oneself), to wear in public.—*vi.* To play, to frolic, to practice the diversions of the field.

spot, spot, *n.* A place discolored; a speck; a blemish; a flaw; a locality.—*vt.* (spotting, spotted). To make a spot on, to stain, to catch with the eye.—*vi.* To act as observer of enemy's position, of effect of gunfire, or of approach of hostile aircraft.

sprain, sprān, *vt.* To overstrain, as the muscles or ligaments of a joint.—*n.* A violent strain of a joint without dislocation.

sprawl, spräl, *vi.* To struggle or show convulsive motions; to lie or crawl with the limbs stretched.

spray, sprā, *n.* A twig; collection of small branches; water or any liquid flying in small drops or particles.—*vt.* To cause to take the form of spray; to treat with spray.

spring, spring, *vi.* (pret. sprang or sprung, pp. sprung). To leap; to start up; to dart; to warp, to become cracked; to originate.—*vt.* To start or rouse, to propose on a sudden; to crack, to jump over.—*n.* A leap; resilience, an elastic body made of various materials, especially steel; cause; an issue of water, source of supply, season of the year when plants begin to grow; a crack in timber.

sprinkle, spring'kl, *vt.* and *i.* (sprinkling, sprinkled). To scatter in small drops, to bedew.—*n.* A small quantity scattered in drops.

spur, spėr, *n.* An instrument with sharp points, worn on horsemen's heels, incitement; stimulus; a sharp outgrowth; a mountain mass that shoots from another.— *vt.* (spurring, spurred). To prick with a spur; to incite; to put spurs on.—*vi.* To travel with great expedition.

spurn, spėrn, *vt.* To drive away, as with the foot, to reject with disdain to treat with contempt.—*vi.* To kick up the heels; to manifest disdain.

spy, spī, *vt.* (spying, spied). To gain sight of; to gain knowledge of by artifice, to explore.—*vi.* To pry.—*n.* One who keeps watch on the actions of others; a secret emissary.

squall, skwäl, *vi.* To cry out; to scream violently.—*n.* A loud scream; a violent gust of wind; a brief storm of wind.

square, skwär, *a.* Having four equal sides and four right angles forming a right angle; just; honest, even; suitable.—*n.* A figure having four equal sides and right angles any similar figure or area; an instrument having one edge at right angles to another, product of a number multiplied by itself; level; equality.—*vt.* (squaring, squared). To make square; to form to right angles; to adjust; to fit; to settle (accounts), to multiply a number by itself.—*vi.* To suit; to spar (colloq.).

squeeze, skwēz, *vt.* (squeezing, squeezed). To subject to pressure; to harass by extortion; to hug.—*vi.* To press; to crowd.—*n.* An application of pressure; compression.

squint, skwint, *a.* Looking obliquely or different ways.—*n.* An oblique look, an affection in which the optic axes do not coincide.—*vi.* To look obliquely.

stable, stā'bl, *a.* Firm; firmly established; steadfast.—*n.* A house for horses, etc.—*vt.* (stabling stabled). To put or keep in a stable.—*vi.* To dwell in a stable.

stack, stak, *n.* A large, regularly built pile of hay, grain, etc.; a number of chimneys standing together; a single tall chimney; a high rock detached.—*vt.* To build into a stack, to pile together.

staff, stäf, *n.*; pl. **staves** or **staffs**, stavz, stafs. A stick or rod; a prop or support; a baton; the five parallel lines on which musical characters are written, a body of officers attached to an army as a whole (pl. *staffs);* a body of persons assisting in any undertaking.

stage, stāj, *n.* An elevated platform; the platform on which theatrical performances are exhibited place of action; a halting-place, distance between two stopping places, degree of progression point reached—*vt.* To put upon the theatrical stage.

stagger, stag'ėr, *vi.* To reel; to totter; to waver.—*vt.* To cause to waver; to amaze; to arrange working hours so that employees enter and leave their place of work at intervals in batches, instead of simultaneously.—*n.* A sudden swaying of the body; *pl.* a disease of cattle, etc., attended with giddiness.

stalk, stäk, *n.* The stem of a plant; part that supports a flower, leaf, fruit, etc., a stately step or walk.—*vi.* To walk in a dignified manner.—*vt.* To watch and follow warily, as game, for the purpose of killing.

stall, stäl, *n.* A place where a horse or ox is kept and fed, division of a stable; a

S

bench or shed where anything is exposed to sale, etc., the seat of a clerical dignitary in the choir; a seat in a theatre.—*vt.* To put into a stall; to plunge into mire.

stamina, sta'mi-na, *n.pl.* Whatever constitutes the principal strength; robustness, power of endurance.

stammer, stam'ėr, *vt.* and *t.* To make involuntary breaks in utterance; to stutter.—*n.* Defective utterance, a stutter.

stamp, stamp, *vt.* To strike by thrusting the foot down; to impress; to imprint; to affix a postage-stamp to, to coin, to form.—*vi.* To strike the foot forcibly downward.—*n.* Act of stamping, an instrument for crushing or for making impressions; mark imprinted; a postage-stamp, character, sort.

stand, stand, *vi.* (standing, stood). To be upon the feet in an upright position, to be on end; to have locality; to stop; to endure; to persevere; to be as regards circumstances, to be equivalent to become a candidate; to hold a certain course, to be valid.—*vt.* To set on end, to endure.—*n.* Act of standing; a stop; a halt; a station; a small table or frame; platform for spectators at gatherings.

standard, stan'därd, *n.* A nag of war, a banner; a rule or measure criterion, test, a certain grade in schools; an upright support.—*a.* Serving as a standard, satisfying certain legal conditions; not trained on a wall, etc., but standing by itself.

star, stär, *n.* Any celestial body except the sun and moon, a heavenly body similar to our sun; a figure with radiating points; a badge of honor; an asterisk, thus *; a brilliant theatrical performer.—*vt.* (starring, starred). To adorn with stars; to bespangle.—*vi.* To shine as a star, to appear as an eminent actor among inferior players.

start, stärt, *vi.* To move with sudden quickness, to wince, to deviate, to set out; to begin; to move from its place.—*vt.* To rouse suddenly; to startle, to originate, to dislocate.— *n.* A sudden motion; a twitch; outset; a handicap.

startle, stärt'l, *vi.* (startling, startled). To move suddenly.—*vt.* To cause to start; to frighten.—*n.* A start, as from fear.

starve, stärv, *vi.* (starving, starved). To perish with cold, to suffer from hunger, to be very indigent.—*vt.* To kill or distress with hunger or cold; to make inefficient through insufficient expenditure.

state, stät, *n.* Condition; situation; rank; pomp; grandeur; an estate (of the realm), a commonwealth, a nation, civil power.—*a.* National public, governmental.—*vt.* (stating, stated). To express the particulars of, to narrate.

stately, stät'li, *a.* Such as pertains to state; august; grand; lofty; dignified.

statistics, sta-tist'iks, *n.* A collection of facts, tabulated numerically; the science of subjects as elucidated by facts.

stay, stä, *vt.* (pret. & pp. stayed or staid). To prop; to stop; to delay; to await.—*vi.* To remain; to reside; to delay; to forbear to act; to stop.—*n.* Sojourn; stop; obstacle; a prop, a rope to support a mast; *pl.* a stiffened bodice worn by females a corset.—**To miss stays,** to fail in the attempt to tack about.

stead sted, *n.* Place or room which another had or might have; assistance: preceded by *in.*—*vt.* To be of use to.

steady, sted'i, *a.* Firm; stable; constant; regular; equable.—*vt.* (steadying, steadied). To make or keep firm.

steal, stēl, *vt.* (pret. stole, pp. stolen). To take feloniously; to pilfer; to gain by address or imperceptibly; to perform secretly.—*vi.* To pass silently or privily; to practice theft.

steam, stēm, *n.* The vapor of water; aeriform fluid generated by the boiling of water.—*vi.* To give out steam: to rise in vaporous form; to sail by means of steam.—*vt.* To expose to steam; to apply steam to.

steel, stēl, *n.* A very hard form or iron, produced by addition of carbon; weapons, swords, etc.; a knife-sharpener, sternness; rigor.—*a.* Made of or like steel; unfeeling; rigorous.—*vt.* To furnish with steel; to harden.

steep, stē p, *a.* Sloping greatly; precipitous.—*n.* A precipitous place; a cliff; process of steeping; liquid in which something is steeped.— *vt.* To soak, to imbue.

stem, stem, *n.* The principal body of a tree, shrub, etc., the stalk stock or branch of a family; the prow of a vessel.—*vt.* (stemming, stemmed). To make way against to press forward through; to dam up; to check.

step, step, *vi.* (stepping, stepped). To move the leg and foot in walking; to walk.—*vt.* To set (the foot); to fix the foot of, as of a mast.—*n.* A pace, a small space; a grade; a rise; footprint; gait; footfall; action adopted something to support the feet in ascending; round of a ladder; *pl.* a step-ladder.

sterile, ste'ril, *a.* Barren unfruitful incapable of reproduction; barren of ideas.

sterling, stèr'ling, *a.* An epithet distinctive of English money; genuine; of excellent quality.

stern, stèrn, *a* Austere, harsh; rigid, stringent.—*n.* The hind part of a ship.

stick, stik, *vt.* (sticking, stuck). To pierce or stab; to fasten by piercing, gluing, etc.; to fix; to set.—*vi.* To adhere, to abide firmly; to be brought to a stop; to scruple.—*n.* A rod or wand; a staff; a stiff, awkward person.

stickler, stik'lèr, *n.* One who stickles an obstinate contender about trifles.

stiff, stif, *a.* Rigid; tense; not moving easily; thick; not natural and easy; formal in manner, stubborn difficult; strong.

stiffness, stif'nes *n.* Want of pliancy; rigidity; viscidness; stubbornness; formality.

stifle, stī'fl, *vt.* and *i.* (stifling, stifled). To suffocate; to smother; to suppress.—*n.* The joint of a horse next to the buttock.

stigma, stig'ma, *n.; pl.* **-mas** or **-mata**. A brand made with a redhot iron; any mark of infamy, part of a flower pistil which receives the pollen, pl. *stigmata.* bodily marks like Christ's wounds impressed supernaturally.

stigmatize, stig'mat-īz, *vt.* To characterize by some opprobrious epithet.

still, stil, *a.* At rest; calm, silent, not loud; soft; not effervescing.—*vt. To* make still; to check; to appease or allay.—*adv. To* this time, always nevertheless; yet.—*n.* A vessel or apparatus for distilling; a distillery

sting, sting, *vt.* (stinging, stung). To pierce, as wasps, etc.; to prick, as a nettle, to pain acutely.—*n.* A sharp-pointed defensive organ of certain animals, the thrust of a sting into the flesh; something that gives acute pain; the biting effect of words.

stingily, stin'ji-li, *adv* In a stringy or niggardly manner; meanly; shabbily.

stink, stingk, *vi.* (stinking, stunk). To emit a strong offensive smell; to be in disrepute.—*n.* A strong offensive smell.

stitch, stich, *n.* A sharp pain, one complete movement of a needle in sewing; a complete turn or link in knitting, netting, etc.—*vt.* and *i.* To sew by making stitches in, to unite by stitches.

stock, stok, *a.* A post; a lifeless mass; stem of a tree; wooden piece of a rifle; a stiff cravat; an original progenitor; lineage; capital invested in any business; money funded in government securities store, animals belonging to a farm; liquor used to form a foundation for soups and gravies, a sweet-smelling garden-plant, *pl.* an instrument of punishment confining the offender's ankles or wrists; timbers on which a ship is supported while building.—*vt.* To provide with a stock, to lay up in store.—*a.* Kept in stock; standing; permanent.

stocking, stok'ing, *n.* A close-fitting knitted covering for the foot and leg.

stone, stōn, *n.* A hard mass of earthy or mineral matter, a pebble; a precious stone; concretion in the kidneys or bladder, a testicle; the nut of a fruit a measure of 14 lbs. avoirdupois.—*a.* Made of stone like stone.—*vt.* (stoning stoned). To pelt with stones; to free from stones; to provide with stones.

stop, stop, *vt.* (stopping, stopped). To stuff up; to close; to arrest the progress of; to put an end to; to regulate the sounds of musical strings by the fingers, etc.—*vi.* To cease from any motion, to come to an end; to stay; to remain.—*n.* Obstruction; interruption; pause; a series of pipes in an organ giving distinctive sounds; a point in writing.

store, stōr, *n.* A large quantity for supply; abundance; a place where goods are kept; a shop; *pl.* necessary articles laid up for use.—*a.* Pertaining to a store; kept in store.—*vt.* (storing, stored). To amass; to supply; to reposit in a store for preservation.

storm, storm, *n.* A violent disturbance of the atmosphere; a tempest; an outbreak; assault on a strong position.—*vt.* To take by assault; to attack.—*vi.* To be in violent agitation; to rage.

straight, strāt, *a.* Stretched tight; direct, correct; upright.—*n.* A straight part or piece; straight direction.—*adv.* Immediately, directly.—*vt.* To straighten.

straightforward, strāt'for-wėrd, *a.* Proceeding in a straight course; candid; honest; frank; open.—*adv.* Directly forward.

strain, strän, *vt.* To stretch tightly; to exert to the utmost; to overtask; to sprain; to carry too far; to wrest, to filter.—*vi.* To exert oneself; to filter.—*n.* Violent effort; excessive stretching or exertion; tenor; theme; a lay; tune; race; family blood: tendency

S

strangle, strang'gl, vt. (strangling, strangled). To choke; to throttle; to suppress or stifle.

strap, strap, n. A long narrow slip of leather, etc.; a plate or strip of metal.—vt. (strapping, strapped). To beat with a strap; to fasten with a strap.

strategic, strategical, stra-tej'ik, stratej'ik-al, a. Pertaining to strategy; effected by strategy.

stray, strā, vi. To go astray; to err; to roam.—a. Having gone astray; straggling.—n. Any domestic animal that wanders at large, or is lost.

streak, strēk, n. A long mark; a stripe, appearance of a mineral when scratched.—vt. To form streaks in.

stream, strēm, n. A river or brook; a current; drift.—vi. and t. To move in a stream, to stretch in a long line, to float at full length in the air.

strength, strength. n. Property of being strong; force or energy; power; support; vigor; intensity; amount or numbers of an army fleet, or the like.—**On the strength of**, in reliance upon, on the faith of.

stress, stres, vt. To put in difficulties, to subject to emphasis.—n. Constraint; pressure; weight; violence. as of weather, emphasis.

stride, strīd, vi. (striding, pret. strode, pp. stridden). To walk with long steps; to straddle.—vt. To pass over at a step.—n. A long step, a measured tread.

strike, strīk, vi. (striking, pret. struck, pp. struck, stricken). To move or turn aside rapidly, to light (upon), to make a blow, to hit, to be stranded; to yield; to quit work to compel better terms.—vt. To smite to mint; to thrust in; to notify by sound; to occur to; to impress strongly, to effect at once, to lower as the flag or sails of a vessel.—n. Act of workmen who quit work to force their employer to give better terms; a strickle.

string, string, n. A small cord; a piece of twine; a line with the things on it; chord of a musical instrument, a series.—vt. (stringing strung). To furnish with string, to put on a string; to make tense.

stroke, strōk, n. A blow, calamity attack, striking of a clock, touch, a masterly effort; a dash in writing or printing a touch of the pen, a line; a gentle rub; the sweep of an oar, a stroke-oar.—vt. (stroking stroked). To rub gently with the hand.

strong, strong, a. Having power or force; robust, not easily broken firm; effectual; earnest, containing much alcohol; glaring; forcible, tending upwards in price, effecting inflection by internal vowel change.

strut, strut, vi. (strutting strutted). To walk with affected dignity.—n. A lofty, proud step or walk; a strengthening piece placed diagonally in a framework.

strychnia, strychnine, strik'ni-a, strik'nīn. n. A vegetable alkaloid poison obtained from the seeds of nux-vomica.

stubble, stub'l, n. The stumps of a grain crop left in the ground after reaping.

stubborn, stub'orn, a. Not to be moved or persuaded; obstinate; intractable.

studied, stu'did, a. Made the object of study; qualified by study; premeditated.

study, stu'di, n. Earnest endeavor application to books, etc.; subject which one studies, apartment devoted to study; a reverie; a preparatory sketch.—vt. and i. (studying, studied). To apply the mind to, to investigate; to have careful regard to.

stuff, stuf, n. Substance indefinitely; material; cloth; a light woolen fabric goods, trash.—vt. To pack, to thrust in, to fill, as meat with seasoning; to fill, as an animal's skin to preserve the form— vi. To cram; to feed gluttonously.

stump, stump, n. The part of a tree, limb, etc., left after the rest is cut off or destroyed; a worn-down tooth; a wicket in cricket.—vt. To lop as trees, to make a tour through, delivering speeches, to put out of play in cricket by knocking down a stump.—vi. To walk stiffly or noisily.

stun, stun, vt. (stunning, stunned). To overpower the sense of hearing of; to stupefy; to make senseless with a blow, to surprise completely.

stupendous, stū-pen'dus, a. Of astonishing magnitude; grand or awe-inspiring.

style, stīl, n. A burin; pin of a sund al, manner of writing with regard to language; a characteristic mode in the fine arts, type; external manner, mode, or fashion; title; in botany, a slender prolongation of the ovary supporting the stigma.—vt. (styling, styled). To term, to designate.

subject, sub'jekt, a. Ruled by another; liable; prone; submissive.— n. One who owes allegiance to a ruler or government; matter dealt with, theme, topic, the nominative of a verb; the thinking agent or principle.—vt. sub-jekt'. To subdue; to make liable; to cause to undergo.

subjective, sub-jekt'iv or sub'jek-tiv, *a.* Relating to the subject; belonging to ourselves, the conscious subject; exhibiting strongly the personality of the author

subjunctive, sub-jungk'tiv, *a.* and *n.* Applied to a mood of verbs that expresses condition, hypothesis, or contingency.

sublimate, sub'li-māt, *vt.* To raise by heat into vapor, as a solid, which, on cooling, returns again to the solid state. to refine; to elevate.—*n.* The product of sublimation.

sublimation, sub-li-mā'shon, *n.* The process or operation of sublimating; exaltation; a highly refined product.

sublime, sub-līm', *a.* High in place or excellence, affecting the mind with a sense of grandeur; noble; majestic.— **The sublime,** the grand in the works of nature or of art; grandeur of style; highest degree.—*vt.* (subliming, sublimed). To render sublime to sublimate.— *vi.* To be susceptible of sublimation.

submit, sub-mit', *vt.* (submitting, submitted). To yield or surrender; to refer, to state, as a claim.—*vi.* To surrender, to acquiesce; to suffer without complaint.

subordinate, sub-or'din-āt, *a.* Inferior, occupying a lower position.—*n.* One who stands in rank, power, etc., below another.—*vt.* To place in a lower order or rank.

subpoena, sub-pē'na, *n.* A writ summoning a witness under a penalty.—*vt.* (subpoenaing, subpoenaed). To serve with a writ of subpoena.

subscribe, sub-skrīb', *vt.* and *i.* (subscribing, subscribed). To append one's own signature to; to promise to contribute (money) by writing one's name; to assent.

subsidize, sub'si-dīz, *vt.* (subsidizing, subsidized). To furnish with a subsidy; to purchase the assistance of another by a subsidy.

subsidy, sub'si-di, *n.* A sum of money granted for a purpose; a sum given by a government to meet expenses.

substance, sub'stans, *n.* That of which a thing consists; material; a body; essence; purport; means and resources.

substantive, sub'stan-tiv, *a.* Expressing existence; independent; real; of the nature of a noun.—*n.* A noun.

substitute, sub'sti-tūt, *vt.* (substituting, substituted). To put in the place of another; to exchange.—*n.* A person or thing in the place of another, a deputy.

subterfuge, sub'tėr-fūj, *n.* An artifice to escape or justify; evasion; a dishonest shift.

subterranean, subterraneous, sub-te-rā'nē-an, sub-te-rā'nē-us *a.* Being under the surface of the earth.

succeed, suk-sēd', *vt.* To follow in order; to take the place of, to come after.—*vi.* To follow in order; to ensue; to become heir, to obtain the end or object desired; to prosper.

succession suk-se'shon, *n.* A following of things in order, series of things; lineage; right of inheriting act or right of succeeding to an office, rank, etc.

successor, suk-ses'or, *n.* One who succeeds or follows another.

suck, suk, *vt.* and *i.* To draw with the mouth, to draw milk from with the mouth, to imbibe, to absorb.— *n.* Act of sucking; milk drawn from the breast.

sucker, suk'ėr, *n.* One who or that which sucks, an organ in animals for sucking; piston of a pump shoot of a plant; the sucking-fish.

suffer, suf'ėr, *vt.* To endure; to undergo; to be affected by, to permit.—*vi.* To undergo pain; to be injured.

sufferance, suf'ėr-ans, *n.* Endurance; pain endured; passive consent, allowance.

sugar, shü'gėr, *n.* A sweet granular substance, manufactured from sugar-cane, maple, beet, etc.; something sweet like sugar—*a.* Belonging to or made of sugar.— *vt.* To season, mix, etc., with sugar; to sweeten.

suggest, su-jest' or sug-jest', *vt.* To hint; to insinuate; to propose; to intimate.

suggestion, su-jest 'yon, *n.* A hint, a tentative proposal; insinuation; intimation.

suit, sūt, *n.* Act of suing; a request; courtship; a suing at law, a set of things.—*vt.* and *i.* To adapt; to fit; to be agreeable to, to agree.

sully, sul'i, *vt.* (sullying, sullied). To soil; to tarnish; to stain or pollute.—*vi.* To be soiled.—*n.* Soil; tarnish, spot.

sulphur, sul'fėr, *n.* Brimstone, a simple mineral substance of a yellow color which burns with a pale blue flame.

Summer, sum'ėr, *n.* The warmest season of the year; a lintel, a girder.—*a.* Relating to summer.—*vi.* To pass the summer.—*vt.* To keep or carry through the summer.

S

summon, sum'un, vt. To call by authority to appear at a place, especially a court of justice; to send for; to call up.

sumptuary, sump'tū-a-ri, a. Relating to expense; regulating expenditure.

sumptuous, sump'tū-us, a. Very expensive or costly; splendid; magnificent.

sun, sun, n. The self-luminous orb which gives light and heat to all the planets, sunshine or sunlight; sunny position; chief source of light, glory, etc.; a year.—vt. (sunning, sunned). To expose to the sun's rays.

sunburn, sun'bérn, vt. To discolor or scorch by the sun; to tan.

sunstroke, sun'strŏk, n. A bodily affection produced by exposure to the sun.

supererogation, sū-pér-e'rŏ-gā'' shon, n. Giving more than enough; performance of more than duty requires.

superficial, sū-pér-fi'shal, a. Being on the surface; shallow; not thorough.

superfluous, sū-pér'flü-us, a. Being more than is wanted; redundant; unnecessary.

superhuman, sū-pér-hū'man, a. Above or beyond what is human; divine.

superintendent, sū-pér-in-tend''ent, n. One who manages and directs; an overseer.—a. Overlooking others with authority.

superior, sū-pē'ri-or, a. Higher; higher in rank or dignity; greater in excellence.—n. One who is superior to another; chief of a monastery, convent, or abbey.

superlative, sū-pér'lat-iv, a. Highest in degree; supreme.—n. That which is superlative; the highest degree of adjectives or adverbs.

superscription, sū-pér-skrip'shon, n. Act of superscribing; that which is written or engraved above or on the outside; address on a letter, etc.

supersede, sū-pér-sēd', vt. (superseding, superseded). To set aside; to take the place of; to supplant.

supersonic, sū-pér-son'ik, a. Faster than sound, above the audible limit.

superstition, sū-pér-sti'shon, n. Groundless belief in supernatural agencies; a popular belief held without reason.

superstructure, sū-pér-struk'tūr, n. Any structure raised on something else.

supervene, sū-pér-vēn', vi. (supervening, supervened). To come, as something extraneous; to happen.

supervise, sū-pér-vīz', vt. (supervising, supervised). To oversee and direct, to superintend; to inspect.

supplicate, sup'li-kāt, vt. (supplicating, supplicated). To beg humbly for; to entreat; to address in prayer.—vi. To beg; to petition; to beseech.

supply, sup-plī', vt. (supplying, sup plied). To furnish, to provide; to satisfy.—n. Act of supplying; quantity supplied; store; pl. stores or articles necessary; money provided for government expenses.

support, sup-pŏrt', vt. To rest under and bear, to prop, to endure; to assist; to second; to maintain; to provide for—n. Act of supporting; a prop; help; sustenance; maintenance.

suppress, sup-pres', vt. To pull down; to crush; to quell, to check; to conceal.

surf, sérf, n. The swell of the sea which breaks on the shore, rocks, etc.

surface, sér'fās, n. The exterior part of anything that has length and breadth; outside; external appearance.—a. Pertaining to the surface; superficial.

surfeit, sér'fīt, n. An overloading of the stomach, disgust caused by excess; satiety.—vt. and i. To feed to excess; to nauseate; to cloy.

surmise, sér-mīz', n. A supposition conjecture; speculation.—vt. (surmising, surmised). To guess; to imagine; to suspect.

survey, sér-vā', vt. To oversee; to examine; to measure and value, as land, etc.; to determine the boundaries, natural features, etc., of.—n. ser'va or ser-va'. A general view examination; determination or account of topographical particulars.

survive, sér-vīv', vt. (surviving, survived). To outlive, to live beyond the life of; to outlast.—vi. To live after another or after anything else.

suspense, sus-pens', n. State of being uncertain; indecision; cessation for a time.

suspension, sus-pen'shon, n. Act of suspending; intermission; abeyance; deprivation of office or privileges for a time.

suspicion, sus-pi'shon, n. Act of suspecting; fear of something wrong; mistrust.

suspicious, sus-pi'shus, a. Mistrustful; inclined to suspect; apt to raise suspicion; doubtful.

sustain, sus-tān', vt. To rest under and bear up; to support, to aid effectually; to undergo; to endure, to hold valid; to confirm; to continue.

swallow, swol'ŏ, vt. To receive through the gullet into the stomach, to engulf, to absorb to believe readily, to put up with.—*n*. The gullet; voracity; capacity of swallowing; a small migratory bird.

swamp, swomp, *n*. A piece of wet spongy land; a fen; a bog.—*vt*. To sink in a swamp, to overwhelm, to overset or fill, as a boat in water.

swarm, swärm, *n*. A large body of small insects, a multitude.—*vi*. To depart from a hive in a body, to crowd; to abound; to climb a tree, pole, etc., by clasping it with the arms and legs.

sway, swā, *vi*. To swing or vibrate; to incline, to govern.—*vt*. To swing to wield; to bias; to influence; to rule.—*n*. Swing or sweep; preponderance; power; rule; ascendency.

swear, swār, *vt*. and *t*. (swearing, pret. swore, pp. sworn). To make a solemn declaration, with an appeal to God for its truth; to make promise upon oath; to cause to take an oath, to curse.

swell, swel, *vi*. (pp. swelled or swollen). To grow larger, to heave, to bulge out; to increase.—*vt*. To expand or increase, to puff up.—*n*. Act of swelling; gradual increase; a rise of ground; a wave or surge; an arrangement in an organ for regulating the intensity of the sound; an important person; a dandy.

swim, swim, *vi*. (swimming, pret. swam, swum, pp. swum). To float; to move through water by the motion of the limbs or fins; to be flooded; to be dizzy.—*vt*. To pass by swimming.—*n*. Act of swimming; distance swum; air-bladder of fishes.

switch, swich, *n*. A small flexible twig or rod; a movable rail at unctions; a device for changing the course of an electric current.—*vt*. To strike with a switch; to shunt.

swivel, swi-vel, *n*. A link in a chain partly consisting of a pivot turning in a hole in the next link; a fastening that allows the thing fastened to turn round freely.—*vi*. (swivelling, swivelled). To turn on a swivel.

sword, sörd, *n*. A military weapon consisting of a long steel blade and a hilt, used for thrusting or cutting; the emblem of justice, authority, war, or destruction; the military profession.

sworn, swŏrn, *p.a*. Bound by oath; having taken an oath; closely bound.

syllable, sil'la-bl, *n*. A sound or combination of sounds uttered with one effort; the smallest expressive element of language.—*vt*. To articulate.

symbol, sim'bol, *n*. A sign; an emblem; a type; a figure; an attribute; a creed or summary of articles or religion.

symbolize, sim'bol-īz, *vt*. To represent by a symbol; to typify; to treat as symbolic.—*vi*. To express or represent in symbols.

sympathy, sim'pa-thi, *n*. Fellow-feeling; compassion; agreement of inclinations; correspondence of sensations or affections.

syndicate, sin'di-kāt, *n*. A body of syndics; office of a syndic; body of persons associated to promote some enterprise. —*vt*. To form a syndicate or body for the use of.

synthesis, sin'the-sis, *n*.; pl. -ses. The putting of things together to form a whole; composition or combination.

syringe, si'rinj, *n*. A tube and piston serving to draw in and expel fluid.—*vt*. (syringing, syringed). To inject by a syringe; to cleanse by injections from a syringe.

S

T

tabby, tab'i, *n.* A rich watered silk or other stuff; a cat of a brindled color, a female cat.—*vt.* To water or cause to look wavy.

tabernacle, tab'ér-na-kl, *n.* A booth, a temporary habitation, a place of worship, a repository for holy things.—*vi.* To sojourn.

table, tā'bl, *n.* A thing with a flat surface; an article of furniture having a flat surface, fare or eatables; persons sitting at a table; a syllabus; index; list.—*vt.* (tabling, tabled). To tabulate, to lay on the table.—*a.* Appertaining to a table.

tabular, ta'bū-lėr, *a.* In form of a table; having a flat surface; set in columns.

tabulate, ta'bū-lāt, *vt.* (tabulating, tabulated). To set down in a table of items.—*a.* tabular.

taciturn, ta'si-tėrn, *a.* Habitually silent, not apt to talk or speak.

tack, tak, *n.* A small nail, a slight fastening; a rope for certain sails; course of a ship as regards the wind; in *Scots law,* a lease.—*vt.* To fasten by tacks; to attach slightly; to append.—*vi.* To change the course of a ship so as to have the wind acting from the other side.

tackle, tak'l, *n.* Gear or apparatus pulleys and ropes for moving weights; ropes and rigging, etc., of a ship.—*vt.* (tackling, tackled). To supply with tackle; to set vigorously to work upon, to seize.

tact, takt, *n.* Touch; nice perception or discernment; adroitness in words or actions.

tail, tāl, *n.* The projecting termination of an animal behind, the hinder or inferior part, the reverse of a coin; limited ownership.

taint, tānt, *vt.* To defile, to infect, to vitiate.—*vi.* To be infected or corrupted.—*n.* Infection; corruption; a stain; a blemish on reputation.

take, tāk, *vt.* (taking, pret. took, pp. taken). To receive or accept, to capture, to captivate, to understand; to feel concerning; to employ; to need; to form or adopt; to assume; to note down; to be infected or seized with, to bear, to conduct, carry, to leap over.—*vi.* To direct one's course; to please; to have the intended effect, to admit of being made a portrait of.

talc, talk, *n.* A magnesian mineral, unctuous to the touch.—*vt.* To rub with talc.

talent, ta'lent, *n.* An ancient weight and denomination of money, a special faculty; general mental power; people of high abilities collectively.

tally, tal'i, *n.* A piece of wood on which notches are cut to keep accounts, anything made to suit another.—*vt.* (tallying, tallied). To record on a tally, to make to correspond.—*vi.* To correspond or agree exactly.

tame, tām, *a.* Having lost its natural wildness; domesticated; spiritless; insipid.—*vt.* (taming, tamed). To make tame; to subdue; to depress.

tandem, tan'dem, *adv.* With two horses harnessed singly one before the other.—*n.* A wheeled carriage so drawn; a cycle for two persons, one behind the other.

tangent, tan'jent, *n.* A straight line which touches a circle or curve, but which, when produced, does not cut it.

tantalize, tan'ta-līz, *vt.* (tantalizing, tantalized). To torment by presenting something desirable which cannot be attained to excite by hopes that are never realized.

tantrum, tan'trum, *n.* A fit of ill-humor; display of temper; chiefly in pl.

tape, tāp, *n.* A narrow strip of woven work, used for strings and the like.

tapioca, tap-i-ō'ka, *n.* A farinaceous substance prepared from cassava meal.

tar, tär, *n.* A thick, dark, viscid substance obtained from pine or fir, coal, shale etc., a sailor.—*vt.* (tarring, tarred). To smear with tar.

tart, tärt, *a.* Sharp to the taste; sour; acid; severe; snappish.—*n.* A species of pastry, consisting of fruit baked in paste.

task, täsk, *n.* A piece of work imposed by another or requiring to be done; burdensome employment; toil.—*vt.* To impose a task upon.

tassel, tas'el, *n.* An ornament consisting of a knob with hanging threads.—*vi.* (tasseling, tasseled). To put forth a tassel or flower, as maize.—*vt.* To adorn with tassels.

taste, tāst, *vt.* (tasting, tasted). To test by the tongue and palate; to perceive the flavor of, to experience, to partake of.—*vi.* To make trial by the tongue and palate; to have a flavor, to have experience.—*n.* Act of lasting; sense of tasting; flavor; intellectual relish or discernment, manner or style.

taunt, tänt, *vt.* To reproach with severe or sarcastic words, to upbraid.—*n.* A bitter or sarcastic reproach.

tax, taks, *n.* A contribution levied by authority; a rate, duty, or impost charged on income or property; a burdensome duty; an exaction.—*vt.* To impose a tax on; to put to a certain effort; to accuse.

tea, tē, *n.* The dried leaves of plants cultivated in China, Assam, Ceylon, etc.; the plant itself; a decoction of tea leaves in boiling water; any decoction of vegetables.—*vi.* (teaing, teaed). To take tea.

teach, tēch, *vt.* (teaching, taught) To instruct; to inform; to make familiar with.—*vi.* To practice giving instruction.

teak, tēk, *n.* An E. Indian tree which furnishes hard and valuable timber.

team, tēm, *n.* A brood; horses or other beasts harnessed together a side in a game, match, etc.

tear, tär, *vt.* (pret. tore, pp. torn). To pull in pieces to rend; to wound; to drag; to pull with violence; to make by rending.—*vi.* To be rent or torn, to rage.—*n.* A rent.

tease, tēz, *vt.* (teasing, teased) To pull apart the fibers of; to annoy; to torment.

tedious, tē'di-us, *a.* Tiresome; wearisome; irksome; fatiguing; dilatory, tardy.

telegraph, tel'e-graf, *n.* Any apparatus for transmitting messages to a distance; an apparatus for transmitting messages along a wire by electricity, but now also wireless.—*vt.* To convey or announce by telegraph.

telepathy, te-lep'a-thi or tel'e-pathi, *n.* Occult communication between persons at some distance.

telescope, tel'e-skōp, *n.* An optical instrument for viewing distant objects.—*vt.* (telescoping. telescoped). To drive the parts of into each other, like the joints of a telescope.

tell, tel, *vt.* (telling, told). To number; to relate, to disclose, to explain; to distinguish; to inform; to bid.—*vi.* To give an account; to take effect

temerity, tē-me'ri-ti, *n.* Contempt of danger, extreme boldness; rashness.

temper, tem'pè r, *vt.* To proportion duly; to moderate, to form to a proper hardness.—*n.* Due mixture; disposition of the mind, temperament; irritation; state of a metal as to its hardness; medium.

temperament, tem'pèr-a-ment, *n.* Due mixture of qualities; combined mental and physical constitution; disposition.

temperance, tem'pèr-ans, *n.* Moderation in indulgence of the natural appetites; sobriety; abstinence from intoxicants.

temperature, tem'pèr-a-tūr, *n.* State with regard to heat or cold climatic heat.

templet, template, tem'plet, tem' plät, *n.* A board whose edge is shaped so as to serve as a guide in making an article with a corresponding contour.

temporal, tem'pō-ral, *a.* Pertaining to time; pertaining to this life, not spiritual or ecclesiastical, secular; pertaining to the temples of the head.—*n.* Anything temporal or secular; a temporality.

tenant, te'nant, *n.* One who occupies lands or houses for which he pays rent.—*vt.* To hold as a tenant.—*vi.* To live as a tenant, to dwell.

tend, tend, *vi.* To move in or have a certain direction; to conduce; to attend.—*vt.* To attend; to guard, to take care of

tender, ten'dèr, *n.* One who attends; a small vessel employed to attend on a larger one a carriage with fuel, etc., attached to a locomotive; an offer of money or service an estimate; thing offered.—*vt.* To present for acceptance.—*a.* Fragile; delicate; compassionate, kind.

tendon, ten'don, *n.* A sinew; a hard, insensible cord or bundle of fibers by which a muscle is attached to a bone.

tennis, ten'is, *n.* A game in which a ball is driven against a wall, and caused to rebound; in ordinary use, lawn-tennis

tenor, ten'or, *n.* A prevailing course or direction; purport; substance, as of a discourse, the highest of the male adult chest voices; one who sings a tenor part.—*a.* Adapted for singing or playing the tenor.

tense, tens, *n.* Inflection of a verb to express time.—*a.* Stretched; tight; strained to stiffness, rigid, not lax.

tension, ten'shon, *n.* Act of stretching; state of being stretched; tightness; strain; intensity; elastic force.

tensor, ten'sor, *n.* A muscle that extends or stretches the part to which it is fixed.

tentacle, ten'ta-kl, *n. sing.* and *pl.* A filiform organ of various animals used for prehension or as a feeler.

tentative, ten'ta-tiv, *a.* Experimental; empirical.—*n.* An essay; a trial.

tenure, ten'ūr, *n.* A holding or manner of holding real estate, condition of occupancy; manner of possessing in general.

term, tèrm, *n.* A limit; boundary time for

which anything lasts; period of session, etc.; day on which rent or interest is paid; a word; a word having a technical meaning; *pl.* conditions; relative position or footing.—*vt.* To name; to call.

terminal, tėr'min-al, *a.* Pertaining to or forming the end; terminating.—*n.* An extremity, the clamping screw at each end of a voltaic battery.

terminate, tėr'min-āt, *vt.* and *i.* (terminating, terminated). To bound; to limit to end.—*a.* Limited.

terminology, tėr-min-ol'o-ji, *n.* The science or theory of technical or other terms; terms used in any art, science, etc.

terminus, tėr'mi-nus, *n.; pl.* -ni. A boundary, a limit, station at the end of a railway, etc.

terrace, te'räs, *n.* A raised level bank of earth, a raised flat area, a row of houses; flat roof of a house.—*vt.* (terracing, terraced). To form into or furnish with a terrace.

territory, te'ri-to-ri, *n.* A definite piece of' land under any distinct administration; a dominion; region, country.

terror, te'ror, *n.* Such fear as agitates body and mind, dread alarm, cause of fear.

terrorism, te'ror-izm, *n.* A system of government by terror; intimidation.

tertiary, tėr'shi-a-ri, *a.* Third, applied to the third great division of stratified rocks, resting on the chalk.—*n.* The tertiary system of rocks.

tessera, tes'e-ra, *n., pl.* -rae. A small cube of marble, ivory, etc. used for mosaic work.

test, test, *n.* A vessel used in trying or refining gold, etc.; a cupel; examination; means of trial; a standard, oath taken before admission to privileges, a hard outer covering.—*vt.* To put to a trial; to refine; to examine; to prove; to attest.

testify, tes'ti-fī, *vi.* (testifying, testified). To bear witness; to give evidence.—*vt.* To bear witness to.

tether, teTH'ėr, *n.* A rope confining a grazing animal with certain limits, scope allowed.—*vt.* To confine with a tether.

tetrahedron, te-tra-hē'dron, *n.* A solid body having four equal triangles as its faces.

text, tekst, *n.* An author's own work as distinct from annotations, a passage of Scripture selected as the subject of a discourse; a topic; a large kind of handwriting, particular kind of lettering.

textile, teks'tīl, *a.* Woven; capable of being woven.—*n.* A fabric made by weaving.

texture, teks'tūr, *n.* A web, that which is woven; a fabric; manner in which constituent parts are connected; the grain or peculiar character of a solid.

thallus, thal'us, *n.* A solid mass of cells, forming the substance of the thallogens.

than, THan, *conj.* A particle used after certain adjectives and adverbs expressing comparison or diversity, as *more, other;* etc.

Thanksgiving, thangks'giv-ing, *n.* Act of giving thanks; public celebration of divine goodness.

that, THat, *a.* and *pron.; pl.* those, THōz. A pronominal adjective pointing to a person or thing mentioned or understood; a demonstrative pronoun; a relative pronoun equivalent to *who* or *which.*—*conj.* Introducing a reason, purpose, or result, a noun clause, or a wish.

theater, thē'a-tėr, *n.* A house for the exhibition of dramatic performances, a place of action, a room for anatomical demonstrations, etc.

theft, theft, *n.* Act of stealing, unlawful taking of another's goods; thing stolen.

their, THār, *pronominal* or *possessive adj.* Pertaining or belonging to them.— **theirs,** possessive case of they, used without a noun.

theme, thēm, *n.* A subject or topic short dissertation by a student leading subject in a musical composition.

then, THen, *adv.* At that time, past or future, soon afterwards.—*conj.* In that case, therefore.

theory, thē'ō-ri, *n.* Speculation; hypothesis to explain something rules or knowledge of an art as distinguished from practice.

thermal, thermic, thėr'mal, thėr' mik, *a.* Pertaining to heat; warm; hot.

they, THā, *pron. pl.* The plural of *he, she,* or *it;* sometimes used indefinitely.

thick, thik, *a.* Having extent measured through; dense; foggy; crowded; close; stupid; gross.—*n.* The thickest part.— *adv.* In close succession; fast or close together.

thicket, thik'et, *n.* A wood or collection of trees or shrubs closely set.

thin-skinned, thin'skind, *a.* Having a thin skin, unduly sensitive irritable.

thirst, thềrst, *n.* The desire or distress occasioned by want of water; eager desire after anything.—*vi.* To feel thirst; to desire vehemently.

thistle, this'l, *n.* A prickly composite plant, the national emblem of Scotland.

thorax, thō raks, *n.; pl.* **-races.** That part of the human body which contains the lungs, heart, etc.; the chest.

thorough-bred, thu'rō-bred, *a.* Bred from pure and unmixed blood, as horses completely bred or accomplished, high-spirited.— *n.* An animal of pure blood.

thoroughfare, thu'rō-fār, *n.* A passage through, unobstructed way; power of passing.

those, THŌz, *a.* and *pron. Pl.* of *that.*

though, THŌ, *conj.* Granting it to be the fact that; notwithstanding that; if.—*adv.* However.

thread, thred, *n.* A fine cord; any fine filament, prominent spiral part of a screw, continued course or tenor; general purpose.—*vt.* To pass a thread through; to pass or pierce through.

threadbare, thred'bār, *a.* Having the nap worn off, worn out, trite hackneyed.

threaten, thret'n, *vt.* To use threats towards; to menace; to show to be impending.—*vi.* To use threats.

threshold, thresh'ōld, *n.* The stone or piece of timber which lies under a door; a doorsill, entrance, outset.

thrill, thril, *vt.* To send a quiver through; to affect with a keen tingling.—*vi.* To quiver, to move trem*ulously.*—*n.* A warbling; thrilling sensation.

throe, thrō, *n.* Extreme pain, anguish of travail in childbirth.—*vi.* (throeing, throed). To struggle in extreme pain.

throne, thrōn, *n.* The seat of a king or ruler, sovereign power and dignity.—*vt.* (throning, throned). To place on a royal seat; to enthrone; to exalt.

throttle, throt'l, *n.* The windpipe or trachea, the throat, the gullet.—*vt.* (throttling, throttled). To choke; to strangle.

through, thrō, *prep.* From end to end of; by means of; on account of; throughout.—*adv.* From end to end, to completion.—*a.* Going with little or no interruption from one place to another.

thumb, thum, *n.* The short thick finger of the hand.—*vt.* To soil or handle awkwardly with the fingers.

thump, thump, *n.* A dull, heavy blow; sound made by such a blow.—*vt.* and *i.* To strike with something thick or heavy.

thwart, thwärt, *a.* Transverse; being across.—*vt.* To cross; to frustrate or defeat.—*n.* The bench on which the rowers sit, athwart the boat.

ticket, tik'et *n.* A label; a card or paper enabling one to enter a place, travel in a railway, etc.—*vt.* To put a ticket on to label.

tickle, tik'l, *vt.* (tickling, tickled). To touch and cause a peculiar thrilling sensation in; to please; to flutter; to puzzle.

ticklish, tik'lish, *a.* Easily tickled; touchy, liable to be overthrown; difficult, critical.

tide, tīd, *n.* Time; season; the rising and falling of the sea; flow; current.—*vt.* or *i.* (tiding, tided). To drive with the tide.—**To tide over,** to surmount.

tidy, tī'di, *a.* Clean and orderly; neat, trim, moderately large.—*vt.* (tidying, tidied). To make tidy.—*n.* A piece of fancy work to throw over a chair, etc.

tie, ti, *vt.* (tying, tied). To bind, to fasten; to oblige; to constrain.—*n.* That which binds or fastens together, a fastening, a neck-tie; bond; obligation; an equality in numbers.

tile, fil, *n.* A slab of baked clay for covering roofs floors, walls, etc.— *vt.* (tiling, tiled) To cover with tiles; to guard against the entrance of the uninitiated.

till, til, *n.* A money box or drawer for money in a shop, etc.—*prep.* To the time of; until.—*vt.* To cultivate; to plow and prepare for seed.

tilt, tilt, *vi.* To run or ride and thrust with a lance; to joust; to lean or slope; to heel over.—*vt.* To set in a sloping position; to cover with an awning.—*n.* Inclination forward; a military contest with lances on horseback; a tilt-hammer; an awning.

timber, tim'bềr, *n.* Wood suitable for building purposes; trees yielding such wood, one of the main beams of a fabric.—*vt.* To furnish with timber.

time, tīm, *n.* The measure of duration; a particular part or point of duration; occasion; season; epoch; present life; leisure; rhythm rate of movement.—*vt.* (timing, timed). To adapt to the time or occasion; to regulate or measure as to time.

tincture, tingk'tūr, *n.* A tinge, tint, or shade; slight quality added to anything; flavor; extract or solution of the active principles of some substance.—*vt.* (tincturing, tinctured). To tinge, to imbue.

tinsel, tin'sel, *n.* Thin, glittering metallic

T

sheets; cloth overlaid with foil; something superficially showy.—*a*. Consisting of tinsel showy to excess.—*vt*. (tinselling, tinselled). To adorn with tinsel.

tissue, ti'shū, *n*. Any woven stuff; a textile fabric; a primary layer of organic substance, a fabrication.

tissue-paper, ti'shū-pā-pėr, *n*. A very thin paper, used for protecting or wrapping.

tithe, tīTH, *n*. The tenth part of anything, tenth part allotted to the clergy; any small part.—*vt*. (tithing, tithed). To levy a tithe on.—*vi*. To pay tithes.

to, tū or tō, *prep*. Denoting motion towards; indicating a point reached, destination, addition, ratio, opposition, or contrast; marking an object; the sign of the infinitive mood.—*adv*. Forward; on.

toad, tōd, *n*. A reptile resembling the frog, but not adapted for leaping.

toddle, tod'l, *vi*. (toddling, toddled). To walk with short tottering steps. *n*. A little toddling walk.

toe, tō, *n*. One of the small members forming the extremity of the foot.—*vt*. (toeing, toed). To touch or reach with the toes.

together, tü-geTH'ėr, *adv*. In company; in concert; without intermission.

toilet, toi'let, *n*. A cloth over a table in a dressing room; a dressing-table; act or mode of dressing; attire.

token, tō'kn, *n*. A mark; sign; indication, souvenir, keepsake a piece of money current by sufferance, not coined by authority.

tolerate, tol'ė-rāt, *vt*. (tolerating, tolerated). To allow or permit; to treat with forbearance, to put up with to allow religious freedom to.

tombstone, töm'stōn, *n*. A stone erected over a grave; a sepulchral monument.

tone, tōn, *n*. Any sound in relation to its pitch, quality, or strength; sound as expressive of sentiment timbre; healthy activity of animal organs; mood; tenor; prevailing character.—*vt*. (toning, toned). To give a certain tone to.—**To tone down,** to soften.

tongue, tung, *n*. The fleshy movable organ in the mouth, of taste, speech, etc., speech, a language strip of land, a tapering flame; pin of a buckle.—*vt*. To utter, to scold; to modify with the tongue in playing, as in the flute.

too, tö, *adv*. Over, more than sufficiently; very; likewise; also; besides.

tool, töl, *n*. Any instrument to be used by the hands; a person used as an instrument by another.—*vt*. To shape or mark with a tool.

toot, töt, *vi*. To make a noise like that of a pipe or horn.—*vt*. To sound, as a horn.—*n*. A sound blown on a horn.

tooth, toth, *n*.; pl. **teeth,** tēth. A bony growth in the jaws for chewing; any projection resembling a tooth.—*vt*. To furnish with teeth, to indent.

top, top, *n*. The highest part of anything, highest rank: platform in ships surrounding the head of the lower masts; a whirling toy.—*a*. Being on the top; highest.—*vi*. (topping, topped). To rise aloft; to be eminent.—*vt*. To cap, to surmount to rise to the top of

topography, to-pog'ra-fi, *n*. The description of a particular place tract of land, etc.

topple, top'l, *vi*. (toppling, toppled). To fall, as with the top first.—*vt*. To throw forward.

toss, tos, *vt*. To pitch, to fling, to jerk, as the head; to agitate.—*vi*. To roll and tumble, to be in violent commotion.—*n*. A throw; pitch throw of the head.

tot, tot, *n*. Anything small or insignificant.—*vt*. (totting, totted). To sum (with up).

total, tō'tal, *a*. Pertaining to the whole; complete.—*n*. The whole; an aggregate.

touch, tuch, *vt*. To perceive by the sense of feeling; to come in contact with, to taste; to reach or arrive at; to refer to; to affect.—*vi*. To be in contact, to take effect, to make mention; to call when on a voyage.—*n*. Act of touching; contact, sense of feeling a trait, a little; a stroke; distinctive handling; in football, etc., part of the field beyond the flags.

toupee, toupet, tö-pē', tö'pē, *n*. A curl or artificial lock of hair; a small wig or upper part of wig.

tournament, tör'na-ment, *n*. A martial sport performed by knights on horseback; contest in which a number take part.

tourniquet, tör'ni-ket, *n*. A bandage tightened by a screw to check a how of blood.

tout, tout, *vi*. To ply or seek for customers.—*n*. One who plies for customers.

tow, to, *vt*. To drag, as a boat, by a rope.—*n*. Act of towing; state of being towed; coarse part of flax or hemp.

toward, towards, to'erd, to'erdz, *prep.* In the direction of, regarding; in aid of; for; about.—*adv.* At hand, going on.

towel, tou'el, *n.* A cloth for drying the skin after washing, or for domestic purposes.

tower, tou'èr, *n.* A lofty narrow building, a citadel, a fortress.—*vi.* To soar; to be lofty; to stand sublime.

trace, trās, *n.* A mark left by anything; footstep; vestige; track; one of the straps by which a carriage, etc., is drawn.—*vt.* (tracing traced). To track out; to follow by marks left; to draw or copy with lines or marks.

trade, trād, *n.* Employment; commerce; traffic; those engaged in any trade.—*a.* Pertaining to trade.—*vi.* (trading, traded). To traffic; to carry on commerce; to have dealings.—*vt.* To sell or exchange in commerce.

tradition, tra-di'shon, *n.* The handing down of opinions, stories, etc., from father to son, by oral communication; a statement so handed down.

tragedy, tra'je-di, *n.* A drama representing an important event generally having a fatal issue, a fatal and mournful event; a murderous or bloody deed.

tragic, tragical, tra'jik, tra'jik-al *a.* Pertaining to tragedy; murderous; calamitous.

trail, trāl, *n.* Something dragged behind; a train; the end of a field gun-carriage that rests on the ground in firing; a path; track followed by a hunter; the position of a rifle when carried horizontally at the full extent of the right arm.—*vt.* To draw behind or along the ground; to drag.—*vi.* To be dragged along a surface; to hang down loosely; to grow along the ground.

trailer, trāl'èr, *n.* One who trails, a plant which cannot grow upward without support; a carriage dragged by a motor vehicle; a series of excerpts advertising coming attractions at the cinema.

train, trān *vt.* To draw, to entice; to rear and instruct, to drill; to bring into proper bodily condition; to shape, to bring to bear as a gun.— *vi.* To undergo special drill.—*n. A* trail; that part of a gown which trails; tail; a series; course; retinue; line of carriages and an engine on a railway; line to conduct fire to a charge or mine.

trance, trans, *n.* A state of insensibility; ecstasy, catalepsy.—*vt.* (tracing, tranced). To entrance; to enchant.

transcribe, tran-skrīb', *vt.* (transcribing, transcribed). To write over again or in the same words; to copy.

transfer, trans-fèr', *vt.* (transferring, transferred). To convey from one place or person to another, to make over.—*n.* trans'fer. Act of transferring; removal of a thing from one place or person to another; something transferred.

transfuse, trans-fūz', *vt.* (transfusing, transfused). To transfer by pouring; to cause to pass from one to another.

transition, tran-zi'shon, *n.* Passage from one place, state, or topic to another.—*a.* Pertaining to passage from one state, etc., to another.

translate, trans-lāt', *vt.* (translating, translated). To remove from one place to another; to transfer; to render into another language.

transmigration, trans-mi-grā' shon, *n.* Act of transmigrating; the passing of a soul into another body after death.

transmission, trans-mi'shon, *n.* Act of transmitting, transference, a passing through any body, as of light through glass, the gear box of an automobile by which engine power is transmitted to the wheels.

transmit, trans-mit', *vt.* (transmitting, transmitted). To send from one person or place to another, to hand down; to allow to pass through.

transparent, trans-pā'rent, *a.* That can be seen through distinctly; not sufficient to hide underlying feelings.

transpire, trans-pîr, *vt.* (transpiring, transpired). To emit through the pores of the skin; to send off in vapor.—*vi.* To exhale; to escape from secrecy, to become public.

transport, trans-pōrt', *vt.* To carry from one place to another, to carry into banishment; to carry away by violence of passion, to ravish with pleasure.—*n.* trans' port. Transportation a ship employed to carry soldiers, warlike stores, etc.; passion; ecstasy.

trap, trap, *n.* A contrivance for catching unawares; an ambush; a contrivance in drains to prevent effluvia rising; a carriage of any kind, on springs; a kind of movable ladder; an igneous rock.—*vt.* (trapping, trapped). To catch in a trap; to ensnare; to adorn.—*vi.* To set traps for game.

trapeze, tra-pēz', *n.* A sort of swing, consisting of a cross-bar suspended by cords, for gymnastic exercises.

traumatic, trä-mat'ik, *a.* Pertaining to wounds.—*n.* A medicine useful in the cure of wounds.

travel, tra'vel, *n.* Act of journeying; journey to a distant country; *pl.* account of occurrences during a journey.—*vi.* (travelling, travelled). To journey; to go to a distant country; to pass; to move.

travelling, tra'vel-ing, *p.a.* Pertaining to, used in, or incurred by travel.

traverse, tra'vėrs, *a.* Transverse.— *n.* Something that is transverse; something that thwarts, a denial.—*vt.* (traversing, traversed). To cross; to thwart; to cross in travelling; to deny.—*adv.* Athwart; crosswise.

travesty, tra'ves-ti, *vt.* (travestying travestied) To transform so as to have a ludicrous effect, to burlesque.—*n.* A burlesque treatment; parody.

tread, tred, *vi.* (pret. trod, pp. trod trodden). To set the foot on the ground; to step; to walk with a measured step, to copulate, as fowls.—*vt.* To plant the foot on; to trample, to dance; to walk on in a formal manner; to copulate with as a bird.—*n.* A step; gait; horizontal part of the step of a stair.

treasure, tre'zhŭr, *n.* Wealth accumulated; great abundance; something very much valued.—*vt.* (treasuring, treasured). To lay up or collect; to prize.

treatise, trē'tiz, *n.* A written composition on some particular subject; a dissertation.

treatment, trēt'ment, *n.* Act or manner of treating; management; usage.

treaty, trē'ti, *n.* Negotiation; agreement between two or more nations.

tremendous, trē-men'dus, *a.* Such as may cause trembling; terrible; extraordinary.

trench, trensh, *vt.* To dig a ditch into turn over and mix, as soil.—*vi.* To cut a trench or trenches; to encroach (with *on* or upon).—*n.* A long narrow excavation; a deep ditch cut for defense.

trepidation, tre-pid-ā'shon, *n.* Confused alarm; perturbation; involuntary trembling.

trespass, tres'pas, *vi.* To enter unlawfully upon the land of another; to do wrong; to offend.—*n.* An offense; a sin; wrong done by entering on the land of another.

tribune, trī'būn, *n.* Among the ancient Romans, a magistrate chosen by the people, to protect them from the patricians; a platform; tribunal, throne of a bishop.

tributary, tri'bū-ta-ri, *a.* Paying tribute to another; subject; contributing.—*n.* One that pays tribute; a stream which falls into another.

tribute, tri'būt, *n.* A sum paid by one prince or nation to another; personal contribution.

trick, trik, *n.* An artifice; a crafty device; fraud; a knack or art; a personal practice or habit, a prank; all the cards played in one round.—*vt.* To deceive; to impose on, to cheat, to draw in outline; to dress; to adorn (often with out).

trident, trī'dent, *n.* Any instrument of the form of a fork with three prongs.

trifle, trī'fl, *n.* Something of no moment or value, a kind of fancy confection.—*vi.* (trifling, trifled). To act with levity; to play or toy; to finger lightly.—*vt.* To waste.

trilith, **trilithon**, trī'lith, trī'lith-on *n.* Three large blocks of stone placed together like door-posts and a lintel, and standing by themselves, as in sundry ancient monuments.

trill, tril, *n.* A shake of the voice in singing; a quavering sound.—*vt.* To sing with a quavering voice, to sing sweetly or clearly.—*vi.* To sound with tremulous vibrations; to pipe; to trickle.

trillion, tril 'yon, *n.* The product of a million multiplied twice by itself.

trilogy, tril'o-ji, *n.* A series of three connected dramas, each complete in itself

trim, trim, *vt.* (trimming, trimmed). To put in order; to embellish, to clip or pare; to adjust.—*vi.* To hold a middle course between parties.—*a.* Set in good order; properly adjusted, neat, tidy.—*n.* Condition; order; mood, dress.

trio, trī'o or trē'o, *n.* Three united; musical composition for three voices or instruments, performers of a trio.

trip, trip, *vi.* (tripping, tripped). To run or step lightly, to skip, to stumble; to err.—*vt.* To cause to fall or stumble; to loose an anchor.—*n.* A stumble, a light short step; an excursion or jaunt, a mistake.

triplicate, tri'pli-kāt, *a.* Threefold. *n.* A third thing corresponding to two others.

Trojan, trō'jan, *a.* Pertaining to ancient Troy.—*n.* An inhabitant of ancient Troy; a jolly fellow; a plucky determined fellow.

troop, tröp, *n.* A collection of people; a company; a body of soldiers; *pl.* soldiers in general, a troupe.—*vi.* To collect in numbers; to march in a body.

trophy, trō'fi, *n.* A memorial of some victory, an architectural ornament representing the stem of a tree, hung with military weapons.

Tropic, tro'pik, *n.* Either of two circles on the celestial sphere, limiting the sun's apparent annual path; either of two corresponding parallels of latitude including the torrid zone, *pl.* the regions between or near these.—*a.* Pertaining to the tropics

trot, trot, *vi.* (trotting, trotted). To run with small steps; to move fast.—*vt.* To cause to trot.—*n.* Pace of a horse more rapid than a walk

troubadour, trö'ba-dör, *n.* one of a class of poets who flourished in S. Europe, especially in Provence, from the eleventh to the end of the thirteenth century.

trouble, tru'bl, *vt.* (troubling, troubled). To disturb, to distress to busy.—*n.* Distress, agitation; affliction; labor.

trowel, trou'el, *n.* A hand-tool for lifting and dressing mortar and plaster etc., a gardener's tool.—*vt.* (troweliing, trowelled) To dress or form with a trowel

troy, troy-weight, troi, troi'wāt, *n.* A weight used for gold and silver divided into 12 ounces, each of 20 pennyweights, each of 24 grains, so that a pound troy = 5760 grains.

truant, trö'ant, *n.* One who shirks duty, one who stays from school without leave.—*a.* Idle; wilfully absenting oneself.

truck, truk, *vi.* and *t.* To barter.—*n.* Exchange of commodities; barter; payment of workmen's wages partly in goods, a small wheel, a barrow with two low wheels; an open railway wagon for goods, a motor driven vehicle used to carry heavy loads or general freight; the cap at the end of a flagstaff or topmast.

true, trö, *a.* Conformable to fact; truthful, genuine, constant, faithful; loyal; honest; exact; correct; right.

trump, trump, *n.* A winning card one of a suit for the time being superior to the others; a person upon whom one can depend, a trumpet.—*vt.* To take with a trump card, to concoct or forge.

trunk, trungk, *n.* The woody stem of a tree; body of an animal without the limbs, main body, chest for containing clothes, etc.; a long wooden tube.

truss, trus, *n.* A bundle, as of hay or straw; a bandage used in cases of rupture, a combination of timbers constitut-

ing an unyielding frame.—*vt.* To put in a bundle; to make tight or fast, to skewer.

trust, trust, *n.* Reliance; confidence; hope; credit; that which is entrusted; safekeeping; care; management.—*vt.* To rely on; to believe, to intrust, to sell to upon credit, to be confident.—*vi.* To have reliance; to confide readily.—*a.* Held in trust.

trustee, trus-tē', *n.* One appointed to hold property for the benefit of those entitled to it.

trustworthy, trust'wėr-THi, *a.* Worthy of trust or confidence, faithful reliable.

try, trī, *vt.* (trying, tried). To test; to make trial of, to afflict; to examine judicially; to attempt.—*vi.* To endeavor.—*n.* The act of trying; a trial, experiment, in Rugby *football*, the right of trying to kick a goal obtained by carrying the ball behind the opponents' goal line and touching it down.

tub, tub, *n.* An open wooden vessel a small cask, a clumsy boat, a vessel used as a bath.—*vt.* (tubbing, tubbed). To set in a tub.—*vi.* To make use of a bathing-tub.

tunic, tū'nik, *n.* A garment of various kinds; an ecclesiastical vestment worn over the alb; a full-dress military coat; a covering membrane; an integument.

turbine, tėr'bīn, *n.* A kind of waterwheel, usually horizontal, made to revolve under the influence of pressure derived from a fall of water; a similar contrivance driven by steam.

turmeric, tėr'mer-ik, *n.* An E. Indian plant of the ginger family yielding a condiment, a yellow dye, and a test for alkalies.

turn, tėrn, *vt.* To cause to move round; to shape by a lathe; to direct; to alter in course; to blunt; to reverse; to change.—*vi.* To revolve; to depend; to change position or course; to return; to have recourse; to become; to become sour; to reel; to become nauseated; to result.—*n.* Act of turning; a revolution; bend; a short walk; an alteration of course; occasion; occasional act of kindness or malice; purpose; character; short spell, as a work; nervous shock.

turnstile, tėrn'stīl, *n.* A post at some passage surmounted by horizontal arms which move as a person pushes through.

turtle, tėr'tl, *n.* A species of small pigeon; the sea-tortoise.

T

tutor, tū'tor, *n.* A guardian; a private instructor; a fellow of an English college who superintend the studies of undergraduates.—*vt.* To instruct.

typesetter, tīp'set-ėr, *n.* One who sets up type; a compositor; a typesetting machine.

typewriter, tīp'rīt-ėr, *n.* A machine used as a substitute for the pen, producing letters by inked types.

typhoon, tī-fön', *n.* A violent hurricane on the coasts of China and Japan.

typical, tip'ik-al, *a.* Pertaining to a type; emblematic; symbolic; representative.

typographic, typographical, tī-pograf'ik, tī-po-graf'ik-al, *a.* Pertaining to typography or printing.

typology, tī-pol'o-ji, *n.* A discourse on types; the doctrine of types in Scripture.

tyranny, ti'ran-i, *n.* Rule of a tyrant; despotic exercise of power; oppression.

U

ubiety, ū-bī'e-ti, n. The state of being somewhere.

ubiquity, ū-bi'kwi-ti, n. Existence everywhere at the same time; omnipresence.

udder, ud'ér, n. The glandular organ of cows, etc., in which the milk is produced.

ugly, ug'li, a. Repulsive; disagreeable in appearance; hateful; ill-omened.

ukulele, ū'kü-lā'lē, n. A small Hawaiian guitar.

ulcer, ul'sér, n. A sore that discharges pus.

ultimatum, ul-ti-mā'tum, n.; pl. -ta or -tums. The last offer, a final proposition which being rejected may be followed by war.

ultra, ul'tra, prefix a. Beyond due limit, extreme.—n. An ultraist.

ultramarine, ul'tra-ma-rēn", a. Being beyond the sea.—n. A beautiful and durable sky-blue.

umbrage, um'brä j, n. Shade; obscurity; jealousy; offense; resentment.

umbrella, um-brel'la, n. A portable shade which opens and folds, for sheltering the person from the sun or rain.

umlaut, um'lout, n. The change of a vowel in one syllable through the influence of a different vowel in the syllable immediately following.

umpire, um'pîr, n. A person to whose decision a dispute is referred; a judge, arbiter, or referee.

unable, un-ā'bl, a. Not able, not having sufficient ability; not equal for some task.

unacceptable, un-ak-sept'a-bl, a. Not acceptable or pleasing; unwelcome.

unadorned, un-a-dornd', a. Not adorned; not embellished.

unadvisable, un-ad-vīz'a-bl, a. Not advisable; not expedient; not prudent.

unaffected, un-af-fekt'ed, a. Not affected; natural; simple; sincere; not moved.

unalterable, un-äl'tèr-a-bl, a. Not alterable; unchangeable; immutable.

unanimous, ū-nan'i-mus, a. Being of one mind; agreeing in determination, formed by unanimity

unauthorized, un-a'thor-ī zd, a. Not authorized; not warranted.

unavailable, un-a-vāl'a-bl, a. Not available, vain; useless.

unbroken, un-brōk'n, a. Not broken: not tamed' not interrupted.

uncalled, un-käld', a. Not called; not summoned; not invited.

uncanny, un-kan'i, a. Not canny mysterious; of evil and supernatural character.

uncared, un-kā rd', a. Not regarded; not heeded; often with for.

uncle, ung'kl, n. The brother of one's father or mother

unclean, un-klēn' a. Not clean; foul; dirty; morally impure, lewd.

uncomfortable, un-kum'fort-a-bl, a. Not comfortable; uneasy; ill at ease.

uncommon, un-kom'mon, a. Not common; rare; strange; remarkable.

unconditional, un-kon-di'shon-al, a. Not limited by conditions; absolute.

unconscious, un-kon'shus, a. Not conscious; not perceiving; un-aware.

unconstitutional, un-kon'sti-tū'' shon-al, a. Not agreeable to the constitution, against the law.

uncover, un-ku'vér, vt. To divest of a cover; to disclose.—vi. To take off the hat.

unction, ungk'shon, n. Act of anointing; an unguent; religious fervor; sham devotional fervor; oiliness.

unctuous, ung'tū-us, a. Oily; greasy; nauseously emotional; oily; fawning.

under, un'dér, prep. Below; beneath; undergoing; affected by; subject to; inferior; during the time of, included in, in accordance with.—adv. In a lower condition or degree.—a. Lower; subject; subordinate.

underclothes, underclothing, un'dér-klōTHz, un'dér-klōTH-ing, n. Clothes worn under others or next to the skin.

undercurrent un'dér-ku-rent, n. A current below another; some movement or influence not apparent.

undergo, un'dér-gō, vt. To bear; to experience; to suffer.

undergraduate, un-dér-grad'ū-āt, n. A student who has not taken his first degree.

underground, un'dér-ground, a and adv. Below the surface of the ground, operating in secret.

undergrowth, un'dér-grōth, n. Shrubs or small trees growing among large ones.

underhand, un'dér-hand, a. Working by stealth; secret; deceitful.— adv. In a clandestine manner.

understand, un-dér-stand', vt. To comprehend; to see through; to suppose to mean, to infer; to assume; to recognize as implied although not expressed.—vi. To comprehend, to learn.

undertake, un'der-tāk, *vt.* To take in hand; to engage in; to attempt; to guarantee.—*vi.* To take upon oneself; to promise; to stand bound.

undertaker, un'der-tāk-er, *n.* One who undertakes; one who manages funerals.

underwear, un'der-wār, *n.* Under-clothes.

underworld, un'der-werld, *n.* The lower world; this world; the antipodes; the place of departed souls; Hades.

underwrite, un-der-rīt, *vt.* To write under, to subscribe one's name and become answerable for a certain amount.

undisturbed, un-dis-terbd', *a.* Free from disturbance; calm; tranquil; not agitated.

undivided, un-di-vīd'ed, *a.* Not divided; whole; entire.

undo, un-dö', *vt.* To reverse what has been done; annul; to loose; to take to pieces; to ruin.

undying, un-dī'ing, *a.* Not dying; imperishable.

unearned, un-ernd', *a.* Not merited by labor or services.—**unearned increment,** the increase in the value of property not due to any expenditure on the part of the owner.

unearth, un-erth', *vt.* To drive or bring from the earth; to uncover; to discover.

unequal, un-ē'kwal, *a.* Not equal inadequate; insufficient; not equable.

unequivocal, un-ē-kwiv'ō-kal, *a.* Not equivocal; not doubtful; clear; evident.

unerring un-er'ing, *a.* Not erring; incapable of error; certain.

uneven, un-ē'vn, *a.* Not even or level, rough; crooked; not fair or just; odd.

unexpected, un-eks-pekt'ed, *a.* Not expected, not looked for; sudden.

unexpired, un-eks-pīrd', *a.* Not expired; not having come to the end of its term.

unexplored, un-eks-plō'rd', *a.* Not explored; not visited by any traveller.

unfading, un-fād'ing, *a.* Not fading; not liable to wither or decay; ever fresh.

unfailing, un-fāl'ing, *a.* Not liable to fail, that does not fail; certain.

unfair, un-fār', *a.* Not honest or impartial; not just; inequitable; disingenuous.

unfamiliar, un-fa-mil'i-er, *a.* Not familiar; not accustomed; strange.

unfasten, un-fäs'n, *vt.* To loose; to unfix.

unforgiving, un-for-giv'ing, *a.* Not forgiving, implacable.

unfortunate, un-for'tŭ-nāt, *a.* Not fortunate; unlucky; unhappy.—*n.* One who is unfortunate; a prostitute.

unfounded, un-found'ed, *a.* Having no real foundation; groundless: idle.

ungrateful, un-grāt'ful, *a.* Not grateful; not thankful, unpleasing, harsh.

ungrounded, un-ground'ed, *a.* Having no foundation or support; groundless.

unguarded, un-gärd'ed, *a.* Not guarded; not cautious; negligent.

unguent, un'gwent, *n.* An ointment.

unhinge, un-hinj', *vt.* To take from the hinges; to unfix; to loosen; to derange.

unholy, un-hō'li, *a.* Not holy; not sacred; unhallowed; profane; impious; wicked.

unicorn, ū'ni-korn, *n.* A fabulous anima; like a horse, with a long single horn on the forehead.

unification, ū'ni-fī-kā"shon, *n.* The act of unifying or uniting into one.

uniform, ū'ni-form, *a.* Having always one and the same form equable; invariable; consistent.—*n.* A distinctive dress worn by the members of the same body.

uniformity, ū-ni-for'mi-ti, *n.* State or character of being uniform; conformity to one type; agreement; consistency.

unify, ū'ni-fi, *vt.* To form into one.

unimaginable, un-im-aj'in-a-bl, *a.* Not imaginable; inconceivable.

unimpaired, un-im-pā'rd', *a.* Not impaired; not diminished; uninjured.

unimpassioned, un-im-pa'shond, *a.* Not impassioned; tranquil; not violent.

unimpeachable, un-im-pēch'a-bl, *a.* Not impeachable; blameless; irreproachable.

uninterrupted, un-in'ter-rupt"ed, *a.* Not interrupted; unintermitted; incessant.

uninviting, un-in-vīt'ing, *a'* Not inviting; unattractive; rather repellent.

union, ū n'yon, *n.* Act of joining; combination; agreement; harmony; marriage; confederacy; a trades-union, a mixed fabric of cotton, flax, jute, silk, or wool, etc.; a certain kind of flag.

uniparous, ū-nip'a-rus, *a.* Producing one at a birth.

unique, ū-nēk', *a.* Without a like or equal, unmatched, unequalled.

unison, ū-ni-son, *n.* Accordance agreement; harmony; concord.

unit, ū'nit, *n.* A single thing or person; an individual; the number 1; a dimension or quantity assumed as a standard.

Unitarian, ū-ni-tā'ri-an, *n.* One who ascribes divinity to God only and denies the Trinity.—*a.* Pertaining to Unitarians.

unite, ū-nīt', *vt.* (uniting, united). To combine, to connect, to associate.—*vi.* To become one; to combine, to concur.

unlike, un-līk', *a.* Not like; dissimilar;

having no resemblance; diverse.

unmanageable, un-man´āj-a-bl, *a.* Not manageable; beyond control.

unmerciful, un-mėr´si-fül, *a.* Not merciful; cruel; merciless.

unmerited, un-mer´it-ed, *a.* Not deserved.

unmindful, un-mī´nd´fül, *a.* Not mindful, regardless.

unnerve, un-nėrv´, *vt.* To deprive of nerve, strength, or composure; to enfeeble.

unnoticed, un-nōt´ist, *a.* Not observed.

unobjectionable, un-ob-jek´shon-abl, *a.* Not liable to objection; unexceptionable.

unobservant, unobserving, un-obzėrv´ ant, un-ob-zėrv´ing, *a.* Not observant.

unobtrusive, un-ob-trö´siv, *a.* Not obtrusive; not forward; modest; retiring.

unorthodox, un-ōr´tho-doks, *a.* Not orthodox; heterodox.

unpleasant, un-ple´zant, *a.* Not pleasant.

unpolished, un-po´lisht *a.* Not polished; rude, plain.

unpopular, un-po´pū-lėr, *a.* Not popular.

unprecedented, un-pre´sē-dent-ed, *a.* Having no precedent; unexampled.

unprincipled, un-prin´si-pld, *a.* Not having settled principles; immoral.

unqualified, un-kwo´li-fīd, *a.* Not qualified, not having the requisite qualifications, not modified by conditions.

unquestionable, un-kwest´yon-abl, *a.* Not to be called in question indubitable.

unravel, un-ra´vel, *vt.* To disentangle; to disengage or separate; to solve.

unreadable, un-rēd´a-bl, *a* Incapable of being read; illegible; not worth reading.

unreal, un-rē´al, *a.* Not real, not substantial.

unreason, un-rē´zn, *n.* Want of reason; folly, absurdity.

unrequited, un-rē-kwīt´ed, *a.* Not requited, not recompensed.

unreserved, un-rē-zėrvd´, *a.* Not reserved or restricted; full; free; open, frank.

unrest, un-rest´, *n.* Disquiet; uneasiness.

unrestrained, un-rē-strān´d´, *a.* Not restrained; licentious; loose.

unrighteous, un-rīt´yus, *a.* Not righteous, not just, wicked.

unripe, un-rīp´, *a.* Not ripe; not mature; not fully prepared; not completed.

unsavory, un-sā´vo-ri, *a.* Not savory; insipid; unpleasing; offensive.

unscathed, un-skāTHd´, *a.* Not scathed, uninjured.

unscrew, un-skrö´, *vt.* To draw the screw from; to unfasten by screwing back.

unscrupulous, un-skrö´pū-lus, *a.* Having no scruples; regardless of principle.

unseasonable, un-sē´zn-a-bl, *a.* Not seasonable; ill-timed; untimely.

unsound, un-sound´, *a.* Not sound; erroneous; not orthodox.

unsparing, un-spār´ing, *a.* Not sparing; profuse; severe, rigorous.

unspeakable, un-spēk´a-bl, *a.* Incapable of being spoken or uttered; unutterable.

unspoken, un-spō´kn, *a.* Not spoken.

unstable, un-stā´bl, *a.* Not stable; inconstant, irresolute, wavering.

unsteady, un-sted´i, *a.* Not steady shaking, fickle; varying.

unstop, un-stop´, *vt.* To free from a stopper, as a bottle; to free from obstruction.

unstrung, un-strung´, *a.* Deprived of strings; having the nerves shaken.

unsuccessful, un-suk-ses´ful, *a.* Not successful; not fortunate in the result.

unsuitable, un-sūt´a-bl, *a.* Not suitable; ill adapted; unfit.

unsung, un-sung´, *a.* Not sung; not celebrated in song or poetry.

untenable, un-ten´a-bl, *a.* Not to be maintained by argument; not defensible.

unthinkable, un-thingk´a-bl, *a.* That cannot be made an object of thought.

unthinking, un-thingk´ing, *a.* Not given to think; not heedful; inconsiderate.

unthread, un-thred´, *vt.* To draw or take out a thread from.

untie, un-tī´, *vt.* (untying, untied). To loosen, as a knot; to undo; to unfasten.

untrue, un-trö´, *a.* Not true; false.

unwieldy, un-wel´di, *n.* Movable with difficulty, unmanageable.

unwilling, un-wil´ing, *a.* Not willing; loath; disinclined; reluctant.

unwise, un-wīz´, *a.* Not wise; injudicious.

unwitting, un-wit´ing, *a.* Not knowing; unconscious; unaware.

unwrap, un-rap´, *vt.* To open or undo, as what is wrapped up.

unwritten, un-rit´n, *a.* Not written; blank; understood though not expressed.

up, up, *adv.* Aloft, in or to a higher position; upright; above the horizon; out of bed, in a state of sedition; from the country to the metropolis; quite; to or at an end.—*prep.* To a higher place or point on towards the interior of.

upland, up´land, *n.* Higher grounds; hillslopes.—*a.* Pertaining to uplands.

upmost, up´most, *a.* Highest; uppermost.

upper, up´ėr, *a.* Higher in place or rank.— *n.* The upper part of a shoe.

upset, up-set', *vt.* To overturn, to discompose completely.—*n.* up'set. Act of upsetting.—*a.* Fixed, determined.—
upset price, the price at which anything is exposed to sale by auction.

upstairs, up'stărz, *a.* or *adv.* Ascending the stairs; in or pertaining to the upper part of a house.

upward, up'wėrd, *a.* Directed to a higher place; ascending.—*adv.* upwards.

Uranus, ū'ra-nus, *n.* The most distant of all the planets except Neptune and Pluto.

urban, ėr'ban, *a.* Of or belonging to a city or town.

urbane, ėr-bān', *a.* Courteous; polite.

urchin, ėr'chin, *n.* A hedgehog; a sea-urchin, a child or small boy.

urine, ū'rin, *n.* An animal fluid secreted by the kidneys and stored in the bladder before being discharged.

urn, ėrn, *n.* A vase swelling in the middle; a vessel for water.

usable, ūz'a-bl, *a.* That may be used.

usage, ūz'ā j, *n.* Act or manner of using; treatment; practice; custom, use.

use, ūs, *n.* Act of employing anything; employment; utility; need; practice, wont.—*vt.* uz (using used). To put to use; to employ; to accustom, to treat.—*vi.* To be accustomed.

usher, ush'ėr, *n.* A door-keeper; an officer who introduces strangers etc.; a subordinate teacher.—*vt.* To give entrance to, to introduce.

utmost, ut'mōst, *a.* Being farthest out; uttermost; extreme.—*n.* The greatest power, degree, or effort.

utter, ut'ėr, *a.* Complete, total, absolute.—*vt.* To give vent to; to put into circulation; to declare; to speak.

uvula, ū'vū-la, *n.* The small fleshy body which hangs over the root of the tongue.

V

vacant, vā'kant, *a.* Empty; void; unoccupied; leisure; thoughtless; inane.

vacate, va-kāt', *vt.* (vacating, vacated;. To make vacant; to leave unoccupied; to annul.

vacuum, va'kū-um, *n.* Empty space, a void; an enclosed space void of air.— **vacuum cleaner**, *n.* An apparatus used for removing dust from carpets, etc., by means of suction.

vagabond, va'ga-bond, *a.* Wandering to and fro; pertaining to a vagrant.—*n.* A wanderer; a vagrant; a rascal.

vagrant, vā'grant, *a.* Wandering; unsettled.—*n.* A wanderer; a vagabond; a sturdy beggar; a tramp.

vain, vān, *a.* Without real value; empty, worthless, ineffectual light-minded; conceited.—**In vain**, to no purpose.

valance, valence, val'ans, val'ens, *n.* The drapery hanging round a bed, couch, etc.

value, va'lū , *n.* Worth; utility; importance; import; precise signification.—*vt.* (valuing, valued). To rate at a certain price; to estimate; to esteem, to prize; to regard.

valve, valv, *n.* A leaf of a folding door; a lid for an orifice, opening only one way and regulating the passage of fluid or air; a separable portion of the shell of a mollusk.

vandal, van'dal, *n.* One who willfully or ignorantly destroys any work of art or the like.

vane, vān, *n.* A weathercock; the broad part of a feather on either side of the shaft; blade of a windmill, etc.

vanity, va'ni-ti, *n.* Quality or state of being vain; worthlessness; vain pursuit; desire of indiscriminate admiration, conceit, a trifle.

variable, vā'ri-a-bl, *a.* That may vary or alter; changeable; fickle; unsteady.

varicose, va'ri-kōs, *a.* Exhibiting a morbid enlargement or dilation, as the veins.

variety, va-rī'e-ti, *n.* State or quality of being varied or various; diversity; a varied assortment; a sort; a kind.

various, vā'ri-us, *a.* Different, several; changeable; uncertain; diverse.

varnish, vär'nish, *n.* A clear solution of resinous matter, for coating surfaces and giving a gloss; outside show;

gloss.—*vt.* To la varnish on; to gloss over.

vary, vā'ri, *vt.* (varying, varied). To change; to diversify.—*vi.* To alter; to change; to differ; to swerve; to disagree.

vascular, vas'kū-lėr, *a.* Pertaining to those vessels that have to do with conveying blood, chyle, etc.

vase, vāz, *n.* A vessel of some size and of various materials and forms, generally ornamental rather than useful.

vast, väst, *a.* Of great extent; immense; mighty; great in importance or degree.—*n.* A boundless space, immensity.

vein, vān, *n.* A blood-vessel which returns impure blood to the heart and lungs, a blood-vessel, a sap tube in leaves; a crack in a rock, filled up by substances different from the rock, a streak; disposition; mood.—*vt.* To fill or variegate with veins.

veneer, ve-nēr', *n.* A thin facing of fine wood glued on *h* less valuable sort, any similar coating; fair outward show.—*vt.* To overlay with veneer; to put a fine superficial show on.

venerate, ve'nė-rāt, *vt.* (venerating, venerated). To reverence, to revere; to regard as sacred.

Venetian, vē-nē'shi-an, *a.* Belonging to Venice, denoting a window blind made of thin slats of wood.

vengeance, venj'ans, *n.* Punishment in return for an injury; penal retribution.

vent, vent, *n.* A small opening; flue or funnel; an outlet; the anus; utterance, expression, sale market.—*vt.* To let out; to publish.

ventilate, ven'ti-lāt, *vt.* (ventilating, ventilated). To winnow to expose to the air; to supply with fresh air to let be freely discussed

venture, ven'tūr, *n.* An undertaking which involves hazard or danger; a commercial speculation; thing put to hazard, chance.—*vi.* (venturing, ventured). To make a venture, to dare.—*vt.* To risk.

venue, ven'ū, *n.* A thrust, the place where an action is laid or the trial of a cause takes place.

verdant, vėr'dant, *a.* Green with herbage or foliage; simple and inexperienced.

verify, ve'ri-fī, *vt.* (verifying, verified). To prove to be true, to confirm, to fulfill.

vermifuge, vėr'mi-fūj, *n.* A medicine that expels intestinal worms.

vermilion, vėr-mil'yon, *n.* Cinnabar or red

sulfide of mercury; a beautiful red color.—*vt.* To color with vermilion.

vermin, vėr'min, *n. sing.* and *pl.* A term for all sorts of small noxious mammals or insects.

versatile, vėrs'a-til, *a.* Readily turning; inconstant; having many accomplishments.

versatility, vėrs-a-til'i-ti, *n.* Aptness to change, facility in taking up various intellectual pursuits.

verse, vėrs, *n.* A line of poetry; meter, poetry, versification, a stanza a short division of any composition.

vertebrata, vėr-te-brā'ta, *n.pl.* The highest division of animals, consisting of those which possess a backbone.

vertebrate, vėr'te-brāt, *a.* Having a backbone.—*n.* One of the vertebrata

vertical, vėr'ti-kal, *a.* Pertaining to the vertex, directly over the head perpendicular to the horizon; upright.

vertiginous, vėr-ti'jin-us, *a.* Giddy or dizzy; affected with vertigo.

vertigo, vėr-tī-gō or vėr'ti-gō, *n.* Dizziness or swimming of the head; giddiness.

very, ve'ri, *a.* True, real; actual.—*adv.* Truly; in a great or high degree.

vesical, ve'si-kal, *a.* Pertaining to the bladder

vesicate, ve'si kāt, *vt.* To blister.

vesicle, ve 'si-kl, *n.* A small bladder-like structure or cavity; a little sac or cyst.

vesper, ves'pėr, *n.* The evening, the evening-star; *pl.* evening worship or service.—*a.* Relating to the evening or to vespers.

vessel, ves'el, *n.* A hollow utensil for holding liquids or solids, a ship a tube or canal for blood or sap; a person.

vest, vest, *n.* Undergarment for the upper part of the body; a waistcoat.—*vt.* To clothe, to endow, to invest.—*vi.* To descend to; to devolve; to take effect, as a title or right.

vested, vest'ed, *a.* Clothed or habited; robed; well settled or established.

veterinary, ve'te-ri-na-ri, *a.* Pertaining to the art of healing the diseases of domestic animals.

veto, vē'tō, *n.* The power or right of forbidding; any authoritative prohibition or refusal.—*vt.* (vetoing vetoed). To forbid, to interdict.

via, vī'a, *prep.* By way of.

viable, vī 'a bl, *a.* Capable of living applied to a new-born child.

vicarious, vī-kā'ri-us, *a.* Pertaining to a substitute; deputed, substituted or suf-

fered for or in the place of another.

vice, vīs, *n.* A blemish; fault; moral failing; profligacy; a fault or bad trick in a horse, an iron instrument which holds fast anything worked upon, a prefix denoting position second in rank.

vicious, vi'shus, *a.* Characterized by vice; faulty; depraved; immoral; spiteful.

vicissitude, vi-sis'i-tūd, *n.* Change or alternation; one of the ups and downs of life.

victim, vik'tim, *n.* A living being sacrificed. a person or thing destroyed; a person who suffers; a gull.

victory, vik'to-ri, *n.* Conquest, a gaining of the superiority in any contest.

view, vū, *n.* A look, inspection; consideration; range of vision; power of perception; sight; scene; pictorial sketch, judgment; intention.—*vt.* To see; to survey; to consider.—*vi.* To look.

vigil, vi'jil, *n.* Act of keeping awake; a devotional watching; the eve or day preceding a church festival.

vignette, vin-yet' or vi-net', *n.* Flowers, head and tail pieces, etc. in books; a wood cut without a definite border; a small photographic portrait; a small attractive picture.

vigorous, vi'gor-us, *a.* Full of vigor; strong; lusty; powerful; energetic.

vindicate, vin'di-kat, *vt.* (vindicating, vindicated). To prove to be just or valid; to maintain the rights of; to defend to justify.

vinegar, vi'nē-gėr, *n.* Diluted and impure acetic acid, obtained from wine, beer, etc.; sourness of temper

vintage, vint'āj, *n.* The gathering of the grape crop; the crop itself the wine produced by the grapes of one season.

vintner, vint'nėr, *n.* One who deals in wine; a wine-seller; a licensed victualler.

violation, vī-ō-lā'shon, *n.* Infringement; transgression; desecration; rape.

violence, vī'ō-lens, *n.* Quality of being violent; vehemence; outrage; injury.

violin, vī-ō-lin', *n.* A musical instrument with four strings, played with a bow, a fiddle.

virgin, vėr'jin, *n.* A woman who has had no carnal knowledge of man, a maid; a sign of the zodiac.—*a.* Chaste; maidenly, unsullied.

Virgo, vėr'gō, *n.* The Virgin in the zodiac.

virile, vi'ril or vi'ril, *a.* Pertaining to a man; masculine; manly; strong.

virility, vi-ril'i-ti, *n.* Manhood; the power

of procreation; masculine action or vigor.

virtual, ver'tū-al, *a.* Being in essence or effect, not in name or fact.

virtue, ver'tū, *n.* Moral goodness; rectitude; morality; chastity; merit; efficacy.

virtuoso, vėr-tū-ō'sō, *n.;* pl. **-osos** or **-osi.** A man skilled in the fine arts or antiquities, curiosities, etc.·

virtuous, vėr'tū-us, *a.* Marked by virtue; morally good; pure or chaste.

visible, vi'zi-bl, *a.* Perceivable by the eye; apparent; open; conspicuous.

visionary, vi'zhon-a-ri, *a.* Pertain-ing to visions; imaginative; imaginary, not real.—*n.* One who is visionary; one who upholds impracticable schemes.

visit, vi'zit, *vt.* To go or come to see to view officially, to afflict.—*vi.* To practice going to see others; to make calls.—*n.* Act of visiting; a call.

vitamin, vī'ta-min, *n.* One of several substances necessary for animal nutrition, and occurring in minute quantities in natural foods; numerous types have been distinguished, and designated by the letters of the alphabet.

vivacious, vī-vā'shus or vi-, *a.* Lively; brisk; sprightly; tenacious of life.

vocal, vō'kal, *a.* Pertaining to the voice; uttered by the voice; endowed with a voice; having a vowel character.

voice, vois *n.* The sound uttered by the mouth; articulate human utterance; state of vocal organs; speech; sound emitted; right of expressing an opinion; vote; a form of verb inflection.—*vt.* (voicing, voiced). To utter or express; to declare.

void, void, *a.* Empty; devoid; ineffectual, null.—*n.* An empty space.—*vt.* To make vacant; to quit; to nullify; to emit; to evacuate from the bowels.

volley, vol'i, *n.* A discharge of a number of missile weapons, as small-arms, emission of many things at once.—*vt.* and *i.* To discharge or be discharged in a volley, to sound like a volley, to strike and return a ball (in lawn-tennis, etc.) before it touches the ground.

volt, vōlt, *n.* A sudden movement in fencing to avoid a thrust; the unit of electromotive force.

volume, vo'lūm, *n.* Something rolled up; a book; a coil; a convolution; mass or bulk; quantity or strength.

voluntary, vo'lun-ta-ri, *a.* Willing; free to act, spontaneous, regulated by the will.—*n.* A volunteer, a supporter of voluntaryism; an organ solo during a church service.

volunteer, vo-lun-tėr' *n.* A person who enters into military or other service of his own free will.—*a.* Pertaining to volunteers.—*vt.* To offer or bestow voluntarily.—*vi.* To enter into any service voluntarily.

vortex, vor'teks, *n.;* pl. **-tices** or **-texes.** A whirling motion in any fluid; a whirlpool or a whirlwind; an eddy.

votary, vō'ta-ri, *n.* One who is bound by a vow; one devoted to some particular service, state of life, etc.

vote, vōt, *n.* Act or power of expressing opinion or choice; a suffrage; thing conferred by vote; result of voting; votes collectively.—*vi.* (voting, voted). To give a vote.—*vt.* To choose or grant by vote.

votive, vō't'iv, *a.* Pertaining to a vow; promised or given, in consequence of a vow.

vowel, vou'el, n. A sound produced by opening the mouth and giving utterance to voice; the letter which represents such a sound.—*a.* Pertaining to a vowel; vocal.

vulgar, vul'gėr, *a.* Pertaining to the common people; vernacular; common; coarse.—**The vulgar,** the common people.

V

W

wad, wod, *n*. A soft mass of fibrous material used for stuffing; material for stopping the charge in a gun.—*vt*. (wadding, wadded). To furnish with a wad or wadding.

waddle, wod'l, *vi*. (waddling, waddled). To walk with a rolling gait; to toddle.

wade, wād, *vi*. (wading, waded). To walk through a substance that hinders the lower limbs, as water to move or pass with labor.—*vt*. To ford.

wafer, wā'fèr, *n*. A thin cake, as of bread; a thin disc of paste for fastening letters.—*vt*. To seal with a wafer.

wagon, waggon, wag'on, *n*. A four-wheeled vehicle for heavy loads.

waif, wāf, *n*. A stray article; a neglected, homeless wretch.

wail, wāl, *vt*. To lament; to bewail. —*vi*. To weep.—*n*. A mournful cry or sound.

wait, wāt, *vi*. To stay in expectation; to continue in patience, to attend; to serve at table.—*vt*. To await.—*n*. Act of waiting; ambush; a musician who promenades in the night about Christmas time.

waiter, wāt'èr, *n*. One who waits; a male attendant; a small tray or salver.

waitress, wāt'res, *n*. A female waiter.

waive, wāv, *vt*. (waiving, waived). To relinquish; to forgo.

walk, wäk, *vi*. To advance by steps without running; to go about; to behave.—*vt*. To pass over or through on foot, to lead about.—*n*. A short excursion on foot; gait; an avenue, promenade, etc.; sphere; way of living; tract of ground for grazing.

wallow, wol'ō, *vi*. To tumble and roll in water or mire; to live in filth or gross vice.

walnut, wäl-nut, *n*. A valuable tree, a native of Persia; the edible nut of the tree.

walrus, wol'rus, *n*. A huge marine carnivorous mammal inhabiting the arctic seas.

waltz, wälts, *n*. A kind of dance for two persons; music for the dance.—*vi*. To dance a waltz.

wand, wond, *n*. A long flexible stick; a rod; a staff of authority; a baton.

wander, won'dèr, *vi*. To ramble here and there, to roam, to rove; to err; to be delirious.—*vt*. To traverse.

wanton, won'ton, *a*. Not kept in due restraint, unprovoked; lustful; frolicsome; rank.—*n*. A lewd person, a trifler.—*vi*. To revel unrestrainedly; to sport lasciviously.

war, wär, *n*. A contest between nations or parties carried on by force of arms, profession of arms; art of war; hostility; enmity.—*vi*. (warring, warred). To make or carry on war, to strive.

wardrobe, wärd'rōb, *n*. A piece of furniture in which wearing apparel is kept, a person's wearing apparel collectively.

warehouse, wär'hous, *n*. A storehouse for goods, a large shop.—*vt*. To deposit or secure in a warehouse.

warn, wärn, *vt*. To caution against to admonish; to advise; to inform previously.

warning, wärn'ing, *n*. Act of one who warns; caution against danger, etc.; admonition; previous notice.

warp, wärp, *vt. and i*. To turn or twist out of shape, to contort; to pervert; to move, as a ship, by a rope attached to something.—*n*. The threads extended lengthwise in a loom; a rope used in moving a ship; deposit of rich mud; twist of wood in drying.

warrior, wä'ri-or, *n*. A soldier; a brave or able soldier.

wart, wärt, *n*. A hard dry growth on the skin.

was, woz, *v*. The first and third person singular of the past tense of to *be*.

waste, wāst, *vt*. (wasting, wasted). To make desolate; to ravage; to wear away gradually; to squander.—*vi*. To decrease gradually.—*a*. Desolate; spoiled; refuse. —*n*. Act of wasting; prodigality; refuse matter, gradual decrease; a desert region.

wasteful, wāst'fül, *a*. Causing waste; destructive, ruinous; lavish; prodigal.

waste-pipe, wāst'pîp, *n*. A pipe for carrying off waste water, etc.

wasting, wāst'ing, *a*. Such as to waste, desolating, enfeebling.

watch, woch, *n*. A keeping awake to guard, etc.; vigilance; a guard; time during which a person is on guard or duty; a small pocket time-piece.—*vi*. To keep awake, to give heed; to act as a guard, etc.; to wait.—*vt*. To look with close attention at or on, to tend to guard.

water, wä'tèr, *n*. A transparent fluid; a fluid consisting of hydrogen and oxygen, the sea, rain, saliva; urine; color or luster of a diamond, etc.—*vt.* To wet or supply with water; to give a wavy appearance to, as silk.—*vi.* To shed liquid matter, to take in water, to gather saliva; to have a longing desire.

water-level, wä'tẻr-le-vel, *n.* The level at which water stands, a levelling instrument in which water is employed.

watt, wot, *n.* The practical unit of power, or rate of conveying energy, used in electricity.

wave, wāv, *vi.* and *t.* (waving waved). To sway or play loosely; to undulate, to brandish, to beckon.—*n.* A swell or ridge on moving water; anything resembling a wave, an undulation, a signal made by waving the hand, a flag, etc.

waver, wā'vẻr, *vi.* To wave gently: to fluctuate; to be undetermined.

wavy, wāv'i, *a.* Rising or swelling in waves; full of waves; undulating.

wax, waks, *n.* A tenacious substance excreted by bees or in the ear; any similar substance; sealing-wax.—*vt.* To smear or rub with wax.—*vi.* To increase; to grow; to become.

wax-work, waks'wẻrk, *n.* Work in wax; figures of persons in wax as near reality as possible.

weakness, wek'nes, *n.* The state or quality of being weak; irresolution; want of validity; a failing.

weal, wēl, *n.* Welfare, prosperity happiness; mark of a stripe; wale.

wealth, welth, *n.* Riches; affluence; opulence, abundance.

wealthy, welth'i, *a.* Possessing wealth; rich; opulent; abundant; ample.

wean, wēn, *vt.* To accustom to do without the mother's milk, to alienate; to disengage from any habit.

wear, wār, *vt.* (pret. wore, pp. worn). To carry as belonging to dress; to have on; to waste by rubbing; to destroy by degrees; to produce by rubbing; to exhibit.—*vi.* To last well or ill, to waste gradually. to make gradual progress.—*n.* Act of wearing; diminution by friction, use, time, etc., fashion.

weather, weTH'ẻr, *n.* The general atmospheric conditions at any particular time. —*a.* Turned towards the wind; windward.—*vt.* To affect by the weather to sail to the windward of; to bear up against and overcome.

web, web *n.* The whole piece of cloth wov'en in a loom; a large roll of paper; membrane which unites the toes of water-fowl, the threads which a spider

spins; a cobweb; anything carefully contrived.

wedge, wej, *n.* A body sloping to a thin edge at one end.—*vt.* (wedging, wedged). To drive as a wedge is driven, to crowd or compress, to fasten or split with a wedge.

week, wēk, *n.* The space of seven days; space from one Sunday to another.

weep, wēp, *vi.* (pret. and pp. wept). To manifest grief, etc., by shedding tears.

weigh, wā, *vt.* To raise; to find the heaviness of; to allot or take by weight, to consider, to balance, to burthen.—*vi.* To have weight; to amount to in weight; to bear heavily.

weight, wāt, *n.* Heaviness; gravity; the amount which anything weighs, a metal standard for weighing; a heavy mass; pressure; burden; importance; moment.—*vt.* To add to the heaviness of.

well, wel, *n.* A spring; a pit sunk for water, perpendicular space in a building in which stairs or a hoist is place.—*vi.* To bubble up; to issue forth.

well, wel, *adv.* In a proper manner; rightly; commendably; considerably.—*a.* Being in health; comfortable; fortunate; convenient; proper.

west, west, *n.* The point where the sun sets, opposite to the east.—*a.* Being in or towards the west, coming from the west.—*adv.* To the west.

what, whot, *pron.* An interrogative pronoun used chiefly of things employed adjectively as equivalent to how great, remarkable, etc., substantively as equivalent to the thing (or things) which.

whelp, whelp, *n.* A puppy; a cub; a young man.—*vi.* To bring forth whelps.—*vt.* To bring forth; to originate.

when, when, *adv.* and *conj.* At what or which time; while; whereas, used substantively with *since* or *till.*

where, whār, *adv.* and *conj.* At or in what place; at the place in which; whither.

whether, wheTH'ẻr, *pron.* Which of two.—*conj.* or *adv.* Which of two or more, introducing alternative clauses.

which, which, *pron.* An interrogative pronoun, used adjectively or substantively, a relative pronoun the neuter of *who;* an indefinite pronoun, any one which.

while, whīl, *n.* A time, short space of time.—*conj.* During the time that; though.—*vt.* whiling, whiled). To cause to pass pleasantly usually with *away.*

whisky, **whiskey**, whis'ki, *n.* An ardent

W

spirit distilled generally from barley; a light one-horse chaise.

whisper, whis'pėr, *vt.* To speak with a low sibilant voice, to converse secretly.—*vt.* To utter in a whisper.—*n.* A low soft sibilant voice; a faint utterance.

whistle, whis'l, *vi.* (whistling, whistled). To utter a clear shrill sound by forcing the breath through the lips; to warble; to sound shrilly.— *vt.* To utter or signal by whistling.—*n.* Sound produced by one who whistles; any similar sound; a small pipe blown with the breath; instrument sounded by steam.

white, whīt, *a.* Being of the color of pure snow; pale; pallid; pure and unsullied.— *n.* The color of snow, a white pigment; white of an egg eye, etc,—*vt.* (whiting, whited). To make white.

who, hö, *pron.*, *possessive* **whose** höz; *objective* **whom,** hom. A relative and interrogative pronoun always used substantively and with reference to persons.

whoever, hö-ev'er, *pron.* Any one without exception; any person whatever.

whole, hōl, *a.* Sound; healthy; healed; intact, entire.—*n.* An entire thing; total assemblage of parts.

wholesale, hōl'sāl, *n.* Sale of goods by the entire piece or in large quantities.—*a.* Pertaining to trade in large quantities; extensive and indiscriminate.

widen, wī'd'n, *vt.* To make wide or wider.—*vi.* To grow wide or wider.

widow, wi'dō, *n.* A woman whose husband is dead.—*vt.* To bereave of a husband.

wield, wēld, *vt.* To manage freely in the hands; to sway; to exercise.

will, wil, *v. aux.* (past. would), expresses futurity in the second and third persons, and willingness, etc., or determination in the first.—*vt.* and *i.* To determine by choice, to wish, to bequeath.—*n.* Wish; choice; determination purpose; legal declaration of a person as to what is to be done after his death with his property; faculty by which we determine to do or not to do something, volition.

win, win, *vt.* (winning, won). To gain, to be victorious in; to allure to reach; to attain.—*vi.* To gain the victory.

wind, wind, in poetry often wīnd *n.* Air in motion, a current of air; breath; power of respiration; empty words, flatulence'.—*vt.* wind (pret. & pp. wound, sometimes winded). To blow, as a horn.—*vt.* wind (pret. & pp. winded). To follow by the scent; to render scant of wind, to let rest and recover wind.

wind, wīnd, *vt.* (pret. & pp. wound). To bend or turn; to twist; to coil.— *vi.* To twine or twist, to crook, to bend; to meander.

window, win'dō, *n.* An opening in a wall for the admission of light or air, the frame (usually fitted with glass) in this opening.

wing, wing, *n.* One of the anterior limbs in birds; organ of flight flight; a lateral extension; side; side division of an army, etc.—*vt.* To furnish with wings; to fly, to traverse by flying; to wound in the wing.

wink, wingk, *vi.* To shut and open the eyelids; to give a hint by the eyelids, to connive, to be willfully blind (with at)—*n.* Act of shutting and opening the eyelids rapidly; a twinkling; a hint given by means of the eye.

winter, win'tėr, *n.* The cold season of the year a year: any cheerless situation.—*a.* Belonging to winter.—*vi.* To pass the winter.—*vt. Ta* keep or feed during winter.

wit, wit, *vt.* and *i.* (pres. tense, wot pret. wist, pres. part. witting and wotting). To know; to be aware.—**To wit,** namely; that is to say.—*n.* Understanding, sense; wisdom; intelligence; faculty of associating ideas cleverly and in apt language; a person possessing this acuity; cleverness.

with, wiTH, *prep.* Against in the company of; among; showing; marked by; immediately after through; by.—*n.* With or with. A withe.

witness, wit'nes, *n.* Testimony; attestation of a fact or event, one who knows or sees anything; one who gives evidence in a trial.—*vt.* To attest; to see the execution of a legal instrument, and subscribe it.—*vi.* To bear testimony.

wolf, wŭlf, *n.;* pl. **wolves,** wulvz. A carnivorous quadruped akin to the dog, crafty and rapacious; a cruel or cunning person.

woman, wŭi'man, *n.;* pl. **women** wi'men. The female of the human race: the female sex: an adult female.

wonder, wun'dėr, *n.* Something very strange; a prodigy or marvel feeling excited by something strange.—*vi.* To be struck with wonder; to marvel; to entertain some doubt and curiosity.

wood, wüd, *n*. A large collection of growing trees; the hard or solid substance of trees; timber.—*vi*. To take in or get supplies of wood.—*vt*. To supply with wood.

word, wérd, *n*. An articulate sound expressing an idea; a term; information, a saying, motto; order, assertion or promise; in *pl.*, talk; wrangle.—*vi*. To express in words.

work, wèrk, *n*. Effort; labor; employment; a task; achievement, a literary or artistic performance; some extensive structure, establishment where labor of some kind is carried on; result of force acting.—*vi*. (pret. and pp. worked or wrought). To put forth effort, to labor, to take effect, to tend or conduce, to seethe, to ferment.—*vt*. To bestow labor upon; to bring about, to keep at work, to influence to achieve, to fashion, to embroider; to cause to ferment.

world, wèrld *n*. The whole creation, the earth, any celestial orb; a large portion of our globe; sphere of existence, a domain or realm mankind; the public; great degree or quantity.

worm, wèrm, *n*. A small creeping animal; an intestinal parasite; *pl.* the disease caused by such parasites; something vermicular or spiral.—*vi*. To wriggle; to work gradually and secretly.—*vt*. To effect by stealthy means; *refl.* to insinuate oneself, to extract cunningly.

worry, wu'ri, *vt*. (worrying, worried). To tear with the teeth, as dogs; to harass; to annoy.—*vi*. To trouble oneself, to fret.—*n*. Trouble; care; anxiety.

worse, wèrs, *a*. Bad or ill in a greater degree, inferior, more unwell; more ill off.—**The worse**, defeat; disadvantage. —*adv*. In a manner or degree more evil or bad.

worship, wèr'ship, *n*. Dignity; honor; a title of honor; religious service, adoration; reverence.—*vt*. (worshipping, worshipped). To adore, to pay divine honors to, to idolize.—*vi*. To perform religious service.

wound, wönd, *n*. A cut or stab etc.injury, hurt or pain to the feelings damage.—*vt*. or *i*. To inflict a wound on.

wrap, rap, *vt*. (wrapping wrapped or wrapt). To fold or roll; to cover by something wound, to envelop. —*n*. An outer article of dress for warmth.

wreck, rek, *n*. Ruin; overthrow; a ruin, destruction of a vessel at sea.—*vt*. To cause to become a wreck; to ruin.

wrench, rensh, *n*. A violent twist; injury by twisting; an instrument for screwing a bolt or nut.—*vt*. To pull with a twist; to distort.

wrestle, res'l, *vi*. (wrestling, wrestled). To contend by grappling and trying to throw down to struggle.—*vt*. To contend with in wrestling.—*n*. A bout at wrestling.

wrinkle, ring'kl, *n*. A small ridge or furrow; a crease; a hint; a notion.—*vt*. and *i*. (wrinkling, wrinkled). To form into wrinkles; to contract into furrows to crease.

writ, rit, *n*. That which is written; the Scriptures; a legal document commanding a person to do some act.

write, rit, *vt*. (writing, pret. wrote, pp. written). To form by a pen, etc.; to set down in letters or words; to cover with letters; to send in writing; to compose.—*vi*. To trace characters with a pen, etc., to be engaged in literary work, to conduct correspondence.

wrong, rong, *a* Not right; not fit; not what ought to be; erroneous.— *n*. What is not right; an injustice; injury.—*adv*. In a wrong manner.—*vt*. To do wrong to; to treat with injustice.

W

X

xanthin, xanthine, zan'thin, *n.* A yellow coloring matter.

xanthous, zan'thus, *a.* Fair-haired.

xerotes, zē'ro-tēz, *n.* A dry habit of the body.

xiphoid, zīf'oid, *a.* Shaped like a sword

x-rays, eks'rā z, or **Röntgen rays,** runt'gen, *n.* Electromagnetic waves of high frequency, which penetrate most substances, except bones, metal, etc., and enable photographs to be taken of these in the living body.

xyloid, zī'loid, *a.* Having the nature of wood; resembling wood.

xylonite, zī'lō-nīt, *n.* Celluloid.

xylophagous, zī-lof'a-gus, *a.* Wood-eating.

xylophone, zī-lo-fōn, *n.* A musical instrument in which the notes are given by pieces of wood struck with hammers

xyst, xystus, zist, zis'tus, *n.* A covered portico or open court for athletic exercises.

Y

yacht, yot, *n.* A light vessel used for racing, pleasure, etc.—*vi.* To sail in a yacht.

yard, yärd, *n.* A standard measure of 3 feet; a long beam slung crosswise to a mast and supporting a sail, piece of enclosed ground.

yard-stick, yärd'stik, *n.* A stick 3 feet in length.

yarn, yärn, *n.* Thread prepared from wool or flax for weaving; a story.

yaw, yä, *vi.* To swerve suddenly in sailing.—*n.* The sudden temporary deviation of a ship.

yawn, yän, *vi.* To have the mouth open involuntarily while a deep breath is taken; to gape.—*n.* A gaping; act of yawning, a chasm.

yea, yā, *adv.* Yes: the opposite of nay.

yean, yēn, *vi.* and *i.* To bring forth young, as a goat or sheep.

year, yēr, *n.* The period of time during which the earth makes one revolution in its orbit; twelve months; *pl.* old age; time of life.

yeast, yēst, *n.* A yellowish substance produced in alcoholic fermentation; barm.

yell, yel, *vi.* To cry out with a loud piercing noise; to scream.—*n.* A loud, piercing outcry.

yellow, yel'ō, *a.* Being of a bright golden color.—*n.* A bright golden color.

yelp, yelp, *vi.* To utter a sharp bark or cry, as a dog.—*n.* A sharp cry of a dog.

yes, yes, *adv.* Even so; expressing affirmation or consent; opposed to no.

yield, yēld, *vt.* To produce in return for labor, etc.; to afford; to grant; to give up.—*vi.* To submit; to comply; to produce.—*n.* Amount yielded; product, return.

yodel, yodle, yō'dl, *vt.* and *i.* (yodeling; yodling; yodeled, yodled). To sing like the Swiss and Tyrolese mountaineers by changing suddenly from the natural voice to the falsetto.

yoke, yōk, *n.* Gear connecting draught animals by passing across their necks, a pair of draught animals; something resembling a yoke; shoulder-piece of a garment supporting the rest; servitude, burden a bond, a tie.— *vt.* (yoking, yoked). To put a yoke on, to couple; to enslave.

young, yung, *a.* Being in the early stage of life. youthful.—*n.* The offspring of an animal.

youngster, yung'stėr, *n.* A young person.

your, yör, possessive corresponding to ye, you. Pertaining or belonging to you.

yours, yörz, *poss. pron.* That or those which belong to you. **yourself,** yor-self' —*pron.;* pl. **-selves.** You, used distinctively or reflexively.

youth, yōth, *n.* State or quality of being young; period during which one is young; a young man; young persons collectively.

youthful, yōth'ful, *a.* Young; pertaining to youth; fresh or vigorous, as in youth.

yowl, youl, *vi.* To give a long distressful or mournful cry, as a dog.—*n.* A mournful cry.

Yule, yöl, *n.* Christmas.

Z

zany, zā'ni, *n.* A buffoon or merry-andrew.

zeal, zēl, *n.* Eagerness; passionate ardour; enthusiasm.

zealot, ze'lot, *n.* One who is zealous; a fanatical partisan; a bigot.

zero, zē'rō, *n.* Number or quantity diminished to nothing: a cipher lowest point.

zest, zest, *n.* Orange or lemon peel, used to flavor liquor; relish; charm; gusto.

zigzag, zig'zag, *n.* Something in the form of straight lines with sharp turns.—*a.* Having sharp turns or bends.—*vi.* (zigzagging, zig-zagged). To move in a zigzag fashion; to form zigzags.

zinc, zingk, *n.* A metal of bluish-white color, used for roofing, to form alloys, etc.

zircon, zėr'kon, *n.* A hard lustrous mineral, one of the gems called also jargon.

zither, zithern, zith'ėr, zith'ėrn, *n.* A flat musical instrument with from twenty-nine to forty-two strings, played with the fingers.

Zodiac, zō'di-ak, *n.* An imaginary belt or zone in the heavens, within which the apparent motions of the sun, moon, and principal planets are confined, divided into twelve equal parts or signs.

zoetrope, zō'ē-trōp, *n.* An optical contrivance by which, when the instrument revolves, certain painted figures inside appear to move in a lifelike manner.

zone, zōn, *n.* A girdle or belt; one of the five great divisions of the earth, bounded by circles parallel to the equator; any well-defined belt.

zoography, zō-og'ra-fi, *n.* The description of animals.

zooid, zō'oid, *a.* Resembling or pertaining to an animal.—*n.* An organism, in some respects resembling a distinct animal.

zoolite, zō'ol-līt, *n.* An animal substance petrified or fossil.

zoology, zō-ol'o-ji, *n.* The science of the natural history of animals.

zymotic, zi-mot'ik, *a.* Pertaining to fermentation; applied to epidemic and contagious diseases, supposed to be produced by germs acting like a ferment.

XYZ

WEBSTER'S
DICTIONARY
AND
ROGET'S
THESAURUS

1999 EDITION

Weston, Florida

32033

Cover Design 1999 - Carol-Ann McDonald

Printed in U.S.A. All Rights Reserved.

ISBN #1-884907-00-8

CONTENTS

Synonyms . . .

Are those words which appear under the
alphabetical listing
All have the same meaning

Antonyms . . .

Are those words which appear under the
alphabetical listing in parentheses
All have the opposite or different meanings

Parts of Speech . . .

Abbreviations:

n - noun
v - verb
adv - adverb
adj - adjective

A

abandon-v depart, go, quit, vacate, evacuate, exit, retire, withdraw, remove, (spring, fly, embark, reach, attain, advent, arrive, join, return, land, get to)

abate-v decrease, diminish, lessen, wane, ebb, decline, descend, subside, melt, die away, subtract, decay, (advance, gain strength, grow, add, enlarge, increase, augment)

abdicate-v resign, give up, vacate, retire, renunciate, abjuration, renounce, disclaim, anarchy, relaxation, loosening, remission, (authorize, influence, despotism, command)

abduct-v take, catch, hook, nab, bag, clutch, sequester, distress, capture, extortion, rapacity, receive, evict, (unclench, release, replevin, return, give, restore, render)

aberrant-adj abnormal, stray, exceptional, deviant, diverge, irregularity, variety, exemption, qualification, (illustrate, conform, adapt, follow, conventional, normal)

abet-v aid, help, support, sustain, uphold, further, advance, nurture, cradle, suckle, relief, rescue, (bar, clog, drag, hinder, stop, impede, obstruct, thwart, frustrate)

abhor-v dislike, loathe, hate, detest, abominate, repel, sicken, reluctance, unwillingness, repugnance, animosity, (care for, like, desire, take to, want, need)

abide-v persist, remain, stay, endure, maintain, keep, continue, sustain, uphold, carry on, keep one's course, (desist, cease, discontinue, halt, pause, rest)

ability-n ableness, cogent, competency, validity, skill, adroitness, craft, proficiency, knack, (bungle, fumble, botch, incompetent, raw, green, disability, impotent)

ablaze-adj afire, burning, fiery, shining, bright, heat, caloric, temperature, warmth, spark, fever, bonfire, (cool, cold, icy, dark, obscure, gloomy, somber, lightness)

able-adj ability, competent, efficient, enablement, capable, competent, dexterous, proficient, (incompetent, unskilled, awkward, clumsy, helpless, exhaust)

abnormal-adj unconventional, oddity, rarity, freak, bizarre, aberration, individuality, idiosyncrasy, (normal, conform, regular, usual)

aboard-adv inhabit, dwell, reside, stay, lodge, presence, occupancy, attendance, inhabit, moored, roost, (absent, void, vacuum, away, gone, missing, lost, elsewhere)

abode-n dwelling, lodging, domicile, residence, address, home, fatherland, quarters, roost, camp, household, native land, inhabit, bivouac, native, cottage, hermitage

abolish-v destruction, dissolution, annihilation, nullify, annul, put an end to, tumble, topple, smash, destroy, break, undo, (produce, do, make, construct, form, fabricate)

abominable-adj evil, bad, sinister, dreadful, dire, horrid, foul, rotten, offensive, hurt, injure, abuse, maltreat, damnify, (super, excellent, good, best, good as gold)

abortion-n failure, fault, miscarriage, blunder, botch,

fall, unsuccessful, lost, cast away, wrecked, addle, stillborn, fruitless, lame (succeed, triumph, gain, attain)

about-*adv* reference, refer, analogy, pertaining, related, connect, associate, near, close, nigh, approximate, around, (disconnected, independent, no relation, irrelevant, remote, far, out of the way)

above-*adv* superior, exceed, transcend, out-do, pass, surpass, top, beat, over, eclipse, precede, ultra, supreme, aloft, overhead, elevated, lofty, upper, (below, underlie, down, ebb, inferior, less, smaller)

abroad-*adv* remote, removed, afar, distant, away, off, yonder, farther, further, beyond, apart, asunder, (earshot, close, near, nigh, bordering, contiguous, adjoining, adjacent, proximate, home, intimate, beside, here)

abrupt-*adj* instantly, sudden, moment, flash, burst, hasty, instantaneously, presto, (eternity, ever, perpetual, flowing, everlasting, continued, evergreen, immortal, undying)

absence-*n* alibi, emptiness, vacuum, void, exemption, hiatus, truant, absent, vacate, withdraw, gone, missing, lost, wanting, omitted, empty, devoid, (presence, occupancy, attendance, fill, pervade, permeate)

absolute-*adj* infinity, greatest, transcend, intense, profound, rank, consummate, supreme, grand, majestic, extreme, towering, perfect, unlimited, stark, complete, unrestricted, entirely, entirety, perfection, ideal, unity, whole, (incomplete, short, meager, uncertain, doubt, hesitation, fallible)

absolve-*v* forgive, pardon, amnesty, conciliation, excuse, exonerate, release, forget, acquit, discharge, free, liberate, immune, clear, (revenge, vengeance, avenge, vendetta, vindictive)

absorb-*v* combine, mix, join, union, unify, synthesize, incorporate, fusion, blending, embody, amalgamate, blend, merge, fuse, consolidate, import, (disperse, disembody, disintegrate, break up, unravel, evict, expel)

abstain-*v* avoid, forbear, evade, elude, reject, eschew, shun, do without, dispense with, do nothing, wait, refrain, (pursue, quest, chase, hunt, follow, engage in, use, consume, employ, perform, operate, do, execute)

abstract-*adj* sole, single, lone, solitary, desolate, by itself, epitome, analysis, digest, brief, summary, draft, note, excerpt, synopsis, textbook, prospectus, (accompanied, appendage, coexistence, company)

abuse-*v* hurt, ill-treat, molest, persecute, harm, injure, victimize, maul, maltreat, do violence, misuse, desecrate, (good, value, virtue, benefit, profit, do a good turn, do no harm, be good)

abut-*v* contiguous, contact, border, adjoin, touch, come in contact with, adhere, end to end, close to, prop, stand, support, bolster, (interspace, gap, hole, opening, far between)

abyss-*n* space, infinite space, roomy, spacious, boundless, vast, bottomless pit, hell, (definite space, region, sphere, area, realm, domain, tract, territory, spot, point, niche, nook, compartment, heaven, paradise, eden)

academic-*adj* teaching, instruction, education,

discipline, lesson, curriculum,
course of study, school,
academy, scholastic, collegiate,
educational, (misinform, render
unintelligible, uncertain,
conceal)

accelerate-v sharpen, quicken,
excite, urge, stimulate, foment,
speed, up, spurt, rush, dash,
bolt, dart, swiftly, hurry, (slow,
languor, drawl, creeping, delay,
move slowly, creep, crawl, lag,
linger, dawdle, apply the brake,
reduce the speed)

accept-v assent, admit, agree,
concur, avow, own,
acknowledge, ratify, approve,
consent, comply, concede,
confirm, allow, grant, give in,
embrace an offer, satisfy,
receive, take, (denial,
contradiction, refuse, give,
donate, bestow, cede, deliver,
endow, invest, award, bequest,
contribute, hand, pass)

access-n approach, path, route,
near, pursue, approximate,
impending, method, manner,
procedure, track, (recession,
withdrawal, deadlock,
retirement, departure, receded,
remove)

accessible-adj possible,
feasible, practical, possible,
conceivable, credible, likely,
performable, achievable,
surmountable, capable, easy,
(impossible, no chance,
absurd, contrary, unlikely,
impracticable, inaccessible,
impassable, difficult, hard)

accessory-n addition, add,
annexation, tack to, append,
also, too, complement,
addendum, supplement,
associated with, auxiliary,
partner, colleague

accident-n occurrence,
misfortune, act of God, mishap,
mischance, disaster, calamity,
contingency, fortune,
haphazard, casualty, tragedy,

adversity, (well, alert,
satisfactory, remedy, utility,
happiness)

acclimatize-v habituate,
accustom, naturalize, inure,
season, tame, domesticate,
breed, tend, break in, train,
cage, bridle, restrain, harden,
familiarize, educate,
(unaccustomed, disuse)

accommodate-v fit, suit,
conform, adjust, adapt, oblige,
furnish, supply, unison,
harmony, concord, concert,
congruity, keeping, fitness,
aptness, relevancy, adaptation,
(discord, dissidence, conflict)

accompaniment-n adjunct,
accessory, appendage,
concomitant, attribute, context,
concomitance, affix, augment,
garnish, sauce, complement,
(remainder, residue, remnant,
rest, relic, leavings)

accomplice-n confederate, ally,
abettor, accessory, assistant,
colleague, recruit, adjunct,
help, partner, mate,
collaborator, friend, confidant,
(opponent, antagonist,
adversary, wrangler)

accomplish-v fulfill, do, achieve,
effect, execute, perform, attain,
feat, acquirement, fulfillment,
performance, realization,
achievement, (destruction,
waste, dissolution, downfall,
ruin, fall, crash)

accord-v tally, harmonize,
concur, grant, bestow,
acquiesce, conformity,
uniformity, agreement,
constancy, level, smooth,
dress, (diversified, varied,
irregular, uneven, rough)

accost-v speak, salute, hail,
address, greet, speech, appeal,
invocation, salutation, make up

account-n score, record, recital,
narration, description,
answerable, explicable, liable,
responsible, amendable,

money matters, finance, bill,
budget, tally, (unaccountable)

accretion-*n* concretion,
adhesion, increment, growth,
accumulation, increase,
enlargement, extension,
development, augment,
(decrease, lessening,
subtraction, reduction,
shrinking, ebb)

accrue-*v* bring in, yield, result,
arise, annexation, increase,
supplement, insertion, affix,
additive, extra, plus, further,
also, (deduction, retrenchment,
amputation, curtailment,
abrasion, deduct)

accumulate-*v* collect, gather,
hoard, increase, assemble,
amass, collection, compilation,
levy, gathering, muster,
assembly, (dispersion,
divergence, scattering,
dissipation, spread)

accuracy-*n* preciseness,
precision, verify, correctness,
just, proper, true, correct,
exact, fact, truth, gospel,
authenticity, veracity, honest,
sober, (error, fallacy,
inexactness, report, mistake,
fault)

accursed-*adj* fated, doomed,
detestable, damnable, diabolic,
charge, slur, incrimination,
imputation, recrimination,
blame, censure, denunciation,
inculpation, plaint, accusation,
(congratulate, compliment,
commendation, praise, eulogy)

accustom-*v* inure, season,
familiarize, habituate, common,
general, natural, ordinary,
track, practice, rut, groove,
precedent, (newness to, leave
off, cast off, break off, violate,
infringe)

ache-*v* smart, shoot, twinge,
hurt, pain, discomfort, suffering,
twitch, headache, spasm,
cramp, crick, thrill, sharp,
gnawing, torment, (pleasure,

physical, sensual, sensuous,
comfort, luxury)

achievement-*n* performance,
fulfillment, accomplishment,
exploit, feat, trace, vestige,
courage, bravery, valor,
boldness, spirit, defiance,
(cowardice, timid, baseness,
fear, faint heart)

acknowledge-*v* grant, concede,
confess, admit, own, assent,
disclose, answer, response,
reply, retort, repartee, discover,
conclusive, satisfy, (inquiry,
search, pursuit, review,
scrutiny, analysis)

acquaint-*v* familiarize, notify,
apprise, inform, tell,
communicate, intimation,
represent, round robin, present,
case, estimate, specification,
report, (conceal, hiding, secret,
screen, disguise, masquerade)

acquiesce-*v* agree, concur,
accede, comply, close with,
admit to, deign, acquirement,
obtainment, grant, gift,
inheritance, donation,
purchase, (expenditure, loss,
penalty, dissent, refusal)

acquittal-*n* exculpation,
clearance, clearing,
exoneration, discharge,
absolution, quietus, reprieve,
pardon, absolve, release,
liberate, let off, (condemnation,
accuse, conviction, restraint)

acrid-*adj* acrimonious, tart,
pungent, bitter, severe, caustic,
biting, keen, sharpness,
roughness, mustard, pepper,
brine, stinging, unsavory,
virulence, spleen, asperity,
(condiment)

act-*n* ordinance, decree, deed,
exploit, statute, law, edict,
scene, perform, do, operate,
behave, play, feign, simulate,
action, doing, (inaction,
passiveness, idle, misbehave,
lax)

advocate-*v* recommend,

counsel, suggest, prescribe, to advise, to support, advise, instruction, charge, enforce, enjoin (intendant, husband, moderator, speaker, proctor)

aeronaut-*n* pilot, flyer, navigator, aviator, airman, aviatrix, scout, balloonist, Iccarus, seaman, skipper, marine, (wayfarer, voyager, passenger, tourist, explorer, straggler, rambler)

aesthetic-*n* artistic, refined, cultured, cultivated, appealing, sensibility, physical, feeling, sensation, impression, cultivate, tudor, (opium, insensible, paralyze, blunt, callous, dull)

afar-*adv* aloof, abroad, away, distant, distance, horizon, reach, spread, remote, mundane, away, yonder, farther, apart, (nearness, proximity, adjacency, breadth, span, close, handy, home)

affable-*adj* approachable, sociable, gracious, friendly, amiable, humility, meek, resignation, modesty, confusion, humble, submit, diminish, (starch, perked, lofty, haughty, mighty, dignified)

affair-*n* event, business, occurrence, matter, concern, question, eventuality, incident, transaction, proceeding, phenomenon, advent, (impending, destined, loom, threaten, await)

affectation-*n* insincerity, pretension, airs, modishness, charlatanism, quackery, artificiality, (modesty, diffidence, timidity, shyness, humility, demureness)

affection-*n* bent, quality, malady, ailment, fondness, tenderness, devotion, nature, spirit, tone, temper, habit, soul, turn, bosom, breast, heart, (experience, response, impression, emotion)

affirmation-*n* ratification, corroboration, allegation, confirmation, assertion, profession, avowal, emphasis, positiveness, dogmatism, (negation, uncertainty, refutation, disclamation)

afraid-*adj* apprehensive, fearful, timorous, alarmed, cowardly, terrified, uncertainty, demure, suspense, caprice, levity, dilly dally, boggle, (determination, resolve, conclude)

agency-*n* causality, method, impelling force, force, function, office, exercise, maintenance, work, swing, action, official, acting, operant, (inaction, powerlessness)

agent-*n* servant, proxy, doer, actor, operator, perpetrator, executor, representative, go-between, mediate, deputy, consignee, trustee, nominee, (deputy, substitute, vice, proxy, minister)

aggravation-*n* heightening, intensification, vexation, annoyance, acridity, irritation, render worse, acerbate, worsen, (relief, alleviation, mitigation, assuagement)

aggregate-*adj* sum total, sum, all, complete, whole, assemblage, compilation, gathering, muster, meeting, assembly, mob, body, tribe, crew, (divergence, scatting, diffusion, dissipation)

aggression-*n* inroad, encroachment, invasion, attack, assault, charge, offense, incursion, invasion against, impugn, assume, harry, invade, (defense, guard, resistance, safeguard)

agile-*adj* quick, lithe, active, nimble, spry, brisk, activity, liveliness, spirit, dash, energy, smartness, alacrity, industry, movement, bustle, stir, fuss, (inactivity, inertness, dullness, languor, sleep, sound)

agitation-*n* jar, jolt, shake, trepidation, shock, flutter, perturbation, disconcertion, confusion, turmoil, turbulence, tumult, stir, ripple, jog, dance, flutter, (order, rest, stability)

agony-*n* anguish, pain, suffering, torment, torture, smart, twitch, spasm, headache, cramp, discomfort, throb, piercing, rack, (pleasure, sensual, comfort, luxury, enjoy, at ease, cozy, snug)

agreement-*n* understanding, accord, keeping, unison, reconcilement, union, harmony, consonance, (disagreement, dissent, inequality, disharmony, unconformity, discord)

agriculture-*n* agrarian, rural, farming, husbandry, cultivation, tillage, gardening, florist, field, meadow, flower, plantation, (taming, breeding, aviary, fishery, trainer)

aid-*n* assistance, help, succor, promotion, cooperation, furtherance, advocacy, defense, patronage, countenance, alleviation, support, lift, advance, relief, rescue, (hindrance, opposition, neglect)

ailment-*n* affection, illness, disorder, disease, malady, sickness, infirmity, complaint, attack, seizure, stroke, canker, virus, plague, pestilence, (health, soundness, vigor, perfect, robust, bloom, recover)

alarm-*n* fear, dread, scare, fright panic, warning, signal, summons, excite, agitate, arouse, startle, affright, terrify, appall, caution, prediction, omen, beacon, give notice, beware, sentinel, watchman

allay-*v* ease, assuage, lessen, mitigate, slacken, pacification, accommodation, arrangement, adjustment, terms,

compromise, armistice, suspension of hostilities, (warfare, fighting, crusade)

allegiance-*n* duty, homage, obedience, loyalty, observance, compliance, submission, passiveness, devotion, obey, control, follow, service, (insubordination, violation, non compliance)

alliance-*n* connection, affinity, compact, league, cooperation, concurrence, complicity, collusion, union, concur, (opposition, antagonism, counteraction, cross-fire, clashing)

allot-*v* divide, share, assign, distribute, apportion, appropriation, portion, contingent, lot, measure, dole, pittance, ration, ratio, quota, allowance

allow-*v* admit, concede, grant, tolerate, let, suffer, permit, permission, leave, concession, grace, dispensation, release, authorization, warranty, (inhibition, disallowance, interdict, embargo)

allowance-*n* salary, grant, stipend, concession, pay, contribution, reward, remittance, discount, apportion, allot, consign, dispensation, division, deal, cast, share, portion, administer

allude-*v* connote, imply, infer, suggest, declaratory, intelligible, literal, synonymous, implied, explicit, latent, expressive, understand, interpret, (nonsense, jargon, gibberish, jabber, mere words)

allure-*v* tempt, attract, draw, desire, wish, fancy, fantasy, want, need, exigency, leaning, bent, partiality, propensity, willingness, liking, love, fondness, relish, (neutral, indifferent, cold, frigid)

almighty-*adj* omnipotent, all-powerful, potency, might, force, energy, arm, authority, strength, ability, ableness, enablement, influence, pressure, (impotence, disability, incapability, ineptitude, palsy)

alms-*n* charity, gratuity, grant, dole, giving, bestowal, donation, presentation, delivery, consignment, dispensation, investment, award, (receiving, acquisition, acceptance, admission)

alongside-*adv* beside, abreast, side by side, broadside on, neck and neck, on a level, parallel, nearness, proximity, adjacency, (distance, remoteness, elongation, offing, background)

aloof-*adj* distant, remote, reserved, unneighborly, secluded, away, afar, beyond, further, abroad, (near, nigh, close, adjoining, handy, intimate)

alternate-*v* periodically, recurrence, succession, taking of turns, changeable, inconsistency, instability, mobility, unstable, (stability, unchangeable, consistent)

altitude-*n* tallness, height, loftiness, perpendicular, distance, elevation, giant, eminence, pitch, loftiness, prominence, (low, flat, level, squat, prostrate)

amateur-*n* novice, dilettante, volunteer, nonprofessional, unaffected, bad taste, dowdy, shabby, ill bred, untamed, (refined, professional, tasteful, pure, dainty)

amatory-*adj* erotic, ardent, amorous, loving, fondness, liking, regard, cherish, hug, prize, adore, suitor, admirer, sweetheart, (hatred, coolness, grudge, bitterness)

ambiguous-*adj* obscure, vague, undefined, equivocal,

uncertainty, doubt, hesitation, suspense, dubious, indecisive, confused, (certainty, surety, reliable, positive)

ambition-*n* resolve, design, aspiration, longing, zeal, pretentious, bold, desirous, zealous, soaring, aspiring, intent, purpose, (speculation, venture, chance, risk)

ambush-*n* ambuscade, trap, pitfall, lurking place, screen, cover, recess, shade, curtain, blind, bloak, cloud, (reveal, lift up, remove, acknowledge, expose, bear)

amendable-*adj* liable, responsible, yielding, accountable, answerable, duty, morality, conscience, decalogue, (fault, nonobservance, nonperformance)

amend-*v* improve, correct, rectify, change, mend, promote, cultivate, advance, forward, enhance, foster, bolster, brighten, (wreck, decay, decline, erosion, blight)

amiable-*adj* kindly, affable, agreeable, pleasant, courtesy, respect, behavior, politeness, gentility, polish, presence, (rude, insult, ill breeding, discourtesy)

ample-*adj* roomy, spacious, large, abundant, considerable, greatness, magnitude, size, immensity, enormity, might, strength, fullness, (smallness, little, diminutive, paltry)

amusement-*n* pleasure, sport, solace, pastime, entertainment, diversion, distraction, relaxation, solace, fun, frolic, merriment, (tedious, weariness, disgust, nausea)

anachronism-*n* error in time, error in chronology, prolapses, misdate, anticipation, disregard, neglect, (chronicle, journal, diary, clock)

analogy-*n* resembling, like, associated, related, correspondent, parallel, similar, semblance, affinity, agreement, look like, (diversity, disparity, difference, novelty)

analysis-*n* decomposition, inquiry, consideration, study, disintegration, break-up, investigation, dissection, resolution, dissolve, (combination, mixture, union, incorporation)

analyst-*n* recorder, historian, chronicler, compiler, notary, clerk, registrar, secretary, scribe, biographer, time keeper, almanac, calendar, journal

anarchy-*n* rebellion, chaos, terrorism, lawlessness, disorder, turmoil, confusion, disarray, jumble, huddle, muddle, hash, (order, regularity, uniformity, symmetry)

ancestry-*n* line, lineage, family tree, family, race, descent, parent, father, dad, pedigree, tribe, clan, descent, parental, forefathers, maternity, mother

anchor-*n* stay, grapnel, safeguard, protection, hold, kedge, killick, link, connective, hyphen, bracket, bridge, (separation, parting, segregation, divorce, break)

anchorage-*n* harbor, safety, roadstead, mooring, refuge, lodgement, establishment, settlement, place, station, (displace, dislodge, exile, remove, unload)

ancient-*adj* aged, hoary, antique, archaic, old, venerable, antiquated, maturity, decline, decay, primitive, classic, (newness, novelty, youth, modernism)

anecdote-*n* story, tale, sketch, account, narrative, description, statement, report, summary, brief, relate, recite, recount,

sum u, tell, give, graphic, epic

angel-*n* divine messenger, ministering spirits, invisible helpers, good man, worthy, model, paragon, hero, demigod,, innocent, saint, (bad man, evil doer, sinner, wicked)

anger-*n* enrage, inflame, arouse, irate, annoy, exasperate, provoke, offend, infuriate, resentment, displeasure, wrath, indignation, (favorite, pet, idol, fondness, love, dear)

angle-*n* guise, aspect, phase, crook, fork, obliquity, cusp, bend, notch, ankle, measurement, elevation, distance, triangle, square, diamond

animate-*v* actuate, excite, cheer, enliven, encourage, inspire, motion, action, intention, inducement, draw, inspire, (dissuade, reluctance, detour, hold, repel)

annex-*v* add, attach, join, affix, junction, union, unite, lump, fix, bind, fasten, stitch, buckle, button, knit, lock, (disjoined, disconnect, disengage, divorce, cut, adrift)

annihilate-*v* exterminate, eradicate, destroy, end, wreck, demolish, extinction, blow, doom, ravage, sacrifice, abolish, perish, (evolve, bring forth, birth, produce, perform)

announce-*v* report, declare, predict, foretell, tell, inform, proclaim, assert, notice, communicate, acquaint, (conceal, hide, mystify, masquerade, cunning)

annoy-*v* trouble, bother, vex, harass, molest, disturb, irritate, tantalize, worry, badness, hurtful, inflict, harm, injure, oppress, persecute, (produce, profit, benefit, goodness, merit)

annul-*v* nullification, diffuseness, cancellation, counter order, invalidation, retraction, repeal,

abolishment, recision,
abrogation, (commission,
delegate, consign, assign)

anoint-*v* rub, lubricate, salve, oil,
divinity, wisdom, goodness,
justice, truth, unity, eternity,
preservation (scourge, halter,
stake, truncheon, stocks)

anonymous-*adj*
unacknowledged, unknown,
unnamed, misnomer, alias,
pseudonym, nickname,
(nomination, designation, title,
head, namesake)

answer-*n* reply, response,
acknowledgement, rebuttal,
retort, return, respond, say,
rebut, acknowledge, echo,
replication, (question, inquiry,
request, search)

antagonism-*n* animosity,
antipathy, hostility, opposition,
enmity, counteraction, polarity,
clashing, collision, resistance,
(concurrence, cooperation,
agreement)

antecede-*v* preexist, precede,
go before, precedence, first,
head, lead, introduce, prefix,
prelude, preface, former,
before, (sequence, after,
succeed, follow, suffix)

anteroom-*n* hall, lobby,
antechamber, receptacle,
enclosure, receiver, apartment,
vessel, portico, porch, veranda,
lobby, hall, vestibule, chamber,
bower

anticipate-*v* expect, await,
forestall, be early, surmise,
predict, preparation, provide,
disposition, forecast, cultivate,
(disqualify, unfitted, shiftless,
unprepared)

antidote-*n* emetic, remedy,
counter poison, help, antiseptic,
corrective, sedative, recipe,
prescription, (poison, virus,
venom, scourge)

antipathy-*n* repugnance,
clashing, opposition,
abhorrence, detestation,

dislike, incompatibility,
reluctance, backward, disgust,
(desire, wish, want, need,
longing)

apathetic-*adj* insensible,
indifferent, cold, unfeeling,
impassive, insensibility, no
desire, disregard, no interest,
(sensible, morale, softness,
warm, tender)

ape-*n* simian, monkey, mimic,
mock, simulate, imitate,
copying, simulation,
semblance, mirror, reflect,
repeat, echo, match, follow,
counterfeit

apostasy-*n* renunciation,
abjuration, recantation,
defection, retraction, disavowal,
revocation, abandonment,
recreancy, relapse

appall-*v* nauseate, revolt,
disgust, terrify, putrefy, painful,
trouble, curse, hurt, displease,
annoy, perplex, tease, irk, vex,
(refresh, comfortable, cordial,
genial)

apparatus-*n* machinery, outfit,
equipment, contrivance,
instrument, engineer,
mechanism, organ, appliance,
gear, tackle, implement, utensil

apparent-*adj* perceptible,
obvious, seeming, clear,
patent, manifest, visible,
appearing, conspicuous,
distinct, evidence, (invisible,
dim, mysterious, confused)

appearance-*n* sight, show,
phenomenon, prospect,
representation, display, stage
setting, exposure, (vanishing,
fading, evanescence,
departure, occultation,
withdrawal)

appease-*v* satisfy, allay, pacify,
placate, quiet, soothe, mollify,
pleasure, moderate, soften,
tranquilize, swag, lull,
compose, (violent, sharp,
quicken, excite, incite)

append-*v* subjoin, add, affix,

attach, annex, supplement, subjoin, reinforce, augment, accrue, introduce, insert, more, include, (subtraction, amputate, abscind, pare)

appetite-*n* passion, craving, want, hunger, longing desire, wish, need, exigency, inclination, greed, covetous, ravenous, (anorexia, apathy, listless)

applause-*n* acclamation, praise, plaudit, acclaim, clapping, approbation, commendation, cheer, good work, blessing, approval, (dislike, reprehend, chide, admonish)

applicable-*adj* convenient, pertinent, suitable, appropriate, relevant, adequate, service, available, ready, tangible, advantageous, (useless, inefficacy, worthless)

appoint-*v* nominate, ordain, assign, establish, prescribe, commission, delegate, consign, authorize, accredit, engage, hire, (annulment, nullification, conceal, cancel)

apportionment-*n* allotment, assignment, consignment, partition, allocation, division, distribution, disperse, spread, intersperse, (crowd, muster, levy, gather, flood)

appraise-*v* rate, judge, estimate, assess, value, survey, reckon, measure, standard, rule, compass, gage, gauge, yard, meter, coordinates, ordinate, latitude

apprehend-*v* arrest, seize, imprison, dread, distrust, perceive, see, understand, known, ascertain, recognize, realize, (ignorant, unexplored, bewilderment)

approach-*v* drawing near, advance, access, advent, admission, convergence, pursuit, drift, gain upon, converge, (avoidance, recession, go away)

approbation-*n* sanction, approval, advocacy, favor, renown, kudos, popularity, commendation, eulogy, homage, (detraction, disrepute, disapprobation)

appropriate-*adj* becoming, fit, suitable, timely, proper, adapted, agreeable, expedient, advisable, convenient, worthwhile, applicable, (undesirable, unfit, clumsy, awkward)

apt-*adj* clever, quick, dexterous, skillful, influence, important, rampant, dominant, regnant, predominant, support, (powerless, uninfluential, irrelevant, inertness)

arable-*adj* productive, fertile, tillable, farming, georgic, agronomy, horticulture, florist, field, meadow, garden, ornamental

arbitrary-*adj* overbearing, imperious, harsh, tyrannical, dictatorial, peremptory, domineering, despotic, austere, (lenient, mild, gentle, tolerant, forbearing)

argument-*n* data, case, discussion, debate, controversy, wangling, contention, dispute, examine, pros and cons, (deceptive, sophistical, irrelevant, evasive)

aristocrat-*n* patrician, lord, noble, nobleman, empire, monarchy, royalty, (democracy, demagogy, republic, magistrate, socialism, anarchy, relaxation, toleration, freedom)

arrangement-*n* provision, preparation, array, assortment, allotment, distribution, analysis, organize, sort, distribute, (disorder, disarrangement, disturb, confuse)

arrive-*v* advent, coming, debarkation, landing, reception, welcome, goal, destination, harbor, haven, port, (egress, departure, embarkation, exit, leaving)

arrogant-*adj* airs, swagger, haughtiness, pretension, ostentation, insolence, take, demand, usurp, appropriate, seize, assume, dignity, pride, self-respect

arsenal-*n* armory, depot, magazine, storehouse, arms, weapons, armament, partisan, battery, gunnery, missile, shrapnel

artful-*adj* adroit, tricky, crafty, designing, sly, shrewd, dexterous, falsity, deception, untruth, lying, misrepresentation, perjury, forgery, (frankness, truthfulness, sincerity)

artificial-*adj* false, sham, unnatural, affected, counterfeit, imitation, deception, untruth, delusion, collusion, treachery, trick, cheat, (truthfulness, veracity, frankness, honesty)

artistic-*adj* talented, beautiful, graceful, accomplished, cultural, exquisite, aesthetic, skillful, clever, ability, ingenuity, capacity, (unskillful, stupidity, indiscretion)

asceticism-*n* austerity, penance, puritanism, abstinence, cynicism, mortification, maceration, flagellation, fasting, ascetic, cynical

ascribe-*v* assign, impute, attribute, refer, theory, reference, pedigree, rationale, (accident, fortune, hazard, chance, random, luck, casualty)

ask-*v* implore, beseech, inquire, interrogate, beg, entreat, request, question, search, research, pursuit, review, scrutiny, sifting, (answer, respond, reply, rebut, retort)

askew-*adj* oblique, crooked, awry, distorted, inclination, slope, slant, leaning, beveled,

tilt, bias, twist, swag, oblique, descend, decline

ass-*n* dolt, booby, donkey, fool, idiot, wiseacre, simpleton, ninny, oaf, lout, loon, addle, innocent, babbler, (sage, wise man, mastermind, thinker, authority)

assassin-*n* cutthroat, killer, murderer, slayer, homicide, manslaughter, slay, butcher, victimize, massacre, strange, stifle, (alive, breathe, respire)

assemblage-*n* collection, concourse, conflux, gathering, mobilization, meet, concentration, compilation, (disjunction, dispersion, divergence)

assert-*v* allege, claim, avow, maintain, state, affirm, belief, credence, credit, assurance, faith, trust, confidence, dependence, (misbelief, discredit, infidelity, dissent, retraction)

astringent-*adj* styptic, sour, tart, austere. binding, contraction, reduction, lessening, shrinking, collapse, decrease, (large, expand, widen, enlarge, grow)

astute-*adj* acute, bright, shrewd, quick, intelligent, capacity, comprehension, intellect, sagacity, judgment, cunning, brains, (imbecility, dull, incompetence, idiocy)

athletic-*adj* acrobatic, strong, robust, powerful, gymnastic, strength, energy, vigor, force, main, spring, elasticity, tone, (weakness, debility, relaxation, languor)

atonement-*n* indemnification, expiation, redemption, conciliation, propitiation, recompense, compromise, (impenitence, obduracy, callousness)

attack-*v* encroachment, onset, onslaught, encounter, assault, charge, aggression, thrust,

kick, punch, assail, invade,
(defense, protection, guard,
shield)

attention-*n* alertness, heed,
observance, inertness, scrutiny,
study, mindfulness, thought,
consideration, reflection,
(inattention, neglect, oversight,
disregard)

audacity-*n* overconfidence, gall,
impudence, temerity, insolence,
rashness, imprudence,
indiscretion, presumption,
(caution, discretion, calculation,
deliberation)

auspicious-*adj* fortunate,
favorable, propitious,
promising, expedient, occasion,
opportunity, suitable, proper,
(unsuitable, improper, lose,
waste)

authority-*n* authorization, power,
warrant, right, dominion,
dictation, command, influence,
facts, evidence, collateral,
(laxity, obedience, servant,
submission)

auxiliary-*adj* assistant,
collaborator, adjuvant, helping,
aiding, ancillary, support, lift,
favor, relief, rescue, ministry,
aid, (prevention, stoppage,
enemy, opponent)

avail-*v* benefit, profit, serve,
succeed, suffice, usefulness,
adequacy, conduce, gainful,
advantageous, valuable,
(inadequacy, unskillful, lost,
seek)

averse-*adj* reluctant, loath,
opposed, counter,
unwillingness, renitency,
reluctance, indifference,
backward, slowness, (willing,
mind, heart, incline, eager)

await-*v* contemplate, impend,
anticipate, expectation,
approach, future, coming,
heritage, posterity, close, next,
eventual, (past, gone, former,
ancient, antiquity)

award-*v* adjudication,

compensation, bestowal,
conferment, decision, giving,
donation, presentation,
accordance, delivery,
endowment, (receiving,
acquisition, acceptance,
admission)

awkward-*adj* unskillful, ungainly,
clumsy, ungraceful,
incompetency, inability,
inexperience, fumble, boggle,
blunder, flounder, stumble,
(skill, expert, craft,
competence)

axion-*n* aphorism, truism,
postulate, rule, proposition,
saying, adage, saw, proverb,
sentence, motto, word, morale,
reflection, (absurdity, imbecility,
nonsense, paradox, muddle)

axle-*n* arbor, pivot, axis, spindle,
rotation, revolution, gyration,
whirl, surge, screw, gimbals,
gyrate, twirl

B

babble-v chatter, prattle, rave, gibber, murmur, gurgle, gossip, empty sound, nonsense, jargon, gibberish, jabber, bombast, (meaning, expression, bearing, substantial)

backsliding-v apostasy, retrogression, lapse, countermovement, regression, retreat, withdrawal, retirement, recession, reflection, (progression, advance, ongoing, headway)

backward-adv delayed, dull, stagnant, tardy, loath, disinclined, reluctant, remiss, retrograde, unwillingness, reluctance, (willingness, punctual, inclination, leaning)

bad-adj sinful, imperfect, rancid, unsuitable, wicked, tainted, hurtful, virulence, injurious, deleterious, noxious, aggrieve, oppress, (good, excellence, merit, virtue, worth)

baffle-v outwit, confound, check, balk, frustrate, foil, nonplus, restrict, restraint, blockade, hindrance, obstacle, drawback, (assistance, help, support, lift, advance)

bag-n container, pouch, sack, protrude, sag, capture, entrap, catch, receptacle, enclosure, receiver, compartment, sac, pocket, sheath

bait-n worry, badger, lure, trap, decoy, harass, deception, falseness, untruth, fraud, deceit, misrepresentation, delusion, juggling, (veracity, truthfulness, sincerity)

balance-n evenness, scales, equilibrium, steadiness, parallel, match, compare, contract, identification, collate, confront, (crooked, uneven, unbalanced)

balk-v shy, stop, back, thwart, disappoint, foil, frustrate, hindrance, deception, falseness, untruth, fraud, deceit, trick, cheat, (true, frank, open, candor, sincerity)

ball-n hop, dance, party, shot, sphere, globe, projectile, roundness, cylinder, drum, rotund

balm-n ointment, balsam, sedative, moderation, gentleness, calmness, relaxation, mitigation, lullaby, (violence, vehemence, might, turbulence)

banish-v expatriate, exile, dismiss, expel, eject, exclude, punish, emission, evacuation, drainage, reject, discard, cut, (admit, introduce, inject, insertion)

bare-adj simple, mere, nude, naked, undraped, empty, destitute, unfurnished, disclose, uncover, reveal, expose, (cover, screen, shake, full, furnish)

bark-n skin, rind, shell, cortex, howl, yelp, yap, bay, cry, growl, yip, roar, bellow, grunt, snort, squeak, purr, mew, croak

barren-adj arid, sterile, unfertile, unprofitable, fruitless, worthless, impotence, waste, desert, unproductive, inoperative, (fertility, multiplication, productive, generate)

barter-v trade, exchange, bargaining, swap, traffic, marketing, interchange, reciprocation, shuffle, retaliate, (substitution, supplanting, alternative)

base-n groundwork, footing, foundation, foothold, substratum, basic, lowest, fundamental, platform,

dishonesty, disgrace,
shabbiness, (integrity, recitude,
honesty, faith)

bashful-*adj* sheepish, modest,
timid, diffident, shy,
constrained, humility,
difference, reserve, nervous,
(conceit, confidence,
approbation)

bear-*v* yield, hold, sustain,
suffer, feel, tolerate, carry,
transport, convey, transfer,
deportation, carriage,
conveyance, delegate, consign

beat-*v* defeat, conquer, pulsate,
throb, hit, strike, bruise, batter,
overcome, accent, rhythm,
pulse, track, course, (break
down, collapse, fail, lose
ground)

beatify-*v* bless, hallow,
consecrate, sanctify, piety, fly,
revere, inspire, (bigot, fanatic,
irreverence)

beauty-*n* loveliness, grace,
elegance, symmetry,
comeliness, fairness,
attractiveness, (ugliness,
deformity, inelegance,
distortion)

becoming-*adj* proper, fit,
attractive, seemly, ornamental,
decorous, beam, bloom, grace,
(unfit, clumsy, awkward,
objectionable)

beg-*v* plead, petition, ask alms,
implore, beseech, crave,
request, motion, overture,
appeal, (depreciation, protest,
receive, mediation)

beginning-*n* start, onset,
commencement, introduction,
prelude, prologue, debut,
outbreak, outset, source,
rudiment, genesis, cause,
introductory, prefatory,
initiative, inaugural, (end, read,
sequel)

belief-*n* faith, assurance,
credence, trust, hope,
dependence, conviction,
persuasion, conclusion, dogma,

theory, principle, (doubt,
unbelief, uncertainty)

belligerent-*adj* disputatious,
pugnacious, quarrelsome,
warlike, fighting, hostilities,
mobilize, armed, combative,
(pacify composed, reconcile)

benefactor-*n* protector, savior,
patron, guardian, guardian
angel, altruist, supporter,
(evildoer, opponent)

benefit-*n* avail, behalf, gain,
profit, advantage, aid, assist,
serve, improve, helpful,
valuable, useful, utility,
(useless, inadequacy, lose,
waste)

benevolence-*n* charity, love,
kindness, unselfishness,
philanthropy, humanity,
tenderness, amiability, mercy,
(malevolence, misanthropy)

bereavement-*n* destitution, loss,
deprivation, affliction, death,
decease, release, departure,
perish, expire, (alive, respire,
living, lively)

besiege-*v* circumscribe, storm,
surround, hedge, beleaguer,
attack, request, ask, beg,
crave, prey, petition, invite,
(depreciation, intercession,
protect, receive)

betray-*v* deceive, divulge,
ensnare, trick, reveal, let slip,
disclosure, discover, breathe,
break, split, acknowledge,
(concealment, cover, screen,
mask, shade)\

bewilder-*v* stagger, daze,
dazzle, perplex, confuse,
mystify, confound, puzzle,
wonder, marvel, astonish,
amaze, (expectance, common,
ordinary)

bewitch-*v* hypnotize, charm,
fascinate, enchant, inveigle,
incentive, provocation, induce,
inspire, stimulate,
(discouragement, damper,
dissuade)

bias-*n* prejudice, tendency,

inclination, warp, slope, prepossession, proneness, bent, turn, tone, conduce, dispose

bid-v invite, ask, proffer, direct, order, enjoin, instruct, summon, call, offer, presentation, tender, motion, present, move, (refusal, rejection, decline, repulse)

bigot-n fanatic, dogmatist, iconoclast, formalist, Pharisee, misconception, bias, warp, twist, partial, narrow, (result, conclusion, judge, deduce, derive)

bind-v restrain, secure, tighten, force, fasten, join, union, junction, associate, closeness, attach, affix, link, fetter, (sunder, divide, sever, cut, cleave)

bisection-n divergence, bifurcation, branching, half, separation, split, (duplication, iteration)

biting-adj nipping, keen, pungent, piquant, sharp, telling, forceful, irritate, pinch, prick, gripe, painfulness, trouble, (pleasurable, agreeable, flatter, enchantment)

blacken-v defame, blot, malign, besmirch, smudge, detract, defamation, scandal, slander, liable, criticism, decry, derogate, (flattery, humor, smooth)

blemish-n deformity, taint, disfigurement, failing, defacement, defect, imperfection, mar, sully, damage, deform, tarnish, (improvement, ornament, perfection)

blend-v compound, combine, mix, fuse, amalgamate, cross, merge, interbreed, union, synthesis, unite, consolidate, (analysis, dissection, decompose, resolve)

blessing-n approbation, boon, Godsend, benefit, benediction,

approval, sanction, advocacy, esteem, (dislike, censure, object, disapprove)

blight-n rot, corruption, decay, impairment, foil, blast, thwart, deterioration, recession, decrease, degenerate, (improvement, mend, elevation, build)

blind-adj sightless, unseeing, inattentive, shade, screen, artifice, ruse, pretext, ambush, subterfuge, (luminary, light, flame, see, sight, candle)

bloat-v puff up, swell, expand, dilate, distend, increase, extend, spread, obesity, inflation, larger, (reduction, lessening, shrinking, collapse)

block-n street, terrace, row, lump, mass, hinder, impede, check, obstruct, prevent, preclude, hindrance, stricture, (support, lift, advance, favor, rescue)

bloom-n prosper, blossom, flower, glow, flourish, thrive, be in health, prosperity, welfare, affluence, luck (adversity, failure, mishap, rot, disaster)

bluff-v brusque, abrupt, ungracious, unceremonious, bank, cliff, headland, brag, hoax, mislead, (lowness, below, debased, down)

blusterer-n braggart, boaster, blower, bluffer, ranter, braggadocio, fanatic, dogmatist, swagger, bully, terrorist

bodily-adj material, physical, corporeal, substantial, entirely, completely, wholly, en masse, (immaterial, spiritual, unearthly)

bogus-adj sham, fake, false, counterfeit, spurious, fraudulent, pretended, deception, untruth, deceit, trick, cheat, (veracity, truth, sincerity, honesty)

bold-adj daring, intrepid, courageous, fearless, forward, dauntless, project, prominence, protrude, (depress, hollow, concave, vaulted)

border-*n* boundary, brim, rim, margin, frontier, edge, verge, brink, flange, side, lip, threshold, portal, fringe, (enclosure, wrapper, barrier)

bore-*v* pierce, drill, cloy, annoy, diameter, caliber, dullard, pest, hole, puncture, perforation, passage, canal, (close, blockade, plug, stop)

bottomless-*adj* unending, abysmal, unfathomable, depth, depression, shaft, well, crater, deepen, buried, (shallowness, shoals, superficial)

bound-*adj* spring, vault, jump, confine, circumscribe, limit, restrain, swiftness, spurt, rush, dash, race, lively, gallop, (slowness, creeping, loiterer, retire)

bounty-*n* subsidy, grant, generosity, liberality, munificence, benevolence, giving, donation, consignment, charity, (receiving, acquire, assigned)

braid-*v* plait, interweave, interface, intertwine, joining, union, unite, bind, attach, fix, splice, truss, tether, (disjoin, disconnect, disengage, separate)

branch-*n* wing, arm, member, ramification, offshoot, limb, bough, twig, fork, divide, bifurcate, diverge, radiate

brand-*n* stamp, stain, sort, kind, grade, stigma, firebrand, burning, cauterization, ignite, (cooling, refresh, congeal, starve)

breadth-*n* broadness, width, expanse, amplitude, spaciousness, tread, span, reach, bore, caliber, thickness

break-*v* fracture, shatter, sever, rend, violate, tame, transgress, infringe, subdue, interruption,

interval, gap, (adjoin, touch, contact, adhere, coincide)

breathe-*v* inhale, respire, live, exist, divulge, utter, whisper, disclose, puff, blow, dust, blast, breeze, gale, blowing, fanning

brevity-*n* briefness, shortness, succinctness, terseness, conciseness, little, curtail, abridge, curt, compact, stubby, (long, length, span, elongate)

bribe-*n* graft, price, allurement, seduction, hush-money, recompense, fee, corrupt, suborn, tempt

brigand-*n* thief, bandit, thug, robber, highwayman, freebooter, filcher, buccaneer, swindler, forger, fence

bright-*adj* vivid, intense, deep, intelligent, apt, clever, lustrous, radiant, luminous, flashing, glistening, glowing, brilliant

brisk-*adj* alert, lively, swift, quick, nimble, velocity, fly, gallop, vanish, brief, quick, sudden, short, spasmodic, cursory, (long, eternity, persistence)

bristling-*adj* sullen, angry, perverse, thorny, spiny, spiked, sharpness, barbed, horned, nib, tooth, (dull, bluntness, obtuse, bluff)

brittleness-*n* frailness, fragility, delicateness, splintery, crack, snap, split, splinter, crumble, (toughness, strength, tenacious, resisting)

broadcast-*v* diffuse, scatter, disseminate, utter, spread, disperse, sow, dispense, disband, dispel, (assemblage, collection, levy, gathering)

broken-*v* shattered, divided, disconnected, docile, infirm, gentle, domesticated, weakness, languor, fragility, (strength, power, energy, vigor)

bubble-*n* sparkle, gurgle, effervescent, foam, boil, nothingness, zero, never,

unsubstantial, burp,
(substantial, article, something,
substance)

buckle-*n* twist, bend, warp,
fastening, fastener, clasp, link,
junction, union, unite, bond,
bridge, braid, hook, girdle,
(disjoin, disconnect, divorce,
cut)

buffoon-*n* pantomimist, fool,
jester, clown, mummer,
comedian, humorist, wag, wit,
dandy, joker, charlatan, mime

bulk-*n* amount, volume,
measure, largeness, mass,
expanse, greater part, whole,
integrity, collectiveness, lump,
(division, segment, fragment,
piece)

bulletin-*n* statement, report,
journal, news, information,
word, advice, dispatch,
publicity, notice, (secret,
mystery, riddle, conundrum)

bully-*n* brawler, tyrant, roisterer,
swaggerer, threaten, bluster,
domineer, browbeat,
combatant, litigant, competitor,
rival, (submissive, surrender,
resignation)

bungler-*n* muddler, lout,
blunderer, fumbler, clown,
duffer, novice, clod, lubber,
muff, swab, yokel, greenhorn,
(proficient, master, veteran,
soldier, experienced)

buoyant-*adj* light, floating,
resilient, springy, sanguine,
foamy, rise, hover, spire, soar,
tower, swim, surge, (descent,
fall, drop, downfall, tumble)

bureaucracy-*n* officialism, red-
tape, authority, influence,
power, command, empire,
sway, (laxity, loose, freedom,
tolerate)

burglar-*n* bandit, robber,
housebreaker, thief, filcher,
swindler, forger, coiner, fence,
smuggler, wrecker

burlesque-*n* buffoonery, farce,
take-off, parody, comedy,

drollery, ridiculous, ludicrous,
preposterous, monstrosity,
(formality, prudery,
demureness, modesty)

burn-*v* sear, parch, char,
destroy, blaze, flame, hot,
swelter, boil, torrid, tropical,
sultry, stifling, stuffy,
suffocating, oppressive, (cold,
cool, chill, frigid, inclement)

burrow-*n* tunnel, mine, dig,
excavate, penetrate, rooted,
inhabit, domesticate, moored,
anchored, established, lodged,
(displacement, banishment,
removal, dislocate)

bushy-*adj* shaggy, hairy,
clumpy, dense, jungle, prairie,
grass, hedge, rush, week,
foliage, growth, woody

business-*n* employment,
occupation, undertaking,
pursuit, avocations, financial
activities, affair, concern, case,
interest, (inaction, inactivity,
leisure)

busy-*adj* occupied, active,
engrossed, employed,
engaged, industrious, diligent,
officious, flurry, rustle, stir,
perturbation, (idle, dawdle,
mope, inactivity, relaxation)

buttress-*n* abutment, prop,
truss, brace, support, aid,
block, anvil, shore, jamb, beam,
rafter, (suspend, hand, fast to,
pensile, hanging)

buy-*v* procure, purchase,
acquire, invest, shop, market,
buyer, vendee, patron,
customer, client, pay, market,
(sell, sale, dispose of,
mortgage, auction)

bygone-*adj* old, former,
departed, antiquated, obsolete,
gone by, past, yore, away,
latter, look back, ancestry,
lapse

byword-*n* proverb, saying,
object of scorn, nickname, pet
expression, by-name

B

C

cab-*n* carriage, hansom, taxicab, hackney, hack, vehicle, conveyance, van, wagon, cart, coach, caravan, car

cabinet-*n* closet, room, repository, case, ministry, council, committee, chamber, board, bench

cackle-*v* chuckle, giggle, cluck, clack, gabble, chit-chat, small talk, babble, gossip, converse, tattle, verbal intercourse, (soliloquize, say, think aloud)

cage-*n* confine, restrain, incarcerate, imprison, enclosure, receptacle, reservatory, compartment, hole, nook, stall

cajole-*v* coax, wheedle, deceive, delude, flatter, praise, soothe, humor, exaggerate, charm, (scandal, defamation, slander, derogate)

calamity-*n* catastrophe, disaster, affliction, casualty, adversity, failure, mishap, accident, trial, tribulation, reverse, (welfare, well being, luck, success)

calculate-*v* estimate, count, reckon, compute, numerate, numbering, enumeration, summation, poll, recite

calefaction-*n* torrefaction, heating, melting, warming, fusion, liquefaction, scarification, cremation, incineration, (cooling, refrigeration, liquefying)

calendar-*n* register, list, almanac, schedule, chronicle, clock, watch, hour glass

caliber-*n* bore, diameter, gauge, capacity, ability, power, force, dimension, bulk, magnitude, big, great, considerable, (smallness, dwarf, pygmy,

minute)

call-*v* muster, assemble, convene, convoke, elect, appoint, summon, invite, shout, yell, designate, signal, invitation, offer, visit, urge, impulse

calling-*n* vocation, outcry, profession, notice, business, occupation, employment, pursuit

callous-*adj* stiff, unfeeling, hardened, obdurate, insensibility, unfeeling, senseless, thick-skinned, dull, numb, dead, (sensible, moral, cultivate, impress)

calm-*adj* placid, serene, impassive, peaceful, composed, tranquil, quiet, rest, still, stagnation, silence, (motion, volatile, restless, mobility, shift)

camouflage-*n* screen, cloak, disguise, concealment

camp-*n* shack, encampment, quarters, tent, locate, encamp, lodge, abode, dwelling, lodging, domicile, nest, (settler, squatter, indigent)

cancel-*v* abolish, repeal, delete, revoke, overrule, abrogation, annulment, stop, disclaim, dismiss, discard, (initiate, commission, start, delegate, consign)

candid-*adj* unaffected, frank, artless, sincere, blunt, outspoken, veracity, sincerity, candor, honesty, fidelity, truthful, (falsify, deception, untruth, lying)

cannibal-*n* anthropophagite, savage, man-eater, brute, ruffian, terrorist, desperado, bully, dangerous, (benefactor, good savior, saint)

canon-*n* law, charge, code, rule, precept, courage, bravery, valor, boldness, gallantry, rashness, confidence, (cowardice, timidity, cower, week-minded)

canopy-*n* tester, awning, overhanging, shelter, dome, vault, sky, cover, tent, umbrella, parasol, sun-shade, envelope

canvas-*n* tent, sailcloth, tarpaulin, painting, picture, covering, gather way, spread sail

canvass-*v* solicit, seek, examine, discuss, request, address, overture, asking, begging, invite, beseech, plead, (depreciate, mediation, protest, intercessory)

cap-*n* headpiece, headdress, skullcap, barrette, fez, completion, achieve, fulfillment, execution, finish, attain reach, (shortcoming, incomplete)

capital-*n* admirable, first-class, excellent, primary, principal, resources, assets, riches, opulence

caprice-*n* humor, notion, fancy, quip, conceit, whim, (permanence, stability)

captious-*adj* fault-finding, hypercritical, carping, sophistical, specious, moodiness, obstinacy, sulk, frown, pout, (endearment, caring, salute, fondle)

captivate-*v* delight, charm, fascinate, enchant, pleasant, pleasurable, agreeable, enrapture, indulge, beatify, (painful, infliction, annoyance, grievance)

capture-*v* apprehend, seize, catch, arrest, secure, taking, hook, nab, bag, receive, accept, distraint, (return, release, replevin, restore)

career-*n* progress, course, path, passage, success, occupation, business, employment, pursuit, undertake, serve

careless-*adj* nonchalant, heedless, easy-going, negligent, thoughtless, reckless, impulsive, indiscreet

caress-*n* fondle, hug, pet, embrace, clasp, cling-to, endearment, kiss, smack, hug, cuddle, gallivant, ogle, sweet upon, (moodiness, sullen, sulky, ill-tempered)

caricature-*n* ridicule, parody, satirize, take-off, repetition, duplication, copy, simulate, mimic

carnage-*n* slaughter, bloodshed, massacre, butchery, killing, homicide, murder, assassination

carouse-*n* feast, debauch, make merry, revel, riot, diversion, reaction, relaxation, pleasure, fun, frolic, prank, (weary, stupid, dry, monotonous, dull)

carry-*v* bear, convey, uphold, sustain, support, purchase, stand, foundation, buttress, stanchion, mainstay

cart-*n* wagon, pushcart, dray, tumbrel, vehicle, transport, displace, displant, unload, empty, transfer, vacate, (lodgement, stow, installation, localize)

carve-*v* quarter, slice, dissect, old, hew, cut, disjunction, separation, parting, divorce, detach, divide, split, (join, unite, close, together)

castrate-*v* neuter, spay, geld, emasculate, purify, cleanliness, lavation, clear, purgative, (impurity, contamination)

casual-*adj* random, accidental, occasional, incidental, contingent, external, conditional, fortuitous

casualty-*n* misfortune, disaster, calamity, mishap, accident, event, adventure, crisis, emergency, contingency, consequence, (loom, await, impend)

cause-*v* birth, beginning, origin, prime, principle, producer, generator, creator, determinant, motive, root, basis, foundation

C

caustic-*adj* pungent, biting, burning, acrimonious, corroding, mordant, repulsive, discourteous, blunt, gruff, harsh, austere, (courtesy, politeness, compliment)

caution-*n* discretion, heed, circumspection, wariness, forethought, vigilance, watchfulness, admonition

cave-*n* grotto, den, cavern, lair, hole, abode, dwelling, domicile, lodging, nest, arbor, cell, retreat, roost

cavil-*v* quibble, haggle, carp, mangle, dissent, dislike, object to, disvalue, outcry, (sanction, advocacy, esteem, repute)

cavity-*n* opening, hole, dent, depression, hollow, excavation, dip, scoop, excavate, tunnel, burrow, (projection, bulge, swell, nob)

cease-*v* discontinue, halt, end, stop, terminate, refrain, closure, desist, pause, rest, interrupt, suspend, cut, (start, continue, initiate, sustain, uphold)

cede-*v* surrender, give up, concede, yield, relinquish, submission, resignation, homage, succumb, submit, (combatant, belligerent, competitor)

celebration-*n* observance, commemoration, jubilation, ovation, triumph, inauguration, honor, installation, coronation

celestial-*adj* holy, unearthly, divine, beatific, Elysian, heavenly, solar, empyreal, starry, otherworldly

celibacy-*n* misogyny, purity, singleness, bachelorhood, virginity, maidenhood, spinster, unmarried, (marriage, wedlock, union, mate)

censure-*n* faultfinding, hypercritical, carping, condemnatory, disesteem, dislike, disapprove, object to, frown, (approval, sanction, esteem, praise)

ceremonial-*adj* ritualistic, formal, pompous, solemn, display, show, parade, ostentatious, showy, grand, flashing

certainty-*n* sureness, certitude, assuredness, safety, inevitable, fact, infallibility, dogmatic, (unbelief, uncertainty)

cessation-*n* discontinuance, interruption, respite, intermission, interval, recess, impediment, halt, lull, suspension, truce

chafe-*v* vex, fret, gall, annoy, rub, warm, pain, suffering, twitch, soreness, crick, sharp, piercing, gnawing, (pleasure, sensual, comfort, luxury)

chaff-*v* refuse, husk, persiflage, raillery, ridicule, deride, travesty, mock, sarcastic, ironical, banter, rally

chagrin-*n* vexation, mortification, painfulness, anxiety, annoyance, irritation, worry, ordeal, trouble, fret, (happiness, enjoyment, comfort, ease)

chance-*n* luck, fortune, unforeseen occurrence, fate, lot, destiny, fortuity, risk, gamble, uncertainty, jeopardy, happen, come, arrive, befall, turn up, (attribution, intention)

channel-*n* duct, waterway, conduit, canyon, chasm, aqueduct, canal, moat, ditch, water gate

chant-*n* melody, song, psalm, canticle, hymn, vespers, mass, prayer, service, vigils

chapter-*n* part, section, division, passage, branch, portion, segment, parcel, piece, detachment, verse, clause, (totality, collectiveness, completeness, bulk)

char-*v* parch, sear, burn, carbonize, scorch, boil, heat, fusion, inflame, roast, toast, cauterize, incinerate,

(refrigerate, cool, fan, refresh)

charitable-*adj* unselfish, generous, liberal, kind, altruistic, donor, eleemosynary, gratis

charlatan-*n* fraud, cheat, impostor, impersonator, quack, deceiver, hypocrite, pretender, humbug

charm-*n* fascination, attractiveness, amulet, talisman, incantation, lure, draw, seduce, conjure, hypnotize

chasm-*n* pit, abyss, gap, fissure, cleft, hold, opening, orifice, passage, channel, gully, mine, gallery, (closure, blockade, shut, obstruct)

chaste-*adj* unaffected, classic, virtuous, undefiled, simple, virginal, symmetry, finish, uniform, balanced, equal, regular, (distortion, warped, irregular)

cheat-*v* swindle, defraud, trick, beguile, dupe, delude, deceive, deception, falseness, fraud, delusion, treachery, (truthful, veracity, frankness, honesty)

checkered-*adj* varied, plaid, irregular, alternating, uneven, barred, checked

cheer-*n* yell, shout, festivity, hospitality, enliven, inspirit, approval, sanction, esteem, praise, applaud, joyous

cheerless-*adj* dismal, somber, gloomy, depressing, sad, dreary, despondent

cherish-*v* prize, treasure, nurture, revere, love, fondness, liking, affection, feeling, tenderness, (hate, alienation, coolness)

chew-*v* grind, eat, crunch, masticate, gulp, gluttony, feed, devour, swallow, take, dispatch, munch, gnaw, (discharge, secretion, ejection)

chief-*n* first, principal, foremost, supreme, main, head, leader,

commander, important, paramount, significant, (insignificant, trivial, nothing, trash)

childish-*adj* simple-minded, infantile, silly, weak, credulous, puerile, youthful, young, shallow, foolish, (wisdom, intellect, cunning, mature)

chivalrous-*adj* knightly, brave, courteous, gallant, war, tenure, courage, honor, generosity

choke-*v* strangle, suffocate, congest, clog, stifle, obstruction, blockage, closure, bolt, seal, clinch, (opening, yawning)

chop-*v* cut, hack, split, hew, dissection, separation, division, fracture, rupture, crack, (attach, fix, affix, join, union, unite)

chronic-*adj* unceasing, survive, lasting, inveterate, constant, eternity, perpetuity, persistent, standing, survival, (transient, passing, fleeting, flying)

chronicle-*n* registry, annals, archives, account, epoch, almanac, calendar, journal, diary, pendulum, (anticipation, disregard, neglect)

cipher-*n* cryptogram, code, monogram, cryptograph, naught, zero, numeration, pagination, recension, summation, (catalog, inventory, schedule, index)

circle-*n* globe, ring, orb, disk, circlet, encircle, circumnavigate, gird, circumscribe, surround, compass, inclose

circulate-*v* spread, report, pass, change hands, propagate, revolve, rotation, revolution, gyration, whir, whirl

circumference-*n* periphery, perimeter, circuit, girth, outline, perimeter, ambit, circuit, lines, contour, profile, zone, belt, (verge, brink, brow, side)

circumscription-*n* bound, limit,

C

confinement, case, restriction, enclosure, restraint, envelope, (perimeter, zone, belt, girth, band)

circumstance-*n* situation, condition, environment, surroundings, position, time, place, occurrence, event, quandary, fix, predicament, dilemma

circumvent-*v* thwart, elude, frustrate, outwit, baffle, prevent, preclusion, interruption, hindrance, (assist, help, promotion, patronage)

cite-*v* arraign, summon, allege, quote, adduce, illustrate, bring forward, charge, imputation, accuse, taunt, (vindication, acquittal, apology, gloss, excuse)

civil-*adj* urbane, well-bred, mannerly, respectful, secular, courteous, behavior, breeding, gentility, (discourteous, ungainly manners, rude, insult)

civilize-*v* polish, refine, cultivate, humanize, breeding, good, polite, conform, admissible, (comical, ridiculous, absurdity, ludicrous)

claim-*v* requirement, plea, assert, content, demand, require, deserve, title, pretense, prerogative, imposition, requisition

claimant-*n* accuser, heir, prosecutor, pretender, petitioner, solicitor, applicant, suitor, beggar, hunter

clamor-*n* outcry, uproar, racket, tumult, din, contention, agitation, cry, shout, roar, cream, cheer, hoot, holler

clamp-*n* fastener, clasp, brace, band, joining, union, connection, unite, attach, affix, (disconnection, disunion, division)

clan-*n* faction, breed, brotherhood, set, sort, family, association, paternity, parent,

father, sire, lineage, pedigree

clash-*v* conflict, collide, dispute, contend, impact, collision, concussion, shock, disagreement, discord, dissidence, (concert, conformity, uniformity)

class-*n* category, division, section, grouping, caste, clique, coterie, order, sort, manner, nature, type, gender, designation

classification-*n* grouping, sorting, systematization, order, allocation, designate, group, tabulate, index, file, systematize, arrange

cleanness-*n* pureness, purity, clearness, neatness, immaculateness, purgation, purification, (impurity, dirty, unclean, decay, corruption)

clear-*adj* bright, unclouded, distinct, intelligible, open, patent, transparent, simpleness, purification, single, sheer, neat

cleft-*adj* fissure, break, gap, crack, crevice, dissection, forking, branching, divide, split, cloven, halve, (double, renewal, twin)

clever-*adj* dexterous, adroit, talented, able, gifted, intelligence, capacity, sagacity, discernment, (shallow, imbecility, incapacity)

climax-*n* zenith, pinnacle, acme, culmination, crest, supremacy, majority, excel, match, culminate, (minority, deficiency, smallness)

clinch-*v* confirm, close, end, fasten, secure, clench, rivet, clamp, grapple, combination, mixture, junction, union, (analysis, dissection, decompose)

clique-*n* coterie, set, group, circle, crowd, party, faction, side, crew, ban, horde, posse, family, clan

clog-*n* hamper, impede, encumber, obstruct, investment, covering, attire, shoe, pump, boot, sandal, slipper, galoche

cloister-*n* abbey, convent, hermitage, monastery, restraint, hindrance, repression, confinement, duress, (liberation, emancipation, dismissal)

clown-*n* jester, rustic, buffoon, fool, boor, humorist, wag, wit, punster, joker, mime, gypsy

club-*n* stick, cudgel, resort, fraternity association, rendezvous, party, faction, side, crew, band, horde

clumsy-*adj* awkward, stupid, unwieldy, bungling, incompetent, unskilled, unfitness, inexpedient, undesirable, inadvisable, (opportunism, graceful, expedient)

clutch-*v* seize, clench, collar, grip, keep, retain, grasp, hold, secure, retentive, inalienable, (release, abandon, dereliction, dispensation)

coagulate-*v* thicken, clot, congeal, curdle, density, solidity, constipation, cohesion, cake, crystallize, (sponginess, rarefactive, expansion)

coarse-*adj* homespun, rough, uncouth, unpolished, crude, rude, vulgar, discord, burr, jangle, creaking, gruff, (refined, cultivated, tact, delicate, good taste, finesse, discriminate)

coax-*v* entice, cajole, persuade, wheedle, motive, intention, inducement, move, draw, inspire, (dissuade, against, warn, indispose)

coerce-*v* make, impel, force, compel, coaction, duress, enforcement, conscription, drive, constrain, (compelling, coactive)

cogent-*adj* forcible, strong, potent, convincing, power, might, force, energy, capable, valid, adequate, almighty, (powerless, incapable, disabled)

cogitate-*v* muse, ponder, consider, meditate, thought, reflection, consideration, speculation, consultation, (vacancy, fatuity, dismiss, thoughtlessness, unoccupied)

cognizant-*adj* conscious, sensible, observant, aware, knowledge, insight, familiarity, leaning, reading, doctrine, (ignorance, blindness)

coherence-*n* adherence, aggregation, accretion, congruity, connection, consistency, harmony, conformity, viscidity

cold-*adj* chilliness, chill, coolness, iciness, gelidity, frigid, biting, piercing, nipping, raw, wintry, anguish, arctic

colleague-*n* ally, partner, associate, companion, mate, helper, hand, friend, cooperator, pal, accomplice, (opponent, antagonist, adversary)

collect-*v* amass, compile, demand, exact, meet, throng, flock, assemble, ligation, gather, compilation, conclave, (dispersion, disjuntion, divergency)

collide-*v* crash, meet, bump, conflict, clash, impulse, impetus, momentum, push, thrust, shove, throw, explode, (recoil, rebound, revulsion, retract)

collision-*n* skirmish, encounter, conflict, interference, shock, impact, discord, resistance, antagonistic, oppose, (concur, conspire, tribute, agree, consent)

colloquial-*adj* conversational, informal, chatty, metaphor, figure of speech, phrase,

C

analogy, irony, personification

colonize-v establish, settle, found, people, place, situate, locate, localize, make a place for, plantation, camp, (displaced, misplaced, exile, removal)

combination-n aggregation, union, mixture, composite, coadunation, synthesis, inosculation, (disjuntion, decomposition)

command-v regulation, order, ordinance, act, bidding, direction, injunction, commandment, ruling, instructions, dispatch, message, (lowness, debasement, depression)

commence-v begin, start, enter upon, outset, inception, genesis, birth, originate, conceive, source, dawn, embarkation, initiate, (end, close, terminate, conclude)

commend-v recommend, praise, acclaim, approve, approbation, applause, clap, esteem, sanction, admiration, appreciate, (dislike, insinuation, ostracism)

comment-n observation, remark, criticism, annotation, interpretation, argument, controversy, debate, reasoning, (mystify, evasion, intuition, instinct)

commission-n warrant, charge, instruction, authorization, mandate, brevet, permit, delegation, consignment, nomination, charter, installation, investiture, accession, (annulment, prohibition)

commit-v perpetrate, consign, intrust, perform, action, doing, performance, exercise, citation, execute, achieve, (inaction, abstinence, passive)

common-adj conventional, usual, prevalent, current,

customary, regular, vulgar, ill-bred, general, universal, (special, designate, realize, determine)

commonplace-adj tedious, prosy, monotonous, ordinary, usual, unimportant, worthless, paltry, (important, prominence, significant, concern)

commotion-n disturbance, tumult, turmoil, disorder, agitation, stir, tremor, shake, ripple, jog, jolt, jar, (oscillation, vibration, liberation)

communion-n intercourse, converse, partnership, association, talk, participation, possession, partaking, (possessor, holder, occupant)

compact-n deal, contract, understanding, bargain, engagement, agreement, stipulation, covenant, terse, condensed, thick, constricted, compressed, dense, (contention, disagreement)

companion-n partner, chum, colleague, associate, accompany, coexist, attend, synchronize, (alone, isolate, disjoin, one, sole, solitary)

company-n association, partnership, group, crowd, cast, syndicate, firm, companionship, assemblage, (dispersion, disjunction, divergence)

compartment-n niche, enclosure, division, part, portion, item, segment, fragment, (collectiveness, completeness, bulk, mass)

compassion-n condolence, sympathy, tenderness, mercy, pity, commiseration, fellow-feeling, yearning, forbearance, (inclemency, severity, malevolence)

compatible-adj harmonious, congruous, suitable, consistent, agreeable, concert, conformity, uniformity, (discord, dissidence, variance, unfitness)

compel-v constrain, force, coerce, impel, drive, compulsion, make, press, coactive, oblige, necessitate

compendium-n epitome, bulletin, review, brief, analysis, recapitulation, summary, excerpt, note, abstract, digest, (dissertation, theme, discourse)

compensation-n repayment, payment, requital, pay, remuneration, reward, honorarium, solatium, mediocrity, generality, compromise

competence-n proficiency, ability, capability, sufficiency, means, rich, luxuriant, affluent, wealthy, abundant, (insufficient, meager, shortcoming, small, scarce)

competent-adj capable, fit, qualified, efficient

competitor-n contestant, rival, entrant, aspirant, claimant, antagonist, adversary, opposition, disputant, enemy, (helper, adjunct, friend, ally, confidant)

compile-v arrange, amass, collect, make, write, assemblage, group, cluster, clump, accumulation, heap, pile, (unassembled, dispersed, sparse)

completion-n attainment, achievement, execution, fulfillment, performance, accomplishment, conclusion

complex-adj complicated, intricate, involved, confused, confusion, disarray, uproar, riot, rumpus, jumble, huddle, (orderly, regular, neat, tidy)

complexity-n entanglement, intricacy, complication, perplexity, compositeness

compliance-n assent, agree, acquiesce, submit, obey, conformity, normal, typical, formal, (abnormal, unusual, eccentric)

complicity-n connivance, conspiracy, collusion, confederacy, cooperate, concur, combine, understand, unite, (opposition, antagonism, counteract, against)

component-n integral part, constituent, ingredient, member, subdivision, radical, intrinsic, inherent, immanent, subsistent, essential, inwrought, innate, inbred, (extraneousness, whole)

compose-v make up, form, construct, fashion, constitute, assuage, calm, improvise, create, reception, (exclusion, omission, reject)

composed-adj serene, calm, unruffled, tranquil, collected, unexcitable

composition-n compounding, constitution, formation, construction, blend, mixture, texture, nature

comprehend-v conceive, grasp, understand, comprise, aware, cognizant, conscious, acquainted, (shallow, unknown, superficial, half-learned)

comprehensive-adj widespread, synoptic, inclusive, extensive, wholesale, full

compress-v condense, reduce, abridge, thicken, squeeze, compact, contract, reduction, lessening, shrinking, (extension, spread, obesity)

comprise-v embrace, embody, contain, comprehend, include, admission, inclusion, enclose, receive

compromise-n settlement, arrangement, adjustment, agreement, composition, commute, compound, arrange, imperil, hazard, jeopardize

compute-v reckon, count, estimate, evaluate, record, note, memorandum, archive, scroll, register, (obliterate, cancel, scratch, erase, trike

C

out)

concavity-*n* hollow, dip, depression, cavity, antrum, trough, furrow, depression, dip, hollow, (rejection, swelling, bulge, protrusion)

concealment-*n* masquerade, secretion, latency, cover, disguise, mask, camouflage, screen, veil, shroud, shelter, secrecy, privacy, secret

concede-*v* assent, yield, acknowledge, surrender, cede, confess, grant, admittance, ratification, acquiesce, (dissent, discordance, disagreement, discontent)

conceit-*n* egoism, epigram, quip, whim, fancy, pride, vanity, complacency, glorification, airs, self-satisfied, (modesty, humility, blushing, reserve, constraint)

conceive-*v* visualize, fancy, devise, realize, grasp, comprehend, form, produce, become pregnant

concentrate-*v* gather, collect, converge, focus, center, fix, assemble, core, nucleus, heart, centralize

concession-*n* permission, acknowledgement, admission, reduction, allowance, grant, gift

conciliate-*v* propitiate, reconcile, satisfy, disarm, placate, mollify, reason, call, inducement, consideration, (dissuade, remonstrate, warn, against, repel)

conciseness-*n* succinctness, brevity, terseness, abridgment, laconicism, condensation, compression

conclude-*v* arrange, finish, settle, terminate, infer, end, deduce, resolve

conclusive-*adj* unanswerable, convincing, indisputable, final, concluding, deduce

concoct-*v* make, hatch, invent, contrive, prepare, falsehood,

untruth, lying, perjury, misrepresentation, forgery, (veracity, sincerity, candor, truthful)

concord-*n* accord, symphony, agreement, harmony, consonance, unison, correspondence, amity, congruence, unanimity, alliance, conciliation

concrete-*adj* solid, definite, substantial, hard, exact, specific, adherence, together, aggregation, consolidation, tenacious, (non-adhesion, loose, relaxation)

condescend-*v* descend, deign, vouchsafe, stoop, humility, meek, submission, resignation, (dignified, stately, proud)

condiment-*n* seasoning, sauce, flavoring, relish, salt, mustard, pepper, spice, relish

condition-*n* stipulation, modification, proviso, situation, plight, fitness, assumption, postulate

condolence-*n* pity, sympathy, commiseration, compassion, consolation, comfort

conduct-*v* deportment, guise, behavior, carriage, comportment, demeanor, operate, work, manage, govern, regulate, supervise

confederate-*n* associate, ally, accomplice, companion, transient, passing, evanescent, fleeting, flying

confer-*v* deliberate, consult, discuss, converse, bestow, advise, consul, suggestion, prompt, recommend

confere-*n* consultation, interview, meeting, parley

confess-*v* acknowledge, admit, divulge, reveal, disclose, assent, accept, accede, concur, (dissent, demur, disagree, protest)

confident-*adj* certainty, trust, self-reliance, spirit, assurance,

confine-*v* restrain, imprison,
incarcerate, cage, bound,
enclosure, limit, inclose,
surround, imprisoned, buried

confirm-*v* endorse, uphold,
corroborate, substantiate,
warrant, vouch, certificate,
facts, record, docket, (disprove,
other side, oppose)

confiscate-*v* sequestrate, seize,
appropriate, taking, capture,
appropriation,catch, nab,
(return, restore, redeem)

conflict-*n* battle, combat,
encounter, discord, dissension,
antagonism, opposition,
counteract, antagonize,
(cooperate, concur, combine)

conformity-*n* agreement,
accord, harmony, resemblance,
congruity, compliance,
observance, acquiescence,
concession, submission,
consent

confound-*v* confuse, jumble,
overthrow, perplex, bewilder,
wonder, marvel, astonish,
admire, (expect, foreseen,
common)

confront-*v* brave, defy, front,
resist, fore, face, outpost,
pioneer, advance, (rear, guard,
stern, behind, after)

confuse-*v* muddle, disturb,
disconcert, fluster, bewilder,
mistake, deranged, mislay,
disorder, unsettle, (arrange,
preparation)

confusion-*n* embarrassment,
discomfiture, tumult, turmoil,
jumble, (dispose, place, pack,
file)

confutation-*n* disproval,
disproof, refutation, refutal,
invalidation, retort, answer,
(demonstrate, prove, establish)

congeal-*v* thicken, set,
condense, coagulate, stiffen,
harden, density, solidness,
mass, cake, (thin, fine,
tenuous, rarefy)

congenial-*adj* sympathetic,
harmonious, adapted,
compatible, agreement, accord,
adapt, fitness, harmonize,
(disagree, hostile, repugnant)

congratulation-*n* best wishes,
felicitation, compliment,
gratulation, condolence

congregation-*n* aggregation,
gathering, fold, flock, brethren,
assemblage, collection, muster,
(dispersed, broadcast, sprinkle)

congress-*n* parliament,
convention, legislature,
assembly, council, committee,
court, chamber, board, staff

conjecture-*n* speculation,
inference, surmise, supposition,
assumption, postulation,
condition

conjugate-*v* coupled, mated,
united, bijugate, paronymous,
verbal, literal, derivation, root,
(corruption, slang, cant)

connect-*v* attach, unite, link,
associate, correlate, relation,
reference, correlation,
similarity, (disconnection,
remote, irrelevant)

conquer-*v* vanquish, subdue,
defeat, overcome, prevail,
success, advance, conquest,
victory, (fail, repulse, rebuff,
defeat, overthrow, slip)

consanguinity-*n* kindred,
relationship, parentage,
paternity, connection,
propinquity, alliance, affiliation,
affinity

conscientious-*adj* scrupulous,
painstaking, exact, faithful,
trusty, upright, duty, obligation,
liability, (relaxation, failure,
evasion)

conscious-*adj* understanding,
aware, keen, sensible,
cognizant, senses, observation,
intuition, judgment, (imbecility,
brutality, without reason)

conscription-*n* impressment, compulsory, enlistment, draft, compel, force, make, drive, coerce

consecrate-*v* hallow, devote, dedicate, apply, utilization, work, yield, manipulate, (disuse, abstain, spare, neglect)

consent-*v* compliance, assent, acquiescence, concurrence, agreement, concession, permission, permit, accession, acknowledgement, (dissent, refusal)

consequence-*n* proceeding, outcome, result, decision, termination, settlement, prominence, self-importance

consequential-*adj* sequential, deducible, derivable, inferable, secondary, supercilious, resultant

consider-*v* regard, notice, heed, believe, adjudge, deliberate, reflect, ponder, (vacancy, thoughtless, absent)

considerable-*adj* extraordinary, intense, notable, weighty, big, massive, substantial

consideration-*n* regard, observation, notice, kindliness, consequence, inducement, deference, esteem, perquisite

consign-*v* delegate, assign, commit, authorize, send, deliver, dispatch, ship, allotment, assignment, charge, task, apportionment

consistent-*adj* compatible, harmonious, conformable, homogeneous, accordant, agreement, accommodate, conventional, (abnormity, infringement, irregular)

consolation-*n* comfort, solace, assuagement, sympathy, encouragement, relief, softening, alleviation, restorative, (aggravated, exasperation, embitter)

consolidate-*v* incorporate, federate, merge, solidify, compact, coherence, adhere, hold fast, tenacity, (looseness, relaxation, freedom, disjunction)

consonance-*n* accordance, tunefulness, concord, harmony, accord

conspicuous-*adj* prominent, famous, renowned, eminent, notable, obvious, glaring, salient, (invisible, concealment, obscure)

conspirator-*n* plotter, accomplice, confederate, traitor, combine, scheme, concur, intrigue, plot

constant-*adj* incessant, unflagging, continual, steadfast, stanch, loyal, agree, uniform, level, smooth, (diversify, varied, uneven)

constitute-*v* establish, set up, found, appoint, form, frame, compose, (exclusion, rejection, omission, separate)

constitution-*n* structure, construction, state, condition, code, law, charter, temperament, disposition, nature

constraint-*n* necessity, coercion, repression, unnaturalness, bind, contract, squeeze, compress

construction-*n* formation, structure build, explanation, translation, erection, creation

consultation-*n* interview, deliberation, conference, council

consume-*v* annihilate, burn, demolish, devour, use up, exhaust, drain, expend, destruction, ruin, downfall, (fabricate, produce, performance, achievement)

consummate-*v* unmitigate, sheer, perfect, finished, profound, intense, complete, fill, replenish, (deficiency, wanting, defective)

contact-*n* meeting, union, conjunction, adhesion, contiguity, proximity, apposition, abutment, touch, adhere, attach, append, adjoin, (interval, distance)

contagion-*n* pestilence, epidemic, transmission, virus, communication, poisonousness, toxicity

contagious-*adj* transmittable, communicable, catching

contain-*v* comprise, embody, include, incorporate, hold, portion, segment, fragment, parcel

container-*n* vessel, utensil, vase, jar, bag, bottle

contaminate-*v* pollute, taint, corrupt, foul, defile, uncleanliness, impurity, decay, filth, dregs, (clean, launder, wipe, mop, disinfect)

contemplate-*v* consider, design, ponder, purpose, reflect, muse, view, sight, glimpse, behold, discover, (blindness, undiscerning)

contempt-*n* scorn, disdain, detestation, abhorrence, despise, disrepute, insignificant, immaterial, trivial, (important, prominence, concern, superior)

contemptuous-*adj* derision, mockery, sneer, spurn, abhor, underestimate (respect, reverence)

contend-*v* hold, maintain, allege, strive, struggle, debate, dispute, reasoning, argument, proposition, (chicane, mystification)

content-*n* real meaning, significance, intent, implication, substance, essence, gist, volume, extent

contention-*n* altercation, struggle, strife, feud, contest, litigation, disagreement, debate, dispute, belligerency

contents-*n* constituents, ingredients, cargo, filling, matter

contingency-*n* prospect, likelihood, situation, case, predicament, incidental, casual, provisional, conditional, accidental

continual-*adj* incessant, repeated, constant, unceasing, perpetuity

continuance-*n* pursuance, maintenance, extension, permanence, duration, perpetuation, stay

contortion-*n* deformation, twist, distortion, crookedness, warp, irregular, unsymmetrical, misshapen, ill-proportioned, stumpy, (symmetrical, shapely, regular, uniform)

contour-*n* form, outline, shape, figure, circumference, parameter, zone, belt

contraband-*n* forbidden, illegal, smuggled, illicit, deception, deceit, juggle, cheat, hoax, decoy, waylay

contract-*n* arrangement, bargain, compact, promise, guarantee, promissory, pledge, (release, absolute, unconditional)

contradict-*v* deny, dissent, refute, disprove, gainsay, (identical, equivalent, the same)

contrariety-*n* antagonism, opposition, repugnance, clashing, disagreement, antipathy, discrepancy, inconsistency, contrast

contrary-*adj* opposed, adverse, opposite, antagonistic, hostile, perverse

contrast-*v* dissimilarity, unlikeness, disparity, antithesis, foil

contribute-*v* conduce, tend, advance, subscribe, donate, giving, consignment, charity, generosity, (acquisition, acceptance, admission)

contrivance-*n* gear, device, apparatus, scheme, trick, stratagem

control-*v* dominion, power, sway, direction, regulation, might, force,energy, pressure, strength, ability, (disability, helplessness)

controversy-*n* dispute, argument, debate, quarrel, altercation, contention, reasoning, discussion, comment, (evasion, quibble, pervert, mystify)

conundrum-*n* puzzle, riddle, enigma, secret, maze, profound, labyrinth, paradox, (information, intelligence, advice, report)

convalesce-*v* recover, rally, improve, revive, restoration, renovation, resume, cure, heal, remedy, (relapse, retrogradation, return)

convenient-*adj* serviceable, suitable, opportune, advantageous, adaptable, expedient, eligible, seemly, becoming, (unfit, undesirable)

convention-*n* caucus, meeting, council, assembly, usage, custom, practice

conventional-*adj* habitual, customary, formal, usual, common, general, familiar, regular, vernacular, (infraction, disuse, violate, infringe)

convergence-*n* confluence, concurrence, concentration, concourse, focalization, meeting, assemblage

conversion-*n* transmutation, change, transformation, metamorphosis, growth, regeneration, assimilation

convey-*v* transport, carry, bear, grant, cede, will, transfer, deportation, carriage, delegate, consign

convict-*v* find guilty, doom, prisoner, captive, criminal, rascal, scoundrel, villain, ruffian, jail-bird, (good man, hero, angel, saint)

conviction-*v* view, opinion, sentence, penalty, belief, credence, faith, assume, esteem, (unbelieving, doubtful, misgiving)

convince-*v* satisfy, assure, convert, persuade, belief, faith, confidence, reliance, certainty, (doubtful, fallible, suspicious)

convoke-*v* collect, muster, gather, convene, summon, assemblage, crowd, throng, mob, hoard, (disperse, scatter, diffuse)

convoy-*v* escort, attend, conduct, guard, watch, support, accompany, custody, safety, security, surety, (insecurity, jeopardy, risk, hazard)

convulse-*v* stir, shake, disturb, rend, wring, pain, suffering, aching, spasm, piercing, sharp, (pleasure, sensual, comfort, luxury)

cool-*adj* wary, unfriendly, self-possessed, chilly, lukewarm, easygoing, placid, compose, calm, freeze, chill, harden

cooperation-*n* combination, joint operation, union, participation, concert, collaboration

coordinate-*n* organize, adjust, harmonize, arrange, preparation, assortment, allotment, catalog, tabulate, (dislocate, disarrange, break up)

copious-*adj* plentiful, full, abundant, profuse, ample, sufficiency, adequacy, enough, fullness, (incompetence, deficiency, poverty)

copy-*n* counterpart, effigy, facsimile, likeness, similitude, semblance, imitation, model, representation, study

cord-*n* string, twine, rope, bond, tie, fastening, shackle, rein, rivet, padlock, anchor

cordial-*adj* hearty, friendly,

genial, warm, sincere,
pleasure, sensual, comfort,
luxury, enjoy, (torment,
anguish, agony)

core-*n* nucleus, kernel, heart,
gist, pith, substance, center,
middle, axis, concentric

corner-*n* niche, nook,
monopolize, control, spot,
point, premises, place, pigeon
hole, compartment

corpse-*n* carcass, dead body,
skeleton, remains, cadaver,
carrion, bones, relic, mummy,
fossil

corpulence-*n* fleshiness,
portliness, obesity, fatness,
bulk, greatness, expanse,
large, big, ample, (small,
pygmy, minute, undersized)

correct-*v* reprove, punish,
chastise, remedy, mend,
discipline, rectify, repair, set
right, strict, accurate, true,
perfect, unerring

correlation-*n* reciprocity,
interdependence, mutuality,
correspondence, comparison,
relative, cognate, (irrelative,
irrespective, arbitrary)

correspondence-*n* letters,
writings, epistle, news,
dispatch, bulletin, accordance,
agreement

corrigible-*adj* tractable,
amenable, submissive, docile,
improvement, better, increase,
ripen, mature, (worse,
deteriorate, degenerate)

corrode-*v* rust, decay, wear,
waste, deteriorate, (improve,
elaborate, promote, cultivate,
advance)

corrupt-*adj* base, dishonest,
tainted, rotten, spoiled,
profligate, dissolute, immoral,
infect, taint, pervert, debase

cost-*n* expense, charge, outlay,
disbursement, expenditure,
expensive, dear, high-priced,
(discount, reduction, allowance,
rebate)

council-*n* committee, court,
chapter, chamber, board,
directorate, syndicate, cabinet,
staff, parliament, (precept,
direction, charge)

count-*v* estimate, consider,
figure, reckon, compute,
enumerate, numbering,
calculation, recite

countenance-*n* expression,
aspect, visage, features,
patronage, favor, front,
foreground, advance, (behind,
rear, stern, run)

counterfeit-*v* fictitious, bogus,
spurious, fake, imitation, false,
copy, duplication, mirror,
reproduce, (original,
unimitated)

counterpart-*n* duplicate,
complement, facsimile, replica,
match, mate, similarity
likeness, affinity

countersign-*v* watchword,
authentication, seal, password,
identification, secondary
evidence, corroboration,
(unattested, unauthenticated)

countless-*adj* innumerable,
uncalculable, numberless,
illimitable, infinite, immense,
immeasurable

country-*n* nation, state, power,
home, territory, district, rural
regions, field, meadow, garden,
ornamental

couple-*n* join, pair, yoke, link,
tie, mate, firm, fast, taut, taught,
secure, set, intervolved,
(sunder, divide, disjoin, dissect,
cut up, carve)

courage-*n* bravery, valor,
fearlessness, hart,
resoluteness, daring, spirit,
boldness, dash, gallantry,
heroism, mettle, nerve, grit,
fortitude, resolution

courier-*n* messenger, runner,
traveler, envoy, emissary,
reporter, informer,
correspondent

course-*n* procedure, path,

behavior, succession, channel, drift, trend, progress, flight, routine, (await, loom, predestine, doom)

court-*n* palace, castle, staff, retinue, train, bar, session, bench, make love, woo, cajole, invite, solicit, praise, (forbearance, refraining, avoidance, evasion, elusion)

courtesy-*n* politeness, refinement, cultivation, gentility, urbanity, culture, elegance, civility, polish, (discourtesy, repulsive, disrespect, impudent)

courtship-*n* suit, courting, wooing, flirtation, endearment, caress, fondling, embrace, salute, kiss, amorous, (glum, morose, frumpish, surly)

cove-*n* inlet, bay, harbor, lagoon, gulf, concavity, depression, dip, hollow indentation, cavity, dent, pit, basin, (convexity, prominence, projection, swelling)

covenant-*n* agreement, pact, compact, bargain, agree, stipulate, undertake, observe, comply, perform, (fail, neglect, omit, elude, evade, ignore, infringe)

covering-*n* screen, shield, shelter, protection, carapace, concealment, seclusion, hide, mystification, (uncover, inform, enlighten, open)

covet-*v* want, crave, envy, long for, desire, wish, greedy, hunger, hanker, solicitude, anxiety, yearning, aspiration, (cold, frigid, lukewarm, careless, listless)

cowardice-*n* graveness, pusillanimity, timidity, timorousness, baseness, effeminacy, abject feat, faintheartedness

cower-*v* shrink, crouch, quail, fawn, grovel, fear, timidity, diffidence, apprehensive,

solicitude, anxiety, misgiving, (trust, confidence, reliance, faith)

coy-*adj* demure, retiring, shrinking, shy, tremble, shake, shudder, nervous, restless, despondent, (hope, trust, aggressive, outspoken, forward)

crabbed-*adj* tempered, surly, cross, perverse, peevish, illegible, intricate, squeezed

crack-*v* burst, break, split, seam, rut, cleft, rip, fissure, sunder, divide, separate, disjoin, isolate, abscind, (attach, fix, join, unite, connect, hold, bind)

craft-*n* handicraft, trade, artfulness, trickery, deceit, vessel, boat, expertness, art, skill, dexterity, adroitness, competence, (quackery, folly, stupidity, indiscretion)

cram-*v* crowd, jam, stuff, choke, guzzle, gorge, assemble, muster, group, cluster, pack, bunch, (disperse, disjunction, scatter, sow, spread)

cramp-*n* hamper, restrain, handicap, paralyze, cripple, incapacitate, contract, reduce, diminish, (expand, extend, augment, develop, swell)

crass-*adj* stupid, raw, elude, gross, ignorant, incomprehension, simplicity, shallow, superficial, green, (instructed, learned, educate, enlightened)

crave-*v* yearn form, long form, beseech, ask, beg, pray, desire, petition, ravening, hungry, famished, desirous

crawl-*v* grovel, fawn, cower, drag, lag, lumber, creep, saunter, plod, trudge, moderate, slow, (speed, scuttle, gallop, rush, velocity)

crazy-*adj* mad, lunatic, sick, crack-brained, shaky, fanaticism, oddity, eccentricity, twist, insane, crazed, frantic, raving, (sanity, soundness, rationality, lucidity)

create-*v* make, originate, form, bring into being, occasion, devise, conceive, invent, breed, propagate, envisage

creation-*n* invention, conception, causation, origination, formation, constitution, cosmos, universe

creator-*n* originator, maker, author, producer, god, supreme being

creature-*n* lower animal, beast, individual, mortal, dependent, slave, being, thing, something, matter, substantial, (nonentity, shadow, phantom, nothing, naught)

credence-*n* reliance, trust, assurance, acceptance, acknowledgement, credit, faith, dependence, (uncertain, doubtful, incredulous)

credibility-*n* belief, believable, trustworthiness, honesty, faith, trust, confidence, reliance, repute, honor, merit, esteem, prestige

credulity-*n* gullibility, infatuation, self delusion, self deception, naivete, silly, stupid, infatuated, simple, (incredulous, skeptical, suspicious, distrustful)

creed-*n* dogma, faith, doctrine, belief, firm, implicit, persuasion, articles, canons, catechism, (doubt, distrust, disputable, unworthy)

crest-*n* culmination, tip, height, top, plume, seal, device, ridge, summit, vertex, apex, zenith, pinnacle, (base, bottom, nadir, foot, fundamental)

crew-*n* mob, company, gang, throng, sailors, squad, crowd, horde, body, tribe, party, clan, brotherhood, (adrift, stray, dishevelled, steaming, scatter)

cringe-*v* flinch, shrink, wince, fawn, grovel, submit, yield, non-resistance, obedience, surrender, succumb, parasite, bow, stoop, servile, supple, (bully, dictate)

cripple-*n* disable, hurt, incapacitate, enfeeble, helpless, prostration, paralysis, palsy, apoplexy, exhaustion, (potent, capable, virtue, qualification)

crisis-*n* emergency, trial, extremity, exigency, crux, full of incident, eventful, stirring, bustling, (loom, await, eventually, forthcoming)

criterion-*n* standard, norm, measure, test, rule, conformation, support, ratification, corroboration, authentication, (oppose, unauthenticated, non-conformity)

critical-*adj* disparaging, faultfinding, judicious, analytical, crucial, turning point, reprove, flay, censure, examine, analyze, judge

crooked-*adj* deceptive, fraudulent, sneaking, warped, awry, twisted, askew, distorted, (symmetrical, shapely, finished, beautiful)

cross-*n* intersection, traversing, decussation, hybridization, passage, entwine, weave, twist, wreathe, dovetail

crouch-*v* bend, stoop, fawn, cower, cringe, low, neap, debased, underlie, slouch, wallow, grovel, depress, (tower, pillar, dome, height, elevate)

crown-*n* diadem, coronet, crest, top, reward, garland, prize, accredit, empower, commission, represent, (dismiss, cancel, repeal)

crucial-*adj* decisive, final, determining, supreme, demonstrate, prove, establish, show, verify, (refute, disprove, expose, rebut)

crude-*adj* unfinished, vulgar, raw, rude, uncouth,

unprepared, unwrought,
incomplete

cruel-*adj* savage, inhuman,
unkind, barbarous, brutal,
merciless, ruthless

crumble-*v* perish, break up, fall
to pieces, decay, degenerate,
deteriorate

crush-*v* press, squeeze,
suppress, overwhelm,
disconcert, shame, bruise

crust-*n* coating, coat, hull, shell,
rind, cover, canopy, bandage,
veneer, inunction, incrustation,
conceal, (uncover, expose)

cry-*v* clamor, shout, outcry,
ejaculation, utterance,
vociferation, call, shriek, howl,
scream, screech, sob, weeping,
lamentation, plaint, whimper

cue-*n* password, catchword, hint,
intimation, inform, acquaint,
communicate, present,
specification, (disguise, screen,
mystify, seclusion)

culprit-*n* offender, victim,
criminal, felon, evildoer, rough,
rowdy, ruffian, bully, hangman,
incendiary, criminal, (model,
paragon, hero, demigod,
innocent, benefactor)

cultivate-*v* develop, work, foster,
till, advance, farm, gardening,
husbandry, agriculture

cultivation-*n* refinement,
breeding, civilization, learning,
education, tillage, agriculture,
husbandry, improvement

cumbersome-*adj* ponderous,
burdensome, unwieldy,
oppressive, clumsy, awkward,
lumbering, bulky,
unmanageable, (expedient,
convenient, suitable)

cunning-*adj* subtlety, deceit,
craftiness, chicanery,
circumvention, guile, knavery,
maneuvering, skill, dexterity

cup-*n* glass, mug, goblet, hollow,
excavation, chalice, tumbler,
tankard, jug

curb-*n* restrain, control, check,

repress, slacken, retard,
confine, duress, custody,
restrict, (liberate, free, unfetter,
untie, loosen, relax)

curiosity-*n* research,
inquisitiveness, thirst for
knowledge, inquiring mind,
interest, (uninterested,
indifferent, impassive)

current-*adj* common, instant,
prevalent, circulating, glow,
stream, draft, existing, present,
actual, present time, (any time,
sometime)

curse-*n* denounce, damn,
swear, blaspheme, bane,
imprecation, anathema, hurtful,
sting, painful, bane, scourge,
(remedy, help, redress,
sedative)

curt-*adj* blunt, brusque, rude,
abrupt, brief, short, succinct,
concise, brevity, abbreviate,
compress, compact, (lengthy,
endlong, interminable

curtail-*v* lessen, reduce,
abridge, abbreviate, cut,
retrench, mutilate, amputate,
abscind, thin, prune, (add,
annex, reinforce, supplement)

curtain-*n* veil, screen, hanging,
blind, drapery conceal, hide,
masquerade, hiding place,
reserve, (mention, acquaint,
informant, outpouring)

custody-*n* imprisonment, care,
bondage, charge, protection,
keeping, confinement, durance,
duress, arrest, (liberate, free,
redemption, acquittal)

custom-*n* rule, fashion,
precedent, practice, patronage,
trade, usage, regular, usual,
habitual, normal

cut-*v* divide, split, sever, shape,
reap, gather, separate, part,
detach, divorce, rupture,
(attach, fix, firm, fast, join,
unite)

cynical-*adj* sardonic, surly,
satirical, contemptuous,
misanthropic, disdainful

D

dabble-*v* trifle, potter, moisten, paddle, splash, dilute, immerse, wash, sprinkle, drench

dagger-*n* stiletto, knife, poniard, sword, weapon, armament, saber, resentment, displeasure, animosity, wrath

dainty-*adj* exquisite, pretty, delicate, particular, meticulous, delicious, appetizing, tasty, attractive, lovely, (annoying, nuisance, infestation, molestation)

dally-*v* philander, flirt, dawdle, prolong, idle, protract, delay, suspend, waive, retard, postpone, procrastinate, (prompt, immediate, haste, sudden)

damage-*n* injure, impair, harm, mutilate, hurt, deteriorate, wane, degenerate, decay, injury, loss, (fructify, ripen, mature, promote)

damp-*adj* humid, moist, foggy, watery, moisture, wet, dank, infiltrate, muggy, drench, dewy, (dry, arid, drought)

dance-*v* prance, glide, move, flutter, perform, party, ball, cotillion, hop, jump, oscillate, agitate, pulsate, effervescence

danger-*n* jeopardy, hazard, peril, risk, insecurity, precariousness, venture, instability, exposure, (safe, secure, impregnability, invulnerability)

dangle-*v* wave, hang, swing, be suspended, droop, sling, pendulum, depend, pensive, loose, flowing, (support, ad, prop, stand, anvil, stay)

dare-*v* challenge, venture, brave, face, defiance, threat, defy, bluster, (agree, accord, sympathize)

darkness-*n* blackness, murk, swarthiness, obscurity, duskiness, gloominess, dimness, dinginess, lightless, opacity, tenebrous

dart-*n* throw, hurl, direct, spurt, shoot, scud, propel, project, fling, cast, pitch, chuck, toss, (pull, haul, draw, lug, rake, drag, tow, trail, train)

dash-*v* break, crush, shatter, depress, discourage, frustrate, imbue, blend, speed, rush, sprint, mark, stroke, line, trace, hint, tinge, grain

daunt-*v* frighten, alarm, cow, discourage, fear, timid, anxiety, solicitude, care, apprehension, (courage, bravery, valor, spirit)

daze-*v* bewilder, dazzle, stupefy, blind, spark, flash, blaze, scintillation, shine, glow, glitter, twinkle, brighten, (dark, obscurity, gloom, dusk, extinction)

dazzle-*v* impress, confound, bedazzle, awe, refraction, distortion, illusion, false light

dead-*adj* lifeless, deceased, defunct, departed, late, inanimate, extinct, fatal, mortal, destructive, murderous

deaden-*v* incapacitate, muffle, paralyze, numb, subdue, invalid, prostration, exhaustion, impotent, (potency, ability, elasticity, magnetism)

deal-*v* allot, distribute, dispense, inflict, give, deliver, administer, arrange, allotment, sort, classify, (derangement, disorder, disorganize)

dearness-*n* expensiveness, high price, costliness, overcharge, extravagance, sumptuous, valuable, (cheapness, dislike, hate, loathe)

debar-*v* hinder, forbid, check, obstruct, exclude, deny, prohibit, bar, stile, barrier, restraint, prevent, impediment, obstacle, (aid, assistance, promote, reinforce)

debase-*v* deprave, degrade, depreciate, lower, dishonor, disgrace, deterioration, degradation, corruption, adulteration

debate-*v* discussion, argument, controversy, contention, conversation, oral communication, reasoning, comment, (answer, response, reply, replication)

debt-*n* liability, debit, obligation, claim, due, deferred payment, deficit, insolvency, (credit, trustworthiness, reliability, reputation)

decay-*v* putrefy, crumble, rot, wither, fall to pieces, decompose, pare, reduce, attenuate, scrape, render, smaller, (expand, spread, extend, overgrown)

decease-*v* demise, dying, departure, passing, death, dissolution, release, rest, extinction, bereavement, (respiration, vitality, animation, subsist)

deceit-*n* falsehood, sham, fraud, treachery, trickery, double dealing, perversion, hollowness, quackery, prevarication, (truthful, veracious, scrupulous)

decent-*adj* ordinary, clean, virtuous, passable, modest, pure, indifferent, middling, mediocre, average, tolerable, (unparalleled, superhuman)

deception-*n* insidiousness, duplicity, deceit, wiliness, sophistry, cunning, dissimulation, falsehood, imposition, misrepresentation, bluff, chicanery, treachery, (veracity, frankness, truth, honesty, sincerity)

decide-*v* resolve, settle, determine, choose, decree, arbitrate, fix upon, judge, result, conclusion, valuation, (misjudge, bias, warped, partiality)

decipher-*v* translate, decode, discover, explain, make out, interpret, definition, explanation, solution, answer, (misrepresent, misinterpret, distort)

decision-*n* resolve, decree, verdict, firmness, will, purpose, judgment, result, conclusion, deduction

declaration-*n* proclamation, avowal, announcement, bulletin, assertion, notice, profess, acknowledge, state

decline-*v* waste, age, die, decay, refuse, repel, shun, spurn, slope, declivity, descent

decomposition-*n* dissolution, break-up, disjunction, disintegration, cariosity, putrefaction, putridity, (cleanliness, combination)

decoration-*n* embellishment, trimming, adornment, ribbon, laurel, medal, ornament, wreath, festoon, (simplicity, plain, homely, unaffected, chaste)

decoy-*n* lure, inveigle, entice, entrap, ensnare, deception, falseness, untruth, fraud, deceit, guile

decrease-*v* diminution, lessening, mitigation, reduction, abatement, shrinkage, contraction, shorten, abbreviate, (increase, augmentation, addition, accumulation)

decree-*n* ordinance, edict, mandate, verdict, decision, regulation, command, order

decrement-*n* diminution, decrease, deduction, attenuation, abatement, waste, loss, (addition, adjunct)

decry-*v* disparage, slander, belittle, underestimate, censure, degrade, depreciation, undervaluing, modesty, (overestimating, exaggeration, vanity)

dedicate-*v* devote, offer, consecrate, inscribe, mark, name, figure, repute, enthrone, celebrate, glorify, (disrepute, discredit, disgrace, stain)

deduction-*n* curtailment, subtraction, removal, excision, abstraction, consequence, implication, derivation, corollary, discount, allowance, (addition, attach, join, interpose, append)

deed-*n* feat, exploit, action, performance, document, evidence, confirmation, warrant, credential, admission, (vindication, counter-protest, oppose, rebut, countervail)

deep-*adj* bottomless, profound, unfathomable, abstruse, astute, designing, cunning, concavity, submerged, (shallow, superficial)

deface-*v* mutilate, distort, injure, disfigure, mar, blemish, deteriorate, shapeless, formless, deform, (conformation, formation, build, trim, fashion)

defame-*v* slander, abuse, disparage, revile, taint, smirch, sully, disrepute, discredit, shame, disgrace, (regard, respect, dignity, splendor)

defeat-*v* vanquish, subdue, conquer, refute, rebut, silence, overcome, failure, abortion, inefficacy, ineffectual, (success, advancement, good fortune, prosperity)

defect-*n* flaw, fault, lack, deficiency, imperfection, weakness, shortcoming, error, failing, blemish, deficient, unsound

defense-*n* security, guard, protection, preservation, resistance, vindication, support, advocacy, plea, espousal, fortification, entrenchment, palisade, (attack, aggression, encroachment, offense, onslaught, assail)

defenseless-*adj* unshielded, powerless, unarmed, helpless, exposed, (strength, adamant, resistless, invincible)

defensible-*adj* impregnable, invulnerable, supportable, maintainable, excusable, justifiable

defer-*v* retard, postpone, delay, procrastinate, adjourn, yield, comply, give in, capitulate

defiance-*n* challenge, threat, provocation, opposition, disobedience, insurgency, rebellion, insubordination, revolt, (obedience, submission)

deficient-*adj* lacking, short, wanting, insufficient, inadequate, shortcoming, inferior, minority, small, subordinate, (superior, supreme, great, advantageous)

define-*v* construe, expound, explain, bound, limit, circumscribe, description, meaning, distinct

definite-*adj* clear, plain, positive, specific, particular, limited, precise, concrete, certain, surety, (doubtful, uncertain, vague, fallibility)

deflect-*v* curve, bend, turn, swerve, diverge, deviation, stray, introvert, divert, digress, departure, (set, undeviating, straight, directly)

deformity-*n* misproportion, disfigurement, ugliness, crookedness, malformation, distortion, (symmetrical, shapely, beautiful, parallel, uniform)

defraud-*v* swindle, hoax, trick, dupe, cheat, deceive, untruth, fraud, guile, misrepresentation, chicane, (truthful, frankness, sincerity, honesty)

defray-*v* settle, meet, liquidate, discharge, pay, acknowledgement, release,

D

receipt, repayment,
satisfaction, reimbursement,
(non-payment, default,
repudiation)

defy-v face, confront, brave,
oppose, challenge, threaten,
dare, defiance, disobey

degrade-v shame, disgrace,
humiliate, dishonor, fall,
abasement, deteriorate,
despicable, unbecoming,
scandalous, (dignity,
stateliness, splendor, noble)

degree-n gradation, grade, step,
extent, measure, point, amount,
mark, rate, standard, height,
range, scope intensity,
strength, (quantity),
instantaneity)

deify-v idolize, venerate,
canonize, immortalize, exalt,
repute, distinction, dedication,
consecration, enthronement,
celebration, (dishonor,
shameful, stain, disgrace)

deity-n omnipotence, god,
omniscience, providence,
supreme being, creator,
almighty, hold, preserve, atone,
redeem

dejection-n despondency,
melancholy, depression,
pessimism, despair, sorrow,
sadness, grief, dolefulness,
distress, weariness,
(cheerfulness, happy, geniality,
gaiety)

delay-v retard, obstruct, linger,
defer, impede, postpone,
procrastinate, put off, adjourn,
late, tardy, belated,
(immediately, briefly, shortly,
quickly)

delectable-adj pleasant,
delightful, tasty, delicious,
pleasurable, savory, relish,
delicacy, appetizing, zestful,
(acrid, repulsive, nasty,
sickening, nauseous)

delegate-v substitute, envoy,
agent, proxy, assign, consign,
entrust, authorize, empower,

commission, assignment,
deputation, (annulment,
nullification, cancel)

delete-v cancel, expunge, erase,
obliterate, efface, (record, note,
register, endorse, memo)

deliberate-v meditate, reflect,
reason, ponder, well-
considered, gradual, voluntary,
leisurely

deliberation-n coolness,
caution, prudence,
deliberateness, slowness,
discretion, prudence,
calculation, foresight,
(impetuous, levity, imprudence,
presumption, audacity)

delicacy-n daintiness, luxury,
elegance, tidbit, discrimination,
tact, culture, sensitiveness,
frailty, infirmity, savory,
palatable, ambrosia

delicious-adj delectable, dainty,
pleasing, luscious, palatable,
tasty, relish, good, ambrosia,
zest, appetizing, sweet,
nectarous, (offensive,
repulsive, nasty, nauseous)

delight-n please, gratify, charm,
enchant, enjoy, pleasure,
fruition, satisfaction, happiness,
rapture, ecstasy, (annoyance,
irritation, worry, plague)

delineate-v block, depict, sketch,
portray, set forth, illustrate,
represent, imitate, sculpture,
engrave, design, draft, trace,
(distort, exaggerate, daub,
scratch)

delinquent-adj derelict, remiss,
neglectful, rough, rowdy,
ruffian, bully, incendiary, thief,
murderer, criminal, (model,
paragon, hero, innocent,
benefactor)

delirious-adj crazed, raving,
mad, insane, light-headed,
lunacy, eccentricity, maniacal,
reasonless, demented, (sanity,
soundness, rationality, sobriety,
lucidity)

deliverance-n liberation,

release, rescue, reprieve, extrication, emancipation, redemption, salvation, (restraint, retention)

delude-*v* dupe, bluff, trick, fool, hoodwink, deceive, false impression, deception, hallucination, fault, blunder, (fact, reality, accuracy, delicacy, rigor)

deluge-*v* downpour, flood, inundation, rainstorm, supersaturate, excessive, superabundant, overflowing, (insufficient, meager, paltry, empty)

delusion-*n* illusion, magic, fallacy, misconception, hallucination, conjuring, infatuation, oddity, (sane, rational, reasonable)

demand-*v* order, impose, ask, exact, question, require, claim, requisition, request, market, ultimatum

demolish-*v* devastate, ruin, overthrow, wreck, crush, explode, invalidate, defeat, (establish, prove, make good, verify)

demonic-*adj* devilish, hellish, possessed, fiendish, vampire, ghoul, fiend, supernatural, weird, unearthly, haunted

demonstration-*n* verification, proof, substantiation, conclusiveness, testimony, exhibition, mass-meeting, (confutation, refute)

demoralize-*v* incapacitate, unnerve, undermine, corrupt, deprave, pervert, render powerless, disqualify, (powerful, puissant, potent, capable)

demur-*v* protest, cavil, object, wrangle, scruple, remonstrance, disbelieve, dissent, unwilling, hesitate, (determination, resolve, vigor, resoluteness)

demure-*v* precise, priggish,

solemn, sad, sedate, shy, bashful, retiring, modesty, reserve, constraint, blushing, (vain, pretentious, conceit, selfishness)

den-*n* sanctum, cave, lair, study, retreat, cell, abode, dwelling, lodging, domicile, residence, habitation

denial-*n* repudiation, negation, contradiction, disallowance, disbelief, disavowal, protest, recusancy, (affirmance, declaration, oath, assurance)

denomination-*n* persuasion, designation, name, side, specification, kind, sect, class, division, category, province, domain

denote-*v* betoken, signify, represent, express, imply, convey, designate, specify, indication, feature, type, characteristic

denounce-*v* arraign, charge, censure, rebuke, blame, curse, damn, accuse, reprehend, chide, admonish, disapprove, (approval, approbation, advocacy, esteem)

density-*n* solidness, body, compactness, thickness, impenetrability, impermeability, coherence, ignorance, crassness, ineptitude, opacity, dullness, obtuseness, (intelligence, rarity)

dent-*n* depression, hollow, indentation, cavity, concavity, dip, cavernous, excavate, burrow, tunnel, (convex, project, swelling, bilge, bulge, protrusion)

denunciation-*n* defiance, condemnation, curse, arraignment, imprecation

deny-*v* differ, protest, contradict, reject, doubt, discredit, dissent, discontent, disagreement, non-conformity, (assent, acquiescence, admission, unanimity)

D

department-*n* jurisdiction, bureau, office, division, part, function, capacity, sphere, orb, field, line, walk, routine

departure-*n* embarkation, start, exit, leaving, egress, parting, withdraw, adieu, farewell, removal, (return, remigration, arrive)

depend-*v* trust, credit, rely, hang, be contingent, uncertain, casual, doubtful, dubious, vague, hesitant, (positive, absolute, definite, decisive, without question)

depict-*v* delineate, portray, represent, picture, describe, mimic, illustrative, imitate, figurative, (distort, exaggerate, misrepresent, daub)

deplore-*v* bewail, lament, regret, mourn, complain, grievous, sad, pitiable, repine, (content, satisfaction, ease, cheerfulness)

deport-*v* banish, transport, exile, remove, send, transit, displace, drift, bring, fetch, transpose

deposit-*v* installment, pledge, payment, alluvium, place, situate, locate, settlement, establish, (displace, eject, removal, unload)

deposition-*n* sworn, evidence, affidavit, allegation, dethronement, expulsion, archive, docket, certificate, (efface, obliterate, erase, cancel)

depository-*n* warehouse, storehouse, vault, store, repository, conservatory, closet, reservoir, cistern

depravity-*n* badness, corruption, perversion, degeneracy, wickedness, impairment, injury, damage, loss, wrong, aggrieve, annoyance, (improvement, amendment, reform, revision)

depreciation-*n* remonstrance, disapprobation, protest, disapproval, mediation,

expostulation, intercession

depreciate-*v* lessen, fall, drop, slight, undervalue, underrate, disparage, slander, affront

depression-*n* sinking, cavity, hollow, dip, diminution, humiliation, abasement, subversion, melancholy, dispiritedness, gloom, despondency, sadness, (cheerfulness, elevation)

deprive-*v* bereave, strip, dispossess, despoil, rob, clutch, capture, distress, divestment, extortion, eviction, (restitution, replevin, redemption, atonement)

depth-*n* profoundness, extent, profundity, intensity, completeness, abundance, (shallowness, veneer, superficiality)

deputy-*n* substitute, proxy, surrogate, delegate, agent, representative, alternate

derangement-*n* discomposure, disorder, confusion, embarrassment, mess, tangle, inversion, mania, insanity, madness, (sanity, arrangement)

dereliction-*n* abandonment, relinquishment, neglect, omission, desertion, failure, fault, evasion, (duty, respect, homage)

deride-*v* disdain, scorn, jeer, mock, ridicule, irruption, snigger, satirize, parody, travesty

derive-*v* secure, get, gain, account for, deduce, infer, etymologize, trace, estimation, valuation, appreciation, assessment, (discover, find, determine, evolve)

derogatory-*adj* scandalous, unbefitting, ignoble, discreditable, disrepute, degrade, dishonor, expel, disgrace, (distinct, repute, dignity, rank, standing)

descend-*v* dismount, slide, go

down, tumble, detail, special,
particular, specific, proper
descent-*n* drop, plunge, fall,
declination, comedown,
gravitate, decline, sink, spring,
issue, (ascent, ascension,
rising, originate, upgrowth)
description-*n* statement,
account, record, report,
summary, outline, depiction,
representation
desert-*n* waste, wilderness,
forsake, abandon, leave, run
away, worth, due, recompense,
meed
deserter-*n* fugitive, truant,
runaway, apostate, changeful,
reactionary, apostatize,
(arbitrary, dogmatic, positive,
uninfluenced)
design-*v* arrangement, make-up,
depiction, drawing, aim, intent,
project, pattern, model
designate-*v* show, specify,
indicate, name, call,
particularize, individualize,
special, proper, detail, definite,
(general, prevail, generic,
collective, broad)
desire-*v* inclination, fancy, wish,
whim, propensity, fondness,
need, want, exigency, urgency,
hunger, necessity, passion,
(dislike, indifference, satiety)
desist-*v* halt, discontinue, stop,
quit, cease, abstain, interrupt,
pause, rest, suspend,
(continue, persistence, sustain)
desolate-*adj* uninhabited,
deserted, waste, forlorn,
miserable, forsaken, lonely,
seclusion, solitude, isolation,
(sociality, visit, welcome,
hospitality)
despair-*n* dejection, misery,
despondency, wretchedness,
anguish, hopelessness,
desperate, relinquish, (hope,
trust, confidence, reliance,
faith)
desperate-*adj* wild, frantic,
frenzied, raging, reckless,

despairing, incurable,
impossible, impervious,
impassible, (practical, feasible,
compatible)
despise-*v* scorn, condemn,
disdain, disregard, hate,
disgust, contempt, derisive,
withering, pitiful, despicable
despond-*v* lament, mourn,
despair, falter, sink,
melancholy, sad, dejected,
depressed, heaviness, dismal,
demure, gravity, (cheerful,
geniality, gaiety, liveliness)
despotism-*n* imperialism,
tyranny, autocracy, oppression,
authority, influence, patronage,
power, prerogative, jurisdiction,
(anarchy, relaxation, remission,
abdication)
destination-*n* port, goal, halting
lace, point, mark, end, close,
termination, conclusion, finale,
consummation, (beginning,
commencement, opening,
outset)
destiny-*n* fortune, fate, lot,
fatalism, prospect, decree,
expectation, impending, future,
(eventuality, incident,
proceeding, advent)
destitute-*adj* poor, penniless,
lacking, bereft, needy,
deficiency, inadequate,
emptiness, poorness,
depletion, (sufficient, adequate,
enough, luxury)
destruction-*n* demolition,
ruination, dissolution,
devastation, cataclysm,
perdition, extermination,
annihilation, extirpation,
(preservation, production)
desultory-*adj* disconnected,
digressive, rambling, fitful,
aimless, erratic, broken,
spasmodic
detach-*v* disconnect, sever,
unfasten, loosen, separation,
segregation, portion, division,
squad, detail, (unite, join,
together, connect)

detail-*n* item, particular, feature, party, patrol, description, account, statement, report, summary, specification, delineation, representation

detain-*v* withhold, delay, retard, secure, retention, retain, detain, keep, custody, tenacity, grasp, gripe

detect-*v* discern, reveal, expose, unearth, perceive, discover, find, determine, evolve, fix upon, (result, conclusion, upshot, deduction)

deter-*v* discourage, hinder, restrain, hold back, dissuade, depreciation, dampen, deport, against, remonstrate, disincline, (induce, entice, allure, bewitch)

deterioration-*n* impairment, detriment, injury, harm, debasement, damage, loss, degeneration, vitiation, dilapidation, disrepair, (improvement, betterment, amendment)

determination-*n* firmness, resolution, resolve, judgment, decree, result, conclusion, evaluate, assess, estimate, (misjudge, positive, intolerant, impracticable)

determine-*v* impel, insure, influence, ascertain, conclude, define, decree, designate, specify

detest-*v* loathe, abhor, abominate, despise, dislike, disgust, disagreeable, disincline, repel, sicken, nauseous, (desire, wish, fancy, fantasy, want, need, inclined)

detraction-*n* derogation, disparagement, scandal, defamation, calumny, contempt, disapprobation, (approbation, flattery)

devastate-*v* ravage, sack, pillage, lay waste, ruin, destructive, subversive, ruinous, incendiary, extinguish, (produce, create, construct,

erect, fabricate)

develop-*v* promote, build, evolve, grow, enlarge, produce, perform, flower, generate, impregnate, prolific, induce, (destruction, dissolution, ruin, annihilate, abolish)

development-*n* consequence, outgrowth, growth, expansion, evolution, effect, eventuality, resulting from, emanate, (cause, origin, source, element, principle)

deviation-*n* divagation, digression, aberration, variation, alteration, diversion, declination, swerve, warp, drift, (continuance, direction, straightness)

device-*n* stratagem, trick, design, contrivance, appliance, emblem, type, figure, representation, characteristic, diagnostic

devious-*adj* circuitous, erring, rambling, indirect, diversion, digression, refraction, departure, aberration, (course, aligned, direct, straight)

devise-*v* create, contrive, scheme, originate, will, bequeath, plan, scheme, design, project, suggestion, resolution

devoid-*adj* destitute, void, lacking, wanting, absent, not present, empty, truant, vacant, elsewhere, inexistent, (present, fill, pervade, permeate, occupy, moored)

devote-*v* destine, preordain, addict, consecrate, dedicate, apply, utilize, resolve, determination, desperation, vigor, (fickle, levity, weakness, waver, hesitate)

devotee-*n* zealot, fanatic, fan, enthusiast, believer, religionist, inclination, desire, magnet, attraction, aspirant, solicitant, (reluctance, lackadaisical, half-hearted)

devotion-*n* loyalty, passion
fidelity, worship, homage,
yearning, gallantry,
benevolence, attachment,
rapture, adoration, (hate,
detest, abominate, abhor)

devour-*v* consume, annihilate,
swallow, masticate, rumination,
gulf, eat, edible, succulent,
potable, bibulous, (eject,
emission, egestion, evacuation)

devout-*adj* sincere, reverent,
pious, religious, holy,
beatification, regeneration,
conversion, veneration,
(irreverence, hypocrisy, bigot,
impiety, sacrilege, blasphemy)

dexterous-*adj* clever, adroit,
expert, proficient, handy,
skillful, dexterity, competence,
facility, mastery, cleverness,
(bungle, unskillful, thoughtless)

diabolic-*adj* impious, infernal,
devilish, satanic, fiendish,
hurtful, injurious, deleterious,
malignity, malevolence,
(goodness, excellence,
beneficial, proficient)

dialect-*n* tongue, speech,
brogue, cant, idiom, vernacular,
colloquialism, slang,
expression, provincialism

dictate-*v* suggest, prescribe,
direct, order, charge, compose,
draw up, advice, council,
instruction, enforce,
recommend

dictatorial-*adj* domineering,
overbearing, autocratic,
peremptory, superiority,
insolence, arrogance,
overbearance, (servile,
obsequious, supple, cringe)

die-*v* fade, expire, perish, depart,
to be killed, mold, seal, punch,
matrix, death, dissolution,
departure, (life, vitality, respire,
vivification, animation)

dietetic-*adj* alimental, dietary,
nutritious, treatment, help,
remedy, medicine, antiseptic,
corrective, restorative,
sedative, (bane, curse, rust,
leaven, poison)

difference-*n* unlikeness,
dissimilarity, variety, diversity,
heterogeneity, dissonance,
disparity, contradiction,
contrast, incongruousness,
dispute, contend, bicker,
(identity, similarity)

differentiate-*v* separate,
discriminate, adapt, distinguish,
set apart, sever, estimate,
refinement, diagnosis,
(uncertain, unmeasured,
overlook)

difficulty-*n* arduousness,
impracticability, hardness,
impossibility, tough, scrape,
entanglement, (smooth,
facilitate, ease, unclog)

diffuseness-*n* verbosity,
amplification, wordiness,
verbiage, loquacity, looseness,
exuberance

digest-*v* classify, settle, arrange,
summarize, assimilate,
transform, endure, think out,
reflect, cogitate, consider,
(vacant, unoccupied,
inconsiderate)

dignity-*n* honor, nobility,
distinction, stateliness, august,
lofty, majestic, haughtiness,
vainglory, supercilious,
(humble, disgrace, service,
submissive)

digress-*v* diverge, swerve,
ramble, wander, deviate, stray,
straggle, sidle, rove, dodge,
meander, veer, (straight,
aligned, undeviating, course)

dilapidated-*adj* crumbling,
decayed, ruined, worn out,
deterioration, debasement,
recession, retrogradation,
(improvement, melioration,
betterment, amendment)

dilate-*v* amplify, stretch,
expatiate, enlarge, expand,
increase, develop, rarefaction,
germination, growth,
(contraction, reduction,

diminution, decrease)

dilemma-*n* perplexity, mess, difficulty, strait, difficulty, impractical, embarrassment, impossibility, tough, hard, (manageable, wieldy, submissive, yielding)

dilute-*v* thin, reduce, weaken, water, declension, delicacy, invalidation, decrepitude, asthenia, fragile, unsubstantial, (strength, power, energy, stamina)

dim-*adj* obscure, dull, hazy, vague, cloudy, faint, blackness, darkness, obscurity, gloom, pale, fade, lackluster, (shine, glow, glitter, shimmer, glimmer)

dimension-*n* extent, area, measurement, expanse, size, proportions, amplitude, mass, capacity, enormity, (intangible, impalpable, inappreciable, infinitesimal)

diminish-*v* curtail, abase, reduce, decrease, weaken, small, slight, little

dip-*v* slope, declivity, decline, inclination, slant, lean, include, distort, oblique, depression, hollow, indentation, cavity, (convexity, prominence, projection, swell)

diplomacy-*n* tact, skill, negotiation, address, politics, chicanery, maneuver, concealment, guile, strategy, (artlessness, simplicity innocence, candor)

dire-*adj* dreadful, shocking, horrible, calamitous, deplorable, fearful, ominous, bad, annoyance, molestation, abuse, (valuable, advantageous, profitable, edifying)

dirty-*adj* soiled, sullied, filthy, stormy, murky, threatening, leaden, contamination, unclean, impure, defilement, (clean, pure, lavation, disinfection)

disable-*v* impair, cripple, incapacitate, maim, helpless, prostration, paralysis, collapse, invalidity, ineptitude, (powerful, mighty, ability, ableness, competence)

disadvantage-*n* hindrance, drawback, detriment, harm, injury, inferior, minority, subordinative, shortcoming, deficiency, (superiority, supremacy, great, exceed)

disagreement-*n* difference, dissonance, discrepancy, inequality, variance, dissent, controversy, inaptitude, impropriety, unsuitability, opposition

disappearance-*n* vanishing, evanescence, dissolution, fading, occultation, eclipse, exit, departure, dissolve, (appearance, visible, show, manifest)

disappointment-*n* frustration, chagrin, bafflement, discontent, failure, disconcerted, miscalculation, (expectation, breathless, anticipation, contemplation)

disapprobation-*n* disapproval, displeasure, disfavor, denunciation, condemnation, rebuke, admonition, reprimand, castigation, objurgation, reprobation

disarrange-*v* disorganize, disturb, disorder, derange, mislay, jumble, shuffle, muddle, dislocate, confuse, (arrange, analysis, digest, classify)

disaster-*n* affliction, cataclysm, calamity, adversity, accident, blow, failure, misfortune, catastrophe, downfall, (prosper, welfare, affluence, success)

disbelieve-*v* discredit, doubt, challenge, lack faith, infidelity, misbelief, dissent, incredulous, suspicious, septic, (credulity, gullible, simple, confident, believing)

discard-*v* abolish, reject, repudiate, cancel, nullify, oversight, absent, abstracted, perplex, bewilder, trash, (observe, scrutinize, study, revise)

discern-*v* appreciate, comprehend, perceive, experience, detect, distinguish, discriminate

discharge-*v* release, exude, absolve, abolish, discard, perform, settle, transact, dismiss, oust, disband, demobilize

disciple-*n* follower, pupil, adherent, student, scholar, apprentice, beginner, recruit, novice, neophyte, apostle, (teacher, trainer, instructor, institutor, master)

discipline-*n* orderliness, subordination, control, obedience, correction, chastisement, development

disclaim-*v* repudiate, deny, disown, renounce, disavowal, contradiction, recusancy, protest, prohibition, (affirmation, allegation, assertion, declaration)

disclosure-*n* divulgence, vent, utterance, exposure, revelation, admission, declaration, confession, avowal, (concealment, ambush)

discomfort-*n* suffering, discontent, soreness, painfulness, disquiet, displeasure, annoyance, (happiness, cheerfulness, refreshment, enchantment)

disconcert-*v* upset, abash, trouble, frustrate, bewilder, perplex, balk, disrepute, discredit, tarnish, degrade, beggar, stigmatize, (dignity, stateliness, solemnity, grandeur)

disconnection-*n* separation, interruption, cleavage, break, dissociation, irrelation,

deviation, sunder, divide, dissect, anatomize, sever, (join, unite, associate, suture, stitch)

disconsolate-*adj* sorrowful, melancholy, hopeless, forlorn, desolate, dejection, depression, prostration, (liveliness, life, vivacity, jocularity, mirth)

discontent-*n* uneasiness, dissatisfaction, regret, disappointment, soreness, mortification, repining, (content, serenity, gratification, happiness)

discontinuity-*n* disunion, fracture, disconnection, cessation, disruption, (continuity, succession, sequence)

discord-*n* dissidence, clash, dissension, disagreement, difference, variance, division, schism, faction, (concord, harmony, agreement)

discount-*v* concession, abatement, allowance, qualification, poundage, rebate, depreciation

discourage-*v* depress, deter, dishearten, daunt, divert, dissuade, deport, remonstrate, warn, disincline, (stimulate, excite, inspirit, persuade)

discourse-*n* discuss, declaim, talk, lecture, expatiate, explain, exercise, task, curriculum, course, elementary, teach, (bewilder, uncertain, mystify, conceal)

discourtesy-*n* incivility, rudeness, impoliteness, tactlessness, rusticity, unmannerly, disrespect, impudence, barbarism, (courtesy, politeness, gentility, refinement)

discovery-*n* ascertainment, detection, exposure, finding, revelation, contrivance, unearthing, invention, device, design, (concealment, veil, cover, camouflage, screen)

D

discredit-*v* shame, debase, disbelieve, disgrace, disrepute, dishonor, tarnish, defile, pollute, humiliate, reproach, (distinguish, elevate, dedicate, ascent, exaltation)

discretion-*n* prudence, option, volition, freedom, wariness, caution, wary, judicious, choice, elect, preference, choose, (indifference, indecision, neutrality)

discrimination-*n* distinction, differentiation, diagnosis, estimation, discernment, acuteness, clearness, acumen, insight

discuss-*v* examine, analyze, reason, argue, debate, consider, study, controversy, inquire, question, investigate, (answer, retort, discover, rationale)

disdain-*v* derision, scorn, haughtiness, arrogance, airs, contempt, insolence, indifference, unconcern, careless, (anxiety, impetuosity, propensity, willingness)

disengage-*v* disentangle, disconnect, sever, free, extricate, clear, liberate, release, emancipation, dismissal, (confine, duress, restraint, repress)

disfigure-*v* deface, impair, mutilate, mangle, mar, ugly, deformity, inelegance, blemish, squalor, eyesore, gaunt, (beauty, elegance, grace, form, gloss)

disgrace-*n* dishonor, shame, degrade, discredit, humiliate, corrupt, recreant, venal, insidious, perfidious, arrange, (upright, honest, equitable, impartial)

disguise-*n* camouflage, mask, concealment, blind, cloak, pretense, hide, mystify, secrecy, reserve, cover, screen, (enlighten, acquaint, knowledge, publicity)

disgust-*v* repugnance, loathing, aversion, repletion, dislike, gall, abomination, sicken, repel, (desire, passion, crave, care for, affect)

dishonest-*adj* fraudulent, false, crooked, dishonorable, deceptive, untruth, guile, misrepresentation, distortion, (veracity, honesty, frankness, truthful, true)

disinfect-*v* purify, cleanse, fumigate, sanitize, ventilate, immaculate, clear, clarify, deodorize, refine, (dirt, filth, soot, contaminate)

disinherit-*v* oust, disown, deprive, cut off, transfer, alienate, assign, limit

disintegrate-*v* break up, crumble, disband, disperse, decompose, powdery, pulverulent

disjunction-*n* disunion, disconnection, parting, partition, break, disengagement

dislike-*v* disinclination, displeasure, disfavor, reluctance, repugnance, abomination, antipathy, abhorrence, hatred

dislocate-*v* disarrange, displace, disjoin, disunite, derange, separate, disjunctive, asunder, distinct, unconnected

dismal-*adj* gloomy, somber, depressing, funereal, sorrowful, mournful, annoyance, grievance, nuisance, vexation, (gratify, delight, gladden, captivate)

dismantle-*v* destroy, undress, strip, disrobe, worthless, inadequate, waste, cripple, lame, useless, (utility, usefulness, conducive, remunerative)

dismiss-*v* send away, banish, discharge, let go, disband, eject, relinquish, abandon, dispense, riddance, (retain, keep, detain, custody, tenacity)

disobedience-*n* unruliness, insubordination, mutiny, intractableness, revolt, obstinacy, noncompliance

disorder-*n* disarrangement, confusion, untidiness, disarray, derangement, anomaly, disunion, anarchy, chaos, clutter

disown-*v* repudiate, deny, renounce, disclaim, reject, retract, dispute, ignore, rebut, disavow, protest, (affirmation, declare, positive, emphatic)

disparage-*v* belittle, decry, discredit, underrate, abuse, scoff at, underestimate, depreciate, modesty, minimize, (oversensitive, exaggerate, vanity, magnify)

dispatch-*v* dismiss, slay, alacrity, expedition, promptness, urgency

dispense-*v* allot, portion, distribute, bestow administer, apportion, disperse, diffuse, shed, spread, dissemination, (assemble, collect, gather, muster, compilation)

dispersion-*n* distribution, scattering, propagation, dissipation, dissemination, allocation, apportionment

displacement-*n* transfer, dislocation, replacement, disturbance, eject, expulsion, dismissal

displease-*v* vex, disturb, annoy, offend, maltreat, sicken, repel, disenchant, disagreeable, distasteful, (pleasant, agreeable, amuse, delectable)

disposition-*n* emotion, temperament, passion, predisposition, tendency, inclination, propensity

disprove-*v* refute, rebut, defeat, confute, negative, expose, invalidation, conviction, clincher, (categorical, decisive)

dispute-*v* clash, wrangle, bicker,

confute, argue, debate, challenge, quarrel

disqualify-*v* incapacitate, disfranchise, unfit, disable, helpless, exhaust, invalid, inefficiency, collapse, (attribute, quality, qualify)

disquiet-*v* turbulence, uneasiness, commotion, anxiety, restlessness, changeable, versatility, mobility, vacillation, (stability, vitality, solidity)

disregard-*v* affront, slight, insult, overlook, underrate, belittle, inconsiderate, escape one's attention, (attention, consideration, reflection, regard)

disrepute-*n* dishonor, discredit, disfavor, disesteem, derogation, abasement, degradation, ignominy, disgrace

dissatisfy-*v* offend, vex, provoke, annoy, anger, displease, chafe, anxiety, concern, grief, bitterness, tribulation, (happiness, felicity, comfort, delight)

dissemble-*v* feign, hide, disguise, mask, simulate, deception, untruth, guile, misrepresentation, pretense, sham, (veracity, truthfulness, frankness, sincerity)

dissent-*v* nonagreement, nonconsent, difference, variance, discordance, schism, disaffection, secession

dissertation-*n* treatise, theme, thesis, essay, discourse, investigation, commentary, lecture, sermon

dissimilarity-*n* unlikeness, divergence, variation, difference, novelty, originality, diversity, disparity, (similarity, resemblance, similitude, semblance)

dissolve-*v* end, destroy, abolish, disintegrate, vanish, evaporate,

D

fade, liquefy, decompose,
disappear, (visible, perceptible,
perceivable, discernible)

dissonance-*n* controversy,
incongruity, dissension,
discordance, harshness,
disagreement, discretion,
(agreement, accord, unison,
harmony)

dissuasion-*n* expostulation,
diversion, remonstrance,
deprecation, constraint, check,
control

distance-*n* remoteness, span,
space, interval, coldness,
frigidity, reservation, aloofness,
outskirts, (nearness, proximity
propinquity)

distasteful-*adj* unsavory,
unpalatable, bitter,
disagreeable, uninviting,
unsatisfactory, painful, irritating,
grievance, (pleasure, attraction,
loveliness)

distinct-*adj* apart, explicit,
separate, characterize, clear-
cut, distinguishable,
disconnected, disjoined, divide,
sever, (attach, entangle, twine,
cohere, incorporate)

distinguished-*adj* famous,
celebrated, noted, illustrious,
eminent, superior, supreme,
majority, (inferior, smaller,
subordinative, deficient)

distortion-*n* deformation,
contortion, twisting, perversion,
irregular, misrepresentation,
misunderstanding,
exaggeration, (interpret,
decipher, understand,
explanatory)

distress-*n* sorrow, agony,
affliction, anguish, grief, misery,
misfortune, pain, concern,
unhappiness, infelicity,
(enjoyment, gratification,
fruition, relish)

district-*n* tract, section,
neighborhood, division,
commune, county, state,
region, sphere, ground, circuit,

territory, (space, expanse,
range, latitude)

distrust-*n* qualm, doubt,
suspicion, apprehension,
disbelief, mistrust, discredit,
infidelity, dissent, doubtful,
(believe, credit, faithful,
dependence)

disturb-*v* upset, muddle, shake,
stir, misplace, worry, trouble,
disquiet, tumult, disorder,
perturbation, derangement,
agitation

disuse-*n* desuetude, non-use,
abandonment, neglect,
relinquishment, discontinuance

divergence-*n* ramification,
furcation, branching,
divarication, separation,
detachment, dispersion,
deviation, disagreement

diversion-*n* recreation, pastime,
variation, break, sport, festivity,
gala, rejoicing, (weariness,
irksome, monotonous)

divert-*v* delight, deflect,
entertain, switch, turn,
inequality, multiformity,
divergence, variation,
dissimilitude

divestment-*n* unstrapping,
unclothing excoriation,
desquamation, excavation,
uncover, strip, bare, denude,
dishabille, (invest, cover,
vesture, array)

divide-*v* assign, separate,
distribute, allot, sunder, cleave,
part, detach, sever, dissect,
mangle, disconnect, (pin, nail,
secure, set, firm, fast, close)

divine-*adj* superhuman, godlike,
celestial, holy, religious,
perfection, indefectibility,
paragon, summit, (imperfect,
inadequate, deficient, fault)

division-*n* rupture, breach, split,
schism, parting, share, portion,
section, apportionment,
system, discord, disjunction

dizzy-*adj* vertiginous, giddy,
light-headed, confused, absent,

abstracted, inattentive, muddle,
disregard, (attentive, observant,
reflective, regardful)

docile-*adj* submissive, gentle,
tractable, obedient, aptitude,
edification, willing, inclined,
geniality, volunteering,
(unwilling, disinclination,
volition)

doctrine-*n* maxim, theory, creed,
dogma, principle, record, note,
register, testimonial,
commemorate, (obliterate,
cancel, delete, erase)

dogmatic-*adj* arrogant,
dictatorial, bigoted,
opinionated, certainty,
necessity, surety, reliability,
gospel, (uncertain, hesitating,
suspenseful, perplexity)

domain-*n* sphere, realm,
territory, dominions, estate,
lands, property, possession,
right, title, claim, possess,
chattel

domestic-*adj* broken, tame,
inland, home, family, inhabitant,
resident, dweller, occupier,
native

doom-*n* judgment, sentence,
fate, fortune, ruin, lot, destiny,
future, impend, destined,
threaten, loom, forthcoming,
(eventual, proceed,
circumstance, casualty)

door-*n* gate, entrance, portal,
obstacle, outlet, inlet, barrier,
begging, inception,
introduction, source, (end,
close, termination, conclusion)

doubt-*v* question, mistrust,
disbelieve, distrust, incredulity,
disbelief, skepticism,
agnosticism

downfall-*n* overthrow, fall,
misfortune, wreck, crash,
destruction, breaking up,
disorganization, desolation,
(productive, flowering, erection,
perform)

downright-*adj* plainly, bluntly,
completely, absolutely, utterly,

simply, innocence, candor,
sincere, honestly, (cunning,
craftiness, artificial,
maneuvering)

downy-*adj* lanate, woolly,
flocculent, soft, fluffy, pliable,
mollify, mellow, relax, mash,
knead, yielding, (hard, rigid,
inflexible, stiff, starched)

draft-*n* sketch, drawing, breeze,
air, select, enlist, impress,
conscript, commandeer

drag-*v* creep, trail, lag, crawl,
elapse, pull, tug, traction, rake,
tow, wrench, jerk, haul, (propel,
project, throw, fling, cast, pitch,
toss)

drain-*v* flow out, leak, discharge,
empty, exhaust, egestion
evacuation, vomit, emission,
effusion, expulsion, (reception,
admission, importation,
ingestion)

draw-*v* lure, attract, fabricate,
describe, sketch, portray, drag,
pull, haul, design, picture, draft,
(misrepresent, distort,
exaggerate, caricature, daub)

dreadful-*adj* horrible, frightful,
tremendous, shocking,
formidable, depressing,
dejected, heaviness, sadness,
(cheerful, genial, gay, good
humor)

dream-*n* vision, reverie, fantasy,
fancy, shadow, inattentive,
absent, bemused, preoccupied

dreary-*adj* somber, gloomy,
depressing, monotonous,
humdrum, dull, solitude,
seclusion, isolation, lonely,
(happy, content, coexist)

dregs-*n* settlings, lees,
sediment, residue, trash,
refuse, riffraff, common, low,
beggarly, uncivilized,
(aristocrat, noble, gentlemen,
distinctive)

dress-*n* attire, clothe, drape,
deck, berate, scold, adorn,
embellish, garments, raiment,
apparel, vesture, garb

D

drink-*v* sip, quaff, tipple, carouse, imbibe, absorb, toast, pledge, libation, potation, draft, gulp, swallow, (eject, emission, emit, evacuate)

drive-*v* impel, oblige, force, urge, steer, manage, control, ride, travel, thrust, aim, compel, enforce

driver-*n* coachman, whip, charioteer, teamster, chauffeur, director, manager, master, taskmaster

droop-*v* despond, decline, sink, wither, fade, hang, lean, drop, decay, retrograde, go down, downhill, (improve, meliorate, betterment, mend)

drop-*v* slide, sink, fall, discontinue, collapse, faint, discard, give up, drip, trickle, descent

drought-*n* parched, aridness, thirst, lack, dearth, scarcity, insufficient, inadequate, scantiness, famine, (sufficient, enough, adequate, fullness)

drown-*v* suffocate, drench, submerge, overpower, overwhelm, deaden, victimize, choke, stifle

drunkenness-*n* inebriety, intemperance, drinking, inebriation, insobriety, intoxication, libations, bacchanalia

dryness-*n* aridity, aridness, drought, parched, desiccation, dehydration, evaporation

dubious-*adj* questionable, doubtful, suspicious, uncertain, hesitation, perplexity, embarrassment, dilemma, (certainty, gospel, reliable, infallible)

ductile-*adj* pliable, pliant, flexible, malleable, tactile, manageable, compliant, docile, tractable

duel-*n* affair of honor, single combat, fight, competition, rivalry, contest, opposition, satisfaction, (peace, harmony, tranquil, concord)

dullness-*n* stupidity, slowness, stagnation, dimness, sluggishness, apathy, obscurity, uninteresting, insipid, unimaginative

dumb-*adj* voiceless, silence, taciturnity, slow-witted, stupid, inarticulate, suppress, mute, (voice, sound, utter, articulate)

dupe-*n* victim, sucker, easy mark, fool, puppet, deceive, trick, fool, delusion, deception, false

duplication-*n* doubling, iteration, renewal, facsimile, copy, imitate, mirror reflect, reproduce, repeat, (original, unmatched, unique)

durability-*n* permanence, continuance, persistence, immutability, stability, unchangeable, constant, (erratic, vagrant, alternating, mobile)

duty-*n* respect, deference, homage, reverence, obligation, service, responsibility, task, commission, charge, trust

dwarf-*n* midget, pygmy, Lilliputian, little, urchin, elf, puppet, shrimp, runt, minute, (mammoth, elephant, hippopotamus, colossus)

dwelling-*n* domicile, abode, house, residence, habitation, housing, home, berth, throne, tenement, barn, mansion, villa, hermitage

dwindle-*v* contract, lessen, shrink, diminish, decline, decrease, abate, depreciate, deteriorate, shorten, (increase, enlarge, expand, augment, raise)

dynamic-*adj* magnetic, power, impelling, driving, energetic, impulse, forcible, active, strong

E

each-*adj* apiece, seriatim, respectively, severally, individual, special, particular, separate, (generally, generic, universal)

eager-*adj* zealous, ardent, earnest, fervent, intent, willing, voluntary, inclined, favorable, ready, forward, (unwilling, renitency, reluctance, indifference)

earliness-*n* promptitude, punctuality, readiness, quickness, haste, speed, swiftness, alacrity, prematureness, precocity, anticipation, hastiness, (lateness, tardiness, delay, deferring)

earnest-*adj* fervent, zealous, ardent, grave, eager, solemn, weighty, serious, determined

ease-*n* enjoyment, readiness, contentment, expertness, cheerfulness, comfort, resignation, satisfaction, (discontent, grief, disappointment, mortification)

easy-*adj* unconcerned, smooth, untroubled, unconstrained, gentle, facile, simple, tractable, manageable, compliant

eat-*v* devour, consume, fare, rust, corrode, erode, masticate, consume, nourishment, subsistence, provision, (excrete, discharge, secrete)

ebb-*v* waste, decay, decline, recede, withdraw, return, reflux, recoil, regress, fall, deteriorate, resilience, (progress, advance, proceed)

eccentric-*adj* irregular, peculiar, odd, deviating, erratic, unsettled, demented, possessed, maddened, moonstruck

ecclesiastical-*adj* religious, priestly, clerical, sacerdotal, scriptural, biblical, prophetic, apostolic, canonical

echo-*n* repercussion, repeat, reverberation, reproduce, resound, ring, reflex, hollow, sepulchral, chime, (dead sound, dampen, muffled, thud)

economy-*n* frugality, thriftiness, savings, prevention of waste, parsimony, retrenchment, careful, saving, sparing, (liberality, generosity, munificent, freely, bountifulness)

edible-*adj* digestible, eating, epulation, masticate, nourishment, sustenance, nurture, subsistence, feed, swallow, gulp, munch, nibble, culinary, nutritive, succulent, potable, bibulous, (discharge, excretion, exude, secrete, emanate, extrude)

edification-*n* performance, achievement, flower, fructify, evolution, development, growth, genesis, bring forth, (destruction, dissolution, consumption, run, breakdown, abolish, annihilation)

education-*v* instruct, tutor, direction, guidance, preparation, discipline, practice, study, lecture, inoculation, impregnate, enlighten, inform, coach, disseminate, (bewilder, perversion, misinformation, deceive, mislead, unedifying)

effect-*n* consequence, result, outgrowth, development, derivative, (cause origin, source, foundation, groundwork)

efficient-*adj* skillful, capable, clever, knowledgeable, adroit, masterful, accomplished, ingenuity, endowed, competent, (unskilled, blunder, inability, stupidity, failure, fumble, disqualify)

E

ego-*n* vanity, conceit, self-esteem, admiration, gaudery, assurance, complacency, praise, glorification, laudation, (modesty, timidity, humility, reserve, demureness, sheepish)

either-*adj* choice, option, alternative, selection, prefer, to set apart, preference, elect, discretion, decision, (neutrality, indifference, waive, abstain, refrain, indecision, neither)

elaborate-*adj* improve, betterment, melioration, amend, elevate, increase, promote, reform, revise, refine, cultivate, enhance, polish, refresh, bolster, revamp, (recede, retrograde, decrease, degrade, deter, impair, deteriorate, degenerate, decline)

elate-*v* cheerfulness, gaiety, geniality, good humor, glee, merriment, hilarity, laughter, rejoice, liveliness, jocularity, mirth, exhilaration, joviality, vivacity, (dejected, depressed, weariness, melancholy, sadness, dismal, despondent, solemnity, sorrowful)

elect-*v* choice, option, discretion, alternative, decision, poll, ballot, vote, selection, pick, choose, cull, separate, prefer, excerpt, (neutral, indifference, waive, abstain, refrain, reject)

elementary-*adj* simple, homogeneity, sheer, neat, unsophisticated, basic, (combined, complicated, developed, complex)

elevation-*n* height, altitude, pitch, loftiness, stature, prominence, mount, tower, soar, surmount, lofty, rise, mountainous, upper, gigantic, picture, drawing, sketch, (lowness, depression, lowlands, underlie, crouch, slouch, grovel, at a low ebb)

eliminate-*v* deduction, retrenchment, removal, mutilation, amputation, curtailment, withdraw, diminish, abscind, prune, subtract, decrease, (addition, annexation, adjection, increase, supplement, inclusive, reinforce)

elude-*n* refraining, forbearance, avoidance, abstain, eschew, shun, keep away from, shirk, dodge, recede, evade, aloof, (pursuit, chase, hunt, follow, leap, seek, engage, quest, prosecute)

emanate-*v* egress, exit, emersiongence, evacuation, distillation, pouring, discharge, drain, emerge, move, pass, evacuate, escape, outlet, export, expatriation, remigration, departure, (ingress, entrance, introgression, influx, intrusion, invasion, import, infiltration)

embark-*v* departure, port of embarcation, outset, start, removal, adieu, farewell, starting point, set out, quit, vacate, (admission, insertion, immigration, insinuation, penetrate)

embarrass-*v* difficulty, dilemma, perplexity, entanglement, awkwardness, quagmire, unwieldy, restriction, hindrance, impediment, restrain, (support, uplift, advance, furtherance, promotion, favor, patronage, advocacy)

embellish-*v* ornament, decoration, architecture, lace, fringe, border, edging, wreath, festoon, garland, pattern, improve, (disfigure, deformity, delete, blemish, flaw, scar)

embitter-*v* aggravate, render worse, exasperation, exacerbation, overestimation, exaggeration, acerbate, heightening, (relief, deliverance, refreshment, easement, softening, alleviation, mitigation, soothing)

emblazon-v bright, vivid, intense, deep, rich, gay, gaudy, showy, flashy, glaring, flaring, inharmonious, ostentatious, pomposity, splendor, (pale, neutral, monochrome, colorless, hueless, faint, dull, muddy, discolored, achromatic)

embolism-n interference, intervention, dovetailing, infiltration, parenthesis, obtrusion, interpenetrate, (surround, beset, encompass, environ, encircle, embrace, circumvent)

embrace-v contain, hold, embody, involve, implicate, inclusion, admission, comprehension, reception, intimate, cordial, devoted, sincere, affection, (alienation, dislike, animosity, hostility, exclusion, rejection, exile, separation, elimination, repudiation)

embroil-v derange, unsettle, disturb, confuse, muddle, fumble, perturbation, inversion, complicate, disorder, involve, convulse, disconsert, dissension, division, rupture, (harmony, agreement, sympathy, unison, accord, reunion, conciliation)

embryo-n beginning, commencement, opening, inception, initial, onset, genesis, birth, start, originate, conceive, initiate, groundwork, foundation, pivot, hinge, (creation, harvest, result, end, termination, conclusion, finale, consummation, death, finality, finish, close, expiration)

emergency-n critical situation, crisis, pinch, quandary, full of incident, circumstance, adventure, contingency, phenomenon, eventuality,

concern, (ease, feasibility, flexibility, smooth, lighten, manageable, submissive, disburden)

emigrate-v migrate, traverse, wander, travel, journey, egress, exit, evacuation, emersion, export, emerge, emanate, evacuate, (ingress, entrance, entry, influx, incursion, invasion, import, infiltration, immigration, admission)

eminence-n high, eminent, exalted, lofty, tall, gigantic, Patagonian, towering, elevated, dignity, importance, primacy, elevation, dedication, glorification, enshrinement, consecration, (disrepute, discredit, tarnish, taint, defilement, degradation)

emit-v ejection, emission, effusion, rejection, extrusion, discharge, expulsion, eviction, excrete, secrete, shed, void, effuse, spend, pour forth (reception, admission, admittance, importation, introduction, absorption, insertion)

emotion-n feeling, affection, suffering, endurance, tolerance, supportance, experience, response, sympathy, sensation, pathos, passion, eagerness, enthusiasm, excitation, (insensitivity, indifference, peacefulness, impassive)

empire-n property, realty, land, acres, ground, command, sway, rule, dominion, sovereignty, government, jurisdiction, (laxity, toleration, anarchy, relaxation, deposition, abdicate, depose, dethrone)

employ-v occupation, function, capacity, place, post, vocation, calling, occupy, undertake, transact, task, engagement, profession, commission, subjection, dependence, subordination, bondage,

E

servitude, (freedom,
independence, play, free,
franchise, liberal, dismissal)

empower-v permission, allow,
liberty, indulge, authorize,
admission, accordance, might,
power, potency, ability, able,
qualify, (impotence, disability,
incapacity, invalidity,
incompetence, helplessness,
collapse, exhaust,
disqualification)

empty-adj void, clear, vacate,
depart, eject, exit, evict,
emission, expulsion, extrusion,
deport, exhaust, spend, use,
consume, impoverish, drain,
disperse, squander, (provide,
supply, fill, furnish, replenish,
recruit, provide, admit, ingest,
absorb, gulp)

emulate-v excellence,
goodness, merit, virtue, worth,
superiority, perfection, prime,
exude, imitate, copy,
simulation, follow, model after,
assimilation, (originality,
unparalleled, mistreat,
injurious, detrimental,
mischievous, nocuous)

enact-v perform, movement,
evolution, perpetration,
execution, deed, proceeding,
participate, put in motion,
achieve, rule regulation,
ordinance, statute,
(unlawfulness, inactivity, idle,
refrain, incomplete, non-
performance, incomplete,
neglect)

enamel-n polish, varnish, gliding,
embellish, lacquer, paint,
veneer, (blemish, disfigure,
deform, injure, tarnish)

enchanting-adj elegant, beauty,
grave, polish, radiance,
splendor, gorgeous, dazzling,
refined, idolatrous, adoration,
(repugnant, shudder, irritating,
revolting, annoying, provoking,
obnoxious, repulsive, offensive)

enclosure-n domain, territory,

district, zone, compartment,
place, spot, document,
envelope, den, cell, dungeon,
(liberate, free, extricate, open,
spacious, boundless,
uncircumscribed)

encounter-v event, occurrence,
incident, affair, phenomenon,
circumstance, accident,
adventure, crisis, emergency,
experience, arrive, (depart,
exodus, await, future,
impending, destiny)

encourage-v induce, persuade,
lure, bribe, prompt, inspire,
beckon, stimulate, tempt,
seduce, coax, tantalize,
fascinate, cajole, support,
promote, accommodate, help,
contribute, expedite, bolster,
uphold, (prevent, obstruct, stop,
interrupt, impede, restrict,
restrain, block, inhibit,
discourage, hamper)

encroach-v trespass, infringe,
extravagate, surpass, overstep,
exceed, invalidate, unlawful,
unauthorized, forfeited,
improper, disfranchisement,
(sanction, warranty, immunity,
franchise, vested interest,
deserve, merit, substantiate)

encumber-v difficulty,
impracticability, tough,
dilemma, perplexity,
entanglement, awkwardness,
delicate, vexed, impossible,
hindrance, restriction,
obstruction, stumbling block,
(ease, flexibility, feasible,
smooth, disencumber)

encyclopedia-n book, volume,
manual, publication,
knowledge, possess
knowledge, learning, instructed,
educational, enlightened,
informed, bookish, scholastic,
profound, (uninformed,
uncultivated, ignorant,
simplistic, unexplored)

end-n terminate, close, finish,
final, conclusion, expire, result,

discontinue, beginning, start,
open, commence, initial,
inaugurate, genesis)
endeavor-*v* pursuit, enterprise,
pursuance, adventure, quest,
exert, labor, resolution,
intention, purpose, determined,
ambition, aim, (indiscriminate,
promiscuous, incidental,
repose, without purpose)
endorse-*v* conformation,
corroboration, support,
ratification, authentication,
admission, indication, attest,
document, refer, substantiate,
verify, acknowledge, concur,
cooperate, agree, affirm,
consent, recognize, avow,
(dissent, discordance, protest,
contradict, disagree, conflicting,
disavow, object)
endowment-*n* cleverness,
talent, ability, ingenuity,
capacity, forte, gift, intelligence,
capability, expertness,
dexterity, adroitness,
proficiency, competence,
excellence, qualification,
bestowal, donation, investiture,
award, (grant, acceptance,
incompetence, inability,
disqualification, unfit,
inexperienced, awkward)
endure-*v* durable, persistent,
lasting, continuing,
permanence, survive, longevity,
prolongation, protraction,
remain, continue, abide,
lingering, eternal, everlasting,
perpetual, stable, established,
unchanged, subsist, (alter,
change, modify, deviate,
transformation, revolution,
short-lived, perishable,
impermanent)
energy-*n* power, might, force,
control, ascendancy, authority,
strength, competency,
pressure, voltaism,
electromagnetism, influence,
enablement, efficiency,
endowment, susceptibility,

friction, potential, intensity,
vigor, elasticity, (inertness,
dullness, inactivity, languor,
quiescence, latency, passive,
torpid, sluggish, slow, tame,
lifeless, uninfluential,
incapacity, inefficacy)
enforce-*v* persuade, prevail,
enlist, engage, animate, incite,
provoke, instigate, actuate,
encourage, dictate, press,
compel, force, compulsory,
constraint, necessitate, oblige,
stringent, duress, coercion,
(loss of right, discourage,
encroach, breach, violate,
forfeit, unsanctioned)
engage-*v* motive, reason,
intention, inducement,
attraction, enticement,
allurement, fascination,
influence, bribe, lure,
campaign, crusade, expedition,
mobilization, tactics, strategy,
battle, combative, militant,
appoint, commission, assign,
commit, authorize, (annul,
cancel, revoke, dismiss,
abolish, retract, rescind,
reverse, disclaim, dissolve,
null)
engrave-*v* memory,
remembrance, retention,
reminiscence, recognition,
keepsake, figure, emblem,
motto, put an indication, label,
imprint, hallmark, inscribe,
(forgotten, unremembered,
obliteration, mindless,
oblivious)
engulf-*v* dive, plunge,
submerge, sink, importation,
admission, ingestion,
absorption, inhalation, suction,
interjection, import, engorge,
inhale, ingest, (ejection,
emission, epulation, spew,
disgorge, dislodge,
expectorate, eviscerate, deport)
enigmatic-*adj* uncertain, doubt,
dubiety, hesitation, perplexity,
dilemma, bewilderment, timid,

E

vacillation, vagueness, obscurity, precarious, casual, random, hypothetical, paradoxical, occasional, provisional, (assurance, reliability, infallible, unerring, positive, dogmatic, explicit, expressive, clear, lucid, precise)

enjoy-v pleasure, sensual, gratification, titillation, comfort, luxury, relish, revel, ask, cordial, palatable, fruition, satisfaction, delight, refresh, happiness, rapture, overjoyed, captivated, ecstasies, entranced, (suffer, pain, ache, displeasure, discomfort, weariness, irritation, worry, infliction, vexation, sorrow, unhappiness)

enlarge-v increase, augment, extend, develop, grow, spread, gain, intensify, enhance, magnify, exaggerate, add, expand, swell, inflate, germinate, larger, amplify, bulbous, (decrease, subtract, reduce, shrink, diminish, contract, shrivel)

enlighten-v inform acquaint, knowledge, communicate, announce, instruct, outpour, report, expound, explain, detect, illuminate, reflect, refraction, shine, glow, glitter, twinkle, gleam, glimmer, sparkle, radiate, (darken, gloom, obscure, shade, dim, eclipse, extinguish, dingy, conceal, disguise, ignore, suppress)

enough-adj sufficient, adequate, full, abundance, copious, profuse, galore, outpouring, abound, exuberate, inexhaustible, ample, commensurate, (insufficient, inadequate, want, lack, require, deplete, empty)

enrapture-v pleasurable, delectability, amusing, inviting,

charm, fascinate, enchanting, amiability, seduction, amenity, loveliness, goodness, flatter, fresh, enliven, attractive, alluring, delightful, felicitous, (annoying, grievance, burden, bother, hurt, displease, disturbing, enraging, disgusting, enrage)

entangle-v attach, affix, bind, clinch, twine, encase, gird, tether, fasten, secure, twist, pinion, string, leash, couple, intervolved, embroil, unsettle, disturb, complicate, ravel, dishevel, tangle, wrangle, breach, (discontinuity, separation, dismemberment, sunder, divide, abscind, rupture, split, disentangle, unleash)

enterprise-n undertaking, engagement, venture, speculate, negotiate, commerce, interchange, quest, pursue, follow, pursuit, course, (abstain, refrain, escape, retreat, reject, disengage, elude, elusive, evasive)

entertain-v observance, attention, application, diligent, recognize, mindful, regardful, examine, scrutinize, consider, social gathering, joviality, hospitality, welcome, festive, fraternize, visit, consort, reception, party, (seclusion, exclusion, privacy, reclusion, isolation, desertion, solitary)

enthusiasm-n emotion, sensation, cordiality, eagerness, zeal, excitation, lively, experience, warm, quick, feverish, flamboyant, fanatical, hysterical, impetuous, impressed, moved, touched, affected, penetrating, (distract, inactive, indifferent, preoccupation, disregard, disconcerted, inattentive)

entrance-n inlet, orifice, mouth, porch, portal, portico, door,

gate, threshold, vestibule,
origin, source, begin,
commence, enter, debut,
inaugurate, ingress, entry,
influx, immigration, (egress,
exit, evacuation, emerge,
discharge, conclude)

entrap-v snare, trap, ambush,
misinform, deceptive, cunning,
deceitful, elusive, insidious,
risk, danger, peril, insecurity,
jeopardy, precariousness,
instability, vulnerability,
endanger, (safety, security,
protect, invulnerable,
defensible, tenable, secure)

entrust-v commission, delegate,
assign, procure, errand,
appoint, nominate, return,
install, employ, empower,
represent, bestow, give,
present, consign, dispense,
endow, award, gift, donation,
grant, benefaction, (acquire,
receive, accept, assign,
beneficiary, admit, cancel,
repeal, dismiss, abolish)

enunciate-v pronounce,
accentuate, aspirate, deliver,
vocal, phonetic, articulate,
distinct, remark, emphatic,
assert, affirm, report, express,
state, communicate, present,
(retract, repudiate, rebut,
silence, mute, suppress, muffle,
raucous, husky, dry)

envoy-n messenger, emissary,
ambassador, marshal, crier,
trumpeter, courier,
representative, functionary,
diplomat, delegate,
commissioner

equal-adj sameness, symmetry,
balance, evenness, monotony,
level, equivalent, match,
capability, capacity, quality,
attribute, endowment, virtue,
gift, qualification, susceptibility,
(helplessness, inability,
incompetence, inept,
unevenness, inequality, partial)

eradicate-v extract, remove,

eliminate, extricate,
exterminate, eject, eviscerate,
(insert, implant, inject, import,
introduce, infuse)

erect-v form, fabricate, produce,
create, construct, manufacture,
build, organize, establish,
achieve, complete, perform,
forge, carve, chisel, constitute,
institute, accomplish, evolve,
(destroy, destruct, dissolve,
break, disrupt, ruin, smash,
annihilate, demolish)

erratic-adj inconstant, versatile,
changeable, unstable, vacillate,
fluctuate, vicissitude, alter,
shifting, unstable, vary, fickle,
restless, spasmodic, divert,
deviate, wandering, (stable,
unchangeable, constant,
immobile, sound, stiff, solid,
established, permanent, firm,
settled)

eruption-n violent, vehement,
impetuous, boisterous,
effervescent, turbulent, severe,
ferocious, raging, exacerbate,
malign, forceful, spastic,
explode, volcanic, rampage,
riotous, (moderate, temperate,
relaxed, gentle, sober, quiet,
calm, tranquil, pacify, sedative,
balmy, smooth)

escape-v release, disengage,
liberate, discharge,
emancipate, dismiss,
deliverance, absolve, extricate,
acquit, free, dismantle, untie,
violate, transgress, derelict,
neglect, evade, (responsible,
accountable, conscientious,
retrain, hinder, coerce, repress,
custody, arrest, incarcerate,
unrestricted)

essential-adj inherent,
important, intrinsic,
quintessence, incarnate,
backbone, principle, main,
major, chief, consummate,
prominent, necessary, required,
indispensable, urgent, exact,
(insignificant, meaningless,

immaterial, minuscule, diminutive, minor, infinitesimal, paltry)

establish-v found, settle, permanent, vested, produce, create, construct, form, fabricate, manufacture, produce, institute, evolve, develop, generate, genesis, contrive, build, accomplish, (ruin, smash, crash, destroy, abolish, suppress, overthrow, demolish, ravage, devastate, wreck, consume)

esteem-v credit, assurance, faith, trust, confidence, presumption, dependence on, reliance, conviction, implicit, unshaken, dogma, credence, credulous, confident, assured, sanctioned, advocacy, approved, (dislike, denunciation, condemnation, scandalous, discredit, suspicious, doubtful, skeptical)

et cetera-adj add, annex, increase, increment, supplement, affix, append, furthermore, along with, insert, and so forth, access, include, upward, (none, naught, deduction, removal, abstraction, curtailment, decrease, abscind, decimate)

eternity-n perpetuity, ever, immortality, everlasting, perpetuation, forever, endless, eternal, ceaseless, evergreen, imperishable, always, lasting, continual, lingering, permanent, (temporary, perishable, briefly, transient, sudden, quick, short)

ether-n buoyancy, lightness, volatility, levity, gossamer, flat, airy, weightless, sublimated, inflation, sponginess, absence of solid, thin, tenuous, hollow, (density, solid, compact, thick, weight, gravity, heaviness, pressure)

etiquette-n rule, standing, order, precedent, routine, mode,

vogue, conformity, practice, custom, habit, manners, breeding, demeanor, gentility, decorum, propriety, carriage, (vulgar, bad taste, awkward, tactless, ill-bred, coarseness, rough, slovenly, ungenteel, gaudy, horrid, obtrusive)

evade-v conceal, secrecy, hide, stealth, mask, disguise, ensconce, muffle, whisper, suppress, veil, evasive, deceive, forge, distort, avoid, escape, retreat, reject, shun, (pursue, chase, scrupulous, frank, open, candid, straightforward, outspoken, undisguised)

event-n occurrence, incident, affair, transaction, proceeding, phenomenon, circumstance, adventure, consequence, happening, encounter, undergo, contest, competition, engagement, tussle, conflict, (uneventful, idle, without incident)

evergreen-adj continuous, progressive, successive, unbroken, uninterrupted, perennial, constant, entire, linear, lasting, persistent, perpetual, (temporary, transient, fleeting, short-lived, impermanent, spasmodic, unsuccessful)

evil-adj harm, hurt, mischief, nuisance, ill, tragedy, badness, bane, outrage, wrong, injure, grievance, oppress, persecute, abuse, overburden, victimize, molest, (goodness, excellence, merit, virtue, value, worth, beneficial, right, commendable)

evoke-v request, motion, apply, canvass, address, appeal, solicit, invite, petition, beseech, plead, implore, invoke, urge, beset, ask, beg, crave, pray, (protest, effect, consequence, ignore)

evolution-n pullulate, bring forth,

create, beget, get, generate,
hatch, develop, produce, form,
make, progress, journey, flow,
move, mobilize, (rest, still,
immobile, hold, halt, remain,
stop, stagnate)

exacerbate-*v* exalt, strengthen,
intensify, enhance, magnify,
aggravate, exaggerate,
increase, growth, advance,
ascend, sprout, exasperation,
impetuosity, effervescence,
turbulence, confusion,
hysterical, (moderate, relax,
remission, mitigation, tranquil,
pacify, soften, decrease,
moderate)

exact-*adj* similar, semblance,
parallelism, likeness, match,
accurate, precise, gospel,
authentic, true, accurate,
actual, definite, right, correct,
punctual, constant, unerring,
(erroneous, untrue, false,
wrong, unsubstantial,
inaccurate, different, incorrect)

exalt-*v* raise, intensify, enhance,
magnify, exaggerate, increase,
enlarge, develop, spread, lift,
sublimate, erect, elevate,
heighten, (depress, lower,
reduce, overthrow, decrease,
diminish, lessen, weaken,
depreciate)

examine-*v* scan, scrutinize,
inspect, review, glance,
consider, account, indicate,
observe, inquire, request,
investigate, seek, search,
explore, ransack, rummage,
(answer, respond, retort,
acknowledge, escape,
unobservant, thoughtless,
careless, inattentive)

example-*n* prototype, original,
model, pattern, precedent,
standard, type, copy, conform,
instance, sample, illustration,
specimen, rule, agreement,
observance, exemplification,
(original, duplicate, imitation,
irregularity, eccentricity,

abnormal, oddity, curiosity,
hybrid, unconventional,
infraction)

exception-*n* abnormal, irregular,
peculiar, unusual, expected,
unconventional, remarkable,
queer, exceptional, informal,
unaccustomed, exclusive,
(typical, normal, formal,
orthodox, sound, rigid, positive,
ordinary, common,
conventional)

excite-*v* energy, intensify, vigor,
strength, pressure, poignancy,
severity, agitation,
effervescence, stir, stimulate,
kindle, exert, inflame, (inert,
dull, inactivity, languor, passive,
slow, lifeless, dormant)

exclusive-*adj* special, particular,
specify, characteristic,
individualize, custom, unusual,
rare, singular, curious, odd,
extraordinary, strange,
remarkable, noteworthy,
eccentric, peculiar, abnormal,
(conventional, ordinary,
conformity, symmetry, regular,
usual)

excuse-*v* forgive, pardon,
condonation, remission,
absolution, amnesty, reprieve,
exoneration, release,
indemnity, forget, acquit,
vindicate, apology, justify,
warrant, advocate, defend,
contend, (accuse, charge,
impute, reproach, denounce,
inexcusable, vicious)

exercise-*n* task, curriculum,
study, lesson, lecture, sermon,
apologue, parable, action,
performance, perpetration,
movement, operation, work,
labor, execution, procedure,
deed, act, proceeding, enact,
(passiveness, nothing,
inactivity, unintelligent,
misinformation)

exert-*v* hold, grasp, grip, reach,
command, use, employ,
exercise, applications,

consume, resort, wield, handle,
manipulate, avail, (abstinence,
relinquish, discard, dismiss,
waive, neglect)

exhaust-*v* disarm, incapacitate,
disqualify, unfit, invalidate,
deaden, cramp, muzzle,
paralyze, fatigue, weariness,
collapse, prostration, (refresh,
restoration, revival, repair,
refection, recover, electricity,
power, energy, magnetism)

exile-*n* remove, eject, unload,
displaced, homeless, seclusion,
privacy, reclusion, recess,
solitude, isolation, loneliness,
estrangement, exclude, repel,
expatriate, outlaw, ostracize,
(companion, community,
welcome, reception, gather,
visiting, social, conviviality,
fellowship)

exit-*n* depart, embarkation,
removal, exodus, valediction,
adieu, farewell, flight, egress,
evacuation, emerge, emanate,
export, (ingress, entrance,
influx, import, invasion,
admission, insertion)

exonerate-*v* disencumber,
disengage, disentangle,
extricate, unravel, untie,
unload, emancipate, manage,
accomplish, absolve, dispense,
release, (prohibit, exclude,
embargo, forbid, restrictive,
difficult, hard, tough, dilemma)

expand-*v* increase, enlarge,
extend, dilate, develop,
augment, gain, ascend, exalt,
intensify, enhance, magnify,
add, develop, spread,
increment, (contraction,
consume, lessen, shrink,
collapse, emaciate, atrophy,
lose, reduce, decrease, limit)

expedient-*adj* desirable, suit,
fitness, agreeable, propriety,
opportunism, befit, conform,
acceptable, convenient,
worthwhile, applicable, useful,
(impropriety, unfit, undesirable,

objectionable, unsatisfactory,
improper)

expel-*v* ejaculate, eject,
discharge, push, fling, throw,
toss, projectile, propel, project,
send, shoot, launch, deport,
emit, reject, banish, extradite,
exit, drain, evacuate,
(reception, admission, admit,
entrance, ingest, absorb,
receive, inhale)

F

fable-*n* fallacy, misconception, error, laxity, mistake, blunder, misprint, delusion, hallucination, deception, mislead, deceive, erroneous, untrue, fallacious, unreal, unauthenticated, (real, actual, veritable, true, exact, accurate, definite, precise, defined)

fabulous-*adj* great, abundant, intense, strong, immense, enormous, vast, extreme, excessive, extravagant, exorbitant, outrageous, preposterous, unconscionable, monstrous, stupendous, astonishing, incredible, marvelous, (small, little, diminutive, minute, paltry, faint, slender, light, slight, scanty, meager, sparing, few, moderate)

face-*n* exterior, surface, outside, skin, superficial, frontal, confront, encounter, clash, contend, confront, brave, dare, summon, meet, stand-up, valiant, resolute, stout, determined, (cowardly, shy, timed, soft, spiritless, skittish, fearful, cower, skulk, flinch, interior, inner, within)

factor-*n* number, symbol, figure, cipher, formula, function, sum, multiplicand, multiple, dividend, prime, director, manager, moderator, taskmaster, delegate, consignee, envoy, merchant, trader, complimentary, positive, negative, formula

fade-*v* vacant, empty, blank, hollow, vanish, evaporate, dissolve, disappear, without, dreamy, shadowy, ethereal, immaterial, nominal, nothing, luminary, (substantial, exist,

full, tangible, essential, material, reappear)

fail-*v* feeble, impotent, relaxed, powerless, weak, soft, fragile, flimsy, unsubstantial, rickety, cranky, drooping, lame, withered, shattered, decrepit, languid, spent, decayed, worn, (strong, mighty, vigorous, forcible, hard, adamantine, stout, robust)

faint-*adj* small, atom, particle, molecule, granule, minimum, diminutive, minute, paltry, slight, scanty, meager, sparing, weak, feeble, debilitate, frail, fragile, languid, decayed, rotten, wasted, (strong, mighty, stamina, muscle, virile, vigor, great, immense, enormous, abundant, considerable)

fair-*adj* colorless, monochrome, pale, blanch, hueless, pallid, dull, muddy, sallow, dingy, ghastly, lusterless, moderate, ordinary, average, indifferent, (unparalleled, ripen, mature, shiny, dark, tone)

faith-*n* belief, credence, credit, assurance, trust, confidence, certainty, conviction, hopeful, optimism, aspire, expectation, confidence, reliance, (hopelessness, despair, despondency, pessimism, forlorn, doubt, misbelief, infidelity, dissent)

fallacy-*n* false, illogical, unsound, invalid, deceptive, evasive, irrelevant, vague, unwarranted, inconsequential, inconsistent, fallacious, (logical, correct, reasonable, rational, controversial, debatable, relevant)

false-*adj* error, fallacy, misconception, mistake, fault, blunder, delusive, deceptive, heresy, untrue, incorrect, lie, guile, perjury, forgery, invention, fabrication, distortion, evade, sham, (truthful,

scrupulous, sincere, frank,
honest, sober, exact, real,
authentic, precise, actual,
certain)

falter-v slow, slack, tardy,
leisurely, deliberate, gradual,
languid, moderate, slouch,
shuffle, totter, stagger, mince,
lumber, linger, loiter, saunter,
plod, trudge, dawdle, (gallop,
canter, trot, hasten, run, race,
whisk, fast, hurry, fly, eloquent)

familiar-adj aware, cognizant,
acquaint, inform, versed,
instructed, learned, lettered,
educated, enlighten, bookish,
accomplished, profound,
recognized, occurrence,
habitual, usual, ordinary,
(unusual, uncomfortable,
ignorant, uninformed, shallow,
empty, illiterate)

family-n kin, relation, fraternity,
paternal, maternal, ancestral,
linear, patriarchal, party,
alliance, linked, banded, united

fancy-n prefer, persuade, option,
select, pick, whim, humor,
drollery, pleasantry, brilliant,
desire, wish, solicitous,
overjoyed, entranced,
enchanted, ravished,
fascinated, captivated,
(afflicted, worried, displeased,
aching, griped, grieve, lament)

fantasy-n desire, wish, fancy,
want, need, inclination,
propensity, liking, fain, anxious,
curious, craving, thirst,
(indifference, neutrality,
coldness, unconcern, apathy,
disdain)

far-adv distance, space, remote,
elongation, remove, span,
away, inaccessible, out-of-
reach, unapproachable,
asunder, unconnected, (close,
tight, taut, firm, inseparable,
near, proximity, vicinity,
confines, alongside)

farce-n absurd, imbecility,
nonsense, paradox,

inconsistency, blunder, muddle,
preposterous, senseless,
inconsistent, ridiculous, foolish,
witty, quick, nimble-witted,
jocular, waggish, whimsical,
playful, pleasant, sparkling,
(dull, dry, commonplace,
pointless, flat, stale)

farewell-n depart, goodbye,
outward, exit, embark,
decampment, forfeiture, loss,
bereavement, deprivation, lose,
bereft, (recover, regain,
retrieve, inherit, arrival, advent,
land, welcome)

fascinate-v influence, prompting,
dictate, impulse, instigate,
encouragement, incentive,
incendiary, provoke, arouse,
stimulate, induce, move,
persuade, prevail, wonder,
astonish, amaze, awe, (expect,
common, ordinary, dissuasion,
disincline, averse, discourage)

fast-adj firm, close, tight, taut,
secure, set, intervolved,
inseparable, indissoluble, fickle,
erratic, afloat, alternating,
speed, hasten, scamper, run,
swift, nimble, agile, expeditious,
galloping, quick, (gradual, slow,
leisurely, tardy, gentle, easy,
deliberate, relax, stagger, plod,
trudge, vary, vacillate)

fat-adj large, big, great,
considerable, bulky,
voluminous, ample, massive,
capacious, comprehensive,
spacious, might, towering,
corpulent, stout, portly, full,
plump, shopping, thundering,
fleshy, burly, vast, (little, small,
dwarf, pygmy, midget, minute,
diminutive, microscopic, petty,
wee, undersized, short,
infinitesimal)

fathom-n length, line, bar, rule,
furlong, examine, study,
consider, calculate, dip, dive,
delve, probe, sound,
conclusion, ascertain, deduce,
derive, gather, collect, (answer,

response, reply, rebut, retort,
rejoin, explain, discover)

fault-*n* interruption, disjunction,
anacoluthon, break, fracture,
flaw, crack, cut, gap, mistake,
blunder, oversight, misprint,
botchery, error, fallacy, fail,
unsuccessful, unfortunate,
(success, fortunate, triumphant,
definite, precise, continuous,
consecutive, progressive,
unbroken, entire)

favorite-*adj* pleasurable,
pleasing, agreeable,
acceptable, welcome,
satisfactory, luscious luxurious,
sensual, attractive, engaging,
captivating, alluring, enticing,
appetizing, charming, delightful,
ravishing, beloved, loving,
adore, enamored, (hate,
alienation, estrangement,
coolness, enmity, animosity,
spiteful, malicious, insulting,
irritating, provoking,
displeasing, annoy, cross,
harass)

fearful-*adj* displease, annoy,
disturb, perplex, sadden,
painful, sicken, disgust, revolt,
nauseate, disenchant, repel,
offend, shock, skulk, slick,
flinch, cower, sneak, timid,
skittish, spiritless, (courage,
bravery, valor, resolute,
boldness, gallant, contempt,
confident, achieve, fortitude,
valiant)

feather-*n* plumage, plume, crest,
tuft, fringe, toupee, nap, pile,
floss, fur, down, light, subtle,
airy, weightless, ethereal,
sublimated, uncompressed,
volatile, buoyant, floating,
(gravity, heaviness, pressure,
ponderous, smooth, polish,
level, glossy, silken)

feature-*n* principle,
characteristic, fixed, incurable,
ineradicable, fixed, invariable,
form, figure, shape,
conformation, construction, cut,

set, build, lineament, posture,
attitude, (disfigure, deface,
mutilate, derange, shapeless,
unfashioned, intrinsic,
subjective)

felicitous-*adj* agreeing, suiting,
accordant, unison, harmonize,
congenial, becoming,
reconcilable, accordance,
consistent, elegant, polished,
classical, graceful, easy,
readable, fluent, flowing,
unaffected, (graceless, harsh,
abrupt, dry, stiff, cramped,
formal, forced, labored,
artificial)

fence-*n* forgery, perjury, false,
untruth, misrepresentation,
lying, invention, fabrication,
subreption, enclosure, refuge,
sanctuary, retreat, shelter,
screen, hiding place, (truthful,
true, veracious, pure, sincere,
candor, honesty, fidelity)

ferment-*v* disorder,
derangement, irregularity,
untidiness, turmoil, disturbance,
convulsion, tumult, uproar,
inert, inactive, passive, torpid,
sluggish, dull, heavy, flat, slack,
dead, uninfluential, latent,
dormant, smoldering, (activity,
agitation, effervescence,
perturbation, orderly, regular,
proper, uniform, methodical,
symmetrical, systematic)

fertile-*adj* productive, prolific,
teeming, fruitful, luxuriant,
pregnant, generate, propagate,
sufficient, ample, abundant,
enough, adequate, copious,
abounding, commensurate,
satisfactory, valid, tangible,
(deficient, inadequate,
imperfect, scantiness, scarce,
poverty, famine, drought)

festoon-*n* curved, linear, lineal,
bowed, vaulted, hooked,
semicircular, crescentic,
lunular, fig-shaped, bow-
legged, oblique, circular,
ornamented, beautified, gilt,

F

tessellated, (simple, plain,
ordinary, homely, eyesore,
straight, direct)

fetch-v bring worth, rate, value,
appraisement, cost, figure,
demand, fare, (reduce,
discount, abatement)

feverish-adj haste, urgency,
acceleration, spurt, rush,
forced, march, dash, flutter,
flurry, hurried, impetuous,
excite, affect, touch, move,
(leisurely, slow, deliberate,
quiet, calm, undisturbed, ease)

fidelity-n veracity, truthfulness,
frankness, sincerity, candor,
honesty, scrupulous, frank,
open, trustworthy, unaffected,
honorable, faithful, loyal,
(violate, lawless, transgressive,
elusive, evasive, false,
deceitful, fraudulent, dishonest,
unfaithful)

field-n spacious, roomy,
expansive, capacious, ample,
wide, vast, uncircumscribed,
boundless, arena, zone,
meridian, territorial, parochial,
provincial, patch, plot, region,
realm, domain, tract, court,
(niche, nook, compartment,
precinct)

fiery-adj violent, vehement,
warm, acute, sharp, rough,
rude, ungentle, bluff,
boisterous, wild, brusque,
abrupt, impetuous, rampant,
turbulent, disorderly, blustery,
raging, uproarious, frenzied,
(moderate, lenient, gentle, mild,
cool, sober, temperate,
reasonable, measured, calm,
quiet, tranquil, still, slow)

fight-v contention, strife, contest,
struggle, belligerency,
controversy, war, litigation,
sparring, competition, rivalry,
opposition, combative,
contending, embattled, militant,
(tranquil, pacific, peaceable,
untroubled, harmony, quiet,
neutrality, conciliatory,

composing, amnesty,
arrangement)

file-v arrange, distribute, sort,
prepare, dispose, organize,
analyze, classify, digest, divide,
catalog, tabulate, index,
systematize, methodize,
regulate, register, consecutive,
continuous, progressive,
successive, linear, (broken,
interrupted, unconnected, gap,
litter, scatter, disarrange,
disorganize)

fill-v complete, entire, replenish,
totally, brimming, plenary,
occupy, inhabit, moored,
domiciled, populous, attend,
dwell, reside, lodge, nestle,
roost, permeate, (absent, away,
gone, missing, lost, omitted,
nonexistent, empty, void,
vacant, devoid)

final-adj end, close, terminate,
dissonance, conclude, finale,
period, term, consummation,
finish, expire, last, complete,
accomplished, culmination,
result, exhaust, (beginning,
commencement, opening,
outset, inception, introduction,
inauguration, embarkation,
initial, first, incipient, leading)

find-v discover, detect, hunt,
determine, evolve, decision,
deduction, gain, acquire,
obtain, purchase, remunerative,
lucrative, (lose, mislay, forfeit,
deprived)

fine-adj thin, narrow, slender,
close, taper, slim, scant, spare,
delicate, incapacious,
contracted, lean, emaciated,
meager, gaunt, lanky, weedy
flimsy, slight, (thick, broad,
dense, widen, ample, extend,
spread)

finesse-n clever, talent, ability,
ingenuity, capacity, endowed,
skillful, dexterous, adroit,
expert, apt, handy, quick, deft,
ready, gain, smart, ready,
proficient, masterful, thorough,

accomplished, able, ingenious,
(bungling, awkward, clumsy,
unskillful, slovenly, gawky,
inept, incompetent, stupid,
unfit)

fire-*n* heat, warmth, hot, torrid,
smoking, burning, alight, afire,
ablaze, unquenched,
smoldering, flow, sweat, sultry,
hellish, inferno, (heavenly,
celestial, cold, cool, frigid,
fresh, keen, bleak, shivering,
bitter, chill, inclement, biting,
icy, glacial, frosty, freezing)

first-*adj* initial, beginning,
commence, opening, outset,
inception, introduction,
inaugurate, manifest, apparent,
entrance, inlet, dawn, genesis,
birth, original, start, front, (end,
last, consummation, finish,
terminate, conclude expire,
definitive)

fish-*n* chase, hunt, sport, pursuit,
prosecution, quest, scramble,
inquire, investigate, unearth,
ferret out, seek, search, track,
trail, feel out, (answer, respond,
reply, acknowledge, discover,
explain, refrain, spare, abstain,
unsought, avoid, neutral,
evasive)

fit-*v* conform, consistent, adapt,
adjust, graduate, assimilate,
match, suit, harmony, unison,
appropriate, deft, apply, meet,
dovetail, (unfit, unsuited,
inconsistent, mismatch,
intrusive, uneven)

fix-*v* join, unite, attach, affix,
fasten, bind, secure, clinch,
twist, tie, string, strap, sew,
lace, stitch, tack, knit, button,
buckle, hitch, lash, truss,
bandage, braid, (sunder, divide,
disjoin, sever, abscind, cut,
saw, snip, nip, cleave, split,
chip, crack, carve)

flagrant-*adj* immoral,
impropriety, scandal,
looseness, demoralization,
corruption, atrocity, infirmity,

weakness, frailty, (virtuous,
merit, worth, excellence, credit,
self-control, self-denial,
fulfillment)

flat-*adj* inert, dull, torpor,
languor, quiescence, inaction,
sloth, obstinacy, passive,
sluggish, slack, tame, slow,
blunt, lifeless, uninfluential,
latent, dormant, low, neap,
debase, nether, crouched,
subjacent, squat, prostrate,
(high, elevated, eminent,
exalted, lofty, tall, gigantic,
towering, soaring)

flatter-*v* cunning, crafty, artful,
skillful, subtle, feline, profound,
designing, contriving, intriguing,
strategic, diplomatic, artificial,
sly, insidious, stealthy,
charming, fascinating,
enchanting, humor, amuse,
gratify, (hurtful, bitter,
displease, annoy, trouble,
disturb, cross, perplex, molest,
tease, tire, irk, bother, pester,
harass, harry, badger, beset,
persecute, heckle)

flaw-*n* discontinue, pause,
interrupt, intervene, break,
interpose, disconnect,
separation, gap, opening, hole,
chasm, crack, slit, fissure, rift,
breach, gash, cut, leak, dike,
fault, erroneous, untrue,
unsound, illogical, inaccurate,
incorrect, (exact, accurate,
definite, precise, well-defined,
just, right, correct, strict, close,
liberal, rigid)

fleece-*v* tegument, skin, pellicle,
fell, fur, leather, hide, pelt,
cover, theft, steal, thievery,
robbery, depredation, plunder,
pillage, blackmail, burglary,
buccaneer, strip, abduct,
confiscate, sequester

fling-*v* propel, project, throw,
cast, pitch, chuck, toss, jerk,
heave, hurl, flirt, fillip, dart,
lance, tilt, sling, send,
discharge, shoot, bolt, (draw,

F

pull, haul, lug, drag, tug, tow,
trail, wrench, jerk, tactile)

float-*v* navigate, sail, nautical,
naval, coasting, afloat,
transport, tender, whaler,
slaver, coaster, yacht, launch,
buoyant, ascend, rise,
(descent, drop, fall, gravitate,
sink, droop, settle, decline,
dismount)

flock-*n* crowd, horde, body,
tribe, crew, gang, band, party,
company, troop, army,
regiment, assemble, dense,
muster, together, collect,
convene, congregate,
accumulate, (disperse, adrift,
stray, disheveled,
dissemination, dissipation,
scatter, disband, disembody,
dispel)

floor-*n* ground, base, foundation,
substructure, pavement, deck,
footing, basis, bottom, nadir,
foot, fundamental, horizontal,
level, even, plan, plat, smooth,
succeed, flushed, victorious,
unbeaten, (unsuccessful,
highest, top, crest, apex,
zenith, uppermost)

flounder-*v* inconstancy,
versatile, unstable, vacillate,
changing, ever-changing,
fluctuating, restless, agitating,
variable, erratic, fickle,
irresolute, capricious,
spasmodic, (fixed, steadfast,
firm, steady, balanced, valid,
immovable, riveted, tethered,
anchored, moored, established)

flourish-*v* prosperity, welfare,
well-being, affluence, success,
wealth, thriving, fortunate,
lucky, flushed, felicitous,
effective, flower, (abortive,
addle, fruitless, bootless,
inefficient, inefficacious, lame,
insufficient, unavailing, useless,
swamp)

flow-*v* elapse, lapse, run,
proceed, advance, pass, roll,
slide, glide, progress, loose,
dependent, stream, flux, run,
course, move, shifting, restless,
nomadic, (still, fixed, stationary,
sedentary, quiet, calm, anchor,
still, restful)

flower-*n* produce, create,
construct, form, fabricate,
manufacture, build, erect, edify,
organize, establish, achieve,
evolve, develop, grow, genesis,
bear, generate, impregnate,
(destroy, destruct, waste,
dissolve, consume, ruin, crash,
smash, extinction, subversive,
suicidal, squash, squelch)

fluctuate-*v* change, inconstancy,
versatility, mobility, instability,
vacillate, alter, restlessness,
fidget, disquiet, agitate,
variable, waver, shift, shuffle,
flitter, totter, tremble, oscillate,
alternate, (tethered, fixed,
steadfast, firm, balanced,
permanent, constant,
unchanged, undeviating,
durable, perennial)

flush-*v* flat, plane, flounder, jet,
spurt, squirt, spout, splash,
rush, gush, deluge, inundation,
stream, flux, flow, brook,
torrent, (gust, blast, breeze,
squall, gale, storm, tempest)

fly-*v* flit, elapse, lapse, flow, run,
proceed, advance, slide, glide,
pass, transient, fleeting,
shifting, spasmodic, wild,
abrupt, impetuous, turbulent,
disorderly, (moderate, gentle,
lenient, still, slow, smooth,
tame, peaceful, standing,
perpetual)

fold-*v* halve, divide, split, cleave,
bisect, enclosed, envelope,
(circumvent, skirt, twine)

follow-*v* succeed, next, ensure,
conform, observe, obey,
comply, supervene,
consecutive, continue, sequel,
behind, attend, pursue, beset,
tread, example, (precede,
forerun, lead, advance, prior,
former, foregoing, before,

advance, start, preliminary)

fool-*n* deceive, false, fraud, guile, delusion, circumvent, overreach, maneuver, cunning, deceptive, counterfeit, pseudo, pretend, feign, tricky, adulterate, rotten, disguise, simulate, disrespect, aweless, irreverent, disparaging, insulting, rude, derisive, sarcastic, (respect, regard, consideration, courtesy, reverence, honor, esteem, estimation, veneration, admiration, approbation)

foot-*n* bottom, nadir, sole, toe, hoof, fundamental, founded, based, ground, broad, support, foundation, base, basis, bearing, hold, landing, aid, prop, stand, shore, truss, beam, rafter, (suspend, hang, pendulum, swing, dangle, swag, flap, loose, flowing)

forbear-*v* refrain, abstain, inaction, neutrality, avoidance, evasion, elusion, seclusion, flight, escape, recoil, reject, unsought, shun, spare, shirk, dodge, parry, fugitive, (pursuit, pursue, enterprise, adventure, scramble, chase, hunt, prosecute)

forbid-*v* prohibit, disallow, bar, forefend, withhold, limit, circumscribe, restrict, taboo, interdict, exclude, dissent, negative, unconsenting, unavowed, discontented, (assent, admission, agreement, affirm, recognition, acknowledge, permit, indulgent, allow)

force-*v* power, potency, might, energy, ascend, control, authority, ability, ableness, competency, efficiency, enablement, influence, capability, almighty, adequate, efficacious, valid, able, (powerless, impotent, unable, incapable, incompetent,

harmless, weaponless, null, void, nugatory, ineffectual, failing, inadequate)

forecast-*v* foresight, deliberation, prevision, longsightedness, anticipation, providence, surmise, foregone conclusion, prudence, foreknowledge, precognition, prediction, announcement, premonition, warning, prognosis, prophecy, horoscope, preparation, rehearsal, provision, arrange, array, (unnurtured, uneducated, premature, undigested, improvidence)

forefathers-*n* paternal, parental, maternal, family, ancestral, linear, patriarchal, descendant, heir, generation, (succeed, ensue, alternate, after, latter, follow)

foreign-*adj* irrelative, irrespective, unrelated, arbitrary, independence, adrift, isolated, insular, extraneous, strange, alien, outlandish, exotic, intrude, emigrant, outsider, inadmissible, (implicate, integral, member, merge, constitute, relative, cognate, referable, akin, family, allied, affiliated, fraternal)

foremost-*adj* superior, supreme, greater, advantage, preponderance, advantageous, prevalence, nobility, preeminence, culmination, transcendence, excess, major, higher, exceeding, distinguished, vaulting, important, (inferior, minority, smaller, minor, less, deficient, subordinate, secondary, least, under, lower, diminish)

forestall-*v* subsequently, afterwards, later, thereafter, thereupon, since, beforehand, anticipate, prior, previous, precede, posthumous, premature, before long,

F

unexpected, postpone,
(adjournment, succeed,
supervene, posterior, following,
after, later, postliminium,
postdate)

forfeit-*v* fail, evasion,
unobservance, omission,
neglect, informality,
infringement, infraction,
violation, transgression, break,
retraction, repudiation,
nullification, protest, lapse,
deprivation, loss, (fulfillment,
satisfaction, faithful, profit,
earnings, proceeds, acquire,
advantageous, gainful,
remunerative, paying, lucrative)

forlorn-*adj* dejected, depression,
prostration, lowness,
oppression, heaviness, gloom,
weariness, melancholy,
sadness, dismal, despondent,
blank, discourage, dispirit,
frown, spiritless, grieve,
affliction, (cheerful, happy,
smiling, blithe, bright, airy,
jaunty, sprightly, vivacious,
sparking, winsome, frisky,
playful, jocular)

form-*n* copy, facsimile,
counterpart, effigy, likeness,
similitude, semblance, cast,
imitation, model,
representation, orderly, regular,
correct, methodical, uniform,
symmetrical, unconfused,
arranged, systematic,
(disorderly, promiscuous,
indiscriminate, chaotic,
complex, intricate, complicated,
perplexed, knotted, tangled,
dislocated)

formula-*n* rule, routine,
uniformity, constancy,
standard, model, precedent,
conformity, principle, steady,
legal process, law, code,
statute, canon, ordinance,
decree, numeral, divisible,
prime, fractional, (irregular,
diversified, indiscriminate,
desultory, difference, illegal,

prohibited, unlawful, illicit,
uncharted, unauthorized,
unofficial)

fortuitous-*adj* casual,
accidental, adventitious,
causeless, incidental,
contingent, undetermined,
possible, unintentional,
haphazardly, random,
speculation, venture, chance,
undesigned, unpremeditated,
indiscriminate, promiscuous,
undirected, without purpose,
(intended, advised, determined,
prepense, undertaking, design,
ambition)

fortune-*n* chance,
indetermination, accident,
hazard, haphazard, random,
fate, lottery, casually, happen,
destiny, foredoom, predestined,
fatalism, wealthy, rich, affluent,
opulent, moneyed, capital,
afford, (poor, indigent, poverty,
needy, necessary, distressed,
bereft, bereaved, reduced)

forward-*adj* early, prime, timely,
punctual, prompt, summary,
discourteous, disrespect,
impudent, ill-bred, vulgar,
unpolished, rude, saucy, harsh,
austere, sarcastic, biting,
caustic, snarling, surly,
(courteous, polite, civil,
mannerly, urbane, well-
behaved, polished, cultivated,
refined, gallant, late, tardy,
slow, behind, behind,
backward)

foundation-*n* stability,
constancy, immobile, sound,
vital, stable, established,
fixture, tower, pillar, fixed,
durable, tethered, anchored,
moored, (unstable, fluctuation,
movable, vicissitude, shake,
totter, fitter, flutter, flounder,
mobile, transient)

fracas-*n* disorder, derangement,
irregular, anomaly, confusion,
disarray, muddle, hodgepodge,
chaos, medley, scramble,

embroilment, whirlwind,
unsymmetrical, untidy, (order,
uniformity, symmetry, series,
routine, method, disposition,
arrangement, discipline)

fracture-*n* separation, parting,
detachment, segregation,
divorce, supposition, divide,
sunder, sever, cut, saw, carve,
dissect, mangle, gash, hash,
slice, whittle, disperse,
apportion, (attach, fix, join,
unite, embody, affix, fasten,
bind, secure, tie, pinion, string,
strap, link, marry)

frail-*adj* weak, relax, languor,
impotence, infirmity, fragile,
declination, loss, dull, spent,
weatherbeaten, decayed,
rotten, worn, seedy, wasted,
defenseless, feeble, debilitate,
unnerved, powerless, flaccid,
nervous, soft, womanly,
unsubstantial, (strong, mighty,
vigorous, forcible, hard,
adamantine, stout, robust,
sturdy, hardy, powerful, potent,
valid, resistless, impregnable,
sovereign, athletic)

frame-*v* support, aid, prop,
stand, anvil, shore, skid, rib,
truss, bandage, stirrup, stilt,
scaffold, skeleton, beam, rafter,
backbone, set, fit, mold, tone,
tenor, turn, trim, guise, fashion,
light, style, character,
structural, organic, model,
formal, (dangle, swag, flap,
trail, flow, suspend, hand, sling,
append, pensive, depend,
swing, loose, flowing)

free-*adj* sunder, divide, sever,
abscind, splinter, chip, crack,
divorce, part, detach, separate,
cut off, adrift, loose,
disentangle, isolate, liberate,
apart, rupture, breach, split,
divulge, section, rift, incision,
fission, (attach, fix, affix, fasten,
pinion, string, gird, tether,
moore, harness, chain, fetter,
join, twine, twist, incorporate,

close, secure, leash, couple,
nail, bolt)

frequent-*adj* repeat, again,
often, anew, over again, once
more, ditto, many, iterate,
harping, recurrence,
succession, monotony, rhythm,
imitate, incessant, perpetual,
continual, constant, habitual,
commonly, (seldom, rarely,
scarcely, hardly, infrequently,
few, never, inconstant)

fresh-*adj* new, novelty, recent,
immaturity, youth, innovation,
renovation, modern,
mushroom, renew, green,
evergreen, raw, virgin, neoteric,
newborn, (old, antiquity,
maturity, decline, decay,
senility, seniority, archaism,
ancient, venerable, prime,
obsolete)

fret-*v* suffer, pain, dolor, ache,
twinge, twitch, gripe, headache,
hurt, cut, sore, discomfort,
malaise, spasm, cramp,
nightmare, throb, agitate,
sharp, piercing, throbbing,
gnawing, anguish, experience,
writhe, (enjoy, luxurious,
sensual, comfortable, cozy,
snug, agreeable, grateful,
refreshing, cordial, genial,
palatable, fragrant, melodious,
lovely, beautiful)

fringe-*n* closure, obstruction,
plug, block, stop, button, shut,
bar, bolt, stop, seal, plumb,
choke, border, (vent, vomiter,
orifice, mouth, throat, portal)

frivolous-*adj* foolish, imbecility,
stolidity, dull, incompetence,
frivolity, irrationality, trifling,
giddiness, eccentricity,
extravagant, absurdity, shallow,
weak, stupid, idiotic, vacant,
bewildered, bovine, silly,
senseless, nonsensical, inept,
giddy, idle, (sober, prudent,
cautious, staid, solid,
considerate, wise, watchful,
provident, intelligent, acute,

F

rational, sound, clever, shrewd, discerning, penetrating)

front-*n* cover, guise, outfit, envelop, involve, sheathe, foreground, face, advance, outpost, countenance, pioneer, insolence, (rear, back, posteriority, guard, nape, stern, rump, breech, dorsal, after, aft, astern, behind, divest, bare, dishabille)

frugal-*adj* economical, saving, thriftiness, retrenchment, prevention, sparing, careful, parsimony, abstinence, moderation, temperance, forbearance, self-denial, restraint, (pleasurable, indulgence, self-indulgence, effeminacy, excess, dissipation, generous, bountiful, liberal, free, unsparing, carte blanche)

frustrate-*v* thwart, disconcert, balk, foil, baffle, snub, override, circumvent, defeat, spoil, mar, cripple, extinguish, dishearten, dissuade, undermine, meddle, encumber, choke, bar, block, barricade, prevent, oppose, (assist, help, lift, advance, favor, advocate, sustain, reinforce, support, uphold, bolster, nurture)

fuel-*n* firing, combustible, coal, anthracite, coke, carbon, charcoal, turf, peat, firewood, bobbing, match, light, incense, brand, torch, fuse, (non-combustible, non-flammable)

fugitive-*n* temporarily, awhile, short, briefly, transient, evanescence, impermanence, fly, gallop, vanish, evaporate, refugee, emigrant, vagabond, nomad, wanderer, adventurer, rover, straggler, rambler, (durable, lasting, permanent, survive, long-standing, persistent, perpetual)

full-*adj* much, great, might, importance, considerable, fair, huge, big, abundant, intense,

strong, sound, heavy, plenary, complete, entirety, perfection, altogether, effectual, wholly, totally, (incomplete, imperfect, fault, short, meager, lame, sketchy, small, minimum, little, diminutive, minute)

fumble-*v* jumble, muddle, toss, hustle, derange, misarrange, misplace, mislay, decompose, disorder, disorganize, embroil, unsettle, disturb, touch, feel, handle, thumb, paw, grope, grabble, twiddle, (arrange, distribute, sort, assort, allotment, apportionment, analyze, classify, digest)

fumigate-*v* vaporize, gasify, evaporate, exhale, volatile, smoke, transpire, emit, clean, purify, defecate, purge, launder, (rot, fester, putrefy, reek, stink, mold, dirty, filthy, grimy, soiled, contaminate, taint, corrupt, liquefied)

function-*n* numeral, symbol, divisible, prime, fractional, decimal, arithmetic, analysis, algebra, integral, calculus, useful, serviceable, subservient, conducive, efficient, effective, applicable, advantageous, expedient, (uselessness, inefficacy, futility, inadequate, inefficient, unskillful)

fundamental-*adj* essential, quintessence, incarnation, intrinsic, inherence, normal, implanted, natural, radical, hereditary, congenital, support, base, basis, bearing, footing, hold, (dependency, suspension, hanging, swing, dangle, append, extrinsically, extraneous, incidental, accidental)

fungus-*n* growth, carbuncle, wart, polypous, fungous, blister, boil, poison, leaven, virus, venom, arsenic, antimony, mildew, dry-rot, cancer, canker,

rust, (remedial, restorative,
nutritious, peptic, curable,
cellular, spongy, infundibular)

furbish-v improve, betterment,
melioration, mend, amend,
advance, elevate, increase,
reform, correct, refine, prepare,
provide, forthcoming,
adornment, embellishment,
japanning, varnish, cosmetic,
(pitted, discolored, imperfect,
impairment, injury, damage,
loss, detriment, decline, decay,
dilapidation, atrophy, collapse)

furnish-v provide, purvey,
reinforce, supply, find, cater,
victual, forage, replenish,
elaborate, mature, ripen,
mellow, season, temper,
anneal, commissariat, reserve,
(shiftless, wasteful, spend,
squander, drain, consumer,
expend, exhaust, disperse)

fury-n violence, inclemency,
vehemence, might, impetuosity,
boisterousness, effervescence,
turbulence, bluster, uproar, riot,
severe, exacerbation, orgasm,
force, outrage, shock,
trepidation, perturbation, ruffle,
hurry, fuss, flurry, fluster, (cool,
passiveness, calmness,
composure, tranquil, serenity,
quiet, staidness, restraint,
submissive)

fuse-v join, junction, attachment,
ligation, corporate, unite, fix,
affix, fasten, bind, secure,
clinch, twist, knit, braid, splice,
gird, tithe, molten, (separate,
disjoin, discontinue, leave,
asunder, adrift, insular, rift,
unconnected, apart)

F

G

gag-*n* render mute, constrained, imprisoned, pent up, stiff, control, repress, smother, suppress, rein, hold, enchain, shackle, bridle, muzzle, pinion, handcuff, secure, (liberate, disengage, release, emancipate, discharge, dismiss, deliver, acquittal)

gage-*n* measure, weigh, survey, appraise, assess, estimate, reckon, gauging, standard, rule, caliper, meter, rod, check, compass, rate

gain-*v* benefit, improvement, advantage, interest, service, behalf, satisfactory, commend, useful, good, blessing, fortune, treasure, happiness, profit, earnings, income, proceeds, fruition, harvest, (lose, forfeit, lapse, privation, bereavement, deprivation, riddance, incur, mislay, minus)

galaxy-*n* assemblage, collection, location, ligation, compilation, levy, gathering, muster, flux, verge, meeting, group, cluster, myriad, multitude, numerousness, profusion, multiple, heavenly bodies, stars, Asteroids, nebulae, milky way, galactic circle, (few, scant, thin, rate, scatter, scarce, infrequent, handful, minority)

gall-*n* torment, torture, rack, discomfort, malaise, twinge, twitch, pained, ache, unsavory, unpalatable, bitter, acrid, rough, offensive, repulsive, nauseous, loath, unpleasant, (palatable, nice, dainty, delectable, gusty, appetizing, exquisite, luscious, pleasurable, gratification)

gamble-*v* chance, accident, fortune, hazard, attribute, imputation, ascription, attribution, rationale, speculation, venture, stake, betting, adventurer, (intentional, knowingly, advisedly, designedly, purposely, studiously, deliberately, attribute

game-*n* beast, brute, animal, fleshy, zoological, pursuit, enterprise, undertaking, adventure, quest, business, hobby, chase, hunt, sporting, follow, prosecute, fun, frolic, amusement, entertain, diversion, relaxation, solace, pastime, pleasure, merriment, laughter, regatta, (weary, disgusting, tiresome, irksome, uninteresting, dry, monotonous, dull, arid, humdrum)

gang-*n* assemblage, gathering, collection, compilation, levy, muster, crown, throng, flood, rush, deluge, horde, body, tribe, crew, band, squad, party, go, moving, mobile, mercurial, restless, shifting, nomadic, unquiet, erratic, (quiet, tranquility, calm, repose, peace, stagnate, unassembled, disperse, sparse, sporadic, adrift, disheveled, streaming)

garble-*v* mutilate, amputate, abscind, excise, pare, thin, prune, decimate, abrade, scrape, file, geld, diminish, curtail, shorten, disseminate, exclude, bar, leave, reject, repudiate, blackball, relegate, segregate, banish, separate, omit, week, (containing, constituting, inclusion, admission, comprehension, reception, addition, annexation, addition, affix, subjoin)

garland-*n* circle, circlet, ring, areola, hoop, bracelet, armlet, round, annular, orbicular, oval, ovate, elliptic, spherical, wreath, fascia, crown, corona, coronet, chaplet, festoon, embroidery, ornamented,

embellish, beautified, adorn,
(simple, plain, homely,
ordinary, unaffected, chaste,
severe, bald, flat, dull)

garrison-*n* occupied,
indigenous, native, domestic,
domiciled, naturalized,
vernacular, domesticated,
domiciliary, safe, utility,
efficacy, serviceable, adequate,
efficient, prolific, shelter,
concealment, fortification,
munition, ditch, entrenchment,
barrier, fence, (aggressive,
attacking, offensive,
obsidianus, incursion, invasion,
encampment, bivouac)

gasp-*v* blow, sneeze,
sternutation, hiccup, cough,
waft, respire, puff, wheeze,
snuff, fan, ventilate,
tempestuous, droop, broken-
winded, fatigue, weariness,
yawning, lassitude, exhaustion,
(refreshed, recuperative,
respire, breathe, reinvigorate,
flow, profluent, effluence)

gather-*v* assemble, collect,
locate, compile, lever, muster,
concourse, verge, hoard, meet,
flock, cumulative, populous,
gainful, profitable, acquire,
remunerative, lucrative, (loss,
forfeit, privation, riddance,
bereaved, dispossessed, quit,
deprivation)

gay-*adj* colorful, hue, tint, dye,
shade, pigment, chromatic,
bright, vivid, intense, deep,
fresh, unfaded, rich, gorgeous,
gaudy, florid, showy, flaunting,
flashy, glaring, flaring,
discordant, (mellow,
harmonious, sweet, delicate,
tender, refined, dismal, somber,
melancholy, dark, gloomy,
dreadful)

gazette-*n* publication, current,
notorious, flagrant, circulated,
propagation, edition,
newspaper, journal, imprinted,
edition, diary, log, book, record,

note, almanac, ledger, archive,
scroll, chronicle, portfolio,
(obliterate, erasure, cancel, out
of print, unregistered, unwritten,
efface)

gear-*n* clothes, things, array,
attire, vesture, garb, apparel,
wardrobe, outfit, equipment,
uniform, regimentals, livery,
accouterment, toggery, handle,
shaft, shank, blade, tiller, helm,
pulley, crank, winch, lever,
(divested, nude, exposed,
thread-bare, bareness,
exfoliation, disrobe, dismantle)

gem-*adj* super-excellence,
superiority, perfection, prime,
flower, cream, goodness, merit,
worth, beneficial, edifying,
satisfactory, jewelry, bijouterie,
trinket, locket, necklace,
bracelet, anklet, previous,
brilliant, (pitted, injured,
deformed, defective, flow, stain,
tarnished, disfigured, hurtful,
noxious, detrimental,
mischievous, malignant)

general-*adj* universal,
miscellany, catholic, every, all,
generic, common, ecumenical,
transcendental, prevalent,
prevailing, always, prescription,
usage, rule, standing order,
precedent, routine, rut, groove,
habitual, conformable, military
authority, marshal, potentate,
sovereign, tyrant, (servant,
subject, retainer, squire, vassal,
slave, unusual, uncommon,
special, disusage,
unconformity, unaccustomed)

genial-*adj* warm, mild, ardent,
aglow, productive, brining forth,
birth, evolution, development,
growth, genesis, perform,
operate, flow, formative,
sensual, voluptuous,
agreeable, cordial, sweet,
melodious, (painful, aching,
sore, gripe, gnaw, torture,
torment, agonize, crucify,
tingle, writher, rack, fall,

G

destroy, dissolution,
consumption, subversive,
ruinous, incendiary,
deleterious)

genius-*n* intellect,
understanding, reason, mental,
rational, subjective, faculties,
senses, consciousness,
observation, percipience,
instinct, conception, capacity,
wit, ability, skillful, dexterous,
adroit, expert, proficient,
masterly, clever, (foolish, inept,
inexperienced, incompetent,
stupid, unqualified, vacant,
thoughtless, diverted, narrow-
minded, dull, thoughtless)

gentle-*adj* moderate, temperate,
sober, calmness, relaxed,
tranquil, mitigate, pacify,
sedative, lessen, slow, smooth,
unexciting, hypnotic, soft,
bland, lenient, reasonable,
peaceful, mild, demure,
imperturbable, enduring,
(vehement, demonstrative,
violent, wild, furious, fierce,
fiery, hot-headed, madcap,
over-zealous, enthusiastic,
impetuous, passionate,
fanatical)

genuflection-*n* bowing,
courtesy, curtsy, obeisance,
depress, drop, sink, fall,
debase, abase, reduce,
prostration, subversion,
precipitation, kneel, surrender,
kowtow, homage,
(disrespectful, aweless,
irreverent, disparaging,
insulting, rude, sarcastic,
elevate, raise, erection,
upheaval)

gestation-*n* production, creation,
construction, formation,
fabrication, manufacture,
building, erection, flowering,
fructify, birth, delivery,
confinement, travail, labor,
midwife, obstetrics, gender,
propagation, impregnation,
(destroy, waste, disruption,

consumption, ruin, smash,
sacrifice, demolish, dispel,
smash, quell, shatter)

ghastly-*adj* pale, uncolored,
achromatic, hueless, pallid,
faint, dull, muddy, dead, dingy,
ashy, cadaverous, ashen,
misshapen, plain, homely, ugly,
deformed, disfigurement,
distorted, graceless, uncouth,
rugged, rough, gross, rude,
awkward, (beautiful, elegant,
graceful, adorned, brilliant,
radiance, splendor, gorgeous,
magnificent, pretty, handsome,
dapper, jaunty, shiny)

giant-*n* gargantuan, monster,
mammoth, whale, behemoth,
leviathan, colossus, whopper,
great, ample, large, corpulent,
stout, fat, huge, immense,
enormous, mighty, stupendous,
infinite, brawny, lumpish,
strong, mighty, robust,
powerful, potent, valid,
resistless, (frail, fragile, shatter,
flimsy, unsubstantial, rickety,
little, dwarf, pygmy, scant,
minute, diminutive, puny,
infinitesimal, atomic)

giddy-*adj* inattentive, absent,
abstracted, distrait, lost,
preoccupied, disconcerted,
napping, dreamy, thoughtless,
scatter-brained, wild, careless,
disregard, heedless, neglectful,
fickle, unsettled, vacillation,
timid, (self-controlled,
determined, decisive, resolute,
vigor, zeal, devotion, self-
possessed, definitive,
peremptory, flinching,
shrinking, firm, relentless)

glid-*v* cover, canopy, bandage,
cutaneous, armor-plated, iron-
clad, sheath, wrap, veneer,
face, coating, paint, anoint,
incrustation, whitewash,
envelop, deceive, falseness,
untruth, fraud, deceit, guild,
misrepresent, trick, cheat,
juggle, collusion, (lie, stuff,

incrust, wad, pad, truth, open)

gird-*v* bind, firm, fast, close,
tight, taut, secure, set, nail,
bolt, hasp, clasp, rivet, solder,.
wedge, miter, attach, affix,
secure, engage, strengthen,
vigor, force, might, robust,
sturdy, hardy, powerful, potent,
dynamic, (weak, feeble,
debilitate, impotent, relaxed,
unnerved, unstrung, flaccid,
soft, effeminate, frail, flimsy)

glad-*adj* gratification, pleasure,
enjoyment, fruition, relish,
satisfaction, happiness, felicity,
bliss, beatitude, joy, gladness,
delight, glee, cheer, comfort,
overjoyed, enchanted,
raptured, ravished, fascinated,
captivated, pleasing, (suffer,
painful, ache, smart, grieve,
mourn, yearn, repine, droop,
languish, despair, displeasure,
annoyance, irritation, infliction,
anxiety, grief, sorrow)

glance-*v* view, look, espial, ken,
glimpse, peep, gaze, stare,
leer, contemplation, visual,
ocular, behold, perceive,
ophthalmic, sight, examine,
cursorily, skim, watchful,
(inattentive, unobservant, blind,
close, dismiss, discard,
discharge, oversight, disregard,
heedlessness, overlook)

glare-*v* garish, blazing, ablaze,
rutilant, meteoric,
phosphorescent, aglow,
shining, luminous, bright, vivid,
splendent, lustrous, flash,
sparkle, scintillate, coruscate,
reflection, refraction,
dispersion, gleam, twinkle,
shimmer, radiate, (dark, dim,
dull, dingy, fade, grimy, shade,
obscure, eclipse, gloom,
extinguish)

glass-*n* transparent, pellucid,
lucid, diaphanous, limpid, clear,
serene, crystalline, vitreous,
hyaline, smooth, polish, gloss,
even, flat, sleek, brittle, fragile,

break, frail, lacerate,
(tenacious, tough, strong,
opaque, film, thick, cloudy,
hazy, smoky, murky, dirty,
rough, rugged)

glide-*v* motion, movement,
move, going, flow, flux, run
course, stir, evolution,
kinematics, step, rate, pace,
tread, stride, gait, port,
cadence, carriage, transitional,
motive, shifting, mobile,
mercurial, unquiet, (still, fixed,
stationary, sedentary, stay,
pause, lull, tranquil, deliberate,
slow, gradual)

glimmer-*n* light, ray, beam,
stream, gleam, streak, moon,
glow, flush, halo, glory,
luminous, lucid, bright, vivid,
lustrous, shimmer, sparkle,
scintillate, radiate, (dark,
obscurity, gloom, eclipse,
shade, sunless, somber, dim,
dingy, gloomy, overcast)

glorify-*v* dedication,
consecration, enthronement,
canonization, celebration,
enshrinement, hero, worthy,
notability, rank, great,
eminence, importance,
elevation, ascent, super,
exaltation, dignify,
aggrandizement, (discredit,
disrepute, bad, disapprobation,
dishonor, disgrace, shame,
humiliation, tarnish, taint,
defilement, pollute)

gloss-*n* smooth, lubricity, velvet,
silk, satin, slide, glass, ice,
plane, file, mow, shave, level,
roll, macadamize, polish,
glabrous, slippery, lubricious,
oil, soft, (render rough, uneven,
knotted, aspergilius, crisp,
gnarled, unpolished, rough-
hewed, gnarled, crumble,
corrugate)

glut-*v* satiety, satisfaction,
saturation, repletion, surfeit,
weariness, spoiled, child, cloy,
quench, slake, pall, gorge,

G

swallow, enough, bolt, devour, gobble up, gulp, raven, greedy, adequacy, omnivorous, over-fed, (fast, starve, clam, famish, perish, unfed, hungry)

go-*v* motion, movement, transit, going, evolution, wander, gone, lost, departed, defunct, negative, elapse, lapse, flow, run, duration, proceed, advance, pass, expire, progress, (stop, admit, absorb, swallow, enter, introduce, receive, import, insert)

Godspeed-*n* depart, go, move, begone, farewell, adieu, goodbye, withdraw, vacate, leave, evacuate, abandon, remove, exit, embarkation, exodus, flight, (arrive, reach, attain, overtake, disembark, welcome, fetch, destined, reception)

good-*adj* savory, well-tasted, tasty, palatable, nice, dainty, delectable, gusty, appetizing, delicate, delicious, exquisite, rich, luscious, ambrosial, relish, zest, virtue, virtuousness, moral, ethic, merit, worth, (scandal, laxity, looseness, demoralizing, depravity, pollution, profligacy, atrocity, infirmity, error, defect, deficiency)

gorge-*v* ravine, break, gap, opening, hole, chasm, cleft, mesh, crevice, creek, cranny, crack, slit, fissure, crevasse, abyss, gulf, inlet, frith, strait, gully, pass, furrow, satiety, satisfaction, saturation, repletion, glut, surfeit, weariness, quench, slake, fatigue, (fastidiousness, nicety, epicure, gourmet, dainty, join, adjoin, touch, meet, osculate, coincide, coexist, adhere)

gorgeous-*adj* beauty, form, elegance, grace, unadorned, symmetry, comeliness, fairness, polish, gloss, good

looks, bloom, brilliancy, radiance, splendor, magnificence, handsome, pretty, lovely, refined, shapely, colored, bright, vivid, (achromatic, hueless, pale, ugly, plain, homely, ordinary, unsightly, deformed, eyesore, frightful, ghastly, graceless, gross)

gospel-*n* certainty, necessary, certitude, surety, assurance, moral, infallibleness, reliability, scripture, positive, dogmatism, sure, solid, absolute, positive, unerring, authentic, official, evident, (uncertain, dubious, hesitation, suspense, perplexity, dilemma, bewilderment, vagueness, confused)

grace-*n* style, elegance, purity, ease, readiness, polished, classical, correct, artistic, chaste, pure, academical, easy, fluent, flowing, tripping, unaffected, natural, unlabored, mellifluous, (stiffness, barbaric, euphuism, graceless, harsh, abrupt, dry, cramped, formal, forced, artificial, mannered)

gradation-*n* degree, extent, measure, amount, ratio, stint, standard, height, pitch, reach, amplitude, range, scope, caliber, shade, tenor, compass, station, rank, order, uniformity, correct, methodical, systematic, (confusion, disorder, jumble, huddle, wrong, fortuitous, perplexed, quantitative, some, more, less, any)

gram-*n* essence, small, little, tenuity, paucity, few, insignificance, mediocre, moderate, atom, particle, molecule, diminutive, minute, paltry, faint, slender, slight, scanty, meager, sparing, modest, mere, low, infinitesimal, stark, bare, (bast, immense, enormous, extreme,

excessive, extravagant,
exorbitant, outrageous,
preposterous)

grammar-*n* punctuate, syntax,
parts of speech, language,
conjugation, cast, declination,
rudiments, elements, outlines,
alphabet, begin, commence,
rise, arise, originate, conceive,
initiate, open, (end, final,
terminal, consummate, finish,
conclude, solecism, bad, false,
slipslop, ungrammatical,
incorrect)

grand-*adj* important,
momentous, serious, earnest,
noble, solemn, impressive,
commanding, imposing, urgent,
pressing, critical, prominent,
grave, superior, instant,
essential, vital, absorbing,
considerable, significant,
telling, (poor, paltry, trifling,
trivial, slight, slender, light,
flimsy, frothy, idle, foolish,
powerless, petty, pitiful)

grant-*v* admit, acknowledge,
avowal, reveal, divulge, allow,
concede, confess, disclose,
transpire, permission,
empower, license, authorize,
absolve, entrust, sanction,
license, privilege, favor,
(prohibit, forbid, disallow,
hinder, restrict, exclude,
withhold, bar, veto, limit,
ambush, conceal, stalk, cover,
recess)

graphic-*adj* intelligent, clear,
explicit, lucid, perspicuity,
legibility, precise, simplify,
understand, comprehend,
distinct, positive, illustrative,
expressive, recognizable,
obvious, (riddle, paradox,
unaccountable, illegible, vague,
loose, ambiguous, obscure,
perplexed, negative, nebulous)

grasp-*v* comprehend,
understand, catch, follow,
collect, master, lucid, luminous,
transparent, plain, distinct,

explicit, positive, definite, take
hold, retain, detain, detention,
custody, tenacity, firm hold,
grip, secure, (relinquish,
abandon, renounce, derelict,
surrender, dispense, resign,
eliminate)

gratuitous-*adj* intuitive,
instinctive, impulsive,
independent, unconnected,
inconsistent, fallible,
groundless, unproved, evasive,
irrelevant, cheap, low,
moderate, reasonable,
depreciated, unsaleable, gratis,
without charge, (expensive,
extravagant, exorbitant,
extortionate, premium,
priceless, precious,
overcharged, rationalistic,
argumentative, controversial)

gravity-*n* force, power, pressure,
elasticity, electricity,
magnetism, galvanism,
capability, voltaism, attraction,
dynamic, energy, friction,
suction, capacity, weight,
heaviness, ponderous, load,
burden, (levity, lightness,
buoyancy, leaven, subtle, airy,
weightless, floating, portable,
powerless, impotent, valid,
effective, influential, productive)

grease-*n* lubricate, smoothly,
anoint, oil, glycerine, lather,
wax, payment, settle,
discharge, quit, acquit,
liquidate, retribution, remit,
installment, (disgorge, repay,
refund, reimburse, insolvent,
bankrupt, gazetted, protest,
dishonor, rub, scratch, scrape,
rasp, scrub, grind, friction)

greed-*n* desire, avidity,
covetous, ravenous, craving,
voracity, gluttony, hunger,
longing, hankering, solicitude,
impatient, impetuous, over-
anxiety, gorge, gormandize,
devour, gobble up, gulp, raven,
guzzle, cram, fill, (fast, starve,
perish, Lenten, unfed, famish,

G

indifferent, cold, neutrality,
unconcern)

gregarious-*adj* social,
companion, comradeship,
conviviality, good fellowship,
festivity, hospitality, heartiness,
cheer, welcome, greetings,
receptive, fraternize,
(seclusion, exclusion, privacy,
retirement, reclusion, recess,
solitude, isolation, loneliness,
estrangement, voluntary exile)

grieve-*v* mourn, anxiety,
concern, grief, sorrow, distress,
affliction, woe, bitterness,
heartache, heaving, aching,
bleeding, misery, tribulation,
wretchedness, desolation,
despair, prostration,
(happiness, felicity, bliss,
beatitude, enchantment,
transport, rapture, ravishment,
ecstasy, paradise, Elysium)

grind-*v* reduce, contract,
decrease, lessen, shrink,
collapse, emaciation,
consumption, atrophy,
condensation, compression,
compact, smaller, squeeze,
lessen, narrow, constrict, crush,
dwarf, (expand, increase,
enlarge, extend, augment,
amplify, spread, increment,
growth, develop)

grip-*n* power, retention, retain,
detention, custody, tenacity,
firm hold, grasp, forfeit, secure,
clutch, swoop, wrench, take,
catch, hook, nab, (return,
restore, reparation, release,
replevin, redemption, recovery,
recuperate, surrender, yield,
forego, renounce, abandon,
expropriate)

gross-*adj* great, magnitude,
size, multitude, immensity,
enormity, infinity, fullness, great
quantity, volume, monstrous,
incredible, whole, total,
aggregate, amount, sum-total,
command, hold, grasp, reach,
clutch, regime, monarchy,

(fractional, fragmentary,
sectional, divided, partial,
compartment, portion, section,
piece)

grotto-*n* alcove, hermitage,
greenhouse, portico, lobby,
court, porch, veranda, arbor,
depression, dip, hollow,
depressed, concave,
cavernous, cave, cove, (cupola,
dome, arch, balcony, eaves,
pilaster)

ground-*n* land, earth, ground,
dry land, continent, mainland,
peninsula, delta, coast, shore,
soil, clay, loam, acres, real
estate, cause, origin, source,
principle, element, reason,
rationale, occasion, derivation,
(consequently, necessarily,
eventually, derivative, sea,
ocean, water, waves, billows)

grow-*v* increase, enlarge,
extension, accession, augment,
gain, strengthen, intensify,
enhance, magnify, redouble,
dilate, exaggerate,
expansibility, germination,
growth, swollen, develop,
amplify, widen, (reduce,
scrape, compress, lessen,
shrink, collapse, emaciate,
atrophy)

guard-*v* protect, preserve,
custody, chaperone, watch,
warden, preserve, shelter,
shroud, flank, secure, trust,
defend, garrison, driver,
coachman, whip, fireman,
(danger, peril, insecure,
jeopardy, risk, precariousness,
exposure, vulnerability,
instability)

gypsy-*n* vagabond, nomad,
Bohemian, wanderer, pilgrim,
emigrant, fugitive, refugee,
runner, courier, comet,
pedestrian, tourist, passenger,
excursionist, explorer,
adventurer, rover, rambler,
straggler, gad-about, (dupe,
dull, credulous)

H

habit-*n* essence, temper, spirit, humor, capacity, constitution, character, type, quality, garment, garb, palliative, apparel, wardrobe, wearing apparel, clothes, array, outfit, morning dress, uniform, (divestment, nudity, bareness, undress, uncover, denude, disrobe, extraneousness, accident, derived from without)

hack-*v* cut, sunder, divide, subdivide, sever, abscind, saw, snip, nib, nip, cleave, rend, slit, split, splinter, carve, cut up, dissect, disintegrate, disperse, separate, discrete, ass, donkey, jackass, mule, horse, (join, attach, unite, fasten, bind, fix, affix, buckle, gird, close)

hackneyed-*adj* dictum, saying, adage, proverb, sentence, perception, enlightenment, glimpse, inkling, trite, reflection, conclusion, golden rule, motto, axiom, maxim, aphorism, (blunder, muddle, absurd, imbecility, farce, rhapsody, sell, pun, ignorance, blindness)

haggard-*adj* fatigue, weariness, yawning, drowsiness, lassitude, tiredness, exhaustion, faintness, collapse, prostration, (refreshed, recover, revival, repair, refection, renew)

hall-*n* welcome, arrive, advent, landing, hither, good day, reach, advent, reception, home, goal, port, haven, sleet, ice, snow, flake, crystal, drift, frost, icicle, (heat, caloric, fire, spark, flash, flame, blaze, bonfire, fireworks, depart, decampment, leave, outward, whence, hence, farewell, adieu, goodbye)

half-*n* bisect, halving, divide, split, cut in two, cleave, dimidiate, separate, fork, bifurcate, cleft, bipartite, fork, prong, gradual, degree, retard, relax, slacken, moderate, rein, curb, leisurely, at half speed, slow, (hurry, accelerate, quicken, haste, rapid, scuttle, scud, gallop, amble, troll, hasten, duplicate, twice, once more, over again, renewal, double)

halt-*v* cease, discontinue, desist, stay, break, leave, hold, stop, stick, interrupt, suspend, enough, truce, weak, debility, stony, loss, drop, crumble, totter, tremble, shake, limp, fade, languish, decline, flag, (strength, power, energy, vigor, force, physical, spring, elasticity, tone, tension, continue, persist, go, sustain, uphold, keep, perpetuate, maintain, preserve)

hammer-*n* repeat, iterate, reiterate, recurrence, succession, monotony, rhythm, recur, revert, reappear, often, blow, dint, stroke, sledge, mall, maul, mallet, flail, batter, pile-driving, punch, bat, axe, (recoil, react, spring, revulsion, rebound, reflex, reverberate, rebuff, repulse, return)

hand-*n* organ of touch, touch, feel, handle, finger, thumb, feel, palpation, tingle, tangible, dextral, right-handed, ambidextrous, right and left, flank, quarter, (numb, intangible, impalpable, insensibility to touch)

handbook-*n* information, enlightenment, acquaintance, knowledge, publication, guide, manual, map, plan, chart, gazetteer, work, volume, tract, pamphlet, circular, portfolio, (conceal, hide, cloak, secrete, cover, screen, cloak, veil, shroud, masquerade)

handsome-*adj* liberal, free,

beautiful, pretty, lovely, graceful, elegant, delicate, dainty, refined, fair, personable, comely, good looking, dapper, jaunty, natty, quaint, (ugly, deformed, inelegance, disfigurement, squalor, monster)

handy-*adj* near, proximity, propinquity, vicinity, nigh, nearby, elongation, background, spread, neighboring, adjacent, adjoining, proximate, intimate, (distant, remote, far, extend, stretch, away, apart, asunder)

hang-*v* dependent, suspending, swing, dangle, swag, draggle, flap, trail, flow, sling, hook up, hitch, fasten, append, strangle, garrote, throttle, choke, stifle, suffocate, smother, asphyxiate, (support, bear, carry, sustain, bolster, hold, shoulder)

hapless-*adj* unfortunate, mishap, unblest, unhappy, unlucky, decayed, poor, adverse, disastrous, calamitous, ruinous, dire, deplorable, anxiety, solicitude, trouble, concern, grief, sorrow, distress, (prosperous, thrive, flourish, smooth, well-being, affluent, success, blessing, lucky)

hard-*adj* strong, strength, power, vigor, force, brute, force, mighty, adamantine, stout, robust, sturdy, powerful, potent, puissant, valid, reinforce, stamina, nerve, muscle, sinew, steel, energy, grip, bone, dynamite, rigid, renitency, inflexible, stubborn, stiff, firm, (soft, pliable, flexible, plasticity, tender, supple, lithe, limber, limp, frail, fragile, flimsy, unsubstantial, rickety, drooping, withered, shattered)

hardly-*adv* scarcely, slight, scanty, limited, sparing, few, low, below, moderate, modest,

inappreciable, infinitesimal, mere, simple, sheer, stark, bare, little, diminutive, nothing, morsel, thimble, trifle, unimportant, insignificant, trivial, paltry, indifference, nonentity, (important, consequence, prominence, considerable, significant, concern, emphasis, great, vast, immense, enormous, extreme, goodly, unsurpassed)

hark-*v* hear, audible, acoustic, listen, catch a sound, attentive, mindful, observant, alive, awakened, behold, breathless, heed, cognizant, recognize, (absent, abstract, disregard, heedless, indifference)

harm-*n* evil, ill, hurt, mischief, nuisance, disaster, accident, casualty, mishap, adversity, tragedy, ruin, destroy, catastrophe, calamity, bale, bad, painful, grievance, injurious, detrimental, noxious, mischievous, nocuous, vile, foul, rotten, (good, excellent, better, superior, above par, nice, fine, genuine, favorable, fair, benefit, advantage, improvement, interest, well, right, satisfactory)

harness-*v* fasten, attach, fix, affix, bind, secure, clinch, twist, tie, pinion, string, strap, sew, lace, stitch, tack, knit, button, buckle, hitch, last, truss, bandage, braid, splice, swathe, gird, tether, moore, picket, chain, fetter, yoke, collar, halter, muzzle, gag, bit, brake, curb, snaffle, bridle, rein, (sunder, divide, subdivide, sever, dissever, abscind, saw, snip, nib, nip, cleave, rend, slit, split, carve)

hatch-*v* produce, create, construct, formation, fabricate, manufacture, build, architect, erect, edification, establish, workmanship, perform,

achieve, complete, flower,
fructify, bring forth, birth,
deliver, evolve, develop, grow,
enclosure, barrier, barricade,
gate, door, hatch, (destroy,
waste, dissolve, disrupt,
consume, nullify, annul,
demolish, deteriorate, perish,
fall)

hateful-*adj* bad, hurtful, evil,
maltreat, abuse, injurious,
deleterious, detrimental,
noxious, pernicious,
mischievous, malignant, vile,
mean, wrong, depraved,
shocking, reprehensible,
disapprove, abominable,
detestable, execrable, cursed,
confounded, damned, infernal,
diabolic, (admirable, estimable,
praiseworthy, pleasing,
tolerable, best, choice, select,
goodness, beneficial, valuable,
serviceable, advantageous,
edifying, favorable)

have-*v* possess, own, hold,
tenure, occupy, depend,
monopoly, heritage,
inheritance, heir, engross,
recreate, acquire, get, gain,
win, earn, obtain, procure,
gather, collect, assemble, pick,
find, reap, secure, draw,
confute, (lose, bereft,
dispossess, rid, minus, deprive,
lapse, forfeit, mislay, exempt)

hazard-*n* chance, accident, haphazard, random, luck, casualty,
contingence, adventure,
probability, possibility, odds,
undetermined, fortuitous,
causeless, incidental,
unintentional, danger, peril,
insecurity, jeopardy, risk,
venture, precariousness,
slipperiness, instability,
defenseless, exposure, imperil,
(safety, security, surety,
impregnability, invulnerability,
safeguard, palladium, guardian)

heap-*n* big, huge, large, ample,
abundant, full, intense, heavy,

plenary, high, zenith, vast,
immense, enormous, extreme,
inordinate, excessive,
extravagant, exorbitant,
outrageous, preposterous,
monstrous, overgrown,
towering, stupendous,
prodigious, astonishing,
incredible, accumulate, lump,
pile, pyramid, (disperse, adrift,
here and there, smallness,
little, few, insignificant,
mediocrity, moderation, atom,
minute, inconsiderable, paltry,
scant, limited, meager, sparing,
few)

heart-*n* love, fondness, liking,
inclination, regard, admiration,
affection, sympathy, fellowship,
tenderness, benevolence,
attachment, passion, devotion,
fervor, adoration, idolatry,
Cupid, lover, amour, betrothed,
fiance, beloved, adorable,
sweet, enchanting, (hate,
disaffection, repugnance,
dislike, antipathy, detest,
abominate, abhor, loathe,
recoil, shatter, shrink, hateful,
irritate)

hearty-*adj* healthy, well, sound,
hale, fresh, green, whole, florid,
flush, staunch, brave, robust,
vigorous, weather-proof, willing,
voluntary, propend, inclined,
geniality, cordiality, goodwill,
readiness, earnestness,
forward, eager, (grudgingly,
unwillingly, adverse, reluctant,
backward, repugnant, delicate,
loss of health, invalidate,
atrophy, decay, decline,
consumption, fatal)

heat-*n* hot, warm, mild, genial,
tepid, lukewarm, unfrozen,
thermal, fervent, sunny, torrid,
tropical, estival, canicular,
close, sultry, stifling, stuffy,
suffocating, oppressive,
reeking, baking, burning,
sweltering, glow, flush, bask,
smoke, stew, simmer, seethe,

H

boil, burn, broil, blaze, flame,
smolder, parch, fume, pant,
content, strife, contest,
struggle, opposition, rivalry,
match, race, steeplechase,
handicap, regatta, (peaceful,
pacific, calm, tranquil, halcyon,
quiet, cold, frigid, ice, snow,
glacial, frosty, freezing, brutal,
hibernal, bitter, chilly, shiver,
fresh, inclement)

heave-v raise, heighten, elevate,
raise, lift, erect, stick, perch, tilt,
upheave, exalt, hoist, cast,
uplift, remain, stay, stand, lie,
bring, draw up, hold, halt, stop,
rest, pause, anchor, (move,
motion, shifting, mobile,
restless, nomadic, lower,
depress, dip, reduce, fall, sink,
trample, duck)

heaven-n god like, kingdom,
throne, paradise, eden,
celestial, resurrection,
supernal, unearthly, beatific,
eternal home, bliss, happiness,
felicity, beatitude, enchantment,
transport, rapture, ecstasy,
Elysium, (grieve, mourn, yearn,
repine, droop, languish, sink,
despair, afflicted, demoniacal,
haunted, supernatural, weird,
uncanny, evil)

hedge-n compensate, equate,
indemnification, compromise,
counter, retaliate, counterbalance, hinder, impede,
prevent, forefend, retard,
slacken, preclude, inhibit,
shackle, obstruct, stop, block,
barricade, (aid, assist, help,
support, lift, advance, further,
promote, relief, advocate,
reinforcement)

heir-n benefactor, grantee,
trustee, holder, generative,
descendant, heredity, descent,
lineage

hell-n abyss, hollow, pit, shaft,
well, crater, bottomless pit,
unfortunate, unblest, unhappy,
unlucky, poor, speculate,

venture, stake, random shot,
adversity, evil, failure, disaster,
gamble, adventure, risk,
hazard, stake, (intention,
purpose, project, design,
ambition, undertake, aim)

helm-n handle, hilt, haft, shaft,
heft, shank, blade, trigger, tiller,
treadle, key, turn screw,
screwdriver, direct, manage,
govern, conduct, order,
prescribe, head, lead, regulate,
guide, steer, pilot, drive, throne,
chair, dais, (anarchy,
relaxation, misrule,
subordinate, dethronement,
deposition, abdication)

hence-adv thence, therefore,
since, on account of, because,
owing to, wherefore, attribute,
impute, refer, derive, theorize,
reason, argue, discuss, debate,
dispute, wrangle, canvass,
comment, (unreasonable,
illogical, false, unsound, invalid,
unwarranted, inconclusive,
casual, fortuitous, accidental,
causeless, incidental,
contingent, undetermined)

herald-n precursor, antecedent,
precedent, predecessor,
forerunner, leader, bell-
weather, harbinger, dawn,
prelude, preamble, preface,
prologue, prefix, introduction,
heading, frontispiece,
groundwork, (sequel, suffix,
successor, tail, train, wake,
trail, rear, retinue, appendix,
postscript)

heritage-n heirs, posterity,
future, next, near, eventual,
ulterior, prospective, tomorrow,
eventual, ultimately, possess,
own occupy, hold, tenure,
depend, retain, inheritance,
revert, engross, (exemption,
absence, devoid, unobtained,
past, gone by, ancient, former,
antiquity, immemorial, bygone,
forgotten, irrecoverable,
obsolete)

hermitage-*n* abode, dwelling, lodging, domicile, residence, address, habitation, berth, seat, lap, housing, quarters, headquarters, tabernacle, throne, ark, home, fatherland, country, homestead, stall, fireside, hearth, stone, household

hesitate-*v* uncertain, suspense, perplexity, embarrassment, doubt, dubiety, vague, haze, fog, obscurity, contingency, puzzle, bewilder, bother, indecisive, ambiguous, questionable, precarious, disputable, (certain, necessary, assured, reliable, gospel, positive, solid, authoritative, authentic, official, evident, infallible)

hinder-*v* impede, prevent, preclude, obstruct, stop, interrupt, retard, embarrass, restrict, retrain, inhibit, interfere, discourage, drawback, stumbling block, foreclosure, prohibit, forbid, disallow, interdict, exclude, unauthorized, (grant, empower, charter, enfranchise, privilege, warrant, sanction, entrust, permit, allow, admit, concede, recognize, favor, license, authorize, aid, helpful, subservient)

hiss-*n* sound, hoot, gibe, flout, jeer, scoff, taunt, sneer, quip, fling, wipe, slap in the face, disrespect, disregard, slight, trifle, discourteous, dishonor, desecrate, insult, affront, outrage, (respect, regard, consideration, courtesy, attention, reverence, honor, esteem, admiration, homage)

hit-*v* blow, dint, stroke, knock, tap, rap, slap, smack, pat, dab, slam, bang, whack, squash, dowse, whop, swap, probability, possibility, contingency, odds, long odds, run of luck, hammer, mall, knock, strike, (duck, recoil, rebound, revulsion, repercussion)

hobble-*v* creep, craw, lag, slug, draw, linger, loiter, saunter, plod, trudge, stump along, move slowly, slouch, stagger, mince, slacken, moderate, easy, leisurely, deliberate, gradual, slow-paced, (trip, speed, hasten, move quickly, scuttle, scud, scamper, race, run, shoot, tear, whisk, sweep, brush, accelerate)

hobby-*n* pursuit, purse, prosecute, enterprise, adventure, quest, game, desire, wish, whim, devotee, aspirant, solicitant, avid, (indifferent, neutral, of no interest, have no desire, cold, frigid, lukewarm, avoid, shun, steer clear, deny)

hollow-*adj* vanish, unsubstantial, incomplete, deficiency, short measure, shortcoming, insufficient, imperfect, concave, dip, indentation, cavity, pit, follicle, depressed, excavate, furrow, trough, basin, valley, (convex, project, sell, bilge, bulge, protrude, tumor, hump, hunch, bulb, node, nodule)

holocaust-*n* kill, put to death, slay, shed blood, murder, assassinate, butcher, slaughter, suffocate, sacrifice, destroy, ravage, (creation, produce, generate, establish, give life to, complete)

homely-*adj* plain, disfigured, blemished, pitted, freckled, discolored, imperfect, injured, simple, ordinary, chaste, severe, (polished, festoon, garland, adorned, decorated, embellished, detailed, fleur-de-lis)

honest-*adj* veracity, truthful, frank, sincerely, candor, fidelity, true, scrupulous, trustworthy, probity, integrity, rectitude,

upright, honor, purity, fair, just,
equity, impartiality, principle,
grace, constancy, faithful,
warrant, apologize, advocate,
plead ignorance, (accuse,
charge, tax, impute, taunt,
reproach, slur, false, deception,
untruth, guile, lying,
misrepresentation, perjury,
forgery, fabrication)

honor-*n* glory, distinction,
reputation, notability, notoriety,
dedication, consecration,
enthronement, canonization,
celebration, enshrinement,
glorification, immortalize, exalt,
glitter, distinguished, great,
eminence, height, important,
(disrepute, discredit, repute,
dishonor, disgrace, shame,
humiliation, scandal, vile,
turpitude, tarnish, disgrace,
degrade, vile, stain, shameful,
degrading)

hoodwink-*v* deception, false,
untruth, fraud, deceit, guile,
misrepresentation, delusion,
trickery, circumvention,
chicane, juggle, hocus, feint,
ignore, bewilderment, shallow,
superficial, empty, half-learned,
uninformed, unaware,
(knowing, aware, cognizant,
conscious, acquainted,
instructed, learned, familiar,
scholastic, profound,
accomplished, ascertained)

hook-*n* attach, fix, affix, saddle
on, fasten, bind, secure, clinch,
twist, tie, string, strap, sew,
lace, stitch, tack, pin, nail, join,
fast, close, tight, taut,
inseparable, entangle, parting,
(sunder, divide, disengage,
subdivide, sever, cut, snip, nib,
nip, cleave, rend, slit, split,
carve, hack, lacerate, mangle,
rupture, shatter, shiver, crunch,
chop)

hop-*v* leap, jump, spring, bound,
vault, station, dance, caper,
curvet, caracole, skip, frisky,

bounce, flounce, agitation, fun,
frolic, merriment, pleasure,
amusement, sport, laughter,
reel, festivity, play, game,
(wearisome, tediousness, drag,
tiresome, uninterested,
monotonous, humdrum, slow,
plunge, dip, dive, duck,
submerge, douse, sink, engulf,
wallow)

hope-*v* desire, expectation, trust,
confidence, reliance, faith,
belief, assurance, reassurance,
promise, optimism, enthusiasm,
encouraging, cheering, bright,
rose-colored, prosperity,
welfare, well-being, affluence,
blessings, thrive, flourish,
(adverse, disastrous,
calamitous, ruinous, dire,
deplorable, unfortunate,
unhappy, unlucky, hapless,
despair, despondence,
abandonment)

horn-*n* receptacle, recipient,
receiver, reservoir,
compartment, vessel, vase,
utensil, sharp, keen, pyramidal,
spindle, needle-shaped, spiked,
thorny, bristling, barbed,
copious, abundant, abounding,
enough, rich, sufficient

horrify-*v* annoyance, grievance,
nuisance, vexation,
mortification, sicken, bore,
bother, plague, pest, sea of
troubles, misfortune, irritation,
painful, disgust, revolt,
nauseate, disenchant, repel,
offend, shock, fear,
apprehensive, solicitude,
anxiety, mistrust, suspicion,
alarm, tremble, shake, shiver,
shudder, (hopeful, trust,
encourage, aspire, optimistic,
pleasant, agreeable, pleasure,
delectable, loveliness, sunny,
bright, sweet, goodness,
satisfy, gratify, satiate, refresh,
attract, allure)

hostile-*adj* disagreeing,
discordant, discrepant,

incompatible, irreconcilable,
inconsistent, uncomfortable,
incongruous, unharmonious,
inapt, unapt,
unaccommodating, opposed,
antagonistic, counteractive,
clashing, conflicting, against,
disfavor, (cooperation,
complicity, participation,
collusion, association, alliance,
confederation, coalition, fusion,
unanimity, combined)

humility-*n* meek, lowliness,
submission, resignation,
modest, blush, suffusion,
confusion, sense of shame,
disgrace, mortification, servile,
condescending, courteous,
pious, faith, holiness, religious,
devout, devoted, reverent,
godly, heavenly, pure, spiritual,
saintly, sacred, solemn,
(wicked, evil, unjust, reprobate,
irreverence, desecration,
sacrilege, dignity, self-respect,
pride, haughtiness, vain,
arrogance, stately, proud)

H

I

idea-*n* notion, conception, thought, apprehension, impression, perception, image, sentiment, reflection, observation, consideration, abstract idea, point of view, theory, fancy, imagination, topic, thesis, text, business, affair, matter, argument, motion, inkling, (indifference, incurious, impassive, ignorance, remote)

identification-*n* identity, sameness, coincidence, exactness, similar, copy, recognize, equality, comparable, deduce, derived, gather, collect, draw an inference, make a deduction, whet, ween, estimate, appreciate, (discover, find, determine, evolve, contrary, oppose, differ, invert, reverse, turn the tables, contradict, antagonize, oppose)

idiosyncrasy-*n* essence, endowment, capacity, capability, moods, declension, features, aspects, peculiarities, diagnostic, principle, nature, specialty, particularity, characteristic, mannerism, specific, singularity, version, state, (general, universal, common, ecumenical, transcendental, prevalent, every all, unspecified, impersonal, implanted, extraneousness)

idle-*adj* shallow, imbecility, incapacity, vacancy of mind, poverty of intellect, weak, wanting, dull, powerless, frivolous, petty, inane, ridiculous, worthless, (paramount, essential, vial, all-absorbing, serious, earnest,

grand, impressive, commanding, imposing)

idol-*n* favorite, pet, spoiled, desire, devotee, aspirant, solicitant, heretic, antichrist, pagan, heathen, bigot, (orthodox, sound, strict, faithful, evangelical)

ignore-*v* neglect, carelessness, trifling, omission, default, inactivity, inattention, nonchalance, insensibility, imprudence, recklessness, inconsiderate, heedless, thoughtless, uninformed, ignored, (knowledge, cognizance, acquaintance, insight, familiarity, intuition, perception, enlightenment)

illegitimate-*adj* illegal, unlawful, smuggling, poaching, prohibited, illicit, contraband, despotic, deceitful, delusive, insidious, untrue, feigned, fraudulent, artificial, unsound, (legal, legitimacy, rule, regulation, equity, enact, vested, constitutional, permitted)

illuminate-*v* light, ray, beam, stream, gleam, streak, sun, aurora, shining, luminous, lucid, bright, vivid, reflection, refraction, lighten, irradiate, color, hue, tint, intense, unfaded, gay, (pale, faded, colorless, decolorize, bleached, tarnished, blanch, dull, muddy, dingy)

illustrate-*v* exemplify, cite, quote, exemplary, example, uniformity, in point, interpretation, definition, explicit, translate, define, construe, decipher, expound, unravel, disentangle, resolve, (misrepresent, pervert, garble, distort, travesty, stretch, aberration, irregularity, exemption)

imbed-*v* locate, place, situation, seat, station, lodge, quarter, post, install, establish, stow, house, fix, pin, root, graft, deposit, vest, pack, give, furnish, afford, supply, lend, support, bottom, found, base, ground, maintain, (depend, suspend, loose, flowing, tail, caudate, hang, displace, vacate)

imitation-*n* copy, duplication, repetition, mirror, reflect, mimic, reproduce, repeat, echo, match, parallel, counterfeit, parody, travesty, caricature, burlesque, imitative, verbatim, duplicate, transcript, shadow, parody, similar, impersonate, (original, prototype, model, pattern, precedent, standard)

immaculate-*adj* perfect, best, pure, good, paragon, unparalleled, supreme, superhuman, divine, approbation, faultless, spotless, impeccable, unblemished, ripen, mature, scatheless, intact, harmless, purity, clean, purify, (decay, corrupt, mold, must, rot, putrefy, fester, rank, reek, stink, dirty, soil, smoke, tarnish, spot, dirty, filthy, grimy)

immature-*adj* new, novelty, recent, youth, innovation, modernism, recent, fresh, neoteric, new-born, young, vernal, renovated, brewing, hatching, forthcoming, (old, ancient, antique, venerable, elder, archaic, classic, seniority, mature, decline, senility)

immense-*adj* great, large, considerable, fair, above par, big, huge, ample, abundant, enough, full, intense, strong, sound, passing, heavy, plenary, high, goodly, noble, previous, might, sad, grave, serious, vast, enormous, extreme, extravagant, preposterous, monstrous, (inappreciable, evanescent, minute,

inconsiderable, paltry, small, diminutive, mere, simple, sheer, scanty, bare)

immortal-*adj* perpetual, eternal, everlasting, perpetuity, continual, endless, unending, ceaseless, incessant, unfading, evergreen, never-ending, enthrone, signalize, consecrate, dedicate, enshrine, (discredit, disrepute, dishonor, disgrace, humiliation, momentary, sudden, instant, abrupt, hasty, quick)

immovable-*adj* stable, unchangeable, constancy, immobile, soundness, stiffness, fixture, rock, pillar, tower, foundation, permanence, remain firm, settle, establish, determined, master over self, self-control, perseverance, tenacity, obstinacy, (vacillating, unsteady, volatile, frothy, weak, feeble minded, inconstancy, versatility, instability, fluctuation, vicissitude, alteration, restless)

impartial-*adj* impartiality, intelligent, keen, acute, alive, discerning, wise, sage, sapient, reasonable, sensible, fair, upright, straightforward, frank, candid, conscientious, scrupulous, (undignified, partial, disloyal, untrustworthy, corrupt, debased, thoughtless, want of intelligence, weak, feeble-minded)

impeach-*v* condemnation, reflection, disparage, ostracism, dispraise, censure, detract, depreciate, exception, rebuke, reprehension, reprobation, admonition, reproach, reprimand, castigate, lecture, disapprove, blame, frown upon, (approbation, approval, sanction, advocacy, esteem, good opinion, praise, applaud, commend, compliment, laudatory)

imperative-*adj* required, need, necessary, essential, indispensability, urgency, prerequisite, uncompromising, inflexible, relentless, peremptory, absolute, unsparing, ironhanded, oppressive, ruthless, (moderate, lenient, moderation, tolerant, mildness, forbearing, compassion, indulge)

imperceptible-*adj* mere, simple, sheer, stark, bare, inappreciable, infinitesimal, diminutive, inconsiderable, slight, scanty, limited, meager, sparing, impalpable, intangible, invisible, molecular, rudimentary, embryonic, (hugeness, enormous, corpulent, fat, plump, squab, full, lusty, strapping consummate, excessive, stupendous, astonishing, inexpressible)

imperious-*adj* command, reign, dynasty, director, dictatorship, authority, influence, patronage, power, jurisdiction, divine right, administration, demagogy, socialism, feudalism, empire, monarchy, royalty, (anarchy, toleration, remission, lax, loose, dethrone, depose, abdicate, remiss, free rein)

impetuous-*adj* boisterous, violence, inclemency, vehemence, might, effervescence, turbulence, buster, uproar, riot, row, rumpus, ferocity, rage, fury, hastily, precipitately, helter-skelter, urgency, acceleration, spurt, forced, march, rush, (leisure, slow, deliberate, quiet, calm, undisturbed, moderation, gentleness, sobriety, quiet, calmness, sedative, lenitive, demulcent, balmy, tranquilize)

imposition-*n* credulity, gull, infatuation, self-delusion, deception, superstition, simple,

green, over-confident, infringe, encroach, exact, arrogate, violate, disfranchise, invalidate, misbehave, undue, unlawful, illicit, unconstitutional, unwarranted, unsanctioned, (due to privilege, prerogative, right, prescription, title, claim, pretension, demand, incredulous, unbelieving, inconvincible, distrustful)

impossible-*adj* impracticable, unachievable, infeasible unsurmountable incompatible, inaccessible, impassible, unobtainable, refuse, rejection, declining, repulse, rebuff, reject, deny, decline, protest, disclaimer, (offer, present, tender, move, start, invite, possibility, potentiality, agree, compatibility, feasibility, practicability, perhaps, perchance, surmountable, accessible, achievable, within reach)

impoverish-*v* weaken, debility, relaxation, languor, impotence, infirmity, femininity, fragility, inactivity, withered, haltered, shaken, crazy, shaky, palsied, decrepit, consumption, expenditure, exhaustion, dispersion, spend, expend, use, consume, (provision, supply, caterer, purveyor, commissary, feeder, reinforcement, strong, might, vigorous, forcible, hard, adamantine, robust, sturdy)

impression-*n* sensation, excite, aesthetic, perceptive, conscious, aware, acute, sharp, keen, vivid, lively, sharpen, cultivate, tutor, idea, notion, conception, thought, apprehension, image, sentiment, reflection, observation, consideration, theory, conceit, fancy, fantasy, imagination, (insensible, unfeeling, senseless, callous,

hardened, case-hardened)
impressive-*adj* sensational,
eloquent, vigorous, nervous,
powerful, command of words,
bold, racy, slashing, pungent,
(feeble, tame, meager, vapid,
dull, dry, languid, monotonous)
imprint-*v* propagate, spread,
advertise, affix, type, figure,
emblem, cipher, device,
represent, motto, circumscribe,
enclose, imbedded
improper-*adj* inapt, unapt,
inappropriate, discordant,
hostile, incompatible,
irreconcilable, inconsistent,
unconformable, exceptional,
unjust, unfair, wrong, encroach,
inequitable, unequal, partial,
unfit, (right, fit, justice, equity,
propriety, impartiality,
reasonable, legitimate,
justifiable)
impudent-*adj* insolence,
haughtiness, arrogance, airs,
overbearance, domineering,
impertinence, sauciness,
flippancy, petulance, bluster,
swagger, presumption,
usurpation, assurance,
audacity, hardihood, front, face,
brass, shamelessness,
effrontery, assumption of
infallibility, (servile, supple, oily,
pliant, cringing, fawning,
groveling, sniveling, mealy-
mouthed, precocious)
impulsive-*adj* impetus,
momentum, push, pulsing,
thrust, shove, jog, jolt, brunt,
booming, throw, explosion,
propulsion, percussion,
concussion, collision, clash,
encounter, deceptive, illusive,
plausible, evasive, hollow,
irrelevant, (reason, argue,
discuss, debate, dispute,
logical, sequence, examine,
question, rebound, reflex,
reverberation, rebuff, return)
inane-*adj* nothing, naught, nil,
nullity, zero, cipher, no one,

nobody, never, no such thing,
insubstantiality, nonsense,
senseless, inexpressible,
undefinable, (intelligent,
clearness, explicitness, lucidity,
perspicuity, legibility, plain
speaking, luminous,
transparent)
inaugural-*adj* precursor,
precedent, forerunner, pioneer
prelude, preamble, preface,
prologue, preliminary,
introductory, (sequel, suffix,
successor, trail, rear, appendix,
postscript, codicil, epilogue)
inauspicious-*adj* untimely,
intrusive, unseasonble, out of
date, inopportune, timeless,
untoward, unlucky,
unpropitious, unfortunate,
unfavorable, unsuited,
inexpedient, hopelessness,
despair, desperation,
despondency, pessimism,
forlorn, (hope, trust, confide,
rely on, harbor, indulge,
confidence, opportune, timely,
well-timed, seasonable,
providential, lucky, fortunate)
incapable-*adj* impotence,
disability, impiousness,
imbecility, inapt, ineptitude,
invalidity, inefficiency,
incompetence, disqualification,
helplessness, prostration,
paralysis, palsy, apoplexy,
exhaustion, collapse,
(capability, capacity, faculty,
quality, attribute, endowment,
virtue, gift, property,
qualification, susceptibility,
puissance, might, force)
incase-*v* cover, superpose,
overlay, wrap, face, veneer,
pave, bind, cap, coat, paint,
incrust, limit, bound,
encystment, imprisoned,
enshrined, (lining, inner
coating, covering, filling,
stuffing, padding)
incendiary-*adj* destructive,
subversive, ruinous,

deleterious, suicidal, deadly, with a crushing effect, demolish, dispel, dissipate, consume, squelch, exterminate, devastate, extinguish, burn, inflame, roast, toast, fry, grill, singe, parch, scorch, cauterize, sear, char, incinerate, (cool, fan, refrigerate, refresh, ice, congeal, freeze, glaciate, solidification, produce, establish, constitute, generate)

incessant-*adj* monotonous, harping, iterative, mocking, chiming, repeatedly, often again, over again, once more, ditto, encore, everlasting, continual, endless, ceaseless, (instantaneous, momentary, sudden, instant, abrupt)

incidental-*adj* casual, fortuitous, accidental, adventitious, causeless, contingent, undetermined, indeterminate, possible, unintentional, haphazard, random probability, possibility, (attribution, theory, ascribe, impute, explanation, ascription, reference to, rationale, imputation)

inclement-*adj* violence, vehemence, might, impetuosity, boisterousness, effervescence, ebullition, turbulence, bluster, uproar, riot, row, rumpus, severe, ferocity, rage, fury, exacerbation, exasperation, malignity, fit, paroxysm, force, convulsion, (moderating, temperateness, gentleness, sobriety, quiet, relaxation, remission, mitigation, tranquilization, assuagement, contemplation, pacification)

inclusive-*adj* addition, annexation, adjection, supplement, subjunctive, annex, affix, superpose, including, inclusive, component, integral, ingredient, element, constituent, contents,

appurtenance, (extraneousness, foreign, alien, intruder, ulterior, excluded, exceptional, deduction, retrenchment)

income-*n* earnings, profit, winnings, proceeds, fruit, crop, harvest, benefit, gaining, acquire, obtain, procure, purchase, inheritance, recovery, retrieval, redemption, salvage, remuneration, wealthy, rich, affluent, opulent, moneyed, (poor, indigent, poverty stricken, impoverished, pauper, ruin, destitution, loss, forfeiture, bereaved, dispossessed, lapse, deprivation)

incomparable-*adj* superior, greater, major, higher, exceeding, great, distinguished, vaulting, ultra, supreme, utmost, paramount, preeminent, foremost, crowning, first-rate, important, excellent, paragon, unparalleled, unequaled, unapproached, unsurpassed, superlative, (inferior, minority, subordinate, shortcoming, deficiency, minimum, smallness, diminished, subordinate)

inconsistent-*adj* illogical, unreasonable, false, unsound, invalid, unwarranted, inconsequential, unscientific, groundless, incorrect, fallacious, unproved, contrary, opposite, counter opposed, contrasted, conflicting, negative, differing, (similar, identical, facsimile, exact, identical, equal)

increase-*v* enlargement, augmentation, extension, dilatation, expansion, increment, accretion, accession, development, growth, ascent, acerbate, sprout, raise, exalt, magnify,

many, several, sundry, various,
profusion, manifold, multiplied,
multiple, multinominal,
populous, (few, paucity, rarity,
handful, minority, scant,
decrease, lessen, subtract,
shrink, wane, reflux)

incredible-*adj* impossible,
absurd, unreasonable,
unfeasible, insurmountable,
unobtainable, inaccessible,
impervious, improbable,
unlikely, contrary, rate,
unimaginable, misbelief,
doubtful, disputable,
questionable, suspect,
inconceivable, hard to believe,
(worthy of, deserving, belief,
credence, assurance, faith,
trust, confidence, presumption,
possible, conceivable, feasible)

increment-*n* augment,
appendage, the addition of,
affix, accrue, expand, extend,
develop, measurement, (pare,
reduce, contract, shrink,
compress, diminish)

incumbent-*adj* inhabitant,
resident, dweller, inmate,
tenant, sojourner, settler,
squatter, citizen, native,
overhanging, overlying
prominent, superimposed,
weighty, burdensome,
cumbersome, heavy,
ponderous, massive, unwieldy,
(light, levity, imponderability,
buoyancy, volatility, sublimated,
floating, low, debasement)

incurable-*adj* hopeless, despair,
despondency, forlorn,
inconsolable, cureless,
remediless, incorrigible,
irreparable, irrecoverable,
ruined, undone, immitigable,
(hope, trust, confident,
presumptuous, feed, foster,
nourish, healthy, sound, hearty,
fresh, unscathed)

indebted-*v* owing, debt,
obligation, liability, arrears,
deficit, default, insolvency,

grateful, thankfulness,
acknowledgement, allegiance,
dueness, propriety, fitness,
sense of duty, recognition,
binding, imperative, behooving,
(ungrateful, credit, trust, tick,
score, tally, account)

indefinite-*adj* uncertain,
incertitude, doubt, suspense,
vague, haze, fog, obscure,
ambiguity, casual, random,
aimless, changeable, fallible,
questionable, precarious,
disputable, invisible,
imperceptible, indistinct,
concealment, confused,
indistinct, (perceptibility,
conspicuousness, appearance,
exposure, manifestation,
obvious, recognizable, certain,
necessity, surety, assurance)

indemnity-*n* compensation,
counteract, balance, hedge,
square, give and take,
compromise, excuse,
exoneration, quitting, release,
acquittal, conciliation,
propitiation, reprieve, reward,
recompense, remuneration,
(penalty, retribution,
confiscation, forfeit, revenge,
vengeance, retaliation, rancor)

indenture-*n* compact, contract,
agreement, bargain, affidavit,
pact, bond, covenant,
stipulation, settlement,
convention, compromise,
cartel, title, deed, authority,
warrant, credential, diploma,
(unattested, unauthenticated,
check, destroy, weaken,
contradict, vindicate, disproof)

indicate-*v* examine, scan,
scrutinize, consider, inspect,
review, rivet, direct, observe,
mean, signify, express, convey,
imply, bespeak, suggest,
allusive, significant, symbolism,
feature, diagnostic, recognize,
(without meaning, senseless,
nonsensical, void, vacant,
insignificant, undefinable)

indigence-*n* insufficiency, inadequacy, incompetence, impotence, deficiency, emptiness, scarcity, want, need, lack, poverty, famine, poor, depletion, vacancy, (sufficient, enough, adequate, commensurate, competent, satisfactory, valid, tangible, copious, abundant, abounding)

individual-*n* human being, person, creature, mortal, body, somebody, earthling, party, head, personal, individuality, special, particular, realize, designate, determine, private, characteristic, originality, (general, universal, miscellaneous, generic, broad, collective, every, all, unspecified)

indomitable-*adj* strong, might, vigorous, forcible, hard, adamantine, stout, robust, sturdy, hardy, powerful, potent, puissant, valid, resistless, irresistible, invincible, impregnable, unconquerable, determined, resolute, (vacillating, unsteady, changeable, cowardly, facile, pliant, reversible, weak)

induce-*v* cause, origin, source, principle, element, genesis, procure, draw down, evoke, entail, provoke, reason, ground, call, principle, keystone, element, consideration, attraction, magnet, enticement, allurement, witchery, cajolery, seduction, (dissuade, deport, against, remonstrate, expostulate, warn, consequence, result, upshot, issue, outgrowth)

indulge-*v* lenient, mild, gentle, soft, tolerant, easy going, clement, compassionate, forbearing, permission, allow, leave, sufferance, tolerance, liberty, law, license, concession, grace, favor,

dispensation, exemption, connivance, (prohibit, disallow, veto, embargo, taboo, restrictive, forbid)

ineffectual-*adj* useless, inefficacy, futile, inaptitude, inadequate, inefficiency, unskillful, inoperative, incompetent, superfluous, dispensable, redundant, unskillful, inadequate, incapable, invalid, helpless, exhaustion, (capable, effective, endowed, virtuous, qualified, powerful, potent)

inert-*adj* dull, inactivity, torpor, languor, latency, sloth, irresolution, obstinacy, passive, sluggish, heavy, tame, slow, blunt, lifeless, dead, uninfluential, latent, dormant, smoldering, insensibility, apathy, lethargic, neutrality, vegetation, (sensitive, impressionable, enthusiastic, spirited, excitable)

inexorable-*adj* unavoidable, necessity, obligation, compulsive, subjection, imperious, iron, adverse, fate, compel, inevitable, irrevocable, impulsive, (volition, voluntary, willful, intended, spontaneity, original, optional, discretionary, willing)

inexperience-*n* ignorance, incomprehensive, simplicity, unexplored, uncertainty, incapable, unknown, bungling, awkward, clumsy, maladroit, incompetent, rusty, without former knowledge, unskillful, disqualification, (skill, dexterity, experience, accomplish, competence, talent, capacity)

infatuation-*n* impulsive, impetuous, passionate, uncontrolled, ungovernable, irrepressible, inextinguishable, burning, simmering, volcanic, vehement, demonstrative, furious, fierce, over-zealous, enthusiastic, impassioned, fanatical, eager, (submission, resignation, fortitude, even tempered, tranquil, tolerance, patience)

infernal-*adj* bad, hurtful, virulence, wrong, arrant, rank, foul, vile, abominable, detestable, cursed, confounded, damned, diabolic, malevolent, grudge, annoy, malicious, rancorous, spiteful, caustic, bitter, envenomed, acrimonious, grinding, galling, (benevolent, benignity, brotherly love, charity, sympathy, tenderness, goodness, excellence, value, merit, virtue, superiority)

infidelity-*n* dishonor, dishonest, disgrace, fraudulent, faithlessness, betrayal, degrade, derogate, stoop, grovel, sneak, unscrupulous, contemptible, abject, untrustworthy, (upright, honest, virtuous, honorable, fair, right, just, equitable, impartial, even handed, square, straightforward, honest)

infiltrate-*v* intervene, interference, introduce, import, throw, insinuate, dovetailing, permeation, passage, transmission, transudation, ingress, instill, mix, join, combine, transfuse, tincture, season, infect, (eliminate, purification, simple, uniform, disentangle, encompass, beset)

infinitesimal-*adj* small, little, tenuity, paucity, fewness, mediocrity, moderation, vanishing point, atom, particle, molecule, diminutive, minute, inconsiderable, paltry, unimportant, slender, meager, few, inappreciable, evanescent, mere, (vast, immense, enormous, extreme, excessive, preposterous,

monstrous, stupendous, astonishing, incredible, marvelous)

influence-*n* change, alteration, mutation, permutation, variation, modification, modulation, mood, qualification, innovation, deviation, turn, diversion, break, transformation, transfiguration, pressure, preponderance, dominance, reign, authority, capability, interest, power, carry, weight, leverage, (impotence, inertness, powerless, irrelevant, permanence, stability, persistence, endurance, persist)

information-*n* knowledge, cognizance, acquaintance, privity, insight, intuition, familiarity, recognition, appreciation, light, enlightenment, learning, lore, scholarly, conceive, comprehend, understand, enlightenment, publicity, communication, intimation, notice, representation, (concealment, hiding, masquerade, secret, recondite, ignorance, uninformed, unconsciousness, incomprehension)

infraction-*n* disobey, violate, infringe, shirk, defiance, uncomplying, unsubmissive, unruly, insubordinate, resisting, insurgent, riotous, unbidden, retraction, repudiation, protest, forfeiture, lawlessness, discard, protest, (observe, perform, compliance, obedience, satisfaction, discharge, acknowledgement, satisfy, fulfill, carry out)

infringe-*v* transgression, trespass, encroach, transcendence, surpass, go beyond, redundance, strain, disobey, violate, shirk defiance,

uncomplying, (obedient,
complying, loyal, faithful,
devoted, restrainable, resigned,
passive, submissive,
henpecked)

infuse-*v* mix, alloy, junction,
combination impregnation,
infiltration, seasoning,
springing, interlard, instill,
imbue, infiltrate, dash, tinge,
tincture, season, sprinkle,
attemper, medicate, blend,
(pure, eliminate, sift, uniform,
homogeneous, single, neat,
clear, sheet)

ingrained-*adj* custom, usage,
use, prescription, practice,
prevalence, observance,
conventional, conformity, rule,
standing, order, precedent,
routine, rut, groove, habit,
combine, unite, incorporate,
amalgamate, embody, absorb,
impregnate, (decomposition,
analysis, dissection, resolution,
unravel, catalytic, disuse,
unusual)

inhibit-*v* restraint, hindrance,
coercion, constraint,
repression, discipline, control,
confinement, durance, duress,
imprisonment, emancipation,
limbo, captivity, blockade,
disallow, interdict, injunction,
embargo, ban, taboo,
proscription, (permit, allow,
sufferance, tolerance, liberty,
law, admit, authorize, warrant,
sanction, entrust)

injury-*n* impairment, damage,
loss, detriment, laceration,
outrage, havoc, contamination,
canker, corruption, adulteration,
alloy, decay, dilapidation,
deteriorate, weaken, hurt,
harm, scathe, injurious,
deleterious, malignant,
nocuous, evil, wrong,
(beneficial, valuable,
advantageous, profitable,
edifying, improve, betterment,
mend, amendment, refine)

inkling-*n* supposition,
assumption, postulation,
condition, hypothesis,
postulate, theory, proposal,
suggestion, conceit, rough
guess, conjecture, surmise,
suspicion, hint, insinuate,
allude, desire, wish, fantasy,
learning, (indifferent, neutral,
unconcern, nonchalance,
earnestness, anorexia, apathy)

innocuous-*adj* good, harmless,
hurt, unobnoxious, beneficial,
valuable, serviceable,
advantageous, profitable,
edifying, salutary, unerring,
above suspicion, impeccable,
(guilty, blame, culpable,
reprehensible, enormity,
atrocity, outrage, deadly,
malpractice)

inoculate-*v* insert, forcible,
ingress, implantation,
introduction, insinuation,
intervention, injection,
importation, infusion,
immersion, submersion, dip,
plunge, interment, imbed,
dovetail, inculcate, indoctrinate,
infuse, instill, infiltrate, ingraft,
(misinform, misdirect,
misrepresent, render,
unintelligible, perversion,
extraction, removal, elimination,
eradication, extirpation, educe,
elicit)

inquisition-*n* inquiry, request,
search, quest, pursuit,
examination, review, scrutiny,
investigation, indication,
exploration, exploitation,
ventilation, sifting, calculation,
analysis, dissection, resolution,
study, tyrannical, extortionate,
grinding, withering, oppressive,
ruthless, (lenient, mild, gentle,
soft, tolerant, indulgent,
forbearing, answer, respond,
reply, rebut, retort, rejoin,
acknowledge, explain)

insidious-*adj* deceitful,
deceived, cunning, delusive,

elusive, covens, untrue, false,
fraudulent, trick, cheat, wile,
blind, feint, sly, stealthy,
underhanded, hidden, crooked,
shrewd, (artlessness, simplicity,
innocence, candor, sincerity,
honesty, frank, open minded,
free, plain, outspoken,
downright)

insinuate-*v* cast reflection,
reproach, disapprove,
disparage, condemnatory,
damnify, denunciate, abusive,
objurgatory, clamorous,
vituperative, defamatory,
satirical, severe, withering,
trenchant, sarcastic,
hypercritical, fastidious, critical,
hint, suggestion, innuendo,
(manifest, apparent, salient,
striking, demonstrative,
prominent, flagrant, notorious,
approbation, approval,
sanctioned, advocate)

insipid-*adj* tasteless, savorless,
flat, stale, fade, mild, gutless,
ingestible, mawkish, indifferent,
cold, frigid, lukewarm, cool,
unconcerned, phlegmatic,
easy-going, (avidity,
greediness, covetous,
grasping, craving, voracity,
taste, savor, smack, gusto)

insist-*v* argue, reason, discuss,
debate, dispute, wrangle,
bandy, controvert, canvass,
rational, argumentative, claim,
warrant, controversial, dialectic,
command, order, ordinance,
act, instruct, dispatch, demand,
imposition, require, charge,
prescribe, (unreasonable,
illogical, false, unsound, invalid,
unwarranted, inconsequential)

insolvent-*adj* destitute,
indigence, penury, pauperism,
want, need, distress,
difficulties, needy, poor,
poverty-stricken, debt,
obligation, liability, arrears,
deficit, impecuniosity,
mendicant, nonpayment,

(credit, trust, tally, account,
accredited, wealth, riches,
fortune, opulence, affluence,
independence)

inspire-*v* encourage, infuse,
give, reassure, embolden,
inspirit, cheer, nerve, put,
enliven, elate, exhilarate,
gladden, animate, raise the
spirits, perk up, give pleasure,
(depress, discourage,
dishearten, dispirit, damp, dull,
deject, lower, sink, dash,
knock-down)

instance-*n* example, specimen,
sample, quotation,
exemplification, illustration,
accommodate, conformity,
illustrate, accordance, cite,
quote, inducement,
consideration, attraction,
enticement, allurement,
(disincline, indispose, shake,
dissuade, remonstrate, warn,
without rhyme or reason)

instant-*n* moment, second,
minute, twinkling, flash, breath,
crack, jiffy, burst, hasty, quick,
flash of lightning, present,
actual, current, important,
consequence, prominence,
consideration, (whenever,
occasion, upon, sooner or later,
perpetual, eternal, everlasting,
immortal, undying)

instinct-*n* intellect, mind,
understanding, thinking,
principle, rationality, faculties,
senses, consciousness,
observation, percipience,
association of ideas,
conception, judgment, wit,
capacity, ability, instinctive,
impulsive, gratuitous,
hazarded, unconnected,
(absence of intellect, imbecility,
argumentative, controversial,
debatable)

institution-*n* school, academy,
university, college, seminary,
alma mater, party, faction, side,
denomination, communion, set,

crew, band, society,
association, alliance, league,
legal, legitimate, link, banded,
bonded, unite, join, associate,
corporation, syndicate,
establishment

instruct-v teach, edification,
education, tuition, guidance,
qualification, preparation,
discipline, exercise, direct,
guide, impress upon, convince,
expound, command, message,
direction, requirement, order,
(misinform, mislead,
misrepresent, lie, bewilder,
deceive, mystify)

insult-v rudeness, discourtesy,
ill-breeding, ungainly manners,
disrespect, impudence,
barbarism, misbehavior, stern,
austerity, modishness,
acrimony, acerbity, irreverence,
slight, neglect, supercilious,
affront, (respect, consideration,
regard, courtesy, attention,
deference, reverence, honor,
esteem, veneration, admiration,
approbation)

integrate-v consolidate, whole,
totality, integrity, entirely,
collectiveness, unity,
completeness, integration,
aggregate, gross amount,
altogether, substantially,
(incomplete, deficient,
shortcoming, insufficiency,
imperfect, defective, unfinished,
fractional, fragmentary,
sectional, divided)

intensify-v increase,
augmentation, enlargement,
extension, dilatation,
expansion, increment, develop,
magnify, enhance, aggravate,
exaggerate, exasperate,
stimulate, activity, agitation,
effervescence, stir, bustle,
perturbation, energize, kindle,
excite, exert, (inertness,
inactive, passive, torpid,
sluggish, dull, heavy,
uninfluential, decrease,

diminish, lessen, shrink, wane)

intercede-v mediate,
intercessor, peacemaker,
negotiator, diplomat, arbitrate,
deprecate, expostulate, protest,
negative request, (request,
motion, overture, demand,
canvass, address, appeal)

interest-n influential, important,
weight, prevailing, rampant,
dominance, predominant,
curious, inquisitive, stare, gape,
lionize, pry, paramount,
essential, vital, all-absorbing,
radical, cardinal, prime,
(indifferent, passive,
irrelevancy, uninfluential,
powerless)

intermediate-adj mean,
medium, average, balance,
mediocrity, generality, middle,
compromise, neutrality, link,
connect, hyphen, bracket,
bridge, bond, tendon, tendril,
intervention, insertion, partition,
septum, diaphragm, midriff,
(circumference, environment,
outskirts, suburbs, precincts)

intermit-adj interrupt, interrupted
sequence, discontinue, break,
fracture, flaw, fault, suspend,
interplay, cease, desist, break
off, hold, stop, stick, pause,
rest, halt, (continue,
persistence, repetition, sustain,
unvarying, unreversed,
unrevoked, unvaried)

interpose-v interject,
intercalated, intersperse,
interweave, intrusive,
(encompass, surround,
circumference, encircle,
embrace, circumvent)

interrupt-v discontinue,
disjunction, break, fault, pause,
disconnect, unsuccessful,
spasmodic, intermittent, few ⟩
and far between, alternation,
patchwork, episode, cessation,
resistance, suspension, stop,
rest, lull, (continue, persist,
repetition, sustain, uphold, hold

up, perpetuate, maintain,
preserve)
intervene-*v* mediate,
peacemaker, negotiator,
diplomat, moderate, time,
duration, period, term, last,
endure, remain, persist, elapse,
while, interim, interval,
intermission, interlude,
(circumvent, around, about,
without, skirt, twin round, lap,
border)
interview-*n* conference,
interlocution, converse,
conversation, confabulation,
talk, discourse, verbal
intercourse, oral
communication, commerce,
chatty, colloquial, parley,
gossip, tattle, visit, call,
assignation, appointment,
(seclusion, privacy, retirement,
reclusion, estrangement,
sequestered, private, snug,
domestic)
intolerance-*n* prejudice, narrow-
minded, intolerant,
impracticable, besotted,
infatuated, fanatical, positive,
opinioned, bigoted, crotchety,
unreasonable, insolent,
impertinence, sauciness,
flippant, petulant, (servile,
obsequious, supple, mealy-
mouthed, settle, pass,
comment, investigate)
intricate-*adj* disorder,
derangement, irregularity,
unconformity, confusion,
confusedness, disarray, jumble,
huddle, litter, complexity,
complexness, implication,
intricacy, perplexity, network,
involved, raveled, entangled,
disarrange, (order, regularity,
uniformity, symmetry,
progression, series,
subordination, systematically,
gradation, uniform)
intrinsic-*adj* inbeing, inherence,
inhesion, subjectiveness,
essence, essentialness,

incarnation, principle, nature,
constitution, character, type,
quality, oral, documentary,
hearsay, external, extrinsic,
internal, demonstration,
(countervail, rebut, refute,
subvert, destroy, check,
weaken, contravene,
objectiveness, extraneousness,
accident, incidental, accidental)
introduce-*v* prefix, place, before,
premise, prelude, preface,
preceding, prior, before, former,
foregoing, aforementioned,
prefatory, introductory,
preamble, prologue,
precession, leading, heading,
precedence, (sequence,
coming after, follower, attend,
beset, succeeding, sequent)
intrude-*v* disagree, discordant,
discrepant, hostile, repugnant,
incompatible, irreconcilable,
inconsistent, interfere, clash,
intervention, partition, midriff,
interpenetrate, permeate,
introduce, import, interpose,
(surround, beset, compass,
encompass, environ, enclose,
encircle, embrace)
inundate-*v* irrigate, deluge,
syringe, inject, gargle, drench,
douse, dilute, dip, immerse,
merge, submerge, redundance,
many, super abundance,
saturation, transcendency,
exuberance, profuseness,
accumulation, (dry, flatulent,
effervescent, atmospheric,
meteorological)
invalid-*n* powerless, impotence,
disability, disablement,
impiousness, imbecility,
incapacity, indocility,
inefficiency, incompetence,
disqualification, helplessness,
prostration, palsy, exhaustion,
inefficacy, failure, (power,
potency, might, force, energy,
ability, capability, faculty,
quality, attribute, valid)
invariable-*adj* uniform,

homogeneity, accordance, agreement, regularity, constancy, always, without exception, like clockwork, symmetry, naturalization, conventionality, example, instance, specimen, typical, normal, illustrative, (exceptional, abnormal, unusual, unaccustomed, rare, varied, diversified, irregular, uneven, rough, multifarious, multiformity)

invasion-*n* attack, assault, assail, charge, impugn, aggression, offense, incursion, inroad, irruption, outbreak, investment, obsession, bombardment, fire, volley, platoon, beset, besiege, beleaguer, (defense, protection, guard, ward, shielding, preservation, guardianship, resistance, safeguard)

inversion-*n* derangement, disorder, eviction, discomposure, disturbance, dislocation, perturbation, interruption, corrugation, complicate, involve, perplex, confound, tangle, litter, scatter, mix, (classify, divide, file, string, together, thread, register, catalog, tabulate, index, graduate, digest, methodize)

invest-*v* purchasing, buying, procure, rent, expenditure, expend, disburse, circulate, remuneration, fee, contingent, quota, (premium, bonus, pension, annuity, jointure, alimony, pittance, proceeds)

invoke-*v* address, allocution, speech, apostrophe, interpolation, appeal, invocation, salutation, request, entreat, beseech, plead, supplicate, implore, conjure, adjure, obtest, evoke, impetrate, imprecate, (deprecation, expostulation, intercession, mediation, protest)

involve-*v* include, contain, hold, comprehend, take in, admit, embrace, embody, implicate, drag into, compose, constitute, form, containing, convoluted, wining, twisted, tortile, intricate, complicated, perplexed, (simple, exclusion, omission, exception, rejection, repudiation, exile, separation, segregation, supposition, elimination, inadmissible, relegate)

irregular-*adj* diverse, unevenness, multiformity, unconformity, varied, rough, disorder, anomaly, disunion, discord, confusion, disarray, jumble, complexity, perplexity, turmoil, ferment, disturbance, convulsion, riot, unsymmetrical, intricate, complicated, (order, uniformity, methodical, symmetrical, uniform, arranged, economy)

irreparable-*adj* hopeless, despair, desperation, despondency, pessimism, forlorn, incurable, cureless, remediless, beyond, remedy, incorrigible, unpromising, unpropitious, threatening, hurtful, painful, pestilence, hurt, harm, (beneficial, valuable, serviceable, advantageous, profitable, edifying, salutary, hope, trust, confidence, reliance, faith, assurance, reassurance, security)

irrevocable-*adj* compulsory, uncontrollable, inevitable, unavoidable, inexorable, involuntary, instinctive, automatic, blind, stable, unchangeable, constancy, established, permanence, fixed, steadfast, firm, valid, irremovable, riveted, rooted, settled, (changeable, mutable, variable, vagrant, alternating)

J

jabber-*v* opacity, talkativeness, garrulity, eloquent, jaw, gabble, chatter, linguistic, declamatory, open-mouthed, fluency, flippancy, flowing, tongue, verbosity, stammer, hesitation, impediment, stutter, falter, mumble, (oratory, elocution, rhetoric, declamation)

jail-*n* bolt, bar, lock, padlock, rail, prison, gaol, cage, coop, den, cell, stronghold, fortress, keep, dungeon, Bastille, bridewell, house of correction, hulks, toll booth, penitentiary, guardroom, (liberate, disengagement, release, emancipate, dismiss, discharge)

jam-*v* squeeze, push, reduce, extricate, express, pulp, paste, dough, curd, pudding, poultice, grume, sugar, syrup, treacle, molasses, honey, manna, confection, nectar, pastry, pie, (sour, vinegar, styptic)

jar-*v* clash, disagree, interfere, intrude, discord, capsule, vesicle, vessel, pod, bottle, decanter, ewer, cruise, carafe, crock, kit, canteen, flagon, demijohn, jug, pitcher, mug, kettle, chalice, tumbler, glass, rummer, horn, saucepan

jargon-*n* paradox, riddle, unintelligibility, incomprehensible, inconceivable, vagueness, loose, beyond comprehension, gibberish, macaronic, confusion of tongues, (verbal, literal, titular, conjugate, derivative, exact, concordance, clear, plain speaking, lucidity, perspicuity, legibility)

jaundice-*n* yellow, gamboge, cadmium, aureate, golden, citron, fallow, sallow, luteous, tawny, bias, warped, twisted, hobby, fad, quirk, one-sided, superficial, partial, narrow, confined, (deduce, derive, gather, collect, judge, umpire, assessor, discover)

jealousy-*n* envious, covet, invidious, rival, suspicion, scruple, qualm, unbeliever, discredit, dissent, (believe, credit, indifference, serene)

jerk-*v* agitate, stir, tremor, shake, ripple, jolt, trepidation, quiver, quaver, dance, disquiet, twitter, flicker, flutter, traction, draw, draught, pull, haul, rake, drag, tug, tow, trail, train, wrench, twitch, tousle, propel, project, throw, fling, cast, pitch, chuck, toss, heave, hurl, flirt, flip, (repulse, repel, abduct, repellent, repulsive, diverge, divaricate, radiate, ramify, diverge)

jetty-*n* projection, prominent, protuberant, convex, nodular, mammillate, papule, arched, bold, bellied, tuberous, tumorous, cornute, odontoid, in relief, raised, salient, roadstead, anchorage, breakwater, mole, port, haven, harbor, pier, seaport, embankment, quay, (precipice, breakers, shoals, shallows, bank, shelf, flat, iron-bound, coast, rock)

jilt-*v* disappoint, disconcerted, aghast, trick of fortune, deception, falseness, untruth, imposition, fraud, deceit, guile, knavery, misrepresentation, delusion, trick, cheat, deceiver, dissembler, hypocrite, shuffler, wolf if sheep's clothing, (dupe, gull, gudgeon, cull, victim, greenhorn, fool)

jobber-*n* tactician, genius, mastermind, head, spirited, cunning, sharp, cracksman, strategist, proficient, expert, merchant, trader, dealer, monger, chandler, salesman, changer, shopkeeper, tradesman, retailer, Chapman, hawker, huckster, haggler, peddler, broker, (bungler, blunderer, fumbler, lubber, duffer, awkward, squad, notice)

jockey-*n* rider, horseman, equestrian, cavalier, rough rider, trainer, breaker, driver, coachman, whip, charioteer, postilion, post boy, carter, wagoner, drayman, cab man, attendant, squire, usher, page, footboy, train-bearer, waiter, tapster, butler, livery servant, lackey, footman, valet, (master, padrone, lord, paramount, commander, captain, chief, sachems, sheik, runner, courier, pedestrian)

jog-*v* push, walk, march, step, tread, pace, plod, wend, promenade, trudge, tramp, stalk, stride, straddle, strut, foot it, stump, bundle, bowl along, toddle, paddle, roving, vagrancy, marching and countermarching, nomad, vagabondism, migration

join-*v* connect, union, attachment, attach, fix, affix, fasten, bind, secure, clinch, twist, pinion, string, strap, sew, lace, stitch, tack, knit, gird, tether, moor, harness, chain, fetter, firm, fast, close, tight, taut, group, cluster, accumulation, assemble, compile, associate, (disperse, dissipate, distribute, apportionment, spread, cut, scatter, sow, disseminate, diffuse, separate, parting, detach)

jolt-*v* impulse, impetus, momentum, push, pulsing, thrust, shove, jog, brunt, booming, throw, strike, knock, tap, rap, slap, flap, dab, pat, thump, beat, bang, slam, dash, punch, thwack, whack, hit,

agitate, shake, convulse, toss, tumble, (recoil, revulsion, rebound, reflection, reflex, reflux, reverberation, rebuff, repulse, return)

journal-*n* almanac, calendar, register, chronicle, annals, diary, chronogram, record, note, memorandum, endorsement, inscription, copy, duplicate, docket, affidavit, certificate, gazette, newspaper, magazine, calendar, ephemeris, diary, log, archive, scroll, (efface, obliterate, erase, scratch, delete, unregistered, undocumented, without)

judgment-*n* instinct, conception, wits, capacity, intellect, understanding, reason, rationality, cogitative, faculties, senses, observation, intuition, discrimination, distinction, differentiation, (indiscrimination, uncertainty. indistinctness, imbecility, without reason)

judicial-*adj* judge, tribunal, municipality, bailiwick, officer, bailiff, sit in judgment, magistrate, authority, prefiguration, auspices, forecast, omen, prognostication, premonition, (weak, feeble-minded, fatuous, idiotic, imbecile, blatant, babbling, bewildered)

jump-*v* sudden change, transilience, leap, plunge, jerk, start, explosion, spasm, convulsion, throe, revulsion, cataclysm, hop, spring, bound, vault, saltation, frisky, skip, dance, caper, curvet, flounce, start, agitation, (submerge, douse, sink, engulf, send to the bottom, plunge, dip, souse, duck)

jury-*n* judge, justice, chancellor, recorder, magistrate, jurat, assessor, arbiter, arbitrator, umpire, referee, archon, tribune, scapegoat, stop-gap

K

keen-*adj* strong, energetic, forcible, active, intense, severe, vivid, sharp, acute, incisive, trenchant, brisk, rousing, irritating, poignant, virulent, caustic, mordant, harsh, stringent, double-edged, (inertness, dull, inert, inactivity, torpor, languor, inaction, lithe, passive, heavy, flat)

keep-*v* retain, retention, custody, tenacity, firm, hold, grasp, grip, clutches, tongs, forceps, pincers, undisposed, tenacious, preserve, safe keeping, conserve, maintain, support, sustentation, salvation, hygienic, (relinquish, abandonment, renunciation, expropriation, dereliction, surrender, dispensation, resignation, riddance, jettison, discard)

key-*n* opener, perforate, wide open, ajar, gaping, patent, tubular, aperient, cause, origin, source, element, principle, occasioned, pivot, hinge, turning point, lever, proximate, cause, ground, reason, rationale, (derived, derivative, hereditary, dependent upon, owing to, resulting, from, due to, closure, occlusion, blockade, shutting, up, obstruction, hindrance, plug, block, cork, bar, shu)

kick-*v* assault, thrust, lunge, pass, push, cut, fire, volley, assail, strike, impulse, whip, attack, aggressive, strike out, fling, insolent, flippant, pert, forward, impertinent, (defense, protect, guard, ward, shield, self-defense, preservation, resistance, safeguard, repel, stand one's ground)

kidnap-*v* take, reception, deglutition, appropriation, prehension, presentation, capture, apprehension, seizure, abduction, subtraction, abstraction, confiscation, eviction, rapacity, extortion, clutch, swoop, wrench, grip, haul, take, catch, scramble, (return, restitution, restoration, reinvestment, recuperation, release, give up, bring back, recoup, reimburse, recuperate, recover, revert)

kill-*v* destroy, violent death, homicide, manslaughter, murder, assassination, massacre, mortal, fatal, lethal, dead, deathly, suicidal, strangle, smother, kill with kindness, consume, burn, idle, trifle, (life, vivacity, spirit, dash, energy, animation)

kindle-*v* excite, affect, touch, move, impress, strike interest, animate, inspire, impassion, smite, infect, stir, provoke, raise up, summon up, arouse, fire, enkindle, apply the torch, set on fire, inflame, stimulate, produce, work, handiwork, fabric, performance, creature, upshot, develop, (tranquil, passive, impassibility, coolness, unexcitable, imperturbable, dispassionate, sedate)

king-*n* potentate, sovereign, monarch, despot, tyrant, crowned head, emperor, majesty, protector, president, judge, empire, royalty, regal, dominant, paramount, supreme, influential, imperial, stringent, (absence of authority, anarchy, relaxation, loosening, remission, misrule, insubordination, depravation of power, remiss, unwarranted)

kiss-*v* endearment, caress, embrace, salute, smack, buss, osculation, courtship, wooing,

K

suit, philander, flirt, obeisance,
bow, courtesy, curtsy, scrape,
loving, love token, (repulsive,
noncomplacent,
accommodating, gallant,
ungentle, rough, rugged, bluff,
blunt, gruff, tart, sour, surly)

kleptomania-*n* steal, theft,
thievery, robbery, deception,
abstraction, pillage, light-
fingered, piratical, predacious,
plunder, rifle, sack, loot,
ransack, spoil, spoilt, despoil,
strip, monomania, eccentricity,
fanaticism, infatuation, craze,
oddity, (sane, rational,
generous, restitution, return,
restore, reimburse, reforge,
recoup, redeem, recuperate,
remit, rehabilitate)

knavery-*n* deception, falseness,
untruth, imposition, fraud, guile,
misrepresentation, delusion,
gullible, conjuring, cunning,
craftiness, subtlety, chicanery,
juggler, concealment, sharp
practice, (natural, pure, native,
simple, plain, inartificial,
untutored, unsophisticated,
unaffected, sincere, frank,
open)

knee-*n* angular, bent, crooked,
aduncous, uncinate, aquiline,
jagged, serrated, furcate,
forked, dovetailed, knock-
kneed, obeisance, homage,
genuflection, courtesy, curtsy,
prostration, kneel to,
(deprecation, expostulation,
intercession)

know-*v* knowledge, cognizance,
acquaintance, privily, insight,
familiarity, appreciation,
intuition, consciousness,
conceive, comprehend, take,
realize, understand, aware,
ascertained, (ignorance,
shallow, superficial, green,
rude, empty, half-learned,
illiterate, unread, uninformed,
empty-headed)

kowtow-*v* bow, depress, lower,

take-down, subvert, prostrate,
level, fell, cast, genuflection,
obeisance, surrender,
succumb, submit, yield, bend,
resign, (elevate, raise, lift,
sublimation, exaltation,
prominence, heighten, erect)

L

labor-*n* work, action, performance, perpetration, movement, operation, evolution, procedure, execution, handicraft, business, deed, act, transaction, job, doings, dealings, proceeding, measure, achieve, inflict, (indolent, lazy, slothful, idle, lust, remiss, slack, inert, torpid, sluggish, languid, supine, heavy, dull, leaden, lumpish, listless, dilatory, laggard)

lack-*n* insufficient, inadequate, impotence, deficiency, imperfection, shortcoming, paucity, stint, scantiness, scarcity, dearth, want, need, poverty, exigency, inanition, starvation, famine, drought, dole, pittance, short-allowance, (sufficient, adequate, enough, satisfaction, competence, fullness, abundance, copiousness, galore, lots, profusion, full measure, rich, luxuriant, ample)

lackadaisical-*adj* indifferent, cold, frigid, lukewarm, cool, unconcerned, insouciant, phlegmatic, easy-going, devil-may-care, careless, listless, half-hearted, unambitious, unaspiring, unsolicitous, inactive, dilatory, laggard, lagging, slow, tottering, irresolute, (active, briskness, liveliness, animation, life, vivacity, spirit, dash, eager, quick, prompt, instant, ready, alert, spry, sharp, spry)

ladle-*n* receptacle, shovel, trowel, spoon, spatula, watch-glass, thimble, receiver, cup, goblet, chalice, soup, decant, draft off, transfuse, spoon, hod, paddle, hoe, spade, spud

lag-*v* linger, slow, retard, relax, slacken, check, moderate, slack, tardy, dilatory, inactive, gentle, easy, leisurely, deliberate, gradual, insensible, imperceptible, languid, sluggish, slow-paced, tardigrade, snail-like, creeping, follow, attendant, shadow, dangler, get behind, (lead, in advance, before, ahead, precede, forerun, introduce)

lame-*adj* incomplete, imperfect, defective, deficient, wanting, failing, meager, half and half, perfunctory, sketch, crude, mutilated, garbled, lopped, truncated, helplessness, prostration, paralysis, palsy, apoplexy, syncope, collapse, exhaustion, emasculation, (ability, ableness, togetherness, faculty, quality, attribute, endowment, virtue, gift, property, qualification, susceptibility, valid, effective

lampoon-*n* censure, scoff at, point at, twit, taunt, satirize, defame, depreciate, find fault with, criticize, disparaging, condemnatory, damnify, denunciatory, reproachful, abusive, objurgatory, clamorous, vituperative, defamatory, satirical, sarcastic, sardonic, cutting, severe, hypercritical, (applaud, praise, laud, good work, homage, blessing, benediction, plaudit, shout, approval)

lance-*n* pierce, perforate, tap, bore, drill, mine, tunnel, enfilade, impale, spike, spear, gore, spit, stab, puncture, stick, prick, riddle, punch, shooter, shot, archer, propel, project, throw, dart, tilt, fling, cast, pitch, chuck, toss, jerk, heave, (repulsion, repulse, abduction, dispel, abduct, repellent, keep at arm's length, send away)

L

land-*n* arrive, reach, attain, get to, come to, overtake, light, alight, dismount, debark, disembark, here, hither, detrain, welcome, converge, meet, completion, earth, ground, continent, coast, shore, mainland, peninsula, delta, soil, globe, clay, loam, acres, real estate, (ocean, brine, water, waves, departure, cessation, decampment, embarkation, outset, start, exit, egress, exodus, farewell)

landscape-*n* agriculture, management of plants, cultivation, husbandry, farming, gardening, horticulture, floriculture, ornamental, flower garden, vineyard, till, scenery, dress the ground, undeformed, undefaced, unspotted, (deformed, defaced, ugly, uninviting)

languid-*adj* weak, poor, infirm, fantasia, sickly, dull, slack, spent, short-winded, effete, weatherbeaten, decayed, rotten, worn, seedy, wasted, washy, laid low, pulled down, frail, fragile, shatter, decrepit, feeble, debilitate, impotent, soft, effeminate, femininity, womanly, colorless, (strength, power, stoutness, strong, might, vigorous, forcible, hard, adamantine, stout, robust, sturdy, hardy)

lap-*n* abode, dwelling, lodging, domicile, residence, address, habitation, berth, seat, sojourn, housing, quarters, headquarters, residence, tabernacle, throne, ark, supporter, aid, prop, stand, anvil, stay, shore, skid, rib, truss, bandage, sleeper, stirrup, stilts, shoe, heel, splint, bar, rod, (suspend, loose, flowing, hang, slip, hitch, fasten to, append)

lapidate-*v* kill, homicide, manslaughter, murder, assassination, attack, assault, onset, onslaught, charge, aggression, offense, incursion, inroad, cut, thrust, fire, volley, platoon, (defend, protect, guard, ward, shield, preservation, guardianship, fortify, resistance)

lapse-*n* elapse, course, progress, process, succession, flow, flux, stream, tract, current, tide, march, run, expire, duration, past, gone, gone by, over, passed away, bygone, foregone, expired, exploded, forgotten, former, pristine, (future, hereafter, approaching, prospectively, hereafter, tomorrow, eventually, ultimately)

large-*adj* quantity, vast, immense, enormous, extreme, inordinate, excessive, extravagant, exorbitant, outrageous, preposterous, unconscionable, swinging, monstrous, big, great, considerable, bulky, voluminous, ample, massive, mass, capacious, comprehensive, spacious, might, towering, fine, magnificent, (dwarf, pygmy, chit, minute, diminutive, microscopic, inconsiderable, exiguous, puny)

lash-*v* enforce, force, impel, push, propel, whip, goad, spur, prick, urge, hurry-on, exhort, advise, advocate, impulsive, seductive, attractive, fascinating, provocative, exciting, violent, vehement, warm, acute, sharp, rough, rude, ungentle, bluff, boisterous, impetuous, rampant, turbulent, (moderation, lenitive, gentleness, quiet, mental calmness, sobriety, relaxing, remission, mitigation, tranquilization, pacification)

last-*n* final, end, close, termination, dissonance, conclusion, period, term, extreme, verge, consummation, finish, conclude, expire, definitive, ending, durable, lasting, standing, permanent, chronic, long-standing, macrobiotic, perpetual, lingering, (transient, impermanence, temporary, brief, quick, brisk, extemporaneous, summary, sudden, momentary)

laud-*v* praise, commendation, approval, sanction, advocacy, esteem, good opinion, admiration, love, worship, benediction, blessing, clap, cheer, hosanna, compliment, complimentary, uncritical, lavish of praise, (disapprove, dislike, lament, reprehension, remonstrance, expostulation, admonition, reproach, rebuke, reprimand, castigation, lecture, curtain lecture, blow up)

laugh-*v* ridicule, derision, sardonic, smile, grin, scoffing, mockery, quiz, banter, irony, squib, satire, skit, quip, quibble, grin, parody, burlesque, satirize, caricature, travesty, giggle, titter, snigger, cheer, chuckle, shout, (lament, wail, complaint, plaint, murmur, mutter, grumble, groan, moan, whine, whimper, sob, sigh, suspiration, mourning, condolence, deplore, grieve)

launch-*v* beginning, commencement, opening, outset, incipience, inception, introduction, initial, inauguration, embarkation, outbreak, fresh start, origin, source, rise, bud, germ, egg, genesis, birth, nativity, cradle, start, (end, close, termination, dissonance, conclusion, period, term, extreme, consummation, finish)

lavish-*adj* profuseness, redundance, too much, super abundance, inordinate, excessive, replete, prodigal, overweening, extravagant, overcharged, supersaturated, drenched, overflowing, superfluous, (receive, take, catch, miser, waste, scrubby, touch, acquire, reception, susceptibility, release)

law-*n* statute, rule, canon, code, rubric, stage, regulation, technicality, precept, direction, instruction, prescription, receipt, golden rule, maxim, permit, give permission, grant, empower, charter, enfranchise, privilege, license, authorize, warrant, sanction, entrust, (disallowance, interdiction, injunction, embargo, ban, taboo, proscription, restriction, hindrance, forbid, disallow, bar, forefend)

lax-*adj* slackness, loose, toleration, anarchy, interregnums, loosening, remission, dead, letter, misrule, dethrone, depose, abdicate, careless, weak, free rein, unbridled, unauthorized, (authority, influence, patronage, hold, rasp, grip, reach, clutch, talons, power, preponderance, credit, jurisdiction)

lazy-*adj* inactive, inertness, obstinacy, idle, remiss, sloth, indolence, indulgence, dawdling, languor, sluggishness, procrastination, torpidity, somnolence, drowsiness, drone, droll, nothingness, slow, slack, moderate, linger, loiter, tortoise, (active, brisk, liveliness, animation, life, vivacity, spirit, dash, energy, nimbleness)

lead-*v* direct, management, government, gubernatorial, conduct, legislate, regulate,

L

guide, steer, pilot, administer, prescribe, cut out work for, head, show the way, authority, influence, patronage, power, jurisdiction, despotism, command, (lax, loose, slackness, toleration, freedom, loosening, remission, misrule, relax, unbridled, unauthorized, dethrone, depose, abdicate)

leak-*n* crack, interval, interspace, separation, break, gap, opening, hole, chasm, interruption, cleft, mesh, crevice, chink, creek, cranny, chap, slit, fissure, scissure, rift, flaw, breach, gorge, defile, transude, run out, strain, distill, perspire, sweat, filter, filtrate, dribble, gush, spout, flow, (excretion, discharge, emanation, exhalation, exudation, extrusion, contiguity, contact, proximity, apposition, join, adjoin, graze, meet, osculate, coincide, adhere, touching)

lean-*adj* thin, narrowness, closeness, exiled, exiguity, tenuity, emaciation, shaving, slip, skeleton, shadow, anatomy, spindle, meager, gaunt, tendency, aptness, proneness, proclivity, bent, turn, tone, bias, set, (breadth, width, latitude, amplitude, diameter, bore, caliber, radius, superficial, thickness, corpulence, dilation, wide, broad, ample, extended, thick)

leap-*v* sudden change, revolution, subversion, break up, destruction, radical, sweeping, transilience, jump, plunge, jerk, start, explosion, spasm, convulsion, throe, revulsion, storm, ascent, ascension, rising, rise, upgrowth, acclivity, hill, rocket, lark, sky-rocket, ascent, rise, mount, climb, clamber, ramp, scramble, (descent, dissension,

declination, fall, drop, cadence, subsidence)

leave-*v* fissure, breach, rent, split, rift, crack, slit, incision, fission, dissection, anatomy, disjoin, disconnect, disengage, sunder, divide, sever, abscind, relinquish, abandon, defection, secession, withdrawal, discontinuance, renunciation, abrogation, resignation, (arrive, reunion, remain, confinement, restrict, forbid, hindrance, taboo, embargo, ban)

leaven-*n* component, integral, element, constituent, ingredient, part and parcel, contents, appurtenance, feature, member, to be implicated in, cause, origin, source, principle, element, agent, groundwork, foundation, (effect, consequence, result, upshot, issue, produce, work, handiwork, fabric, performance, creature)

ledge-*n* shelf, support, ground, foundation, base, basis, bearing, fulcrum, footing, prop, stand, anvil, shore, skid, rib, truss, bandage, stirrup, silts, tower, pillar, column, obelisk, monument, steeple, spire, escarpment, edge, brae, height, (lowness, neap, debased, nether, flat, level with the ground)

left-*adj* residuary, remaining, remainder, residue, remnant, rest, relic, leavings, heel-tap, odds and ends, surplus, overplus, excess, complement, sinistrality, left-handed, port, (dextral, right-handed, ambidextrous, adjunct, affix, appendage, reinforcement, accompaniment, adjective)

leg-*n* support, travel, wayfaring, journey, excursion, expedition, tour, trip, grand tour, circuit, peregrination, discursion, ramble, pilgrimage, course, ambulation, march, step, tread, pace, plot, wend, promenade

legal-*adj* permit, leave, allow, sufferance, tolerance, liberty, law, license, concession, grace, indulgence, favor, dispensation, exemption, release, connivance, vouchsafement, authorization, warranty, accordance, admission, warrant, sanction, (forbid, prohibit, disallowance, injunction, embargo, ban, taboo, hindrance, bar, forefend)

legend-*n* record, trace, vestige, transactions, proceedings, debates, chronicles, annals, history, biography, tabulation, entry, booking, signature, identification, recorder, journalism, register, (efface, obliteration, erasure, cancellation, circumscribe, deletion, expunge, cancel, blot, deface)

legion-*n* multitude, numerousness, multiplicity, profusion, host, enormous, number, array, sight, army, sea, galaxy, scores, peck, bushel, shoal, armed force, troops, soldiery, military, standing army, volunteers, (few, paucity, small number, small quantity, rarity, infrequency, handful, minority, thin)

leisure-*n* spare time, slow, deliberate, quiet, calm, undisturbed, slack, tardy, dilatory, gentle, easy, gradual, insensible, imperceptible, languid, sluggish, slow-paced, tardigrade, creeping, (speed, velocity, celerity, swiftness, rapidity, expedition, eagle speed, haste, spurt, dash, race, lively)

lend-*v* loan, advance, accommodation, federation, mortgage, investment, pawnbroker, money lender, usurer, advance, intrust, invest, let, lease, demise, aid, assistance, help, support, lift, patronage, countenance, favor, interest, advocacy, (prevention, preclusion, obstruction, stoppage, interruption, restriction, borrow, pledge, hire, rent, farm brace, touch, hold up)

lenient-*adj* moderate, temperateness, gentleness, sobriety, quiet, mental calmness, relaxation, remission, mitigation, tranquilization, assuagement, contemplation, pacification, measure, (violence, inclemency, vehemence, might, impetuosity, boisterousness, uproar, riot, severity)

lessen-*v* decrease, subtraction, reduction, abatement, declination, shrinking, abridgment, diminish, abridge, shrink, fall away, waste, wear, wane, ebb, decline, subside, compression, compactness, collapse, emaciation, atrophy, (expansion, enlargement, extension, augmentation, growth, development, increase, additional, undiminished, exaggerate, exasperate)

let-*v* permit, leave, allow, tolerance, liberty, law, license, concession, grace, indulgence, favor, dispensation, exemption, release, connivance, vouchsafement, authorization, warranty, lend, advance, accommodate, (prohibition, disallowance, borrow, interdict, injunction, embargo, ban, taboo, restriction, release, hindrance, exclusive)

lethargic-*adj* inactivity, inaction, inertness, obstinacy, drowsiness, nodding, hypnotism, heaviness, sleep, coma, trance, nap, doze, snooze, relaxation, idle, drone,

L

droll, dawdle, insensibility,
(active, briskness, liveliness,
animation, life, vivacity, spirit,
dash, energy, nimbleness,
agility, quickness)

letter-*n* mark, character,
hieroglyphic, writing, printing,
abc's, consonant, vowel,
diphthong, mute, liquid, labial,
dental

levity-*n* lightness,
imponderability, buoyancy,
volatility, feather, dust, mote,
down, thistle down, flue,
cobweb, gossamer, straw, cork,
bubble, float, ether, air, leaven,
ferment, barm, yeast, (gravity,
weight, heaviness, specific
gravity, ponderous, pressure,
load, burden, ballast,
counterpoise, lead)

libation-*n* drunkenness,
intemperance, drinking,
inebriety, insobriety,
intoxication, tipsy, sot, potable,
draught, carousel, nourishment,
sustenance, nurture, (excretion,
discharge, exhalation,
exudation, extrusion, secretion,
sobriety, teetotaler)

liberty-*n* freedom,
independence, immunity,
exemption, emancipation,
franchise, liberalism,
permission, leave, allow,
sufferance, tolerance, law,
concession, grace, indulgence,
favor, dispensation, release,
(prohibit, disallowance,
interdict, unlicensed,
contraband, subjection)

lick-*v* eat, feed, fare, devour,
swallow, take, gulp, bolt, snap,
dispatch, pick, peck, crunch,
chew, masticate, nibble, gnaw,
mumble, strike, deal a blow to,
smite, slap, face, smack,
(discharge, emanation,
exhalation, exudation,
extrusion, secretion, effusion,
saliva, outpour)

limbo-*n* purgatory, hell,

bottomless pit, place of
torment, everlasting fire,
torment, Gehenna, abyss,
inferno, mental suffering, pain,
ache, smart, displeasure,
vexation of spirit, (pleasure,
gratification, enjoyment,
fruition, relish, zest,
satisfaction, heavenly,
paradise, eden, celestial)

limit-*n* restrain, hindrance,
restraint, coercion, constraint,
repression, discipline, control,
confinement, durance, duress,
imprisonment, end, close,
termination, conclusion, finish,
(begin, commence, originate,
conceive, initiate, open, dawn,
liberation, disengagement, free,
deliverance)

linear-*adj* continuity,
consecutive, progressive,
gradual, serial, successive,
immediate, unbroken, entire,
uninterrupted, unremitting,
perennial, paternity, parentage,
consanguinity, maternal, family,
ancestral, patriarchal,
(discontinue, pause, interrupt,
intervene, break, disconnect,
break)

liniment-*n* ointment, linseed,
unguent, glycerine, stearin,
grease, suet, remedy, help,
redress, antidote, antiseptic,
corrective, restorative,
sedative, physic, medicine,
drug, potion, (bane, curse, evil,
hurtfulness, painfulness,
scourge, sting, fang, thorn)

link-*n* pin, nail, bolt, hasp, clasp,
clamp, screw, rivet, impact,
solder, set, weld, fuse together,
wedge, rabbet, mortise, mire,
jam, dovetail, encase, graft,
ingraft, inosculate, close, tight,
taut, (sunder, divide, subdivide,
sever, dissever, abscind, saw,
snip, nib, nip, cleave, rive, rend,
slit)

lion-*n* courage, hero, demigod,
tiger, panther, bull dog,

prowess, heroism, chivalry, manliness, nerve, pluck, mettle, game, spunk, face, virtue, prodigy, phenomenon, potent, (coward, timidity, effeminacy, poltroonery, baseness, dastardliness, sneak, recreant, shy)

liquid-*n* fluid, inelastic, liquor, humor, juice, sap, serum, blood, serosal, succulent, sappy, flowing, soluble, lymph, (atmospheric, airy, aerial, meteorological, weather-wise, ventilate, climate)

list-*n* catalog, inventory, schedule, register, account, file, index, book, ledger, synopsis, bill of lading, prospectus, statistics, directory, score

listless-*adj* inattentive, inconsiderateness, absent, abstracted lost, preoccupied, engrossed, napping, dreamy, disconcerted, (attention, mindfulness, observance, consideration, notice, regard)

literary-*adj* lingual, dialectic, vernacular, polyglot, book, writing, work, volume, publication, portfolio, periodical, style, diction, phraseology, wording, manner, strain, literary

litigation-*n* citation, arraignment, prosecution, impeachment, accusation, apprehension, arrest, committal, writ, summons, subpoena, strife, warfare, outbreak, disagreement, variance, difference, (concord, accord, harmony, symphony, agreement, sympathy, response, union, unison)

litter-*n* disorder, irregularity, anomaly, unconformity, anarchy, confusion, disarray, jumble, huddle, lumber, mess, mash, hodgepodge, (order, regularity, uniformity, symmetry, gradation, progression, series,

subordination, routine, method, disposition)

little-*adj* small, quantity, vanishing, diminutive, minute, inconsiderable, paltry, faint, unimportant, weak, slender, light, slight, scanty, scant, limited, mere, simple, sheer, stark, bare, dwarf, pygmy, chit, (corpulent, stout, fat, plump, squab, full, lusty, strapping, bouncing, portly, burly, huge, immense)

live-*v* exist, being, entity, subsistence, reality, actuality, positiveness, fact, matter of fact, real, actual, absolute, true, permanence, persistence, endurance, standing, maintenance, present, occupying, inhabiting, dwell, reside, stay, sojourn, abide, lodge, (absence, inexistent, empty, void, vacant, extinction, annihilate, nullify, abrogate, destroy, negative, blank, missing)

livery-*n* outfit, equipment, uniform, regimentals, canonical, gear, harness, turn out, accouterment, caparison, suit, rigging, trappings, traps, slops, masquerade, color, hue, tint, tinge, dye, complexion, shade, tincture, cast, coloration, glow, flush, tone, key, (hueless, pale, pallid, muddy, leaden, nudity, bareness, undress, dishabille, molting, exfoliation, divest, uncover, denude)

load-*n* cargo, contents, lading, freight, shipment, bale, shipload, stuff, oppress, care, anxiety, solicitude, trouble, trial, fiery ordeal, shock, blow, dole, fret, burden, (pleasure, gratification, enjoyment, fruition, relish, zest, gusto, satisfaction, complacency, well-being)

loathe-*v* dislike, repugnance,

L

disgust, queasiness, turn,
nausea, averseness, antipathy,
abhorrence, horror, hatred,
detestation, animosity,
hydrophobia, insulting,
irritating, provoking,
abomination, aversion, (love,
fondness, liking, inclination,
affection, sympathy,
tenderness)

local-*adj* location, lodgement,
reposition, stow, package,
settlement, installation, fixation,
insertion, anchorage, mooring,
encampment, plantation,
colony, place, situate, locate,
localize, station, house,
(displacement, transposition,
eject, exile, removal,
dislocation, unload, empty)

lock-*v* fasten, attach, fix, affix,
bind, secure, clinch, twist,
string, strap, firm, close, knot,
shackle, rein, padlock, rivet,
stake, hook, latchet, resistance,
stand, front, oppugnant,
opposition, reluctant, (separate,
parting, detachment,
segregation, divorce, divide,
unlock, detach, isolate)

locomotion-*n* moving, stream,
flow, flux, run, course,
evolution, kinematics, step,
transitory, shifting, movable,
mobile, mercurial, restless,
nomadic, erratic, cadence,
(quiet, tranquility, calm, repose,
peace, dead calm, immobility,
fixed, stay, stagnate, rest,
pause, lull)

lodge-*n* location, place, situate,
locate, localize, put, lay, set,
seat, station, quarter, post,
install, house, stow, establish,
fix, pin, root, graft, plant,
people, inhabit, dwell, reside,
stay, sojourn, live, abide,
nestle, present, (absent,
missing, empty, void, vacant,
devoid, truant, displacement)

lofty-*adj* height, altitude,
elevation, eminence, pitch,

sublimity, colossus, tall,
gigantic, Patagonian,
vehement, impassioned, poetic,
eloquent, petulant, (feeble,
tame, meager, vapid, trashy,
cold, frigid, dull, dry,
monotonous, weak, careless,
inexact)

log-*n* fuel, firing, combustible,
coal, anthracite, culm, coke,
carbon, charcoal, turf, peat,
firewood, bobbing, faggot,
cinder, record, note, minute,
register, roll, list, entry,
memorandum, document,
deposition, affidavit, certificate,
(efface, obliterate, erase,
expunge, cancel, blot, scratch)

long-*adj* durable, lasting,
permanent, chronic, long-
standing, protracted,
prolonged, lengthy, drawn out,
profuse, verbose, copious,
exuberant, rambling, broad,
wide, ample, extended, thick,
dumpy, streak, outstretched,
elongate, extend, stretch,
(short, little, abbreviated, brief,
curt, compact, stubby,
temporary, cursory, short-lived,
deciduous, mortal, summary,
concise, terse)

longevity-*n* age, oldness,
senility, anility, climacteric,
declining years, decrepitude,
caducity, seniority, eldership,
matronly, anile, ripe, mellow,
wrinkled, (youth, juvenility,
cradle, nursery, green,
budding)

longitude-*n* situation, position,
locality, status, footing,
standing, standpoint, post,
stage, aspect, attitude, posture,
place, site station, seat, length,
span, linear, measure of length,
(shortness, brevity, littleness,
shortening, abbreviation,
abridgment, concision,
retrenchment, curtailment)

look-*v* see, vision, sight, view,
glance, glimpse, peep, gaze,

stare, leer, contemplation, squint, visual, ocular, optic, appear, aspect, phase, guise, complexion, color, image, apparent, seeming, ostensible, (invisible, imperceptible, conceal, blind, sightless)

loop-hole-*n* hole, perforation, opening, vent, orifice, path, thoroughfare, escape, avocation, elopement, flight, evasion, retreat, narrow, hair-breadth, impunity, reprieve, livery, liberation, refugee, elude, (closure, occlusion, blockade, shutting up, obstruction, plug, block, shut, bolt, stop, seal, unopened)

loose-*adj* detach, sunder, divide, subdivide, sever, dissever, abscind, saw, snip, nib, nip, cleave, rupture, shatter, shiver, lacerate, scramble, mangle, gash, hash, slice, whittle, carve, dissect, liberate, disengagement, release, enlargement, emancipation, enfranchisement, discharge, dismissal, (restraint, hindrance, coercion, compulsion, constraint, repression, discipline, control)

lose-*v* loss, depredation, forfeiture, lapse, privation, bereavement, deprivation, dispossession, riddance, lost, irretrievable, hopeless, farewell, adieu, failure, miscarriage, repulse, rebuff, defeat, fall, downfall, defeat, rout, overthrow, (success, fulfillment, advance, progress, surmount, overcome, triumph, proficiency, gain, attain, carry, acquire, obtainment, purchase, descent, inherit)

love-*v* desire, wish, fancy, fantasy, want, need, exigency longing, hankering, inkling, solicitude, anxiety, yearning, coveting, aspiration, liking, fondness, relish, passion,

range, mania, ambition, eagerness, zeal, ardor, breathless, impatience, impetuosity, (indifferent, cold, frigid, lukewarm, cool, careless, listless, lackadaisical, half-hearted, apathy, insensibility)

lucid-*adj* luminous, lighten, enlighten, shine, glow, slitter, glisten, twinkle, gleam, flare, glare, beam, shimmer, glimmer, flicker, sparkle, scintillate, dazzle, transparent, pellucid, diaphanous, limpid, clear, serene, crystalline, glassy, hyaline, (opacity, opaqueness, film, cloud, dim, turbid, thick, muddy, opaques, obfuscated, cloudy, hazy, misty, foggy, vaporous, dark, black, shade, shadow, extinction)

lush-*adj* vegetation, rank, drunkenness, intemperance, drinking, inebriety, insobriety, intoxication, tipsy, guzzle, swill, soak, sot, lush, bib, carouse, (sobriety, teetotaler, abstainer)

luxury-*n* enjoyment, pleasure, gratification, relish, complacency, comfort, ease, cushion, joy, gladness, delight, glee, cheer, sunshine, happiness, felicity, bliss, paradise, ecstasy, Elysium, indulgence, high living, excess, sensuality, (temperance, moderation, forbearance, self-denial, frugality, total abstinence, sufficient, care, anxiety, solicitude, concern)

lymph-*n* fluid, liquid, liquor, humor, juice, sap, serum, blood, transparent, pellucid, lucid, relucent, limpid, clear, serene, crystalline, vitreous, watery, aqueous, aquatic, lymphatic, drenching, diluted, week, set, moist, (airy, ventilate, flatulent, effervescent, windy, opaque, smoky, murky, dirty, opaque)

L

M

maceration-*n* saturation, water,
serum, serosal, lymph, rheumy,
delude, dilution, dip, immerse,
submerge, plunge, souse,
duck, drown, soak, steep,
pickle, sprinkle, atonement,
reparation, compromise,
composition, compensation,
quitting, expiation, redemption,
(atmospheric, airy)

mad-*adj* insane, disordered,
lunacy, madness, mania,
mental alienation, aberration,
demented, frenzy, raving,
incoherence, wandering,
delirium, calenture of the brain,
delusion, hallucination, vertigo,
dizziness, fanaticism, (sanity,
soundness, rationality, sobriety,
lucidity, senses, sound mind)

madcap-*n* buffoon, humorist,
wag with, repartee, life of the
party, wit-snapper, joker, jester,
farceur, tumbler, acrobat,
harlequin, clown, motley,
motley fool, zany, dandy,
caricaturist, lunatic, maniac,
dreamer, excitable,
impetuosity, boisterousness,
impatience, (passive, coolness,
calmness, serene)

madrigal-*n* solo, duet, duo, trio,
quartet, descent, glee, catch,
round, chorus, antiphon,
accompaniment, composer,
musician, perform, attune,
instrumental, vocal, choral,
lyric, operatic, harmonious,
poetry, versification, rhyming,
(unpoetical, unrhymed)

magistrate-*n* authority,
influence, patronage, power,
preponderance, credit,
prestige, jurisdiction, divine
right, despotism, command,
empire, auspicious, propitious,
master, padrone, paramount,
(servant, subject, retainer,
follower, henchman, menial,
attendant, squire, usher, page,
footboy)

magnetism-*n* power, potency,
puissance, might, force,
energy, almightiness,
omnipotence, authority,
strength, ability, ableness,
competency, efficiency, validity,
cogency,enablement, pressure,
elasticity, gravity, electricity,
galvanism, (impotence,
disability, disablement,
impiousness, imbecility,
incapacity)

magnificent-*n* grand,
ostentation, display, show,
flourish, parade, pomp, array,
state, solemnity, dash, splash,
glitter, strut, pomposity,
magnificence, splendor,
demonstration, celebration,
pageant, spectacle, form,
elegance, brace, beauty,
unadorned, symmetry, refined,
delicate, (ugly, graceless,
inelegant, ungraceful, ungainly,
uncouth, stiff, rugged, rough,
gross, rude, awkward, clumsy)

magnify-*v* increase, augment,
enlargement, extension,
expansion, increment,
accretion, accession,
development, intensify,
enhance, redouble,
exaggerate, exasperate,
heighten, overestimate,
oversensitive, vanity, overrate,
(underestimate, depreciate,
detraction, undervalue,
modesty)

magnitude-*n* size, quantity,
dimension, amplitude, mass,
amount, quantum, measure,
substance, strength, more or
less, greatness, multitude,
immense, enormity, infinity,
might, volume, help, (minimum,
particle, molecule, corpuscle,
small, diminutive, minute,
inconsiderable)

main-*adj* important, consequence, moment, prominence, consideration, mark, materialistic, import, significance, concern, emphasis, interest, gravity, seriousness, solemnity, conduit, channel, duct, (unimportant, insignificant, nothingness, immaterial, triviality, levity, frivolity, minor detail, nonsense)

maintain-*v* sustain, act upon, perform, play, support, strain, take effect, quicken, strike, preservation, safekeeping, conservation, keep, prophylactic, unimpaired, unbroken, continue, persist, perpetuate, undying, unvaried, (discontinue, cease, desist, stop, slacken, decay, deteriorate, suspend, interrupt)

major-*adj* greater, supreme, higher, exceeding, distinguished, vaulting, utmost, paramount, foremost, crowning, first-rate, excellent, transcendent, sovereign, superlative, inimitable, incomparable, potentate, lord, sovereign, monarch, autocrat, despot, tyrant, (servant, subject, flunky, inferior)

make-*v* constitute, composition, combination, inclusion, admission, comprehension, reception, form, compose, contain, embrace, embody, involve, implicate, produce, create, fabricate, manufacture, establish, perform, achievement, (destruction, waste, dissolution, ruin, annihilation)

makeshift-*n* substitute, supplanting, supersession, stop-gap, jury-mast, dummy, scapegoat, double, alternative, representative, supersede, replace, ostensible motive, ground, plea, pretext, pretense,

lame, excuse, (interchanged, reciprocal, mutual, communicative, intercurrent)

malaise-*n* pain, suffering, bodily, physical pain, dolor, ache, smart, twinge, twitch, ripe, headache, hurt, cut, sore, discomfort, spasm, mental suffering, annoyance, irritation, infliction, plague, (happy, blest, blessed, blissful, beatified, comfortable, overjoyed, entranced, enchanted)

malaria-*n* contagious, infectious, catching, taking, epidemic, insalubrious, noxious, deleterious, pestilent, poisonous, bane, curse, evil scourge, leaven, virus, mephitis, (remedy, help, restorative, corrective, tonic, therapeutic, sedative)

malformation-*n* distortion, twist, crookedness, grimace, deformity, monstrosity, misproportion, contort, twist, warp, writhe, irregular, unsymmetrical, awry, askew, ugliness, misshape, (symmetry, shapeliness, finish, beauty, proportion, uniformity, regular, uniform, balanced, parallel, coextensive)

malign-*v* bad, hurtful, virulence, bane, malevolence, ill-treatment, annoyance, molestation, abuse, oppression, persecution, outrage, misusage, injury, damage, wrong, aggrieve, (goodness, excellence, merit, virtue, value, worth, price, beneficial, profitable, edifying, healthful, salutary)

man-*n* adult male, he, manhood, gentlemen, sir, master, yeoman, swain, fellow, blade, beau, chap, gaffer, good man, husband, masculine, manly, hero, demigod, bully, courageous, lion-hearted

manager-*n* director, governor,

M

rector, comptroller,
superintendent, overseer,
inspector, surveyor, moderator,
monitor, taskmaster, leader,
conductor, property man,
machinist, prompter, call-boy,
(unmanaged, abandoned,
without direction)

mangle-v separate, part,
detachment, segregation,
divorce, fissure, breach, split,
rift, crack, slit, incision, sunder,
divide, haggle, lacerate, gash,
hash, slice, scramble, whittle,
impairment, injury, damage,
infect, (improve, mend, revise,
refine, rectify, enrich, mellow,
elaborate, fatten)

mania-n disordered, abnormal,
unsound, derangement,
insanity, lunacy, madness,
mental alienation, aberration,
demented, frenzy, raving,
incoherence, wandering,
hallucination, dizziness,
kleptomania, dipsomania,
hypochondriasis, hysteria,
(sane, rational, reasonable)

manifold-adj multiform, variety,
diversity, multifariousness,
many-sided, omnifarious,
irregular, diversified, different,
all sorts and kinds, many,
several, sundry, divers, various,
profusion, populous, numerous,
(fewness, paucity, small
number, rarity, infrequency,
handful, maniple, minority,
scattered)

manner-n description,
denomination, designation,
character, stamp, predicament,
sort, genus, species, variety,
family, race, tribe, clan, type,
kit, sect, assortment, feather,
kidney, suit, range, style, mode
of expression, method, way,
manner, wise, gait, form, mode,
fashion, tone, guise

mannerism-n special, particular,
individual, specific, proper,
personal, original, private,

respective, definite,
determinate, especial,
characteristic, ideocracy,
distinctive feature, (general,
universal, miscellany,
collective, common, prevalent,
transcendental)

many-adj frequent, repetition,
many times, incessant,
perpetual, continual, constant,
numerous, multiplicity,
profusion, plenty, majority,
huge numbers, several, sundry,
various, manifold, multiplied,
thick, studded, (fewness,
reduction, weeding, elimination,
decimation, scanty, thin)

marble-n hard, rigid, stubborn,
stiff, firm, starched, stark,
unbending, unlimber,
unyielding, inflexible, tense,
indurate, adamantine, concrete,
stony, granitic, vitreous, (soft,
tender, supple, pliant, lithe)

march-v advance, precession,
leading, heading, precedence,
priority, forerun, proceed,
progress, roving, vagrancy,
countermarching, nomad,
vagabondism, (regression,
withdrawal, retirement,
recession, follow, pursue,
shadow, trail, lag)

margin-n edge, verge, brink,
brow, brim, border, skirt, rim,
flange, side, space extension,
extent, expanse, room, field,
way, expansion, compass,
sweep, play, swing, spread,
capacity, stretch, range,
latitude, scope, (center, interior,
surface, climate, zone,
meridian)

mark-n indication, sign, symbol,
type, figure, emblem, cipher,
representation, epigraph,
motto, characteristic, pointer,
not, token, line, stroke, dash,
score, witness, voucher,
position, place, period, pitch,
stand, (insignificant, disregard,
non-representative, without

affirmation)

market-*n* purchase, buying, shopping, bribery, patron, client, customer, invest in, procure, rent, spend, mart, place, bazaar, staple, exchange, hall, stall, booth, wharf, office, chambers, warehouse, establishment, (sale, seller, vendor, dispose of, dispense, merchant, vent)

marry-*v* combine, unite, incorporate, amalgamate, embody, absorb, re-embody, blend, merge, fuse, melt into one, consolidate, cement in a union, impregnate, matrimony, wedlock, union, nuptial, tie, match, betrothment, bridal, spouse, join, couple, betroth, (divorce, separate, widowhood, decomposition, dissection, resolution, dissolution, corruption, dispersion)

marital-*adj* warfare, fighting, hostilities, war, arms, battle array, campaign, crusade, expedition, mobilization, battle, campaigning, service, havoc, tribunal, court, board, bench, law, arbitration, inquisition, (pacification, conciliation, reconciliation, accommodation, terms, compromise, amnesty)

martyrdom-*n* unselfishness, self-denying, sacrificing, devoted, generous, liberal, benevolence, elevation, loftiness of purpose, exaltation, magnanimity, chivalry, heroism, sublimity, (selfishness, indulgence, worldliness, self-seeking, mean, narrow-minded, mercenary, earthly, mundane)

marvelous-*adj* great, wonderful, admire, surprise, astonish, amaze, astound, dumbfound, dazzle, wondrous, overwhelming, stupendous, indescribable, inexpressible, awesome, aghast, agape, spellbound, (common, ordinary,

expected, foreseen, astonished at nothing)

mash-*v* mix, blend, tincture, sprinkle, cross, alloy, amalgamate, compound, adulterate, infect, instill, infiltrate, confusion, disorder, disarray, jumble, huddle, litter, lumber, mess, muddle, hash, hodgepodge, (uniformity, symmetry, orderly, neat, tidy, well-regulated, correct, methodical)

mask-*v* conceal, hide, mystification, seal of secrecy, screen, disguise, masquerade, stealthiness, reticence, reserve, evasion, suppression, white lie, cover, blind, gauze, veil, mantle, cloud, mist, shade, shadow, (inform, acquaint, announce, tell, impart, mention, make known, enlighten, specify)

master-*v* understand, comprehend, take in, catch, grasp, follow, collect, make out, easily understood, clearness, simplify, explain, plain, distinct, explicit, positive, precise, graphic, expressive, conceive, accomplished, profound, book-learned, (shallow, superficial, rude, empty, illiterate, uninformed)

mate-*n* similar, resemblance, likeness, affinity, approximation, parallelism, sameness, fellow, analog, pair, twin, double, counterpart, likeness, wife, espouse, marry, join, spousal, bridal, helper, auxiliary, recruit, assistant, associate, midwife, colleague, (opposition, enemy, adversary, dissimilar, unlike, unmatched, unlikeness, diversity, dissemblance, difference)

matter-*n* substance, body, flesh and blood, thing, object, article, tangible, material, essential, physical, sensible, ponderable,

M

palpable, objective, impersonal, neuter, unspiritual, subject, idea, argument, text, sum and substance, gist, suggestive, (immaterial, unextended, disembodied, personal, subjective, groundless, nothingness, nonentity, unsubstantial)

mature-*adj* old, age, antiquity, decline, decay, seniority, eldership, tradition, custom, venerable, time-honored, prime, adolescent, pubescent, of age, grown up, virile, adult, (new, novel, recent, fresh, young, green, immature, virgin, modern, late, neoteric)

maze-*n* convolution, winding, circumvolution, wave, undulation, tortuosity, coil, roll, curl, buckle, spiral, helix, corkscrew, worm, volute, tendril, dilemma, embarrassment, perplexity, intricacy, entanglement, awkwardness, mesh, (ease, feasibility, flexibility, smoothness, round, rounded, oval)

meager-*adj* small, little, tenuity, paucity, few, mediocrity, moderation, minute, slight, limited, sparing incomplete, insufficient, immature, deficit, omission, lack, hollow, (complete, large, entirety, full, sufficiency, replenish, whole, quantity, volume, unlimited, vast, immense, enormous, extreme)

mean-*adj* contemptible, wretched, vile, scrubby, pitiful, sorry, trashy, worthless, medium, intermediate, average, balance, mediocrity, generality, compromise, neutrality, commonplace, (gravity, seriousness, solemnity, pressure, urgency, stress, matter of life and death)

meander-*v* winding, convolution,

sinuosity, undulation, tortuosity, twirl, snake-like, involved, intricate, complicated, perplexed, stray, straggle, sidle, diverge, trailing, digress, wander, twist, rove, drift, go astray, adrift, (bearing a straight course, set, directly, straight, point blank, straightforward)

measure-*n* computer, survey, valuation, appraisement, assessment, estimate, reckoning, gauging, standard, rule, compass, calipers, gage, meter, scale, coordinates, degree, extent, amount, ratio, intensity, strength, quantity, mass, comparative, gradual, limits

mediocrity-*n* mean, medium, average, generality, intermediate, neutral, compromise, imperfect, deficiency, inadequacy, fault, defect, weak point, flaw, blemish, indifferent, middling, ordinary, passable, secondary, limited, (perfect, faultless, model, standard, complete, intact, inimitable, harmless, immaculate, impeccable)

medley-*n* alloy, mixture, jumble, sauce, mash, instill, infiltrate, blend, cross, amalgamate, compound, infect, complex, intricacy, perplexity, disarrange, entangled, deranged, haphazard, random, luck, (orderly, regularity, subordination, methodical, unconfused, arranged)

meet-*v* assemble, crowd, throng, flood, rush, deluge, rabble, mob, horde, body, tribe, crew, gang, group, cluster, muster, convene, gather, converge, concur, come together, unite, concentrate, expedite, convenient, due, proper, eligible, seemly, (exit, emergence, burst, evacuation,

diverge, repel, push, dispel,
leave, depart, disperse,
dismember)

mellow-*adj* advance, ascend,
increase, fructify, ripen, pick up,
come about, rally, better,
improved, enrich, cultivate,
enhance, render, elaborate,
season, bring to maturity,
mature, nurture, (crude, raw,
virgin, unprepared, improvise,
coarse, deteriorate,
degenerate, impair, weaken)

melt-*v* convert, pervert, render,
mold, form, merge, liquefy,
dissolve, solvent, boil, heat,
calcination, ignite,
inflammation, adust, incendiary,
caustic, smelt, digest, stew,
cook, seethe, simmer, (cool,
fan, refrigerate, refresh,
congeal, freeze, glaciate,
benumb, starve, quench,
extinguish)

memory-*n* remembrance,
retention, tenacity, readiness,
reminiscence, recognition,
recurrence, recollection,
retrospect, reminder, memento,
souvenir, keepsake, relic,
memorandum, memorabilia,
tenacious, (oblivion,
forgetfulness, short, efface,
mindless, insensible, escape,
failing memory)

menagerie-*n* collection, clan,
brotherhood, association, gang,
swam, shoal, school, convey,
flock, herd, drove, array, bevy,
vivarium, zoological garden,
aviary, aquarium,
domestication, breeding,
(disperse, scatter, disseminate,
diffuse, shed, spread)

mendicant-*adj* beggar, sturdy,
cadger, canvasser, touter, loss
of fortune, pauper, poor,
indigent, penniless, insolvency,
(wealth, richness, fortune,
affluence, sufficiency,
livelihood)

mental-*adj* intellect,

understanding reason,
rationality, cogitative, faculties,
senses, consciousness,
observation, percipience, under
consideration, thought, reflect,
consider, deliberate,
(unendowed with reason,
imbecility, vacant, thoughtless,
diverted, irrational)

mercy-*n* leniency, moderation,
tolerance, mildness,
gentleness, favor, clemency,
forbearance, compassion,
tolerance, pity, commiseration,
sympathy, ruthful, humane,
exorable, melt, thaw, relent,
unhardened, (severity,
strictness, harshness, rigor,
stringency, austerity,
inclemency, relentless)

merge-*v* combine, mixture,
union, unification, synthesis,
incorporation, amalgamation,
embodiment, coalescence,
fusion, blending, absorption,
centralization, impregnate,
ingrained, (decompose,
analysis, dissect, catalysis,
dissolution, corruption, unravel,
disperse)

merit-*n* goodness, excellence,
virtue, value, worth, price,
perfection, prime, flower, cram,
champion, beneficial, profitable,
advantageous, salutary,
favorable, good, superior, fine,
genuine, admirable,
praiseworthy, (vile, oppressive,
burdensome, malign,
corrupting, corrosive,
destructive, destroy)

merriment-*n* cheerful, geniality,
gaiety, cheer, good humor, high
spirits, liveliness, vivacity,
animation, joviality, jollity,
jocularity, mirth, hilarity,
exhilaration, laughter, rejoicing,
elate, exhilarate, gladden,
inspire, perk up, delight,
(dejection, depression,
lowness, heaviness,
melancholy, sadness, dismal)

M

mesh-*v* interval, interspace, separation, break, gap, opening, hole, chasm, interruption, interstice, cleft, crevice, chink, rime, creek, cranny, crack, chap, slit, flaw, breach, rent, gash, cut, crossing, intersection, transversely, network, web, twill, skein, chain, braid, entanglement, (coexist, adhere, graze, touch, meet, osculate, contact, proximity, meeting)

mess-*n* mixture, combine, intermix, mingle, shuffle, knead, brew, impregnate with, instill, imbue, infiltrate, compound, infect, among, amongst, amid, amidst, miscellaneous, dilemma, embarrassment, perplexity, intricacy, entanglement, awkwardness, delicacy, maze, vexed, quandary, (ease, facilitate, smooth, emancipate, free, manageable, light, simple, eliminate, single, pure, clear)

messenger-*n* envoy, emissary, legate, ambassador, diplomat, marshal, flag-bearer, herald, crier, trumpeter, courier, runner, errand boy, reporter, mail, telephone, wireless, heliograph, subject, retainer, follower, henchman, menial, help, attache, handmaid, secretary, assistant, (master, lord, padrone, paramount, commander, captain, chief, authority, corporal)

meteor-*n* heavenly body, cosmically, mundane, terrestrial, solar, heliacal, lunar, celestial, sphere, starry, stellar, luminary, light, flame, spark, phosphorescence, star, blazing, (shade, sunshade, gauze, veil, mantle, mask, cloud, mist, umbrageous)

mettle-*n* sensible, impressionable, susceptive, impassion, gushing, warm-

tender, soft-hearted, romantic, enthusiastic, high-flying, spirited, vivacious, lively, expressive, mobile, trembling, excitable, fastidious, (insensible, inertness, apathy, dull, frigid, cold-hearted, indifferent, lukewarm, careless)

middle-*n* midst, half-way, navel, equidistance, dissection, half-distance, equator, diaphragm, midriff, intermediate, equatorial, midship, compromise, compensation, middle term, meet one half way, give and take, arrange, adjust, agree, moderate, average, mediocrity

midst-*n* centrality, center, core, kernel, nucleus, heart, ole, axis, navel, backbone, marrow, symmetry, center of gravity, bring to focus, intermediate, intervention, introduce, (surround, beset, encompass)

mild-*adj* moderate, temperate, relaxation, remission, mitigation, tranquilization, pacification, gentleness, sobriety, quiet, contemplation, appease, soothe, lull, swag, calm, cool, hush, quell, tame, (violent, fury, storm, rough, vehement, warm, acute, sharp, rude, impetuous, rampant)

mill-*v* reduce, grind, pulverize, comminute, granulate, triturate, levigate, scrape, file, abrade, rub down, grate, rasp, pound, bray, bruise, contuse, beat, crush, crunch, crumble, disintegrate, (lubricate, oil, glycerine, lather, grease, smooth)

millennium-*n* period, second, minute, hour, day, week, month, quarter, year, decade, lifetime, generation, century, age, prospectively, hereafter, eventually, ultimately, whereupon, (lapse, elapse, advance, progress, succession, proceed, slip, slide, past, gone,

foregone, extinct, forgotten,
over)

mince-*v* cut up, separate,
sunder, divide, subdivide,
rescind, segregate, keep apart,
sever, abscind, chop, chip,
crack, snap, break, tear, burst,
rend, wrench, rupture, shatter,
shiver, hack, slash, mangle,
slice, tear, whittle, (join, unite,
annex, attach, hinge, seam,
suture, stitch, link, miter, close,
combine)

mind-*n* intellect, understanding,
reason, thinking, rationality,
cogitative, faculties, senses,
consciousness, observation,
percipience, intuition,
association of ideas, instinct,
conception, judgment, wits,
capacity, genius, ability,
thoughtful, reflect, speculate,
contemplate, consider

mine-*n* sap, destroy, waste,
dissolution, breaking up,
disruption, consumption,
disorganization, fall, downfall,
ruin, perdition, annihilation,
demolition, overthrow,
subversion, suppress, abolish,
ruinous, incendiary,
deleterious, (produce, perform,
operate, form, construct,
fabricate, frame, contrive,
forge)

minister-*n* subserve, mediate,
intervene, instrumental, useful,
give, bestow, donation,
presentation, accordance,
delivery, consignment,
dispensation, communication,
endowment, award, generosity,
liberality, offering, bequest,
legacy, devise, deliver, present,
(receive, acquire, accept,
assign, admit)

minor-*adj* inferior, shortcoming,
deficiency, minimum,
smallness, less, lesser, minus,
lower, subordinate, second-
rate, least, lowest, diminished,
decrease, infant, babe, youth,

youngster, master, (veteran,
old, seer, patriarch, superior,
supreme, major, great, noble,
higher, exceeding)

minute-*adj* small, little,
diminutive, inconsiderable,
paltry, faint, slender, light,
slight, scanty, limited, sparing,
inappreciable, infinitesimal,
mere, simple, sheer, stark,
bare, period of time, duration
of, moment, instant, second,
twinkling, flash, breath, burst,
sudden, instantaneous, hasty,
quick, lightning, (perpetuity,
eternity, ever, everlasting,
great, magnitude, considerable,
ample)

mirror-*n* imitate, copy, repetition,
duplication, quotation,
reproduction, mimicry,
simulation, reflector, speculum,
looking glass, pier, model,
standard, pattern, best,
inimitable, paragon,
unparalleled, supreme, perfect,
(imperfect, faulty, unsound,
deficient, unimitated, original,
unmatched)

misbehave-*v* coarse,
indecorous, ribald, gross,
unseemly, unpresentable,
ungraceful, ill-mannered,
underbred, ungentlemanly,
unladylike, unpolished,
uncouth, heavy, rude,
awkward, (good taste,
cultivated, delicacy, refinement,
gust, finesse, nicety, polish,
elegance, grace, connoisseur)

miscalculate-*v* misjudge,
prejudgment, foregone
conclusion, narrow-minded,
intolerant, besotted, dogmatic,
opinioned, unreasonable, false
judgment, weak, feeble, poor,
flimsy, loose, vague, irrational,
foolish, frivolous, (logical
sequence, good sense,
deduce, conclusive)

mischief-*n* evil, harm, hurt,
nuisance, disaster, accident,

M

casualty, mishap, calamity,
bale, mental suffering, outrage,
wrong, injury, foul play,
grievance, disastrous, bad,
aggrieve, oppress, persecute,
inflict, maltreat, abuse,
(goodness, admirable,
estimable, praise-worthy,
satisfactory, favorable)

misconduct-*n* mismanage,
misapplication, absence of rule,
bungling, blunder, unskillful,
quackery, mistake, misguided,
foolish, inconsistent, ignorant,
(accomplished, expert, skillful,
competent)

miserable-*adj* suffering, pain,
dolor, ache, smart, displeasure,
dissatisfaction, discomfort,
discomposure, malaise,
uneasiness, dejection,
annoyance, irritation, worry,
infliction, visitation, care,
anxiety, solicitude, trouble, trial,
ordeal, shock, burden,
unhappiness, misery,
tribulation, (pleasure,
gratification, enjoyment, well-
being, comfort, ease, joy,
gladness, delight, mind at
ease)

misfortune-*n* adversity, evil,
failure, bad fortune, trouble,
hardship, curse, blight, blast,
load, pressure, mishap,
disaster, calamity, catastrophe,
accident, casualty, ruin, failure,
affliction, (prosperity, welfare,
well-being, affluence, wealth,
success, thrift, roaring, prosper,
thrive)

mishap-*n* source of irritation,
annoyance, grievance,
nuisance, vexation,
mortification, bore, bother,
plague, pest, infestation,
molestation, (pleasant, inviting,
attractive, lovely, enchantment,
seduction)

misjudgment-*n* bias, warp,
twist, hasty conclusion,
preconceived, partisanship,

partial, narrow, blind side,
confined, error, fallacy, laxity,
mistake, fault, blunder,
(accuracy, exactness, honest,
precise)

mismatch-*v* different, diverse,
varied, modified, various,
dissimilarity, disagreement,
disparity, discord, unconformity,
conflict, unfitness, inaptitude,
impropriety, inconsistency,
disjoining, (conformity,
uniformity, concert, relevancy,
admissibility, compatibility,
relation)

misrepresent-*v* lie, falsehood,
deception, untruth, guile,
mendacity, perjury, forgery,
invention, fabrication,
suppression of truth,
perversion, distortion,
exaggeration, misinterpretation,
misconstrue, mistake, parody,
equivocation, evasion, fraud,
(veracity, truthfulness,
frankness, sincerity, honesty)

miss-*v* girl, lass, wench, damsel,
maiden, virgin, fail,
unsuccessful, labor, toil in
vane, miscarry, omission,
oversight, slip, trip, stumble,
mess, mishap, misfortune,
collapse, (success, advance,
lucky, fortunate, prosperity,
triumph, gain, advantage,
conquest, victory)

mist-*n* cloud, bubble, foam,
froth, head, spume, lather,
spray, surf, yeast, barm, vapor,
fog, haze, stream,
effervescence, fermentation,
nebulous, (semi-fluid,
stickiness, viscidity,
adhesiveness)

mistake-*n* error, fallacy,
misconception, miss, fault,
blunder, oversight, misprint,
slip, blot, flaw, trip, stumble,
heresy, hallucination, laxity,
miscount, untrue, false, unreal,
ungrounded, failure,
unsuccessful, mishap, split,

collapse, (true, infallible,
successful, fortunate,
prosperous)

mitigate-v abate, moderate,
soften temper, mollify, leniency,
dull, take off the edge, blunt,
obtund, sheathe, subdue,
chasten, sober, tone, smooth
down, lessen, palliate,
tranquilize, assuage, appease,
(violent, sharpen, quicken,
excite, explode, convulse,
infuriate, madden, lash)

mix-v combine, instill, imbue,
transfuse, join, intermix, mingle,
shuffle, knead, brew,
impregnate, infiltrate, dash, stir-
up, together, compound,
adulterate, (simple, purity,
homogeneity, eliminate)

mob-n crowd, assemblage,
throng, flood, rush, press,
crush, horde, body, tribe, crew,
gang, knot, squad, band, party,
swarm, school, covey, flock,
herd, drove, array, bevy,
galaxy, company, troop, group,
cluster, clump, (disperse,
scatter, sow, disseminate,
diffuse, shed, spread,
disembody)

mobile-adj motion, movement,
going, unrest, stream, flow, run,
coarse, stir, evolution,
kinematics, step, transitional,
motor, motive, shifting,
mercurial, unquiet, restless,
nomadic, inconstancy,
versatility, mobility, unstable,
restlessness, fidget, disquiet,
agitation, (stable, constant,
immobility, stand, established,
fixture, foundation,
permanence, durable)

mock-v imitate, copy, mirror,
reflect, reproduce, repeat,
echo, catch, transcribe, match,
mimic, ape, simulate,
impersonate, counterfeit,
parody, modeled after,
verbatim, word for word,
repetition, sameness, pair,

mate, double, parallel,
(dissimilar, unlike, unmatched,
originality, different kind)

mode-n state, condition,
category, estate, lot, case, trim,
mood, plight, aspect, schuss,
tone, tenor, trim, guise, light,
complexion, style, character,
structural, organic, method,
way, manner, fashion, form,
habit, (infraction of usage,
unaccustomed, leave off,
unusual, unaccustomed)

model-n represent, imitation,
illustration, delineation,
depiction, imagery, portraiture,
design, art, personation,
impersonation, image, likeness,
(misrepresent, distort,
exaggerate, daub)

moderate-adj small, allay, slow,
sufficient, cheap, temperate,
low, reasonable, inexpensive,
depreciated, nominal, bargain,
sufficient, adequate, enough,
satisfactory, competent,
mediocrity, fill, (scarcity, want,
need, lack, poverty, insufficient,
inadequate)

modesty-n humility, timidity,
diffidence, bashfulness,
blushing, self-knowledge, shy,
nervous, skittish, coy,
sheepish, shamefaced,
unpretending, reserved,
constrained, demure, private,
without ceremony, (vanity,
conceit, self-confidence, airs,
pretension, egotism, gaudery,
elation, ostentation)

mold-n frame, fabric, constitute,
habitude, stamp, set, fit, mode,
form, shape, tone, tenor,
prototype, original, model,
pattern, precedent, standard,
type, rush, weed, fungus,
mushroom, toadstool, lichen,
moss, conferva, growth, (result,
copy, facsimile, duplicate)

molestation-n wrong, aggrieve,
oppress, persecute, trample,
tread, run down, victimize,

overburden, maltreat, abuse, ill-use, ill-treat, buffet, bruise, scratch, smite, scourge, violate, destroy, hurt, harm, (admire, excellent, best, choice, select, praiseworthy, beneficial, serviceable, edifying, salutary)

monotonous-*adj* uniform, consistent, even, invariable, always, without exception, regularity, routine, conformity, equal, even, match, symmetrical, (uneven, countervail, varied, diversified, irregular)

monstrous-*adj* huge, giant, gargantuan, mammoth, corpulent, stout, fat, plump, immense, enormous, might, vast, stupendous, monstrous, gigantic, (small, dwarf, pygmy, inconsiderable, puny, atom)

monument-*n* memorial, cenotaph, shrine, grave, tombstone, hatchment, slab, tablet, trophy, achievement, obelisk, pillar, column, monolith, commemoration, celebration, (obliterate, erasure, cancellation, deletion)

mood-*n* affection, character, disposition, nature, spirit, tone, temper, idiosyncrasy, propensity, humor, grain, mettle, sympathy, passion, temperament, vein, tendency, aptness, prone

more-*adj* added, addition, annex, affix, extra, plus, likewise, furthermore, further, including, inclusive, besides, to boot, et cetera, supplement, accessory, appendage, reinforce, (subtract, deduct, retrench, minus, without, except, diminish)

mortal-*adj* fatal, kill, assassination, massacre, butcher, slayer, lethal, dead, deathly, suicidal, internecine, transient, impermanence, fugacity, caducity, mortality,

temporary, (durable, lasting, permanent, long-standing, chronic, perennial)

mortar-*n* cement, glue, gum, paste, size, wafer, solder, lute, putty, bird-lime, stucco, plaster, grout, arms, weapon, missile, bolt, projectile, shot, ball, canister, cannon, grenade, shell, bomb, rocket

mortification-*n* humility, meek, lowness, modesty, blush, suffusion, confusion, disgrace, condescend, demean, stoop, submissive, service, affable, resigned, abashed, ashamed, brow-beaten, (dignified, stately, proud, haughty, lofty, high, mighty, vainglorious, arrogant)

motion-*n* movement, going, stream, flow, flux, run, course, stir, evolution, kinematics, progress, offer, proffer, presentation, tender, bid, overture, proposal, invitation, advances, (refusal, rejection, projection, disclaimer, dissent, revocation, remain, stay, stop, stagnate, halt)

motley-*adj* variegated, mottled, marbled, dappled, clouded, mosaic, pled, diverse, variety, multifariousness, manifold, heterogeneous, epicene, indiscriminate, (uniform, constant, routine, custom, standard, conformity, punctual)

mount-*v* ascend, rising, ascension, upgrowth, leap, acclivity, ladder, arise, apprise, climb, escalate, soar, display, show, flourish, parade, magnificence, splendor, mountain, hill, elevate, high, (low, neap, debased, flat, under, descent, declination, fall, drop, lapse, downfall, slip, tilt, trip)

mournful-*adj* melancholy, sadness, depression, dejection, prostration, despondency, dismal, spiritless, unhappy,

somber, dark, gloomy,
lamenting, dreadful,
(cheerfulness, geniality, gaiety,
good humor, glee, light,
liveliness, vivacity, merriment,
hilarity, exhilaration, animation,
jovial)

mouth-*n* entrance, beginning,
opening, outset, incipience,
inception, inchoation,
introduction, initial, origin,
source, receptacle, recipient,
receiver, reservoir, gizzard,
ventricle, bread-basket, (end,
close, termination, dissonance,
conclusion, consummation,
finish, terminate, conclude)

muddy-*adj* moist, damp, watery,
undried, humid, wet, dank,
muggy, dewy, swampy, soft,
sodden, swashy, soggy,
dabbled, reeking, dripping,
soaking, (dry, anhydrous, arid,
dried, undamped)

multifarious-*adj* disconnection,
independence, strange, alien,
foreign, outlandish, exotic,
diverse, variety, diversity,
manifold, motley, mosaic,
indiscriminate, irregular,
(regularity, uniformity, constant,
punctual, routine, normal,
natural, ordinary, steady)

multitude-*n* numerous,
multiplicity, profusion, legion,
host, great, enormous, quantity,
number, array, army, sea,
galaxy, scores, peck, bushel,
shoal, swarm, many, several,
sundry, various, (few, small
quantity, rarity, infrequency,
handful, maniple, minority,
reduction)

musical-*adj* melody, rhythm,
measure, rhyme, pitch, tone,
modulation, temperament,
syncopation, song, glee,
madrigal, compose, perform
strains, (discord, harshness,
tuneless, unmusical,
dissonance)

mute-*adj* silent, stillness, peace,

hush, lull, solemn, dead,
render, hold one's tongue,
stifle, muffle, muzzle, inaudible,
faint, suppress, smother, dumb,
(vocal, cry, utter, exclaim,
pronounce)

mysterious-*adj* obscure, dark,
muddy, dim, nebulous,
undiscernible, invisible,
indefinite, perplexed, confused,
undetermined, vague, loose,
ambiguous, mystic,
transcendental, occult,
recondite, undefinable,
(intelligent, clear, explicit, lucid,
perspicuity, legibility, plain
speaking, understandable)

M

N

name-*n* imprint, label, indicate, symbolize, mark, note, stamp, earmark, ticket, docket, score, dash, trace, print, appoint, nominate, return, charter, ordinate, install, inaugurate, investiture, accession, coronation, enthronement, (countermand, disclaim, abolish, dissolve, dismiss, nullify, annul, cancel)

napping-*v* dull, unentertaining, depress, humdrum, monotonous, inactive, heaviness, absent, bemused, dreaming, unreflective, (attentive, observant, absorption of mind)

native-*adj* inhabitant, resident, dweller, occupier, household, lodger, inmate, tenant, incumbent, sojourner, settler, squatter, indigent, aborigines, free, plain, outspoken, blunt, downright, (cunning, craft, artful, skillful, subtle, alien, foreign)

naught-*n* nothing, zero, cipher, none, nobody, complete absence, insubstantiality, vacant, vacuous, empty, blank, hollow, nominal, null, inane, (numerous, many, several, some, profuse, multiple)

near-*adv* loom, impending, destined, about to happen, coming, eventually, prospective, approaching, future, precipitation, anticipation, premature, soon, shortly, (now, occurring, happening, immediate)

necessity-*n* requirement, need, want, have occasion for, needful, essential, indispensable, prerequisite, demanding, urgent, obligatory,

involuntary, compulsive, inevitable, (willing, volition, free-will, voluntary, optional, discretionary, intentional, spontaneous)

neglect-*v* abandon, negligent, careless, omit, default, thoughtless, remiss, perfunctory, inconsiderate, reckless, (care, watchful, vigilant, survey, alert, regardful, cautious, considerate, prepared)

negotiate-*v* mediate, intervene, peacemaker, diplomat, moderate, arbitrate, intercede, bargain, agree, promise, stipulate, barter, compromise, settle, conclude, come to an understanding

net-*n* remainder, residue, remains, remnant, rest, relic, leavings, result, left, unconsumed, sedimentary, surviving, exceeding, over and above, outlying, superfluous, (adjunct, addition, addendum, affix, appendage, augment, increment)

neutralize-*v* opposition, contrariety, antagonism, polarity, clashing, compensation, cross, interfere, conflict, with, jostle, antagonize, withstand, counterpoise, retroactive, reactionary, contrary, (concur, conspire, cooperate, agree, consent)

nice-*adj* pleasing, savory, good, fastidious, agreeable, delectable, lovely, beatify, satisfy, refreshing, comfortable, genial, glad, sweet, luxurious, voluptuous, sensual, attractive, enticing, appetizing, charming, (annoying, painful, grievance, vexation, mortification, bother, displeasing, disturbing)

nightmare-*n* fright, affright, m alarm, dread, awe, terror, horror, dismay, consternation, panic, scare, stampede, intimidation, terrorism, reign of terror, demonic, scarecrow

nil-*n* inexistent, negative, annihilation, extinction, destruction, abrogate, destroy, take away, perish, blank, missing, omitted, absent, exhausted, gone, lost, departed, defunct, dead, (subsist, presence, positive, realty, actuality, live, breathe, real, actual, positive, substantial)

nip-*v* cut, destroy, shorten, sunder, divide, subdivide, sever, dissever, abscind, saw, snip, nib, cleave, rive, rend, slit, split, splinter, crack, snap, carve, dissect, hinder, impede, obstruct, stop, (attach, join, hinge, seam, suture, stitch, link, miter, close, combine, fix, affix, fasten)

noble-*adj* great, virtuousness, morality, ethical, rectitude, integrity, cardinal virtues, merit, worth, desert, excellence, credit, self-control, resolution, self-denial, exemplary, saintly, seraphic, godlike, commendable, praiseworthy, (wicked, immoral, impropriety, weak, fault, deficient, vicious, sinful)

nod-*v* signal, wag, gesture, wink, glance, leer, shrug, beck, touch, nudge, oscillate, undulate, wave, eat, waggle, bob, curtsy, play, dangle, assent, acquiescence, admission, accordance, agreement, recognition, acknowledgement, avowal, (dissent, discordance, contradiction, protest, non-compliance)

nomination-*n* commission, delegation, assignment, procuration, deputation, legation, mission, embassy, agency, appointment, return, charter, ordination, installation,

inauguration, investiture, accession, coronation, enthronement, (dismiss, abolish, dissolve, cancel, repeal, revocation, annul)

nonsense-*n* absurdity, vagary, tomfoolery, mummery, imbecility, blunder, muddle, farce, absence of meaning, meaningless, empty, jargon, gibberish, balderdash, insanity, (significant, expression, substantial, literal, plain, simple, suggestive, convey, imply, indicate)

nook-*n* limited space, lieu, spot, pint, dot, niche, hole, compartment, premises, station, abode, angle, cusp, bend, fold, notch, for, corner, recess, oriel

noose-*n* snare, trap, pitfall, decoy, bait, cobweb, net, meshes, mouse trap, mine, scaffold, block, axe, guillotine, stake, cross, gallows, gibbet, drop, rope, halter, bowstring

normal-*adj* regular, intrinsic, fundamental, implanted, inherent, essential, natural, innate, inborn, inbred, radical, incarnate, thoroughbred, immanent, instinctive, (extraneousness, incidental, accidental)

note-*n* remark, examine, scan, scrutinize, consider, revise, pour over, inspect, review, indication, observe, look, see, view, notice, regard, give, heed, contemplate, attentive, mindful, watchful, (inattentive, blind, deaf, inconsiderate, absent, abstracted, lost, overlook, disregard, dismiss)

noteworthy-*adj* exceptional, non-conformity, unconventional, unusual, uncommon, extraordinary, unparalleled, fantastic, exceptional, (conventional, usual, common, ordinary,

N

natural)

notorious-*adj* famous, notability,
notoriety, vogue, celebrity,
renown, popular, glory, honor,
illustriousness, regard, respect,
reputable, respectable, dignity,
stateliness, solemnity,
grandeur, splendor, noble,
majesty, sublime, (shameful,
disgrace, tarnish, blot, taint,
discredit, degrade, vilify)

null-*adj* powerless, impotent,
disable, impiousness, invalidity,
inefficiency, incompetence,
disqualification, helplessness,
prostration, paralysis, palsy,
apoplexy, exhaustion,
emasculation, (power, potency,
ability, ableness, energy, force,
control, authority, strength,
influence, magnetism)

nurture-*n* feed, food,
nourishment, nutriment,
sustenance, fodder, provision,
ration, keep, commons, board,
commissariats, pasture,
dietary, eatable, edible,
culinary, succulent, potable,
(stave, excrete, deject,
perspire, sweat, diarrhea,
salivation, discharge)

O

oak-*n* strong, mighty, vigorous, forcible, hard, adamantine, stout, robust, sturdy, hardy, powerful, potent, puissant, valid, courage, brave, valor, resolute, bold, gallant, intrepid, defiant, (coward, timid, poltroonery, baseness, dastard, sneak, weak, relaxed, frail, fragile, shatter, flimsy)

oar-*n* paddle, navigate, fin, flipper, natation, handle, hilt, haft, shaft, heft, shank, blade, trigger, tiller, helm, treadle, key, turn screw, screwdriver

oasis-*n* separation, parting, detachment, segregation, divorce, supposition, deduction, discerptible, unconformable, exceptional, abnormal, continent, mainland, peninsula, delta, isthmus, (attach, fix, affix, fasten, bind, secure, clinch, twist, pinion)

obdurate-*adj* obstinate, tenacious, stubborn, case-hardened, inflexible, immovable, inert, unchangeable, severe, strictness, harshness, rigor, stringency, austerity, inclemency, (lenitive, moderation, tolerance, mildness, gentleness, favor, indulgence, clemency, mercy)

obey-*v* rules, observance, compliance, submission, subjection, resignation, allegiance, loyalty, fealty, homage, deference, devotion, complying, (violate, infringe, shrink, insubordination, disobedient)

object-*n* thing, matter, body, substance, stuff, element, principle, material, article, something, still life, decision,

determination, resolve, purpose, ultimatum, resolution, motive, intention, advise, (speculation, venture, stake, game of chance, risk, hazard, fortuitous, indiscriminate)

oblige-*v* accommodate, consult the wishes of, humor, cheer, encourage, nurture, cultivate, foster, cherish, support, sustain, uphold, bolster, compulsive, coercion, coaction, constraint, duress, enforcement, press, conscription, (prevention, preclusion, obstruction, interruption, hindrance)

obnoxious-*adj* source of irritation, annoyance, grievance, nuisance, vexation, mortification, bore, bother, burdensome, oppressive, sinister, maltreat, abuse, persecute, abomination, (excellence, merit, virtue, value, worth, beneficial, advantageous, edifying, pleasant, agreeable, enchanting)

obscure-*adj* dark, murky, gloomy, extinguish, cloudy, confused, indistinct, shadowy, indefinite, ill-defined, opaque, (visible, conspicuousness, distinct, exposure, discernible, apparent, perceptible)

observation-*n* understanding, reason, rationality, cogitative, intelligence, intuition, association of ideas, instinct, conception, judgment, wits, capacity, ability, attention, mindfulness, intentness, thought, consideration, (abstraction, absorption, preoccupation, distraction, disregard)

obstruct-*v* hinder, prevent, preclude, stoppage, interruption, retard, embarrassment, restriction, impede, obstacle, drag, stay,

stop, shut, blockage, bar, bolt,
seal, choke, occlusion, (open,
vent, vomiter, perforate, pierce,
puncture, support, lift, advance,
assist, promote, favor, relief,
rescue)

obtain-v get, acquisition,
gaining, procuration, purchase,
descent, inheritance, gift,
recover, retrieval, redemption,
salvage, gain, remuneration,
proceeds, harvest, benefit,
(deprived, loss, lapse, bereft)

obtrude-v interfere, intervention,
introduce, import, insinuate,
smuggle, infiltrate, ingrain,
partition, interpenetrate,
permeate, insert, implantation,
inoculation, immersion, imbed,
(removal, elimination,
extrication, eradication,
evolution, wrench, evulsion)

occasion-n opportunity,
opening, room, suitable,
proper, tempestuous, crisis,
turn, juncture, conjuncture,
turning point, given time, timely,
providential, lucky, fortunate,
happy, favorable, propitious,
auspicious, critical, (unsuitable,
ill-timed, intrude, premature,
intrusion)

occult-adj concealed, hidden,
secret, recondite, mystic,
cabalistic, dark, cryptic, private,
privy, auricular, clandestine,
close, inviolate, stealthy,
skulking, surreptitious,
(informant, enlightenment,
case, specification,
communicative, advice,
monition, statement,
affirmation)

occupation-n business,
employment, pursuit, affair,
concern, matter, case, task,
work, job, errand, commission,
mission, charge, care, duty,
vocation, calling, profession,
industry, trade, officiate, serve,
capacity, handicraft

occupy-v presence, attendance,

where, permeation, pervasion,
diffusion, dispersion,
omnipresence, inhabit, dwell,
reside, stay, sojourn, live,
abide, lodge, nestle, roost,
perch, locate, fill, domiciles,
(truant, absent, absence,
inexistent, emptiness, void,
vacant, deserted, devoid)

occur-v eventuality, event,
occurrence, incident, affair,
transaction, proceeding,
phenomenon, advent, concern,
circumstance, casualty,
accident, adventure, passage,
crisis, pass, emergency,
contingency, consequence,
(impending, threaten, loom,
await, approach, destined,
approaching)

odd-adj individuality,
idiosyncrasy, originality,
mannerism, exception,
peculiarity, infraction, violation,
infringement, eccentricity,
bizarre, monstrosity, rarity,
freak, remainder, residue,
remains, relic, (supplement,
continuation, rider, off-shoot,
conformity, symmetry,
conventionality, pattern,
specimen)

ode-n poetry, poetics,
versification, rhyming, making
verses, prosody, song, ballad,
lullaby, anthology, assonance,
accentuation, laureate, lyrist,
(prose, unpoetical, unrhymed)

offensive-adj unsavory,
repulsive, nasty, acrid,
acrimonious, rough, sickening,
nauseous, loathsome,
unpleasant, displease, annoy,
discompose, trouble, disquiet,
disturb, cross, perplex, molest,
(refreshing, comfortable,
cordial, genial, glad, sweet,
delectable, good, palatable,
nice, dainty)

offer-v proposal, presentation,
tender, bid, overture, motion,
invitation, candidature, move,

start, gift, donation, present, fairing, favor, benefaction, grant, oblation, sacrifice, (receive, acquire, reception, acceptance, release, admission, refusal, rejection, denial, decline, repulse, rebuff, discountenance)

official-*adj* authoritative, influence, patronage, power, preponderance, absolute, command, empire, rule, dominion, sovereign, hold, grasp, certain, necessity, surety, unerring, infallible, reliability, (uncertainty, doubt, dubiety, hesitation, precariousness, unfortunate, fallible, adverse, disastrous)

offset-*n* compensate, equate, commutation, indemnification, compromise, neutralization, nullification, counteraction, counterpoise, equivalent, consideration, offshoot, ramification, descendant

often-*adv* repetition, iteration, reiteration, harping, recurrence, succession, monotony, rhythm, repeat, echo, frequent, many times, repeatedly, perpetually, continually, constantly, incessantly, (sometimes, occasionally, at times, rarity, fewness, seldom, scarcely)

ogle-*v* look, view, espial, glance, ken, glimpse, peep, gaze, stare, leer, contemplation, survey, speculation, watch, sightseeing, longing, hankering, inkling, solicitude, anxiety, yearning, coveting, (indifferent, cold, frigid, lukewarm, cool, unconcerned, blind, hoodwink, dim-sighted)

oil-*n* lubricate, anointment, glycerine, grease, lather, grease, soap, wax, ointment, unctuous, slippery, oleaginous, adipose, sebaceous, fatty, (pulpy, paste, dough, curd, jam, poultice, watery)

old-*adj* age, ancient, antique, long standing, time-honored, venerable, eider, prime, primitive, igneous, primordial, seniority, maturity, decline, decay, senility, ripe, mellow, longevity, decrepitude, (young, youthful, juvenile, green, callow, budding, new, novel, recent, fresh, modern, recent, immature)

omission-*n* exclusion, exception, rejection, repudiation, exile, seclusion, separation, segregation, supposition, elimination, bar, leave, shut, reject, repudiate, blackball, banish, (include, admit, consist of, embrace, embody, involve, implicate, contain, constitute, complete, entire, supplement)

one-*adj* whole, total, integrity, collectiveness, unity, complete, indivisibility, integration, aggregate, main, essential, identity, sameness, monotony, identical, (inversion, contrariety, contrast, part, portion, division, segment, fraction, parcel, piece, morsel)

oneself-*n* identity, sameness, coincidence, facsimile, similar, alter ego, identification, self, monotony, exactness, identical, (opposite, reverse, inverse, converse)

only-*adj* small, unity, individual, sole, single, solitary, apart, alone, unaccompanied, isolation, seclusion, lone, lonely, desolate, dreary, simple, purity, homogeneity, uniform, neat, (mixture, tinge, tincture, compound, infusion, combination, matrimony, accompany, coexist, attend, part)

ooze-*v* emerge, exit, issue, emersion, burst, emanation, evacuation, perspiration, sweating, leakage, percolation,

O

distillation, gush, outpouring, effluence, effusion, disclose, divulge, split, acknowledge, allow, (screen, cover, mask, masquerade, ingress, enter, influx, invasion, import)

opalescent-*adj* semitransparent, opalescence, milkiness, pearliness, gauze, muslin, film, mist, cloud, variegation, iridescence, play of colors, polychrome, maculation, spottiness, spectrum, rainbow, (transparent, pellucid, lucid diaphanous, relucent, limpid, clear, serene, crystalline, vitreous)

open-*adj* divulge, reveal, break, split, disclose, resection, unveiling, deferred, revelation, exposition, acknowledgement, avowal, confession, disclose, allow, concede, grant, admit, (ambush, screen, cover, shade, blinker, veil, curtain, blind, cloak, cloud, mask, visor, disguise, masquerade, dress)

operate-*v* cause, groundwork, foundation, support, spring, genesis, descent, produce, perform, fabricate, frame, construct, manufacture, contrive, forge, coin, carve, build, raise, edify, rear, erect, constitute, (extinction, annihilation, destroy, ruin, demolish, overturn, sacrifice, subvert)

operator-*n* agent, doer, actor, agent, performer, perpetrator, executor, practitioner, worker, stager, bee, ant, artisan, handicrafts, workman, artisan, craftsman, mechanic, operative, maker, journeyman, pursuit, pursuing, prosecution, (abstain, refrain, spare, eschew, maintain, spare)

opinion-*n* persuasion, conviction, convince, self-conviction, certainty, mind, vie, conception, impression,

surmise, conclusion, judgment, tenet, dogma, principle, popular belief, (misbelief, discredit, miscreant, infidelity, dissent, retraction, doubt, skepticism, misgiving, demur, mistrust)

opponent-*n* antagonist, adversary, adverse party, opposition, enemy, assailant, obstructive, brawler, wrangler, disputant, malcontent, demagogue, reactionary, rival, competitor, (helper, recruit, assistant, midwife, colleague, partner, mate, collaborator, ally, friend, confidant)

opportunity-*n* occasion, opening, room, suitable time, proper time, crisis, turn, juncture, turning point, timely, lucky, fortunate, happy, providential, favorable, propitious, auspicious, suitable, (untimely, intrusive, inopportune, unlucky, inauspicious)

oppose-*v* contrary, contrast, antithesis, contradiction, antagonism, inversion, opposite, invert, diverse, conflicting, hostile, diametrically opposite, crossfire, clashing, collision, conflict, resistance, restraint, hindrance, (cooperation, association, alliance, conference, coalition, fusion)

oppressor-*n* tyrant, severe, strictness, harshness, rigor, stringency, austerity, inclemency, arrogance, arbitrary power, despotism, dictatorship, autocracy, tyranny, domineering, assumption, usurpation, inquisition, reign of terror, disciplinarian, despot, inquisitor, extortioner, (lenient, mil, gentle, clement, tolerant, indulgent, easy-going, forbearing)

oral-*adj* voice, vocal, organ,

lungs, bellows, cry, utterance,
breathe, ejaculate, rap out,
articulate, distinct, stertorous,
melodious, enunciate,
pronounce, accentuate,
aspirate, deliver, (stammer,
hesitation, impediment,
titubation, whisper, lisp, drawl,
twang, accent, stutter, mumble,
mutter, whisper)

oratory-*n* speaking, speech,
locution, talk, parlance, verbal
intercourse, oral
communication, oration,
recitation, delivery, lecture,
harangue, sermon, formal
speech, rhetoric, declamation

orb-*n* region, sphere, ground,
soil, area, realm, hemisphere,
quarter, district, beat, circuit,
circle, department, domain,
tract, territory, country, canon,
county, shire, province, parish,
township, arena, precincts,
walk, clime, climate, zone,
meridian, (spacious, roomy,
extension, extent, superficial
extent)

orbit-*n* world, creation, nature,
universe, earth, globe, wide
world, cosmos, sphere,
heavens, sky, firmament,
celestial spaces, starts,
asteroids, nebulae, galaxy,
milky way, path, way, manner,
method, gait, form, mode,
fashion, tone, guise, procedure

orchestra-*n* music, concert,
strain, tune, air, melody,
instrumental music, full score,
minstrels, band, concerted,
piece, stringed instruments,
wind instruments, vibrating
surfaces

ordain-*v* appointment,
nomination, return, charter,
installation, inauguration,
investiture, accession,
coronation, enthronement,
vicegerency, regency,
regentship, viceroy, consignee,
commission, accredit,

(abrogate, annul, cancel,
destroy, abolish, revoke,
repeal, rescind, reverse,
retract, recall)

ordeal-*n* concern, grief, sorrow,
distress, affliction, woe,
bitterness, heartache, broken
hearted, anxiety, solicitude,
trouble, fiery ordeal, shock,
blow, dole, fret, burden, load,
(happiness, felicity, bliss,
beatitude, enchantment,
transport, rapture, ravishment,
ecstasy, paradise, pleasing)

order-*n* regular, uniformity,
symmetry, gradation,
progression, routine, method,
disposition, arrangement, array,
system, economy, discipline,
orderliness, rank, place,
methodically, systematically,
periodically, (disorder,
derangement, irregularity,
confusion, complexity,
perplexity)

ordinary-*adj* indifferent,
middling, mediocre, average,
tolerable, fair, passable,
decent, admissible, bearable,
secondary, inferior, second-
rate, second-best, typical,
normal, orthodox, regular,
steady, (irregular, abnormal,
unconventional, unusual,
perfect, impeccability, model,
paragon)

organize-*v* arrange, plan,
preparation, distribution,
allocation, sorting, assortment,
allotment, apportionment, taxis,
graduation, organization,
analysis, classification, division,
digestion, atlas, (disorder,
disturbance, dislocation,
perturbation, interruption,
shuffling, inversion, misplace,
mislay)

original-*n* prototype, model,
pattern, precedent, standard,
scanting, type, protoplasm,
module, exemplar, example,
ensample, text, (imitation, copy,

O

transcription, repetition,
duplication, mimicry)

orthodox-*adj* conformity,
observance, symmetry,
naturalization, conventionality,
custom, agreeable, example,
quotation, exemplification,
illustration, typical, normal,
formal, canonical, sound, strict,
rigid, positive, uncompromising,
(unusual, unaccustomed,
uncommon, remarkable,
extraordinary, curious)

oscillation-*n* motion, vibration,
liberation, motion of a
pendulum, nutation, undulation,
pulsation, pulse, alternate,
wave, rock, swing, pulsate,
beat, waggle, fluctuate, dance,
curvet, reel, change,
inconstancy, vicissitude,
(stable, constant, established,
fixture, permanence, solidity,
firm, steadfast)

osculation-*n* contact, contiguity,
proximity, apposition,
juxtaposition, touching,
abutment, meeting,
coincidence, adhesion, (gorge,
defile, ravine, crevice,
separation, interval, opening,
leak)

ostensible-*adj* probable, likely,
hopeful, to be expected, in a
fair way, plausible, specious,
colorable, well-founded,
reasonable, credible,
presumable, presumptive,
apparent, apparently,
seemingly, (improbability,
unlikelihood, unfavorable,
possibility, incredibility, rare,
infrequent, inconceivable)

oust-*v* eject, emit, exit, dispatch,
exhale, excerpt, excrete,
secrete, secern, extravagate,
shed, void, evacuate, effuse,
spend, expend, pour forth,
squirt, spurt, spill, slop,
perspire, exude, (admit,
receive, import, introduce,
ingest, absorb, suction,

sucking, insertion)

outburst-*n* violence, inclemency,
vehemence, might, impetuosity,
effervescence, turbulence,
ferocity, rage, fury,
exacerbation, exasperation,
(moderation, lenitive,
gentleness, sobriety)

outcome-*n* profit, earnings,
winnings, innings, pickings, net
profit, proceeds, return,
harvest, benefit, get back,
recover, regain, retrieve,
redeem

outlandish-*adj* ridiculous,
ludicrous, comic, droll, funny,
laughable, grotesque, farcical,
odd, whimsical, fanciful,
fantastic, queer, eccentric,
strange, awkward, (tasteful,
unaffected, cultivated, refined)

outline-*n* origin, source, rise,
but, germ, egg, rudiment,
genesis, birth, title page,
heading, rudiments, elements,
grammar, alphabet, begin,
commence, inchoate, arise,
originate, conceive, initiate,
open, (end, close, finish,
terminate, conclude, expire,
consummation, definitive)

outlying-*adj* remaining,
unconsumed, sedimentary,
surviving, net, exceeding, over
and above, outstanding, cast
off, superfluous, redundant,
surplus, overplus, excess,
(augment, appendage, adjunct,
addition, affix, reinforcement,
supernumerary, accessory)

outmaneuver-*v* deception,
falseness, fraud, deceit, guile,
fraudulence, knavery, cunning,
misrepresentation, delusion,
gullible, juggle, defeat,
conquer, vanquish, overcome,
silence, quell, checkmate,
(fruitless, ineffectual, inefficient,
impotent, efficacious)

outrage-*n* bad turn, affront,
disrespect, atrocity, ill usage,
intolerance, persecution,

malevolent, grudge, abolish,
malign, molest, worry, harass,
haunt, wreck, impair, wane,
(benevolent, kind, well-
meaning, amiable)
outrageous-*adj* violent,
vehement, warm, acute, sharp,
rough, rude, ungentle, bluff,
boisterous, wild, brusque,
abrupt, impetuous, excite,
incite, urge, lash, stimulate,
irritate, inflame, kindle,
(tranquilize, assuage, appease,
swag, lull, soothe, compose,
still, calm, cool, quiet, hush,
quell)
outrival-*adj* superior, exceed,
excel, transcend, outdo,
outweigh, dominate, prevail,
come first, culminate,
distinguished, vaulting,
greatest, paramount, foremost,
crowning, excellent, important,
(inferior, minority, subordinate,
shortcoming, deficiency,
minimum, smallness, diminish)
outset-*n* beginning,
commencement, opening,
incipience, inception,
inchoation, introduction, alpha,
initial, inauguration,
embarkation, outbreak, onset,
brunt, initiative, fresh start,
(end, close, finish, terminate,
conclude, be all over with,
expire, final, crowning,
complete, hinder)
outside-*n* exterior, surface,
eccentricity, face, superficial,
skin-deep, frontal, external,
outward, covering, extramural,
(interior, inside, interspace,
innermost, indoor, inward,
enclosed)
outstanding-*adj* remainder,
residue, remains, remnant,
rest, relic, leavings, heel-tap,
odds and ends, left,
unconsumed, sedimentary,
surviving, exceeding, outlying,
(adjunct, addition, affix,
appendage, augment,

increment, reinforcement,
supernumerary, accessory,
item, garnish, sauce)
outweigh-*v* exceed, excel,
transcend, out-balance, out do,
pass, surpass, get ahead of,
cap, beat, eclipse,
preponderate, predominate,
prevail, proceed, take
precedence, come first, render
larger, (inferior, smaller,
decrease, contract, hide, lower,
minor, less, lesser, deficient,
minus)
ovation-*n* celebration,
solemnization, jubilee,
commemoration, triumph,
jubilation, keep, signalize,
rejoice, (nonobservance,
evasion, failure, omission,
neglect, laxity, informality)
overburden-*adj* redundant,
luxury, excess, surplus, margin,
remainder, duplicate,
surplusage, extravagance,
lavishness, superfluous,
unnecessary, needless

O

P

pack-v arrange, dispose, place, form, collocate, marshal, size, rank, group, parcel out, allot, distribute, dispose of, assign, assort, classify, divide, file, string, assembled, closely packed, dense, swarming, (dispersion, divergence, scattering, dissemination, misplace, mislay, disorder)

paddle-v walk, march, step, tread, pace, plod, wend, promenade, trudge, tramp, stalk, stride, straddle, strut, stump, bundle, handle, hilt, haft, shaft, heft, shank, blade, trigger, tiller, helm, treadle, key

padlock-n fasten, bolt, latch, latchet, tag, tooth, hook, holdfast, rivet, anchor, grappling, stake, post, tie, strap, tackle, rigging, brace, girder

page-n numeration, numbering, pagination, tale, recension, enumeration, summation, reckoning, computation, check, prove, demonstrate, balance, audit, part, issue, number, album, portfolio, periodical, serial, magazine, circular, paper, bill, sheet, broadsheet

pair-n couple, duality, duplicity, two, deuce, brace, cheeks, twins, duplex, analog, the like, match, similarity, resemblance, likeness, affinity, pendant, fellow, mate, double, counterpart, (dissimilar, unlike, disparate, of a different kind, unmatched, nothing of the kind)

palatable-adj savoriness, zest, dainty, delicacy, ambrosia, nectar, appetite, relish, like, smack the lips, well-tasted, good, nice, dainty, delectable, gusty, appetizing, lickerish,

delicate, delicious, exquisite, rich, luscious, (offensive, repulsive, nasty, sickening, nauseous, loathful, unpleasant)

pale-adj dimness, darkness, half-light, glimmer, nebulosity, aurora, duck, twilight, shades, moonlight, lackluster, dingy, dark, pallid, tallow-faced, faint, dull, cold, muddy, leaden, discoloration, neutral tint, monochrome, (pigment, color, dye, tinge, illuminate, emblazon, bright, vivid, intense, deep)

pall-n cloak, mantle, mantlet, mantua, shawl, wrapper, veil, cape, tippet, kirtle, plaid, muffler, comforter, coffin, shell, sarcophagus, urn, bier, hearse, catafalque, offensive, repulsive, nasty, sickening, nauseous, loathful, unpleasant, (dainty, delicacy, ambrosia, nectar, game, relish, like)

palpable-adj material, bodily, corporeal, physical, somatic, sensible, tangible, ponderable, substantial, objective, impersonal, neuter, unspiritual, plain, distinct, definite, well-defined, marked, in focus, recognizable, (invisible, non-appearance, concealment, dim, confused, indistinct)

palpitate-v tremble, agitation, stir, tremor, ripple, jog, jolt, jar, jerk, shock, succussion, trepidation, tingle, thrill, heave, pant, throb, quiver, flutter, twitter, shake

pamper-v indulge, high, living, self-indulgence, voluptuousness, dissipation, sensuality, animalism, carnality, pleasure, effeminacy, silkiness, luxury, piggish, gluttony, greed, epicurism, gorge, overfed, omnivorous, (fast, starve, clam, famish, perish, Lenten, unfed, frugality, moderation)

panel-n partition, septum,

diaphragm, midriff, party-wall,
vail, between, betwixt,
sandwich, parenthesis, list,
catalog, inventory, schedule,
register, account, bill, calendar,
index, table, contents,
(surround, beset, compass,
encompass, environ, inclose,
enclose, encircle, embrace)

paper-*n* write, pen, copy,
engross, write out, fair,
transcribe, scribble, scrawl,
scrabble, scratch, interline,
stain paper, write down, record,
sign, compose, indite, draw up,
dictate, inscribe

paradox-*n* absurdity, imbecility,
nonsense, inconsistency,
blunder, muddle, bull, farce,
rhapsody, farrago,
extravagance, romance,
obscure, dark, muddy, dim,
nebulous, shrouded in mystery,
invisible, (plain, distinct,
explicit, positive, definite,
graphic, expressive, illustrative,
lucid)

parallel-*adj* similarity,
resemblance, likeness,
similitude, semblance, affinity,
approximation, agreement,
analogy, brotherhood,
repetition, uniformity, imitation,
copying, transcription,
duplication, quotation,
(unimitated, unmatched,
unparalleled, original,
dissimilar, unlike, disparate)

paramount-*adj* supreme,
essential, vital, all-absorbing,
radical, cardinal, chief, main,
prime, primary, principal,
leading, capital, foremost, over-
ruling, of vital importance,
significant, telling, trenchant,
emphatic, pregnant, urgent,
pressing, critical, (poor, paltry,
pitiful, contemptible, sorry,
mean, meager)

paraphrase-*n* explanatory,
expository, explicative,
exegetical, polyglot, literal,

significative, synonymous,
equivalent, interpret, explain,
define, construe, translate,
phrase, expression, set phrase,
sentence, paragraph, figure of
speech, periphrase,
(misrepresent, pervert, garble,
falsify)

parody-*n* ridicule, derision,
sardonic, smile, grin, scoffing,
mockery, quiz, banter, irony,
raillery, chaff, joke, twit, quiz,
satirize, caricature, burlesque,
travesty, servile, copy,
imitation, counterfeit,
deception, faithful, (prototype,
original, model, pattern,
precedent, standard, scanting,
type, paradigm)

paroxysm-*n* passion,
excitement, flush, heat, fever,
fire, flame, fume, blood boiling,
tumult, effervescence,
ebullition, boiling, whiff, gust,
storm, tempest, scene breaking
out, agony, explosion, burst,
(submission, resignation,
suffer, forbearance, fortitude,
compose, appease)

part-*n* divide, portion, dose, item,
particular, aught, any, division,
warm, subdivision, section,
chapter, verse, article, clause,
count, paragraph, passage,
sector, segment, fraction,
fragment, parcel, (whole,
totality, integrity, entirety,
aggregate, gross amount, sum
total, bulk, mass, lump,
altogether)

particular-*adj* exact, accurate,
definite, precise, well-defined,
just right, correct, strict, close,
rigid, rigorous, punctual,
genuine, authentic, legitimate,
orthodox, pure, natural, sound,
sterling, (error, fallacy,
misconception, mistake, miss,
fault, blunder, oversight,
misprint, slip, blot, flaw, loose
thread)

partner-*n* companion,

P

accompany, coexist, attend,
fellow associate, escort,
consort, spouse, colleague,
satellite, concomitant,
accessory, spouse, mate,
yokefellow, husband, man,
consort, goodman, squaw,
lady, matron, wedded pair,
husband, wife, (separation,
divorce, unity, oneness)

pass-*v* move through,
transmission, permeation,
transudation, infiltration,
endosmose, ingress, egress,
opening, journey, perforate,
penetrate, thread, conduit,
gone, last, latter, bygone,
foregone, elapsed, lapsed,
expired, (future, prospectively,
impending, next, stay,
eventual)

passion-*n* emotion, character,
qualities, disposition, nature,
spirit, tone, temper,
idiosyncrasy, soul, pervading,
spirit, humor, mood, grain,
mettle, sympathy, desire, wish,
fancy, fantasy, want, need,
exigency, inclination, leaning,
(indifferent, cold, frigid,
lukewarm, unconcerned,
careless, listless)

passive-*adj* inert, dullness,
inactivity, torpor, languor,
quiescence, latency, inaction,
sloth, sluggish, heavy, flat,
slack, tame, slow, blunt,
lifeless, dead, uninfluential,
dormant, (strong, energetic,
forcible, active, intense, severe,
keen, vivid, sharp, acute,
incisive, trenchant, brisk,
poignant, caustic)

paste-*n* bond, tendon, tendril,
fiber, ribbon, rope, cable, line,
hawser, painter, mooring, wire,
chain, fasten, tie, strap, tackle,
rigging, adhere, fuse

pat-*v* blow, stroke, knock, tap,
rap, slap, smack dab, fillip,
slam, bang, hit, whack, thwack,
cuff, squash, dowse, whop,

swap, punch, thump, pelt, kick,
cut, thrust, lunge, hammer,
batter, (recoil, retroaction,
revulsion, rebound, rebuff,
reflux, reverberation, return)

patch-*n* plot, enclosure, close,
arena, precincts, tract, territory,
country, canton, county, shire,
domain, blemish,
disfigurement, deformity,
defect, flaw, injury, stain, blot,
spot, speck, freckle, mole,
blotch, disfigure, pitted,
(spacious, roomy, extensive,
expansive, capacious, ample,
boundless)

patience-*n* perseverance,
resolution, determination,
desperation, devotion, tenacity,
obstinacy, self-control,
submission, resignation,
forbearance, longanimity,
fortitude, (ruffle, hurry, fuss,
stew, ferment, fit, violence,
rage, fury, desperation,
madness, distraction, raving,
delirium, frenzy, hysterics)

patter-*v* rap, snap, tap, knock,
click, clash, crack, crash, pop,
slam, bang, clap, rustle,
loquacity, talkativeness,
garrulity, eloquent, jaw, gabble,
jabber, chatter, orate, fluent,
(silence, mute, mum, still,
reserved, reticent, conceal,
hush)

pause-*v* rest, lull, respite, truce,
drop, interregnums, abeyance,
cessation, resistance,
intermission, interruption, stop,
halt, arrival, closure,
discontinue, quiet, tranquil,
calm, repose, stand still,
stagnate, quell, stationary,
anchor, (move, motion,
transitorily, restless,
changeable, nomadic)

pay-*v* remunerate, reward,
recompense, meed, quitting,
compensation, reparation,
redress, retribution, reckoning,
acknowledgement, requital,

amends, salvage, perquisite, allowance, salary, (penalty, fine, forfeit, escheat, amerce, sconce, confiscate, punishment, penalty, atonement)

peace-*n* concord, accord, harmony, symphony, agreement, love, response, union, unison, unity, assent, unanimity, friendship, alliance, understanding, conciliation, fraternize, (dissension, odds, discord, disagreement, division, split, quarrel, squabble, altercation, wrangling, strife, embroilment)

peak-*n* summit, top, vertex, apex, zenith, pinnacle, acme, culmination, meridian, utmost height, pitch, maximum climax, tip, crown, garret, ceiling, pediment, (bottom, base, basement, foundation, substructure, ground, earth, pavement, floor)

peck-*n* multitude, numerous, multiplicity, profusion, plenty, legion, host, large, enormous, array, army, sea, scores, bushel, sundry, dilemma, stumbling block, pickle, stew, hot water, (smooth, unload, emancipate, easiness, capability, fewness, paucity, small number, handful, minority, scanty)

peculiar-*adj* unusual, unexpected, monstrous, wonderful, remarkable, noteworthy, nondescript, curiosity, abnormal, exception, infraction, distinctive, specific, original, respective, (general, generic, universal, every, unspecified, impersonal, conformity, conventional)

pedigree-*adj* continuity, sequence, succession, round, suite, progression, series, train, chain, entire, linear, uninterrupted, unbroken,

paternal, maternal, family, ancestral, patriarchal, line, genealogy, descent, extraction, forefathers, (broken, discontinue, unsuccessful)

peep-*v* short sight, sharp, quick, piercing, penetrating, look, glance, glimpse, gaze, stare, leer, regard, watch, peer, pry, visible, perceptible, exposed to view, (invisible, obscure, misty, veiled)

peer-*n* equal, even, level, monotonous, coequal, symmetrical, coordinate, on a par, balanced, match, reach, keep pace with, peerage, house of lords, temporal, spiritual, grandee, aristocrat, (common, plebeian, bourgeois, peasantry, masses, inferior, unequal, uneven, disparate)

pelt-*n* skin, covering, pellicle, fleece, fell, fur, leather, hide, cuticle, scarf, mask, concealment, shield, stone, lapidate, hurl, beset, besiege, beleaguer, cut and thrust, kick, strike, impulse, (protect, guard, safeguard, shield, preserve)

pen-*n* enclosure, envelope, case, wrapper, receptacle, paddock, pound, net, wall, rail, railing, barrier, barricade, gate, door, hatch, restraint, hindrance, coercion, confinement, imprisonment, captivity, (liberation, release, emancipation, dismissal, discharge, free, unfetter, disengage, acquit)

penalty-*n* retribution, punishment, pain, amercement, forfeit, sequestration, confiscation, damage

penchant-*n* disposition, willing, inclination, leaning, humor, mood, vein, bent, aptitude, desire, geniality, cordiality, goodwill, readiness, earnestness, forwardness, (unwilling, grudgingly,

P

indifferent)

pensive-*adj* thoughtful, thinking, meditative, reflective, museful, wistful, contemplative, speculative, deliberative, studious, sedate, introspective, (vacancy, unintellectual, unoccupied, thoughtless)

people-*n* mankind, human race, species, nature, humanity, mortality, flesh, generation, human being, person, individual, creature, mortal, body, somebody, soul, living soul, earthling, party, persons, folk, general public, national, realm, population

pepper-*n* pungent, strong taste, twang, sharp, rough, unsavory, seasoning, palatable, spice, full-flavored, condiment, high-tasted, biting, spicy, herb, (insipid, weak, flat, vapid, tasteless, mawkish)

perch-*n* place, locate, situate, localize, put, lay, set, seat, station, lodge, quarter, post, install, house, stow, camp, root, shelve, deposit, reposit, cradle, moor, tether, picket, pack, vest, (displace, eject, set aside, remove, unload, empty, dispel, banishment, exile, vacate, cart-away)

perchance-*adv* possibility, potentiality, compatibility, agreement, practicability, feasibility, practicable, contingency, compatible, chance, feasible, (impossible, no chance whatever, hopeless)

perdition-*n* destruction, fall, downfall, ruin, crash, smash, havoc, waste, dissolution, breaking up, disruption, consumption, (production, creation, construction, formation, fabrication, manufacture)

peremptory-*adj* asserting, declaratory, predictor, pronunciation, affirmative, positive, certain, express, explicit, absolute, emphatic, flat, broad, confident, (negation, denial, disavowal, contradict, prohibit)

perennial-*adj* continual, consecutive, progressive, gradual, successive, immediate, unbroken, entire, evergreen, constant, (discontinue, pause, interrupt, intervene, spasmodic, intermission, alternate)

perfect-*adj* great, faultless, immaculate, spotless, impeccable, flawless, inimitable, paragon, unparalleled, supreme, superhuman, divine, (fault, weak, imperfect, deficient, defective, cracked)

perform-*v* achieve, accomplish, completion, fulfillment, execution, dispatch, consummation, culmination, finish, conclusion, close, issue, (incomplete, shortcoming, unfulfilled, neglect)

perhaps-*adv* possibly, potentiality, feasibility, conceivable, credible, compatible, achievable, chance, contingency, practicable, within reach, accessible, surmountable, (impossible, absurd, contrary)

perish-*v* die, death, decease, demise, dissolution, departure, release, rest, loss, bereavement, end, cessation, extinction, death rattle, (life, vitality, animation, vivification, alive, respire, subsist, revive)

permeate-*v* pervade, fill, present, occupy, inhabiting, moored, domiciled, omnipresent, dwell, reside, diffusion, haunt, revisit, sojourn, abide, lodge, nestle, roost, (empty, vacuum, truant, absent, vacate)

perplex-*v* distressing,

bothersome, afflicting, unlucky, uncomfortable, disheartening, depressing, distasteful, unpleasant, unpopular, thankless, (refreshing, comfortable, cordial, genial, glad, pleasant, delightful, lovely, felicitous)

persecute-*v* oppress, wrong, aggrieve, trample, tread, overburden, weigh down, victimize, molest, maltreat, abuse, ill-use, ill-treat, harm, injure, (goodness, merit, beneficial, valuable, profitable)

persist-*v* continue, last, endure, go on, remain, intervene, elapse, continue, seize an opportunity, permanent, duration, pending, interval, (never, nevermore, at no time, hesitant, doubtful)

persuade-*v* induce, prevail, overcome, carry, bring round, procure, enlist, engage, invite, court, tempt, seduce, entice, allure, captivate, fascinate, (discourage, dampen, restrain, reluctance)

pertinent-*adj* relative, bearing, reference, connection, concern, correlative, cognate, association, nearness, interest, relevancy, comparison, correlation, (incidental, parenthetical, remote, far fetched)

pervert-*n* misrepresent, garble, distort, travesty, retort, stretch, strain, misinterpreted, hardening, backsliding, declination, reprobation, (elected, adopted, regenerated, inspired, consecrated, converted)

pessimism-*n* underestimate, depreciate, detract, undervalue, modest, underrate, disparage, minimize, (overestimation, oversensitive, vanity)

petrify-*v* density, solidity, solidness, constipation, solidified, compact, thickset, substantial, massive, impenetrable, impermeable, (rare, subtile, thin, fine, tenuous, compressible, flimsy, slight, spongy)

phantom-*n* imaginary, fancy, conceive, deal, realize, create, originate, devise, invent, fabricate, improvise, fertile, unreal, ideal, legendary, whimsical, fairy-like, mythological, illusory, fallacious

photography-*n* representation, illustration, delineation, depiction, portraiture, engraving, daguerreotype, image, likeness, facsimile, (misrepresent, distort, exaggerate, daub)

physical-*adj* materialistic, substantiality, condition, matter, body, substance, stuff, element, principle, object, article, (immaterial, disembody, spiritualize, extramundane, earthy, pneymatolysis)

pick-*v* select, choice, option, discretion, volition, alternative, dilemma, adoption, decision, judgment, election, poll, ballot, exception, preference, (indifferent, neutral, abstain, refrain)

picket-*n* place, situate, locate, moore, tether, pack, tuck in, imbed, vest, make a place for, put, lay, set, seat, station, lodge, quarter, post, sentinel, watch, parol, vedette, bivouac, scout, spy, spiel

pickle-*n* preserve, maintain, keep, embalm, dry, cure, salt, season, bottle, pot, tin, can, macerate, dilution, humectant, dilemma, embarrassment, perplexity, (easy, facile, feasible, easily managed)

picture-*n* description, set forth, portray, represent, characterize, particularize, narrate, relate, recite, recount,

P

graphic, appearance, aspect, color, image, (vanish, disappear, missing, lost, departure)

piercing-v shrill, harsh sounds, acute, high note, scream, discordant, cry, roar, shout, hoop, whoop, yell, bellow, howl, scream, screech, shriek, (muffled, dead silence, melodious)

pile-v heap, exaggerate, magnify, aggravate, amplify, overestimate, hyperbolize, overestimate, accumulation, congeries, lump, mass, pyramid, drift, acervate, conglomeration, quantity, greatness, (disperse, scatter, disseminate, diffuse, shed, spread, overspread, distribute, dispel)

pilot-n guide, direct, manage, govern, conduct, order, prescribe, regulate, steer, take the helm, superintend, sailor, mariner, navigator, skipper, gondolier, steersman, seaman

pin-v fasten, restraint, hindrance, coercion, compulsion, constraint, repression, discipline, control, confinement, durance, duress, imprisonment, (liberate, disengagement, release, dismissal)

pinch-v requirement, need, want, necessities, stress, exigency, essential, indispensability, urgency, pain, suffer, ache, smart, bleed, tingle, hurt, chafe, (pleasure, bodily enjoyment, gratification, luxury)

pioneer-n precursor, antecedent, precedent, predecessor, forerunner, vancourier, prodrome, outrider, leader, herald, prelude, prior, groundwork, (sequel, suffix, successor, tail, train, wake, rear)

pitch-v degree, grade, extent,

measure, amount, ratio, stint, standard, reach, amplitude, range, scope, gradation, shade, tenor, station, comparative, gradual, limit, height

pith-n gist, intrinsically, inherence, inhesion, subjectiveness, ego, essence, essential part, quintessence, incarnation, quiddity, marrow, sap, lifeblood, backbone, heart, soul, (outward, incidental, extrinsic, extraneous, accidental, objective, derived from without)

place-v arrange, prepare, plan, disposal, distribute, sort, assort, allotment, apportionment, analysis, classification, division, digest, (disorder, misarrange, disturb, confuse, perturb, jumble, muddle)

placid-adj passive, tranquil, coolness, calmness, composure, serenity, quiet, peace of mind

plagiarism-n steal, theft, thievery, borrowed, forgery, imitator, echo, transcribe, match, parallel, simulate, impersonate, represent, counterfeit, parody, travesty, caricature, burlesque

plain-adj simple, plain, homeliness, undress, chastity, unaffected, chaste, severe, bald, flat, dull, unvaried, monotonous, unornamented, blank, (ornate, florid, rich, flowery, elegant)

platform-n pulpit, desk, reading, theater, amphitheater, forum, stage, rostrum, hustings, tribune, plan, scheme, design, project, proposal, suggestion, sketch, skeleton, outline, draught, draft

plausible-adj probable, likelihood, hopeful, specious, ostensible, founded, reasonable, credible, presumable, presumptive,

apparent, most likely,
(improbable, unlikely, long
odds, unfavorable)

plea-*v* vindication, justification,
warrant, exoneration,
exculpation, acquittal,
whitewashing, extenuation,
softening, mitigation, reply,
(accusation, charge,
imputation, slur, libel)

pleasant-*adj* flatter, adulator,
eulogist, euphemism, optimist,
encomiast, laudatory,
whitewasher, toady, sycophant,
courtier, puffer, touter, amuse,
entertain, diversion, relaxation,
solace, fun, frolic, merriment,
laughter, labor of love,
(weariness, lassitude, disgust,
nausea, loathing)

pledge-*v* promise, undertaking,
word, troth, plight, parole, word
of honor, vow, oath, affirmation,
assurance, warranty,
guarantee, insurance, contract,
borrow, (demise, lease,
advance, loan)

plenty-*n* sufficient, adequate,
enough, withal, satisfaction,
ample, copious, abundant,
abounding, replete, rich,
luxuriant, affluent,
inexhaustible, liberal, (scarcity,
want, need, lack, poverty, dole)

plod-*v* slow, languor, slow-goer,
linger, loiter, sluggard, snail,
dawdle, creep, crawl, lag,
drawl, saunter, trudge, stump
along, retard, slacken, (move
quickly, trip, speed, hasten,
scuttle, scud)

pluck-*v* take, catch, hook, nab,
bag, sack, pocket, receive,
accept, assume, possess, take
possession of, ravish, seize,
pounce, assault, intercept,
scramble for, snatch, (return,
restore, recuperate, reinvest,
reparation, remit, rehabilitate)

plump-*adj* huge, immense,
enormous, might, vast,
stupendous, monstrous,

colossal, gigantic, infinite, large
as life, hulky, unwieldy,
lumpish, whopping, (dwarf,
pygmy, atom, microscopic,
gaunt, molecular, thin,
inconsiderable)

pocket-*n* receptacle,
compartment, hole, corner,
niche, recess, nook, crypt, stall,
chest, box, coffer, caddy, case,
basket, pouch, sack, wallet,
scrip, poke, knit, knapsack,
haversack, satchel

point-*v* mark, topic, food for
thought, subject matter, theme,
thesis, text, business, affair,
argument, motion, resolution,
inquiry, problem, question,
(notion, conception, reflection,
observation, idea)

polemic-*n* combatant, disputant,
controversial, litigant,
belligerent, competitor, rival,
contention, strife, opposition,
rivalry, handicap, contest,
match, race, (peace, amity,
friendship, harmony)

polished-*adj* polite, courtesy,
respect, good manners, good
behavior, good breeding,
urbanity, presence, obeisance,
politeness, amiability,
complacency, (impudence,
disrespect, sternness)

pommel-*v* rotund, round,
circular, cylindrical, columnar,
spherical, ball, boulder, oblong,
oblate, drop, vesicle, bulb,
bullet, barrel, drum, rolling pin,
rundle, cone

ponderous-*adj* judgment, result,
conclusion, upshot, deduction,
inference, egotism, illation,
corollary, porism, estimation,
valuation, appreciation,
assessment, (detection,
discovery, find, determine,
trace)

poor-*adj* poverty, indigence,
penury, pauperism, destitution,
want, need, lack, necessity,
distress, difficulties, bad,

P

embarrassed, reduced, circumstances, slender, stricken, (wealth, rich, fortunate, opulence, affluence, provision, livelihood, maintenance, dowry, means, resources)

pop-*v* abruptly, unexpectedly, plump, unaware, without notice, startle, take aback, electrify, stun, stagger, astonish, surprise, (expected, anticipating, reckoning, suspense, waiting, abeyance)

popular-*adj* celebrated, distinction, mark, name, figure, repute, reputation, fame, renown, approbation, notoriety, illustriousness, hero, nobility, glory, honor, (disgrace, shame, humiliation, tarnish, scandal)

portable-*adj* transit, transition, passage, removal, conveyance, relegation, portage, carting, shoveling, freight, convoy, bring, fetch, reach, send, consign, deliver, transpose, movable, contagious

portfolio-*n* book, part, issue, number, album, magazine, periodical, serial, annual, journal, paper, bill, broadsheet

positive-*adj* certain, necessity, certitude, surety, assurance, infallibleness, reliability, gospel, scripture, absolute, unqualified, inevitable, infallible, unchangeable, impeachable, conclusive, authoritative, (uncertain, doubtful, dubious, indecisive, value, ambiguous, undefined, confused)

possess-*v* ownership, tenure, occupancy, holding, tenancy, heritage, inheritance, enjoy, labor under, come to pass, conditional, (circumstance, situation, phase, position)

posthumous-*adj* late, tardy, slow, behind, belated, unpunctual, backward, slowly, leisurely, deliberately, delay,

postponement, adjournment, prorogation, retardation, (punctual, promptitude, prematurity)

posture-*n* form, figure, conformation, make, formation, feature, lineament, turn, phase, aspect, situation, locality, latitude, footing, standing, standpoint, stage, aspect, attitude

potentiality-*n* possibility, compatibility, agreement, practicability, feasibility, feasible, performable, achievable, accessible, superable, surmountable, obtainable, contingent, (impossibility, absurd, unreasonable, incredible, inconceivable, improbable, prodigious, impervious)

potpourri-*n* fragrant, aromatic, redolent, spicy, balmy, scented, sweet-smelling, perfumed, muscadine, ambrosial, scent, mixture, join, combine, intermix, mingle, instill, compound, medicate

pout-*v* moody, discourteous, displacency, grim, sullen, peevish, acrimonious, surly, rough, blunt, gruff

poverty-*n* indigence, penury, pauper, destitution, want, need, necessity, privation, distress, needy, difficulties, beggar, (wealth, riches, fortune, opulence, affluence, livelihood)

practical-*adj* operative, efficient, efficacious, effectual, maintaining, practice, procedure, practical joking, ridicule, sarcasm, mockery, discourtesy

praiseworthy-*adj* commendable, praise, laud, good work, tribute, eulogy, homage, benediction, blessing, applause, complimentary, uncritical, (frown upon, reprehend, admonish, reprimand, chastise, castigate, lash out, trounce)

precedent-*n* coming before, lead, superiority, antecedent, anterior, prior, former, foregoing, prefatory, introductory, precursor, (sequence, coming after, succeed, follow, ensure, alternate)

precious-*adj* valuable, dear, extravagance, exorbitance, superiority, goodness, excellence, worth, rare, expensive, costly, beneficial, serviceable, advantageous, edifying, (cheap, depreciated, bargain)

precipice-*n* slope, obliquity, inclination, slant, crooked, leaning, bevel, tilt, bias, twist, swag, cant, lurch, rise, ascent, gradient, rising ground, dip, fall downhill, steepness, cliff, escarpment

precocious-*adj* flippant, pert, cavalier, saucy, forward, impertinent, malapert, assuming, bluff, brazen, shameless, aweless, unblushing, unabashed, bold, bare, impudent, audacious, presumptuous, (servile, obsequious, supple, soapy, oily, groveling, sniveling, mealy-mouthed, beggarly, prostrate)

pregnant-*adj* productive, fertility, luxuriance, puberty, pullulating, fructify, multiplication, propagation, procreation, superfetation, generate, (sterile, waste, barren, addle, unfertile, arid)

prejudice-*adj* misjudgment, miscalculation, hasty conclusion, foregone conclusion, narrow-minded, confined, illiberal, intolerant, besotted, infatuated, fanatical, positive, dogmatic, bias, underestimate, overestimate, (solve, resolve, render right, be near the truth, recognize, realize, verify, make certain)

prepense-*v* predetermination, premeditation, deliberation, foregone conclusion, resolve, propend, intention, project, redesigned, advised, calculated, well-laid, (impulse, sudden)

prerogative-*n* right, privilege, prescription, title, claim, pretension, demand, birthright, immunity, license, liberty, franchise, vested interest, sanction, authority, (impropriety, emptiness, illegality)

prescribe-*v* advice, counsel, suggestion, recommendation, advocacy, instruction, charge, direct, manage, govern, conduct, order, lead

present-*v* bestowal, donation, delivery, consignment, dispensation, endowment, investment, almsgiving, generosity, liberality, charity, dispensation, (receive, acquire, admission, benefactor)

pretend-*v* feign, assume, make believe, false, simulate, counterfeit, sham, malign, deceitful, dishonest, evasive, hollow, insincere, forsworn, fabricate, prevaricate, (veracity, truth, frankness)

primary-*adj* important, significant, concern, emphasis, greatness, superiority, notability, gravity, seriousness, solemnity, no laughing matter, urgent, prominence, (trivial, frivolous, paltry, small)

privacy-*n* seclusion, exclusion, retirement, reclusion, recess, snugness, solitude, solitary, isolation, loneliness, voluntary exile, aloofness, convent, exile, ostracism, (social, companionship, association, acquaintance, conversable, convivial, jovial, hospitable)

P

probation-*n* verification, test, assay, proof, diagnostic, crucial test, check, ordeal, experiment, answerable, prove, establish, make good, show, conclusiveness, (refutation, answer, disproof, conviction, invalidation, retort, negative, parry, argument)

procreate-*v* productive, prolific, teeming, fertile, fruitful, frugivorous, luxuriant, pregnant, generative, life-giving, spermatic, multiparous, (sterility, infertility, waste, desert, unprofitable)

profession-*n* part, cue, province, function, lookout, department, capacity, sphere, orb, field, line, routine, career, race, vocation, calling, craft, trade, actively employed, employment

promise-*v* undertaking, work, troth, plight, pledge, parole, affirmation, vow, oath, profession, assurance, warranty, guarantee, insurance, obligation, contract, (release, liberation, absolute, free)

pronounce-*v* utter, breathe, give, ejaculate, vocalize, prolate, articulate, enunciate, accentuate, aspirate, deliver, mouth, phonetic, oral, (silence, render mute, muzzle, muffle, suppress, smother)

propagate-*v* productive, prolific, teeming, fertile, fruitful, circulate, promulgate, spread, publish, known, information, put forward, proclaim, announce, advertise, (sterile, unproductive, unfertile)

propitiate-*v* forgiveness, pardon, condonation, grace, remission, absolution, amnesty, oblivion, indulgence, reprieve, conciliation, reconciliation, pacification, (revenge, vengeance, avenged)

prosecute-*v* accuse, charge, imputation, slur, inculpation, elation, criminative, argument, condemnation, defendant, prisoner, charge, (vindication, justification, warrant, exoneration)

provide-*v* supply, purvey, commissariats, grist, resource, caterer, furnish, find, cater, victual, prepare, anticipate, foresight, arrange, ripening, maturation, evolution, (waste, expenditure, dispersion, consumption, exhaustion)

province-*n* region, sphere, ground soil, area, realm, hemisphere, quarter, district, beat, orb, circuit, circle, domain, tract, territory, country, canon, county, shire, parish, (abyss, free space)

prune-*v* retrench, cut short, scrimp, cut, chop up, hack, hew, clip, dock, lop, shear, shave, mow, reap, crop, snub, truncate, pollard, stunt, nip, curtail, (long, lengthy, outstretched, elongate)

pulsate-*v* agitation, stir, tremor, shake, ripple, jog, jolt, jar, jerk, shock, succussion, trepidation, quiver, quaver, dance, twitter, flicker, flutter, disquiet, perturbation, commotion, turmoil, stagger

punctual-*adj* accuracy, exact, precise, delicacy, rigor, mathematical, clockwork precision, genuine, authentic, legitimate, substantial, tangible, valid, undistorted, (laxity, indefinite, erroneous, untrue)

pure-*adj* innocent, spotless, clear, immaculate, clean, not guilty, irreproachable, virtuous, above suspicion, exceptional, without flaw, blameless, (guilt, atrocity, fault, sin, error, transgression)

purpose-*n* intent, project, predetermination, design, ambition, contemplation, mind, view, proposal, study, decision, resolve, settled, resolution, wish, motive, deliberate, (speculation, venture, chance)

pursue-*v* continue, persist, keep, stick to, maintain, carry on, uninterrupted, sustain, uphold, hold up, perpetuate, preserve, harp upon, repeat, (cease, discontinue, desist, pause, rest, respite)

push-*v* propulsion, ejaculation, ejection, throw, fling, toss, shot, discharge, missile, projectile, motion, dart, lance, flirt, flip, shoot, launch, send forth, (draw, pull, haul, lug, rake, drag, tug, tow, trail)

P

Q

quackery-*n* unskillful, incompetency, inability, disqualification, folly, stupidity, indiscretion, neglect, thoughtless, absence of rule, blunder, (skill, dexterity, clever, talent, ability)

quadrant-*n* angular, measurement, elevation, distance, velocity, sextant, miter, obtuse, salient, fusiform, wedge-shaped, cuneiform, triangular, rectangular, multilateral, cubical, pyramidal

quagmire-*n* marsh, swamp, morass, moss, fen, bog, slough, sump, wash, mud, squash, slush, embarrassing, awkward, unwieldy, unmanageable, intractable, (ease, feasibility, smooth)

quake-*v* flutter, trepidation, feat and trembling, perturbation, tremor, quivering, shaking, trembling, throbbing, palpitation, fright, affright, quiver, quaver, twitter, twirl, writhe, toss

qualify-*v* change, mutate, permutation, variation, modification, modulation, innovation, metastasis, deviation, turn, diversion, beat, transform, transfigure, metamorphosis, convert, alter, vary, diversity, (stable, permanent, persist, endure, standing, maintain, preserve, conserve)

qualm-*n* misbelief, discredit, infidelity, dissent, change of opinion, doubt, uncertainty, skepticism, misgiving, demure, suspicion, jealousy, scruple, unbeliever, (credence, assurance, faith, trust)

quantity-*n* magnitude, amplitude, mass, amount, quantum, measure, substance, strength, quantitative, some, any, more or less, (comparative, gradual, shading, range, scope, caliber)

quantum-*n* dividend, portion, contingent, share, allotment, lot, measure, dose, dole, meed, pittance, ration, ratio, proportion, quota, mess, allowance, (insufficient, inadequate, scarce, lack, famine)

quarrel-*n* dispute, tiff, squabble, altercation, words, big words, wrangling, jangle, babble, cross questions, strife, broil, brawl, row, racket, embroilment, (accord, peace of mind, comfort, harmony, unison, agreement)

quarter-*n* quadratic, quartile, tetracid, four, tetrad, quartet, abode, dwelling, lodging, domicile, residence, address, habitation, berth, seat, lap, sojourn housing, headquarters, throne

quasi-*adj* imitate, copy, mirror, reflect, reproduce, repeat, do ike, echo, catch, transcribe, match, parallel, mock, mimic, simulate, impersonate, counterfeit, (original, unique, unimitated)

quell-*v* becalm, hush, lull to sleep, lay an embargo on, remain, stay, stand, resting place, bivouac, anchor, rest, cast, quiet, tranquility, repose, (motion, stream, flow, restlessness, nomadic)

quench-*v* dissuade, deport, cry out against, remonstrate, expostulate, warn, contraindicate, disincline, repel, damp, cool, calm, quiet, deprecate, (persuade, prevail, overcome, carry, procure)

question-*n* inquiry, examination, review, scrutiny, investigation, exploration, sifting, calculation, analysis, dissection, resolution, induction, (answer, respond, reply, rebut, retort, rejoin)

questionable-*adj* doubtful, mistrust, suspect, raise a question, unbeliever, refuse to admit, harbor, demure, suspicious, have one's doubts, inconceivable, (belief, credence, credit, reliability, assurance)

quibble-*v* sophism, solecism, paralogism, quirk, fallacy, subterfuge, subtlety, quilled, inconsistency, mockery, pervert, equivocate, mystify, evade, elude, the absence of reason, evasion, (logical sequence, good cause, sound, valid)

quick-*adj* hurry, hasten, accelerate, quicken, swift, rapid, eagle speed, acceleration, spurt, rush, dash, fast, speedy, nimble, agile, expeditious, express, (slow, dawdle, retard, slacken, falter)

quid-*n* barter, exchange, truck system, tit for tat, give and take, blow for blow, measure for measure, recrimination, accusation, revenge, (resist, rebuff, opposition, reluctant, withstand)

quiet-*adj* moderation, lenitive, temperate, gentle, tranquilize, assuage, appease, hush, quell, sober, soothe, compose, lull, calm, pacify, (loud, violent, ear-breaking, blast, fury)

quip-*n* cranks, jest, joke, conceit, quirk, merry, bright, happy, flash of wit, scintillation, witticism, work-play, riddle, smartness, retort, repartee, ridicule, (dull, uninteresting, unlively, stupid, slow, flat)

quirk-*n* amusement, entertainment, reaction, relaxation, solace, pastime, sport, labor or love, fun, frolic,

merriment, jollity, heyday, laughter, (weariness, lassitude, fatigue, disgust, loathing)

quit-*v* relinquish, abandon, desertion, defection, secession, withdrawal, break off, desist, stop, vacate, renounce, forego, discard, abandon, discontinue, resignation, retirement

quiz-*v* question,m interrogate, interpolation, challenge, examination, cross-examination, inquire, investigate, seek, search, rummage, explore, (answer, respond, reply, rebut, unriddle)

quota-*n* appointment, dividend, contingent, allotment, measure, dose, dole, meed, pittance, ration, proportion, allowance, share, portion, assign, appropriate

quote-*v* example, instance, specimen, sample, exemplification, illustration, case in point, pattern, agreement, illustrative, invariable, instance, cite

Q

R

rabid-*adj* longing, hankering, inkling, solicitude, anxiety, yearning, coveting, aspiration, ambition, eagerness, zeal, ardor, breathless, impatience, over-anxiety, (indifferent, cold, frigid, lukewarm)

race-*v* run, spurt, rush, dash, steeplechase, lively, gallop, cantor, trot, round trot, scamper, lightening, rocket, arrow, dart, torrent, hustler, gazelle, (creep, crawl, shuffle, saunter, delay, sluggish)

rack-*n* care, anxiety, solicitude, trouble, trial, ordeal, shock, blow, dole, fret, burden, load, vessel, vase, bushel, barrel, canister, utensil, hamper, crate, cradle, (well-being, good, snugness)

racket-*n* loudness, power, loud noise, din, clang, clatter, bombination, roar, uproar, peal, swell, blast, boom, resonance, vociferation, hullabaloo, thunder, resound, (whisper, inaudible, low, dull, muffled)

radical-*adj* cause, original, primary, aboriginal, embryonic, germinal, having a common, review, improve, refine upon, rectify, enrich, mellow, elaborate, fatten, promote, cultivate, advance

rage-*n* resentment, displeasure, animosity, anger, wrath, indignation, exasperation, violence, vehemence, impetuosity, boisterousness, effervescence, row, (calm, moderate, gentle, sobriety)

raise-*v* increase, augment, enlarge, extend, expand, increment, accretion, accession, develop, aggravate, ascent, acerbate, spread, exalt, deepen, (decrease, diminution, lessen, subtraction)

rake-*v* drag, draw, pull, haul, lug, tug, tow, trail, train, take in tow, wrench, jerk, twitch, tousle, traction, rascal, scoundrel, villain, miscreant, wretch, reptile, viper, scamp, (model, paragon, good example)

rampant-*adj* influential, important, weighty, prevailing, prevalent, rife, dominant, regnant, predominant, run through, pervade, (impotence, inertness, irrelevant, uninfluential, powerless)

random-*adj* indiscriminate, aimless, promiscuous, undirected, drift, causeless, without purpose, casually, by the way, accidental, speculate, unintentional, (intentional, purpose, decision, motive)

ransack-*v* plunder, pillage, rifle, sack, loot, spoil, spoilt, despoil, strip, steal, abstract, appropriate, plagiarize, seize, poach, swindle, peculate, embezzle

rapid-*adj* advance, proceed, progress, move quickly, trip, speed, hasten, spank, scuttle, hurry, accelerate, quicken, fast, swift, quick, nimble, agile, expeditious, express, (relax, slow, regress, retreat, retrograde, withdraw, short, halt)

rapture-*n* love, fondness, liking, inclination, regard, admiration, affection, sympathy, yearning, tender passion, flame, devotion, (hate, detest, abominate, abhor, loathe, revolt against)

rare-*adj* unusual, extraordinary, singular, unique, curious, odd, strange, monstrous, unexpected, remarkable, noteworthy, queer, quaint, nondescript, original, (typical, normal, ordinary, conventional)

rate-v estimation, valuation, appreciation, judicature, result, conclusion, upshot, deduction, ponderous, assessment, deduce, derive, gather, collect, (result, discover, find, determine, evolve)

ratio-n degree, grade, extent, measure, amount, stint, standard, height, pitch, reach, amplitude, range, scope, caliber, gradation, shade, rate, sort, comparative, (absolute, quantity, mass)

rational-n intellect, mind, understanding, reason, thinking, principle, rationality, cogitative, faculties, senses, consciousness, observation, intuition, soul, spirit, (imbecility, brutality, brute-instinct)

rattle-v repeated noise, roll, drum, rumble, clatter, patter, clack, hum, trill, shake, chime, peal, toll, tick, beat, ding-dong, tantara, whir, rat-a-tat, rub-a-dub, racket, clutter, cuckoo, repetition, devil's tattoo

ravenous-adj appetite, sharp appetite, keenness, hunger, stomach, twist, thirst, avidity, greed, covetous, grasping, craving, voracity, gluttony, (earnestness, anorexia, inappetence, apathy)

raw-adj immaturity, crudity, abortion, disqualification, improvisation, dismantle, extemporize, non-preparation, neglect, improvidence, (preparation, ripen, maturation, evolution, elaboration, gestation)

reaction-n counteraction, opposition, contrariety, antagonism, polarity, clashing, collision, interference, resistance, renitency, friction, neutralization, recoil, compensation, hindrance, (concurrence, cooperation, cogency, union, agreement, consent)

ready-adj prepare, providing, provision, anticipation, foresight, precaution, rehearsal, note of preparation, arrangement, clearance, tuning, array, ripening, (extemporize, improvise, undress)

reap-v acquire, get, gain, win, earn, obtain, procure, gather, collect, assemble, find, receive, replevy, redeem, advantageous, gainful, remunerative, paying, lucrative, (loss, privation, bereavement, deprivation, dispossession, riddance, deprived, bereft, irretrievable)

reason-n wisdom, sapience, sense, common sense, rationality, judgment, solidity, depth, profundity, caliber, enlarged views, genius, inspiration, aptitude, (shallow, wanting, weak, idiotic, vacant, blatant)

reassure-v hope, confident, trust, rely on, presume, optimism, enthusiasm, aspiration, secure, encouraging, cheering, inspiriting, looking up, bright, roseate, (hesitate, falter, funk, cower, crouch)

rebuff-v repulse, defeat, rout, overthrow, discomfiture, beating, drubbing, nonsuit, subjugation, fall, downfall, ruin, perdition, wreck, fail, unsuccessful, (success, speed, advance, progress, good fortune)

recede-v recession, move from, retirement, withdrawal, retreat, retrocession, departure, recoil, flight, avoidance, remove, shunt, shun, shrink, depart, (approach, approximate, near, access)

receive-v acquisition, exception, introduction, susceptibility,

R

acceptance, admission,
assignee, devisee, donor,
grantee, take in, (give, gift,
donation, delivery,
dispensation, generosity)

recess-*v* regress, retreat,
withdrawal, retirement,
recession, refluence, ebb,
return, reflection, recoil,
deterioration, recede,
retrograde, (progression,
advance, improvement,
proceed, forward, onward)

reciprocate-*v* interchange,
exchange, transposition,
shuffling, casting, barter,
retaliation, bandy, shuffle,
permute, in exchange, vice
versa, (consideration,
substitute, supersede, replace,
redeem)

reckon-*v* discharge, settle, quit,
acquit, account, balance,
square up, disgorge, make
repayment, repay, refund,
reimburse, retribute, make
compensation, (default,
defalcation, protest,
repudiation)

recognize-*v* see, behold,
discern, perceive, have in sight,
descry, sight, make out,
discover, distinguish, spy,
witness, contemplate,
speculate, cast, (blind,
hoodwink, dazzle, screen from
sight)

recommend-*v* approval,
approbation, sanction,
advocacy,m esteem,
estimation, good opinion,
admiration, appreciation,
regard, account, popularity,
credit, repute, (reprehension,
admonition)

reconcile-*v* forgiveness, pardon,
condonation, grace, remission,
absolution, amnesty, oblivion,
indulgence, reprieve,
conciliation, excuse, exonerate,
(revenge, ruthless, avenging,
retaliation, feud)

recovery-*n* restitution,
restoration, return,
reinvestment, recuperation,
rehabilitation, reconstruction,
reparation, atonement, release,
regurgitate, (dispossession,
relapse, deterioration, return,
retrogression, confiscate,
eviction)

rectify-*v* restoration, renovation,
revival, refresh, renaissance,
redress, recovery, restitution,
return to original state, curable,
heal, repair, (deterioration,
relapse, retrograde, recidivism)

redeem-*v* recover, retrieval,
replevin, salvage, trove, find,
foundling, compensate, equate,
indemnity, compromise,
neutralization, nullification,
retaliation, equalize

reduce-*v* decrease, diminish,
lessen, abridge, shorten,
shrink, contract, discount,
depreciate, extenuate, lower,
weaken, fritter away, subtract,
(increase, enlarge, extend,
augment, magnify, gain)

reek-*v* unclean, impurity,
defilement, contamination,
abomination, taint, decay,
corruption, mold, must, mildew,
dirty, filthy, grimy, soiled, stink,
rank, (clean, immaculate,
spotless, neat, tidy, trim)

refinement-*n* improvement,
betterment, melioration,
amendment, mend,
advancement, cultivate,
reformation, correction,
elaboration, purification, repair,
(deterioration, impairment,
injury, damage)

reflux-*v* recoil, refluent, react,
spring, rebound, revulsion,
ricochet, elasticity, reflection,
reverberation, resonance,
boomerang, (impulse, impetus,
momentum, push, thrust,
hammer, punch)

refrain-*v* avoidance,
forbearance, inaction,

abstention, neutrality, evasion, elusion, seclusion, avocation, flight, escape, retreat, recoil, departure, (pursuit prosecution, enterprising, undertaking)

refresh-v restoration, rehabilitation, reproduce, renovation, revival, resuscitation, renaissance, second youth, rejuvenescence, new birth, regeneration, (relapse, fall back, retrograde, return)

regard-v view, look, espial, glance, point of view, see, behold, discern, perceive, descry, make out, discover, distinguish, recognize, contemplate, speculate, (blindness, undiscerning)

register-v digest, synopsis, compendium, table, analysis, classification, division, atlas, classify, methodize, regulate, systematize, coordinate, settle, fix, (litter, scatter, mix, entangle, ravel, dishevel)

regret-v self-reproach, penitence, contrition, compunction, repentance, remorse, self-accusation, be sorry for, confess, reclaimed, disclose, (induration, obduracy, impenitence, uncontrite, shiftless)

rehabilitate-v restore, reinstatement, renovation, revival, refreshment, renaissance, redress, retrieval, reclamation, recovery, convalescence, resumption, recuperate, curative, remedial, recover

rehearse-v repetition, iteration, reiteration, harping, recurrence, succession, monotony, rhythm, chimes, imitation, reverberation, recur, reappear, renew, repeated, often, again, over gain, ditto

reinforce-v aid, assist, help, appellation, support, lift,

advance, furtherance, promotion, relief, sustenance, nutrition, ministry, accommodation, supply, (present, preclude, obstruct, stop, block)

rejoice-v bless, beatify, satisfy, gratify, desire, slake, satiate, quench, indulge, humor, flatter, regale, refreshing, comfortable, cordial, glad, cheering, exciting, (annoyance, grievance, nuisance, bother)

relax-v loose, incoherence, immiscibility, looseness, laxity, loosening, freedom, disjunction, slacken, detach, disheveled, segregated, unconsolidated

relentless-adj resolved, determined, strong-willed, resolute, self-possessed, decided, definitive, peremptory, obstinate, persevering, (fickleness, levity, weakness, demur, hesitating, vacillation)

relief-n aid, assist, oblige, accommodate, humor, cheer, encourage, rescue, deliverance, refreshment, easement, softening, alleviation, mitigation, palliation, soothing, consolation, (aggravate, embitter)

relish-n desire, wish, fancy, want, need, exigency, mind, inclination, bent, longing, hankering, inkling, solicitude, anxiety, yearning, coveting, aspiration, (indifference, cold, frigid, halfhearted, neutrality)

remarkable-adj paramount, essential, vital, all-absorbing, radical, cardinal, chief, main, prime, primary, principal, leading, foremost, vital, significant, emphatic, (ordinary, petty, frivolous, insignificant)

remiss-adj careless, neglect, trifling, omission, default, supineness, reckless, inconsiderate, slovenly, erroneous, nonchalant,

R

inactive, abandoned, disorderly, (care, heed, watchful, exact, attentive, vigil)

remote-*adj* distant, far, elongation, background, removed, telescopic, yonder, father, further, beyond, apart, asunder, wide apart, (nearness, nigh, close, adjacent, intimate, adjoin)

remove-*v* extract, elimination, extrication, eradication, evolution, extermination, ejection, egress, extirpation, export, evolve, squeeze out, (insertion, introduction, insinuation, injection, immersion)

render-*v* restitution, return, restoration, reinvestment, recuperation, rehabilitation, reparation, release, replevin, redemption, remit, revert, (take, catch, capture, seizure, subtraction, reception)

renovate-*v* restore, reinstate, cure, repair, reparation, recruit, disinfection, redemption, deliverance, restitution, relief, recover, return to original state, (deterioration, retrogress, fall back, relapse)

repair-*v* improve, amend, betterment, mend, advancement, progress, ascent, promotion, elevation, increase, reform, correct, refinement, elaborate, (deteriorate, impair, injure, damage, loss, detriment)

repel-*v* depart, cessation, removal, exit, egress, valediction, farewell, outward bound, repulsive, abduction, chase, dispel, (attract, magnetism, gravity, draw, adduce)

replace-*v* substitute, commutation, supplant, supersession, make-shift, alternative, supersede, in lieu of, redeem, change, equivalent,

shift, (exchange, reciprocation, transposition, shuffling, barter, swap)

report-*v* description, account, statement, exposure, disclosure, specification, particulars, abstract, narrative, history, memoir, memorials, annals, chronicle, relate, recount, descriptive

repose-*v* rest, sleep, relaxation, breathing time, halt, pause, respite, unbend, slacken, lie down, recline, unstrained, cessation, vacation, recess, holiday, (exertion, effort, strain, tug, pull)

represent-*v* express, exposition, demonstration, exhibition, production, display, showing, indication, publicity, disclosure, indicate, manifest, proclaim, (allusive, dormant, hidden, invisible, imply, conceal)

repress-*v* restraint, hindrance, coercion, compulsion, repression, discipline, control, confinement, durance, duress, imprison, restrict, (liberate, disengage, release, enlarge, dismiss)

reprieve-*v* forgive, pardon, condonation, grace, remission, absolution, amnesty, oblivion, indulgence, conciliation, reconciliation, pacification, excuse, exonerate, (revenge, vindictive, unforgiving, ruthless, retaliation, rancorous)

repudiate-*v* dissent, discordance, disagreement, difference, diversity of opinion, non-conformity, protest, contradiction, rejection, demur, (ratification, confirmation, corroboration, approval)

require-*v* need, want, necessary, essential, indispensable, urgent, requisition, exactness, demanding, compel, force, make, drive, coerce, enforce, oblige, (depletion, vacancy, low, empty, insolvency)

rescind-*v* abrogation, annulment, canceling, repeal, dismiss, depose, abolish, retraction, destroy, ignore, repudiate, reconsecrate, divest, (commission, delegate, assign, ensign, entrust)

resist-*v* refuse, reject, denial, decline, peremptory, repulse, rebuff, discountenance, protest, dissent, revocation, disclaim, (present, bid, propose, move, advance, start, invite)

resolute-*adj* determined, strong-willed, decided, definitive, peremptory, obstinate, steady, intense, serious, relentless, inflexible, persistent, stability, (vacillating, changeable, weak, fluctuate, hesitate)

resolve-*v* interpret, explain, define, construe, translate, render, find out, illustrate, exemplify, unfold, expound, comment upon, annotate, popularize, disentangle, (misrepresent, garble, distort)

respect-*n* courtesy, good manners, behavior, breeding, politeness, gentility, polish, presence, humor, humility, obeisance, (disrespect, rude, insult, repulsive, bitter, acrimonious, sarcastic)

response-*n* answer, reply, replication, rejoinder, rebut, retort, repartee, rescript, examination, acknowledgement, password, discover, solution, explanation, rationale, respond, (question, analysis, query, problem, exploration, review, exploitation, ventilation, sifting, search, inquire, calculation, analysis)

restless-*adj* disturbance, fidget, disquiet, agitation, unstable, vacillation, fluctuate, vicissitude, alteration,

oscillation, unrest, agitation, (stable, stand, keep, remain firm, establish, settled, solid)

restore-*v* repair, reparation, recruit, reaction, redemption, restitution, relief, reconstruct, redeem, redress, resuscitate, renovate, renew, reestablish, (deteriorate, mutilate, disfigure, blemish, deface)

result-*n* conclusion, upshot, deduction, inference, corollary, estimation, valuation, appreciation, estimate, deduce, derive, gather, collect, settle, (discover, detect, find, determine, evolve)

retain-*v* retention, keep, detention, custody, tenacity, firm hold, grasp, gripe, grip, clinch, clench, secure, withhold, detain, hold, reserve, possess, entail, settle, (relinquish, abandon, dispense)

retire-*v* seclusion, privacy, reclusion, recess, snugness, sequestered, delitescent, hermit, estrangement, voluntary, exile, solitude, isolation, loneliness, (social, companionship, comradeship, hospitality)

retort-*v* retaliation, reprisal, retribution, reciprocation, recrimination, accusation, revenge, reaction, turn upon

retreat-*v* regress, retirement, withdrawal, recede, counter-motion, remigration, recession, recidivation, deterioration, (progression, advance, improvement, proceed, forward, forth)

return-*v* succession, revolve, pulsate, alternate, intermit, steady, punctual, arrive, disembark, advent, reception, welcome, recursion, remigration, (departure, cessation, removal, exit)

revenge-*n* vengeance, avenged, rancor, vindictiveness,

R

implacability, malevolence, ruthlessness, unforgiving, rankling, (forgiveness, pardon, conciliate, condone, acquit, pacify)

reverse-*v* contrary, opposite, counter, differing, diametrically opposed, inverse, antipodal, against, annulment, dismissal, remission, abolish, retract, recall, dissolve, (inaugurate, accredit, engage)

revolt-*v* resistance, stand, front, oppugnant, opposition, renitency, reluctant, repulse, rebuff, insurrection, against, strong, obstinate, stubborn, (retaliate, retort, turn upon, reciprocate)

rich-*adj* sufficient, adequate, enough, satisfaction, competence, ample, abundant, wealthy, luxuriant, fertile, affluent, pregnant, inexhaustible, (insufficient, deficiency, incomplete, shortcoming)

rid-*v* liberate, disengage, release, free, disband, discharge, unfetter, untie, loose, relax, escape, redeem, deliver, extricate, emancipate, acquit, escape, (confine, imprison, repress, control, hinder)

riddle-*n* instrument for sorting, sieve, screen, arrange, dispose, place, form, put, collocate, pack, marshal, range, size, rank, group, enigma, puzzle, charade, maze, (news, information, advice, word)

ride-*v* chase, give chase, course, hunt, hound, tread, rush upon, run, direct, pursue, quest, follow, prosecute, prowl, engage in, endeavor, search, (retreat, recoil, depart, avoid, evade, seclude)

ridiculous-*adj* folly, frivolity, irrationality, trifling, ineptitude,

negaters, inconsistency, conceit, giddiness, inattention, eccentricity, absurd, idiotic, imbecile, (wise, sapient, reasonable, rational, sensible)

rift-*n* fissure, breach, rent, split, crack, silt, incision, dissection, decomposition, cutting instrument, sharp, divorce, part, detach, separate, rescind, segregate, (attach, fix, bind, secure, join, hinge)

right-*n* privilege, allow, sanction, warrant, authorize, ordain, prescribe, constitute, charter, enfranchise, prescribe, presume, absolute, indefeasible, unalienable, merit, (infringe, encroach)

rigid-*adj* obstinate, tenacious, stubborn, obdurate, case-hardened, inflexible, hard, immovable, inert, arbitrary, dogmatic, positive, bigoted, prejudiced, (recant, retract, revoke, rescind, recall, withdraw)

rile-*v* annoy, grieve, nuisance, vexation, bore, bother, blow, distressing, afflicting, disheartening, depressing, deplorable, undesirable, causing pain, haunt, (pleasant, charming, fascinating)

ring-*n* resonance, loud, clang, clatter, noise, roar, uproar, racket, sonorous, powerful, thundering, ear-splitting, deafening, (inaudible, scarcely, low, dull, faint, soft, soothing, melodious)

riot-*n* violence, row, rumpus, inclemency, vehemence, impetuosity, boisterousness, rage, ferocity, fury, exacerbation, turbulent, disorderly, uproarious, frenzied, (tranquil, mild, reasonable, calm, still)

ripen-*v* completion, accomplish, achieve, fulfillment, performance, execution, dispatch, consummation, culmination, conclusion, close, final, finished, (incomplete, neglect, undone)

rise-*v* ascend, grow, begin, slope, progress, stir, revolt, rocket, climb, clamber, mount, aspire, tower, soar, hover, spire, excelsior, up hill, flight, (decline, fall, drop, lapse, tumble, dip, descend, sink)

risk-*v* danger, chance, speculation, venture, stake, blind bargain, gamble, fate, hazard, wager, game, accidental, indiscriminate, random, (decision, determination, purpose, resolution)

ritual-*n* rite, ceremony, observance, duty, solemnity, sacrament, service, worship, duty, officiate, transfiguration, consecration, ostentation, showy, pretentious, pompous, palatial, theatrical, dramatic

rival-*n* competition, contest, opposition, strive, struggle, scramble, wrestle, spar, square, exchange, belligerent, combative, unpeaceful, quarrelsome, pugilistic, (harmony, peace, concord, tranquil)

rivet-*v* attach, join, close, tight, taut, taught, secure, set, intervolved, hinge, unite, connect, fix, bind, tie, string, pin, nail, bolt, hasp, clasp, fuse together, jam, (separate, rupture, shatter, carve, cut)

roast-*v* heat, calefaction, increase of temperature, melt, burn, combustion, ignition, warm, chafe, stove, kindle, toast, inflame, stew, cook, seethe, simmer, (cool, fan, refrigerate, refresh, congeal)

robust-*adj* strong, mighty, vigorous, forcible, hard, adamantine, stout, sturdy, hardy, powerful, potent,

puissant, valid, resistless, invincible, impregnable, able-bodied, (weak, delicate, soft, limp, feeble)

rogue-*n* cheat, knave, scamp, bad man, wrong-doer, evil doer, sinner, rascal, scoundrel, villain, wretch, viper, serpent, monster, devil incarnate, (paragon, hero, demigod, saint, benefactor, angel)

rollick-*v* cheerful, genial, gaiety, good humor, liveliness, vivacity, animation, jovial, pleasing, laughter, amusement, rejoicing, smile, rejoice, enliven, exhilarate, (depressed, dejected, gloom, weariness)

romantic-*adj* impressionable, sensitive, gushing, impassioned, tender, warm, enthusiastic, highflying, spirited, mettlesome, vivacious, lively, expressive, excitable, (nonchalance, unconcern, callousness)

room-*n* spacious, extensive, expansive, capacious, ample, wide-spread, vast, world-wide, uncircumscribed, boundless, capacity, stretch, absence

root-*n* base, basement, plinth, dado, wainscot, foundation, support, substructure, substratum, ground, earth, pavement, floor, paving, flag, carpet, fundamental, built-on, (summit, apex, zenith, pinnacle)

rose-*n* fragrant, aroma, redolence, perfume, bouquet, sweet, aromatic perfume, sachet, scent, spicy, balmy, muscadine, ambrosial, fragrant as a rose, (stench, stick, unclean, offensive, rank)

rot-*v* deteriorate, debase, wane, ebb, recess, retrogradation, decrease, degenerate, impairment, injury, damage, loss, detriment, outrage, pollution, poison, (relieve,

R

refresh, infuse, reform,
enhance)

rotation-*n* periodically,
intermittent, beat, oscillation,
bout, round, revolution, turn,
cycle, sated time, routine
succession, return, revolve,
pulsate, alternate, (uncertain,
capricious, flicker, ramble,
spasmodic)

rough-*adj* uneven, scabrous,
knotted, gnarled, unpolished,
rugged, grain, texture, ripple,
corrugated, ruffle, crisp,
crumble, (smooth, even, plane,
shave, level)

round-*adj* circle, rotund, circlet,
ring, areola, hoop, roundlet,
annulet, bracelet, annulet,
ringlet, eye, loop, wheel, cycle,
orb, orbit, ellipse, oval,
necklace, collar, noose

rouse-*v* stimulate, excite, inspirit,
animate, incite, provoke,
instigate, induce, move,
prompt, attract, beckon, bribe,
lure, inspire, encourage, solicit,
(discourage, dampen, hinder,
restraint, repel)

routine-*n* custom, habit, rule,
standing order, precedent, red
tape, rut, groove, usual,
general, accustom, naturalize,
repeat, prevalent, vogue,
etiquette, order of the day,
(breached, spontaneous)

row-*v* discord, disagreement, jar,
clash, shock, broil, brawl,
racket, hubbub, embroilment,
disturbance, commotion,
quarrel, dispute, embroil,
entangle, (harmony,
agreement, conciliation, peace,
accord)

rub-*v* friction, attrition, rubbing,
scratch, scrape, scrub, fray,
graze, curry, scour, polish, rub
out, gnaw, file, grind, difficult,
hard, tough, laborious,
awkward, unwieldy, (lubricate,
smooth, pat, gentle touch)

rude-*adj* graceless, inelegant,

harsh, abrupt, dry, stiff,
cramped, formal, forced,
labored, artificial, mannered,
ponderous, turgid, affected,
barbarous, uncouth, (graceful,
easy, temperate, gentle)

ruin-*n* waste, destroy,
dissolution, breaking up,
consumption, fall, downfall,
perdition, crash, smash, havoc,
extinct, annihilation, demolish,
suppress, abolish, ravage,
devastate, (rectify, flower,
evolve)

rumple-*v* disorder,
derangement, confusion,
disarray, jumble, huddle, litter,
lumber, mash, muddle,
complex, intricate,
unsymmetrical, unsystematic,
untidy, slovenly, (order,
uniform, symmetry, arranged)

runagate-*n* absence of pursuit,
abstention, forbearance,
refrain, inaction, neutrality,
avoidance, evasion, elusion,
seclusion, flight, escape,
retreat, departure, rejection,
(pursuit, chase, hunt, follow)

rush-*v* haste, urgency,
acceleration, spurt, forced,
march, dash, velocity,
precipitancy, impetuosity, hurry,
drive, scramble, bustle, fuss,
fidget, flurry, (leisurely, slow,
deliberate, quiet, calm)

rusty-*adj* moldy, musty,
mildewed, moth-eaten, mucid,
rancid, bad, gone bad, touched,
effete, rotten, corrupt, tainted,
unclean, dirty, filthy, sooty,
turbid, (wash, clean, pure,
disinfect, neat)

ruthless-*adj* revenge,
vengeance, vendetta,
retaliation, rancor,
vindictiveness, implacability,
malevolence, avenge,
unrelenting, rigorous, (forgive,
pardon, conciliation,
reconciliation, absolution)

S

sack-*n* bag, receptacle, enclosure, recipient, receiver, reservoir, sac, knapsack, satchel, take, catch, hook, gain, acquire, procure, collect, assemble, bring home, secure, derive, draw

saintly-*adj* piety, religious, holiness, sanctimony, reverence, humility, veneration, devotion, prostration, worship, grace, unction, edification, consecration, spiritual existence, (hypocrisy, irreverence, sin)

salute-*v* respect, regard, consideration, courtesy, attention, deference, reverence, honor, esteem, estimation, veneration, admiration, homage, command, (dishonor, desecrate, insult, affront, outrage)

salvage-*v* get back, recover, regain, retrieve, replevy, redeem, come by one's own, come by, receive, inherit, succeed, realize, treasure up, clear, produce, (loss, incur, rid, forfeit, lapse)

sanctify-*v* moral, ethical, casuistical, conscientious, amenable, liable, accountable, responsible, answerable, allegiance, (exempt, release, acquit, discharge, remise, remit, free)

satiate-*v* satisfy, saturate, replete, glut, surfeit, weariness, cloy, quench, slake, pall, gorge, tire, enough, complete, altogether, wholly, totally, laden, (exhaustive, regular, consummate, sheer)

saunter-*v* creep, ramble, dawdle, drawl, slacken, mincing, steps, linger, loiter, sluggard, tortoise, snail, move slowly, crawl, lag, plod, lumber, drag, grovel, waddle, shuffle, (move quickly, speed, hasten)

savage-*adj* cruel, brutal, inhuman, barbarous, fell, untamed, truculent, incendiary, bloodthirsty, murderous, atrocious, fiendish, demoniacal, diabolic, devilish, (benevolent, consideration, ind)

save-*v* economy, frugality, thrift, care, husbandry, retrenchment, prevention of waste, parsimony, sparing, invest, miserly, tightfisted, mercenary, venal, greedy, (liberal, generous, charitable, bounty)

say-*v* speech, locution, talk, parlance, verbal intercourse, oral communication, spoken, lingual, phonetic, unwritten, eloquent, talkative, mouthpiece, language, (stammer, stutter, falter, mumble)

scaffold-*n* support, foundation, base, bearing, footing, hold, place, platform, block, rest, sustentation, aid, prop, stand, truss, stilt, staff, shaft, pediment,)pendant, hanging, dependent, suspended, loose)

scatter-*v* dispersion, disjunction, divergence, dissemination, diffusion, dissipation, distribution, apportionment, spread, sow, strew, dismember, interspersion, (accumulate, heap, lump, pile, stack)

scold-*v* execrate, beshrew, anathematize, denounce, execration, proscribe, excommunicate, fulminate, threaten, abuse, cross, grumpy, glum, morose, (hug, cuddle, address with affection, serenade)

scourge-*v* rod, cane, stick, switch, truncheon, ship, last, strap, thong, cowhide, pillory, stocks, whipping-post, brank,

triangle, wooden horse,
thumbscrew, guillotine,
(reward, satisfy, compensate)

scratch-*v* mark, line, stroke,
dash, score, stripe, streak, tick,
dot, point, notch, nick, asterisk,
red letter, jotting, print, imprint,
note, annotation, maltreat,
abuse, bruise, hurtful, injurious

scruple-*n* probity, integrity,
rectitude, uprightness, honesty,
faith, honor, good faith, purity,
clean, fairness, fidelity, loyalty,
trustworthiness, candor, dignity,
(dishonesty, moral turpitude,
disloyalty)

scrutiny-*n* attention,
mindfulness, intentness,
thought, observance,
consideration, reflection, heed,
notice, regard, circumspection,
study, (abstract, absence,
preoccupation, reverie)

scuttle-*n* destroy, move quickly,
trip, fisk, speed, hasten,
accelerate, quicken, whisk,
bolt, bound, scamper, run,
spank, scour, scamper, run like
mad, fly, race, (slow, slack,
tardy, gentle, easy, leisurely)

secure-*v* hope, desire, sanguine,
expectation, trust, confidence,
reliance, faith, belief, affiance,
assurance, reassurance,
promise, well-grounded,
presumption, anticipation,
(despair, lose, desperate)

seduction-*n* desire, wish, fancy,
fantasy, want, need, exigency,
mind, inclination, attraction,
magnet, allurement, temptation,
fascination, devotee, solicitant,
(indifferent, cold, frigid, half-
hearted)

see-*v* view, vision, sight, optics,
look, espial, glance, ken,
glimpse, peep, gaze, stare,
leer, point of view,
demonstrate, eye, field of view,
contemplation, regard, survey,
(close, blind, shut, cataract)

seethe-*v* hot, glow, flush, sweat,

swelter, bask, smoke, reek,
stew, simmer, boil, burn, broil,
blaze, flame, smolder, parch,
fume, pant, sunny, torrid,
tropical, estival, canicular,
sultry, oppressive

seize-*v* reception, carry, bear
sway, abstract, hurry off,
abduct, steal, ravish, size,
pounce, spring upon, swoop,
assault, confiscate, sequester,
despoil, strip, (restitution,
return, restoration, atonement)

send-*v* delegate, consign,
relegate, turn over to, deliver,
ship, embark, waft, shunt,
transpose, propel, project,
throw, fling, cast, pitch, chuck,
toss, jerk, heave, shy, (draw,
pull, haul, lug, rake, drag, tug)

sensation-*n* pleasure, bodily
enjoyment, animal gratification,
luxuriousness, dissipation,
titillation, gusto, comfort, ease,
refreshment, voluptuous, cozy,
snug, agreeable, (torment,
torture, rack, agonize)

senseless-*adj* absurd, imbecility,
nonsense, paradox,
inconsistency, blunder, muddle,
bull, slip-slop, anticlimax, farce,
rhapsody, farrago, jargon,
fustian, twaddle, no meaning,
(wise, perception, belief)

sensuous-*adj* feeling, warmth,
glow, unction, gusto, fervor,
heartiness, cordiality,
earnestness, eagerness, ardor,
zeal, passion, enthusiasm,
blush, flush, penetrating,
absorbing, impetuous

sequence-*n* coming after, going
after, order, following,
consecutive, succession,
posteriority, continuation,
sequential, alternate, latter,
posterior, subsequently, (litter,
scatter, confound, tangle)

service-*n* useful, utility, efficacy,
efficiency, adequacy, use,
stead, avail, help, applicability,
subservience, instrumentality,

function, value, worth,
productive, (worthless,
inefficient, unskillful)

settle-*v* pay, discharge,
clearance, liquidation,
satisfaction, reckoning,
arrangement, reimbursement,
retribution, reward,
expenditure, defray, quit,
acquit, (repudiate, protest,
dishonor, nullify)

several-*adj* many, numerous,
multitude, profusion, large,
enormous, array, scores,
bushel, majority, multiplication,
diverse, various, populous,
crowd, manifold, (few, small,
handful, paltry, minority)

severe-*adj* strict, harsh, rigor,
stringent, austere, inclemency,
absolute, tyrant, disciplinarian,
stickler, despot, hard master,
oppressor, inquisitor,
extortioner, vulture, (moderate,
lenient, tolerant, mild, soft)

shabby-*adj* poor, paltry, pitiful,
contemptible, sorry, meager,
miserable, wretched, vile,
scrubby, scrannel, weedy,
scurvy, putrid, beggarly,
worthless, cheap, trashy,
(essential, vital, prime, main)

shade-*n* cover, screen, cloak,
veil, shroud, screen from sight,
draw close, curtain, eclipse,
mask, disguise, ensconce,
muffle, smother, whisper,
conceal, (enlighten, open,
impart)

shake-*v* oscillate, vibrate,
liberate, nutation, undulation,
pulsation, alternation, flow, flux,
wave, swing, beat, wag, dance,
lurch, dodge, fluctuate, to and
fro, brandish, (steady, unfurl,
unfold, without motion)

shame-*n* disgrace, dishonor,
tarnish, stain, discredit,
degrade, debase, defile, expel,
punish, stigmatize, vilify,
defame, slur, reprehend,
despicable, unworthy, (worthy,

glorification, hero, elevate)

shape-*n* form, figure, fashion,
carve, cut, chisel, hew, cast,
sketch, block, hammer, frame,
stamp, build, mold, contour,
phase, posture, attitude, sculpt,
type, (destroy, shapeless,
unformed, deface, mutilate)

shield-*n* defend, protect, guard,
ward, preservation, resistance,
safeguard, shelter, fortification,
hold, armed, screen, shroud,
fence, ward off, hinder, asylum,
(attack, invade, outbreak,
assault, siege)

shift-*v* deflect, divert, shunt,
wear, draw aside, crook, warp,
stray, straggle, sidle, diverge,
digress, drift, wander, twist,
meander, veer, rove, adrift,
yaw, (direct, aligned, straight,
straightforward)

shock-*n* false expectation,
disappointment, discalculation,
surprise, sudden, burst,
thunderclap, blow, wonder, bolt
of the blue, electrify, astonish,
abrupt, startling, (foresight,
anticipate, reckon, waiting)

shoot-*v* death blow, finish
stroke, execution, gallows, fast,
speedy, rapid, quick, fleet,
nimble, agile, expeditious,
express, active, swift, (slow,
languor, drawl, retard, relax,
slow, slack, tardy)

short-*adj* concise, brief, terse,
close, to the point, exact, neat,
compact, laconic, curt, pithy,
trenchant, summary,
compendious, compress,
summarize, (amplify, profuse,
drawn out, ramble)

shrewd-*adj* cunning, crafty,
subtle, sharp, diplomatic, artful,
skillful, feline, profound,
designing, contriving, intriguing,
strategic, underhanded, hidden,
(free, outspoken, direct,
downright, candid)

shrivel-*v* reduce, lessen, shrink,
consume, condense,

S

compress, compact, squeeze, strangle, corrugate, astringent, dwindle, narrow, collapse, deteriorate, (expand, swell, wide, fat, bulbous)

shudder-v cold, shiver, gooseflesh, quake, shake, tremble, diddle, quiver, chill, frigid, nipping, piercing, icy, glacial, frosty, freezing, wintry, bitter, (sunny, torrid, tropical, seethe, broil)

shut-v close, enclose, surround, imprison, enfold, buy, encase, enshrine, confine, desist, stop, give over, break, relinquish, abandon, renounce, defect, withdraw, renounce, desert, forsake

sick-adj ill, disease, ailing, infirmity, seizure, stroke, atrophy, disorder, malady, sore, fever, ulcer, corruption, abscess, consumption, eruption, rash, (healthy, sound, vigor, staunch, robust)

siege-n attack, assault, assail, aggression, offense, incursion, invasion, outbreak, storming, obsession, bombardment, fire, volley, beset, besiege, beleaguer, (defend, forefend, shield, screen)

signal-n insignia, banner, flag, colors, streamer, standard, eagle, post, rocket, important, momentous, salient, prominent, memorable, stirring, eventful, (subordinate, inferior, respectable, tolerable)

simple-adj mere, sheer, stark, bare, faint, light, slight, scanty, limited, meager, insufficient, sparing, so-so, modest, tender, subtle, inappreciable, unimportant, (extraordinary, important)

sincere-adj veracity, truthful, frank, candor, honesty, fidelity, plain dealing, genuineness, scrupulous, honorable, pure, unfeigned, outspoken, undisguised, (sham, pretense, false, forgery)

sink-v plunge, dip, souse, duck, dive, plumb, submerge, douse, engulf, bottom, wallow, descent, decline, fall, drop, cadence, subsidence, tumble, (ascent, rise, mount, arise, aspire, climb, clamber)

situation-n circumstance, phase, position, posture, attitude, place, point, terms, regime, footing, standing, status, occasion, predicament, event, juncture

skepticism-n disbelieve, discredit, doubtful, uncertainty, misgiving, demur, distrust, suspicion, jealousy, qualm, refuse to believe, dissent, hesitate, (believe, confide, assured, positive, satisfied)

sketch-n picture, drawing, draught, draft, trace, copy, photograph, image, likeness, icon, portrait, representation, illustration, delineation, depict, personification, (misrepresent, distort, bad)

skim-v recapitulation, resume, review, abbreviation, contraction, shorten, compress, abridge, abstract, epitomize, summarize, run over, (dissertation, essay, theme, discourse, memoir)

skittish-adj cowardly, fearful, shy, timid, poor spirited, soft, effeminate, weak-minded, weak, cower, skulk, sneak, slink, frightened, dastardly, (dare, venture, bold, affront, confront, aweless)

slender-adj thin, small, trifling, narrow, close, fine, thread-like, finespun, taper, slim, slight-made, scanty, emaciated, lean, meager, delicate, gaunt, skinny, (thick, broad, wide, ample, extended)

slink-v retreat, turn-tail, fly, desert, elope, scamper, sneak, flip, steal away, decamp, flit, abscond, levant, skedaddle, escape, abandon, depart, (pursue, follow, quest, hunt, seek)

slippery-*adj* dangerous, precarious, critical, ticklish, tumble down, threatening, ominous, alarming, crumbling, waterlogged, top-heavy, unsafe, hazardous, (safe, secure, sure, shelter)

slow-*adj* idle, drone, droll, dawdle, mope, truant,lounge, loaf, indolent, lazy, slothful, lust, remiss, slack, inert, torpid, sluggish, languid, supine, heavy, dull, leaden, listless, (fast, hasten, lively, agile)

smash-*v* failure, blunder, mistake, fault, omission, miss, oversight, slip, trip, stumble, claudication, botchery, scrape, mess, mishap, collapse, blow, explosion, misfortune, (fortunate, attain, secure)

smite-*v* maltreat, abuse, ill-use, buffet, bruise, scratch, maul, scourge, violent, stab, pierce, outrace, mischief, nocuous, malignant, noxious, injurious, deleterious, (beneficial, valuable, serviceable)

smother-*v* repress, suppress, restrain, stifle, hush, bury, sink, keep from, withhold, reserve, ignore, silence, hoodwink, mystify, puzzle, deceive, (set right, awaken, overhear, understand)

snag-*v* hindrance, obstruction, interruption, blockade, obstacle, impediment, knot, bar, stile, barrier, shackle, restrain, bolt, cramp, hamper, (relief, rescue, help, aid, assist, give a hand)

sneak-*v* contemptible, abject, mean, shabby, little, paltry, dirty, scurvy, scabby, groveling, scrubby, rascally, low-minded, corrupt, venal, mongrel,

dishonest, (upright, honest, veracious, honorable)

snub-*v* short, brevity, abbreviated, curtailment, retrench, cut short, scrimp, chop up, hack, hew, clip, dock, prune, shear, shave, mow, crop, compact, (long, span, streak, prolong)

sober-*adj* moderate, wise, sane, grave, temperate, abstinent, serious, sedate, staid, solemn, demure, grim, visage, rueful, wan, long-faced, disconsolate, forlorn, (cheerful, happy, smiling, blithe)

soft-*adj* pliable, flexible, sequacity, malleability, plasticity, flaccidity, laxity, clay, wax, butter, dough, pudding, cushion, pillow, feather-bed, mollify, mellow, relax, temper, mash, (hard, rigid, durable)

solace-*n* relief, deliverance, refreshment, easement, softening, alleviation, mitigation, palliation, soothing, consolation, comfort, encouragement, (aggravation, exasperation, embitter, sour)

solution-*n* interpretation, definition, explanation, answer, rationale, meaning, translation, rendering, key, secret, clue, illustration, literal, translate, render, define, (distort, misrepresent, question)

soothe-*v* relieve, moderation, tranquilize, assuage, appease, swag, lull, compose, still, calm, cool, quiet, hush, quell, sober, pacify, alleviate, (violent, impetuous, uproar, riot, ferocity, rage, fury, row)

sore-*adj* pain, suffering, dolor, ache, smart, shooting, twinge, twitch, gripe, headache, hurt, cut, discomfort, spasm, cramp, torture, rack, agonize, (refreshed, regale, relish, treat, comforting, cordial)

sorry-*adj* trifling, care, anxiety,

S

solicitude, trouble, grieved, concern, distress, affliction, woe, bitterness, heartache, broken-hearted, tribulation, desolation, despair, anguish, (overjoyed, entranced, at ease)

sound-*n* stable, unchangeable, constancy, immobility, vitality, fixed, steadfast, firm, fast, steady, balanced, confirmed, valid, immovable, riveted, rooted, settled, (restless, agitated, fitful, spasmodic)

span-*n* length, from end to end, outstretched, lengthy, wiredrawn, stretch out, extend, reach, stretch, elongate, prolong, (cut, chop, hack, hew, crop, shave, mow, reap, nip, foreshorten)

spasm-*n* transilience, jump, leap, plunge, jerk, start, explosion, throe, revulsion, storm, cramp, nightmare, convulsion, throb, agitation, pang, (comfort, sensuous, palatable, cozy, snug)

spatter-*v* unclean, dirty, spot, smear, daub, blot, blur, smudge, slobber, slime, grime, contaminate, taint, leaven, corrupt, sooty, smoky, thick, turbid, (clean, rinse, wring, flush, full, wipe, mop, sponge)

special-*adj* individual, particular, peculiar, specific, proper, personal, original, private, respective, definite, determinate, certain, esoteric, (general, universal, impersonal, miscellaneous)

speculate-*v* supposition, assumption, postulation, condition, hypothesis, postulate, theory, proposal, suggestion, surmise, chance, venture, stake, (decision, determination, design, ambition, intentional)

spicy-*adj* fragrant, aromatic, redolent, balmy, scented, sweet-smelling, perfumed,

thuriferous, muscadine, ambrosial, (smell, odor, stench, stink, rancid, unclean, skunk, bad smell, foul)

spiritless-*adj* dejected, depressed, prostration, lowness, oppression, gloom, weariness, disgust of life, melancholy, sad, dismal, doldrums, vapor, despondent, (cheerful, amusing, hilarity, happy, glad)

splendor-*n* form, elegance, grace, beauty, unadorned, symmetry, comeliness, fairness, polish, gloss, good effect, bloom, brilliancy, radiance, gorgeous, magnificent, (ugly, deformed, disfigured)

split-*v* divide, sunder, sever, abscind, cut, saw, snip, nib, nip, cleave, rend, slit, splinter, chip, crack, snap, break, tear, burst, rend, rupture, lacerate, mangle, gash, (join, unite, attach, affix, bind, secure)

spout-*n* running water, jet, spurt, squirt, splash, rush, gush, stream, course, flow, profluent, spring, overflow, pour out, discharge, shower down, drench, (ingress, entrance, influx, import, insert)

spread-*v* disperse, scatter, sow, disseminate, diffuse, shed, overspread, dispense, disband, disembody, dismember, distribute, strew, straw, cast, (assemble, collect, locate, compile, levy)

spring-*v* hurry, hasten, accelerate, leap, jump, hop, bound, vault, saltation, dance, caper, curvet, caracole, capriole, demivolt, buck, trip, bob, bounce, flounce, start, (plunge, dip, souse, duck, dive)

sprout-*v* expand, grow, offspring, posterity, progeny, breed, issue, brook, litter, seed, furrow, spawn, family, grandchildren, child, son, daughter, shoot, olive branch, spirit, descendant, heir, heredity

squat-*v* place, situate, locate, localize, put, lay, set, perch, hive, bivouac, burrow, encamp, establish, reposit, cradle, moor, tether, imbed, inhabit, settle, abode, (displace, eject, exile, abnegate, remove)

staff-*n* director, manager, governor, rector, comptroller, supervisor, intendant, attendant, squire, usher, page, servant, footman, flunky, valet, orderly, messenger, herdsman, maid, housekeeper

stagger-*v* disincline, indispose, shake, discourage, deter, hold, restrain, repel, turn aside, deviation, chill, blunt, calm, quiet, quench, deprecate, dissuade, (stimulate, inspirit, arouse, animate, incite)

stand-*v* exist, behave, subsist, live, breathe, obtain, occur, event, have place, prevail, find oneself, vegetate, real, actual, positive, absolute, substantial, (perish, annihilated, extinct, exhausted, gone)

stare-*v* take an interest, gape, prick up the ears, see sights, lionize, pry, curious, inquisitive, burning with curiosity, curiosity, inquiring mind, (indifference, impassive, have no curiosity)

start-*v* begin, commencement, open, outset, incipience, inception, introduction, initial, inauguration, rising of the curtain, origin, source, rudiment, genesis, (end, close, terminate, conclude, finale, edge)

state-*n* condition, affirmation, statement, allegation, assertion, predication, declaration, work, averment, remark, observation, position, certify, (contradictory, deny, dispute, impugn, repudiate)

station-*n* rank, standing, brevet rank, precedence, place, position, status, order, degree, condition, greatness, eminence, height, importance, primacy, dedication, (disconcert, humble, disgraced)

stay-*v* prolong, defer, delay, lay over, suspend, shift, waive, retard, remand, postpone, adjourn, procrastinate, dally, protract, lengthen out, temporize, linger, loiter, (premature, early)

steel-*n* strong, mighty, vigorous, forcible, hard, adamantine, stout, robust, sturdy, hardy, powerful, resistless, impregnable, sovereign, valid, potent, (frail, fragile, shatter, flimsy, unsubstantial, feeble)

step-*n* pace, rate, tread, stride, gait, port, cadence, carriage, velocity, angular velocity, progress, locomotion, journey, voyage, transit, nomadic, motor, erratic, (remain, stay, stand, ride, pause, rest)

stereotype-*n* indication, mark, note, stamp, earmark, label, ticket, docket, dot, spot, score, dash, trace, chalk, print, imprint, engrave, symbolize, typify, represent

stiff-*adj* rigid, hard, stubborn, firm, starched, stark, unbending, unlimber, unyielding, inflexible, tense, indurate, gritty, proof, petrify, crystallization, (soft, pliable, flexible, relax, tender, supple, pliant)

stimulate-*v* excite, provoke, arouse, inspirit, animate, incite, instigate, actuate, encourage, influence, sway, incline, persuade, overcome, engage, invite, procure, (discourage, dampen, hinder, repel)

stock-*v* accumulate, amass, hoard, fund, garner, save,

S

reserve, keep, deposit, stow,
stack, load, harvest, heap,
collect, preserve, conserve,
(spend, expend, use, consume,
swallow up)

stoop-v low-minded, disgrace,
dishonor, demean, degrade,
derogate, grovel, sneak, lose
caste, sell oneself, dishonest,
unscrupulous, fraudulent,
(scrupulous, respectful,
reputable, candid)

story-n narrative, history,
memoir, memorials, annals,
chronicle, tradition, legend,
tale, journal, life, adventures,
experiences, confessions,
anecdote, work of fiction

stow-v place, situate, locate,
localize, put, lay, set, seta,
station, lodge, quarter, post,
install, house, establish, fix, pin,
root, graft, plant, insert,
(displace, exile, transposition,
remove, transfer, banish)

straggle-v deviate, stray, sidle,
diverge, digress, wander, wind,
twist, meander, veer, ramble,
rove, drift, adrift, step aside,
scent, shift, shunt, wear, draw
aside, crook, warp, (align, level,
toward)

straight-adj rectilinear, direct,
even, right, true, in a line,
unbent, undeviating, inflexible,
align, (deviating, errant,
desultory, rambling, stray,
curved, arch)

strange-adj exceptional,
abnormal, irregular, arbitrary,
informal, wandering, eccentric,
unusual, uncommon,
remarkable, noteworthy,
monstrous, wonderful,
unexpected, (typical, normal,
ordinary)

streak-n variegated, iridescence,
play of colors, spottiness,
spectrum, rainbow, stripe,
speckle, sprinkle, stipple,
maculate, dot, tattoo, inlay,
polychromatic

stress-n labor, work, toil, travail,
manual labor, exertion, effort,
strain, trouble, operoseness,
drudgery, slavery, flagging,
hammering, hardworking,
strenuous, (repose, rest, sleep,
relax, unbend, slacken)

strict-adj exact, accurate,
definite, precise, well-defined,
just right, correct, close,
rigorous, religiously, punctual,
mathematical, faithful, constant,
authentic, (erroneous, untrue,
false, fallacious, unsound)

strive-v endeavor, attempt,
speculation, probation,
experiment, tempt, attempt,
venture, adventure, try hard,
push, exertion, contend,
contest, (tranquil, calm,
peaceable, harmony)

stronghold-n hold, asylum,
refuge, sanctuary, retreat,
fastness, keep, last resort,
ward, prison, covert, shelter,
screen, wing, shield, umbrella,
anchor, (attack, assault,
charge, aggression)

strut-v ostentatious, showy,
dashing, pretentious, jaunty,
grand, pompous, palatial, high-
sounding, splendid,
magnificent, sumptuous,
theatrical, gaudy, flaunt,
(modest, diffident, humble,
timid, bashful)

stumble-v tumble, trip, titubate,
lurch, pitch, swag, topple, tilt,
sprawl, plump down, descend,
fall, drop, gravitate, slip, slide,
settle, decline, set, sink, (climb,
clamber, escalade, surmount,
tower, soar)

style-n tone, tenor, state,
condition, category, estate, lot,
case, trim, mood, pickle, plight,
fashion, light, complexion,
character, structure, format,
(inconsequential, unconformity,
unrelated)

sublime-adj height, altitude,
elevation, eminence, pitch,

loftiness, tallness, stature, prominence, colossus, giant, tower, soar, (low, depressed, underlie, squat, prostrate)

substance-*n* matter, body, stuff, element, principle, materialistic, object, article, thing, something, tangible, substantial, unspiritual, sensible, physical, (immaterial, spiritual, disembodied, subjective)

subterfuge-*n* untruth, evasion, white lie, juggle, device, plot, maneuver, strategy, artful dodge, trickery, deception, shift, intrigue, contriving, artificial, (innocence, candor, sincerity, honest, guileless)

subvert-*v* destroy, demolish, overthrow, suppression, abolish, sacrifice, ravage, devastate, revolution, incendiarism, deterioration, ruin, dispel, (flower, fructify, teem, build, raise, edify, erect, establish)

succulent-*adj* eatable, edible, esculent, comestible, alimentary, dietetic, culinary, nutritive, potable, bibulous, tasteful, delicacy, gusto, (rank, tasteless, repulsive)

sudden-*adj* instantaneous, abrupt, moment, second, minute, momentary, instant, hasty, lightning, spur of the moment, (perpetual, eternal, everlasting, continual, endless, ceaseless)

suggest-*v* advice, council, recommendation, advocacy, persuasion, mention, acquaint, instruct, inform, authorize, inform, (conceal, suppress, evasion, silence, mystery)

summary-*n* short, brief, curt, compendious, compact, concise, curtail, squat, reduce, (long, lengthy, outstretched, prolong, extend)

sunshine-*n* shine, glow, glitter, glisten, twinkle, gleam, flare, glare, beam, shimmer, glimmer, flicker, sparkle, scintillate, flash, glance, bright, reflect, sunny, cloudiness, meteoric, phosphorescent

S

T

tackle-*v* undertake, engage, embark, volunteer, promise, contract, take upon one's shoulders, begin, fasten, tie, ligament, strap, rigging, standing, trace, harness, yoke, bandage, brace, roller

tactic-*n* game, policy, execution, manipulation, treatment, campaign, career life, course, conduct, behavior, carriage, demeanor, manner, direction, transact, execute, dispatch, proceed

tale-*n* description, account, statement, report, specification, particulars, summary of facts, catalog, information, fable, parable, apologue, narrative, novel, work of fiction, journal, recital, sketch

talk-*n* speech, locution, parlance, verbal intercourse, oral communication, word of mouth, oratory, elocution, rhetoric, recitation, formal speech, (stammer, hesitation, impediment, stutter, falter)

tame-*adj* domesticate, acclimatize, breed, tend, break in, train, cage, bridle, restrain, pastoral, bucolic, veterinary art, teach, instruct, edify, school, tutor, cram, (bewilder, uncertain, misinform, deceive, mislead)

tangible-*adj* material, bodily, corporeal, physical, somatic, sensible, ponderable, palpable, substantial, objective, impersonal, neuter, unspiritual, (personal, subjective, spiritualize, disembody)

task-*n* exercise, curriculum, explanation, teach, instruct, edify, fatigue, weariness, yawning, drowsiness, lassitude, tiredness, exhaustion, sweat, faintness, (restore, refresh, revive, repair, relief)

tattler-*n* narrator, scandal-monger, tale-bearer, gossip, many-tongued, rumored, currently, reported, glad tidings, eavesdrop, (observe, swear, hide, close-mouthed)

tear-*v* separate, destroy, overturn, nullify, annul, demolish, crumple up, sunder, divider, cut up, carve, dissect, pull, disintegrate, nip, nib, cleave, snap, break, (join secure, inseparable)

tease-*v* annoy, displease, incommode, discompose, trouble, disquiet, disturb, perplex, molest, tire, irk, vex, mortify, harass, harry, badger, persecute, harrow, (please, agreeable, amusement, charm, delight)

technical-*adj* artistic, scientific, businesslike, talent, ability, ingenuity, cleverness, endowed, skillful, experienced, efficient, qualified, handy, capable, smart, proficient, (stupidity, inexperienced, ignorant)

tell-*v* influence, weight, pressure, preponderance, prevalence, sway, predominance, ascendancy, dominance, reign, authority, (impotence, inertness, irrelevancy, uninfluential, unconducing)

temper-*n* pervading, penetrating, absorbing, strong, sharp, acute, cutting, piercing, incisive, caustic, violent, vehement, warm, rough, boisterous, rampant, (moderate, gentle, mild, cool, sober, calm)

tempt-*v* seduce, entice, allure, captivate, fascinate, bewitch, carry away, charm, conciliate, coax, lure, tantalize, cajole, deceive, bribe, influence, prompt, instigate, (dissuade, discourage, hinder)

tender-*adj* offer, proffer, present, bid, propose, move, advance, start, invite, hold out, put forward, overture, bribe, give, (refuse, reject, repulse, rebuff, deny, decline, nill, repudiate)

tendril-*n* filament, line, fiber, fibril, funicle, vein, hair, capillary, gossamer, wire, string, threat, packthread, twine, ribbon, splinter, yarn, hemp, jute, strand

tenor-*n* direction, bearing, course, set, drift, tendency, incidence, bending, trending, dip, tack, aim, collimation, steer, bend, trend, verge, incline, (deviation, swerve, digress, depart, aberration, sweep)

tenure-*n* possession, ownership, occupancy, monopoly, retention, sanction, authority, warranty, charter, permission, constitution, security, claimant, appellant, (infringe, encroach, exact, relax)

term-*n* time, duration, period, stage, space, span, spell, season, era, limit, boundary, confine, frontier, word, vocabulary, name, nomenclature, verbal, literal

terrorist-*n* coward, poltroon, dastard, sneak, recreant, weak-minded, effeminacy, timidity, oppressor, tyrant, firebrand, incendiary, anarchist, destroyer, iconoclast, savage, (benefactor, savior, courage)

text-*n* copy, design, type, matter, subject, meaning, signify, convey, imply, breathe, indicate, bespeak, expressive, declaratory, (nonsense, jargon, gibberish, jabber, absurd, vague, balderdash, trash)

thankless-*adj* bitter, distasteful, uninviting, unwelcome, undesirable, obnoxious, unacceptable, unpopular, distressing, disheartening, depressing, (bless, beatify, satisfy, gratify, thankful, flatter)

thaw-*v* melt, liquefy, heat, dissolution, run, dissolve, resolve, fuse, burn, combustion, ignition, inflammation, roast, singe, incinerate, smelt, boil, (cool, refrigerate, refresh, congeal, freeze, chill)

thesis-*n* supposition, assumption, postulation, condition, hypothesis, postulate, theory, proposal, plan, association of ideas, topic, proposition, (perception, image, sentiment, reflection, abstract idea)

thick-*adj* dense, solid, impenetrable, cohesion, constipation, consistence, condense, substantial, lump, massive, (rarefy, expand, dilate, subtilize, sponginess, thin, fine, flimsy, slight)

thin-*adj* insufficient, inadequate, deficiency, imperfection, scarcity, want, need, lack, scanty, small, stingy, meager, poor, spare, starve, stricken, (sufficient, ample, abundant, enough, adequate, full)

thorn-*n* point, spike, spine, needle, pin, prick, spur, rowel, barb, spit, cusp, horn, antler, snag, tag, bristle, nib, tooth, tusk, spoke, cog, ratchet, barbed, spurred, (blunt, obtund, dull)

thoughtless-*adj* negligent, omission, careless, inattentive, nonchalance, insensibility, heedless, remiss, perfunctory, unmindful, inconsiderate, (careful, regardful, prudent, considerate, provident, cautious)

thread-*n* pass, perforate, penetrate, permeate, enfilade, traverse, journey, worm, passage, wire, string, slip, strip,

T

filament, line, fiber, splinter, ribbon, soft, fragile, inactivity

threaten-*v* inspiring fear, alarming, formidable, perilous, danger, portentous, fearful, dread, shocking, terrible, horrid, ghastly, revolting, awful, terrorize, startle, (hopeful, confident, secure, enthusiastic)

threshold-*n* beginning, entry, inlet, orifice, mouth, portal, portico, door, gate, vestibule, border, edge, commence, rise, arise, conceive, initiate, open, dawn, (end, close, terminate, conclude, finale, finish)

thrill-*n* provoke, summon, raise, rouse, arouse, stir, fire, kindle, inflame, excite, stimulate, inspire, infect, agitate, passion, stun, astound, electrify, galvanize, (insensible, disregard, neglect, unaffected)

throw-*n* fling, toss, discharge, shy, propel, project, cast, pitch, chuck, jerk, heave, hurl, dart, lance, tilt, ejaculate, send forth, expel, shot, (draw, drag, tug, tow, trail, train, pull together)

tickle-*v* please, cause pleasure, delight, gladden, make cheerful, captivate, fascinate, enchant, entrance, enrapture, regale, amuse, stimulate, excite, (irritate, annoy, grieve, vex, displease)

tidy-*adj* orderly, regularity, uniformity, symmetry, methodically, ship-shape, routine, arrangement, array, series, neat, spruced, primp, prepared,. classified, (disorderly, derange, ruffle, untidy, shapeless)

tight-*adj* firm, fast, joined, close, taut, secure, set, intervolved, drunk, tipsy, intoxicated, inebriation, mellow, groggy, (sobriety, teetotaler, water drinker, separate, scission, loose)

tilt-*v* obliquity, incline, slope, slant, crooked, leaning, bevel, bias, list, twist, swag, can, lurch, distorted, bend, recumbent, skew, (parallel, coextension, alongside, straight)

timid-*adj* modest, humble, diffident, timorous, bashful, shy, nervous, skittish, coy, sheepish, shamefaced, blushing, reserved, constrained, demure, quiet, private, (self-satisfied, airs, pretentious)

tinsel-*n* luster, sheen, shimmer, reflection, gloss, spangle, brightness, brilliancy, splendor, lucid, illuminate, shine, glow, glimmer, sparkle, dazzle, (dark, dim, dingy, gloomy, shady, obscure, black)

title-*n* name, style, baptism, appellation, designation, surname, description, call, term, denominate, entitle, christen, characterize, specify, distinguish, label, (anonymous, nameless, misnomer, pseudonym, alias, nickname)

tolerate-*v* lenient, mild, gentle, soft, indulgent, easy-going, clement, compassion, forbearing, favor, moderation, merciful, spoil, (severe, strict, harsh, domineer, rigid, stern, rigorous, uncompromising)

tone-*n* state, condition, category, estate, lot, case, trim, mood, pickle, plight, temper, aspect, appearance, tenor, turn, guise, fashion, light, complexion, style, character, (circumstantial)

tonic-*n* remedy, help, redress, antidote, prophylactic, antiseptic, corrective, restorative, sedative, cure, physic, medicine, potion, salve, ointment, (poison, leaven, virus, venom, arsenic, fungus, rot, canker)

tool-*n* instrument, organ,

implement, utensil, machine, engine, lathe, gin, mill, gear, tackle, apparatus, appliance, equipment, harness, hammer, fittings

top-*n* supreme, superior, major, greatest, higher, exceed, distinguished, vault, important, first-rate, excellent, unparalleled, culmination, foremost, (inferior, smaller, bottom, diminish, short-coming)

topple-*v* unbalanced, unequal, difference, uneven, countervail, disparate, over-balanced, top-heavy, lop-sided, inferior, (equal, matched, reach, balanced, equate, adjust, accommodate, level)

torture-*v* punish, chastise, castigate, cruelty, brutality, savagery, ferocity, barbarity, unhumanity, vivisection, outrage, persecution, atrocity, (benevolent, kind, well-meaning, amiable, obliging)

total-*n* complete, integration, entirety, perfection, entire, whole, full, thorough, plenary, undivided, altogether, beginning to end, saturated, limit, sufficient, (deficient, shortcoming, omit, incomplete)

totter-*v* fluctuate, vary, waver, flounder, flicker, flitter, flit, flutter, shift, shuffle, shake, tremble, vacillate, wamble, sway, oscillate, changing, alternating, mobile, (fixed, steadfast, firm, immovable, tethered)

touch-*v* contact, abutment, osculation, meet, close, adjoin, graze, coincide, coexist, adhere, deed, act, overt act, gesture, transaction, job, maneuver, (remote, distant, far off, away, apart, asunder)

tower-*n* pillar, column, obelisk, monument, steeple, spire, minaret, campaniles, turret, dome, cupola, pole, pikestaff,

maypole, flagstaff, mountain, height, (low, depress, concave, lowland, underlie)

trace-*v* discover, recognize, realize, verify, make certain of, identify, get at, solve, resolve, unriddle, unravel, interpret, disclose, unearth, (obliterate, extinct, no trace of, deletion)

trade-*n* commerce, buying and selling, bargain, sale, traffic, business, custom, shopping, commercial enterprise, speculation, jobbing, dealing, transaction, negotiate

tradition-*n* old, ancient, antique, maturity, prescription, prime, primitive, customary, immemorial, old-fashioned, time honored, long standing, (new, novel, recent, fresh, green, young, immature, late)

train-*v* prepare, make ready, educate, novitiate, cultivate, mature, evolve, pioneer, instruct, edify, tutor, direct, guide, qualify, drill, practice, explain, lecture, task, school, (deceive, conceal, misrepresent)

trample-*v* destroy, waste, dissolve, break up, consume, disorganize, fall, downfall, ruin, crash, smash, annihilation, demolish, ravage, devastate, (produce, perform, operate, construct, fabricate)

tranquil-*adj* calm, moderate, relax, remission, mitigation, gentleness, sedative, assuage, appease, swag, lull, soothe, compose, still, cool, quiet, hush, quell, sober, (fury, dragon, demon, tiger, violent)

transcendent-*adj* super-excellence, goodness, superiority, perfect, complete, immaculate, spotless, unblemished, sound, scathless, intact, harmless, paragon, (indifferent, middling, secondary)

T

transport-*v* ship, tender, transit, remove, displace, relegation, deportation, conveyance, draft, carriage, transition, send, delegate, consign, relegate, (hold, store, retain, keep, preserve)

transpose-*v* exchange, interchange, reciprocate, shuffle, castling, barter, retaliate, commute, mutual, communicative, intercurrent, (substitute, supplant, supersede, instead of, redeem, equivalent)

trash-*n* useless, inefficacy, futile, inaptitude, inadequate, insufficient, unskillfulness, unproductive, litter, rubbish, lumber, refuse, rubble, (useful, value, worth, fruitful, serviceable, prolific)

travesty-*n* imitate, mock, mimic, ape, simulate, impersonate, act, represent, counterfeit, parody, caricature, burlesque, plagiarism, forgery, echo, duplication, repeat, (originality, unique)

tremor-*n* agitation, stir, shake, ripple, jog, jolt, jar, jerk, shock, succussion, trepidation, quiver, quaver, disquiet, perturbation, commotion, turmoil, turbulence, fuss, racket, fits, (calm, quiet, disentangle)

trenchant-*adj* strong, energetic, forcible, active, intense, deep-dyed, severe, keen, vivid, sharp, acute, incisive, brisk, rousing, irritating, poignant, caustic, corrosive, (inert, inactive, passive, torpid, dull)

trespass-*v* transgression, infringement, transcendence, redundance, surpass, go beyond, over-step, exceed, surmount, encroach, infringe, (default, collapse, extricate, eliminate)

tribute-*n* observe, respectful, deferential, decorous, obsequious, regard, revere, venerate, worship, duty, devotion, salute, inspire, impose, dazzle, (ridicule, disrespectful, irreverent, disparaging)

trickle-*v* ooze, emerge, emanate, issue, pass, pour out, pass off, evacuate, spout, gush, dribble, perspire, vent, filter, filtrate, distill, discharge, extravagate, (absorb, ingest, inhale, swallow, engulf)

trim-*v* equalize, match, balance, cope with, dress, adjust, poise, fit, accommodate, adapt, establish, equality, readjust, coordinate, (unequal, countervail, advantage, disparate, partial, over-balanced)

trip-*n* journey, excursion, expedition, tour, grand tour, circuit, peregrination, discursion, ramble, pilgrimage, course, ambulation, march, walk, promenade, constitutional, (rest, pause, lull, bivouac)

trouble-*n* difficulty, irksome, laborious, arduous, awkward, unwieldy, unmanageable, impossible, complicated, impracticable, hopeless, embarrassing, perplexing, (easy, facilitate, smooth, submissive)

true-*adv* verify, gospel, authentic, veracity, accuracy, exactness, precise, delicacy, rigor, mathematical, punctuality, plain, honest, sober, naked, real, actual, (mistake, fault, blunder, error, fallacy, untrue)

trump-*n* perfect, faultless, immaculate, spotless, impeccable, sound, superior, transcendence, model, best, inimitable, paragon, superhuman, divine, (bearable, imperfect, below par, indifferent)

trunk-*n* house, stem, tree, stock, stirps, pedigree, lineage, line, family, tribe, sect, race, clan, genealogy, descent, extraction, birth, ancestry, forefathers, patriarchs

truss-*n* support, aid, prop, stand, anvil, stay, shore, skid, rib, bandage, sleeper, stirrup, stilts, shoe, sole, heel, splint, outrigger, (suspend, hang, sling, hook up, hitch, fasten to, append)

trust-*n* believe, credit, give faith, credence, esteem, confide, certain, sure, assured, positive, unhesitating, convinced, accredited, persuasive, impressive, (disputable, uncertain, unworthy)

try-*v* experiment, endeavor, tempt, attempt, venture, adventure, speculate, tempt fortune, assay, content, contest, strive, struggle, scramble, wrangle

tube-*n* channel, passage, way, path, pipe, vessel, tubule, canal, gut, fistula, chimney, flue, tap, funnel, gully, tunnel, shaft, alley, mine, (closure, occlusion, blockade, obstruction)

tug-*v* effort, exertion, strain, pull, stress, throw, stretch, struggle, spell, spurt, labor, work, toil, travail, drudgery, trouble, pains, duty, exert, strict, (repose, rest, slacken, inactive, recline, halt, pause)

tumble-*v* trip, stumble, titubate, lurch, pitch, swag, topple, tilt, sprawl, plump, descend, dismount, alight, swoop, stoop, titubation, drop, (climb, clamber, surmount, scale, tower, soar, hover. spire)

tumultuous-*adj* violent, inclemency, vehemence, might, impetuosity, boisterousness, effervescence, turbulence,

severity, ferocity, rage, fury, exacerbation, strain, (moderation, relaxation, tranquilize)

turbulence-*n* disquiet, perturbation, commotion, turmoil, tumult, hubbub, rout, bustle, fuss, racket, spasm, throe, throb, palpitation, convulsion, disturbance, disorder, restlessness

turgid-*adj* expanded, increase, enlarge, extension, augmentation, amplification, spread, increment, growth, development, pullulating, dilatation, inflation, (condense, lessen, shrink, collapse, atrophy)

turn-*v* rotate, revolution, gyration, circulation, convolution, whir, vortex, whirlpool, whirligig, roll, axis, axle, spindle, pivot, mandrel, swivel, (vibration, alternation, up and down, fluctuation)

turpitude-*n* dishonor, disgrace, shame, humiliation, scandal, baseness, vileness, improbity, infamy, tarnish, taint, defilement, pollution, stain, blot, blur, (elevate, ascent, dignify, consecrate, enthrone)

turret-*n* tower, pillar, column, obelisk, monument, steeple, spire, minaret, dome, cupola, pole, pikestaff, maypole, flagstaff, top, mast, skyscraper, (low, debased, underneath, below, flat, level)

tutelage-*n* sage conduct, escort, convoy, guard, shield, defense, guardian, angel, deity, protector, warden, preserver, custodian, chaperon, sentinel, sentry, (danger, peril, insecurity, jeopardy, risk)

twist-*v* distort, contort, warp, writhe, deform, misshape, contortion, crooked, grimace, irregular, unsymmetrical, grotesque, deformed,

T

misbegotten, (symmetrical, shapely, uniform, classic, uniform)

type-*n* form, figure, shape, conformation, make, formation, frame, construction, cut, set, build, trim, stamp, cast, mold, fashion, contour, outline, structure, feature, lineament, posture, attitude

tyranny-*n* assume, usurp, arrogate, domineer, bully, inflict, wreak, sever, strict, hard, harsh, rigid, stiff, stern, rigorous, uncompromising, (lenient, tolerant, mild, indulgent, clement, compassionate, forbearing)

U

ugly-*adj* deformity, inelegance, disfigured, blemish, squalor, eyesore, frightful, hideous, odious, uncanny, forbidding, repellent, repulsive, shocking, (form, elegance, grace, beauty, gorgeous)

ulterior-*adj* extraneousness, extrinsically,m foreign, alien, strange, ultramontane, excluded, inadmissible, exceptional, (component, integral, element, constituent, ingredient)

ultimatum-*n* decision, determination, resolve, purpose, resolution, with motive, settled, intent, undertaking, predetermination, design, ambition, (speculation, venture, stake, gamble, chance)

unabashed-*adj* bold, spirited, daring, audacious, fear, daunt, dread, aweless, undaunted, enterprising, adventurous, ventures, dashing, chivalrous, soldierly, fierce, (courage, bravery, valor, resolute)

unadorned-*adj* simple, plain, homely, ordinary, unaffected, chaste, severe, ungarnished, disarrange, untrimmed, unvarnished, bald, flat, dull, (ornamented, beautified, ornate, rich, gilt)

unanswerable-*adv* categorical, decisive, crucial, demonstrated, proven, deducible, consequential, inferential, following, established, verify, (refutation, answer, disproof, conviction, invalidation)

unassisted-*adv* encumber, stop, prevent, load, burden, lumber, pack, difficulty, dampen, obstruct, stay, bar, bolt, unaided, hinder, block, impede, (assist, aid, rescue, help, contribute, furnish, relief)

unaware-*adv* uninformed, ignore, unexplored, unknown, blind, unconsciousness, shallow, superficial, (aware, cognizant, conscious of, acquainted, versed, learned, instructed, proficient)

unblushing-*adj* dignity, self-respect, pride, haughtiness, vainglory, arrogance, supercilious, disdainful, bumptious, magisterial, imperious, overweening, consequential, (humble, lowly, meek, modest)

unborn-*adv* non-existence, absence, abeyance, nullity, negative, annihilation, extinction, destruction, abrogate, uncreated, perished, exhausted, gone, lost, departed, (real, actual, positive, absolute)

uncertain-*adv* incertitude, doubt, dubiety, hesitation, suspense, perplexity, embarrassment, dilemma, bewilderment, timidity, fear, vacillation, indetermination, vague, obscure, (certain, unerring, infallible)

unclog-*v* liberate, disengage, release, enlarge, emancipate, enfranchise, discharge, dismiss, deliver, redeem, extricate, acquit, absolve, set free, unfetter, untie, (confine, restraint, hinder, repress)

uncommendable-*adj* dispraise, disapprobation, censure, obloquy, detract, condemnation, ostracize, criticism, sarcasm, insinuation, innuendo, poor, (approval, sanction, advocacy, applause)

uncomplying-*adj* refuse, reject, deny, decline, nil, negative, discountenance, recusancy, abnegation, protest, disclaimer, dissent, revocation, unconsenting, (offer, present, tender, advance, invite, bid)

unconditional-*adj* unrestricted, unlimited, absolute, discretionary, unassailed, unforced, unbiased, spontaneous, free, autonomous, unclaimed, (dependence, employ, constraint, liability)

unconscious-*adj* insensible, impassive, blind to, unimpressionable, unfeeling, apathetic, phlegmatic, dull, frigid, cold, obtuse, inert, torpid, sluggish, inactive, languid, (sentimental, sensible, romantic)

uncouth-*adj* bad taste, vulgar, awkward, coarse, indecorum, misbehavior, low life, boorishness, gaudy, unkempt, unpolished, incondite, rude, outlandish, (tasteful, pure, chaste, classical, artistic)

uncover-*v* divulge, reveal, break, split, utter, blab, acknowledge, allow, concede, grant, admit, own, avow, disclose, transpire, confess, visible, (ambush, hide, mask, disguise, masquerade)

under-*v* low, underneath, below, down, neap, crouched, squat, prostrate, horizontal, depress, concave, molehill, underlie, wallow, (high, elevated, eminent, exalted, tall, gigantic)

underhand-*adj* reticence, reserve, mental, suppression, evasion, white lie, silence, misprison, secretive, seclusion, hidden, sneak, skulk, prowl, (inform, enlighten, acquaint, communicate)

undermine-*v* cunning, crafty, artful, skillful, subtle, feline, profound, contriving, intriguing, strategic, diplomatic, artificial, insidious, stealthy, hidden,

underhand, (free, plain, outspoken, blunt, direct)

understand-*v* knowledge, acquaintance, insight, familiarity, apprehension, recognition, appreciation, intuition, perception, enlightenment, impression, philosophy, (ignorance, bewilder, uncertain)

underwrite-*v* execute, stamp, sign, seal, evidence, grant, lease, hold in pledge, security, acceptance, authentication, verification, warrant, certificate, voucher, docket, records, discharge, release

undone-*v* lost, ruined, broken, bankrupt, dead beat, destroy, frustrated, crossed, unhinged, disconcerted, dashed, unattained, uncompleted, (succeed, prosper, triumphant, flushed, well-spent)

unearthed-*v* exhume, disinter, autopsy, examination, inhume, lay out, mummify, look, inquire, peer, hunt, leave no stone unturned, seek, search, explore, rummage, ransack, (answer, reply, respond)

unerring-*adj* unblamed, blameless, above suspicion, irreproachable, venial, harmless, pure, virtuous, innocent, model, paragon, perfection, impeccable, (guilt, misbehave, sinful, fault, failure, atrocity)

uneven-*adj* diverse, varied, irregular, rough, multifarious, multiform, various kinds, all sorts, not uniform, lop-sided, unequal, different, partial, over-balanced, (even, level, equal, balance, monotony)

unexplored-*v* hidden, silence, mystery, concealed, darkness, unknown, invisible, impenetrable, undisclosed, unexposed, dormant, unsuspected, (apparent, prominent, flagrant, notorious, distinct)

unfamiliar-*adj* unusual, uncommon, rare, remarkable, unexpected, unaccountable, unconventional, unparalleled, newfangled, grotesque, outlandish, (conventional, ordinary, common, usual)

unfit-*adj* objectionable, unreasonable, unallowable, unjustified, improper, illegal, immoral, wrong, inequitable, partial, unfair, injustice, (right, fit, impartial, moral, reward, recompense, good, just)

unforeseen-*v* miscalculation, unexpected, unaware, pounce, abrupt, sudden, startle, instantaneous, surprised, shock, wonder, fall upon, (expect, foreseen, prospective, impending, prepared, count on)

unfortunate-*adj* unsuccessful, abortive, at fault, inefficient, ineffectual, foiled, defeated, ruined, broken, unattained uncompleted, frustrated, disconcerted, (successful, prosperous, triumphant, victorious)

unfriendly-*adj* hostile, inimical, discord, alienation, estrangement, dislike, hate, heartburning, animosity, malevolence, disaffected, (familiarity, intimacy, fellowship, friendly, welcome, harmony)

unguided-*v* extemporaneous, impulsive, improvised, unprompted, unnatural, unguarded, spontaneous, voluntary, flash, spurt, improvisation, (predetermined, aforethought)

unhappy-*adj* mope, brood, fret, sulk, pine, yearn, repine, regret, despair, refrain from laughter, depressed, gloomy, unlively, melancholy, dismal, somber, (cheering, inspiriting, jovial, hilarious)

uniform-*adj* homogeneous, consistency, conformity, agreement, regularity, constancy, routine, even tenor, monotony, assimilate, level, smooth, dress, invariable, (diversified, varied, uneven, rough)

union-*n* combination, mixture, junction, unification, synthesis, incorporation, amalgamation, embodiment, coalescence, fusion, blending, (decompose, separate, dissect, unravel)

unique-*adj* non-conformity, unconventional, abnormal, eccentricity, rarity, freak, individual, originality, exceptional, exclusive, eccentric, irregular, (conform, typical, normal, formal, ordinary)

unite-*v* gather, assemble, collect, convene, draw, conclave, accumulate, heap, converge, pile, pyramid, conglomeration, muster, meet, join, cluster, (unassembled, broadcast, stray, disperse, sow)

unlucky-*adj* unfortunate, ill-timed, intrusive, inopportune, inauspicious, unfavorable, unsuited, inexpedient, premature, unpunctual, (opportune, timely, well-timed, fortunate, lucky, suitable)

U

V

vacant-*adj* absence, inexistent, nonresidence, absenteeism, empty, void, vacuum, truant, unoccupied, uninhabited, devoid, deserted, (present, occupied, inhabited, dwell, fill, domiciled)

vacate-*v* depart, cessation, decampment, embarkation, outset, start, removal, exit, egress, exodus, flight, valediction, adieu, farewell, goodbye, abandon, leave, (arrive, welcome, reception, return)

vacillate-*v* unsteady, changeable, unsteadfast, fickle, capricious, volatile, frothy, light, giddy, weak, feeble-minded, fidgety, tremulous, hesitate, uncertain, (steady, sound, inflexible, hard, resolute)

vacuous-*adv* absent, not present, away, non-resident, gone from home, missing, lost, wanting, omitted, nowhere to be found, nonexistent, empty, void, vacant, untenanted, (fill, pervade, permeate, present)

vagabond-*n* bad man, wrong-doer, worker of iniquity, evil-doer, sinner, bad example, rascal, scoundrel, villain, miscreant, wretch, reptile, viper, serpent, scamp, (model, paragon, hero, saintly)

vagrant-*n* roving, vagrancy, marching, nomad, gadding, flitting, migration, travel, journey, take wing, emigrate, prowl, roam, range, patrol, traverse, wander, (stagnate, stick, pause, anchor)

vague-*adj* indefinite, indistinct, perplexed, confused, undetermined, loose, ambiguous, mysterious, mystic, transcendental, occult, recondite, abstruse, crabbed, (understand, comprehend, grasp)

vain-*adj* vanity, conceit, self-conceit, self-complacency, self-confidence, selfishness, airs, pretensions, mannerism, egotism, priggish, gaudery, vainglory, elation, (modest, reserved, demure, blushing)

value-*n* price, amount, cost, expense, prime cost, charge, figure, demand, damage, fare, hire, wage, remuneration, dues, duty, toll, tax, impose, tallage, levy, gabelle, excise, assessment, benevolence

vanish-*v* disappear, dissolve, fade, melt away, pass, go, avant, be-gone, leave, no trace, retire from sight, efface, evanescent, missing, lost, gone, (appear, view, vista, spectacle, guise, look, visible)

vary-*v* differ, diverse, heterogeneous, distinguishable, modified, other, another, unequal, not the same, unmatched, distinct, characteristic, (uniform, regular, level, always, without exception)

vast-*adj* great, immense, enormous, extreme, inordinate, excessive, extravagant, exorbitant, outrageous, preposterous, swinging, monstrous, over-grown, (small, diminutive, minute, paltry)

veer-*v* change, alter, vary, wax and wane, modulate, diversity, qualify, tamper with, turn, shift, tack, chop, shuffle, swerve, warp, deviate, turn aside, overt, introvert, resume, (permanent, stationary)

vehemence-*adv* feeling, emotion, excitability, impetuosity, boisterousness, turbulence, impatience, intolerance, non-enduring, irritability, agitation, (serene, calm, placid, composure, quiet, tranquil)

vein-*n* trend, contribute, conducive, lead, dispose, incline, verge, bend to, trend, affect, carry, gravitate, promote, subservient, instrumental, nature, temperament, mood, drift, cast

velocity-*n* speed, swiftness, rapidity, expedition, activity, acceleration, haste, spurt, rush, dash, race, lively, gallop, move quickly, hasten, whisk, sweep, (retard, relax, slacken, gentle, easy, linger)

vent-*v* divulge, reveal, break, split, tell, breathe, utter, allow, acknowledge, concede, grant, admit, own, confess, avow, disguise, transpire, come to light, (screen, cover, shade, blinker, veil, curtain)

ventilate-*v* gust, blast, breeze, squall, gale, storm, tempest, hurricane, whirlwind, wind, blow, fan, respire, breathe, waft, flatulent, issue, bellows, blow-pipe

venture-*n* trial, endeavor, attempt, essay, adventure, speculation, probation, experiment, try, strive, tempt, gamble, bet, risk, hazard, accidental, (intend, purpose, design, propose)

verdict-*n* result, conclusion, upshot, deduction, inference, egotism, illation, estimation, valuation, appreciation, judicature, assessment, ponderous, judgment, (discover, find, determine, evolve)

verge-*n* edge, brink, brow, brim, margin, border, skirt, rim, flange, side, mouth, jaws, cops, chaps, lip, muzzle, threshold, marginal, conducive, tend, incline, affect, gravitate toward, promote

vernacular-*n* indigenous, native, domestic, domiciled, naturalized, home, indoor, endemic, interior, intrinsic, closed, inward, within, (exterior, outside, surface, skin, superficial, external)

versatile-*adj* changeable, mutable, checkered, ever changing, inconstant, unsteady, fluctuate, restless, agitated, erratic, fickle, irresolute, capricious, vagrant, vibratory, alternating

very-*adv* fact, reality, existence, nature, truth, gospel, authenticity, veracity, accuracy, exactness, precise, unalloyed, regularity, principal, (error, fallacy, mistake, fault, blunder, heresy, deceit)

vessel-*n* receptacle, enclosure, recipient, receiver, reservoir, compartment, vase, bushel, barrel, canister, jar, bottle, basket, hopper, crate, cradle, bassinet, hamper, douser, cistern

vexation-*n* disappointment, mortification, cold comfort, regret, repining, taking on, inquietude, soreness, heartburning, lamentation, hypercriticism, malcontent, (comfort, resignation, content)

vibrate-*v* fluctuation, vacillation, swing, beat, shake, wag, see-saw, lurch, dodge, oscillate, alternate, undulate, pulsate, beat, dance, curvet, reel, (fixed, steadfast, firm, fast, steady, balanced)

vicious-*adj* vice, evil-doing, wickedness, iniquity, demerit, sin, immorality, impropriety, indecorum, scandal, laxity, infirmity, weakness, frailty, imperfection, (virtuous, good, innocent, meritorious, deserving)

victim-*n* pigeon, April fool, laughing stock, flat, greenhorn,

V

fool, dupe, gull, gudgeon, cull,
deceived, swallow up, bit,e,
credulous, mistaken, (cheat,
swindler, thief, knave, rogue,
decoy-duck, trickster)

view-*v* see, observe, watch,
attend to, eye, survey, scan,
inspect, glance, behold,
discern, perceive, discover,
distinguish, recognize, spy,
contemplate, (blind, hoodwink,
dazzle, dim-sighted, wall-eyed)

vigilance-*n* watchful,
surveillance, vigil, look out,
care, solicitude, heed,
alertness, activity, attention,
prudence, circumspection,
caution, preparation, accuracy,
(neglect, carelessness, trifling,
omission)

vigor-*n* healthy, well, sound,
hearty, hale, fresh, green,
whole, florid, flush, hardy,
stanch, staunch, brave, robust,
unscathed, perfect, excellent,
(fever, calenture, inflammation,
ailing, disease sick)

villain-*n* rascal, scoundrel,
miscreant, wretch, reptile,
viper, serpent, urchin,
delinquent, criminal,
malefactor, culprit, thief,
murdered, jail-bird, (good,
paragon, hero, innocent, good
example)

vincible-*adj* powerless,
impotent, unable, incapable,
incompetent, inefficient, inept,
unfit, disqualified, harmless,
defenseless, unfortified,
indefensible, pregnable,
(powerful, puissant, potent,
capable)

vinaigrette-*n* fragrance, aroma,
redolence, perfume, bouquet,
sweet smell, aromatic perfume,
incense, musk, frankincense,
spicy, balmy, ambrosial,
perfumed, (stench, stink, fetid,
strong smelling, putrid,
suffocating, nidorous)

vindicate-*v* justification, warrant,

exoneration, exculpation,
acquittal, whitewashing,
extenuation, softening,
mitigation, reply, deference,
recrimination, (accusation,
charge, imputation, slur,
inculpation, exprobation)

vindictive-*adj* resentful,
cantankerous, pugnacious,
perverse, querulous, fiery,
peppery, passionate, choleric,
shrewish, quick, hot, testy,
touchy, animosity,
exasperation, bitterness

violate-*v* seduction, defloration,
defilement, abuse, rape, incest,
social evil, adultery, harem,
intrigue, debauch, defile,
rampant, lustful, carnal, erotic,
voluptuous, (pure, undefiled,
modest, delicate)

viper-*n* snake, serpent, asp,
vermin, beast, poison, leaven,
virus, venom, arsenic,
antimony, nicotine, demon,
sting, fang, (remedial,
restorative, corrective,
palliative, balsamic, narcotic)

virgin-*n* new, immaculate,
immaturity, novel, recent,
youth, restore, evergreen,
untried, modern, neoteric, new
born, (old, ancient, antique,
long-standing, prime, primitive)

virile-*adj* strength, power,
energy, force, physical force,
stamina, muscle, sinew, vitality,
athletic, adamant, steel, iron,
oak, might, stout, robust,
(weak, frail, fragile, languid,
poor, rickety, cranky)

virtual-*adj* inexistence, negative,
blank, missing, omitted, absent,
unreal, potential, baseless,
unsubstantial, vain, uncreated,
exhausted, annihilated, gone,
lost, departed, (actual, real,
positive, absolute, prevalent)

virtue-*n* good, innocent,
meritorious, reserving, worthy,
correct, moral, righteous, well-
intentioned, creditable,

laudable, commendable, praiseworthy, admirable, (vicious, corrupt, atrocity)

visible-*adj* perceptibility, conspicuousness, distinctness, appearance, exposure, manifestation, ocular, ocular evidence, demonstrate, field of view, (invisible, indistinct, conceal, hidden)

visit-*n* courtesy, light, alight, dismount, debark, disembark, cast anchor, arrive, land, reception, welcome, destination, harbor, haven, port, refuge, (depart, removal, exit, egress, adieu, farewell)

vitality-*n* life, ability, animation, vital, spark, flame, respiration, wind, breath of life, existence, vivification, nourishment, subsist, quick, tenacious, (die, expire, meet one's death, end, pass away)

vivacious-*adj* cheerful, genial, gaiety, good humor, glee, light-hearted, mirth, merriment, hilarity, exhilaration, amusement, winsome, pleasing, (dreary, flat, dull, mournful, dreadful, depressing)

vivid-*adj* strong, energetic, forcible, active, intense, deep-dyed, severe, keen, sharp, acute, incisive, trenchant, brisk, rousing, exciting, (inert, inactive, passive, torpid, sluggish, dull, heavy, flat, slack)

vixen-*n* shrew, virago, termagant, dragon, scold, porcupine, spit-fire, fire-eater, blusterer, fury, violent person, irascible, bad, ill-tempered, irritable, susceptible, excitable, fretful, fidget, hasty, passionate

vocabulary-*n* word, term, vocable, name, phrase, root, etymon, derivative, part of speech, grammar, dictionary, lexicon, index, glossary, thesaurus, concordance, literal, verbal, titular, conjugate, exact

vocation-*n* calling, profession, cloth, faculty, industry, art, industrial arts, craft, mystery, handicraft, trade, commerce, perform, observe, fulfill, obligation, (exempt, free, neglect, relax, excuse, fail)

vociferation-*n* hullabaloo, loud noise, clang, clatter, noise, bombination, roar, uproar, racket, hubbub, raucous, resonance, thunder, bellow, powerful, (inaudible, low, muffled, hoarse, husky, gentle, soft)

void-*n* vacant, vacuous, empty, eviscerated, blank, hollow, nominal, null, inane, vanish, evaporate, fade, dissolve, melt away, disappear, nothing, (substantial, exist, object, tangible, being, substance)

volatile-*adj* gaseous, aeriform, ethereal, aerial, airy, vaporous, evaporation, flatulent, distillation, sublimation, exhale, transpire, emit, fume, reek, (dissolve, resolve, liquate, liquefied, soluble)

volcano-*n* reverberatory, forge, fiery furnace, brazier, salamander, heater, warming pan, boiler, cauldron, kettle, crucible, alembic, still, furnace, (refrigerate, cool, dampen, freezing, mixture)

volitant-*n* aeronautics, balloon, flying, flight, voyage, sail, put to sea, navigate, warp, luff, scud, boom, drift, course, cruise, row, paddle, pull, maritime, (walk, march, step, tread, pace, plod, wend)

volley-*n* shower, storm, cloud, group, cluster, clump, repeated sounds, report, thud, burst, explosion, discharge, detonation, squib, cracker, rap, snap, (rolling, monotonous)

volume-*n* size, magnitude, dimension, bulk, large, great, quantity, expanse, amplitude,

V

mass, proportions, mammoth,
capacity, ton, obesity, (small,
little, thin, dwarf, pygmy,
minute, microscopic)

voluntary-*adv* willing,
disposition, inclination, leaning,
mood, vein, free, without
reluctance, graciously, assent,
spontaneous, unasked,
unforced, (unwilling, grudgingly,
under protest, qualm)

voluptuous-*adj* impure,
concupiscent, prurient,
lickerish, rampant, lustful,
carnal, lewd, lascivious,
lecherous, social, evil, smut,
unchaste, wanton, debauched,
(vestal virgin, prude, pure,
undefiled)

vouch-*v* assert, declaratory,
predictor, pronunciation,
affirmative, positive, certain,
express, explicit, absolute,
emphatic, distinct, decided,
confident, dogmatic, (dispute,
impugn, traverse, rebut, deny)

vow-*v* promise, undertake,
engage, commit, assure,
warrant, guarantee, covenant,
bear witness, troth, plight,
pledge, word of honor, oath,
affirmation, compromise,
votive, obligation

vulnerable-*adj* expose, risk,
hazard, venture, precarious,
instability, defenseless, forlorn,
hopeless, threaten, tottering,
ominous, unprepared, (safe,
sure, guard, shield, protect,
precaution, refuge)

W

wade-*v* gather, learn, acquire, gain, receive, drink in, obtain, collect, knowledge, information, peruse, pore, industrious, studious, (teach, instruct, edify, tutor, enlighten)

waggle-*v* oscillate, alternate, undulate, wave, rock, swing, pulsate, beat, nod, bob, courtesy, curtsy, play, fluctuate, dance, curvet, reel, quake, shake, flicker, wriggle, roll, toss, pitch, flounder

wait-*v* put off, defer, delay, lay over, suspend, shift, waive, retard, remand, postpone, adjourn, procrastinate, dally, prolong, protract, knee back, (early, prime, timely, punctual, forward, prompt)

wall-*n* bar, barrier, turnstile, gate, portcullis, barricade, defense, breakwater, bulkhead, block, buffer, stopper, dam, weir, drawback, objection, stumbling block, (relief, rescue, lift, aid)

wallop-*v* strike, punic, chastise, castigate, slap, smack, spank, thump, beat, swing, buffet, thresh, thrash, pummel, drum, leather, trounce, baste, belabor, pelt, stone, lapidate, torture

wander-*v* move, motion, transitional, motor, motive, shifting, mobile, mercurial, unquiet, restless, nomadic, erratic, drift, flow, stream, (remain, stay, stagnate, rest, pause, lull, stop, repose)

want-*v* desire, wish, fancy, fantasy, need, exigency, mind, inclination, leaning, bent, longing, hankering, inkling, solicitude, anxiety, yearning, coveting, aspiration, (indifferent, cool, unconcerned)

wanton-*adj* capricious, erratic, eccentric, fitful, hysterical, full of whims, maggoty, inconsistent, fanciful, fantastic, whimsical, crotchety, particular, humorism, freakish, skittish, wayward, contrary, arbitrary

ward-*n* region, sphere, ground, soil, area, realm, hemisphere, quarter, district, beat, orb, circuit, circle, pale, limit, department, domain, tract, territory, parish, (boundless, uncircumscribed, extensive)

warehouse-*n* storehouse, closet, depository, repository, stock, accumulate, hoard, stack, promontory, reservoir, receptacle, amass, collect, harvest, save, reserve, (spend, expend, use, consume, spill)

warn-*v* discourage, dampen, disincline, indispose, stagger, repel, quench, deprecate, induce, deter, dissuade, obstinate, restrain, keep back, (prompt, deter, dissuade, obstinate, retrain, keep back, (prompt, persuade, bribe, lure, stimulate)

warrant-*n* dictate, mandate, caveat, decree, writ, ordination, bull, edict, decretal, dispensation, citation, permit, authorize, admission, grant, empower, (prohibit, forbid, disallow, bar, withhold, shut)

wash-*v* lavatory, laundry, clean, pure, purification, defecation, lustration, abstersion, ablution, disinfect, fumigate, deodorize, immaculate, (mud, mire, quagmire, sludge, slime, slush)

watch-*v* observe, attend to, peep, peer, pry, look, witness, contemplate, speculate, cast, discover, distinguish, recognize, spy, behold, demonstrate, (blind, hoodwink, undiscerning, dim-sighted)

way-*n* method, manner, wise,

W

form, mode, fashion, tone,
guise, procedure, path, road,
route, course, trajectory, orbit,
track, beat, means of access,
channel, passage, avenue,
approach, artery, lane

weak-*adj* feeble, insipid, illogical,
frail, fragile, flimsy,
unsubstantial, rickety, cranky,
drooping, tottering, broken,
lame, withered, shatter,
shaken, crazy, shaky, (strong,
might, vigorous, forcible, hard)

wear-*v* impair, injure, damage,
loss, detriment, laceration,
outrage, havoc, deteriorate,
degenerate, decay,
dilapidation, rotten, blight,
(improve, refine, rectify, enrich,
mellow, elaborate)

weave-*v* produce, perform,
operate, do, make, form,
construct, fabricate, frame,
contrive, manufacture, forge,
twine, entwine, twist, interlace,
(destroy, ruin, dilapidation,
deteriorate, wreck)

wedge-*n* fusiform, wedge-
shaped, triangular, angular,
bent, crooked, firm, fast, close,
tight, taut, secure, hinge, tether,
pin, nail, rivet, jam, dovetail,
(sunder, divide, sever, carve,
dissect, detach)

ween-*v* think, hold, opinion,
conceive, trow, fancy,
apprehend, embrace, assured,
positive, satisfied, confident,
nurture, credence, secure,
impress, (dispute, fallible,
uncertain, untrue, distrust,
doubt)

weight-*v* influence, tell, have a
hold upon, magnetize, bear
upon, pervade, prevail,
dominate, gain, important,
rampant, regnant, reign,
(irrelevant, unconducive,
impotence, inert, powerless)

well-intentioned-*adj* merit,
worth, excellence, credit, self-
control, resolution, self-denial,

virtuous, creditable, laudable,
commendable, exemplary,
(vicious, sinful, wicked,
immoral, lawless)

wheedle-*v* coax, persuade,
prevail, bring round, tempt,
seduce, entice, allure,
captivate, fascinate, bewitch,
carry away, charm, conciliate,
lure, tantalize, (remonstrate,
dissuade, discourage, averse)

where-*v* seek, inquire, search,
look for, scan, reconnoiter,
explore, sound, rummage,
ransack, pry, peer, hunt,
canvass, investigate, examine,
probe, fathom, scrutinize,
(answer, respond, reply, rebut)

whet-*v* sharpen, hone, strop,
grind, point, aculeate, picul, set,
acute, prickly, thorny, bristling,
studded, spike, cutting edge,
(obtuse, dull, bluff, render
blunt)

whim-*n* caprice, fancy, humor,
crotchet, quirk, freak, maggot,
fad, vagary, prank, erratic,
eccentric, fitful, hysterical,
frivolous, fickle, giddy, volatile,
skittish, inconsistent, fanciful,
fantastic, whimsical

whine-*v* complain, lament,
murmur, mutter, grumble,
groan, whimper, sob, sigh,
mourn, grieve, weep, complain
without cause, frown, scowl,
(smile, giggle, titter, cheer,
chuckle, shout, sing,
triumphant)

whisk-*v* sweep, rapid, speed,
hasten, rush, dash, race, lively,
swift, gallop, skim, hurry,
accelerate, quicken, spring,
fast, agile, expeditious,
instantaneous, (gradual, slow,
languid, sluggish, slow-paced)

whisper-*n* inaudible, low, dull,
stifled, muffled, husky,
melodious, speak imperfectly,
mutter, undertone, faint sound
hoarse, gentle, (blast, loud,
swell, clang, holler, scream,

piercing, deafening)

whittle-*v* sunder, divide, subdivide, sever, abscind, cut, snip, nib, rip, cleave, rend, slit, split, rupture, shatter, shiver, crunch, cop, hack, hew, slash, haggle, hackle, lacerate, scramble, mangle, slice

whole-*n* entire, total, integral, complete, one, individual, unbroken, wholly, altogether, sum total, gross amount, embody, (fractional, fragmentary, section, divided, break, piece, compartment)

wholesale-*adj* trade, commerce, market, buying and selling, bargain, traffic, business, commercial enterprise, speculation, jobbing, broker, negotiation, dealing, transaction, (retail, over the counter)

whopping-*adj* huge, enormous, giant, immense, monstrosity, corpulent, stout, fat, plump, thumping, thundering, overgrown, puffy, mighty, stupendous, infinite, (small, little, dwarf, unimportant)

wide-*adj* broad, ample, extended, expanded, breadth, latitude, amplitude, diameter, thickness, crassitude, expansion, thicken, dumpy, squab, squat, (narrow, coarctate, taper, slim, scanty)

wield-*v* agitate, shake, convulse, toss, tumble, bandy, brandish, flap, flourish, whisk, jerk, hitch, jolt, joggle, buffet, hustle, disturb, stir, hake up, churn, jounce, wallop, whip, vellicate, palpitate

will-*n* voluntary, volitional, free, optional, discretionary, freedom, spontaneity, originality, of one's own accord, by choice, purposely, deliberately, (compulsory, necessary, needful, compel, requisite)

win-*v* triumph, exultation, proficiency, skill, conquer, victor, succeed, gain, attain, secure, accomplish, master, conquest, carry, secure, effect, complete, (failure, lose, ruined, defeated, broken down)

wince-*v* pain, suffering, physical pain, aching, smart, twinge, twitch, gripe, headache, hurt, sore, discomfort, malaise, spasm, cramp, nightmare, convulsion, writhe, agonize, (sensual, sensuous, pleasure, bodily enjoyment, gratification, creature comforts)

winch-*n* lever, crane, derrick, instrument, tool, implement, utensil, handle, hilt, haft, shaft, shank, blade, trigger, helm, treadle, capstan, lift, heighten, elevate, (crouch, stoop, bend, bow, sink, reduce)

wing-*n* leave, depart, exit, egress, exodus, farewell, goodbye, quit, retire, withdraw, remove, wing one's flight, spring, fly, flit, outward bound, (arrive, welcome, here, return, overtake, join)

winsome-*adj* charming, delightful, felicitous, exquisite, lovely, beautiful, ravishing, rapturous, heart-felt, thrilling, ecstatic, beatific, seraphic, heavenly, attractive, (repel, disgust, revolt, nauseate, sicken)

wipe-*v* dry, soak, up, sponge, swab, drain, parch, anhydrous, napkin, cloth, handkerchief, towel, sudary, doily, duster, mop, wash, launder, spruce, tidy, (sludge, slime, slush, grime)

wise-*adj* intelligent, keen, acute, alive, awake, bright, quick, sharp, sage, sapient, sagacious, reasonable, rational, sound, sensible, judicious, strong-minded, unprejudiced, calculating

W

wish-*n* desire, fantasy, want, need, grasping, longing, hankering, anxiety, yearning, aspiration, vaulting, ambition, eagerness, zeal, ardor, impatience, (indifferent, undesired, neutral)

wistful-*adj* thinking, thoughtful, pensive, meditative, reflective, museful, contemplative, speculative, deliberate, studious, sedate, introspective, philosophical, (vacant, unintellectual, unoccupied)

wither-*v* decrease, dwindle, shrink, contract, narrow, shrivel, collapse, lose flesh, fall away, waste, wane, decay, deteriorate, lessen, pare, reduce, strangle, restrain, file, (expand, spread, extend, develop)

withstand-*v* resist, repugn, reluctant, stand up, strive, bear up, stand firm, refractory, oppose, strike, revolt, front, repulse, insurrection, (reprisal, retort, reaction, reciprocate)

witness-*n* spectator, beholder, observer, onlooker, eye witness, bystander, passer-by, sightseer, spy, sentinel, be present, contemplate, survey, curiosity, (retire from sight, disappear, vanish)

woe-*n* beshrew, confusion, damn, confound, blast, curse, devil take, hang, plague, scold, denounce, proscribe, excommunicate, fulminate, threaten, (benevolent, kind, well-meaning, amiable, obliging)

wonder-*v* astonish, amazement, marvel, bewilder, admiration, awe, stupor, fascination, sensation, surprise, wondrous, electrify, stun, confound, dazzle, baffle, stupendous, miraculous, overwhelming

word-*n* maxim, aphorism, saying, adage, saw, proverb, sentence, motto, axiom, reflection, conclusion, term, name, phrase, part of speech, vocabulary, literal, concordance

work-*v* labor, toil, travail, manual labor, sweat of one's brow, trouble, pains, sweat, drudge, slave, wade through, strive, strain, pull, exert, effort, struggle, (relax, unbend, slacken, refresh, sleep, rest)

workmanship-*n* produce, perform, operate, flower, bear fruit, fructify, create, beget, generate, hatch, develop, form, prolific, labor, build, edify, pride, (destroy, perish, demolish, tear up, dispel, nullify)

worldly-*adj* atheist, septic, unbeliever, deist, infidel, heathen, alien, gentile, freethinker, rationalist, materialistic, agnostic, disbelieve, doubt, (worship, inspire, revere, adore, bow down and worship)

worn-*v* weak, battered, shattered, pulled down, seedy, altered, fatigued, weary, drowsy, drooping, haggard, toil, footsore, weatherbeaten, faint, exhausted, prostrate, (reinvigorate, freshen up)

worse-*adv* deteriorate, degenerate, wane, decrease, retrograde, decline, droop, sink, from bad to worse, recession, decay, decrepitude, (improve, mend, advance, reform, ripen, better, correct)

worthy-*adj* virtuous, good, innocent, meritorious, deserving, righteous, well-intentioned, creditable, laudable, commendable, praiseworthy, excellent, admirable, sterling, pure, noble, admirable

wrangle-*v* discord, quarrel, dispute, tiff, squabble, altercation, words, jangle, babble, broil, brawl, racket, disturbance, dissent, dissension, (agree, accord, harmonize, concord, united, allied)

wreck-*n* smash, crash, quell, squash, squelch, shatter, sink, swamp, scuttle, shipwreck, engulf, submerge, raze, level, lay waste, ravage, gut, dismantle, (create, construct, form, put together)

write-*v* record, pen, scribe, transcribe, copy, scribble, scrawl, scrabble, scratch, interline, write down, compose, print, publish, compositor, manuscript, shorthand, handwriting

wry-*adj* slope, slant, lean, incline, shelve, stoop, decline, descend, bend, heel, careen, sag, swag, slouch, cant, sidle, poke, askew, askant, oblique, (parallel, coextension, alongside, laterally)

W

Y

yarn-*n* exaggeration, expansion, hyperbole, stretch, strain, coloring, caricature, extravagance, nonsense, fringe, embroidery, traveler's tale, overestimate, wire, string, thread, twine, cord, rope

yawn-*n* nod, get sleepy, snooze, nap, dream, sleepy, indolent, lazy, slothful, idle, lust, remiss, slack, inert, sluggish, languid, supine, heavy, dull, leaden, listless, (active, quick, prompt, alert, spry, sharp)

yearling-*n* infant, babe, child, youth, stripling, youngster, younker, weanling, papoose, bambino, seedling, whipper-snapper, (veteran, old man, seer, patriarch, centenarian, old stager, forefathers)

yearn-*v* pity, compassion, commiseration, sympathy, tenderness, forbearance, humanity, mercy, clemency, leniency, charity, touched, soften, (unmerciful, uncompassionate, severe, unrelenting)

yeast-*n* leaven, ferment, barm, light, subtile, airy, imponderable, astatic, weightless, ethereal, sublimated, uncompressed, volatile, buoyant, floating, portable, (heavy, massive, lead, millstone)

yell-*v* cry, vociferate, raise, shout, roar, bawl, rawl, hop, whoop, bellow, howl, scream, screech, screak, shriek, squeak, squall, whine, pule, pipe, cheer, hoot, grumble, moan, groan

yield-*v* succumb, submit, bend, resign, defer, submissive, surrender, capitulate, retreat, downtrodden, pliant, undefended, permit, relinquish, sanction, (overpower, struggle, unbending, forbid, refuse)

yoke-*n* lock, latch, belay, brace, hook, grapple, leash, couple, accouplement, link, bracket, bridge over, span, pin, nail, bolt, hasp, clasp, clamp, (sever, rupture, segregate, breach, rescind, divide)

yokel-*n* bungler, blunderer, marplot, fumbler, lubber, duffer, awkward, squad, greenhorn, clod, muff, (proficient, expert, adept, connoisseur, veteran)

yokemate-*n* spouse, consort, husband, wife, better half, mate, helpmate, match, betrothment, promise, (unmarried, bachelor, virgin, single, celibacy)

yonder-*adj* distant, far-off, remote, telescopic, distal, stretching, ulterior, transmarine, span, stride, faraway, farther, further, beyond, far and wide, (near, close, no great distance, nigh, within reach)

yore-*adj* formerly, of old, last, latter, retrospective, ancient, time, immemorial, olden, forgotten, extinct, gone by, ancestral, (anticipate, millennium, advent, look forward, eventual)

young-*adj* youthful, juvenile, green, callow, budding, sappy, beardless, under age, junior, infant, minor, pupilage, puberty, prime, rising generation, (seniority, elder, longevity, aged, antiquated, decay)

Z

zany-*adj* fool, idiot, tomfoolery,
    wiseacre, simpleton, witling,
    donkey, ass, ninny,
    nincompoop, lout, loon, gabby,
    trifler, babbler, dullard, doodle,
    clod, lack-wit, (authority,
    luminary, wise man)
zeal-*adj* quick, prompt, yare,
    instant, ready, alert, spry,
    sharp, smart, fast, swift,
    expeditious, awake, forward,
    eager, strenuous, enterprising,
    industrious, diligent, (indolent,
    lazy, slothful, idle, remiss)
zealot-*n* bigot, intolerant,
    obstinate, immovability,
    inflexibility, prejudgment,
    opinionist, enthusiast,
    tenacious, (changeful, idle,
    withdraw from, relinquish)
zealous-*adj* eager, animated,
    resolute, steadfast, vivacious,
    diligent, fiery, brisk
zero-*n* nothing, naught, cipher,
    none, no one, nobody, never,
    unsubstantial, blank, void,
    immaterial, groundless,
    nonentity, (substantial, thing,
    object, something, being)
zest-*n* pleasure, gratification,
    enjoyment, fruition, delectation,
    relish, gusto, satisfaction,
    content, well-being, snugness,
    comfort, amusement,
    happiness, (concern, grief,
    sorrow, distress, affliction, woe)
zigzag-*v* diversion, digression,
    departure, aberration,
    divergence, detour, circuit,
    wander, vagrant, by-paths and
    crooked ways, oblique motion,
    deviate, swerve, (toward, aim,
    line, path, road, range)
zone-*n* region, sphere, clime,
    climate, meridian, latitude,
    territorial, local, arena,
    precincts, district, domain, tract,

parish, province, township,
field, plot, (unlimited space,
wilderness, waste, free space)

Z